CISTERCIAN STUDIES SERIES: NUMB

C000132284

Alexander Golitzin

Mystagogy

οὐκ οἴδατε ὅτι ναὸς θεοῦ ἐστε καὶ
τὸ πνεῦμα τοῦ θεοῦ οἰκεῖ ἐν ὑμῖν;
1 Cor 3:16

καὶ ἐμφανίσω αὐτῷ ἐμαυτὸν . . .
καὶ πρὸς αὐτὸν ἐλευσόμεθα καὶ
μονὴν παρ᾽ αὐτῷ ποιησόμεθα.
John 14:21-23

CISTERCIAN STUDIES SERIES: NUMBER TWO HUNDRED FIFTY

Mystagogy

A Monastic Reading of
Dionysius Areopagita

By

Alexander Golitzin

with the collaboration of

Bogdan G. Bucur

Edited by

Bogdan G. Bucur

α

Cistercian Publications
www.cistercianpublications.org

LITURGICAL PRESS
Collegeville, Minnesota
www.litpress.org

This monograph has evolved out of the author's extensive revisions of his earlier book *Et introibo ad altare Dei: The Mystagogy of Dionysius Areopagita* (Thessaloniki, Greece: George Dedousis Publishing Co., 1994). Original sections are used with permission.

A Cistercian Publications title published by Liturgical Press

Cistercian Publications
Editorial Offices
Abbey of Gethsemani
3642 Monks Road
Trappist, Kentucky 40051
www.cistercianpublications.org

2	3	4	5	6	7	8	9

Library of Congress Cataloging-in-Publication Data

Golitzin, Alexander.
    Mystagogy : a monastic reading of Dionysius Areopagita : 1 Cor 3:16, John 14:21-23 / Alexander Golitzin ; (with the collaboration of Bogdan G. Bucur) edited by Bogdan G. Bucur.
        pages   cm. — (Cistercian studies series ; no. 250)
    Includes bibliographical references.
    ISBN 978-0-87907-250-6 — ISBN 978-0-87907-760-0 (e-book)
    1. Pseudo-Dionysius, the Areopagite.   I. Title.

BR65.D66G65   2013
230'.14092—dc23   2013024765

Contents

Author's Note

This monograph has evolved out of the work of revising my earlier book, *Et introibo ad altare Dei: The Mystagogy of Dionysius Areopagita*. That text has been revised and restructured, several chapters have been eliminated, and much other material has been added, reflecting my engagement with more recent scholarship and further reflection on the *Corpus Dionysiacum* and its reception in the Christian East in a number of studies that I have published between 1993 and 2009.[1] For this editorial work, as well as for a

1. The articles in question are, in chronological order, the following: "The Mysticism of Dionysius Areopagita: Platonist or Christian?" *MQ* 19 (1993): 98–114; "Hierarchy Versus Anarchy: Dionysius Areopagita, Symeon the New Theologian, Nicetas Stethatos, and Their Common Roots in the Ascetical Tradition," *SVTQ* 38 (1994): 131–179; "Liturgy and Mysticism: The Experience of God in Eastern Orthodox Christianity," *ProEccl* 8 (1999): 159–186; " 'A Contemplative and a Liturgist': Father Georges Florovsky on the Corpus Dionysiacum," *SVTQ* 43 (1999): 131–161; "Revisiting the 'Sudden': Epistle III in the Corpus Dionysiacum," *SP* 37 (2001): 482–491; " 'Earthly Angels and Heavenly Men': The Old Testament Pseudepigrapha, Nicetas Stethatos, and Interiorized Apocalyptic," *DOP* 55 (2001): 125–153; "The Demons Suggest an Illusion of God's Glory in a Form: Controversy over the Divine Body and Vision of Glory in Some Late-Fourth, Early-Fifth Century Monastic Literature," *StudMon* 44 (2002): 13–43; "A Testimony to Christianity as Transfiguration: The Macarian Homilies and Orthodox Spirituality," in *Orthodox and Wesleyan Spirituality*, ed. S. T. Kimbrough (Crestwood, NY: St Vladimir's Seminary Press, 2002), 129–156; "Dionysius the Areopagite in the Works of Gregory Palamas: On the Question of a 'Christological Corrective' and Related Matters," *SVTQ* 46 (2002): 163–190; " 'Suddenly, Christ': the Place of Negative Theology in the Mystagogy of Dionysius Areopagites," in *Mystics: Presence and Aporia* (ed. M.

number of paragraphs in the introduction, the first chapter, and the conclusions, credit and my profound gratitude goes to Bogdan Gabriel Bucur, my former student and now colleague in academia.

I am especially grateful to Dr. James Miller, a former student at Marquette University, whose hard work of recuperating the text of my 1994 book from ancient diskettes made this project possible; to Mr. Benjamin Burkholder for his proofreading of several versions of the old manuscript; to Mr. Ignatius (Harry) Green for his very careful first proofreading; to Mr. Justin Pearl for compiling the index; and to Mr. Dan Octavian Botez, who generously donated the photograph on the book cover. Many thanks to Fr. Mark Scott and Hans Christoffersen at Cistercian Publications for all their efforts in bringing this project to fruition, and for their patience and kindness all along the way.

Kessler and C. Sheppard; Chicago: University of Chicago Press, 2003): 8–37; "Dionysius Areopagita: A Christian Mysticism?" *ProEccl* 12 (2003): 161–212; "Christian Mysticism over Two Millennia," in *The Theophaneia School: Jewish Roots of Christian Mysticism*, ed. Andrei Orlov and Basil Lurie (Saint Petersburg: Byzantinorossica, 2007), 17–33; "Heavenly Mysteries: Themes from Apocalyptic Literature in the Macarian Homilies and Selected Other Fourth Century Ascetical Writers," in *Apocalyptic Themes in Early Christianity* (ed. Robert Daly; Grand Rapids: Baker Academic, 2009), 174–192.

Abbreviations

Ps-Dionysius

CD	*Corpus Dionysiacum*
CH	*Celestial Hierarchy*
EH	*Ecclesiastical Hierarchy*
MT	*Mystical Theology*
DN	*Divine Names*

Primary Source Collections

ACW	*Ancient Christian Writers*
ANF	*A Select Library of the Ante-Nicene Fathers of the Christian Church*
CSEL	*Corpus Scriptorum Ecclesiasticorum Latinorum* (Louvain)
CSCO	*Corpus Scriptorum Christianorum Orientalium* (Louvain)
GNO	*Gregorii Nysseni Opera* (ed. W. Jaeger et al.)
Lampe	*A Patristic Greek Lexicon* (ed. G. H. W. Lampe: 1963)
LCC	*Library of Christian Classics* (Philadelphia)
Loeb	*Loeb Classical Library* (Cambridge, MA)
NPNF	*A Select Library of the Nicene and Post-Nicene Fathers of the Christian Church*
PG	*Patrologia Graeca*
PL	*Patrologia Latina*
PO	*Patrologia Orientalia*
SCh	*Sources chrétiennes*

Journals and Other Collections

AnBoll	*Analecta Bollandiana*
APQ	*American Philosophical Quarterly*
AfR	*Archiv für Religionsgeschichte*
AHDLM	*Archives d'histoire doctrinale et litteraire du Moyen Age*
AOC	*Archives de l'orient chrétien*
Aug	*Augustianum*
BAGB	*Bulletin de l'association Guillaume Budé*
Bib	*Biblica*
BLE	*Bulletin de littérature ecclésiastique*
Byz	*Byzantion*
ByzZ	*Byzantinische Zeitschrift*
COr	*Cahiers d'Orientalisme*
CambHist	*The Cambridge History of Later Greek and Early Medieval Philosophy* (ed. A. H. Armstrong [Cambridge: Cambridge University Press, 1967])
CH	*Church History*
Cist Stud	*Cistercian Studies*
ClassQ	*Classical Quarterly*
CPhilog	*Classical Philology*
DOP	*Dumbarton Oaks Papers*
DRev	*Downside Review*
DSp	*Dictionaire de Spiritualité* (Paris: Beauchesne, 1932–)
EB	*Études Byzantines*
ECQ	*Eastern Churches Quarterly*
ECR	*Eastern Churches Review*
EO	*Échos d'Orient*
EOB	*East of Byzantium: Syria and Armenia in the Formative Period* (ed. N. G. Garsoian, T. F. Mathews, R. W. Thompson [Washington, DC: Dumbarton Oaks Center for Byzantine Studies, 1982])
EphL	*Ephemerides liturgicae*
EtPG	*Études de philologie grecque*
FZPT	*Freiburger Zeischrift für Philosophie und Theologie*
GOTR	*Greek Orthodox Theological Review*
Greg	*Gregorianum*

HistJ	*Historisches Jahrbuch*
HTR	*Harvard Theological Review*
IPQ	*International Philosophical Quarterly*
Ir	*Irenikon*
JEH	*Journal of Ecclesiastical History*
JJS	*Journal of Jewish Studies*
JRS	*Journal of Roman Studies*
JTS	*Journal of Theological Studies*
LuthQ	*Lutheran Quarterly*
MAev	*Medium Aevum*
MS	*Mediaeval Studies*
MessPR	*Messager de l'exarchat du Patriarchat Russe en Europe Occidentale*
Mus	*Le Muséon*
NAWG	*Nachrichten der Akademie der Wissenschaften in Göttingen*
OC	*Oriens Christianus*
OCA	*Orientalia Christiana Analecta*
OCP	*Orientalia Christiana Periodica*
OStud	*Ostkirchliche Studien*
OSyr	*Orient Syrien*
ParO	*Parole d'Orient*
PBR	*Patristic and Byzantine Review*
Philog	*Philologus*
PJ	*Philosophisches Jahrbuch*
PSB	*Princeton Seminary Bulletin*
RAM	*Revue d'ascétique et de mystique*
RBPH	*Revue belge de philologie et d'histoire*
REA	*Revue des études augustiniennes*
REB	*Revue des études byzantines*
RHE	*Revue d'histoire ecclésiastique*
RHLR	*Revue d'histoire et de littérature religieuse*
RHPR	*Revue d'histoire et de philosophie religieuse*
RHR	*Revue de l'histoire des religions*
RMfP	*Rheinisches Museum für Philologie*

RP	*Recherches de philosophie*
RSP	*Recherches des sciences philosophiques*
RSPT	*Recherches des sciences philosophiques et théologiques*
RSR	*Recherches de science religieuse*
RT	*Revue thomiste*
RTL	*Revue théologique de Louvain*
SacE	*Sacris erudiri*
Schol	*Scholastik*
Sob	*Sobornost*
SP	*Studia Patristica*
SuCD	*Studien über christliche Denkmäler*
SVSQ	*St Vladimir's Seminary Quarterly*
SVTQ	*St Vladimir's Theological Quarterly*
SymbO	*Symbolae Osloensis*
TAV	*A Tribute to Arthur Vööbus* (ed. R. H. Fischer [Chicago: Lutheran School of Theology, 1977])
Teol Vida	*Teología y vida*
TU	*Texte und Untersuchungen*
TVM	*Théologie de la vie monastique* (Paris: 1961)
TWNT	*Theologisches Wörterbuch zum Neuen Testament* (ed. G. Kittel; Stuttgart: Kohlhammer, 1932–1973)
TZ	*Theologisches Zeitschrift*
VC	*Vigiliae Christianae*
VerC	*Verbum Caro*
ZAM	*Zeitschrift für Askeze und Mystik*
ZFDA	*Zeitschrift für deutsches Altertum und deutsche Literatur*
ZKT	*Zeitschrift für Katholische Theologie*
ZKG	*Zeitschrift für Kirchengeschichte*
ZRG	*Zeitschrift für Religions- und Geistesgeschichte*
ZPhTh	*Zeitschrift für Philosophie und Theologie*

Introduction

1. A Controversial Figure: A Brief Look at Dionysius' Ecclesial and Scholarly Reception[1]

The first clearly datable reference to the Dionysian corpus[2] comes to us from the minutes of the colloquium, between opponents and defenders of the Council of Chalcedon, convoked by the Emperor Justinian in 532 in order to put an end to the quarrel over Christology, or at least so the emperor hoped. The hope was in vain, as it turned out, but in the course of discussion the anti-Chalcedonians cited one Dionysius the Areopagite who, they said, had lent apostolic-era approval to their position on the single nature of the incarnate Word by writing in his fourth epistle of Christ's "single, divine-human activity." Metropolitan

---

1. I have provided a more thorough and extensive *Forschungsbericht* in A. Golitzin, *Et introibo ad altare Dei: The Mystagogy of Dionysius Areopagita* (Thessalonica: Patriarchal Institute, 1994), 21–42. See also the introductory studies by G. Reale ("Introduzione: Il *Corpus Dionysiacum* e i grandi problem che suscita per la sua interpretazione") and E. Bellini ("Saggio introduttivo") in *Dionigi Areopagita: Tutte le opere. Testo greco a fronte* (trans. P. Scazzoso and I. Ramelli; introd. G. Reale; introductory essay, notes, and indices by E. Bellini; complementary essay by C. M. Mazzucchi; Milan: Bompiani, 2009), 11–29 and 33–73 (esp. 33–42).

2. I will be referring to the Greek text of Dionysius in two editions, Migne's *Patrologia Graeca*, vol. 3, with the column numbers, and, in parentheses, the page and line numbers of the critical edition: *De divinis nominibus* (vol. 1 of *Corpus Dionysiacum*; ed. B. R. Suchla; Berlin: de Gruyter, 1990), and *Corpus Dionysiacum II*, containing the treatises on the hierarchies, the *Mystical Theology*, and the *Epistles* (ed. G. Heil and A. M. Ritter; Berlin: de Gruyter, 1991).

Hypatius of Ephesus, speaking for the pro-Chalcedonian side, replied tartly that, since none of the earlier fathers had mentioned this "apostolic source," he was not about to admit it into evidence, either.[3] In spite of the good Metropolitan's hesitations, Dionysius proved to be an immediate "hit" in the Chalcedonian and even Nestorian (!) worlds as well. The terms he invented, most notably the word "hierarchy" and the phrase "mystical theology," spread with remarkable speed.[4] Ten or twenty years after the colloquium, Bishop John of Scythopolis in Palestine would write the *Scholia* on the corpus which cemented its reputation and which have accompanied it ever since.[5] Even sooner, perhaps contemporaneously with or even a little before the colloquium, Sergius of Reshaina would translate Dionysius into Syriac,[6] where he immediately

3. *Acta Concilium Oecumenicorum* (ed. E. Schwartz; Berlin: de Gruyter, 1914), IV.2, 173:13–18.

4. See, e.g., J. Stiglmayr, "Über die Termini Hierarch und Hierarchia," *ZKT* 22 (1898): 180–187.

5. See B. R. Suchla, *Die sogennanten Maximus-Scholien des Corpus Diony-siacum Areopagiticum* (NAG; Göttingen: Vandenhoeck & Ruprecht, 1980), 31–66; idem, *Eine Redaktion des griechischen Corpus Dionysiacum im Umkreis des Johannes von Skythopolis, des Verfassers von Prolog und Scholien: Ein dritter Beitrag zur Überlieferungsgeschichte des Corpus Dionysiacum* (NAG; Göttingen: Vandenhoeck & Ruprecht, 1985), 1–18; P. E. Rorem and J. C. Lamoreaux, *John of Scythopolis and the Dionysian Corpus: Annotating the Areopagite* (Oxford: Oxford University Press, 1998), esp. 7–45.

6. Thanks to the labors of the scholars listed below, the text appears to have been recovered (most of it in the late sixth- or early seventh-century *Sinai Syriacus* 52, and several scattered fragments) and will hopefully be edited soon. On the Syriac transmission of Dionysius, see J.-M. Hornus, "Le corpus dionysien en Syriaque," *ParOr* 1 (1970): 69–93; G. Wiessner, "Zur Handschrift-enüberlieferung der syrischer Fassung des Corpus Dionysiacum," *NAWG* (1972): 165–216; I. Perczel, "Sergius of Reshaina's Syriac Translation of the Dionysian Corpus: Some Preliminary Remarks," in *La diffusione dell'eredità classica nell'età tardo-antica e medievale. Filologia, storia, dottrina. Atti del Semi-nario nazionale di studio, Napoli-Sorrento, 29–31 ottobre 1998* (ed. C. Baffioni; Alessandria: Edizioni dell'Orso, 2000), 79–94; idem, "The Earliest Syriac Re-ception of Dionysius," in *Re-Thinking Dionysius the Areopagite* (ed. S. Coakley and C. M. Stang; Malden, MA: Wiley-Blackwell, 2009), 27–41; P. Sherwood, "Sergius of Reshaina and the Syriac Versions of the Pseudo-Dionysius," *SE* 4 (1952): 174–184; M. Quaschning-Kirsch, "Ein weiterer Textzeuge für die

shows up in the writings of the rather strange Syrian Christian mystic, Stephen bar Sudaili.[7] In the following century the greatest theologian of the later Byzantine era, the monk and saint Maximus the Confessor, would hold Dionysius in the highest regard. The Areopagite appears everywhere in Maximus' oeuvre, as he does in that of John Damascene a century later.[8]

If 532 provides the *ad quem* of the Areopagitica, the *a quo* is usually set at 487, the death of the pagan Neoplatonist philosopher

---

syrische Version des Corpus Dionysiacum Areopagiticum: Paris B.N. Syr. 378," *Mus* 113 (2000): 115–124; A. Palmer and I. Perczel, "A New Testimony from India to the Syriac Version of Pseudo-Dionysius (Pampakuda, Konat Collection, Ms. 239)," *Iran & the Caucasus* 6 (2002): 11–26; P. Géhin, "Manuscrits sinaïtiques dispersés, I: Les fragments syriaques et arabes de Paris," *OC* 90 (2006): 23–43. For a French translation of Sergius' own remarks on his translation, idem, "Mimro de Serge de Rešayna sur la vie spirituelle," *OrSyr* 5 (1960): 433–457; 6 (1961): 95–115, 121–156.

7. R. A. Arthur (*Pseudo-Dionysius as Polemicist: The Development and Purpose of the Angelic Hierarchy in Sixth-Century Syria* [London: Ashgate, 2008], esp. 138, 155, 160, 184, 186–187, 197) thinks that the Areopagitica are composed by Sergius of Reshaina in direct response to "men like bar Sudhaili and probably to him in person." Perczel ("The Earliest Syriac Reception of Dionysius," 34) seems convinced that the *CD* was "a joint work of Sergius and his (most probably younger) "assistant" . . . and Stephen Bar Sudhaili," although he also warns, only a few lines later, against imagining "some monk sitting in a hidden monastery and writing under divine inspiration" ("The Earliest Syriac Reception of Dionysius," 34). For a translation and introduction to Stephen bar Sudaili, see *The Book Which is Called The Book of the Holy Hierotheos: With Extracts From the Prolegomena and Commentary of Theodosios of Antioch, and From the Book of Excerpts and Other Works of Gregory Bar-Hebraeus* (ed. and trans. F. S. Marsh; London: Williams and Norgate, 1927).

8. See L. Thunberg, *Microcosm and Mediator: The Theological Anthropology of Maximus the Confessor* (2d ed.; Chicago: Open Court, 1995), throughout, though esp. 192–195, 408–410, 413–418, 423–426; P. M. Blowers, *Exegesis and Spiritual Pedagogy in Maximus the Confessor: An Investigation of the Quaestiones ad Thalassium* (Notre Dame: University of Notre Dame Press, 1991), esp. 11–12, 184–185, and 252–253; Y. de Andia, "Transfiguration et théologie négative chez Maxime le Confesseur et Denys l'Aréopagite," in *Denys l'Aréopagite et sa posterité*, 293–328; A. Louth, "St Denys the Areopagite and St Maximus the Confessor: A Question of Influence," *SP* 27 (1993): 166–174; A. Louth, "St Denys the Areopagite and the Iconoclast Controversy," in *Denys l'Aréopagite et sa posterité*, 329–339.

Proclus Diadochus. Here we arrive at the question of Dionysius' Christianity. An anonymous scholiast of Dionysius had noticed, along with others, the strong resemblances—not to say occasional word-for-word matches—between Proclus and the disciple of Saint Paul, Dionysius. The scholiast argued that the pagan had cribbed from the Christian master.[9] After Marsilio Ficino's admiring reference to Dionysius (in a piece entitled, significantly, *The Praises of Philosophy*) as *Platonicus primo, deinde Christianus*, came Martin Luther's explicit dismissal of Dionysius (again, significantly, in the treatise *On the Babylonian Captivity of the Church*) as *plus platonisans quam christianizans*, and his warning to "stay away from that Dionysius, whoever he was!"[10] I am myself expert in neither the Reformation generally nor Luther in particular, but I think it not inaccurate to say that he read Dionysius as perhaps the advocate *par excellence* of a *theologia gloriae*, in opposition to his own *theologia crucis*, which is to say, a theological perspective which effectively makes superfluous the Incarnation and atoning death of God the Word, and which does so because it assumes that the human mind of itself is capable, at least in potential, of achieving direct contact with the deity. The great doctor of the Reformation saw this pernicious attitude especially embodied in the *Mystical Theology*, which he read as an example less of truly Christian piety than of an appeal to the autonomous human intellect; hence: "Shun like the plague that *Mystical Theology* and other such works!" Ever since Luther, though here I should add that I am over-simplifying somewhat, Dionysius has been by and large a "non-starter" for Protestant theology and devotion, while Protestant scholarship, insofar as it deals with him at all, remains generally—or even emphatically—unsympathetic.[11]

9. *PG* IV, col. 21D.

10. *Marsilii Ficini Opera* (Turin: Bottega d'Erasmo, 1959) 1:768; *Luthers Werke* (Weimar: Böhlau, 1888) 6:562.

11. On the Protestant reception, see K. Froehlich, "Pseudo-Dionysius and the Reformation of the Sixteenth Century," in *Pseudo-Dionysius: The Complete Works* (trans. C. Luibhéid and P. E. Rorem; New York: Paulist, 1987), 33–46; P. E. Rorem, "Martin Luther's Christocentric Critique of Pseudo-Dionysian Spirituality," *LuthQ* 11 (1997): 291–307.

The Roman Catholic approach to the Areopagite is somewhat different. During the Middle Ages, from the twelfth and especially the thirteenth centuries on, he was widely popular, even sensationally so.[12] Thomas Aquinas quoted him nearly as often as Scripture, something over a thousand times.[13] Apologists for Papal authority saw in his treatises on the hierarchies, *The Celestial* and *The Ecclesiastical Hierarchy*, apostolic-era support for the vision of church order they were seeking to establish and defend. The mystics of the late medieval Rhineland and England (e.g., Meister Eckhart and the author of *The Cloud of Unknowing*), and, later on, the great spiritual writers of Counter-Reformation Spain,

---

12. H. F. Dondaine, *Le corpus dionysien de l'université de Paris au XIII· siècle* (Rome: Storia e letteratura, 1953); L. M. Harrington, *A Thirteenth-Century Textbook of Mystical Theology at the University of Paris* (Leuven: Peeters, 2004), 1–38; Rorem, "The Early Latin Dionysius: Eriugena and Hugh of St. Victor," in *Re-Thinking Dionysius*, 71–84.

13. For Aquinas' use of Dionysius, see F. O'Rourke, *Pseudo-Dionysius and the Metaphysics of Aquinas* (Leiden: Brill, 1992); P. Kalaitzidis, "*Theologia*: Discours sur Dieu et science théologique chez Denys l'Aréopagite et Thomas d'Aquin," in *Denys l'Aréopagite et sa posterité en orient et en occident: actes du colloque international, Paris 21–24 septembre 1994* (ed. Y. de Andia; Paris: Études Augustiniennes, 1997), 457–487; E.-H. Weber, "L'apophatisme dionysien chez Albert le Grand et dans son école," in *Denys l'Aréopagite et sa posterité*, 379–403; W. J. Hankey, "Dionysian Hierarchy in Thomas Aquinas," in *Denys l'Aréopagite et sa posterité*, 405–438; D. Burrell and I. Moulin, "Albert, Aquinas, and Dionysius," in *Re-Thinking Dionysius*, 103–119; T.-D. Humbrecht, "Noms divins: les sources de saint Thomas au XIIIe siècle," *RT* 105 (2005): 411–434, 551–594; M. B. Ewbank, "Diverse Orderings of Dionysius's *triplex via* by St. Thomas Aquinas," *MS* 52 (1990): 82–109; J. D. Jones, "An Absolutely Simple God? Frameworks for Reading Pseudo-Dionysius Areopagite," *Thomist* 69 (2005): 371–406; idem, "(Mis?)-Reading the Divine Names as a Science: Aquinas' Interpretation of the Divine Names of (Pseudo) Dionysius Areopagite," *SVTQ* 52 (2008): 143–172; D. B. Twetten, "Aquinas's Aristotelian and Dionysian Definition of 'God,' " *Thomist* 69 (2005): 203–250; B. G. Bucur, "The Theological Reception of Dionysian Apophatism in the Christian East and West: Thomas Aquinas and Gregory Palamas," *DRev* 125 (2007): 131–146; idem, "Dionysius East and West: Unities, Differentiations, and the Exegesis of Biblical Theophanies," *Dionysius* 26 (2008): 115–138; A. Hofer, "Dionysian Elements in Thomas Aquinas's Christology: A Case of the Authority and Ambiguity of Pseudo-Dionysius," *Thomist* 72 (2009): 409–442.

such as Theresa of Avila and especially John of the Cross, were likewise well disposed to Dionysius, especially, once more, to his *Mystical Theology*.[14] Yet, it is also the case that Dionysius was never approached so to speak *in toto* by any of his medieval and post-medieval Western admirers (or detractors, for that matter). Rather, bits of his thought—for example, the appeal of his long treatise on *The Divine Names*, with its *exitus-reditus* scheme of creation and return to God, to Thomas and other masters of speculative divinity; or the notion of hierarchy to the canonists; or the *Mystical Theology* to the enthusiasts of mystical piety—were broken off and applied, as it were, piecemeal to the several interests of his different admirers. Put briefly, it is an effectively fractured Dionysius that we find at the end of the Western Middle Ages, with larger or smaller chunks of his oeuvre tacked on to—or, as with Aquinas, assimilated with magisterial elegance into—an already well-established and secure theological *Gestalt*.[15] With the Reformation and its aftermath, Catholic attention shifted into a defensive mode, and the Areopagite became one element among many—though not a very important one—in the to and fro of

14. C. Taylor, "The Cloud-Author's Remaking of the Pseudo-Dionysius' *Mystical Theology*," *MAev* 75 (2006): 202–218; K. Ruh, "Die 'Mystica Theologia' des Dionysius Pseudo-Areopagita im Lichte mittelalterlicher Kommentatoren," *ZFDA* 122 (1993): 127–145; M. J. Will, "Dionysian Neoplatonism and the Theology of the Cloud, Author I; Author II," *DRev* 379 (1992): 98–109; 380 (1992): 184–194. See also the essays in the above-mentioned volume *Re-Thinking Dionysius*: B. T. Coolman, "The Medieval Affective Dionysian Tradition," 85–102; P. J. Casarella, "Cusanus on Dionysius: The Turn to Speculative Theology," 667–678; D. Turner, "Dionysius and Some Late Medieval Mystical Theologians of Northern Europe," 121–135; L. M. Giron-Negron, "Dionysian Thought in Sixteenth-Century Spanish Mystical Theology," 163–176.

15. Rorem (*Pseudo-Dionysius: A Commentary to the Texts and an Introduction to Their Influence* [Oxford: Oxford University Press, 1993]) touches throughout on Dionysius' appropriation by the medieval Latin West, if from a perspective not at all friendly to Dionysius himself. See also J. Leclercq, "Influence and Noninfluence of Dionysius in the Western Middle Ages," in *Pseudo-Dionysius: The Complete Works*, 25–34; A. Louth, *Denys the Areopagite* (Wilton, CT: Morehouse-Barlow, 1989), 121–126; idem, "The Influence of Denys the Areopagite on Eastern and Western Spirituality in the 14th Century," *Sob/ECR* 4 (1982): 185–200.

debate over the sources and witnesses to tradition. Catholic interest at this point was focused chiefly on defending what is now recognized as indefensible: the apostolic-era provenance of these writings. With the advent of modern scholarship, particularly the past century or so, Catholic scholars—with some notable exceptions—became generally much more ambivalent, and on occasion actively hostile, toward the *Corpus Dionysiacum*.

Modern scholarship on Dionysius dates properly from two German scholars, Hugo Koch and Josef Stiglmayr. Independently of each other, both published important articles in 1895 comparing the teaching on evil in *DN* IV.17–33 with Proclus' *De malorum subsistentia* and noting the striking parallels. Their subsequent research, followed by many others to this day, has documented in exhaustive detail the lexical, literary, and notional parallels between the *CD* and the writings of late antiquity dealing with religion and philosophy.[16]

Scholarly research on Dionysius, however, has continued to be determined by a *theological* appraisal of Dionysius' relationship to Late Neoplatonism and, following from that, of his ostensible allegiance to the faith of Saint Paul and the Gospels. To borrow from

16. H. Koch, "Proklus als Quelle des Pseudo-Dionysius Areopagita in der Lehre vom Bösen," *Ph* 54 (1895): 438–454; idem, *Pseudo-Dionysius Areopagita in seinen Beziehungen zum Neuplatonismus und Mysterienwesen* (Mainz: Kirschheim, 1900); Stiglmayr, "Der Neuplatoniker Proklos als Vorlage des sog. Dionysius Areopagita in der Lehre vom Übel," *HJ* 16 (1895): 253–273, 721–748. See also the latter's equally important article, "Das Aufkommen der ps.-dionysischen Schriften und ihr Eindringen in die christliche Literatur bis zum Lateranconcil 649: Ein zweiter Beitrag zur Dionysios-Frage," *IV Jahresbericht des öffentlichen Privatgymnasiums an der Stella matutina zu Feldkirch* (Feldkirch: Sausgruber, 1895), 3–96, which places the Dionysian corpus in Syro-Palestine at the turn of the sixth century. See also C. Steel, "Proclus et Denys: de l'existence du mal," in *Denys l'Aréopagite et sa postérité*, 89–116; S. Lilla, "Pseudo-Denys l'Aréopagite, Porphyre, et Damascius," in *Denys l'Aréopagite et sa postérité*, 117–152; R. Griffith, "Neo-Platonism and Christianity: Pseudo-Dionysius and Damascius," *SP* 29 (1997): 238–243; and the series of articles by Saffrey: "Un lien objectif entre le Pseudo-Denys et Proclus," *SP* 9 (1966): 98–105; "Nouveaux liens objectifs entre le Pseudo-Denys et Proclus," *RSPT* 63 (1979): 3–16; "Le lien le plus objectif entre le Pseudo-Denys et Proclus," in idem, *Le néoplatonisme après Plotin* (Paris: Vrin, 2000), 239–252.

Tertullian: given the massive presence of "Athens" in Dionysius' thought, was there any real room—aside from purely verbal acknowledgements—for "Jerusalem"? Put another way: to what degree is Late Neoplatonism compatible with Christianity, and how successful was the Areopagite in making the match? For those of Reformed or Lutheran background, from Anders Nygren in the 1930s to Paul Rorem in the 1980s and 1990s, Dionysius is at best a failed Christian, if not a pagan wolf in Christian sheep's clothing. Nygren, indeed, sees in the reception of the corpus proof that the Christian world had already and for far too long been drinking much too deeply at Plato's well. That the Medieval West would follow the East—much later and a little disjointedly (recall my remarks above)—in receiving Dionysius with, if anything, even greater enthusiasm, served the Swedish bishop as proof for the need for Luther's rediscovery of Galatians and the Reformation's recovery of Pauline Christianity.[17] While this confessional, not to say polemical, current is nearly invisible in Rorem's recent works, it is nonetheless the case that both men, together with nearly all the Protestant scholarship of the sixty years between the two of them, understand Neoplatonist philosophy and Christian faith as mutually antithetical.[18]

Catholic and Orthodox scholars display more variety. Hans Urs von Balthasar, Louis Bouyer, and, more recently, William Riordan on the Catholic side, with Vladimir Lossky, Andrew Louth, and John Romanides for the Orthodox, applaud the *Corpus Dionysia-*

---

17. A. Nygren, *Agape and Eros* (trans. P. S. Watson; rev. ed.; Philadelphia: Westminster, 1953), esp. 576–593, where Dionysius appears as the climax of the betrayal of Christianity to Platonism initiated by the second- and third-century Alexandrians.

18. Most of Rorem's works are studiously neutral, at least in their formal presentation. He does, however, specifically mention his belonging to the Lutheran communion in his *Commentary* (239), and has expressed himself more openly on Dionysius from a Lutheran perspective in "Luther's Christocentric Critique of Pseudo-Dionysian Spirituality," noted above, and "Empathy and Evaluation in Medieval Church History and Pastoral Ministry: A Lutheran Reading of Pseudo-Dionysius," *PSB* 19 (1998): 99–115.

cum as both profound in itself and faithful to prior tradition.[19] Another Catholic, René Roques, together with the Orthodox scholars Georges Florovsky and John Meyendorff, maintain certain reservations, particularly with regard to the Dionysian hierarchies and Christology.[20] Ysabel de Andia's study "Transfiguration et théologie negative" (cited above) was followed by a monograph that is much less negative in tone regarding Dionysius' fundamental Christianity, and most commendably sensitive to his patristic background.[21] The Belgian Jesuit Jean Vanneste sees in Dionysius less the Christian than the pagan philosopher, even metaphysician.[22] For Werner Beierwaltes and Christian Schäfer, Dionysius is not, despite his indebtedness to Proclus, a disguised Neoplatonist, but rather *Christianus simulque vere Platonicus*.[23] By contrast, the scholars who produced the massive annotated Italian translation

19. H. von Balthasar, *Herrlichkeit: Eine theologische Ästhetik* (Einsiedeln: Johannes, 1964), 2:228–289; L. Bouyer, *The Spirituality of the New Testament and the Fathers* (New York: Seabury, 1982), 384–392; W. Riordan, *Divine Light: The Theology of Denys the Areopagite* (San Francisco: Ignatius, 2008), esp. 75–76, 136–151; V. N. Lossky, "La notion des 'analogies' chez Denys le pseudo-Aréopagite," *AHDL* 5 (1931): 179–209; and throughout his epochal book, *The Mystical Theology of the Eastern Church* (Cambridge: Clarke, 1968); A. Louth, *Denys the Areopagite*; and J. Romanides, "Notes on the Palamite Controversy and Related Topics," *GOTR* 6 (1960/61): 186–205; 9 (1963/64): 225–270.

20. R. Roques, *L'univers dionysien* (Paris: Aubier, 1954); G. Florovsky, *The Byzantine Ascetic and Spiritual Fathers* (vol. 10 of *The Collected Works of Father Georges Florovsky*; Vaduz: Büchervertriebsanstalt, 1987), 204–229; J. Meyendorff, *Christ in Eastern Christian Thought* (Washington, DC: Corpus, 1969), 75–84.

21. De Andia, *Henôsis: L'union à Dieu chez Denys l'Aréopagite* (Leiden: Brill, 1996). See, e.g., *Henôsis*, 303–373, for an impressive assembly of patristic parallels to Dionysius' treatment of Moses in *Mystical Theology* I.3.

22. J. Vanneste, *Le Mystère de Dieu* (Bruges: Desclée de Brouwer, 1959); idem, "Is the Mysticism of Pseudo-Dionysius Genuine?" *IPQ* 3 (1963): 286–306.

23. W. Beierwaltes, "Dionysius Areopagites—ein christlicher Proklos?," in Beierwaltes, *Platonismus im Christentum* (Frankfurt am Main: Klostermann, 2001), 44–84, at 50, 84. This is the general position of C. Schäfer (*The Philosophy of Dionysius the Areopagite: An Introduction to the Structure and the Content of the Treatise on the Divine Names* [Leiden/Boston: Brill, 2006]), who proposes "a reassessment of Dionysius' philosophy *and* the Pauline ways of thinking" (167; see also 7, 170–171).

and the accompanying studies are united in their view that Dionysius is best characterized as *non Christianus, sed vere Platonicus*.[24]

Excursus: A Word on Conspiracy Theories

This brings us to some of the more extravagant views about the *Corpus Dionysiacum*. In his article, noted above, Mazzucchi argues that the author of the CD produced his "grandioso falso storico" with such "cynical confidence" and "such shrewdness and resolute impudence" that any and all Christian elements must be regarded as the very proof of a masterful dissimulation: the seemingly Christian doctrine is no less a mask than the "Dionysius" *persona*.[25] The author of the CD was in fact none other than Damascius, who, having lost all hope of a political restoration of paganism, embarked on a grand project of reversing the episode of Acts 17 and transforming Christianity into Neoplatonism.[26] He disseminated the CD in Alexandria—the beating heart of Christian culture—in order to make sure that the "virus" would soon

---

24. The formula, paraphrasing Beierwaltes (who paraphrases Ficino) is that of Reale, in his introduction to the same volume ("Introduzione," *Dionigi Areopagita: Tutte le opere*, 21). Indeed, Reale judges that the CD lacks the very axis of Christian theology—Christ and the Cross—so that Dionysian thought and Pauline theology are utterly dissonant, even contradictory (28, 29). Similarly, for Mazzucchi ("Damascio, autore del *Corpus Dionysiacum*, e il dialogo ΠΕΡΙ ΠΟΛΙΤΙΚΗΣ ΕΠΙΣΤΗΜΗΣ," *Dionigi Areopagita: Tutte le opere*, 709–762), the CD has no place for the personal God of the Christian faith—the addressee of the Lord's Prayer (724), and substitutes the abstract "fatherhood" and "sonship" for the Father, Son, and Spirit of Christian orthodoxy (749, 753).

25. Mazzucchi, "Damascio, autore del *Corpus Dionysiacum*," 736, 724.

26. Mazzucchi, "Damascio, autore del *Corpus Dionysiacum*," 736, 743, 747. The "Damascius hypothesis" is not new. For Hathaway also (*Hierarchy*, 25–29) Damascius is a very plausible candidate, given Dionysius' "audacity" (xvii) to "mimic" Christian traditions (27) in an attempt at "refounding Christian thought and theology on the basis of Neoplatonic philosophy" (xxiv) in a time—around the edict of 529—when, "the ultimate Christian victory was inevitable" (26). Beierwaltes (*Platonismus im Christentum*, 83n. 117) rejects the hypothesis.

be "circulating in the body of the Church"; it is even possible that he gave the impulse for Sergius' Syriac translation *and* for the annotated edition by John of Scythopolis.[27] To prove this imaginative hypothesis, Mazzucchi notes that Damascius possessed the ability, the motivation, and the character to produce the forgery,[28] and points to the following wordplay, which comprises no less than the *sphragis* of our forger: "Παῦλος—Πρόκλος; Ἱερόθεος—Ἰσίδωρος; Διονύσιος—Δαμάσκιος: same initial letters, same final letters, same number of syllables, same accentuation." There is thus "no doubt" that the relation between Paul, Hierotheus, and Dionysius is the fictional analogue of the philosophical tradition of Proclus, Isidore, and Damascius.[29] Tradition has, in conclusion, adopted and cherished the sophisticated forgery designed to be "the ultimate weapon (*l'arma estrema*) in the battle against Christianity,"[30] a work designed to subvert the very essence of Christian faith and thought.

The Hungarian Orthodox scholar István Perczel argues, somewhat similarly, that the Areopagite was a cunning and deliberately deceptive heretic of the most extreme sort: a crypto-Nestorian as well as a Protoctist/Tetradite Origenist, whom Leontius of Byzantium knew very well and criticized severely (without naming him, however, since Leontius was concealing his own [Isochrist] brand of Origenism); Dionysius would have authored the anonymous *De Trinitate* (usually ascribed to Didymus), a work in which the polemic against Arianism, when properly decoded, reveals a fierce critique of Cyrillian Christology; a number of proper names that occur in the *CD* are in fact codes for real persons: e.g.,

27. Mazzucchi, "Damascio, autore del *Corpus Dionysiacum*," 759.

28. Mazzucchi, "Damascio, autore del *Corpus Dionysiacum*," 746–747.

29. Mazzucchi, "Damascio, autore del *Corpus Dionysiacum*," 748. Moreover, Dionysius' Θεολογικαὶ στοιχειώσεις is barely concealing a reference to Proclus' Θεολογικὴ στοιχείωσις (here the Proclus-Paul equivalence being impossible to maintain), while the *Divine Names* corresponds to the *One Book Concerning Divine Names* by Porphyry (751).

30. Mazzucchi, "Damascio, autore del *Corpus Dionysiacum*," 736.

"Bartholomew" is Origen, "Apollophanes" is Proclus,[31] "Simon Magus" is Jerome, "Elymas" is Theophilus of Alexandria; the text in *DN* III.2 describing, according to the scholiast, the apostles' gathering at the funeral service for Mary Theotokos, would refer to a council in which Dionysius took part, "possibly the council of Chalcedon"—and, again, "James" stands for the bishop of Jerusalem, "Peter" for the Pope of Rome, etc.; the term "theology" is a coded reference to the teachings of Origen, Eusebius, and Evagrius, while "Trinity" conceals a christological "triad" in the Origenistic-Evagrian tradition; conversely, christological affirmations are to be read as cryptic references to the Trinity.[32]

Finally, Rosemary Arthur thinks that "Dionysius is at home with the [alchemic] colour symbolism of stones and metals," and that his "insistence on the precise performance of ritual, together with a repeated stress on the necessity of excluding certain categories of persons might be indicative of involvement in some magical circle or other"; in her conclusions, Arthur appears firmly convinced of "Ps-Dionysius' knowledge of alchemy, magic and theurgy."[33]

What is one to make of such claims? It is probably best to withhold judgment until Perczel publishes his promised monograph on

---

31. Cf. Mazzucchi ("Damascio, autore del *Corpus Dionysiacum*," 750), who thinks that "Apolophanes" is in fact the Neoplatonist Asclepiades (Mazzucchi offers the same irrefutable argument: "stessa iniziale e finale . . . isosillabia, isotonia").

32. Perczel, "Le Pseudo-Denys, lecteur d'Origène," in *Origeniana Septima: Origenes in den Auseinandersetzungen des vierten Jahrhunderts* (ed. W. A. Bienert and U. Kühneweg; Leuven: Peeters, 1999), 674–710; "Une théologie de la lumière: Denys l'Aréopagite et Évagre le Pontique," *REAug* 45 (1999): 79–120; "Once Again on Dionysius the Areopagite and Leontius of Byzantium," in *Die Dionysius-Rezeption im Mittelalter: Internationales Kolloquium in Sofia vom 8. bis 11. April 1999 unter der Schirmherrschaft der Société internationale pour l'étude de la philosophie médiévale* (ed. T. Boiadjiev, G. Kapriev, A. Speer; Turnhout: Brepols, 2000), 41–85; "Pseudo-Dionysius and Palestinian Origenism," in *The Sabbaite Heritage in the Orthodox Church from the Fifth Century to the Present* (ed. J. Patrich; Leuven: Peeters, 2001), 261–282; " 'Théologiens' et 'magiciens' dans le Corpus dionysien," *Adamantius* 7 (2001): 55–75; "The Christology of Pseudo-Dionysius the Areopagite: The Fourth Letter in Its Indirect and Direct Text Traditions," *Mus* 117 (2004): 409–446.

33. Arthur, *Ps.-Dionysius as Polemicist*, 38, 186.

the hidden doctrines of the Areopagite, and until the Syriac translation of the Corpus is edited (since much of Perczel's argument is based on the divergence between the Syriac and the Greek—or the current Greek—text). The idea, however, that there exists a coherently encoded message in the CD, that "beneath the surface . . . lies a tapestry of codes and allusions whose meaning can be detected by those for whom they are intended, and by others who belong to the same group,"[34] and that *no one*, from the sixth century up until now, ever realized the fact (let alone deciphered the message!) strikes me as highly problematic: it implies that Dionysius outsmarted himself, by concealing his subversive theology so well that his attempt to convey it to anyone failed miserably.[35]

Let us return to the mainstream of scholarship. Vanneste raised in sharpest form the question of Dionysius' mysticism—or, rather, the lack of it. For Vanneste, the Areopagite is not a mystic, but a religious philosopher who is less interested in the details of a "vital experience" than in "the exact and tight articulations of [his] conceptual structure."[36] The very symmetry and rigor of his thought, a point which both Vanneste and Rorem bring out in their analyses of, in particular, the *Mystical Theology*, argue for them against this treatise as the report or fruit of any actual experience. With this assertion we come up against another question which has greatly exercised Dionysian scholarship: the coherence or, more precisely, the perceived incoherence of the corpus. On the one hand, we have the apparent advocacy of direct encounter and union with God which we find in the *MT's* account of Moses' ascent, and which Dionysius repeats in at least a dozen passages in his longest treatise, the *Divine Names*. On the other hand, in the

---

34. Arthur, *Ps.-Dionysius as Polemicist*, 191.

35. In fact, after his enthusiastic presentation of Mazzucchi's theory, Reale does note ("Introduzione," 24) that the CD's *Wirkungsgeschichte* was quite the opposite of what the supposedly anti-Christian author had intended.

36. Vanneste, "Is the Mysticism of Pseudo-Dionysius Genuine?," 290.

two treatises on the hierarchies, *CH* and *EH*, we find a repeated insistence on what Georges Florovsky has referred to as "the staircase principle,"[37] that is, that knowledge of divine things is necessarily mediated. It percolates downward from the orders of angels around the divine throne through the lower angelic ranks to our hierarchy, to our sacraments and clergy and, finally, through the latter, to the baptized laity. In terms of Dionysius' four treatises, what do the *DN* and especially the *MT* have to do with his meditations on the hierarchies of men and of angels? What is the relation, if any, between the public worship of the Christian Church, its sacraments and ordained ministers, and the direct encounter with God in "the darkness of unknowing"? And, relatedly, what is the connection between his ostensible profession of Christian faith and the obvious use he makes of the late Neoplatonists?

The answers different scholars give once again vary considerably. Vanneste and, to a lesser degree, Roques suggested a bifurcation in Dionysius' thought between the "dispensation" or "theurgy" of the hierarchies and the "theology," i.e., matters pertaining to the divinity itself, of the *DN* and *MT*.[38] Once the Areopagite's thought is thus divided, there is considerable room allowed—and, in Vanneste's case, insisted upon—for his non-Christian Neoplatonism, and so for the autonomy of the human intellect in its inherent capacity for a "natural union" with divinity that is independent of the Christian appurtenances of Scripture, sacraments, and, indeed, of Christ himself and the Holy Trinity.[39] More recently, Rorem has argued in several books and articles that, to the contrary, Dionysius' thought is altogether united and coherent; but it is this very coherence which he understands as giving the lie to any protestations of Christianity in the corpus.

---

37. Florovsky, *Byzantine Ascetical and Spiritual Fathers*, 221.

38. Roques, *L'univers dionysien*, 29–30; Vanneste, *Mystère de Dieu*, 32–35.

39. Vanneste, *Mystère de Dieu*, 182–217, perhaps esp. 195–197. Cf. also, on a "natural mysticism" in Dionysius and the late Neoplatonists, J. R. Rist, "Mysticism and Transcendence in Later Neoplatonism," *Hermes* 92 (1964): 213–225, at 219. I am happy to add, however, that Rist has subsequently withdrawn this accusation.

According to his reading, the apophatic "methodology" of the *MT* lies at the center of the corpus and properly precedes the reading of the *CH* and *EH*, an ordering of the treatises (*DN, MT, CH, EH*) which is reflected in the Rorem-Luibheid translation of the *CD* for *Classics of Western Spirituality*. Placed thus as, in Rorem's words, the "methodological prologue" to the reflections on Scripture and liturgy in the *CH* and *EH*, the *MT* acts as a kind of solvent, burning away the outward Christian trappings in order to reveal, beneath them all, the "timeless" relationship obtaining between the divine as cause and the intellect as effect.[40] Rorem therefore insists on the *CD* as purely a kind of "head trip," "fundamentally an epistemology," and is likewise obliged to assert—frequently, I might add, in defiance of the text—that Dionysius is simply "devoid of eschatology."[41]

2. The *Corpus Dionysiacum*: Christian Mysticism and Monastic Mystagogy

We do know roughly the region which Dionysius writes from, Syria-Palestine, but we cannot pinpoint it more exactly. We simply

40. The adjective, "timeless," i.e., as indicating the fundamentally "natural" and philosophical or ahistorical—as opposed to Christian—thrust of Dionysius' thought, appears often in Rorem's many works. See, e.g., *Commentary*, 120, 123, 125, 171, and 239; and on the *MT* as a "methodological prologue" to the treatises on the hierarchies, 209, and "The Place of *The Mystical Theology* in the Pseudo-Dionysian Corpus," *Dionysius* 4 (1980): 87–98. His other works on Dionysius, in chronological order, include: "Iamblichus and the Anagogical Method in Pseudo-Dionysius' Liturgical Theology," *SP* 18 (1979): 543–60; "The Place of the Mystical Theology in the Pseudo-Dionysian Corpus"; *Biblical and Liturgical Symbols within the Pseudo-Dionysian Synthesis* (Toronto: Pontifical Institute of Mediaeval Studies, 1984); "Moses as the Paradigm for the Liturgical Spirituality of Pseudo-Dionysius," *SP* 18 (1989): 275–279; "The Uplifting Spirituality of Pseudo-Dionysius," in *Christian Spirituality* (vol. 1 of *Origins to the Twelfth Century*; ed. B. McGinn, J. Meyendorff, and J. Leclercq; New York: Crossroad, 1988), 132–151; P. E. Rorem and J. C. Lamoreaux, "John of Scythopolis on Apollinarian Christology and the Pseudo-Dionysius' True Identity," *ChH* 62 (1993): 469–482, and *John of Scythopolis and the Dionysian Corpus: Annotating the Areopagite*.

41. Rorem, *Commentary*, 122.

do not know who he was, nor, barring new evidence, will we ever know. Various candidates have been advanced over the past hundred years for the authorship of the corpus, ranging from Chalcedonian writers to "Monophysites" to pagans, yet none of these proposals have ever succeeded in persuading anyone save their particular scholarly advocate.[42] These factors, the anonymity, the only very approximate location, and the near half-century between 487 and 532, make it next to impossible to agree on Dionysius' *Sitz im Leben*. Why was he writing at all? For whom? What, as we say nowadays, was his agenda? To these I would add: why was he so readily and enthusiastically received in the Christian East? I wrote earlier about the "fractured Dionysius" that we find, at the end of the Western Middle Ages, tacked on to, or assimilated into, an already well-established and secure theological *Gestalt*. What we do not find practically anywhere is much of any true sense of the Dionysian writings *as a whole*, i.e., what they were, what they were trying to say, and to whom. I will argue in the chapters to follow that the chief reason we find no conflict over them in the Christian East (or at least not until the influence of Western scholarship during the twentieth century) is that Dionysius is an Eastern Christian writer and, moreover, a monastic one: he wrote to and for monks, and monks in turn—Eastern ones, at least—have always recognized that fact. They understood him then, and in general they still understand him now, because he and they shared and still share common concerns and a common theological, liturgical, and spiritual *Gestalt*.[43]

---

42. For a listing of the various attempts to identify Dionysius with one or another figure in pagan or Christian antiquity, see R. Hathaway, *Hierarchy and the Definition of Order in the Letters of Pseudo-Dionysius: A Study in the Form and Meaning of the Pseudo-Dionysian Writings* (The Hague: Nijhoff, 1970), 31–35.

43. This is a point not generally appreciated in the scholarly literature. There is only one article, to my knowledge, devoted to Dionysius' concept of the monk: Roques, "Éléments pour une théologie de l'état monastique chez Denys l'Aréopagite," in *Théologie de la vie monastique: Études sur la tradition patristique* (ed. G. Lemaître; Paris: Aubier, 1961), 283–314. For all its general excellence, Roques' article is still primarily concerned to relate Dionysius' treatment of the monk's "singleness" to Neoplatonic themes, and in consequence it misses entirely important echoes of prior Christian traditions. I

I maintain that there is no need for question marks over Diony-sius' Christianity and mysticism. Perhaps it is worth considering one of the few reports of direct experience which we do find in this mysterious author, and where we may also be fairly certain that he is not writing in order to support his pseudonym. Here he is speaking of his own baptism:

> It was this sacrament which first gave me [the power] to see, and, by means of its ruling light, to be led up in light to the vision of the other sacred things.[44]

Elsewhere in the same treatise, the *Ecclesiastical Hierarchy*, he re-turns to this idea on at least two other occasions. In chapter 2 he speaks of baptism supplying a spiritual capacity for the sight or vision of the divine light informing Christian worship.[45] In chapter 3, while discussing the formation of catechumens in the "womb" of the Church's "Liturgy of the Word," he notes that, because they are not yet fully formed, they have not yet received "the organs" capable of spiritual sight which are given in baptism.[46] The at least implicit doctrine of the "spiritual senses" here, associated with and indeed given by the Christian sacrament, recalls Origen of Alexandria three hundred years before, as well as much of the ascetic literature in the intervening centuries, e.g., in Evagrius of Pontus (+399) and in the late fourth-century *Macarian Homi-lies*. I will return to the latter in a further chapter, but for now I would like to stress, first, that Dionysius, at least in the *EH*, places repeated emphasis on the "divine birth" of baptism, and thus, second, appears to establish the context of whatever "vision" or "experience" of God he may ultimately espouse firmly within the liturgical and sacramental life of his local church.

---

must confess that I am nearly unique in drawing attention to the latter, and quite unique in stressing it as I do.

44. *EH* III.1, 425AB (80:1–4).

45. *EH* II.3.3, 400AB (74:15–75:9).

46. *EH* III.3.6, 432D–433A (85:11–21): literally, "the [organs] capable of receiving light" (τὰ δεκτικά).

The chapters to follow seek to present Dionysius' thought as a coherent vision centered upon the Incarnation. I quite agree with Rorem's assertion of the *CD*'s unity, but decidedly not with his understanding of it. First of all, there are the quite physical facts that (a) in *none* of the ancient manuscripts we possess does the *MT* precede the treatises on the hierarchies, and (b) that in *all* of the Greek manuscripts the ordering is just as we find it in Migne: the *CH*, *EH*, *DN*, *MT*, and finally the ten *Epistles*. Second, and relatedly, there is the now established fact that the *CD* comes down to us in this order, accompanied by the *Scholia* of John of Scythopolis, from within a generation or two, and perhaps even less, of the corpus' actual composition.[47] Third, as I have noted above, Dionysius himself grounds his very capacity for the vision of "sacred things," by which I take him to mean both the physical sight (not allowed to catechumens) of the sacraments and the spiritual perception of the Presence which informs them, in the grace he received at the "divine birth" of baptism. This in itself would certainly seem to place the *EH* before the *DN* and *MT*, and therefore, fourth, it seems to me clear that we are to read the treatises, including the epistles, in precisely the order in which they have been handed down to us, beginning with the *CH* and ending, not with the *MT*, but with the tenth *Epistle*. Fifth, I maintain that doing so will reveal the *CD* as a deliberately progressive "mystagogy," that is, as at once the explication of and the entry into the one and unique mystery, Christ.

While arguing that the *EH* constitutes the core and pivot of the Dionysian system, I will also deal with those questions that scholars have raised chiefly with regard to the other treatises, especially the *DN* and *MT*. Such is the unity of Dionysius' thought that any one aspect necessarily includes the rest, and certainly the points bearing on monism, mysticism, the intelligibles (νοητά), and generally the whole "Christian versus Platonist" debate are not irrelevant either to the hierarchies or to the question of their

---

47. See B. R. Suchla, *Eine Redaktion des griechischen Corpus Dionysiacum*; and on the proximity of John of Scythopolis' *scholia* to the first appearances of the *CD*, Rorem and Lamoreaux, *John of Scythopolis and the Dionysian Corpus*, 22–39.

patristic antecedents. I will thus limit my remarks to the most prominent landmarks, as it were, of the Dionysian vision rather than trying to draw a comprehensive and detailed map of his theology. Given the volume of literature already devoted to the Neoplatonism of the *CD*, I hope I can be excused for not following the same path. I do, however, refer to the Neoplatonists and to relevant studies when touching on the central issues: Dionysius' use and transformation of the μονή-πρόοδος-ἐπιστροφή ("abiding-procession-return") cycle and the related theme of microcosm/macrocosm, monism, the intelligibles (νοητά), and theurgy.

The "Cook's Tour" of the Dionysian corpus that I propose in the first chapter contains the essential articulation of my thesis, which will be further developed in the subsequent chapters. The second chapter opens with a review of the *MT* and *DN*, and covers the Dionysian apophaticism, the Trinity, and the essence/energies distinction underlying the treatment of the divine names. In the third chapter I move to consider the reason-endowed creatures, angels and humans, as each a reflection or icon of the divine energies and the capacity of each for union with God. With the fourth and fifth chapters I arrive at, first, a discussion of "hierarchy" in general as the reflection on a given plane of being (intelligible: the *CH*, and the sensible: the *EH*) of the activity of God *ad extra* and, secondly, to a focus on the ecclesiastical hierarchy as the locus of the human encounter with God through his Incarnation in Christ. Chapter 5 will endeavor to draw the connection or parallel between the human soul and the structures of grace embodied in the Church as, truly, the "body" of Christ, a single divine-human organism.

Chapters 2, 3, and 4 are thus at once moving outward—from the core of the hidden divinity to the energies, to the reason-endowed beings, and finally to the world as intended by God, hierarchy—and, at the same time, inward: from God the unutterably distant, to the "extension" of the divine energies, to the world, to humans, and finally to the core of the human soul, the point of contact between humanity and God. In Chapter 5 I discuss the simultaneous presence of all the circles in our world and ourselves. Moreover, I submit that this "centering" is a function of the Incarnation: Jesus as God in the flesh is at once the unfathomable mystery of the divine darkness at the infinite center and the power both embracing and irradiating the walls of the world about us, his flesh, the Church. This in turn, I argue, supports the contention that the Church as a "body," a single whole, both images forth and enables the individual soul in achieving its divinely intended vocation: to reflect, so far as possible, the presence and activity of God, to become a mirror through participation of the divine and aboriginal light. The latter I view as essential to Dionysius' transformation of both the pagan images of macro-microcosm and the Origenist-Evagrian vision of the whole visible cosmos as the (temporary) vehicle of salvation which at once reveals the νοῦς -demiurge, Christ, and mirrors the structures of the fallen soul.

The sixth and final chapter will discuss those elements in the Christian patristic tradition that were most important in the elaboration of the *CD*. Having offered a broader treatment in my earlier book—the New Testament, pre-Nicene writers, the Cappadocians, the mystagogies of Cyril of Jerusalem, Theodore of Mopsuestia, and John Chrysostom, and finally the Syrian writers of the fourth and fifth centuries—I will here confine my discussion to the Egyptian desert tradition and Evagrius Ponticus, on the one hand, and the Syrian ascetic tradition and the Macarian Homilist, on the other.

In the concluding remarks I argue that the *CD* is first of all a coherent and unified structure, and secondly that, as such, it evidences both a striking originality and a remarkable fidelity, the latter not applying primarily to the pagans, from whom Dionysius did indeed borrow, but to the already long-established currents in Greek Christian speculation—and meditation—on the mystery of God in Christ from which we insist the Areopagite took first of all. His originality derives from a re-combination of those elements which, set in the frame of the Antiochene mystagogy and ascetic (especially Syrian-inspired) appropriation, effected a synthesis whose power continues to influence—indeed, to shape—the Orthodox East to this day.

Chapter 1

The Christian
Mysticism of
Dionysius Areopagita

1. *Epistle* X, "To the Apostle John at Patmos," as an Introduction to the *Corpus Dionysiacum*: A Response to Apocalyptic Literature and Visionary Practices Directed to a Monastic Audience

Before I take up the *Celestial Hierarchy* and embark on the brief "Cook's Tour" of the *Corpus* which I propose for this first chapter, I would like first to begin at the end of *CD*: the brief *Epistle* addressed to none other than Saint John the Divine, the author—for Dionysius, at least—of both the Fourth Gospel and, as the address of the epistle indicates ("To John at Patmos"), of the Apocalypse. I do so because I believe that, read correctly, this little piece reveals a great deal about Dionysius' purposes in writing, at once something of his context and of those who served as both his addressees and his targets.

It is surely curious that a writer "devoid of eschatology" should address his concluding remarks to the author of the one and only full-blooded apocalypse to find its way into the NT canon, and do so, moreover, against the background of a Syrian Church which did not accept this book as canonical until very late indeed. Neither is this the first time Dionysius has mentioned the author of the

Apocalypse. In the course of his description of the "Liturgy of the Word" in *EH* 3, he concludes his list of the books of Scripture read in the Church with a reference to "the hidden and mystical vision of that inspired man who was the most beloved of the disciples," and then to "his transcendent theology concerning Jesus," which I take to be references, respectively, to the Apocalypse and to the Fourth Gospel.[1] More remarkably still, he asserts at the beginning of *Epistle* X that John is especially dear to him—"more so than for the many," he says—and then again, toward the end, that he is "at present engaged in remembering and renewing the truth of your theology."[2] What, it may fairly be asked, does this writer, whom many see as the most rarified and abstract in all of patristic literature, see in the wild and profuse imagery of the Apocalypse? The attractiveness of the high Christology of the Fourth Gospel, together with the latter's stress on the divine indwelling, is easily comprehensible, but the Apocalypse—with its candlesticks and thrones and seals and cups and descending cubical city fifteen hundred miles on a side decorated with precious stones, furnished with flora (the "trees of life"), fauna (the Lamb and "the four living creatures" of the throne), and waterworks (the "river of life")—what can this strange book mean to the advocate *par excellence* of negative theology, of the denial of even the most exalted ideas to the hidden divinity, let alone the lushly tangible iconography of the Seer of Patmos?

The answer, I think, lies in three elements, two of which are contained or at least suggested in the text itself of the epistle, while the third, though not stated, is, I believe, assumed. The first comes early in the epistle: "Truly," Dionysius writes, "visible things (τὰ ὁρατὰ) are the manifest images [or icons] of the invisible." This is an allusion to Rom 1:20, which Dionysius has referred to twice before, once in *DN* IV with reference to "light" as a worthy image of God, and once in *Epistle* IX with reference to "fire" in the same context.[3] Light and fire are, indeed, constantly present throughout

---

1. *EH* III.3.4, 429D (83:21–23).

2. *Ep. X*, 1117A and 1120A (208:4–5 and 209:12).

3. *Ep. X*, 1117B (208:9–10); cf. *DN* IV.4, 700C (149:7–8); and *Ep.* IX.2, 1108B (199:15–200:1).

the *CD*. Much more than the famous "darkness"—about which more anon—it is fire and especially light which are associated throughout the corpus with the *visio dei*.

This is so in turn, I think, because of that unspoken element I just mentioned. The Apocalypse of John, as with the majority of apocalypses characteristic of the Second Temple and early Christian eras, turns around a vision of the divine throne and the heavenly court, imagery which itself derives from the post- and even pre-exilic cultus of the Jerusalem Temple.[4] John's cubical New Jerusalem, for example, finds its ancestry in the eschatological Jerusalem of Ezekiel 40–48, while the latter in its turn takes from the cubical dimensions of the inner sanctuary of Solomon's temple (cf. 1 Kgs 7). It is at least arguable that John himself is aware of this—for want of a better word—liturgical aspect. He has his vision, after all, "on the Lord's day," the day of the Eucharist, and may have understood his portrait of the reconciliation and ultimate identity between the heavenly throne and the world to come as already anticipated in the worship of the local church. The brilliant and fiery Glory of God, the *kevod YHWH* of the Hebrew and δόξα τοῦ κυρίου of the Greek, surrounded by the dark cloud, is the center of the great theophany on Sinai, and likewise at the literal heart of the Temple, as in 1 Kings 8; Isaiah 6; Ezekiel 1; 9–11; 43, and in many of the psalms.[5] It is also therefore the subject of

4. See, for example, C. Rowland, "The Visions of God in Apocalyptic Literature," *JSJ* 10 (1979): 137–54; and at greater length, idem, *The Open Heaven: A Study of Apocalyptic in Judaism and Early Christianity* (New York: Crossroad, 1982), esp. 78–93 and 193–248; M. Himmelfarb, *Ascent to Heaven in Jewish and Christian Apocalypses* (New York: Oxford University Press, 1993), esp. 9–46; R. Elior, *The Three Temples: On the Emergence of Jewish Mysticism in Late Antiquity* (Oxford: Littman Library of Jewish Civilization, 2005). On the "Glory of God" in the cult tradition of, particularly, the "Priestly" strain of the Pentateuch, see T. D. N. Mettinger, *The Dethronement of Sabaoth: Studies in the Shem and Kabod Theologies* (Lund: CWK Gleerup, 1982), esp. 80–123; J. P. Fossum, "Glory," in *Dictionary of Deities and Demons in the Bible* (ed. K. van der Toorn, B. Becking, and P. W. van der Horst; 2d rev. ed.; Leiden: Brill, 1999), 348–352.

5. On the importance of the book of Ezekiel for later apocalyptic visions of God and the heavenly temple, see again Himmelfarb, *Ascent to Heaven*, 9–28, and Elior, *Three Temples*, together with J. D. Levenson, specifically on Ezekiel

the throne visions of Daniel 7, of 1 and 2 *Enoch*, of Revelation 4–5 and 21–22, and, just for example, of the early Christian apocalypse, *The Ascension of Isaiah*.[6] I believe that it is no accident that the biblical texts Dionysius discusses throughout his corpus are predominantly, not to say overwhelmingly, associated with these throne visions and related theophanies. This leads me to what I take him to mean when he says he is "carrying on" John's work. He understands himself, in sum, to be linking the liturgical and Glory imagery of the Apocalypse to the interiority of the Fourth Gospel. Put another way, and to anticipate my argument later on in this essay, for Dionysius the Glory of God, the heavenly fire, and especially the divine light, is present in Christ, who in turn appears on the altar of the consecrated eucharistic elements and in the heart—or intellect—of the baptized Christian.

If we allow Dionysius this background and purpose, and I will be providing further evidence for them along the way, then we must ask why he believes it necessary to "renew" the Apostle's teaching. I think that we have an important clue in my third element, a passage which comes from close to the middle of *Epistle* X:

40–48 in *Theology of the Program of Restoration of Ezekiel 40–48* (Missoula, MT: Scholars, 1976); and more broadly on the Temple, in "The Jerusalem Temple in Devotional and Visionary Experience," in *Jewish Spirituality* (vol. 1 of *From the Bible to the Middle Ages*; ed. A. Green; New York: Crossroad, 1988), 32–62. For a reading of the book of Revelation as fundamentally liturgical, see P. Prigent, *Apocalypse et liturgie* (Neuchâtel: Delachaux et Niestlé, 1964); J. Fekkes III, *Isaiah and the Prophetic Traditions in the Book of Revelation: Visionary Antecedents and Their Development* (Sheffield: JSOT Press, 1994), esp. 42, with numerous references. On the "Glory" and *visio dei* in the Psalms, see M. S. Smith, "Seeing God in the Psalms: The Background to the Beatific Vision in the Bible," *CBQ* 50 (1988): 171–183; and, more broadly, including Isaiah 6, Ezekiel 1, and the theophanies of Exodus: J. M. Vincent, "Aspekte der Begegnung mit Gott im alten Testament: Die Erfahrung der göttlichen Gegenwart im Schauen Gottes," *RB* 103 (1996): 5–39.

6. On the *Ascension of Isaiah*, see A. Acerbi, *L'Ascensione di Isaia: Cristologia e profetismo in Siria nei primi decenni del II secolo* (Milan: Vita e pensiero, 1989), esp. 50–59 and 138–148. For a translation of the text, see J. H. Charlesworth, ed., *The Old Testament Pseudepigrapha* (Garden City, NY: Doubleday, 1985), 2:164–76.

We also see others who are, here and now, already (ἤδη) with God, since they are lovers of truth and withdraw (ἀναχωροῦσι) from the passion for material things. They depart with complete freedom from every evil, and with divine love (ἔρως) for every good thing, they love (ἀγαπῶσι) peace and holiness. They abandon this present life by living in a way (ἐμπολιτευμένοι) which is of the [life] to come, like angels in the midst of [other] men, with total dispassion (ἀπάθεια), with invocation of the divine name, and with sanctity (ἁγιότητι) and everything else that is good.[7]

Who are these angels among men? Two key terms, withdrawal (ἀναχωρέω) and abandonment (ἀποχή), should immediately alert us to the fact that Dionysius is talking about monks. Similarly, the verb, πολιτεύομαι, here meaning "to live a [disciplined] way of life," together with the nouns, ἀπάθεια or dispassion, ἔρως, and the latter's effective equation with ἀγάπη, both meaning love here, place this passage—as well as other, lengthier ones in the *CD*—in a long prior line of patristic thought to do with asceticism and mysticism, one which runs from Clement and Origen in Alexandria through Gregory of Nyssa in Cappadocia to the great Desert Father and mystic, Evagrius of Pontus. The term sanctity, ἁγιότης, I would take to be Dionysius' Greek rendering of the Syriac word, *qaddishuta*, a *terminus technicus* in the Syrian Church for consecrated celibacy.[8] Finally, the constant "invocation of the divine name" is tantalyzingly reminiscent of later

---

7. *Ep.* X, 1117B (208:12–209:4).

8. On early Syriac technical terms for consecrated celibacy, including *qaddishuta*, see S. Griffith, "Asceticism in the Church of Syria: The Hermeneutics of Early Syrian Monasticism," in *Asceticism* (ed. V. L. Wimbush and R. Valantasis; New York: Oxford University Press, 1995), 220–245. For *qaddishuta* in relation to the asceticism of Qumran and the latter's possible relevance for early Christian ascetical terminology in Syriac, see A. Guillaumont, "À propos du célibat des Esséniens," in idem, *Aux origines du monachisme chrétien* (Bégrolles en Mauges: Abbaye de Bellefontaine, 1979), 13–23. On monasticism as "the angelic life," see P. Suso Frank, *Angelikos Bios: Begriffsanalytische und begriffsgeschichtliche Untersuchung zum "engelgleichen Leben" im frühen Mönchtum* (Münster: Aschendorff, 1964). The latter, however, seems quite without any awareness of the fact that joining the angelic priesthood was already extant

Byzantine hesychasm, or at least of the preoccupation with 1 Thess 5:17, "pray unceasingly," which we find throughout early monastic literature.[9]

It is the connection with Syria, in particular with Syrian Christian asceticism, which I believe is virtually the royal key to unlocking the mystery which the *CD* has posed for its modern interpreters. One reason, to be sure, that no one has noticed this is that no one to date has thought to look there, with a few partial exceptions.[10] The first puzzle this connection explains is why Dionysius, given his first-century pseudonym, should speak of "monks" at all, and even make the seemingly ludicrous claim that the title itself, μοναχός, had originally been given them by the Apostles.[11] The anachronism fades, however, when we take into account a NT apocryphon which is also a document of Syrian provenance, the second-century *Gospel of Thomas*, which we know continued to be read by Syrian monks throughout the fourth

in Jewish apocalyptic literature. See thus, again, M. Himmelfarb, *Ascent to Heaven*, 29–46; Elior, *Three Temples*, 58, 93, 99, 171.

9. See D. Burton-Christie, *The Word in the Desert: Scripture and the Quest for Holiness in Early Christian Monasticism* (New York: Oxford University Press, 1993), esp. 107–33 for constant "rumination" and "repetition" of selected Scriptures; and specifically on the "invocation of the name [of Jesus]" in early monasticism, A. Guillaumont, "Une inscription Copte sur la prière de Jésus," *OCP* 8 (1977): 187–203; repr. in *Aux origines du monachisme chrétien*, 310–25. Repetition of the divine name(s) as means to ascent to heaven appears as early as apocalyptic literature, e.g., *Apocalypse of Abraham*, 17–18, on which see I. Gruenwald, *Apocalyptic and Merkabah Mysticism* (Leiden: Brill, 1980), 29–72, esp. 56–57.

10. On the Syrian connection, see most notably W. Strothmann, *Das Sakrament der Myron-Weihe in der Schrift de ecclesiastica hierarchia des Pseudo-Dionysios in syrischen Übersetzungen und Kommentaren* (Wiesbaden: Harrassowitz, 1978). See also A. Louth, *Denys the Areopagite*, 63–64, 69–70, and 78–98; Golitzin, *Et introibo*, 354–392.

11. *EH* VI.1.3, 532D–33A (116:15–16): "Whence our divine leaders reckoned them worthy of sacred names, some calling them 'servitors' [or "ministers," θεραπευταί], and others 'monks' [μοναχοὶ] . . ." Note that John of Scythopolis' *Scholia* pick up on the use of the word, θεραπευταί, for Jewish ascetics in Philo's *De vita contemplativa* (see PG IV, 528A–29B), but that John is conspicuously silent about trying to supply first-century credentials for μοναχός, apparently unaware of the Syrian traditions discussed below.

century. In *Thomas*, it is the Lord Jesus no less who speaks of "solitaries," μοναχοῖ, or, in the possible Syriac original, of *ihidaye* (from the Syriac *had*, "one").[12] Later on in the fourth century, in the *Demonstrations* of Aphrahat of Persia and the *Hymns* of Ephrem Syrus, we meet bands of these *ihidaye*, the "sons of the covenant" (*b'nai qeiama*), whose relation to the local church precisely matches the Dionysian sketch of the monastic order presented in *EH* VI and *Ep*. VIII.[13] These Syrian ascetics are neither grouped in separate communities, in the style of Egypt's Pachomius, nor living away from the towns like the semi-anchorites of Scete or the hermits of Anthony's type. Both Aphrahat's *ihidaye* and Dionysius' monks live in the larger community, take part in and are assigned a special place at the liturgical assembly of the local church, receive their tonsure from the ordained clergy (unknown in Greek monastic literature prior to Dionysius) in a way that is connected with their baptism, and—in Dionysius' case most emphatically—are subject to the direction of the local bishop.[14]

12. "Jesus said, 'Many are standing at the door, but it is the solitary [μοναχός] who will enter the bridal chamber,'" *Gospel of Thomas*, 75 in *The Nag Hammadi Library* (ed. J. M. Robinson; trans. T. O. Lambdin; rev. ed.; San Francisco: Harper & Row, 1988), 134 (see also *logia* 16 and 49). On the presence of *Thomas* in two fourth-century Syrian ascetical authors, see A. Baker, "The Gospel of Thomas and the Syriac *Liber Graduum*," *NTS* 12 (1965): 49–55; idem, "Pseudo-Macarius and the Gospel of Thomas," *VigChr* 18 (1964): 214–225; and G. Quispel, "The Syrian Thomas and the Syrian Macarius," *VigChr* 18 (1964): 226–235. On the relation, perhaps, of origin between the Syriac word, *ihidaya*, and the Greek term, μοναχός, see esp. F.-E. Morard, "Monachos, Moine: Histoire du terme grecque jusqu'au IVe siècle," *ZPhTh* 20 (1973): 332–411, at 362–377. Note also her references to Dionysius in 335–356 and 405–406, and cf. M. Harl, "À propos du *Logia* de Jésus: le sens du mot μοναχός," *REG* 73 (1960): 464–74 (here 473–474); and A. Guillaumont, "Monachisme et éthique judéo-chrétienne," in *Aux origines du monachisme*, 47–66 (here 58), who also relate this archaic use of the term, "monk," in the *Gospel of Thomas* specifically to Dionysius.

13. See Golitzin, *Et introibo*, 354–359.

14. On Dionysius as the first to assign monastic tonsure to priestly activity, thus placing it under the authority of the hierarchy, see K. Holl, *Enthusiasmus und Bussgewalt beim Griechischen Mönchtum: Eine Studie zum Symeon dem Neuen Theologen* (Leipzig: Hinrichs, 1898), 205–207. This is correct, so far as I know,

There is no question about the emphatic quality of Dionysius'
insistence on this subordination. He devotes time to it in his description of the monks in *EH* VI and, at much greater length, in
his eighth epistle.[15] The addressee of the latter is a certain monk
Demophilus, whose name I take to mean something like "beloved by the mob." Demophilus has transgressed the hierarchical order, τάξις, by breaking up the confession of a great sinner.
He has beaten the sinner up and chased the confessing priest
out of the sanctuary, where he now stands guard over the "holy
things," presumably the reserved sacrament, in order to prevent
their profanation a second time.[16] Dionysius uses this scenario
to expand at length on the virtues of meekness (πραότης), mercy,
and love, which in a very traditional way (reminiscent, in fact,
of Evagrius) he understands as the prerequisites for the *visio dei*.
Moses, David, and Christ himself are the exemplars, over against
Demophilus' appeal to Elijah.[17] He goes on, secondly, to the ne-

---

with respect to *Greek* Christian literature, but simply wrong if applied to early
Christian writers in Syriac. On the very ancient linkage in Syriac-speaking
Christianity between ascetical and baptismal vows, and thus for dedication to
sacred "singleness" (*ihidayuta*) as occurring in a decidedly ecclesiastical and
liturgical context, see R. Murray, "An Exhortation to Candidates for Ascetical
Vows at Baptism in the Ancient Syrian Church," *NTS* 21 (1974): 59–80, perhaps
esp. 77–80, and note thus Dionysius' explicit parallelism between Baptism
and monastic tonsure in *EH* VI.3.4, 536B (118:12–15).

15. *EH* VI.3.1, 533C (117:19–22); and esp. *Ep.* VIII in its entirety, 1084B–
1100D (171–192). See also Roques, "Théologie de l'état monastique," esp.
297–304, on relations between monks and clergy.

16. *Ep.* VIII.1, 1088BC (175:4–13).

17. *Ep.* VIII.1, 1084B-88B (171:3–175:4); and 5–6, 1096C–1100C (186:8–192).
On the importance of meekness (πραότης), mercy (ἔλεος), and love (ἀγάπη)
in Evagrius Ponticus (+399), perhaps the most important architect of Eastern Christian spiritual theory, see G. Bunge, *Geistliche Vaterschaft: Christliche
Gnosis bei Evagrios Pontikos* (Regensburg: Friedrich Pustet, 1988), 42–44, and
idem, "Palladiana II: La version copte de l'*Histoire Lausiaque*," *StMon* 33
(1991): 117–118. The latter is an account of a heavenly ascent Evagrius experiences, and the counsel he receives from a divine voice quite matches the
advice Bishop Carpus gets from Christ in the story of the bishop's throne
vision which concludes Dionysius' epistle, 1100A–C (190:5–192): God wants
"meekness and mercy."

cessity of maintaining the order (τάξις) given by God. Monks have no authority to enter the altar area, which is here apparently separated off from the nave by a wall and curtain, and even less either to lay hands on the "holy things" or to correct the ordained clergy, even if the latter are in the wrong. This transgression of hierarchy, and thereby of the three great virtues just cited, has come about because Demophilus' own, *inner* hierarchy is itself out of alignment. The latter is instead "to give due place *within himself* to reason, anger, and to desire." This, Dionysius continues, is "the proper inner order (τάξις)" without which no one can hope to rule himself, let alone others.[18]

Here we arrive at a second and even a third key to the *CD*. The second is the coordination between inner and outer. Implied here, as will become clear when I turn to the opening of the *CH*, is the thought that the visible *pattern* (a term to which I will return) of Church order—by which Dionysius means primarily the Church as we see it at worship, with its sacraments and its ordered sequence of bishops, priests, deacons, monks, laity, and catechumens, stretching from the inner sanctuary to the church porch—is a divinely given image or icon of the order which is properly to obtain within the soul. The third key lies in Demophilus' very assumption of authority, together with the suggestion of popular approval which his name seems to imply. Now, examples of monastic zealotry are legion in the Christian East, both then and now, but I think we must look a little deeper. What was the source for the authority which this and other monastic zealots

---

18. See *Ep.* VIII.1, 1088C (176:3) on Demophilus overturning the "divinely-given τάξις" of the Church's hierarchy; and 3, 1093A (186:7–8) for his having wronged his own, inner τάξις. On τάξις in prior monastic literature as employed for the inner-ordering of the soul, see G. Gould, *The Desert Fathers on Monastic Community* (Oxford: Clarendon, 1993), 151–152. Behind both uses of the word here in Dionysius, I would see the notion of the divine "pattern" of worship which I discuss below. Note the use of OT tabernacle and temple examples—Uzziah (2 Chr 26), the entry of the high priest behind the veil (Lev 16:3-4, Exod 30:10, etc.)—in 1089 B.C. (178:1–179:10). Interestingly, in his *Paradise Hymns*, Ephrem Syrus uses much the same imagery for Adam's transgression; see *Hymns on Paradise* (trans. S. Brock; Crestwood, NY: St Vladimir's Seminary Press, 1990), 93–96 (for *Hymn* 3:7–16).

claimed? What did they think gave them the mandate to overrule
ordained clergy?

This claim to authority derived from the popular belief, universal throughout the East and especially concentrated in Syria,
that the monks were the successors of the seers and prophets of
old.[19] More than the local priest, more even than the bishop, who
may have been perceived fairly often (and with occasional justice)
as less a holy man than a politician, it was the monk who was
the Spirit-bearer, the link in his own person between this world
and the one to come. In Syria, particularly, this was a very old
tradition. Quite possibly, it lies behind the early second-century
Christian apocalypse I cited above, *The Ascension of Isaiah*.[20] Likewise, as recent scholarship has sought to demonstrate, the μοναχοῖ
in the *Gospel of Thomas* may have represented precisely the same
ascetic and visionary currents as run throughout the assorted
Apocryphal Acts of the Apostles which were popular reading
in the East (and West) in the Early Church, and which retained
their popularity well into the fourth and fifth centuries, and even
beyond.[21] The *Acts of Judas Thomas* continued to be regular fare
in the Syrian Church into early medieval times. It is also in the
late fourth century that we find, orginating once again in Syria,
a monastic movement which, at least according to its accusers,
preached indifference or contempt for the sacraments, and more
so for the leadership of the bishops, while holding that the sole
access to God was through constant prayer—hence the move-

19. See P. Escalon, *Monachisme et église, le monachisme syrien du IVe au VIe
siècle: un monachisme charismatique* (Paris: Beauchesne, 1999), esp. 71–123, and,
on tensions with the hierarchy, 267–394.

20. See Acerbi, *L'Ascensione di Isaia*, 217–253 and 289–290.

21. On the *Gospel of Thomas* and *Acts of Thomas* in the *Macarian Homilies*, see
G. Quispel, *Makarius, das Thomasevangelium, und das Lied von der Perle* (Leiden:
Brill, 1967), esp. 8–13, 37–64, and 114–118; on the possible setting of the *Gospel
of Thomas* in Jewish mystical traditions of ascent and vision, see A. DeConick,
Seek to See Him: Ascent and Vision Mysticism in the Gospel of Thomas (Leiden:
Brill, 1996), esp. 43–125; and for the same in the *Acts of John*, see J. Fossum,
"Partes Posteriori Dei: The Transfiguration of Jesus in the *Acts of John*," in *The
Image of the Invisible God: Essays on the Influence of Jewish Mysticism on Early
Christology* (ed. J. Fossum; Freiburg: Universitätsverl, 1995), 95–108.

ment's name, "Messalianism," from the Syriac, *tslo'*, to pray.[22] Lastly, at least for our purposes, these monks claimed the possibility of a vision of the Trinity which they said was accessible to their physical eyes.[23] While the movement was condemned in a series of regional episcopal councils beginning in Antioch in the 390s and culminating in the Ecumenical Council of Ephesus in 431, it seems to have continued to exist in the land of its origins, Syria, well into the sixth century, which is to say, into the era of the *CD* itself.[24]

I hope it is clear by now why I have taken so much time over one brief epistle. Dionysius had a problem: he was confronted, as I read him, by a tradition of ancient provenance which, in its extreme form, threatened the Church of the sacraments and bishops. Here, I think, is one very good reason, perhaps even the reason, for his adoption of a sub-apostolic pseudonym.[25] Another reason, surely, lies in his appeal to philosophical culture in the face of ascetics and their supporters who had no use, in Ephrem Syrus' words, for "the poison of the Greeks." Dionysius thus sets out to write his very own New Testament pseudepigraphon, precisely in reply to other pseudepigrapha and apocrypha such as those mentioned above.[26] He is "fighting fire with fire," and his choice

22. On the Messalians, see esp. C. Stewart, *Working the Earth of the Heart: The Messalian Controversy in History, Texts, and Language to A.D. 431* (Oxford: Clarendon, 1991); K. Fitschen, *Messalianismus und Antimessalianismus: Ein Beispiel ostkirchlicher Ketzergeschichte* (Göttingen: Vandenhoeck & Ruprecht, 1998).

23. For citation of the texts containing these claims, and commentary on them, see Fitschen, *Messalianismus*, 202–205 and 228–229.

24. On the durability of the sect in Syria, see again Fitschen, *Messalianismus*, 286–310.

25. Cf. Arthur, *Ps.-Dionysius as Polemicist*, 16: "Bar Sudhaili was a danger to the stability of the Church; if he would not accept the authority of his own bishops, perhaps he would accept the authority of St Paul?"

26. It is noteworthy that Sergius of Reshaina states, in his introduction to the Syriac translation of the *CD*, that the sacred books of the Areopagite set forth the very ἄρρητα ῥήματα (2 Cor 12:4) that Paul received when, in the course of his ascension into the third heaven, he was led into the divine *didaskaleion* (*bayt yulpānā*) of the region of Paradise: heavenly mysteries, words not lawful for a man to utter, which, however, are now to be spoken of in a divine manner

of pseudonym fits neatly into his intentions: as the philosopher-disciple of Saint Paul, he at once invokes the authority of the Apostle and sustains the legitimacy of deploying the wisdom of the pagans. To use Schäfer's very apt formulation, the pseudonym "is to be taken as the programmatic key for the understanding of his writings. . . . In the Corpus of his writings, 'Dionysius the Aareopagite' is not so much the subject that produced them, but one of the topical subjects the writings treat of."[27]

Dionysius deliberately takes over the esoteric language and air of an adept communicating privileged data to a chosen disciple, "Timothy" (intended to recall the addressee of the Pastoral Epistles), in order to "de-gauss," as it were, the apparatus and appeal of the apocryphal and esoteric works circulating among Christian monks of the area. His "secrecy" is in fact a pose: he intends his work to be read by many.[28] It is public, and the esoterica he espouses in, for example, the *DN* turn out in sum to be the "names" of Christian or, more precisely, of scriptural theology. This is the point of his insistence in *DN* I on Scripture as the exclusive source of the names he will discuss and, in *EH* I, on Scripture as the οὐσία of "our hierarchy." It is quite reminiscent of Paul's "Nothing beyond what is written!" (1 Cor 4:6). Thus, we have the pseudonymic effect that he wishes to obtain: the

---

(Sherwood, "Mimro de Serge de Resayna," CXVI [146/147–148/149]). This would make the *CD* an equivalent of the *Apocalypse of Paul*. It is amazing (and unfortunately characteristic of much of Dionysian scholarship) that Hathaway can read this passage and completely miss the Pauline reference: for him, "everything that one is not permitted to say, and that which a man is prohibited from speaking about" would refer to "philosophy, and especially the writings of Proclus and Damascius" (Hathaway, *Hierarchy*, 25).

27. Schäfer, *Philosophy of Dionysius*, 164, 170. Schäfer's argument, of course, is quite different from mine—he thinks that the *CD* intended to show that "a Christian adaptation and re-interpretation of pagan lore (and of Greek philosophy in particular) was the necessary and mandatory next step" for pagan Neoplatonism, while I think the intended audience to have been radical Christian ascetics.

28. *Pace* Perczel, who believes that "the original *CD* was never meant to be widely read but was instead produced for a select, esoteric audience of Origenists" ("The Earliest Syriac Reception of Dionysius," 35).

philosopher-disciple of Saint Paul, initiated into the esoterica of the latter's mystical experiences (e.g., 2 Cor 12), writes down his revelations, and we are led to discover in turn that the latter are nothing other than the common faith of the Great Church, sacramentally based and theologically orthodox. Like Irenaeus, therefore, for Dionysius there really is no esoteric revelation; all is public and open. The *CD*, among other things, is in substance an anti-esoteric work, and this message is conveyed all the more forcefully by the device of the pseudonym. I might note as well that Dionysius' modesty is too seldom pointed out. He was, after all, much more successful than Iamblichus in hiding his personal identity, doing so in order, precisely, to accentuate his message.[29]

It was also in the philosophical culture of the era, specifically in the late Neoplatonism of Iamblichus and Proclus, that Dionysius doubtless saw the potential for a reasoned balance and harmony between the subjective experience of ascetic seers, whose capacity for vision I think it clear that he affirmed (recall the "hear and now already with God" of *Ep.* X above), and the objective, visible liturgy of the Church through which God's presence in Christ is mediated to us. The key here lay in late Neoplatonism's denial of the soul's inherent capacity to ascend—or return—to the One. The latter doctrine had been held by the earlier philosopher and mystic, Plotinus, who also, as Porphyry his biographer tells

---

29. Dionysius' pseudonymity provides a great impetus for the "herme-neutic of suspicion" practiced by his modern interpreters. The imposture must be hiding something dubious. I do not agree that the matter of pseudonym-ity should of itself justify this suspicion. See with regard to the philosophi-cal culture of the day, B. D. Larsen, *Jamblique de Chalcis, exégète et philosophe* (Aarhus: Universitetsforlaget I Aarhus, 1972), 157, on Iamblichus' choice of a pseudonym for his *De mysteriis Aegypti*: "Derrière la pseudonymie dans la littérature philosophique se prouve justement la conception que ce qui est décisif, ce n'est pas *qui a dit* ceci ou cela, mais au contraire, *ce qui est dit*" (emphasis added), i.e., it served to highlight the content rather than the author. On the pseudonymity of scriptural works and of apocryphal litera-ture, see the essays edited by N. Brox, *Pseudepigraphie in der heidnischen und jüdisch-christlichen Antike* (Darmstadt: Wissenchaftliche Buchgesellschaft, 1977), and by K. von Fritz, *Pseudepigrapha I: Pseudopythagorica, lettres de Platon, littérature pseudépigraphique juive* (Geneva: Fondation Hardt, 1971).

us, had had in consequence no particular use for the rites of the temples and cults. In contrast, Iamblichus and Proclus believed that it was only through the "ineffable rites" handed down from antiquity that the inherent "weakness of the soul" could be bolstered sufficiently to participate in the divine realm.[30] Now, Neoplatonist theurgy was in practice worlds away from Christian liturgy. Dionysius clearly had no interest whatever in its sacred stones, crystals, unpronounceable names, seances, ectoplasm, and moving statues.[31] In the notion, however, of a traditional and ancient worship which claimed to communicate a saving knowledge and communion, and which could moreover demonstrate that it had been received from a divine revelation vastly better documented and more consistent than Proclus' sad appeal to the spurious antiquity of the *Chaldaean Oracles*,[32] I think Dionysius must have seen not only the possibility of a missionary appeal to the pagans (which is the usual account one gets from sympathetic scholars) but, and even more importantly, a way of reconciling the occasionally clashing claims of bishops and monks, of liturgy

---

30. Porphyry, *Vita Plotini*, 10. On late Neoplatonist denial of human autonomy, see Rist, "Pseudo-Dionysius, Neoplatonism, and the Weakness of the Soul," in *From Athens to Chartres, Neoplatonism and Medieval Thought* (ed. H. J. Westra; Leiden: Brill, 1992), 135–161; and on Iamblichus and theurgy in particular, G. Shaw, *Theurgy and the Soul: The Neoplatonism of Iamblichus* (University Park, PA: Pennsylvania State University Press, 1995), esp. 237ff.; idem, "Neoplatonic Theurgy and Dionysius the Areopagite," *JECS* 7 (1999): 573–599; G. Luck, "Theurgy and Forms of Worship in Neoplatonism," in *Religion, Science, and Magic: In Concert and in Conflict* (ed. J. Neusner et al.; Oxford: Oxford University Press, 1989), 185–228. For older, but still useful considerations of theurgy, see E. R. Dodds, "Theurgy and its Relation to Neoplatonism," *JRS* 37 (1947): 55–69; P. Boyance, "Théurgie et télèstique néoplatonicienne," *RHR* 247 (1955): 189–209; C. Zintzen, "Die Wertung von Mystik und Magie in der neuplatonischer Philosophie," *RM* 108 (1965): 71–100; A.-J. Festugière, "Proclus et la réligion traditionelle," in *Études de philosophie grecque* (Paris: Vrin, 1971): 575–584; Louth, "Pagan Theurgy and Christian Sacramentalism in Denys the Areopagite," *JTS* 37 (1986): 432–438.

31. *Pace* Arthur, *Ps.-Dionysius as Polemicist*, 38–39, 186.

32. See H. Lewy and M. Tardieu, *The Chaldaean Oracles and Theurgy: Mysticism, Magic, and Platonism in the Later Roman Empire* (rev. ed.; Paris: Études Augustiniennes, 1978).

and mysticism. Even here, though, where he is apparently very "Neoplatonist," he will in fact also be drawing on the thought of Syrian Christian ascetics who had lived over a century before him.

To all of the above, I would add Charles Stang's suggestion, which I see as perfectly complementary to my own approach: the very practice of writing under a pseudonym is "integral to the ascetic and mystical enterprise described in the *CD*"; "like the ecstatic God with whom he seeks to suffer union, as a writer he simultaneously remains where he is and stretches outside himself," and, like Moses on Sinai, he is "neither oneself nor someone else" (*MT* I.3 1001 A).[33] For the author of the *CD*, pseudonymous writing is thus not merely a literary exercise but a devotional practice aiming at refashioning oneself into Dionysius, an "imitator of Paul" (Gal 4:16) seeking, like the Apostle, to share his own self with Christ (Gal 2:20) by rendering his own self "cleft open, split, doubled, and thereby deified."[34]

2. The *Celestial Hierarchy*: Coordination between Heaven, the Liturgy, and the Soul—A Theme from the Ascetical Literature of Early Syrian Christianity

This brings me at last to my promised "Cook's Tour," and so to the opening chapter of the *CH*. The latter begins by quoting James 1:17, "Every perfect gift is from above coming down to us from the Father of lights." We therefore begin with light and its procession to us from God the Father who seeks to "gather us" back to himself.[35] Let me pause here to note the presence of this word, συναγωγός, "gatherer," applied to the Father and, as we shall see, its echo of the liturgy. The means whereby the Father gathers us to himself, Dionysius then tells us, is "Jesus, the light of the Father, 'the true light enlightening every man coming into

33. Stang, "Dionysius, Paul and the Significance of the Pseudonym," in *Re-Thinking Dionysius the Areopagite*, 11–25, at 18, 21, 22. The thesis is developed in Stang's recent monograph *Apophasis and Pseudonymity in Dionysius the Areopagite: "No Longer I"* (Oxford: Oxford University Press, 2012).

34. Stang, "Significance of the Pseudonym," 22–23.

35. *CH* I.1, 120B–121A (7:3-8); συναγωγοῦ on ll. 6–7.

the world,' through Whom we have obtained access (προσαγωγή) to the Father."[36] The combination here of the Fourth Gospel and Saint Paul is worth noting in itself, but I should like particularly to underline the word "access," προσαγωγή. It is in Christ, for Dionysius, that we discover our unique entry into the presence of divinity. The same word will appear again in a key text from the *EH*, and will be presumed when we come to the *MT* and the first five epistles concluding the corpus.

In the following paragraph, *CH* I.3, we arrive at the manner and means of that access which Christ has given us. This is arguably the most important passage in the entire *CD*:

> It would not be possible for the human intellect (νοῦς) to be ordered with that immaterial imitation of the heavenly minds [i.e., the angels] unless it were to use the material guide that is proper to it, reckoning the visible beauties as reflections of the invisible splendor, the perceptible fragrances as impressions of the intelligible distributions, the material lights an icon of the immaterial gift of light, the sacred and extensive teaching [of the Scriptures] [an image] of the intellect's intelligible fulfillment, the exterior ranks of the clergy [an image] of the harmonious and ordered state (ἕξις) [of the intellect] which is set in order (τεταγμένας) for divine things, and [our partaking] of the most divine Eucharist [an icon] of our participation in Jesus Christ.[37]

Dionysius is obviously talking about the liturgy, with its candles, incense, Scripture readings, orders of clergy, and sacraments. The whole is a symbol, which for him means always a kind of incarnation, a "real presence" of God and heaven coming to us in and through the material forms and objects—bread and wine, oil and water—which we have received from the teachings of Christ and the traditions of the Apostles. This symbol, which is the liturgy, unites three different levels: the visible and material elements of our worship, the invisible and spiritual (or "intelligible," νοητός)

---

36. *CH* I.2, 121A (7:9–11).
37. *CH* I.3, 121C–124A (8:19–9:6).

world of the angelic liturgy about the throne of God, and the inner world of the believer's soul or intellect (νοῦς). The first two together, that is, the Church's worship as a reflection of and participation in the worship of heaven, is a very old idea, perhaps even, as I noted above, reflected in the Apocalypse of John. It is in the third level, in the coordination between the interior hierarchy of the soul and the liturgy, that Dionysius offers us his apparently "novel" contribution.

My reasons for the quotation marks around "novel" will appear in a moment. For now, I should like to stress that this coordination between the "inner" and the "outer" hierarchies of the soul and Church appears throughout the treatises on the hierarchies. For example, two chapters later, in *CH* III, Dionysius gives us his definition of hierarchy as

> a sacred order [τάξις], knowledge [ἐπιστήμη], and activity [ἐνέργεια] assimilated so far as possible to the form of God [τὸ θεοειδής] and leading up in due proportion to the illuminations given it by God.[38]

Its purpose (σκοπός), he continues, is to make its members "images (ἀγάλματα) of God . . . clear and spotless mirrors reflecting the primordial light,"[39] which is to say that "hierarchy" refers both to the collective, that is, in our case to the worshipping Church, and to the individual Christian. Both—with the Christian arriving at hierarchy in and through the worshipping Church—are called to be the *imago dei*, and thus to become vessels of the divine light. Recall in my citation of *CH* I.3 above that he called the ranks (διακοσμήσεις) of the clergy an image or icon of that condition or state, ἕξις (like the Latin *habitus*), of the inner man which is open to—literally, "set in order for"—the reception of divine things. Now remember our examination above of the problem posed in *Ep.* VIII by the monk, Demophilus. The latter disrupted the sacred order, τάξις, of the Church, which Dionysius consistently refers to as "our hierarchy" (the collective), because the inner

---

38. *CH* III.1, 164D (17:3–5).
39. *CH* III.2, 165A (17:10–18:4).

order, τάξις, of his soul (the individual) was already out of order. Demophilus had, in short, refused to allow the shape or *pattern* of the liturgy precisely to shape or form his inner man, and had thus, as *Ep.* VIII also makes clear, rendered himself opaque to the vision of God. The liturgy is therefore for Dionysius not merely a sign—a "symbol" in the weak, modern sense—but a shaping force without which no one can attain to the encounter with God within. It is in this sense that we are to understand his insistence in the *CH* and elsewhere on the "hierarchic principle," for example in *CH* VIII: "that beings [here, angels] of the second rank receive enlightenment from God through the beings of the first rank,"[40] a principle which, applied to "our hierarchy," means the authority of the clergy. Two chapters later, however, we find the same principle applied to the inner life: "Every being endowed with intelligence . . . has its own set of primary, middle, and lower orders and powers."[41] Likewise, and a final example, in *EH* III, which is devoted to the Eucharist, Dionysius refers to this sacrament as the σύναξις, from συνάγω, to gather together (and recall in *CH* I.1 above the Father as συναγωγός, gatherer). At one point he applies this to the individual: the Eucharist is that sacrament which "gathers together into unity the divisions *within* us,"[42] and then, later in the chapter, to the collective, where it is the function of the Eucharist to bring us together without divisions "*among* ourselves."[43]

I could multiply examples, but these must suffice to illustrate my point: Dionysius does not believe in the autonomous human intellect. The latter is neither capable of, nor free to approach, the Godhead on its own. It requires the liturgy, the community of the Church, to form it and render it *capax dei*. Here, to be sure, we can certainly point to a parallel in the late Neoplatonist notion of theurgy, the "ineffable" and immemorial rites which alone can afford the presence of the gods to a soul too weak by nature

40. *CH* VIII.2, 240D (34:14–16).
41. *CH* X.3, 273C (40:23–41:2).
42. *EH* III.1, 424C (79:9–12).
43. *EH* III.3.8, 437A (88:13–18).

to ascend to them by itself. The parallel is obvious, and I freely grant that Dionysius made use of it. It may even have been what attracted him to Proclus and company in the first place. Let me add two caveats, however. There is first the certainty that Dionysius felt that he had a superior revelation and better—much better—rites. The pagans were obliged to turn Plato into holy writ and to rely on the dubious and late mystagogy of the *Chaldean Oracles*. The Christian writer, by contrast, could and did point to the incontestably revelatory claims of Scripture, together with a liturgy that could document a pedigree going back to the Apostles, and still further to an even more distant, if transformed, ancestry in the cult of the Jerusalem Temple and, indeed, even before Solomon, to the worship of the tabernacle revealed to Moses on Sinai (Exod 25:9ff.) as, exactly, the divinely-given *pattern* of worship.[44] The imagery of the Old Testamental Temple, not accidentally I think, is ubiquitous throughout the *CD*.[45]

---

44. "In accordance with all that I show you concerning the pattern [Hebrew *tabnit*, LXX παράδειγμα] of the tabernacle and of all its furniture, so shall you make it" (Exod 25:9, NRSV). Cf. Dionysius' discussion of the "three hierarchies"—the "legal hierarchy" (ἡ κατὰ νόμον ἱεραρχία), "our hierarchy" (ἡ καθ' ἡμᾶς ἱεραρχία), and the angelic hierarchy—in *EH* V.1.2–4, 501B–503A (104:15–107:12). The discussion is in great part based on, and flows out of, Exodus 25:9ff., thus the explicit reference to Sinai and the tabernacle in V.1.2, 501C (105:11–16). Throughout, the assumption behind the discussion supposes the modeling of human worship on the liturgy of heaven, less perfectly in the case of the OT cultus, more perfectly in the Christian, and cf. Heb 10:1, the distinction between "shadow," σκιά, and "image," εἰκών. That Dionysius is in accord here with ancient and contemporary traditions (esp. lively in Syria) concerning the tabernacle/temple and Christian Church, see for example N. Séd, "Les *Hymnes sur le paradis* de saint Ephrem et les traditions juives," *Mus* (1968): 455–501, here 458–465 and 476–477; B. Bucur, "The Mountain of the Lord: Sinai, Zion, and Eden in Byzantine Hymnographic Exegesis," in *Symbola Caelestis: Le symbolisme liturgique et paraliturgique dans le monde chrétien* (ed. B. Lourié and A. Orlov; Piscataway, NJ: Gorgias, 2009), 139–182. For the OT and later Jewish thought, see again J. D. Levenson, "The Jerusalem Temple in Devotional and Visionary Experience"; idem, *Sinai and Zion: An Entry into the Jewish Bible* (Minneapolis: Winston, 1985), esp. 89–184; and R. Patai, *Man and Temple in Ancient Jewish Myth and Ritual* (2d ed.; New York: Ktav, 1967).

45. See *CH* I.3, 124A (our hierarchy assimilated to the angelic priesthood); 4.3, 180C (angels as initiators); VII.2, 208A (highest angels as "gates," προθύροι,

My second caveat refers back to the quotation marks I placed around Dionysius' "novel" contribution regarding the coordination of the inner and outer liturgies, and thus to my earlier remark that he was drawing upon a Syrian Christian literature that antedated him by over a century. Here I have in mind primarily three fourth-century Syrian writers, Ephrem Syrus (+373), and the anonymous authors of the *Liber Graduum* (*Book of Steps*) and the *Macarian Homilies*.[46] The first two wrote in Syriac and the third in

---

to the sanctuary of divinity); VII.4, 212B (echoes of Ezek 3:12 and Isa 6:3, also angels as the "place" of divine "rest"); VIII.2, 241A–C (angels as priests, echoing Ezek 9; 10:6-8; and Zech 1:3 and 2:4); XIII.4, 304C–305B (Isaiah's "initiation" into the liturgy of heaven); XV.4, 333AB (angels with priestly vesture); *EH* I.1, 372AB (Jesus established our priesthood); IV.3.5–6, 440B–D (seraphim around Christ as priests around the bishop); V.1.2, 501BC (see above, n. 68); V.1.7, 508CD (clergy as icon of divine energies); *DN* I.8, 597AB ("visions" enlightening "prophets in the holy places," echoing Ezek 9–11, Exod 24 and 33–34, and Rev 4–5); IV.2, 696B ("to reflect the light glowing in the inner sanctuary," i.e., the heavenly *debir*); IV.22, 724B (an angel as a "mirror . . . enlightening within itself . . . the goodness of the silence of the inner [heavenly] sanctuaries"); V.2, 816C (Godhead's foundation "in a secret place," cf. Ps 80:8); V.8, 821C (highest angels as again προθύροι of the Trinity); *MT* I.1, 997AB (a likely echo of the darkness of the *debir* in the "brilliant darkness of the hidden silence"); I.2, 1000AB ("darkness his hiding place," cf. Pss 18:11 and 80:8); I.3, 1000CD (the "place of God" to which Moses ascends, cf. Exod 24:10); *Ep.* V, 1073A–6A (the "darkness" and "unapproachable light" in which God dwells, cf. 1 Tim 6:16); *Ep.* VIII.1, 1089BC (see above, n. 48); VIII.6, 1100AC (appearance of Christ on heavenly throne, "shining flame," surrounded by angels). To these I might add *CH* II, esp. 1–2 and 5, 137A–137D and 145B (almost exclusively devoted to Ezekiel 1); the entirety of chapters XIII, 300B–308B, on Isa 6:1-6; and XV, esp. 2-5, 328C–340B (again almost exclusively devoted to Ezek 1 and 9–11); *DN* IX.5, 912D–13B (alluding to the OT theophanies in bodily form); and X.2, 937B (echoing Dan 7:9 and 13). This list does not claim to be comprehensive. I am merely noting the passages which most forcibly struck me.

46. For Ephrem, see the translation by Brock, *Hymns on Paradise* (cited above, n. 48). For the *Liber Graduum*, see M. Kmosko's edition of the Syriac text with facing Latin translation in *PS* 3 (Paris: Firmin-Didot, 1926); English translation: *The Book of Steps* (trans. R. A. Kitchen and M. Parmentier; Kalamazoo: Cistercian Publications, 2004). Macarius' homilies and letters exist in four medieval collections, three of which enjoy critical editions. The most broadly circulated was the collection of fifty homilies: *Die 50 geistlichen Homilien des*

Greek. The last two in particular were also concerned especially with what I argued in my discussion of *Ep.* VIII was Dionysius' fundamental goal: the reconciliation of ascetics, especially of ascetic visionaries, to the liturgy and sacraments of the Church. These earlier Syrian writers were themselves involved with the ascetic movement—or, perhaps better, bundle of traditions—which was later to be condemned as Messalianism, and they, too, were anxious to propose a solution to the dangers which they saw in that movement, with which they had much in common, posing for the life of the Great Church.[47] The outlines of their solution

Makarios (ed. H. Dörries, E. Klostermann, and M. Kröger; *PTS* 6; Berlin: de Gruyter, 1964); English trans. G. Maloney, *Pseudo-Macarius: The Fifty Spiritual Homilies and the Great Letter* (New York: Paulist, 1991). Added later to the fifty, we have the seven additional homilies first edited by G. L. Marriott, *Macarii Anecdota: Seven Unpublished Homilies of Macarius* (Cambridge, MA: Harvard University Press, 1918). These two collections I will henceforth refer to as (II). Perhaps the most important and certainly the largest collection (sixty-four homilies) is *Makarios/Symeon, Reden und Briefe: Die Sammlung I des Vaticanus Graecus 694B* (2 vols.; GCS; Berlin: Akademie-Verlag, 1973), henceforth (I). Finally, *Pseudo-Macaire: Oeuvres spirituelles I. Homélies propres à la Collection III* (*SC* 275 ; introd., trans., and notes by V. Desprez; Paris: Cerf, 1980). I will also refer to W. Jaeger, *Two Rediscovered Works of Ancient Christian Literature: Gregory of Nyssa and Macarius* (Leiden: Brill, 1965), 233–301, for the text of the "Great Letter," henceforth Jaeger. The "Symeon" referred to in Berthold's edition of (I) represents a scholarly enthusiasm, lasting some two generations, and based on H. Dörries' identification of "Macarius" with the Messalian writer, Symeon of Mesopotamia, condemned at Ephesus in 431: *Symeon von Mesopotamia. Die Überlieferung des messalianischen Makarios-Schriften* (Leipzig: Hinrichs, 1941). Dörries later rejected the "Messalian" label: *Die Theologie des Makarios-Symeon* (Göttingen: Vandenhoeck & Ruprecht, 1978).

47. See below, chapter 4.3. For long both the *Liber* and, especially, Macarius were themselves confused with the Messalian heresy (see previous note). For Macarius as "Messalian," see, e.g., A. Louth, *The Origins of the Christian Mystical Tradition: From Plato to Denys* (Oxford: Clarendon, 1981), 113–125. It is the great merit of Stewart, *Working the Earth of the Heart*, and Fitschen, *Messalianismus and Antimessalianismus* (both cited above), to have cleared up this confusion. See also M. Plested, *The Macarian Legacy: The Place of Macarius-Symeon in the Eastern Christian Tradition* (Oxford: Oxford University Press, 2004), 16–27. Most scholars today would doubtless follow Stewart's summary of the Macarian writings as "the emergence into the Greek-speaking

match those of Dionysius. Indeed, the match is on occasion virtually exact, as in the following from Macarius, which my citation from *CH* I.3 echoes over a century later:

> Because visible things are the type and shadow of hidden ones, and the visible temple [a type] of the Temple of the heart, and the priest [a type] of the true priest of the grace of Christ, and all the rest of the sequence of the visible arrangement [a type] of the rational and hidden matters of the inner man, we receive the visible arrangement and administration of the Church as a pattern (ὑπόδειγμα) [of what is] at work in the soul by grace.[48]

Once again, we find the language of a divinely given *pattern* of worship. Christ came, the same writer says a little earlier, and gave us the "icon of the Church" in order that "faithful souls might be made again and, having received transformation (μεταβολή), be enabled to inherit everlasting life."[49] The liturgy is thus not merely

---

environment of language and imagery rooted in the Semitic earth of Syriac Christianity" (Stewart, *Working the Earth of the Heart*, 169; cf. also 234–235).

48. *Makarios/Symeon: Reden und Briefe*, homily 52.2.1, vol. II: 140, lines 3–8. For further discussion of Macarius, see Plested, *Macarian Legacy*, and Golitzin, "A Testimony to Christianity as Transfiguration: The Macarian Homilies and Orthodox Spirituality," in *Orthodox and Wesleyan Spirituality* (ed. S. T. Kimbrough; Crestwood, NY: St Vladimir's Seminary Press, 2002), 129–156; idem, "Heavenly Mysteries: Themes from Apocalyptic Literature in the Macarian Homilies and Selected Other Fourth Century Ascetical Writers," in *Apocalyptic Themes in Early Christianity* (ed. Robert Daly; Grand Rapids: Baker Academic, 2009), 174–192; "Dionysius the Areopagite in the Works of Gregory Palamas: On the Question of a 'Christological Corrective' and Related Matters," *SVTQ* 46 (2002): 163–190; "'A Contemplative and a Liturgist': Father Georges Florovsky on the Corpus Dionysiacum," *SVTQ* 43 (1999): 131–161; "Hierarchy Versus Anarchy: Dionysius Areopagita, Symeon the New Theologian, Nicetas Stethatos, and Their Common Roots in the Ascetical Tradition," *SVTQ* 38 (1994): 131–179; "Christian Mysticism over Two Millennia," in *The Theophaneia School: Jewish Roots of Christian Mysticism*, ed. Andrei Orlov and Basil Lurie (St. Petersburg: Byzantinorossica, 2007), 17–33; "Revisiting the 'Sudden': Epistle III in the Corpus Dionysiacum," *SP* 37 (2001): 482–491.

49. *Makarios/Symeon: Reden und Briefe*, homily 1.6, 139:30–140:2. The "transformation," μεταβολή, is here a deliberate evocation of the change of the

a sign or projection of the soul outward, but, as in Dionysius later on, a transforming force molding the soul from within.

The *Liber Graduum*, whose author is confronted by certain ascetics living away "off on the Mountain" and disdaining the liturgy and sacraments, offers an exactly similar coordination between, as he puts it, the "three churches": the heavenly church, the earthly church of sacraments and clergy, and the "little church" of the heart. It is the middle term, he insists, the earthly church, which enables the Christian "to find himself in the Church of the heart and [thence] in the Church on high."[50] Finally, and apparently outside of any controversy, Ephrem Syrus' *Hymns on Paradise* offer a striking set of parallels between: (1) the Paradise Mountain; (2) Sinai; (3) the Jerusalem Temple; (4) the Christian Church; and (5) the human being. On the peak of the Paradise Mountain enthroned on the Tree of Life, on the summit of Sinai, within the holy of holies of the Temple, on the altar of the Church, and in the innermost chambers of the human spirit we find Christ.[51] Ephrem also, on at least one occasion, refers to Christ's presence as the *Shekinta*, i.e., he deploys the same word (in its Syriac form) as the *Shekinah* of the Rabbis, who in their turn use it to mean the radiant manifestation of God, the divine Glory abiding in Israel. For Ephrem, and I think also for Dionysius, though he never uses that term, this radiance and splendor of God in Christ abides in the

---

eucharistic elements. On Macarius' frequent use of liturgical imagery and terminology for the inner condition of the soul, see Golitzin, "Liturgy and Mysticism," 177–179, and at greater length Chapter 6.3.3 below.

50. *Mimra* 12.2, *PS* 3:288.20–289.8. English translation, *The Syriac Fathers on Prayer and the Spiritual Life* (trans. S. Brock; Kalamazoo: Cistercian Publications, 1987), 45–53, here 46–47. The similarity between Macarius and the *Liber* in their effort to coordinate the worship of heaven, the church, and the soul was first noted by R. Murray, *Symbols of Church and Kingdom: A Study of Early Syriac Tradition* (London: Cambridge University Press, 1975), 262–276.

51. On these parallels, see Brock's "Introduction" to the *Hymns on Paradise*, 46–57, esp. the chart he supplies on p. 54; see also the detailed analysis in N. Séd, "Les hymnes sur le Paradis de saint Éphrem," and the chart on p. 463.

Church and in the Christian.[52] It is the secret within the complementary sanctuaries of the Church and the heart.

There are in fact a number of fascinating echoes of Saint Ephrem in the *CD*, including the former's use of another word, *raza*, which he employs in a way very akin to the Dionysian use of σύμβολον, symbol, both for what we might call the symbolic discourse of Scripture, the names of God in particular, and for the sacraments themselves.[53] In both writers there is a continual to and fro between the poles of hidden and revealed, God present in His "symbols" or "mysteries" and at the same time veiled by them. For our purposes, though, it is particularly Ephrem's parallels between Sinai, Church, and the soul that I should like us to bear in mind, since I think that they provide us with a key that unlocks the relationship which obtains for Dionysius between the two treatises, the *EH* and, especially, the ascent of Moses up Sinai which begins the *MT* and provides the setting for the latter treatise's concluding series of negations.

52. *Hymns on Paradise* 2.11, Brock, 89. For the Syriac, see E. Beck, ed., *Des heiligen Ephraem des Syrers: Hymnen de Paradiso*, CSCO 174, p. 7, line 28. The term, *šekinta*, turns up with some frequency in Christian writers in Syriac. I have come across it in Aphrahat (fl. 340s), Jacob of Serug (+521), and Isaac of Nineveh (+ca. 690), where each time, I believe, it signals the presence of Christ. To my knowledge, however, this usage has not yet attracted any scholarly attention. For the rabbinic usage of *šekinah*, see A. M. Goldberg, *Untersuchungen über die Vorstellung der Shekinah in der frühen rabbinischen Literatur* (Berlin: de Gruyter, 1969); and in the targumim, D. Muñoz-Leon, *Gloria de la Shekina en los targumim de Pentateuco* (Madrid: Consejo Superior de Investigaciones Científicas, 1977). For its use in Jewish mystical texts, see I. Chernus, *Mysticism in Rabbinic Judaism: Studies in the History of Midrash* (Berlin: de Gruyter, 1982), esp. 74–87. On echoes of these traditions in Dionysius, see my discussion of *MT* 1.3 and *Epistles* I–V in chapter 1.6, and, in more detail in Golitzin, "Revisiting the 'Sudden': *Ep.* III in the *Corpus Dionysiacum*," *SP* 37 (2001): 482–491, esp. 482–483n. 3.

53. See E. Beck, "Symbolum-Mysterium bei Aphrahat und Ephräm," *OC* 42 (1958): 19–40; and R. Murray, "The Theory of Symbolism in St. Ephrem's Theology," *ParOr* 6–7 (1975/76): 1–20.

3. The "Architecture" of the Church at Worship in the *Ecclesiastical Hierarchy*: "Bracketing" All of Christian Life

We turn then to the *EH*, "our hierarchy," the Church. By the latter, Dionysius means essentially the Church at worship. It is composed of three triads, like the three triads of the angelic orders in the *CH*, save that in our case the first triad is composed of the sacraments of baptism, eucharist, and the consecration of the sanctifying perfumed oil, the μύρον, used to anoint the newly baptized and to consecrate the altar. It might strike us nowadays as unusual to rank the consecration of the oil as a sacrament, but this was apparently commonly believed in the Syrian Church of the era.[54] Likewise, the bottom triad of monks, baptized laity, and catechumens/penitents also might appear odd or contrived, but once more we see exactly the same sequence of three grades in Ephrem's *Paradise Hymns*.[55] In between, mediating the sacraments to the laity, we find the triad of sacred ministers—bishops, presbyters, and deacons (whom Dionysius calls hierarchs, priests, and ministers: λειτουργόι)—familiar to us from at least the days of another Syrian, Ignatius of Antioch (+115), who is, interestingly enough, the only Church Father whom Dionysius feels free to cite by name.[56] Every one of these triads is therefore traditional, though the *EH* is the first to assemble them in precisely this sequence. One reason for this assembly, aside from the undoubted Neoplatonism of triads within triads (which has drawn most of the scholarly attention), is surely Dionysius' wish to emphasize the mediating role of the clergy, particularly with respect to the monks.

It is on the design or "architecture" of the *EH* that I should like to dwell here, while recalling the mountain imagery we saw in Ephrem and will see in the *MT*. The treatise features two primary movements, the first into the mystery of the altar and culminating

---

54. See esp. Strothmann, *Myron-Weihe*.

55. See *Hymns on Paradise* 2.10–11, Brock 88–89; and, for comment on this triad, Murray, "The Theory of Symbolism in St. Ephrem's Theology," 9.

56. *DN* IV.12, 709B (157:10–11). For Ignatius' triad of clergy, see for example his letter *To the Philippians*, 4.

in the meditation on it at the end of chapter 4 on the μύρον, and the second moving away from the altar as the reader is led through successive meditations on clerical ordination, accomplished within the sanctuary in chapter 5, to monastic tonsure, done in front of the sanctuary gates in chapter 6, to the concluding chapter 7, on Christian burial, which begins in the nave and finishes by taking us out of the church building on the way to interment. We thus enter the Church through baptism, commune at the Eucharist, reflect on the altar itself, and then trace the movement of divine grace moving down from the altar in order to finish once again "outside the doors" of the Church in hope of the Resurrection. Chapters 2, on baptism, and 7, on burial, constitute a kind of "bracket" which encloses the whole of Christian life. Dionysius speaks in fact of two births and two deaths. The first birth is of course the "divine birth" of baptism where, as we saw above, we receive the "eyes of the mind" capable of perceiving divine things, and which we are given through participation in the figurative death of baptismal immersion, in imitation of Christ's death and burial. The literal death of the Christian in chapter 7 looks forward to the "rebirth" (παλιγγενεσία) of the resurrection precisely in fulfillment, as Dionysius is careful to stress, of the baptismal promise.[57] Thus, while describing the sacramental rites and offices of the visible church, the *EH* simultaneously represents, enclosed within those brackets, the Christian's existence, hope of the world to come, and possibility of communion with God in this life. Once more, in short, we find that principle of coordination between macrocosm and microcosm, outer and inner, objective and subjective, institutional and personal, which I stressed above in connection with *CH* I.3 and the latter's background in Syrian ascetical literature.

Space permits me to dwell only on one text from the *EH*, but I think it an essential one. It is the passage referred to above at the

---

57. *EH* II.1, 392AB (69:3 and 7) for Baptism as ἀναγέννησις and γέννησις; and VII.1 and 3, 553A and 556B (120:23 and 123:15) for the παλιγγενεσία of the Resurrection anticipated in Christian burial. Note also Dionysius' specific indication of the funeral service's appeal to, and parallel with, the "divine birth" (θεῖα γέννησις) of Baptism in VII.3.8, 565A (129:15–22).

conclusion of *EH* IV. This is simultaneously the climax of the first movement, the entry or "introit" into the mystery of the Church and, if I may borrow from Saint Ephrem's imagery, the summit of the ascent of the Church as the mountain of God. Given the latter image, I think this passage also has a direct relation to Dionysius' use of Mount Sinai in the *MT*. After describing the rite of the sacred oil's consecration, an action which takes place entirely within the veiled sanctuary (and hence, perhaps, one reason he has chosen this sacrament as the background for his concluding reflections on the movement into the mystery), Dionysius begins his contemplation, θεωρία, with a lengthy discussion of the saints. It is these people, he tells us, who "*are* the truly divine images of that infinitely divine fragrance"[58] which has taken up its lodging "within their minds," and, as he makes clear a few paragraphs later, that fragrance is the presence of Jesus.[59] After an extended consideration of the seraphim gathered about Christ in heaven, as typified by the clergy around the bishop at the altar, and following repeated reflections on the Incarnation, he sums up his remarks on the altar and on our participation in Christ with the following:

> The theurgy [by which term Dionysius always means the Incarnation] transcends the heavens and is superessential. It is the origin, essence, and perfecting power of all our divinely-worked sanctification. For if our most divine altar is Jesus, Who is [both] the divine consecration of the heavenly intelligences [i.e., the angels] [and He] in Whom we, according to the saying, being at once consecrated and in mystery wholly consumed [lit. become whole burnt offerings, ὁλοκαυτώμενοι], have our access (προσαγωγή) [to God], let us gaze with supramundane eyes on this most divine altar, by whom all that is being perfected is perfected and sanctified, made perfect by him who is himself [also] the most divine myron.[60]

58. *EH* IV.3.1, 473B (95:21–96:5).

59. *EH* IV.3.4, 480A (99:8–14).

60. *EH* IV.3.12, 484D-5A (103:4–9). Cf. the description of the sanctified believer as a "holocaust" (ὁλοκαύτωμα), offered up by Christ the High Priest and consumed by "spiritual fire," in Homily 7.2 in Collection III of the Macarian homilies: *Pseudo-Macaire. Oeuvres spirituelles*, 118–121, esp. 118:1–12, with

In this passage, we find, first of all, the reference to the holy man whom Dionysius sees as typified by the sacrament; second, the coordination between heaven and earth, the liturgies around the divine throne and the Christian altar; and, third, the identification of both altars, on high and here below, with the God-man, Jesus. Thus we encounter, yet again, the harmony or mutual reflection established between not only the liturgies of heaven and earth but as well between both the latter and, to borrow from the *Liber Graduum*, the "little church" of the individual Christian. I have a fourth point, too, and that lies in what I take to be the relation—indeed, perhaps even the functional identity—between the passage quoted here and Moses' entry into the divine darkness in the *MT*. We enter into God through God, and God for Dionysius here means Christ. We do so as both "consecrated and, in mystery, wholly consumed." I cannot help but see a direct relation between this holocaust on the peak of the "Mountain of the Church" (borrowing now from Saint Ephrem's imagery), and the divine darkness on Sinai into which Moses plunges in the *MT*, stripped of every concept and of all human knowing. In both passages, we must be "burned up" altogether, as it were, in order to enter fully into God. Put in more pedestrian terms, I take this passage as the context, so to speak, for the apophaticism of the *MT*. It is the Church, the body of Christ, which is for Dionysius the divine milieu, the "place" of encounter with God, the τόπος θεοῦ, and therefore also the place for our considerations of the following treatises, the *DN* and the *MT*. But what then of that "dazzling darkness" of divinity which we shall meet in the latter treatise? That too, as we shall see, is Christ.

---

lines 4 and 10 for ὁλοκαύτωμα and ὁλοκάρπωμα, resp. The image is also reminiscent of second-century descriptions of the Christian martyr as sacrificial offering and, indeed, as a kind of sacrament making God present. See, e.g., Ignatius himself in *Romans* and Polycarp in the *Letter of the Smyrneans*. For citation and discussion of the latter texts, see Golitzin, *Et introibo* 243–247, together with R. D. Young, *In Procession before the World: Martyrdom as Public Liturgy in Early Christianity* (Milwaukee: Marquette University Press, 2001), esp. 9–24.

4. The *Divine Names*: Notes of Eschatological Anticipation and "Spiritual Fatherhood" as Illustration of the Trinity

The long treatise of the *DN*, which has fascinated so many generations of theologians, especially the great Scholastics, will not detain us as long as it should. The first three chapters do, however, require a brief consideration.

Chapter 1 sets out the basis of discussion, beginning with an opening appeal to the apophaticism which also closes the treatise in chapter 13 and leads naturally into the *MT*: "God is properly known through an "unknowing" (ἀγνωσία) beyond mind and speech.[61] Dionysius moves on to declare that the treatise is to be limited entirely to "what Scripture has disclosed" in the "hidden depths" of the names it has given God,[62] names which, as he implies elsewhere, are, we might say, sacramental in their character.[63] They carry the divine presence. Section 3 of the chapter asks its readers to "lift up" their eyes to this "divine light," and continues its praise of the light in ways which, to my ear, recall key terms of Syrian Christian asceticism. The divine light of Scripture is "safety for those who stand . . . simplicity for those turning toward simplicity."[64] The fourth section is also one of the keys to

61. *DN* I.1, 585D–8A (108:4, for ἄγνωστος, and 9, for ἀγνωσία "beyond reason [λόγος] and intellect [νοῦς]"), and for the closing appeal to apophaticism, see XIII.3, 981AB (229:15–230:5).

62. *DN* I.2, 588C (110:2–4), repeating what he has already said in 1.1, 588A (108:6–8).

63. See, e.g., *DN* I.8, 597BC (121:4–15), where Dionysius speaks of interpretation of the divine names in terms and phrases which deliberately evoke the *disciplina arcana* traditionally (at least from the fourth century) applied to the sacraments, e.g., "holy things are for the holy" (121:9–10), still sung today in the Orthodox Church prior to the fraction and priest's communion. Cf. also IX.1, 909B (207:8), on the divine names as θεῖα ἀγάλματα, "divine images" or "icons," and, for discussion, Golitzin, *Et introibo*, 70–74.

64. *DN* I.3, 589A–589C (111:3–112:6), with esp. 589C (121:16–112:2) for the terms which remind me of the lexicon of Syrian asceticism: "those who stand" (111:16), "simplicity" and "oneness of those being unified" (112:2). The first, "standing," recalls the *qeiama*, "covenant," of the ascetics, but whose root is "stand" (*qwm*), while the last two evoke the *ihidaya*, or "single one," the root

the treatise and, indeed, to the entire corpus. Dionysius begins
it by recalling the Trinity, God as monad and triad, and then the
Incarnation, where God "became complex" by entering "into our
human nature."[65] In what follows, this "complexity," the "vesture"
we might say of the incarnate God—or, in Dionysius' phrase, the
"veils" of God's love for humanity (φιλανθρωπία)—are specifically equated with the Scripture and liturgy (= "the hierarchical
traditions") which establish the possibility of our approach to the
divine mystery "now," i.e., in this life. "But *then*," as he continues,
in the age to come:

> We shall . . . be filled, on the one hand, with pure contempla-
> tion of His most visible theophany, shining round us with
> manifest brilliance as it shone round His disciples at the divine
> Transfiguration, and, on the other hand, we shall [also] par-
> ticipate in His noetic gift of light with our intellects grown
> passionless and immaterial; and [finally we shall share] in the
> union which transcends the [created] intellect through the
> unknowable and blessed impulsions of [His] supra-luminary
> rays in a more divine imitation of the heavenly intellects be-
> cause, as Scripture says, "we shall be equals to the angels and
> sons of God, being sons of the Resurrection."[66]

Let me underline three things here: first, the explicit affirmation of
three levels or aspects of the beatific vision: body, intellect (νοῦς),
and beyond the created frontiers of both the latter in union with
the "supraluminary rays" of divinity. Second, we find the appeal to the Transfiguration's portrait of Christ's own transformed
body.[67] Third, the entire human composite is thus to be redeemed

---

of which is *hd*, "one." On the several resonances of *qeiama* and *ihidaya*, see
again Griffith, "Asceticism in the Church of Syria," esp. 223–234.

65. *DN* I.4, 589D–92B (112:7–114:7).

66. *DN* I.4, 592BC (114:7–115:5). On this passage, see Golitzin, " 'On the
Other Hand': A Response to Father Paul Wesche's Recent Article on Dionysius," *SVTQ* 34 (1990): 305–323, esp. 310–316.

67. On the importance of the Transfiguration in Eastern Christian thought,
see J. McGuckin, *The Transfiguration of Christ in Scripture and in Tradition* (Lewistown: Mellen, 1986), esp. 99–143; A. Andreopoulos, *Metamorphosis: The Trans-*

and transfigured, which affirmation is quite in accord with what we have seen elsewhere, particularly in the *EH*.

This is not, however, the end of the passage which, up to this point, has been bracketed by a now (νῦν)/then (τότε) construction reminiscent of 1 Corinthians 13:12 ("now in a glass darkly, but then face to face"). Dionysius also admits the real, if fleeting and partial, possibility of a glimpse of eschatological realities in this life, and here he is again in complete accord with his ascetic sources. The *Liber Graduum* likewise insists on the possibility of vision "in this world" (*bhan alma*), as do the *Macarian Homilies* (ἀπὸ τοῦ νῦν, "right now"), and Evagrius Ponticus.[68] "As for now" (νῦν δὲ), Dionysius thus continues, we use the analogies and symbols given us in the tradition, rise to the perception of the presence— the unity and simplicity, as he puts it—which informs them, and then cease the exercise of our own powers altogether in order to allow those of Another to take over, the "ray beyond being."[69] This is exactly the sequence he uses later in describing the ascent of Moses in the *MT*, and to which he also returns nearly a dozen times in the *DN*. The mysteriously impelling force which takes us over in this ascent is, as he spells out at length in *DN* 4, nothing more nor less than God's own love, his ἔρως or ἀγάπη, which

---

figuration in Byzantine Theology and Iconography (Crestwod, NY: St Vladimir's Seminary Press, 2005).

68. For the *Liber's bhan alma*, see *Mimra* 15.16, *PS* III, 373:12–13, and relatedly, "the migration" to the heavenly church "while still in this present life" in 12.2, 288:20–289:8; trans. in Brock, *Syriac Fathers on Prayer*, 46–47. For Macarius' ἀπὸ τοῦ νῦν: see, e.g., Collection I, homilies 33.3.6 (Berthold II:31, line 14); 34.1 (II:34, lines 4–5); 50.2.3 (II:127, line 1); 54.4.6 (II:157, line 12); and 58.2.5 (II:184, line 25). In the last-named, note as well Macarius' insistence on the divine and objective nature of the light which appears—not a νόημα, a product of the intellect, but an ὑποστατικόν φῶς, "substantial light" (II:183, lines 14–15). For Evagrius, see the texts assembled and analyzed by G. Bunge, "Nach dem Intellekt leben? Zum sogennanten 'Intellektualismus' der Evagrianischen Spiritualität," in *Simandron, der Wachklopfer: Gedenkschrift für Klaus Gamber* (ed. W. Nyssen; Cologne: Luthe, 1989), 95–109; together with N. Séd, "La Shekinta et ses amis araméens," *COr* 20 (1988): 230–242, esp. 240-242; and below Chapter 5.2.3 ("Eschatology or Ecstasy? Dionysius and Evagrius on the Experience of God").

69. *DN* I.4, 592C–3A (115:6–18).

moved him to create us and this world in the first place, and, in the second, to redeem his creatures in the Incarnation.[70]

For anyone familiar with patristic literature dealing with the Trinity, particularly the thought of the great Cappadocian fathers of the fourth century, there are no surprises whatever in *DN* II. It is straight Cappadocian triadology, together with, chiefly in its concluding section, a continuation and intensification of the essence/energy distinction which Basil the Great and Gregory of Nyssa had adumbrated over a century before Dionysius.[71] Bearing in mind, however, the links between the *CD* and the ascetic tradition which I have sought to establish, I should also point out *DN* II.8. The subject here is the relation of the Trinity to the process of deification, θέωσις, as the latter is realized in the uniquely intimate relationship obtaining between a "spiritual father" and his disciple, or "son." "Fatherhood and sonship of this kind," Dionysius writes, "are brought to perfection in a spiritual fashion . . . and this is the work of the divine Spirit."[72] He does not state that this relationship is uniquely monastic, which indeed it need not be, but there is equally no question that the mysterious bond between a Christian elder (γέρων) and his (or her!) disciple were highlighted in a new and peculiarly powerful way precisely in the literature of fourth-century monasticism.[73] Dionysius sees in

70. *DN* IV.10–17, 705D–13D (154:7–162:5).

71. See C. Pera, "Denys le mystique et la *theomachia*," *RSR* 25 (1936): 5–75, esp. 36–49; A. Louth, *Denys the Areopagite*, 89–91; Golitzin, *Et introibo*, 289–304. For the theology of divine operations, which equates the divine *energeiai* in the Cappadocians and the divine processions in Dionysius, see D. Bradshaw, *Aristotle East and West: Metaphysics and the Division of Christendom* (Cambridge: Cambridge University Press, 2004), 153–186 ("The Formation of the Eastern Tradition"). See for instance 181–182, on the Cappadocians and Dionysius, and 190–191 on the Cappadocians, Dionysius, and Maximus the Confessor.

72. *DN* II.8, 645BC (132:5–13).

73. To scratch the surface of a large and growing bibliography: for a sensitive, if somewhat dated, analysis of the relationship between spiritual father and son in Eastern Christian ascetical literature, see I. Hausherr, *Spiritual Direction in the Early Christian East* (trans. A. Gythiel; Kalamazoo: Cistercian Publications, 1990), esp. 1–98 and 123–151, together with K. T. Ware's "Forward," vii–xxxiii. See also H. J. M. Turner, *St. Symeon the New*

this relationship, further, an image—arguably for him even *the* image—of the Trinity itself, while adding, in a phrase we should remember when coming to the negations of *MT* V, that, as with all other images, "the Father and the Son supremely transcend all divine fatherhood (πατριώτης) and sonship (υἱότης)."[74] Let alone the physical begetting of sons, even this exalted image derived from a purely spiritual begetting is, in the last analysis, inadequate to its prototype in the divine life. I might add that I have never seen this passage connected with its obvious roots in Christian ascetical tradition in any of the scholarly literature, including— prior to this essay, at least—my own.

DN chapter 3 takes up yet another theme emphasized in ascetic literature, especially in Evagrius of Pontus: prayer.[75] It is prayer which constitutes the privileged path to divine encounter, the way *par excellence* through which we, in Dionysius' own terms, become present to God. Again, this phrasing and the marked emphasis he places on human passivity in the higher reaches of

---

Theologian and Spiritual Fatherhood (Leiden: Brill, 1990), esp. 37–189. On the presence of the ascetic holy man in late antique society, see P. Brown, "The Rise and Function of the Holy Man in Late Antiquity," *JRS* 62 (1971): 80–101, and P. Rousseau, *Ascetics, Authority, and the Church* (Oxford: Oxford University Press, 1978), esp. 18–67. On the holy man as "theophanic," see M. S. Burrows, "On the Visibility of God in the Holy Man: A Reconsideration of the Role of the Apa in the Pachomian *Vitae*," *VigChr* 41 (1987): 11–33; S. A. Harvey, "The Sense of a Stylite: Perspectives on Symeon the Elder," *VigChr* 42 (1988): 376–394; A. Golitzin, "Earthly Angels and Heavenly Men: The Old Testament Pseudepigrapha, Nicetas Stethatos, and the Tradition of Interiorized Apocalyptic in Eastern Christian Ascetical and Mystical Literature," *DOP* 55 (2001): 125–153.

74. *DN* II.8, 645C (132:11–13).

75. *DN* III.1, 680B–D (138:2–139:16), and 680B (138:7–9) on "becoming present" to the Trinity. For Evagrius' *On Prayer*, see the translations of the Greek text in Nicodemus of the Holy Mountain's *Philokalia* 1:176–89 (under the name of Nilus of Sinai), and the slightly different MS tradition in J. P. Migne's *Patrologia Graeca* LXXIX: 1165–99C, by, respectively, K. T. Ware, P. Sherrard, and G. W. Palmer, eds., *The Philokalia: The Complete Text* (London: Faber & Faber, 1979), 1:28–71; and J. E. Bamberger, *The Praktikos and Chapters on Prayer* (Kalamazoo: Cistercian Publications, 1970), 52–80. Note the Evagrian "apophaticism" in *On Prayer*, 67–68, 73–74, and 114–117.

prayer places him, I think, squarely in the company of the earlier
desert fathers in general and, once more, of Evagrius in particular.
The passive note of the experience of God is specifically underlined earlier, in chapter 2, where Dionysius speaks of his spiritual
father, Hierotheos, "suffering" the mystery of the Incarnation,
παθὼν τὰ θεῖα.[76] Hierotheos appears again in chapter 3, where he
is presented as having wholly departed himself, ἐξεστηκός, and
communed with the divine things on the occasion of his participation in the funeral of the Mother of God—for which feast, by
the way, Dionyius provides us with one of our earlier witnesses
(it was very popular in Syria).[77] In the latter experience, of course,
we find mystical ecstasy once again set in a liturgical context,[78]
but I do not think that this takes away from the debt to ascetical
literature. Hierotheos' "suffering" in the preceding chapter has
no such ecclesiastical context.

5. The *Mystical Theology*: Ascending the "Mountain of the Church" to Approach the Light of Christ, the *Shekinah*

These remarks brings us at last to the matter of the little treatise
called the *Mystical Theology*, where I think we might do well to
pause a moment to consider the meaning of that title, which is
Dionysius' own coinage. We do well, too, to bear in mind the fact
that the term "mysticism," as used today, is of relatively recent
vintage, not much over three hundred years old. Anyone approaching this little work in expectations of the sort of detailed,

76. *DN* II.9, 648B (134:2).

77. *DN* III.2, 681D–684A (141:11–14). For bibliography on the feast of the
Mother of God's falling asleep, see Harvey, "Incense Offerings in the Syriac
Transitus Mariae: Ritual and Knowledge in Ancient Christianity," in *The Early
Church in its Context: Essays in Honor of Everett Ferguson* (ed. A. J. Malherbe, F.
W. Norris, and J. W. Thornton; Leiden: Brill, 1998), 175–191.

78. Cf. also Isaiah's vision in the Temple, the subject of all of *CH* XIII, and
Bishop Carpus' reception of visions prior to celebrating every liturgy, *Ep.*
VIII.6, 1097BC (188:11–13), together with Moses' ascent of Sinai in *MT* I.3 as
freighted with liturgical overtones. On the latter, see Rorem, "Moses as the
Paradigm" and my discussion below in chapter 5.1–2.

personal accounts of supra-normal experience which one meets in, say, the great Counter-Reformation mystics is going to be disappointed—as was Vanneste forty years ago.[79] Dionysius delivers nothing of the kind. Does this mean that he was not a "mystic," in our modern sense? It does not. I would myself say that he was writing about something he knew from experience, but I would have to add that this is an opinion which cannot be proven from the text. What is evident, though, and even obvious, is the fact that he believed that such an experience is possible.

This leads me back to the title. "Mystical" for our writer carries essentially its general, patristic meaning. It signifies "hidden," "secret," perhaps with overtones of "spiritual"—as in Origen of Alexandria's phrase, the "mystical sense" of Scripture—and "invisible."[80] What then would a hidden, secret, spiritual or invisible *theology* be? As a glance at Lampe's *Patristic Greek Lexicon* will tell us, our current understanding of the word "theology" as "rational discourse about divine things" stands at the very bottom of a long list of meanings. By contrast, at the top of that list we find the following: (1) God, especially as in the inner life of the Trinity; (2) the experience of God in Trinity, i.e., the mystical (in the modern sense) encounter, also the beatific vision; (3) divine praise, liturgy, as in the worship of: (a) the angels and (b) the Church; and (4) the Scripture.[81] It seems to me that this sequence, including its assignments of relative importance, gives us a pretty good idea of Dionysius' project. His subject, I take it, is the life of the Trinity as we may experience it in this life, recalling at the same time his stress on the liturgy and sacraments as supplying the whole context of our life in Christ, and his general attention to the Scriptures. Only at the very end, last and least, do we have

79. See in this respect Louth, "Mysticism: Name and Thing," *Archaeus* 9 (2005): 9–21.

80. See the sources and meanings listed for μυστικός in G. W. H. Lampe, *A Patristic Greek Lexicon* (Oxford: Clarendon, 1972), 893–894; together with B. McGinn, *The Foundations of Christian Mysticism: Origins to the Fifth Century* (New York: Crossroad, 1991), esp. 117ff.

81. *Patristic Greek Lexicon*, 627–628.

a technical, philosophically based discussion of the ascent to God, in this instance of the apophatic way or *via negativa*.

It is therefore no surprise that the *MT* is—again my favorite word—"bracketed" by the Trinity. Dionysius begins and ends with it. The *MT* opens with a prayer to the "supraessential Trinity," which I quote in slightly amended form from the Paulist Press translation:

> Lead us beyond unknowing and light, up to the furthest, highest peak of the mystical Scriptures, where the mysteries of theology lie simple, absolute, and unchanging in the brilliant darkness (γνόφος) of a hidden silence. Amid the deepest shadows they pour out overwhelming light.[82]

Here we should note particularly the terms "silence" (σιγή) and "darkness" (γνόφος). The latter, based on Exodus 19–20 and 24, will be the term of Moses' ascent two paragraphs later, while the former Dionysius understands as the terminus of all theological discourse, of all our words and images, as indicating that moment when we are, as it were, confronted with God himself. I will return to Moses and the darkness in a moment, but for now let me turn rather to the end of the treatise, where Dionysius moves to the application of the *via negativa* whose theory he has just finished sketching in chapters 2 and 3. He begins in chapter 4 by stating that God is not a body nor anything approachable by the senses (recall the Messalians' claim to a physical sight of the Trinity)[83] and then addresses the higher, intelligible names of God:

---

82. *MT* I.1, 997A (141–142:3); *Pseudo-Dionysius: The Complete Works*, 135.

83. *MT* IV, 1040D (148). See above and nn. 52–53 for the Messalians. In view of the latter, and more broadly of the pseudepigraphic and apocryphal literature that I understand Dionysius to be confronting, I would see these negations directed against the notions of God having a body, a "place," a "form" (μορφή) and "shape" (εἶδος), etc., as quite relevant to Dionysius' readers. These were ancient ideas, based on the biblical throne visions, and, in both Jewish and Christian circles, long-lived. On their presence in Jewish literature roughly contemporary to Dionysius, see for example G. Scholem, *Jewish Gnosticism, Merkabah Mysticism, and Talmudic Tradition* (New York: Jewish Theological Seminary of America, 1960), 36–42; and in early Christian

> Moving yet higher, we say that He is . . . neither soul nor
> mind; neither has He imagination nor opinion nor reason
> (λόγος) nor intuitive knowing (νόησις); neither is He reason
> nor intuition, neither can He be reasoned nor intuited. He is
> neither life nor does He live; neither is He essence, nor eternity,
> nor time . . . He is neither oneness, nor deity, nor goodness.
> He is not spirit, as we understand [the term], nor sonship nor
> fatherhood . . . He is no one of the things which are not, nor
> any one of those which are . . . beyond affirmation . . . and
> beyond negation is the transcendence of Him Who, simply, is
> beyond all things and free.[84]

It may be argued that I have been a little perverse here in choosing
to use as pronoun the masculine singular, "he," and in assigning
the place of the last word to "free," ἀπολελυμένον, when the Greek
actually ends with "beyond (ἐπέκεινα) them all." Both moves are
frankly interpretative, that is, intended to emphasize what I take
to be Dionysius' central concerns. On the other hand, to use the
pronoun "it," as the Paulist Press text does, is itself equally an
interpretation, and one which, given the English associations with
the neuter pronoun, is inevitably a negative one.[85] In light of my
prior discussion, I think it fair to say that we can dispense with
the question mark over Dionysius' Christianity, and thus use "He"
both to underline the personal quality of the encounter with God,
and, with an eye toward my discussion of the epistles following
the *MT*, to point toward Christ. Likewise, I understand "free" to
signal the real thrust of these negations. Their point is that God is

---

literature, G. G. Stroumsa, "Form(s) of God: Some Notes on Metatron and
Christ," *HTR* 76, no. 3 (1983): 269–288; together with A. DeConick, *Seek to See
Him*, esp. 95–125, and J. Fossum, "Partes Posteriori Dei" (both cited above).

84. *MT* V, 1045D–1048B (149–150).

85. Note that, although the negations begin in *MT* IV and carry on through
most of V speaking of "the cause of all," ἡ τὸν πάντον αἰτία, admittedly an
impersonal phrase and with attendant pronouns in the feminine (for αἰτία),
they conclude with: "the transcendence of *him* [or "it"] who, simply, is beyond
all things and free" (ἡ ὑπεροχὴ τοῦ πάντων ἁπλῶς ἀπολελυμένου καὶ ἐπέκεινα τῶν
ὅλων), where τοῦ and ἀπολελυμένου indicate either a masculine or a neuter
genitive singular. I have opted for the former.

subject to absolutely none of our conceptions. Even the revealed names—Father, Son, and Spirit—are finally icons, images, drawn from human experience in the world. They are, indeed, *given* us in order to point to a reality in the Godhead, in fact to a divine *community*, but that community in and for itself escapes definitition altogether. Note, too, Dionysius' careful qualification: "not spirit *as we understand* [*the term*]," and recall as well that we have already seen him denying the adequacy of sonship and fatherhood to God in *DN* II.8 while discussing "spiritual fatherhood." Again, even the most exalted and refined of our relations with one another are only pointers to a reality which transcends us. They are, surely, "like" God in some sense, but the divine reality is not simply equivalent to our experiences with each other. God can only be known in the experience of His presence, His light, His darkness—in short, in the special kind of "unknowing" which we also saw begin the *DN*.

All this brings me, at long last, to the ascent of Moses in *MT* I.3, which I quote at length in my own translation:

> Moses is bidden first of all to be purified himself, and then to separate himself . . . and, after complete purification, he hears the many-voiced trumpets, he beholds many lights . . . then . . . with the chosen priests he arrives at the summit of the divine ascents. And yet in these he still meets not with God, for he sees not Him—since He is not to be seen—but the place [τόπος] where He stands. And this I take to mean the highest and most divine of the things which are seen and grasped by intuitive knowing, which are certain basic principles [λόγοι] of the things subordinate to Him Who transcends all things, through which His Presence [παρουσία] is indicated which is above any conception, and which is mounted upon the spiritual summits of His most holy places. And then, abandoning both what is seen and those who see them, he enters into the truly secret darkness [γνόφος] of unknowing, according to which he closes [his eyes] to all perceptions open to knowledge, and enters into Him Who is altogether untouchable and invisible and beyond all things. Beyond all things, and belonging to nothing else, whether to himself or to any other, he is, in accordance with what is greater and by a complete cessation

of all his own activity of knowing, united to Him Who is wholly unknowable, and by knowing nothing, knows in a manner beyond intellect.[86]

It is difficult for me to say that this is not a properly "mystical" text, whether of Dionysius' own experience or else taken from the experience of others, such as Evagrius, who uses Exodus 24:10 in a very similar way.[87] Nothing known is God. The notional iconography of the divine names carries us up to "the place where God stands" (so Exod 24:10 in the LXX), which I understand to mean, on the basis of the Exodus text and its interpretation, to just beneath the divine throne. The one phrase which has given pause to some is the "in accordance with what is greater," κατὰ τὸ κρεῖττον. By this "greater" something, Moses is joined to the unknowable God, and with all his own, human activities of mind at a standstill, quiescent. Is this "greater" an inherent faculty? It might be, equivalent in fact to the term, ἕνωσις or union, which Dionysius uses elsewhere and seems to as to understand as the human capacity for receiving God.[88] If so, however, it is a wholly passive capacity, once more reminiscent of Evagrius Ponticus and the "susceptibility" which the latter sees as the highest faculty of the created intellect, the νοῦς, i.e., that whereby the intellect may become a vessel ready to receive the "light of the Trinity." It is that in us which answers, again in Evagrius as in Dionysius, to the Church's altar.[89] The last act of the human approach to God is thus an openness, a surrender, in order to enter into the Presence,

---

86. *MT* I.3, 1000C–1A (143:18–144:15).

87. For Evagrius' use of Exodus 24:10, see esp. the sixty chapters supplementary to his *Kephalaia Gnostica* edited by W. Frankenberg, *Evagrius Ponticus* (Berlin: Weidmann, 1912), particularly chs. 2, 21, and 25 (Frankenberg, 425, 441, and 449), together with letters 29, 33, esp. 39 (Frankenberg, 587, 589, and 593).

88. J. Vanneste, *Mystère de Dieu*, 183–217; de Andia, *Henôsis*.

89. "The intelligible temple is the pure intellect which now possesses in itself the Wisdom of God . . . the temple of God is he who is a beholder of the sacred unity, and the altar of God is the contemplation of the Holy Trinity," in *Kephalaia Gnostica* (PO 28; ed. A. Guillaumont; Paris: Firmim-Didot, 2003), 213. Cf. also supplementary chapters 37 and 45 (Frankenberg, 459 and 461).

the παρουσία in Dionysius' terms, or, as I like to think of it, into the darkness which is at the same time the "unapproachable light" of the *Shekinah*.

I will make my reasons for referring to light, and even to the *Shekinah*, clear in a moment, I hope. For now, let me also recall the discussion above on the liturgy in, particularly, *CH* I.3 and *EH* IV.3.12. The liturgical tonality of Moses' ascent, in both the biblical texts themselves and in Dionysius, should be obvious. Moses, as Rorem has pointed out, is certainly a type of the Dionysian hierarch, of the bishop standing before the altar, but he is also a type of the Christian soul.[90] The *ascensus montis Dei* is at the same time an *ingressus ad altare Dei*, a movement into the living core of the Christian mystery: to Christ in heaven, on the altar, and within the heart. Taken by itself, as it has too often been taken, this passage in tandem with the "nots" of *MT* V might well suggest, as again Rorem thinks is the case, a "loveless" and "christless" mysticism.[91] And, in fact, the words "Christ," "Jesus," and "love" do not occur at all in the *MT*, so how can I maintain their presence, even if unspoken? I reply that I can, first, because we have already seen in the *CH* and, especially, in the *EH* that Christ, in the Church, is our divine milieu. He is the one in whom we receive the "eyes of the intellect" and, in whom, as "our most divine altar," "wholly consumed," we discover our access to God. Second, because that same consummation, on the peak of the "Mountain of the Church," must surely discover its correlate experience here, in the darkness of the mount of revelation and theophany, Sinai, a correlation that we have already met in Ephrem Syrus: the Church as Sinai. Third, Christ is also himself the μύρον that consecrates and consumes, the substance of the gift received through the very access which he himself offers us. Fourth, regarding love, Dionysius

90. Rorem, "Moses as the Paradigm." The bishop as Moses, with echoes of Dionysius' *MT* I.3, is taken up with delight by Patriarch Germanos of Constantinople in the early eighth century. See *St. Germanos on the Divine Liturgy* (trans. P. Meyendorff; Crestwood, NY: St Vladimir's Seminary Press, 1990), 90–93.

91. Expressed perhaps most forcefully in his "Uplifting Spirituality of Pseudo-Dionysius," 144.

has already told us in the *DN*, and at length, that divine ἔρως is the power which returns us all to God. It is thus necessarily that force which drives the *ascensus-ingressus* of Moses here in the *MT*.

6. Completing the Context of the *Mystical Theology*: *Epistles* I–V and Christ the "Sudden"

The first five epistles of the *CD* function as a kind of chiasm, and together serve to round out and complete the thought of the *MT*.[92] Let me proceed according to what I take to be the chiasm, with *Ep.* I matching up with V, *Ep.* II with IV, and *Ep.* III tying them up and together. *Ep.* I continues the themes of divine darkness and unknowing which preoccupy the *MT*: God's transcendent darkness (here σκότος) is "hidden by the light of knowledge," Dionysius says, while "complete unknowing is the knowledge of him who is known to transcend all things."[93] Very good, but then this is met and countered by the opening of *Ep.* V: "The divine darkness [γνόφος] *is* the unapproachable light in which God is said to dwell."[94] God's dwelling place, κατοικητήριον, recalls—and not, I think, accidentally— the place of the divine throne which, in the ancient traditions of apocalyptic literature, and in the later Christian apocalypses and apocryphal materials which I mentioned above in connection with the monks (or, for that matter, in the Rabbinic mystical texts of the *merkabah*, the divine chariot-throne), is always characterized by overwhelming light. Light is both the Presence, the *Shekinah* himself, and the stream which proceeds from him.[95] Thus we find Dionysius continuing in *Ep.* V:

92. I have made this argument before, in *Et introibo*, 222–227, and, with larger range of supporting texts, in "Revisiting the 'Sudden': *Epistle* III in the *Corpus Dionysiacum*," *SP* 37 (2001): 482–491.

93. *Ep.* I, 1065A (156–157).

94. *Ep.* V, 1073A (162:3–4), and cf. *DN* VII.2, 869A (196:11–12) for the same equation of the thick cloud of Sinai (γνόφος) with the "unapproachable light" (ἀπρόσιτον φῶς) of 1 Timothy 6:16.

95. For the fire and/or light of the Presence in the ancient apocalypses, see *I Enoch* 14:17-22 and 71:2-6; Daniel 7:10; *2 Enoch* 20:1 and 22:1; *3 Enoch*

> And if it [i.e., the unapproachable light] is invisible because
> of its superabundant clarity, and unapproachable because of
> its transcendent outpouring of light, yet it is here that everyone
> enters [γίγνεται] who has been made worthy of seeing and
> knowing God.[96]

He then goes on to cite David and, especially, Paul as examples
of this experience. Let me draw our attention to two other points
here. First, the "entering into" the divine presence deploys the
same verb (γίνομαι) as Dionysius uses in *Ep.* X concerning those
holy ascetics who, even in this life, "are already with God" (μετὰ
τοῦ θεοῦ γιγνομένους). Second, an ancient marginal note to *Ep.*
V here will help us in identifying a key theophany to which I
believe Dionysius will shortly be alluding in the central *Ep.* III.
On the phrase, "unapproachable light," the scholiast makes the
seemingly humdrum observation that the experience of the *visio
dei* might be compared to trying to stare at the sun's disk at noon
(μεσημβρία).[97]

The "transcendent outpouring of light" leads us to the matter
of God's self-communication, which I take to be the subject of
both *Ep.* II and *Ep.* IV. In the former, Dionysius alludes back to a
distinction that he had touched on in *DN* II and XI, between God
in se and *ad extra*. God truly gives himself, the Areopagite states in

---

36, among Jewish sources, and cf. the Christian *Martyrdom and Ascension of
Isaiah* 8:1–2, 21–26; and 9:6. On the Rabbis, see again Chernus, *Mysticism in
Rabbinic Judaism*, 74–87, and for personal transformation, W. F. Smelik, "On
the Mystical Transformation of the Righteous into Light in Judaism," *JSJ* 27
(1995) 122–144; C. R. A. Morray-Jones, "Transformational Mysticism in the
Apocalyptic-Merkabah Tradition," *JJS* 43 (1992): 1–31; and in the early Christian *Gospel of Thomas*, see again DeConick, *Seek to See Him*. For the "blessed
light of the Holy Trinity" in Evagrius, see A. Guillaumont, "Les visions mystiques dans le monachisme oriental chrétien," in *Aux origines du monachisme*,
136–147; N. Séd, "La Shekinta et ses amis araméens," 240–242; G. Bunge,
"Nach dem Intellekt Leben?," and for the same notes in Evagrius' teacher,
Gregory of Nazianzus, J. A. McGuckin, "Perceiving Light from Light in Light
(Oration 31.3): The Trinitarian Theology of Gregory the Theologian," *GOTR*
39 (1994): 7–32.

96. *Ep.* V, 1073A (162:4–6).
97. *PG* IV:536B.

Ep. II, and truly deifies, but, while he is himself the deifying gift, θεοποιῶν δῶρον, he yet transcends all the relations he enters into. He gives of his actions (ἐνέργειαι) or powers (δυνάμεις), but not of his essence (οὐσία).⁹⁸ *Ep.* IV makes it clear that the source of this gift of divine energy or power is Christ. In Jesus, Dionysius tells us, transcendence and immanence (here ἀπόφασις and κατάφασις, respectively) have met and been joined. Those things, he goes on, "which are affirmed of Jesus' love for humanity preserve the force of transcendent negation." Therefore, he concludes,

> [Christ] did not do what is divine as God, nor what is human as man, but instead [as] God having become man, He has administered to [or, arranged for] us a certain, new divine-human activity [καινήν τινα τὴν θεανδρικὴν ἐνέργειαν ἡμῖν πεπολιτευμένος].⁹⁹

My translation is different from the usual rendering of this text, which applies the "theandric activity" entirely to Jesus (as in the Paulist Press version: "He accomplished something new in our midst—the activity of the God-man"). Whether strictly accurate or not, however, it still serves to convey something which Dionysius believes is true and fundamental, and that is that the Incarnation affords us a real participation in God's own actions and gifts. Let us recall the definition of hierarchy, which I quoted earlier from *CH* III.1–2, and which included the description of a hierarchy's members as "spotless mirrors of the primordial light." We might add, in *EH* I, the reference to Jesus Who "makes our life, disposition, and activity (ἐνέργεια) something divine."¹⁰⁰ I could multiply examples, but these will suffice to make my point: Christ's divine-human activity comes even to us, and it does so specifically in the

---

98. See *DN* XI.6, 953C–956B (222:3–223:3), and also V.2, 816C (181:7–15), together with John of Scythopolis' σχόλιον on *Ep.* II in PG IV, 529B–D, where John rightly discerns the importance of Dionysius' distinction between the powers/activities which God shares with us, and the incommunicable essence, for understanding the Areopagite's "deifying gift" in *Ep.* II.

99. *Ep.* IV, 1072BC (161:4–10).

100. *EH* I.1, 372AB (63:12–64:6).

divine polity and way of life—the ἔνθεος πολιτεία, as Dionysius puts it elsewhere[101]—of the Church. It is in the latter that we receive the "deifying gift" mentioned in *Ep.* II, just as it is in and through the Church that we are led to encounter the mystery of Christ's divinity in a "transcendent outpouring of light." These several points, together indeed with the entire *CD* itself, are summed up by the center and "punchline" of the chiasm, *Ep.* III, which I translate in full:

> "Suddenly" [ἐξαίφνης] means that which comes forth from the hitherto invisible and beyond hope into manifestation. And I think that here the Scripture [lit., "theology"] is suggesting the philanthropy of Christ. The super-essential has proceeded out of its hiddenness to become manifest to us by becoming a human being. But He is also hidden, both after the manifestation and, to speak more divinely, even within it. For this is the hidden of Jesus, and neither by rational discourse nor by intuition can His mystery [μυστήριον] be brought forth, but instead, even when spoken it remains ineffable, and when conceived with the intellect, unknowable [ἄγνωστον].[102]

The first thing to notice is the reprise of the themes I have been discussing: divine unknowability and ineffability, together with the tension between transcendent hiddenness and revelation. Secondly, there is the sacramental echo in the reference to the μυστήριον of the Incarnation. Christ is *the* sacrament, both at the center and terminus of the divine processions to us and to our world, and, simultaneously, the vehicle and goal of our return, or ascent.

The real force and key to the coalescence of Dionysius' thought here lies in the word "suddenly" (ἐξαίφνης), which opens the epistle. On the one hand, and as has often been noted by modern scholarship, the "sudden" has a long ancestry in the Platonic tradition. Plato himself uses it three times: in the *Parmenides* to indicate the

---

101. For ἔνθεος πολιτεία, see *EH* II.2.4, 396A (71:5); III.3.11, 441C (91:23); and *Ep.* IX, 1113A (206:2).

102. *Ep.* III, 1069B (159:3–10).

timeless moment of intersection between the eternal, unmoving realm of the Forms and the world of serial time and flux; again in the *Symposium*, to signify the end and goal of the ascent of ἔρως to the vision of Beauty; and lastly, in Ep VII of Plato's corpus, for the "sudden" conclusion of the philosopher's quest in, perhaps, the vision of divinity (a passage which is alluded to, in fact, in *CH* XV). All these—ἔρως, beauty, stasis/motion, eternity/time—are also important Dionysian themes. Plotinus, too, in an even closer approximation to the thought of the *CD*, uses the "sudden" in *Enneads* V.3.17; 5.7; and VI.7.36 to signal the vision of the One in light. I have no doubt that Dionysius was aware of these passages.[103]

It is at this point, however, that modern scholarship has always stopped. It thus remains entirely insensitive to the resonances which the "sudden" has in the Scriptures and in later Christian literature, all of which I believe Dionysius also intended to evoke.[104] I have in mind especially four appearances in the NT of the word ἐξαίφνης, together with certain passages in early ascetical literature and, again, Ephrem Syrus. The NT texts are Acts 9:3, 22:6, Luke 2:13, and Mark 13:36. The first two are both descriptions of Paul's conversion on the Damascus Road and are functionally identical. I quote from the second: "And it happened that as I was travelling . . . at around midday [μεσημβρία] a great light from heaven flashed suddenly [ἐξαίφνης] around me." The light, of course, is Christ, who sends Paul on to his life's work, the apostolate to the gentiles. I note the themes of light, personal encounter with Christ, the "midday" we saw above signaled by the anonymous

---

103. For discussion of the Platonist background of the "sudden" in *Ep.* III, see W. Beierwaltes, *"Exaiphnes*, oder die Paradoxie des Augenblicks," *PhJ* 84 (1966/67): 271–282; idem, *Platonismus im Christentum*, 80–84; R. Mortley, *From Word to Silence*, vol. 2: *The Way of Negation* (Bonn: Hanstein, 1986), 236–240.

104. To give but one example, Mazzuchi judges that the adverb carries no special semantic weight in the biblical occurrences ("Damascio, autore del *Corpus Dionysiacum*," 737–738n. 125), which allows him to consider the connection with *Parm.* 156 exclusively, and to find yet another indication that the author of the *CD* must have been the well-versed commentator of the passage, Damascius.

scholiast, and, perhaps not least, the mission to the "Greeks."[105]
Luke 2:13 links the "sudden" to the angelic liturgy, the *gloria in
excelsis*, which appears around the shepherds near Bethlehem
at the moment of the Incarnation. The fourth text, Mark 13:36,
occurs at the end of the eschatological discourse. Be watchful,
Christ warns his listeners, lest returning "suddenly," the Master
find them sleeping. The NT therefore ties the "sudden" to Christ,
light, the angelic liturgy, ascetical "watchfulness," and the eschaton. Surely, this set of associations is at least as important for
Dionysius as the ones I listed above from the pagans.

The appearances of the "sudden" which follow from the later
Christian literature are not the result of any thorough inquiry on
my part. I have made no systematic search, yet each of the following works—the *Acts of Judas Thomas* (popular in the Syrian
Church at least into the sixth century), Athanasius' *Life of Anthony*,
and the works of Saint Ephrem—are all texts with which Dionysius could easily have been familiar. In the third-century *Acts of
Thomas*, the "sudden" occurs at the climactic point of the "Hymn
of the Pearl," when the speaker encounters the "robe of glory"
woven for him in heaven:

> But suddenly [Gr. ἐξαίφνης, Syr. *men shel'*], when I saw it over
> against me, the splendid robe became like me, as my reflection
> in a mirror . . . so that we were two in distinction, and again
> one in a single form. . . . And the likeness of the King of Kings
> was completely embroidered all over it. . . . I clothed myself
> with it, and mounted up to the gate of greeting. . . . I bowed
> my head and worshipped the splendor of the Father [meaning
> Christ here] Who had sent the robe to me.[106]

105. The scholiast's remark in any case appears to have been rooted in a
tradition, perhaps even one based on the story of Paul's vision on the road to
Damascus. Μεσημβρία, "noonday," occurs elsewhere in the ascetical literature,
in contexts that have overtones of the mystical vision. See, for example, Basil
the Great, *Longer Rules* 2, PG 31:909; Evagrius, *Epistle* 33 (Frankenberg, 589).

106. *Acta Thomae* 112, in *Acta Apostolorum Apocrypha* (ed. M. Bonnet;
Hildesheim: Olms, 1959), II.2, 223:7–13; translation in W. Schneemelcher,
ed., *New Testament Apocrypha* (trans. R. McL. Wilson; Louisville: Westminster
John Knox, 1992), 2:384–385.

The robe here is the "heavenly double" and "luminous image," familiar from both Jewish and Christian literature, in which the speaker recognizes the form or shape of his own true being. Christ as the "Splendor" (φέγγος) of the Father again recalls the Glory and *Shekinah* traditions, just as the scene itself partakes of the classical patterns of the ascent to heaven in apocalyptic literature.[107]

In the *Life of Anthony*, the "sudden" occurs early in the narrative, after "the father of monks" has grown weary and battered from his struggles with the demons. Near despair, Anthony cries to God for help and, "suddenly," the roof of the tomb where he is staying opens up and a beam of light descends to surround him. The light carries the presence of Christ, who expels the demons and comforts the ascetic.[108] This account clearly recalls the CD's third epistle. Perhaps even more so, it bears a striking resemblance to Carpus' vision in *Ep.* VIII where we also find the "sudden" (here ἄφνω) opening of the roof and vision of Christ in light.[109] But in the latter case it is a bishop who receives the visitation, and Dionysius tells the story in order to admonish a not very holy monk.

Ephrem mentions the "sudden" three times to my knowledge, once in his *Hymns on Nature* and twice in the *Paradise Hymns*, to which I have already referred several times. In the first, it is Christ Who is the "star of light Who shone forth suddenly" in the Incarnation.[110] In the *Paradise Hymns* the "sudden" occurs first in reference to the angelic liturgy. The thrice-holy hymn (τρισάγιον) of the seraphim "suddenly" breaks the silence before the Presence

---

107. For a similar use of the "sudden" (ἐξαίφνης), see the *Acta Phillipi*, Bonnet, *Acta Apocrypha Apostolorum* II.2, 10:26–11:5 (Christ appears "suddenly," more radiant than the sun); and in an early Manichean document, *The Cologne Mani Codex: Concerning the Origin of His Body* (ed. R. Cameron and A. J. Davey; Missoula, MO: Scholars, 1979), 55:12–57:16, pp. 42 and 44 (a "sudden" rapture to heaven). On the latter text as indicative of continuing traditions of apocalyptic ascent in Syro-Mesopotamian Christian and para-Christian circles, see J. C. Reeves, *Heralds of that Good Realm: Syro-Mesopotamian Gnosis and Jewish Traditions* (Leiden: Brill, 1996), 5–30.

108. *Vita Antonii* 10; PG XXVI, 860A.

109. *Ep.* VIII, 1100A (190:5ff).

110. Ephrem Syrus, *De natura* 6.7, CSCO 186, 52; ET: K. McVey, *Ephrem the Syrian: Hymns* (New York: Paulist, 1989), 112.

in Eden, and, interestingly enough in light of our discussion of Sinai, Ephrem brings up the angelic worship here in parallel to a reference to the thunder of theophany on Sinai.[111] The second appearance of the "sudden" in the *Paradise Hymns*, and perhaps the most apposite of all considering our reflections on Dionysius so far, occurs during Ephrem's obviously eucharistic allusion to the supper of the risen Jesus with the two disciples at Emmaus in Luke 24:29-31:

> When the disciples' eyes were closed, bread too was the key whereby their eyes were opened to recognize the Omniscient One: darkened eyes beheld a vision of joy and were suddenly filled with happiness.[112]

It seems to me, just on the basis of these nine texts, that we have evidence of a certain tradition or at least current in Christian literature which links the "sudden" to Christ, to light, and to both the heavenly and earthly liturgies.[113] Assuming that Dionysius knew Syriac, there is perhaps an additional play on this word. The Syriac phrase which renders the Greek ἐξαίφνης is *men shelya*. *Men* is simply the preposition "from," like the Greek ἐκ. *Shelya*, on the

111. Ephrem, *Hymnen de Paradiso* 5.11, *CSCO* 174, 18:6–11 (*men shel* on line 7); S. Brock, *Hymns on Paradise*, 106.

112. Ephrem, *Hymnen de Paradiso* 15.4, 63:3–8 (*men shel* on line 8); Brock, *Hymns on Paradise* 183. I was alerted to the importance of the "sudden" in Ephrem by M. Schmidt, "Alttestamentliche Typologien in Paradies Hymnen von Ephräm der Syrer," in *Paradeigmata: Literarische Typologie des Alten Testaments* (ed. F. Link; Berlin: Duncker & Humboldt, 1989), 55–81, here 75, together with the explicit parallels she draws between Ephrem and Dionysius in 64–65.

113. M. N. A. Bockmuehl notes (*Revelation and Mystery in Ancient Judaism and Pauline Christianity* [Tübingen: Mohr, 1990], 66), that "the theme of heavenly revelation out of silence is common in ancient Jewish thought," citing in particular the *Wisdom of Solomon* 18:14–15, which is worth quoting here: "For while gentle silence [ἡσύχια σιγῆς] enveloped all things . . . your all-powerful word [λόγος] leaped from heaven, from the royal throne, into the midst of the land . . ." (NRSV). Note the movement of the divine word from the throne, and from silence, into the world; note also that the Syriac Old Testament, the *Peshitta*, has thus the word (*melta*) moving "from . . . silence" (*men . . . shelya*).

other hand, has interesting associations. It contains the meanings "rest," "silence," and "stillness" and is usually connected in Christian Syriac with the hermits, as is ἡσυχία in Christian Greek.[114] It may also, though, be used, as Dionyius' precise contemporary, the distinguished scholar and bishop Philoxenus of Mabbug, uses it, to signify the divine being or essence.[115] As a bilingual pun playing off of these several resonances—thus: "from silence," "from stillness," "from the divine being" etc.—the "sudden" fits indeed very well into the intentions and associations of the *CD*, and particularly of the *MT*, which I have been at pains to underline so far.[116]

Here I am reminded, again, of the Syrian whose works we know Dionysius knew—Ignatius of Antioch. Ignatius characterized Christ as the Word Who proceeds from the Father's silence, σιγή. Ignatius elsewhere offers a remark that, again, echoes some of the themes we touched on in the *MT* and in the epistles: "It is better to keep silence and to be, than to talk and not to be. . . . He that truly possesses the word of Jesus is able to listen to His silence."[117] I would therefore suggest that the silence which concludes the *MT* is neither empty nor impersonal, but instead the presence of the light of Christ.

But I have not yet cited the scriptural text which the σχόλια of John of Scythopolis tell us Dionysius is actually quoting in *Ep. III*. This is Malachi 3:1: "And suddenly the Lord Whom you seek will come into His temple, and the Angel of great counsel whom

114. See J. Payne Smith, *A Compendious Syriac Dictionary* (Oxford: Clarendon, 1903; repr., 1990), 580.

115. See R. Chestnut, *Three Monophysite Christologies: Severus of Antioch, Philoxenus of Mabbug and Jacob of Sarug* (Oxford: Oxford University Press, 1976), 63n.2, and 105, for *shelya* in Philoxenus of Mabbug. In her first example, it denotes the simplicity of the divine essence, and in her second signals the inner condition of the soul—quiet, silence—necessary for the encounter with God.

116. Thus "from the simple divine being" and the "stillness" around the divine throne (cf. the discussion of Wis 18:14-15 in the note above), hence a reference to the Incarnation, and "from the silence *within*," and so the mystical perception of the divine Presence.

117. Ignatius, *Magnesians* 8 and *Ephesians* 15. For the Greek text, see the edition by P. Camelot, *Lettres. Martyr de Polycarpe* (SC 10; Paris: Cerf, 1969), 86 and 70–72, respectively.

you desire."[118] The incarnational allusion that John sees in this text is doubtless part of Dionysius' intention, but, given the other resonances of "temple" which we have seen in the course of this essay, the continual coordination between the temple of the liturgical assembly and the temple of the Christian's body and soul, together with the resonances of mystical experience and especially of a theophany of light attached to the word "sudden," we can surely say that Dionysius intends to signify as well the presence of Christ on the eucharistic altar, his body after all, together with his visitation—"beyond hope," "ineffable," "unknowable," to cite *Ep.* III—within the temple of the soul. This, the sudden flash of the "unapproachable light" within, is, I submit, the very content of the "darkness" (γνόφος) into which Moses ascends in *MT* I.3, as well as of the "consummation" and "access" of *EH* IV.3.12, where Christ is both the way and the goal. *Ep.* III is the *Corpus Dionysiacum* in concentrated form: christological, liturgical, and mystical. The worship of the heavenly and earthly churches, the experience of the transcendent God, the hope of the Christian, all meet on the altar which is Christ.

7. A Reply to the Critics: The Revealed "Pattern" of Public Worship and Private Prayer

I affirmed earlier that there is no need for question marks over Dionysius' Christianity and mysticism. The Areopagite is both Christian and mystic, or, regarding the last, is at the very least a theologian who places the mystical encounter at the center of his thought. But, it is fair to ask, is "my" Dionysius the real one? Here I can do no more than suggest that the hypothesis which offers the best, most rounded and elegant account of the phenomenon under investigation ought to be preferred. I think that my accounting here best matches that description. My Dionysius belongs and

---

118. *PG* IV:532AB. In fact, the text John cites appears to be a conflation of Mal 3:1 and Isa 9:6 (LXX). The second half of Mal 3:1 actually reads "and the angel of the covenant," unless there is a variant version of which I am unaware. John's version, of course, accentuates the echo of the Incarnation.

contributes to a continuum. On the one hand, we have the long tradition of Christian Platonism, beginning as early as, say, the Epistle to the Hebrews and continuing through Christian Alexandria to the Asia Minor of the Cappadocians, and then going on through Dionysius to Maximus Confessor, John Damascene, and, still further, to the end of the Byzantine era.[119] Similarly, the ascetico-mystical line begins at or in the setting of Second Temple Judaism, even before Christian origins, carries on in the second- and third-century texts of, for example, the Thomas tradition, sees its encratism and centrifugal tendencies corrected by other, primarily Syrian, ascetics in the fourth century (thus Aphrahat, the *Liber*, Macarius, and Ephrem), and then runs through Dionysius to Maximus, especially to the latter's profound little treatise, *The Mystagogy*, which sets out—precisely as Maximus says he is going to do—in explicit fashion nearly all the very same connections which I have been obliged to tease out of the *CD*,[120] and then, beyond Maximus, to Symeon the New Theologian and Nicetas Stethatos in the eleventh century, and on to Gregory of Sinai and Nicholas Cabasilas in the fourteenth.[121] Dionysius fits exactly

119. On the Christian Platonist tradition in the East, if from a Roman Catholic perspective and hence not always especially friendly to certain aspects of Eastern tradition, see the still very useful study by E. von Ivanka, *Plato Christianus: Übernahme und Umgestaltung des Platonismus durch die Väter* (Einsiedeln: Johannes Verlag, 1964), together with Golitzin, *Et introibo*, 255–317.

120. For an account of Maximus' *Mystagogy* which appears—and quite strikingly so, since it is to the best of my knowledge, a wholly independent work—as a near exact duplicate of the reading of Dionysius in my earlier book, *Et introibo*, particularly on the relation between the *EH* and *MT*, see A. Louth, *Wisdom of the Byzantine Church: Evagrios of Pontos and Maximus the Confessor* (1997 Paine Lectures in Religion; Columbia, MO: University of Missouri-Colombia, 1998), esp. "Apophatic Theology and the Liturgy in St. Maximos the Confessor," 34–45.

121. See in regard to this chain esp. A. Golitzin, "Hierarchy versus Anarchy? Dionysius Areopagita, Symeon the New Theologian, Nicetas Stethatos, and their Common Roots in Ascetical Tradition," *SVTQ* 39 (1994): 131–179; together with the brief sketch of the Dionysian reception in idem, *Et introibo*, 401–413. On the "inner liturgy" in the Byzantine Hesychast, Gregory of Sinai, see M. van Parys, "La liturgie du coeur selon saint Grégoire le Sinaïte," *Ir* 51 (1978): 312–337, though the author, while citing Maximus' liturgy of the

into these two continua. He is "bracketed," to use that word one last time, by tradition on all sides. It was for this reason, far more than for any aura which may have attached to his sub-apostolic pseudonym, that he was accepted so quickly and so wholeheartedly in the East, and especially so by the monks. Put another way, they welcomed in him what they had known already and accepted in others before him; they recognized him for what he was, a spokesman of the Great Tradition. Put more simply still, the monks have always known better.

Dionysius as an anomaly, a sort of "lonely meteorite" blazing oddly across the night sky of patristic thought, to use an image coined by Vanneste, is too embedded in the scholarly consensus—to the degree that we can speak of any consensus at all—to be rooted out easily.[122] Yet the very fact that Dionysius was accepted by contemporaries of the highest stature and intellectual attainment—Severus of Antioch, John of Scythopolis, and the Alexandrian Christian philosopher John Philoponus in the sixth century, Maximus Confessor in the seventh, and John Damascene in the eighth, to name but a few of the most prominent—suggests at the least that he was not so odd to them as he seems nowadays to us. To hold in any case that men of the degree of intelligence, learning, and spiritual accomplishment as those whom I have just listed were simply gulled by the pseudonym is frankly ludicrous. They had to have seen something they liked and, to repeat myself, which they recognized. Long-standing scholarly shibboleths have also played their part in modern dismissals of the Areopagite. Here I think especially of the nineteenth- and early twentieth-century argument for a "Hellenization" of the Gospel put forward with such force by such scholars as Adolph von Harnack, a thesis which still on occasion, and to no good effect, intrudes into and obfuscates the study of the Early Church. Confessional attitudes have also played a role in the assessment of Dionysius, whether explicitly (Nygren) or implicitly (Rorem),

heart, seems quite unaware of the presence of his theme in the fourth-century Syrians, in Dionysius, and in Symeon and Nicetas.

122. Vanneste, "Is the Mysticism of Pseudo-Dionysius Genuine?," 288–289.

and have in their turn as often obscured the picture as they have illumined it. Put crudely, Dionysius, according to this particular confessional approach, amounts to a kind of justification for the Reformation. More broadly, however, the Dionysian "problem" is itself but one particular instance of a generally prevailing—even today—"occidentalism" in patristic scholarship, which is to say that Dionysius continues to be read through the lense of the great Western tradition which owes so profoundly to Augustine of Hippo. It is the latter who contributed essentially to that larger *Gestalt* of Western theology which I touched on in my introduction, a *Gestalt* which remained fundamentally unaltered in its basic outline even in a setting, such as that of the medieval Schoolmen, where the Areopagite could be heartily welcomed. The result, as I also noted in the Introduction, was a kind of kaleidoscopic splintering and fragmentation of the *Corpus Dionysiacum* into different elements, one or another of which might then be incorporated into the extant form and concerns of Western theology. One had only to rotate the tube, as it were, to find a pattern that would please.

In spite of how my last remarks may appear, I really do not wish to indulge here either in a cheap bout of Augustine-bashing (especially since I have come more and more over the years to appreciate him as one of the great Fathers) or in yet another instance of an equal and opposing "orientalism." Either or both would be quite as limited and provincial as what I am criticizing here. Indeed, and too typical of much Orthodox literature, this would simply be to engage in a theology of reaction, defensive in mode, condemnatory in tone, no whit better than the sort of polemic, conscious or unconscious, that I am deploring, and in the last analysis little more than a kind of mirror-image opposite of its target. Understandable as such an attitude might be in light of the massive weight—indeed, all-prevailing dominance—of Western thought throughout the world, it remains a futile and sterile self-indulgence. The problem is not with bad will, as it were, on the part of past Dionysian exegetes, including as far back as the Scholastics themselves, but rather that the lense through which they read Christianity itself has been shaped by the Augustinian inheritance. What fits that lense, perhaps especially as it was refined by the Reformers—e.g., the great dichotomies of law and gospel, nature and grace, and the overarching principle of justification by faith—does not really fit Dionysius or, indeed, much of the Christian East, and thus what I do want to do, and what I hope I have at least begun to do, is to enter the plea that we look—really *look*—at a strange (to us) body of theological literature and try to see it anew, to place it in the context for which I believe it was intended. If we do that, and if we make use, exactly, of those same splendid tools which Western scholarship makes available to us (and for which I daily give thanks), then I think we will begin to perceive the lineaments of a Christian accounting of the liturgy, of ascetical striving, of mystical vision, and—above and before all else—of Christ, which, for all the oddity of its rococo vocabulary, should strike us as at once powerful, deeply moving, and—even—strangely familiar.

That familiar element, to put things in a nutshell, derives most basically from the biblical traditions of tabernacle and temple, the two classical *loci* in the Hebrew Scriptures of divine presence and theophany. Put, I hope, a little more precisely still, it turns around the "pattern" for divine worship, the tabernacle, which God reveals to Moses as, arguably, the very climax of the Sinai narrative in Exodus 25:9ff.[123] Dionysius, quite consciously (see *EH* V.1.2–4), applies that "pattern" to *both* the Christian assembly at worship, *and* to the Christian soul, and he does so in order to keep both anchored in each other and thus, mutually, in the revelation given once-for-all, ἐφάπαξ, in Christ. My echoing of Hebrews is intentional here. In the latter's distinction (Heb 10:1) between "shadow" (σκιά) and "image" (εἰκών), we can arguably discern the germ of the *Areopagitica*. In fact, I think we can see a certain fundamental kinship between Dionysius and the whole Pauline corpus,[124] particularly when we bear in mind that the Apostle, as

123. On the importance of the temple traditions for early Christianity, see M. Barker, *On Earth as It Is in Heaven: Temple Symbolism in the New Testament* (Edinburgh: T&T Clark, 1995), esp. 7–11, 13–25, and 61–72; C. R. Koester, *The Dwelling of God: The Tabernacle in the Old Testament, Intertestamental Literature, and the New Testament* (Washington, DC: Catholic Biblical Association of America, 1989); and R. E. Clements, *God and the Temple* (Philadelphia: Fortress, 1965).

124. *Pace* Arthur, *Ps.-Dionysius as Polemicist*, 3.

is becoming increasingly clear in at least some recent scholarship, was often confronting claims to visionary authority very much akin to what I have argued here Dionysius was seeking to correct, corral, and finally harness to an ordered and responsible living-out of the Faith: sacramentally based, community-centered, long-suffering, humble, non-judgmental, and suffused with charity.[125]

This places Dionysius within a tradition extending back into Christian origins. As I have also argued, he was drawing at the same time, and again very consciously, on more proximate Christian sources, notably fourth-century Syrian ascetical literature, whose own roots go back, in all probability, to the earliest forms and sites of Christianity: the Jewish-Christian villages and communities of Aramaic-speaking Palestine. These fourth-century sources as well—from Aphrahat and the *Liber Graduum* in the Persian empire east of the Tigris, to Ephrem and the *Macarian Homilies* in Roman Mesopotamia—were all likewise struggling with the same issues and drawing on the same or very similar

---

125. See, for example, the following: J. A. Fitzmeyer, "Glory Reflected in the Face of Christ (2 Cor 3:7–4:6) and a Palestinian Jewish Motif," *TS* 42 (1981): 630–644; J. Blank, "Gnosis und Agape: Zur christologischen Struktur paulinischer Mystik," in *Grundfragen christlicher Mystik* (ed. M. Schmidt and D. R. Bauer; Stuttgart: Fromann-Holzboog, 1987), 1–13; J. Tabor, *Things Unutterable: Paul's Ascent to Heaven in its Greco-Roman, Judaic, and Early Christian Contexts* (Lanham, MD: University Press of America, 1986), esp. 11–21 and 83–97; A. Segal, *Paul the Convert: The Apostolate and Apostasy of Saul the Pharisee* (New Haven: Yale University Press, 1990), esp. 9–22 and 34–71; M. Hengel, " 'Setze dich zu meiner Rechten!' Die Intronisation Christi zur Rechten Gottes und Psalmen 110:1," in *Le trône de Dieu* (ed. M. Philonenko; Tübingen: Mohr, 1993), 108–194; C. R. A. Morray-Jones, "Paradise Revisited (2 Cor 12:1-12): The Jewish Mystical Background of Paul's Apostolate," *HTR* 86 (1993): 177–217; 265–292; J. M. Scott, "The Triumph of God in 2 Cor 2:14: Additional Evidence of Merkabah Mysticism in Paul," *NTS* 42 (1996): 260–281; together with a series of articles by M. Goulder, arguing not for Paul as mystic (to which idea Goulder is allergic), but certainly that he is using the vocabulary of, while arguing against, vision and ascent traditions among Jewish-Christians: "Sophia in 1 Corinthians," *NTS* 37 (1991): 516–534; "The Visionaries of Laodicea," *JSNT* 43 (1991): 15–39; "Vision and Knowledge," *JSNT* 46 (1994): 53–71; and "The Pastor's Wolves: Jewish-Christian Visionaries behind the Pastoral Epistles," *NT* 38 (1996): 242–256.

sources in both canonical and extra-canonical literature.[126] It is in
this Syrian, very Semitic, context, and with regard to this theme
(the working-out of the Christian meaning of "temple," of the
locus of theophany) that we are also to place Dionysius' recourse
to late Neoplatonism, specifically to the latter's concern to defend
"ancient rites" and piety against claims lodged in favor of the autonomous intellect. Overall, I think, at least as judging from his
subsequent reception and the use to which he was put in the East,
Dionysius' move here—for which he also had precedents in the
long history of Jewish (e.g., the *Wisdom of Solomon* and Philo) and
Christian Platonism—was generally understood and applauded.
The bottom-line in any event is that he was *not*—even emphatically not—the proponent of a *theologia gloriae* in the Lutheran
sense. Luther misread him, though I would not particularly blame
the great doctor of the Reform for his error. His Dionysius was,
after all, already the product of centuries of prior misconstrual and
of consequent mutation. On the other hand, the real Dionysius
was hardly the advocate of a classically Lutheran *theologia crucis*,
either, but then I cannot think offhand of *any* figure in the patristic
age who would precisely meet that standard. Historical inquiry
can do a great deal to clear up our differences, but it cannot simply
dissolve them. They remain, yet even so I do not believe that they
are enough to justify our dismissal of the *Corpus Dionysiacum* as
a passing—or perniciously influential—anomaly.

---

126. Aphrahat, whom I have not touched on here, is strikingly insistent
throughout his work on the Christian as the temple of God, and on internal-
izing the ascent traditions of the apocalypses and (perhaps) contemporary
hekhalot literature in the portrait he offers of the transfigured Christian sage
who has become himself the *locus gloriae* and site of the heavenly liturgy. For
comment, see Golitzin, "The Place of the Presence of God: Aphrahat of Persia's Portrait of the Christian Holy Man," in *ΣΥΝΑΞΙΣ ΕΥΧΑΡΙΣΤΙΑΣ: Studies
in Honor of Archimandrite Aimilianos of Simonos Petras, Mount Athos* (Athens:
Indiktos, 2003), 391–447; also, S. K. Skoyles Jarkins, *Aphrahat the Persian Sage
and the Temple of God: A Study of Early Syriac Theological Anthropology* (Piscataway, NJ: Gorgias, 2008).

8. A Closing Illustration: The Mosaic of the Transfiguration at Saint Catherine's, Sinai[127]

In the mid-sixth century, the same emperor who convoked the colloquium of 532, Justinian I, built a fortress monastery in the Sinai at the foot of Jebel Musa, the by-then traditional site associated with the theophanies of Exodus and, in consequence, already a longtime haunt of Christian ascetics.[128] In the monastery church, imperial artisans assembled several mosaics, including one depicting the Transfiguration. The latter is located in the apse, directly above the altar. Here already, as Jas Elsner has pointed out in a remarkably perceptive essay in his recent book *Art and the Roman Viewer*,[129] we find the assemblage in a single glance of the major Dionysian themes: the God-man Christ in light, the altar of the Eucharist, the Sinai of Moses' ascent, the Tabor of the Transfiguration, and the suggestions at once of mystical vision in this life open to the monks (and pilgrims) who form the worshipping body, and of the eschaton.

What I should like particularly to focus on, and which Elsner does not cover, is what I take to be elements from our discussion just now of the *Epistles*, and especially of *Ep.* III, reflected in the portrayal of Christ in this mosaic—which, by the way and to the best of my knowledge, is the prototype for all subsequent Orthodox iconography of the Transfiguration. Christ is depicted clothed in brilliant white and gold. Rays shoot out from his Person to strike Elijah and Moses at his right and left, together with the stunned disciples at his feet—including, as Elsner points out, the figure of Peter, directly below, who is awakening from sleep into mystical vision. With the force of the rays we might also recall the

---

127. I have deployed the example of the Sinai mosaic in a number of earlier publications, at greatest length in "'A Contemplative and a Liturgist': Father Georges Florovsky on the *Corpus Dionysiacum*," *SVTQ* 43 (1999): 131–161, at 158–161.

128. For the dating of the mosaic, see V. Beneševi, "Sur la date de la mosaïque de la Transfiguration au Mont Sinai," *Byz* 1 (1924): 145–172; and for an analysis, E. Kitzinger, *Byzantine Art in the Making* (Cambridge, MA: Faber & Faber, 1977), 99–104, though the latter has been deepened by J. Elsner, *Art and the Roman Viewer* (Cambridge: Cambridge University Press, 1995).

129. Elsner, *Art and the Roman Viewer*, 94–125.

μεσημβρία ("midday") pointed out by the anonymous Scholiast and certainly presumed in the Christophany to Saint Paul, as well as the "ray" imagery so generally prominent in the *CD*. In addition, the mandorla around Christ has a curious feature, also usually reproduced in later Byzantine icons. It is banded. At its outer edge a pale shade, roughly the same hue as the rays, its several rings of color grow increasingly dark as we move inward until, immediately around the Person of Christ, the innermost ring is a midnight blue verging on black. At least two explanations have been proposed for this feature, both of which have a certain cogency. In one, the blue denotes the color of the firmament beneath God's feet in Exodus 24:10, a text which Evagrius takes up in his portrayal of the azure light of the intellect awaiting the descent of the uncreated light of the Trinity. In the other explanation, the mandorla represents both the bright cloud overshadowing the disciples at the Transfiguration and the dark cloud on Sinai into which Moses enters. I think both of these apply, but I would go further than Elsner, who stops at the *MT*. In the epistles we saw a certain alternation, especially in *Ep.* I and V, between dark and light. In *Ep.* III we met the paradox of Christ's sudden manifestation: light, overpowering, coming forth from the depths of silent divinity and, still, hidden even in the manifestation. The Sinai mosaic strikes me, in short, as a portrayal of the ἐξαίφνης ("suddenly"). The latter, with its simultaneous evocation, via Malachi 3:1, of the twin temples of the altar and the heart also matches the image, a depiction of mystical vision sited directly over the table of the Eucharist. It is, in fact, the *MT* located at the heart of the *EH*, with both united in the Person of Jesus.[130] Whoever, I think, commissioned that image knew his Dionysius very well indeed.

---

130. Thus the point of Louth, *Wisdom of the Byzantine Church*, 38: "Apophatic theology as Maximos envisages it . . . is the realization in the Christian soul of what is accomplished and celebrated in the Church's liturgy."

Chapter 2

The Mystery of God

Transcendence and Presence

Dionysius' treatises on the *Mystical Theology* and the *Divine Names*, the latter providing the basis of the following discussion, are the least original works of his corpus. While this statement will come as no surprise to those for whom the two treatises represent little other than thinly veiled Neoplatonist metaphysics, I contend that the Areopagite's want of originality here derives less from his imitation of the pagan masters than from his fidelity to patristic teaching on the Trinity and the divine names or attributes. That teaching stresses with respect to the Trinity, first, that It is a revealed mystery. God is known as both Three and One, yet how he is so remains forever hidden. Thus, secondly, the nature of each divine person and of their unity is utterly irreducible to any of the schemes or analogs derived from human thought and ways of being. Regarding the "names" of God, I distinguish the following points: (1) apophatic or negative theology, what we cannot know of God, is always the preferred approach, while (2) positive or cataphatic theology, statements about God, can only point to the, as it were, "periphery" of God's being. Therefore, (3) the names themselves refer rather to the activities or powers of God in creation than to his forever-secret inner life, his essence. In spite, then, of being human constructs, (4) the "names" can still, as *given* through either scriptural revelation or the "natural" revelation of the Creator in his creation (e.g., Rom 1:19-20), carry or impart some communication of the divine. In short, as "notional icons," they bear a certain sacramental power and participate in the mystery of God's revelation in Christ.

This patristic, primarily Cappadocian (though not entirely, as my research into Ephrem has shown) teaching is at the heart of the *DN*.[1] It is furthermore the key to that treatise's parallels with, particularly, the late Neoplatonists' commentaries on Plato's *Parmenides*—parallels which, as I noted above, have been so ably documented by Corsini. I do not intend to repeat the latter's work but will instead confine myself here to noting how the *DN* corresponds to the points just outlined. In so doing I hope to show that the *DN* represents at once a real break from the thought of the late Neoplatonists and their understanding of the intelligibles (νοητά), and the exploitation of those elements in their vision which were most open to development by a Christian thinker. As a full discussion of the *DN/MT* texts is impossible in the space I have allotted it, I will concentrate on the central chapter, *DN* II, and on certain aspects of the discussion flowing from it as vital not only to the *DN* but, bearing as the latter does on the notion of the divine powers, to Dionysius' whole understanding of our participation in God. Let me open the discussion by turning first to his understanding of that mystery as it exists for and in itself.

1. Reciprocal Ecstasies: A Preface

In his very short treatise on the *Mystical Theology* Dionysius concludes discussion of the apophatic way with the following, sweeping series of negations:

> [The divine] is neither soul nor mind; neither has it imagination, nor opinion, nor reason, nor intuition, neither is it reason nor intuition, nor can it be reasoned or intuited . . . it is neither

---

1. See Golitzin, *Et introibo*, 291–304 (Cappadocians), 359–362 (Ephrem). Bradshaw states, similarly, that "the work of Dionysius that most clearly shows his affinity to the Cappadocians is *The Divine Names*" (*Aristotle East and West*, 180).

life nor does it live; neither is it essence, nor eternity, nor time
. . . it is neither one nor oneness, nor deity, nor goodness. It
is not spirit, as we know it, nor is it sonship, nor fatherhood
. . . it is no one of the things which are not, nor is it any of
those which are . . . beyond all affirmation . . . and beyond
negation is the transcendence of him who, simply, is free of
all things and beyond them all.[2]

There is then evidently very little indeed that one can say when
attempting to speak of the deity as it is in itself. Dionysius takes
this point up specifically, and notes that all such discussion has
silence, a cessation of both discourse and of intuition, as its final
outcome: "and entering now into the darkness beyond mind
[we find] not brevity of speech but a total want of speech and
thought."[3] At the terminus of the ascent one is to become "wholly
speechless" in order "to be united to the unutterable."[4] The deity
as it is in itself remains wholly outside the realm of discourse—
and of everything. It is wholly unknowable, ineffable, incommunicable. It is other. God may be "known," as it were, through
an act of "unknowing" alone: "to see and to know through un-
seeing and unknowing . . . through the negation of all things
known and seen."[5] Our sole access to the "darkness of the secret
silence" lies through an act of ecstasy.[6] The creature approaches
the "super-essential ray of divine darkness" by means of "the
complete and pure departure from itself and from all things."[7]
It is an out-going from self, a departure from the state of creaturely being, shedding all (πάντα ἀφελῶν) in accordance with the
demands of "a union (ἕνωσις) which exceeds the creaturely powers of intellect and intuition."[8] God dwelling in unapproachable
light permits no other mode of approach.

2. *MT* V 1045D–1048B (149:1–150:9).
3. *MT* III 1033BC (147:8–10).
4. *MT* III 1033C (147:11).
5. *MT* II 1025A (145:2–5).
6. *MT* I.1 997B (142:2).
7. *MT* I.1 997B–1000A (142:9–10).
8. *DN* I.1 585B–588A (108:3–5).

While I will return in the chapter following to the *MT*, I should like at this point to indicate that there is little, in the passages just cited, that is new with respect either to patristic writers[9] or to the late Neoplatonists.[10] Dionysius is here surely touching on a point where Christians and Neoplatonists converge. The latter, too, require an ἔκστασις or "out-passing" of the mind in order to approach the transcendent divinity.[11] Their stress on divine transcendence is also both consistent and unequivocal[12]—so much so in fact that it is difficult, at best, to see in them any thoroughgoing monism.[13] The Neoplatonist philosophers insist on apophasis and so on the vast chasm between the ineffable One and everything else.[14] So great, indeed, did they see that gulf that their greatest difficulty lay in explaining just how the rest of existence, the realm of being, comes to be at all. Thus we find in Plotinus that the descent of the Second Hypostasis, the Νοῦς, is occasionally spoken of in terms reminiscent of nothing so much as original sin.[15]

9. See my discussion of, particularly, Clement of Alexandria and the Cappadocians, in *Et introibo*, 261–262 and 314–316 respectively. See esp. Gregory of Nyssa on the darkness and silence, 292nn. 57–58.

10. See Koch, *Beziehungen*, 123–134 and 147–174.

11. See, for example, Plotinus, *Enneads* III.8.9–10 and VI.7.34–36; as well as Proclus, *In Tim.* I.212 (cited by Beierwaltes, *Proklos: Grundzüge seiner Metaphysik* [Frankfurt am Main: Klostermann, 1965], 319).

12. See Plotinus, *Enn.* I.7.1 (citing Plato's *Republic* 509B); Iamblichus, *De mysteriis* (ed. des Places) I.5 (see also Dillon *Iamblichi in Platonis Dialogos Commentariorum Fragmenta* [1973], 29–33); and for Proclus: Beierwaltes, *Proklos*, 343–348.

13. Such as is maintained by Bernhard Brons, *Gott und die Seienden: Untersuchungen zum Verhältnis von neuplatonischer Metaphysik und christlicher Tradition bei Dionysius Areopagita* (Göttingen: Vandenhoeck & Ruprecht), 229–236.

14. See, for example, S. Gersh, *From Iamblichus to Eriugena: An Investigation of the Prehistory and Evolution of the Pseudo-Dionysian Tradition* (Leiden: Brill, 1978), 37. For a study of apophatic or negative theology, see esp. R. Mortley, *From Word to Silence* (Bonn: Hanstein, 1986), in particular 2:97–127 for Proclus and Damascius, and 221–241 for Dionysius himself.

15. For the descent of Νοῦς from the One as τόλμα, see *Enn.* VI.5.13; VI.7.9; and, relatedly, VI.8.5.

Dionysius' insistence on the divine transcendence raises the problem of God's immanence. If divinity *in se* is utterly removed from the sphere of creaturely being, what then is or can be the nature of God's relation to the creation? Indeed, how is it that creation comes to be at all? Further, assuming that there is a relationship between Creator and created, how, and employing which modes, is the divine and super-essential reflected in created essences in such a manner that it can and does become accessible, in a finite way, to the limited capacities of creaturely knowing? For while the *MT* does insist ultimately upon the creature's ecstatic move (ἔκστασις), it nonetheless presupposes an ascent through degrees of knowing prior to the final leap into "unknowing" (ἀγνωσία).[16] What, then, is the shape of the process, the παιδεία, proper to the creature both by essence and, as we shall see, by grace? What, particularly, is the nature of the corresponding condescension of the deity that enables the creature's ascent?

It is here that we approach one of Dionysius' fundamental, and Christian-inspired, adjustments of pagan thought. The key lies in the term ἔκστασις itself. If the created mind encountering divinity in the transcendent darkness proper to the latter is no longer creature *qua* creature ἐν ἐκστάσει, deity in commerce with creation is no longer divinity *in se* but God outside of himself. Dionysius' ἔκστασεις are reciprocal.[17] In reference to God the word is used twice, once in adjectival form and once as a participle. Describing the process whereby the divine is brought into relation with creation, Dionysius declares that the Godhead "descends to immanence *by means of an ecstatic and super-essential power* while remaining within itself."[18] The second usage of the term, ἐξεστηκῶς, refers rather to God's transcendence than to his immanence.[19] Finally, however, Dionysius uses a related term, ἔκβασις, to describe

---

16. See the account of Moses' ascent, *MT* I.3 1000C–1001A (143–144).

17. See Roques' remarks on the divine love, ἔρως and ἀγάπη, in his "Introduction" to the *Hiérarchie Céleste* (SC 58), xliii–xliv; and his article, "Symbolisme et théologie négative chez le Pseudo-Denys," *BAGB* 1 (1957): 97–112, esp. 12. See also, more recently, Bradshaw, *Aristotle East and West*, 181.

18. κατ᾽ ἐκστατικὴν ὑπερούσιον δύναμιν, *DN* IV.13 712B (159:13–14).

19. *Ep.* IX.5 1112C (205:5).

the action whereby God creates: "He brings essences into being by means of an *out-going* from essence."[20] I do not think Gersh justified in reading this application of ἔκστασις to God as an "unqualified emanation metaphor" highly suggestive of "automatism."[21] The metaphor seems to me considerably removed from the impersonal note he finds elsewhere in the pagans.[22] Neither, for that matter, can we find any of the philosophers using ἔκστασις to describe *God's* action.[23] The lower levels of being may move *up* to union with transcendence via an "out-passing," but a downward ecstasy is nowhere stated. While the metaphor is certainly a bold one, it appears to me that Dionysius is using it in order to accentuate at once the gap between God and creation, and the former's own, personal action in moving to create—it is, after all, persons and not "things" who are the subjects of ecstasies.

We arrive then at the following fundamental equation of Dionysian thought: if the creature may only encounter God as the latter is in his transcendence through "passing out" of its proper being, then, conversely, God may enter into relationship, including the act of creation, only through a kind of "self-transcendence." Moved to create—and we shall see below that he is so moved because he desires it—God "leaves" in a sense the state of being, or "super-being," proper to him. He goes "outside" his hidden essence, ἔξω ἑαυτοῦ γίνεται.[24] It is this divine "out-passing" that is the foundation or subject of the *DN* and, insofar as they are the mirrors of God, of the Celestial and Ecclesiastical Hierarchies as well. God as he is known in his names and in his creation is God "outside," as it were, of his essence.

20. κατὰ τὴν ἀπὸ οὐσίας ἔκβασιν, *DN* V.8 824C (188:6).
21. Gersh, *From Iamblichus to Eriugena*, 20.
22. Gersh, *From Iamblichus to Eriugena*, 17–26.
23. See Beierwaltes, *Proklos*, 212, 319 and 379 for ἔκστασις in Proclus.
24. *DN* IV.13 712B (159:11).

2. The One and the Many in God: The Divine Differences

In the second chapter of the *DN* Dionysius draws the distinction that I, following Lossky,[25] understand as crucial to his system. As Dionysius tells us himself, his discussion here of the divine διακρίσεις ("differences") will provide the context of the whole treatise following.[26] That discussion has as its aim at once the maintenance of the patristic doctrine of God in Trinity and in his energies, and therewith a radical readjustment of the Neoplatonist philosophers' teaching concerning the One and the intelligible world.[27]

Let us first ask after the nature of the problem Dionysius confronted in the Neoplatonists and those aspects of their system that he may have felt capable of exploiting in accordance with an already established Christian theology. I have already mentioned the crucial one: that ambiguity or gap between the ineffable One

25. See esp. Lossky, "La théologie négative dans la doctrine de Denys l'Aréopagite," *RSPT* 28 (1939): 204–221; "Apophasis and Trinitarian Theology" and "Darkness and Light in the Knowledge of God," both in Lossky, *The Image and Likeness of God* (ed. and trans. J. Erickson and T. E. Bird; Crestwood, NY: St Vladimir's Seminary Press, 1974), 13–29; 31–43.

26. *DN* II.4 640D (126:4–5).

27. E. Corsini, *Il trattato 'De divinis nominibus' dello Pseudo-Dionigi e i commenti neoplatonici al Parmenide* (Torino: Giappichelli, 1962), 39–42, 140ff. Here I take issue particularly with Corsini, Gersh, and Brons. The first, in spite of his close analysis of the texts, misses the point of the *DN* in reading the intelligibles (νοητά) as existing entities, the created principles of the world. Gersh, on the other hand, denies the distinction between essence and powers entirely (166–167n. 184). He thus finishes struggling to see the difference between the Persons of the Trinity and the intelligible names (187n. 269). This line of argument somewhat resembles the approach taken up and repeatedly stressed by Brons. The latter states flatly that the *DN* represents indeed the destruction of Proclus' "metaphysisch-architektonische Kunstwerk," but only at the cost of leaving in its wake chaotic plurality within a Godhead whose unique claim to unity lies in its being "cause [αἰτία]" of all things (165–166). Gersh's remark reveals the source of each of these scholars' difficulties: the "distinction . . . made between God's essence and God's energies . . . [was] explicitly rejected by the Athenian school of Neoplatonism which is Pseudo-Dionysius' source" (166–167n. 184). The false assumption is that Proclus and his predecessors provided Dionysius with, effectively, his unique source.

and the Many, with the latter including the realm of the intelligibles, the νοητά. Thus, for example, in Plotinus the One is above thought, not equivalent even to the intelligible one of mathematics.[28] Indeed, the "One" and "Good" are only names, pointers to a transcendent reality.[29] The One is above all free of our distinctions.[30] It is other and infinite.[31] The same sentiments may be found echoed in both Iamblichus[32] and Proclus.[33] As Armstrong has noted, this transcendent freedom from concepts and numerical reckoning opens, for a Christian theologian, the Neoplatonist "One" to a possible trinitarian reading.[34] Following the lead of J. Trouillard,[35] Armstrong draws another interesting conclusion from the One's transcendence and its lack of a real connection with the hierarchy of intelligibility: "It seems to me that this [apophatic] side of Plotinus' thought . . . must lead in the end . . . to nothing less than the abolition of the *kosmos noetos* . . . to the denial of an eternal, unchanging intelligible reality."[36] Once this consequence is accepted, he continues, one is free to move from the worship, as idols, of the intelligibles to their veneration as icons.[37] These are exactly the outlines of Dionysius' response. On the one hand, he was not bound as a Christian either to the traditional intellectualism of Greek thought, or to the essentially religious conservatism

28. *Enn.* VI.9.5.

29. *Enn.* V.5.6.

30. *Enn.* VI.9.4.

31. *Enn.* V.5.6; V.8.9. See A. H. Armstrong, "Plotinus' Doctrine of the Infinite and Christian Thought," *DRev* 73 (1954–1955): 47–58. For Dionysius' use of "infinity" as taken not from Plotinus and later Neoplatonists, but from Gregory of Nyssa, see also S. Lilla, "The Notion of Infinitude in Pseudo-Dionysius Areopagita," *JTS* 31 (1980): 93–103, esp. 101–102.

32. See Dillon, *Iamblichi*, 32, and *De myst.* VII.2 (des Places), 195–196.

33. See *Théologie Platonique* (ed. Saffrey/Westerink), II.1–6, 1–43.

34. Armstrong, "The Escape of the One: An Investigation of some Possibilities of Apophatic Theology Imperfectly Realized in the West," *TU* 116 (1971): 77–87.

35. Trouillard, "Raison et Mystique chez Plotin," *REA* 20 (1974): 3–14.

36. Armstrong, "Escape from the One," 84.

37. Armstrong, "Escape from the One," 88–89; see also his "Negative Theology," *DRev* 95 (1976): 188–189.

that together constrained the later philosophers to include, as a kind of reflex, both Plato's Ideas and Aristotle's *Nous* in their accounts of reality.[38] Neither was he under their compulsion to make his own that intellectual portrait of a perfectly continuous spectrum, of a descent "without leaps"[39] which characterized their own attempts—whether in the form of Plotinus' broad sweep or the more "cinematic"[40] approach, featuring a marvelously complex and heavily populated intelligible universe of interlocking triads,[41] taken up by the latter's successors in order to fill the spaces left between his three primary Hypostases.[42] Quite to the contrary, Dionysius was free to abandon their elaborate machinery of emanation while exploiting the opportunity that, as Armstrong has indicated, was present in their doctrine of transcendence. On the other hand, their religious tone, a corollary of the insistence on transcendence—as well as a sign of the times—and their stress on communion with the divine[43] must certainly have appeared to our author as points of potential convergence which he, already equipped with the patristic theology of divine transcendence and immanence, was able fully to exploit. Here then is the foundation of the *DN*: God is transcendent as both One and Three, yet is fully immanent to creation in his powers whose presence we may discern in the notional icons of his names given in revelation.

38. See the articles by Armstrong and A. C. Lloyd in *CambHist*, esp. 212–214, 236–237, 275–282, and 320–321.

39. Lloyd, *CambHist*, 281–282.

40. Both the contrast and the phrase are Gersh's, *From Iamblichus to Eriugena*, 120–121.

41. See E. R. Dodds, *Proclus, The Elements of Theology* (2nd ed.; Oxford: Clarendon, 1963), xxvi–xxxiii; also, for Iamblichus, Dillon, *Iamblichi*, 33–38; and for detail on Proclus, Beierwaltes, *Proklos*, 48–164.

42. For reasons why Plotinus' simple triad failed to satisfy his successors, see Armstrong, "Eternity, Life, and Movement in Plotinus' Accounts of *Nous*," in *Le Néoplatonisme* (ed. C. J. de Vogel; Paris: Centre National de la Recherche Scientifique, 1971), 67–74.

43. See E. R. Dodds, *Pagan and Christian in an Age of Anxiety* (Cambridge: Cambridge University Press, 1965), 70–100.

2.1. God *in se: The One and the Three*

Dionysius stresses in *DN* II.1 that the names of God belong indivisibly (οὐ μερικῶς) to the Godhead.[44] He goes on, however, to insist that there is nonetheless no confusion (σύγχυσις) of differences within God. Scripture, he declares, "delivers some things in a unified fashion (ἡνωμένως) and some in a differentiated manner (διακεκριμένως), and it is neither lawful to divide the unified nor to confuse the differentiated."[45] There is then a certain real plurality in God's own mode of being. As the first and truly primary example of this plurality he points of course to the Trinity. While those "unities" (ἡνωμένα) such as the "beyond-good" (ὑπεράγαθον), "beyond-being" (ὑπερούσιον), and so forth, whence are derived the "Good," "Being," etc., which we receive as gifts of God, must be predicated on the whole divinity (τῆς ὅλης θεότητος), the διακεκριμένως of the three divine persons are no less proper to God as he is in himself.[46] Unity and difference are simultaneous and intrinsic to the very *esse* of divinity. Dionysius illustrates this antinomy of the Many subsisting in the deeps of the One, the Trinity, with the image of a house having many lamps that project a single light, "united in difference and distinguished in unity."[47]

While this has the appearance of trinitarian orthodoxy, there are many who contend it is appearance alone. Vanneste, for example, argues that Dionysius' Three are irrelevant to, and finally disappear into, his transcendent One.[48] He is echoed in Brons' assertion that the "more general" is the more real for Dionysius, although the German writer also adopts a slightly different line in seeing the difference between the powers *ad extra* and the Persons as purely a "verbal" one.[49] The Latin Christian criteria for trinitarian

44. *DN* II.1 636C (122:7).
45. *DN* II.2 640A (125:6–7).
46. *DN* II.3 640C (125:19–21).
47. *DN* II.4 641AB (127:5–7).
48. Vanneste, *Mystère de Dieu*, 18–19, 28–29, and 149–150; see also Otto von Semmelroth, "Gottes überwesentliche Einheit: Zur Gotteslehre des Pseudo-Dionysius Areopagita," *Schol* 25 (1950): 209–234," at 213.
49. Brons, *Gott und die Seienden*, 109; 88.

theology are not altogether applicable to Dionysius.[50] Yet it is also undeniable that certain texts might appear to indicate a primary emphasis on the divine unity. In *DN* XIII he asserts that the name of the One is to be considered as the highest or most important (κρατερώτατον) of the divine titles.[51] More troubling still, he tells us at the end of *DN* II that the unities take precedence over the differentiations.[52] If the Persons of the Trinity are to be identified exclusively with the "differences," then the Neoplatonist One does prevail.

Such is not the case, however. Corsini has himself shown that this simple identification is impossible.[53] One may point first to the very beginning of chapter 2: Dionysius follows his declaration that the "unities" (ἡνωμένα) must be predicated indivisibly on the whole Godhead by listing a series of examples, "good," "being," "life," "lordship," and then goes on to apply these attributes to the divine Persons severally.[54] Again, below, we find the same repeated: "whatever is proper to the divine unity or super essentiality is united to the Trinity which is source of unity [τῇ ἐναρχικῇ Τριάδι]." This list includes "the unity beyond the source of unity, that which is ineffable, that which is given many names, that which is unknown, that which is eminently conceptual, that

---

50. Golitzin, *Et introibo*, 39–40. I might add that Brons' desire to see Dionysius use the Neoplatonists' intelligible triad οὐσία - ζωή - νοῦς, after the manner of Augustine (*Gott und die Seienden*, 36) precisely misses the point which I maintain Dionysius saw in the philosophers' transcendence doctrine and which, in accord with prior tradition (see Golitzin, *Et introibo*, 285–317), he felt free to exploit. Brons is perhaps also reflecting Beierwaltes' approval of Meister Eckhardt's vision of "die Entfaltung der trinitarischen Rationalität . . . die Selbstidentität seines [Gottes] Seins und Denkens"—i.e., a triumph of cataphatic theology—as opposed to Proclus' "impersonal" ἀπόφασις (see *Proklos*, "Exkurs IV," 397–398). The identification of the Trinity with, effectively, the Neoplatonists' νοῦς would have been anathema for Dionysius, as indeed it was for his predecessors (see Golitzin, *Et introibo*, 287–289 and 297ff.

51. *DN* XIII.1 977B (226:6–7); see also XIII.3 980A–D (228–229).

52. *DN* II.11 652A (157:5–6): αἱ ἑνώσεις τῶν διακρίσεων ἐπικρατοῦσι καὶ προκατάρχουσι.

53. Corsini, *Il tratto*, 39ff.

54. *DN* II.1 636C–637C (122–124).

which is beyond all affirmation and negation" (ἡ ὑπὲρ ἐναρχίαν ἑνότης, τὸ ἄφθεγκτον, τὸ πολύφωνον, ἡ ἀγνωσία, τὸ παννόητον . . . τὸ ὑπὲρ πᾶσιν καὶ θέσιν καὶ ἀφαίρεσιν).[55] Finally we may point to the statement that "these [i.e., the Persons] are the unities [ἑνώσεις] and differences [διακρίσεις] according to the [divine] ineffable union and existence."[56] Thus, all of the divine unities and differences, the latter referring to the processions, belong to each of the persons[57]—the sole exception being of course the Incarnation[58] with which Father and Spirit communicated only through the consent of the common divine will.[59] The "whole divinity," in other words, belongs to each.

If each person is a unity, each is also the One. The same chapter 13 which exalts the latter name immediately adds: "and One [εἷς] God is the Father, and One [εἷς] Lord Jesus Christ, and One [ἕν] and the same Spirit."[60] The divine "arithmetic" is thus thrice one equals one, and it is surely with that in mind that Dionysius concludes: "divinity above all things, hymned as monad and as triad, is neither any monad nor triad [οὐδὲ μονὰς οὐδὲ τρίας] of the sort known to us."[61] God above gods is ultimately unknowable in terms of number (ἀριθμός) or unity (ἑνότης) or any other way of reckoning, and we must therefore confess our ignorance at the last and admit with Scripture the superior propriety of ἀπόφασις ("negation") in confronting the revelation of the unknowable God.[62]

Each of the Three is unity and each the One, yet, although each is identical to the others,[63] there is no exchange (ἀντιστροφή) among them of personal identity.[64] Each is therefore absolute. Here we appear to be at the opposite extreme from a resolution of

---

55. *DN* II.4 641A (126:14–127:2).
56. *DN* II.5 641D (128:14–15).
57. *DN* II.1 637C (124:4–11).
58. *DN* II.3 640C (125:21–126:2) and II.6 644C (130:8–9).
59. *DN* II.6 644C (130:8–9).
60. *DN* XIII.3 980B (228:8–9).
61. *DN* XIII.3 980D (229:6–8).
62. *DN* XIII.3 981AB (229:10–230:5).
63. *DN* II.4 641A (126:14–127:4).
64. *DN* II.3 640C (125:20) and II.5 641D (128:11).

the three into the One. Rather than teaching the priority of unity, we must ask instead how Dionysius avoids tritheism.

As I have shown in greater detail elsewhere, he does so through the use of four arguments familiar from the fourth century.[65] The first is his articulation of trinitarian περιχώρησις ("mutual indwelling"): "the abiding and foundation of the ruling persons in one another" (ἡ ἐν ἀλλήλαις τῶν ἐναρχικῶν ὑποστάσεων μονή καὶ ἵδρυθσις).[66] Dionysius argues secondly from the unity of the divine activity.[67] The same list I cited above as comprising DN II.1 concludes with: "as much as is said of the Father and of Him [i.e., the Son] also applies commonly [κοινωνικῶς] and unitedly to the divine Spirit."[68] None of the attributes or functions—save, again, the Incarnation—ascribed to God can be referred to any one of the Three as distinct from the others. The divine πρόοδος ("procession"), or δύναμις ("power"), or ἐνέργεια ("activity"), or πρόνοια ("providence") is ultimately one and the same, and the "whole divinity" refers thus to the united and indivisible activity of the Three.[69] Thirdly, the Father is the "unique source" [μόνη δὲ πηγή] of the super-essential divinity."[70] His is the monarchy of

65. See Golitzin, Et introibo, 297–302.

66. DN II.4 641A (127:2–3), repeated in MT III 1033A (146:4–7). See the perceptive article by V. Harrison, "Perichoresis in the Greek Fathers," SVTQ 35 (1991): 53–65.

67. See Golitzin, Et introibo, 269–271, on Gregory of Nyssa's On Why There Are Not Three Gods. This was one of the keys both to the Cappadocians' defense of the Trinity as one, and to their refutation of "polytheism" which was, at least potentially, inherent in Origen's division of functions within the Trinity—thus see Golitzin, Et introibo, on both Origen (270–273) and Basil (289–290). I also note that this is a point of Greek triadology which Brons seems completely to miss (Gott und die Seienden, 101, 108–109, and 122–125). It serves, finally, to explain why Dionysius is free to use "Providence," "Spirit," "Jesus," "Thearchy," etc., in identical contexts: the action of God is proper to each Trinitarian person and to all.

68. DN II.1 637C (124:6–7).

69. For the unity of the πρόοδος, see for example DN II.5 641D (128:15); for δύναμις, VIII.3 892B (201:17–21); for ἐνέργεια, IX.5 912D (210:9); and for πρόνοια, CH IX.4 261B–D (39:1–24).

70. DN II.5 641D (128:11); see also II.7 645B (132:1).

origins and he alone is θεόγονος, source of divinity.[71] His relation
of origin to the other co-eternal Persons serves simultaneously as
the uniquely revealed mode of distinction among them.[72] Lastly,
there is the appeal to ἀπόφασις ("negation") I noted concluding
DN XIII. The modes of divine union and difference in the hidden
life of God are forever unknowable. They escape all categories.
Number no longer applies and the very names themselves of the
divine persons, taken from our human ways of being, can do no
more than to direct us to the mystery of the tri-unity.[73] Like the
Incarnation itself, whence we know of the Trinity, the latter is an
irreducible given, revealer of its providence to us, but itself in
itself ever mysterious.[74]

In reply to the questions posed concerning the Dionysian Trinity, I may thus list the following: (1) the Three are severally and
together, inseparably and unconfusedly, the "whole divinity";
(2) each is the One; (3) each is not the other; (4) they are together
One through their coinherence; (5) their single origin is from the
Father; (6) their activity is united and single; and (7) their unity
is beyond thought and number. There can be no doubt that these
points constitute a fully orthodox triadology according to the
criteria of the Cappadocians.[75] It must, equally, be admitted that
Dionysius' is a very brief account of the Trinity, little more than
a bare outline. In his defense, though, I stress that it is an outline
fully capable of expansion, that the Three are not the declared
subject of the *DN*, and furthermore, that he does promise a fuller
treatment in the *Outlines of Divinity*.[76] There appears to me to be
no compelling reason to dismiss the latter as a fraud, and I be-

---

71. For the Father as θεόγονος, see *DN* II.1 637B (123:9); II.7 645B (132:2);
XIII.3 981A (229:8); and *Ep.* IX.1 1104C (194:8); and as, by implication, the
divine γονιμότης, see *DN* I.4 592A (113:1).

72. *DN* II.3 640C (125:19–21); II.5 641D (128:12–13); II.7 645B (132:1–3).

73. See *DN* II.7 and II.8 645A and C–D (130–132); *MT* V 1048A (150:4);
and *Ep.* IX.1 1104C–1105A (194:7–195:2).

74. *DN* III.1 680B (138:2–4).

75. See again Golitzin, *Et introibo*, 297–302.

76. *DN* I.1 585B (107:3); II.1 636C (122:11); and *MT* III 1033A (146:9).

lieve it wisest to accept his sketch in the *DN* as a true indication of his mind.[77]

2.2. God ad extra: *The Divine Differences and Immanence*

We arrive at the subject proper of the *DN*. If in the Trinity we discover the One and the Many enshrined ineffably in the (super-) essence itself of God, we are led to see the same principle of distinction applied to the opposition between God *in se* and *ad extra*. Dionysius is careful to distinguish the "differences" (and "unities") which are the divine Hypostases from this second kind of διάκρισις.[78] "Difference" in the latter case signifies a mode of existence that is other than the essential. It is equivalent to God's ecstatic movement we discussed above: "divine difference is the beneficent procession [πρόοδος] of the divine unity multiplying itself in goodness and in a manner transcending unity."[79] While he uses qualifiers such as ὑπερηνωμένως (Jones: "beyond every way of unity") in referring to this self-multiplication of God, Dionysius' point remains clear: there is a structure in God that has a decisively real character.[80] To put it another way, it is the same God who at once abides ineffably removed in his proper transcendence and perfectly present through his own act of "self-transcendence," his procession.

2.2.1. Procession: a lesser God? The use of this term has often been raised to accuse the Areopagite of pagan philosophizing: "the principle of unity and distinctions in God . . . does not derive from Christian Revelation but from Neoplatonism . . . the

---

77. As does Vanneste, *Mystère de Dieu*, 20.

78. *DN* II.5 641D (128:15). Note Dionysius' use of μὲν . . . δὲ: on the one hand, the Hypostases of the Trinity; on the other, the distinctions which are not in the essence.

79. *DN* II.5 641D (128:15).

80. *DN* II.5 641D–644A (128); see von Semmelroth's remarks in "Geeinte Vielheit: Zur Gotteslehre des Pseudo-Dionysius Areopagita," *Schol* 25 (1950): 389–407, at 394.

unity of the being in itelf and the plurality of emanation."[81] It is
undeniable that the late Neoplatonist triad of abiding, procession,
and return (μονή-πρόοδος-ἐπιστροφή) does occupy a central place
in the *CD* as a whole.[82] God's μονή is in the transcendent Trinity,[83]
while his πρόοδος and ἐπιστροφή, as I will argue, accomplish respectively the establishment and salvation of his creatures. The
latter again—especially the reason-endowed—both individually
and collectively mirror this double movement. While it is certainly
true that this cycle is a major theme in the pagans' philosophy as
at once a theory of causation and a morphology of mind,[84] i.e., of
the microcosm mirroring the macrocosm,[85] it is also the case that
it had already undergone a considerable and progressively more
transforming adaptation at the hands of Christian writers beginning particularly with Origen.[86] The whole account of Dionysius'
own use will become clearer in the course of my exposition.

Dionysius uses πρόοδος to signify the presence of God as "outside" his essence.[87] Its use in the singular refers to the unified
quality of the procession as a single out-flowing, as well as to the
unity of its source. The plural usages doubtless point both to the

81. Vanneste, *Mystère de Dieu*, 38–39.

82. For a brief history of this triad in Neoplatonist thought, see Dodds,
Elements, 220–221.

83. The only other use of this term as applied to God and in reference
generally to his transcendence is in *Ep.* IX.3 1109C and D (202:13, 203:4).

84. See esp. Gersh, *From Iamblichus to Eriugena*, 27–120, and Beierwaltes,
Proklos, 118–164. For a harsh judgment on the absurdity to which the equivalence mind/world led Proclus, see Dodds, *Elements*, xxv.

85. A key theme from the origins of Neoplatonism in Plotinus onward.
See J. Moreau, *L'idée d'univers dans la pensée antique* (Turin: Societa editrice
internazionale, 1953), esp. 24, for the shift in Plotinus from the demiurgic
creation model of the *Timaeus* to the biological one of the Stoa: the universe
as one thing. Still, for qualification, see Rist, *Plotinus: The Road to Reality*
(Cambridge: Cambridge University Press, 1963), 66–83. For the doctrine of
thought (θεωρία) as *the* reality of the universe, see *Enn.* III.8.5–7.

86. See my discussion in *Et introibo*, 280–282.

87. Cf. Bradshaw, *Aristotle East and West*, 181: "The *proodoi* both *are* God
and *manifest* God, who remains beyond them as their source. As Dionysius
later remarks, God is 'a manifestation of Himself though Himself' [ἔκφασιν
ὄντα ἑαυτοῦ δι'ἑαυτοῦ, DN IV.14 712C]."

varied effects to which the procession gives rise and to the mul-
tiple causes (αἰτίαι) of the creatures. The expression thus generally
describes the movement of the Godhead that both gives rise to
the creature's being, "the essence-creating procession to all things
of the divine source of essence,"[88] and also offers the creature
its hope of ascent back and up to its source—its hope granted it
by nature and grace. There is thus a fundamental link between
πρόοδος and revelation. The "names" of God which Dionysius
offers as the subject of his treatise are on several occasions specifically linked to the processions. At the end of DN II's discussion
of the διακρίσεις, the author declares it his intent to "celebrate
these . . . common and unified differences of the whole divinity, or beneficent processions, from the divine names expressing
them in Scripture."[89] The Scripture, as divine and unique source
of true knowledge,[90] reveals those names of God which reflect in
greater or lesser degree the divine processions. The names do not
and cannot lend expression to the super-essence, to God in se.[91]
They are instead associated, even down to a certain parallelism
in Dionysius' writing, with the other mode of divine being, the
processions.[92] While his essence remains ineffable and unknowable, God may therefore be truly known, and known truly as God,
in his processions. That which permits him to be active "outside"
his essence sets up the created being's hope of knowledge of (and,
finally, union with) him. The processions (πρόοδοι) are thus finally
the gifts (δωρεαί) he makes of himself.[93]

88. DN V.1 816B (180:13); note also the use of the plural in IX.5 913B (211:12).
89. DN II.11 652A (137:8–10).
90. DN I.1 588A (108:6–8); although note Roques' qualification, "Introduction," xxv.
91. Dionysius is careful to note (in V.1 816B [180:8–9]) that the object of
his treatise On the Divine Names is "not to manifest the being beyond being"
(τὴν ὑπερούσιον οὐσίαν), inasmuch as "this is ineffable, unknown, completely
non-manifest . . ."
92. DN V.2 816D (181:18–19), where the one God is declared source of
both "the benevolent processions" and "those divine names celebrated by
us." See also Lossky, "Apophasis and Trinitarian Theology," 26.
93. DN II.5 644A (129:2).

The equivalence of "gift" to πρόοδος is significant not only with respect to that gracious quality of God's out-passing to which I will return shortly but also for a text important to my argument concerning the nature of this procession. In *DN* III.1 Dionysius refers to "the good gifts which are gathered togethered around it [i.e., the Trinity]," (τὰ πανάγαθα δῶρα τὰ περὶ αὐτὴν ἰδρυμένα).[94] The use of περί with the accusative links the *DN* specifically with a way of discussing God's immanence particularly developed by the Cappadocians: the divine πρόοδοι exist as a kind of radiance or "penumbra" about the transcendent essence.[95] The image of the sun as a "visible [ἐμφανής] icon of the divine goodness"[96] is thus taken up in *DN* IV's discussion of the name of the "Good." As the sun sheds its light, so God "sends forth the rays [ἀκτῖναι] of the all-goodness to all."[97] God's light or "rays" illumine all the reason-endowed creation and conform it thereby to his likeness; they grow into the form of the Good (ἀγαθοειδεῖς).[98] God as the Good thus takes on the name of "intelligible light [φῶς νοητόν]," or "overflowing outpouring of light [ὑπερβλύζουσα φωτοχυσία]," bringing all intelligences into, and uniting them in, "a single, true, pure, and uniform knowledge."[99] The terminology bearing on light (ἀκτίς, φωτοχυσία, μαρμαρυγή, αἴγλη, etc.) is consistent throughout the whole *CD*. When not describing an operation on the level of the creature, it should be taken as referring to God *ad extra*, to the divine πρόοδοι—as the expressions themselves would clearly seem to indicate: "ray," "effusion of light," "radiance," and so forth.[100]

---

94. *DN* III.1 680B (138:6).

95. See Golitzin, *Et introibo*, 296 and n. 98.

96. *DN* IV.4 697C (147:11). This is, of course, far from an original image. See Plato, *Rep.* 506ff., and, for its subsequent use in the Neoplatonists and the importance of light imagery generally, esp. Armstrong, "Emanation in Plotinus," *Mind* 46 (1937): 61–66.

97. *DN* IV.1 693B (144:5).

98. *DN* IV.1-2 696A (143:15) and 696B (145:7).

99. *DN* IV.6 701A (150:2–3).

100. We hear of the γνόφος ("darkness," "thick cloud") in *MT* I.3 1001A (144:10) and *Ep.* V 1073A (162:3), and in *MT* I.1 1000A (142:15) and *Ep.* I 1065A (156:3) of God's σκότος ("darkness"). Yet we note that *Ep.* V defines

The language of "rays" directs us finally to the, as it were, non-substantial character of the πρόοδοι and thus to Dionysius' fundamental—and already traditional—alteration of the pagans' emanation scheme. For the latter, πρόοδος refers primarily to the effect's departure from its cause,[101] i.e., the next level of existence down the scale of being. If such were truly Dionysius' view, then indeed we should have to speak of "lesser gods." For the *DN*, however, God's πρόοδοι have no reality independent of his essence, are in no way a *Zwischenwesen*.[102] Instead they refer back directly to their transcendent source. Like the sun's rays they have a certain "oblique" reality, but the viewer (or contemplator) gazing—by grace—directly up at them encounters the blinding "darkness" described in the *MT*. The Dionysian πρόοδοι represent in short the elimination of the pagan κόσμος νοητός ("intelligble world"). All the elaborate structures of intermediary "henads" and intelligible gods[103] vanish at a stroke. This exorcism is more-over conscious and deliberate:

> For we do not say that being-in-itself is any sort of divine or angelic essence [οὐσία] . . . nor that which produces life any divinity other than the God above all things . . . nor, to be brief, that there are [other] principles of being and demiurgic

the γνόφος as God's ἀπρόσιτον φῶς ("unapproachable light"). Cf. *MT* I.1 1000A we find "the ray of divine darkness, which is above everything that is" (τὴν ὑπερούσιον τοῦ θείου σκότους ἀκτῖνα), and again in *MT* II 1025A (145:1) as a "super-abundance of light [ὑπέρφωτος γνόφος]." The way of negation does not then lead to an absence, but rather to the sense of an overwhelming presence. I would also connect the "ray" language here with the divine energies pointing us to their source. Dionysius does not speak of a vision of the essence—see Lossky, "Théologie négative," 219. See also the article by H.-C. Puech, "La ténèbre mystique chez le pseudo-Denys l'Aréopagite," in *En quête de la gnose* (2 vols.; Paris: Gallimard, 1978), 1:119–141, esp. 120–129, vs. an over-emphasis on the darkness theme in Dionysius.

101. See J. Rosán, *The Philosophy of Proclus* (New York: Cosmos, 1949), 74, commenting on propositions 33 and 35 of the *Elements*; Gersh, *From Iamblichus to Eriugena*, 48–49; and H. Dörries, "Ὑπόστασις: Wort- und Bedeutungsgeschichte," *NAG* 3 (1955): 35–92, at 72.

102. See von Semmelroth, "Geeinte Vielheit," 392–393.

103. See *Elements*, propositions 113–183 (Dodds, 100–161 and 257–294).

> essences and subsistences . . . we say rather that being-in-itself and life-in-itself and divinity-in-itself are, on the one hand, principally and divinely and causally the one transcendent and super-essential source and cause of all, and, on the other hand, [that they are] participably the providential powers given from God the imparticipable.[104]

The processions are neither lesser gods nor less God. They are instead God, as it were, in transit, transcendent communications, "imparticipably participated."[105] God *ad extra* is fully God, yet the distinction remains. While it may be a distinction difficult for many to accept,[106] it is still evident from the texts. Nor, in the face of the quotation above and of its twin,[107] do I understand how Corsini can maintain his thesis of created intelligibles (νοητά). While he points to the use of ὑποστάτης ("subsistence") in the lines immediately following the above passage,[108] I do not see how that term, any more than ἐπικρατέω or προκατάρχω,[109] necessarily refers the processions to a lower level of *subsistent* being

---

104. *DN* XI.6 953C–956A (222:6–16). Exactly the same proviso appears earlier in the *DN*, see V.2 816D–817A (181:16–21).

105. *DN* II.5 644A (129:3). The phrase τὰ ἀμεθέκτως μετεχόμενα is admittedly echoed in Proclus' *Elements*, esp. prop. 23. Proclus is here, however, clearly speaking about the sort of intermediate entities we have just seen Dionysius specifically reject. The Dionysian μετεχόμενα are instead God communicating himself in his energies which, "in the measure that these transcend all created participations . . . remain united in the super-essence" (Lossky, "Apophasis and Trinitarian Theology," 26–27). Thus see *DN* II.11 649B (133:14–15): the divine διάκρισις is given to all and is overflowing the participations of all that are good (δωρουμένη . . . πᾶσι τοῖς καὶ ὑπερέχουσα τὰς τῶν ὅλων ἀγαθῶν μετουσίας).

106. See, for example, R. D. Williams, "The Philosophical Structures of Palamism," *ECR* 9 (1977): 23–44, esp. 36–38; B. Schultze, "Grundfragen des theologischen Palamismus," *OS* 24 (1975): 105–135, esp. 133–134.

107. *DN* V.2 816C–817A (181:7–21, esp. 16–21).

108. Corsini, *Il tratto*, 140. The passage is *DN* XI.6 953C (221:16): God is simultaneously life itself and power itself, and the support of life itself and power itself.

109. *DN* II.11 652A (137:6), "the unities prevail and have precedence over [ἐπικρατοῦσι καὶ προκατάρχουσι] the differences."

than the divine. God indeed gives his πρόοδος reality,[110] hence the priority of his essence, but not separate existence. Dionysius' point is clear, in fact reiterated immediately after ὑποστάτης,[111] and to deny it would be precisely to fail to recognize him as having fully exploited that ambiguity or gap in pagan thought between the transcendent and the intelligibles (νοητά). He has taken the step suggested by Armstrong,[112] and eliminated the independent intelligibles as unnecessary, thus freeing himself in the process to use the pagan terminology as he chooses.

2.2.2. Δύναμις and ἐνέργεια. Here I deal with two expressions that are both familiar in Neoplatonist as well as early Christian usage,[113] but allied in Dionysius to the altered sense of πρόοδος and διάκρισις. Thus, DN II.7 states that

> if we should call the super-essential hiddenness by the name of God, or life, or essence, or light, or reason, we in fact conceive of nothing other than the powers proceeding out to us

110. So see the definition of ὑποστάτης given in Lampe's *Patristic Greek Lexicon*, 1461.

111. *DN* XI.6 956B (223:10–12).

112. See Armstrong, "Negative Theology," 184n. 9.

113. For δύναμις as a divine reality in late antique religion, see Hans Lewy, *Chaldean Oracles and Theurgy*, 77–78. For its use in Proclus, see Gersh, *Κίνησις ἀκίνητος: A Study of Spiritual Motion in the Philosophy of Proclus* (Leiden: Brill, 1973), 24–48. For δύναμις in Philo and early Christian literature, see J. Pépin, *Théologie cosmique et théologie chrétienne* (Paris: PUF, 1964), 378–379; C. Termini, *Le Potenze di Dio: Studio su δύναμις in Filon di Alexandria* (Rome: Institutum Patristicum Augustinianum, 2000); H. F. Hägg, *Clement of Alexandria and the Beginnings of Christian Apophaticism* (Oxford: Oxford University Press, 2006), 239–240 (Philo), 246–251, 260–267 (Clement); M. R. Barnes, *The Power of God: Δύναμις in Gregory of Nyssa's Trinitarian Theology* (Washington, DC: Catholic University of America Press, 2001). For ἐνέργεια in Proclus, see Rosán, *Proclus*, 69–74; Gersh, *Κίνησις ἀκίνητος*, 81–101; and in the Neoplatonists generally, Gersh, *From Iamblichus to Eriugena*, 37–44. The most extensive treatments of ἐνέργεια from Aristotle to Palamas are those of H. Schaeder, "Die Christianisierung der aristotelischen Logik in der byzantinischen Theologie repräsentiert durch Johannes von Damaskus (ca. 750) und Gregor Palamas (ca. 1359)," *Theologia* (1962): 1–21, and Bradshaw, *Aristotle East and West*.

from it, whether they be deifying, or creative of essence, or
life-giving, or granting wisdom . . .[114]

It is evident from the above that "power" (δύναμις) is practically
synonymous with "procession" (πρόοδος), practically because we
seem further along the road to the actual contact of the uncreated with the creature, to the processions of God as we receive
them. If his procession is the origin, the fount of our being and
beatitude, then power or virtue is on the way to the realization
of that being and beatitude, to God as we receive him, thus the
μεθεκτῶς ("in a participated way") of *DN* XI.6 956A (222:16).[115] It
is the same God who is communicated in his powers and transcendent in his essence. While all being and all virtue in creation
derive "from [his] super-essential power,"[116] yet "in no way are
the infinite and infinitely created powers ever able to blunt the
super-infinite activity of his power that causes power to be."[117]
By means of his δύναμις God grants his creatures the potential for
communion with himself, for "deification itself."[118] The antinomy
is stated again clearly in the following from *CH* XIII: "the divine
power unceasingly advances and penetrates all and yet to all is
invisible, not only as transcending everything in super-essential
manner, but also as hiddenly sending forth among all things its
providential energies."[119]

The concluding term above, "activity" (ἐνέργεια), is the last of
the basic terms employed by Dionysius to express God *ad extra*.
It is used several times in a manner equivalent to πρόοδος.[120] We
note in particular *DN* IX.9: God moves to creation "by means of

114. *DN* II.7 645A (131:7–10).
115. See Lossky, "Darkness and Light," 41; idem, "Théologie négative,"
240; von Semmelroth, "Erlösung und Erlöser im System des Ps.-Dionysius
Areopagita," *Schol* 20–24 (1949): 367–379, at 369.
116. *DN* VIII.3 892B (201:21); see also VIII.6 893CD (204:2).
117. *DN* VIII.2 889D–892A (201:7–10).
118. *DN* VIII.5 893A (202:22).
119. *CH* XIII.3 301A (44:17–20).
120. See *DN* IX.5 912D (210:9): God proceeds to all things κατ᾽ ἐνέργειαν μίαν.
Note the use of the singular also in *CH* III.2 165B (18:16–17) where it is the
vocation of the reason-endowed creature to reveal the divine activity in itself.

his providential processions and energies."[121] In the same passage, however—indeed in almost the same breath—Dionysius goes on to speak of God's motion (the subject of the passage) as "the unswerving procession of the energies." This would appear to imply something of a distinction between the two terms. I suggest that the distinction is of the same nature as that between πρόοδος and δύναμις, only, as it were, more so. Ἐνέργεια represents something concrete, present or realized,[122] although I stress that here I am speaking not of the effects of God's activities, but of himself in action. Thus, there appears to be a sequence or progression to the three terms. Πρόοδος to δύναμις to ἐνέργεια might be taken as parallel in the mode of God *ad extra* to the creaturely triad given in the *CH* of οὐσία - δύναμις - ἐνέργεια:[123] the progress from essence to potential to expression. The parallel can certainly not be pushed too far since in God such distinctions cannot be too clearly drawn and the terms do tend to shade one into the other. Nonetheless, it does appear to me to be a useful one in light of the distinction of modes of being in God. The divine essence is totally transcendent and Dionysius will thus never, as would for example Augustine, speak of a naturally trinitarian image imprinted on the creature.[124] Yet, as we see in chapter 3 below, the creature's mode of being is called to become a reflection of God's. This can then only be of God *ad extra*, and therefore my suggested parallel. Ἐνέργεια, in any case, while used occasionally like πρόοδος, appears far more often, and usually in the plural, to denote concrete activity. It is

121. *DN* IX.9 916C (213:14).
122. See Gersh, *Κίνησις ἀκίνητος*, 91n. 1.
123. *CH* XI.2 284D (42:1–2).
124. In this Dionysius is typical of Greek triadology generally; see, for example, von Balthasar's critical remarks in *Kosmische Liturgie* (2nd ed.; Einsiedeln: Johannes-Verlag, 1961), 91–92. On Augustine's triadology, see his reluctance regarding the use even of the term *persona* for the persons of the Trinity, *de Trinitate* V.9–10, *PL* XLII 916–918. For the *vestigia Trinitatis* in the human soul, see, for example, *de Trin*. X and XIV, *PL* XLII 971–984 and 1035–1058, as well as *Civitas Dei* XI.26.23–26, *PL* XLI 339–340. Jerome provides an amusing example of Latin difficulties with the Greek ὑπόστασις in *Ep*. 15, *PL* XIII 180B–185B.

God in his energies who is present and active in his creation.[125] In *CH* XIII he brings the first rank of angels into being and so into "participation of his providential energies."[126] God "extends" in *DN* XIII to all things "by means of his unfailing gifts and unceasing energies."[127] The particular association of the term with God active in creation is again borne out by the frequency of its appearance in the *CH* and *EH*,[128] precisely the treatises dealing specifically with the structures and ways of created being. Of the terms so far discussed, ἐνέργεια is the one most often and most intimately linked with the divine Providence,[129] and it is God as Providence that is the subject of the *DN*.

Before turning to Dionysius' use of πρόνοια, let me summarize my discussion so far. God as God is totally other, outside any and all categories of being and non-being, neither one nor many. The emphasis on transcendence so characteristic of late Neoplatonism is taken up and exploited in order to allow for the Trinity of Revelation and, by means of another distinction in God's being, creation and revelation. God is God both as the infinitely "other," the Three persons in unity, and as God "outside" God, differentiated indivisibly and extended "ecstatically" into immanence. This second mode, and second only in a certain logically subordinate sense, at once does away with the pagans' emanations of intermediate deities and provides the foundations for human existence, knowledge, and hope of participation in God. It is the ground of creation, of revelation, and of beatitude. Both the names of God

125. See von Semmelroth, "Gottes ausstrahlendes Licht: Zur Schöpfungs- und Offenbarungslehre des Pseudo-Dionysius Areopagita," *Schol* 28 (1953): 481–503, esp. 483.

126. *CH* XIII.4 308A (49:7); see also XIII.4 305C (48:15–16), where the first ranks of angels share in distributing God's purifying energies.

127. *DN* XIII.1 977B (227:1).

128. E.g., *CH* III.2 165B (18:16); XIII.4 305C (48:16); XIII.4 308A (49:11); XV.2 329C (53:3–4); *EH* V.1.7 508C (109.22); V.1.7 509A (110:3–4); *Ep.* IX.3 1109D (302:4).

129. Note *Ep.* IX.3 1109C (202:11–203:5): God is paradoxically abiding in himself even while going forth to all, "having his providential energies in his steadfastness [τὰς προνοητικὰς ἐνεργείας ἐν μονημότητι], and his abiding in his providential activity [τὴν μονὴν ἐν τῷ προνοεῖν]."

and the hierarchies of men and of angels are thus the expressions, as I will note, of the divine out-passing, which the Areopagite has labeled with the terms just discussed, and of God's "return [ἐπιστροφή]" to himself. God in "extension" and "return" is finally God as love, the fundamental origin and hope of created being. We turn then to the discussion of this cycle of God in relation, and to the one term that Dionysius understands as yielding the whole range of meanings of God *ad extra*: πρόνοια.

2.3. Πρόνοια: *God's Love in Motion*

We find Dionysius using πρόνοια to denote all of God's activities in creation. In *DN* III.1 it appears in parallel with Πρόοδος.[130] Again, in *DN* V, the Providence of God is linked with his procession in explicit opposition to God *in se*: "it is, then, the intent of this treatise to celebrate all the revelatory names of Providence, and not to express the super-essential goodness . . . but Providence which has been declared good and creative of good."[131] The divine names are the manifestation (ἐκφαντικήν) of the one Providence. Comprehending God in all of his relations with the creature, at once embracing all while abiding in itself transcendent, Providence is God so far as the creature is concerned.[132] It is without beginning or end, in procession while abiding unchanged in itself, both all-pervasive and wholly ineffable.[133] All things share somehow in Providence as their universal source (ἀρχή) and cause

---

130. *DN* III.1 680B (138:1–4).

131. *DN* V.2 816C (181:7–8, 11–12).

132. *DN* XII.2 969C (224:13–225:1): Θεότης ἡ πάντα θεωμένη πρόνοια ("divinity is the providence which contemplates all"). Note also in the same text Dionysius' derivation of θεότης ("divinity") itself from θεάω ("to contemplate"). This equivalence of "divinity" with a divine activity is paralleled in the Cappadocians (Golitzin, *Et introibo*, 285–317). For πρόνοια as God, see von Semmelroth, "Geeinte Vielheit," esp. 401.

133. *Ep.* IX.3 1109B–D (202:1–203:5). See the comments in Lossky, *Mystical Theology*, 72; Roques, *L'univers*, 114; and Hathaway, *Hierarchy*, 112–114.

(αἰτία):[134] "the divine Providence is in all things and no one of the things which are is without it."[135]

All of the terms so far mentioned find their inclusion and summation in Providence. In a passage concerning God's ἔρως (to which I will return), Dionysius declares that God moves "outside himself . . . by means of [his] providences with regard to all things."[136] Again, in the *CH*, he speaks of Providence as "gushing forth [ἐκβλυζομένη]" from God.[137] Providence is then inclusive of the divine ἔκστασις, God's "super-essential ecstatic power." As the "benevolent procession" of God outside himself, "by goodness multiplied without division" in creation,[138] Providence is equivalent to both the divine διάκρισις and the divine πρόοδος. As that in which all things participate,[139] as causing all (πανάιτιος) through pre-containing all,[140] and as cause of both the being and well-being of creation through its embrace, indwelling, and lending of itself to all,[141] Providence stands as well for δύναμις and ἐνέργεια. It enables and operates all things, manipulates even evil to the good, and dispenses itself in accord with the proper and varied goods of its different creatures (ἀναλογικῶς).[142] It stands for the whole cycle of exodus and return.

Does this mean that it is therefore little better than—once more—poorly disguised, and poorly adapted, Neoplatonism? Now it is certainly true that this term figured prominently in later, post-Plotinian Neoplatonism as belonging to the gods above Νοῦς and no longer, as in Plotinus, to the lower realms of Soul and Fate.[143] Neither will I deny the parallels which exist between

134. *CH* IV.I 177C (20:7, 11); and VII.4 212C (32:11).
135. *DN* IV.33 733B (178:7–8).
136. *DN* IV.13 712B (159:11).
137. *CH* IV.1 177C (20:14–15).
138. *DN* II.5 641D–644A (128:15–129:3).
139. *CH* IV.1 177C (20:13–14).
140. *DN* I.7 597A (120:7).
141. *Ep.* IX.3 1109C (202:7–9); see also *CH* VII.4 212C (32:11–12).
142. *DN* IV.33 733C (178:17).
143. For πρόνοια in Plotinus as governing only the lower realms beneath Soul, see *Enn.* III.2.1; 1.9; 2.2–3; and 3.1. It is equivalent to ἀνάγκη, the basis of karma; see also the article by Müller, "Plotinos über die Vorsehung," *Philog.*

Dionysius and his pagan predecessors.[144] Here again, though, we see Dionysius as using certain points of convergence in Neoplatonist thought in order to express what was for him a traditional vision of the Christian mystery, one that does not overlook sin and the Cross—and Dionysius does not ignore the Fall[145]—but which looks primarily to Christ as the highest expression at once of God's love and of the deepest reality of created being itself. In other words, for Dionysius God's Providence and the created nature that it sustains and draws to itself both presuppose the Incarnation. In order to express this, the Areopagite freely exploited the pagans. It is, for example, by no means clear in the latter where Providence belongs, i.e., to which level of the gods.[146] There is no such ambiguity in the *CD*. Providence, as πρόοδος, is from God. We shall see below the same process at work in the understanding of divine love.

---

26 (1913): 338–357. For its role, much expanded, in Proclus, see *Elements*, prop. 120, 104–106, and for comment, the article by Beierwaltes, "Pronoia und Freiheit in der Philosophie des Proklos," *FZPT* 24 (1977): 88–111. I do not, however, feel bound to accept Beierwaltes' conclusions (110–111) concerning the "necessary" conflict between the Neoplatonists' Providence and the Incarnation of Christ in Dionysius—thus my argument following.

144. See esp. Koch, *Beziehungen*, 74–86, and for ἔρως, 66–72. Brons' contentions, in an article devoted specifically to πρόνοια in the *CD* ("Πρόνοια und das Verhältnis von Metaphysik und Geschichte bei Dionysius Areopagita," *FZPT* 24 [1977]: 165–186) again appear to me as extreme. He claims, rightly, that the term encapsulates the Dionysian vision (165–166). He goes on, however, to declare that the effect on Dionysius' Christian pretensions is disastrous (167–171; 175–177). The Incarnation in particular falls victim to the generalized scheme of procession—return, cause and effect, and becomes merely a timeless "doublet" of the larger plan. It brings nothing new to the world (178–185). The last phrase reveals, I think, Brons' own tradition, for if the coming of Christ is understood as something entirely new and fundamentally unrelated to the world rather than first and most deeply the fulfillment of created being, then indeed Dionysius must be judged inadequate. In my eyes, though, he is not so, but instead an exponent of the same tradition expressed in the quotation from Maximus the Confessor opening this book and, for example, in Gregory of Nyssa. See Golitzin, *Et introibo*, 285–317.

145. See above (2.1, "The Fall and the Devil").

146. Thus see Gersh, *Κίνησις ἀκίνητος*, 93–94, esp. 93n. 1.

For now, let me move briefly from Providence in the *DN* to note where and how Dionysius employs the term in the treatises concerning the hierarchies. In so doing we move from the abstract to the concrete, to the history of God's dispensation as set forth in Scripture. In every hierarchy each being is given its proper share (ἀναλόγως) of the divine light (θεῖον φῶς) through the action of Providence.[147] The same divine light, together with its distribution and the enabling of the creature to participate in it, comes under the heading of Providence. The latter's immediacy is never compromised. In dealing with the guardian angels allotted to the nations, Dionysius carefully qualifies the doctrine: "God has not divided his governance of us among other gods or nations," rather that governance remains always a property of the "unique Providence directing all things [τῆς μιᾶς ἁπάντων]."[148] There are no intermediary divinities. Again, in discussing Israel's unique fidelity to God—and I note that Dionysius' failure to deny other nations some share in divine revelation need not be read as pagan systematizing but instead as a certain faithfulness to God's generosity and to his own Christian tradition[149]—Dionysius observes that while angels indeed act as guides, "the source [ἀρχή] and Providence of all is one."[150] Finally, Providence in the hierarchies remains ever itself above essence (ὑπερούσιος) and transcendent (ὑπεριδρυμένη) with regard to all, directing our angelic initiators to guide us to the knowledge of itself as "itself the proper source" of all (ἐπ᾽ αὐτὴν ὡς οἰκείαν ἀρχήν).[151]

If one of the modes of its expression toward humanity in the old dispensation was this assignment of angelic guides and guardians, then, as I have just stressed, the expression of Providence in the new dispensation (and so *par excellence* of God as he comes forth from himself to his creation) is Jesus himself:

147. *CH* XIII.3 301D (46:1).
148. *CH* IX.4 261C (39:12).
149. See my remarks concerning Clement of Alexandria and the latter's attitude to Greek thought, in *Et introibo*, 263–264 (vs. Brons, *Gott und die Seienden*, 58–59).
150. *CH* IX.4 261C (39:5–6).
151. *CH* IX.4 261C (39:5–6).

> What might one say concerning the philanthropy according
> to Christ which has poured out peace . . . but indeed that we
> might effect divine things together with them [the angels] in
> accordance with the Providence of Jesus who works all in all,
> and creates peace ineffable . . . and reconciles us to himself
> in the Spirit and through himself and in It [the Spirit] to the
> Father.[152]

Jesus is the expression of God's Providence revealed and proclaimed in the Scripture, and mystically or symbolically—a serious
term in Dionysius to which I will return in following chapters—
realized in the Church's liturgy. It is Jesus as Providence who is
recalled by the bishop at the altar: "the divine hierarch, standing
before the holy altar, hymns the . . . sacred theurgies of Jesus, our
most divine Providence."[153]

I note the two other terms appearing in the texts above as synonymous with God's dispensation in Christ: φιλανθρωπία ("love
for mankind") and θεουργία ("work of God"). While the latter
is of distinctly pagan provenance, it is once again a term that
Dionysius has taken and put to his own use.[154] First, "theurgy"
expressed pagan antiquity's desire, and awareness of the need, to
transcend merely intellectual communication with the divine.[155]
Thus, secondly, it stressed the grace and gift of God or the gods.[156]
Dionysius, certainly aware of the potential convergences thus
carried by the word, further transformed it, such that, in Rorem's
words, it no longer denoted "works addressed to the gods . . .
[but] God's mighty acts."[157] It is thus used most often as an

152. *DN* XI.5 953A (221:5–10).

153. *EH* III.3.12. 441C (92:5–7).

154. See my earlier note on theurgy in chapter 1.1.

155. Thus see Iamblichus, *de Myst.* I.3 and II.1 (des Places) 41–43 and 95–97
respectively. For comment, see Larsen, *Jamblique*, esp. 176–178. On Dionysius'
relationship to Iamblichan theurgy, see my comments in the Introduction
and Rist, "Pseudo-Dionysius, Neoplatonism, and the Weakness of the Soul."

156. See Iamblichus, *de Myst.* I.3 and II.1 (des Places) 41–43 and 95–97
respectively, and Larsen *Jamblique*, 178–181 and 184–185. See also Proclus,
Théol. Plat. I.25 (Saffrey/Westerink) 109–113.

157. Rorem, *Symbols*, 14–15.

expression for the dispensation of Christ, and for Christ himself as our Providence.[158]

Concerning φιλανθρωπία, it is surely mistaken to reject Dionysius' use of this traditionally Christian word as "unbiblical" because it is "merely" the application of the more general divine ἀγαθότης ("benevolence") to our level of being.[159] This simply misses Dionysius' point, which is that both divine goodness and God's φιλανθρωπία in Christ are a function of God's love. Christ is the supreme expression of the overflowing love that raised us up even when fallen,[160] and φιλανθρωπία is generally used exclusively in reference to the Incarnation.[161] To say that he is also expressive of the love that God as Providence holds for all of creation is hardly an un-Christian idea.[162] Providence is therefore incarnate in Jesus who both ordains and is expressed in the Church's liturgy,[163] but the Incarnation is as well the result—I might almost

---

158. See *CH* IV.4 181B (22:3); VII.2 208CD (29:11–12, 18); VII.3 209B (30:8); XIII.4 305C (48:18); *EH* I.1 369A (63:4) and 372A (64:1); I.2 372B (64:13); I.5 377B (68:13); III.2 425D (81:5–6, 8); III.3.5 432B (84:18); III.3.10 440B (90:9) and ff; III.3.12 441CD (92:3, 6, 12); III.3.15 445BC (94:13, 17); IV.3.4 477D (99:6); IV.3.12 484D (103:3) and 485B (103:21); V.1.3 504C (106:20); V.1.4 504D (107:3); V.3.7 513C (113:22); *DN* I.4 592B (113:12); II.1 637C (124:7); and II.2 644C (130:5–10).

159. Brons, "Πρόνοια," 176.

160. *DN* VI.2 856D (191:16).

161. For φιλανθρωπία in direct reference to the Incarnation, se *CH* I.3 124A (9:8); IV.4 181B (22:23); VII.3 209B (30:10); *EH* II.1.1 393A (70:5); III.3.3 429AB (82:23–83:1, 9); III.3.8 437A (88:10); III.3.11 441A (91:9); III.3.12 444A (92:23); III.3.13 444C (93:17); V.3.5 512C (112:9–10); *DN* I.4 592A (113:6); II.3 640C (126:1–2); II.6 644C (130:9); II.10 648D (135:2); VI.2 856D (191:16); IX.5 953A (221:5); *Ep.* III 1069B (159:4); and *Ep.* IV 1072B (160:8). It is used twice in reference to the Old Testament Economy: *CH* VIII.2 240D (34:17) and 241B (35:5–6). Elsewhere it stands for divine clemency or mercy with regard to sinners: *EH* VII.3.7 561D (127:21); and *Ep.* VIII.4 1093D (184:10). Finally, Dionysius speaks of the angels sharing in Jesus' "philanthropic virtue," *CH* VII.2 208C (112), and of their "philanthropy" in watching over and guiding us, *Ep.* VIII.I 1085C (173:7) and VIII.6 1100D (192:1).

162. For the same view, see Rist, "A Note on Eros and Agape in Ps.-Dionysius," *VC* 20 (1966): 235–243, esp. 236.

163. Note *CH* I.3 121C–124A (8:1—9:15) together with I.1–2 120B–121A (7:3–11).

say the inescapable result—of that movement of God that weaves together all the Dionysian universe.[164]

2.3.1. The divine ἔρως. Here is the key to Dionysius' Providence and, with it, to his understanding of God *ad extra* and the whole of the *CD*. Providence and love are in a sense identical.[165] Dionysius' ἔρως is the "motor" of Providence,[166] the origin of God's movement giving role in creation. "It [God's ἔρως] did not suffer itself to remain infertile in itself, rather it moved itself."[167] The movement of love[168] brings about love's diffusion: God, "on account of an overflowing of loving goodness [ἐρωτικῆς ἀγαθότητος]," moves outside himself, "bewitched, as it were, by goodness and charity and love."[169] Thus does he introduce himself into the realm of contingent beings as creator, sustainer, and ultimate goal. Here is the source of the divine ἔκστασις, and thence of all God's πρόοδοι. This is his "super-essential, ecstatic power." He moves into creation because, simply, he desires it.

Dionysius, as I noted, uses circular imagery for πρόνοια,[170] i.e., the cycle of abiding, procession, and return. Here, too, we discover the basic role of ἔρως as the expression and definition of divine Providence. Just as through love God moves to create, so is it also through love that he works in creation to bring the latter to himself. He himself works, in other words, the ἐπιστροφή

---

164. It is important to note that this "places Dionysius firmly within the theological tradition of Irenaeus, Tertullian, Maximus the Confessor, Isaac of Nineveh, and Nicholas Cabasilas" (Bucur, "Unities, Differentiations, and the Exegesis of Biblical Theophanies," 118; for details see Bucur, "Foreordained from All Eternity: The Mystery of the Incarnation According to Some Early Christian and Byzantine Writers," *DOP* 62 [2008]: 199–215).

165. See von Semmelroth, "Die Lehre des Pseudo-Dionysius Areopagita vom Aufstieg der Kreatur zum göttlichen Licht," *Schol* 29 (1954): 24–52, at 33.

166. *DN* IV.14 712C (160:6–7).

167. οὐκ εἴασεν αὐτὸν ἄγονον ἐν ἑαυτῷ μένειν, *DN* IV.10 708B (155:18-19); for the use of ἄγονος here, see chapter 3 below (1.1., "Emanationism?").

168. Dionysius goes to some pains to justify his use of ἔρως as the equivalent of ἀγάπη, *DN* IV.11–12 708C–709D (156–158).

169. *DN* IV.13 712AB (159:10–14).

170. *DN* XII.2 969C (225:1).

("return") of his creatures. The latter is a feature of Dionysian thought that is clearly revealed in our author's use of the verb ἐπιστρέφω. When used of God it is in the active voice indicating his activity,[171] and, when referring to the creatures, we find the passive (middle) voice.[172] We recall that the divine and creaturely ἔκστασεις are reciprocal, and understand thus that the activity or ἐνέργεια of the divine ἔκστασις is this same divine love working in the creature to bring about the ἔκστασις of the latter. God pours himself into immanence in order that the realm of contingent being may transcend itself in and through him. The circle imagery is indeed apt, suggesting both the process of divine activity proceeding outward to bring all back to itself[173] and the principle of the double ἔκστασις having its beginning and end in God.[174] Providence as ἔρως is thus

> a certain single and simple power [δύναμις] which impels itself toward a kind of unifying mingling, from the Good to the last of those which are, and from the last of those which are back again (through all things) to the Good; from itself and through itself and towards itself circling round itself, and ever retracing itself identically towards itself.[175]

---

171. Thus see *CH* I.1 120B (7:6); *DN* IV.4 700AB (148:9, 15); IV.6 701B (150:11); IV.10 708B (155:16); VI.2 856D (192:1); IX.6 913C (211:17); X.1 937A (214:15); XI.1 948D (217:8); and *Ep.* VIII.6 1097C (188:13).

172. So see *CH* VIII.1 240A (33:15); IX.1 257B (36:7); IX.2 257C (36:17); IX.3 261A (38:13); XII.3 293B (43:17); XV.9 340A (59:2); *EH* III.3.10 440A (89:17, 18); IV.3.1 476A (97:2); *DN* IV.4 700B (148:15, 20); IV.10 705D (154:22); IV.14 712C (160:11) (God as love being returned to himself); VI.1 856C (191:8); IX.6 913C (211:16–17); IX.6 913C (211:17); XIII.3 980C (228:14); and *Ep.* VIII.1 1088A (175:1). I am grateful to Professor Rorem for having been directed to this distinction, present as well in such important and related verbs as ἀνάγω and ἀνατείνω.

173. *DN* IV.14 712C–713A (160:5–15); and concerning the "eternity" of this circle (*DN* IV.14 712C–713A [160:12–13]), see my discussion in chapter 3 (2.1.1., Στάσις: Ever-Moving Repose).

174. See G. Horn, "Amour et extase d'après Denys l'Aréopagite," *RAM* 6 (1925): 278–289," esp. 288.

175. *DN* IV.17 713D (162:1–5).

While there can be no doubt that this circular scheme, and the important role of ἔρως in particular, owes much to the forms of late Neoplatonism,[176] the degree of that debt is still open to some debate. I have chosen, after Dionysius' own arguments[177] and in the light of the tradition he represents,[178] to call his ἔρως simply "love." In my view he has once again, and here most strikingly, exploited the parallels in pagan usage and accentuated them in favor of a Christian interpretation. It is true that, especially, Proclus makes considerable use of the ἔρως theme as the moving principle of his system,[179] but not at all clear, as Gersh has demonstrated,[180] that the pagan's is a downflowing love coming from God, and certainly not an ἔρως ἐκστατικός.[181] Rist expresses my own feelings admirably: "It would seem merely perverse to deny that Dionysius' Christianity is the direct case of this adaptation."[182]

2.3.2. Κίνησις. Dionysius speaks often of motion in relation to God's out-passing and Providence, for example that God "moved

176. See Koch, *Beziehungen*, 66–72, and Beierwaltes, *Proklos*, 165–239, esp. 165–191.

177. *DN* IV.11–12 708C–709D (156–158).

178. For Origen's understanding of ἔρως as equivalent to the New Testament ἀγάπη, see Golitzin, *Et introibo*, 314–315; and Rist, *Eros and Psyche: Studies in Plato, Plotinus, and Origen* (London: Oxford University Press, 1964), esp. 206–208.

179. See Beierwaltes, *Proklos*, 306–312.

180. Gersh, *Κίνησις ἀκίνητος*, 123–127, here directly in opposition to Nygren, *Eros and Agape*, 569–570. Armstrong ("Platonic Eros and Christian Agape," *DRev* 79 [1961]: 105–121, at 117), while not in apparent agreement with Gersh's later view, also takes opposition to Nygrens' basic dichotomy; similarly, Beierwaltes, *Platonismus im Christentum*, 15–16 (16n.8 mentions Nygren explicitly) and 73–75. It would appear to me that Nygren's thought lies behind many of the assumptions fundamental to Brons.

181. Rist, "Eros and Agape in Ps.-Dionysius," 239. See esp. the argument by C. J. de Vogel, "Greek Cosmic Love and the Christian Love of God," *VC* 35 (1981): 57–81; esp. 61–68 and 71–72 for the most thorough demonstration of Dionysius' independence from Proclus and debt to his Christian sources in the use he makes of ἔρως.

182. Rist, "Eros and Agape in Ps.-Dionysius," 239.

himself [ἐκίνησε αὐτόν]" out of love to create.[183] Motion in God is linked directly to love and thereby to Providence, to the *ad extra*, in another passage worth quoting at some length. Dionysius is endeavoring to explain how God is both lover and beloved, the love which causes motion and the love which is moved:

> by the one he is moved and by the other moves; or, that he is himself both sent forth from himself and cause of motion [in others]. They call him at once both beloved and desired in as much as he is the Good and Beautiful, and both desire and love as a power at once setting in motion and leading up to itself. The same is alone on its own account both the Good and the Beautiful. . . . [He is] a manifestation of himself through himself and [he is] both beneficent procession and loving [yearning] motion of the transcendent unity . . . self-moving . . . pre-existing in the Good, and gushing forth from the Good to those things which are, and again returning to the Good.[184]

This is a splendid summary of my discussion so far. God as love is both moved and moves his creature insofar as he is source, sustainer, and goal of his creation. Motion is inclusive, as a name of Providence, of that cycle of abiding, procession and return that characterizes Dionysius' thought. The text is a description of both God *in se* and *ad extra*. The transcendent God leaps forth from himself and becomes in a sense motion, movement, both proceeding outward into immanence and bringing all back with itself to rest in him. In the statement that he becomes a "manifestation of himself," we have an indication pointing toward the development of the hierarchies and, particularly, to Christ and the ecclesiastical hierarchy. God departs from himself in order to reveal himself. The act of revelation, the revealer and the revealed are one and the same: God loving and loved, the divine Providence.

---

183. *DN* IV.10 708B (155:19).
184. *DN* IV.14 712C (160:3–11).

Motion is the paradox essential to Dionysius' thought, one which, I might add, has both Neoplatonist roots[185] and specific sources and "targets" in the Christian tradition.[186] It is a paradox because the divine is by definition fixed, immobile (ἀκίνητος). "How," our author asks, "can the theologians [the writers of Scriptures] speak of the divine as at once unmoving yet also in motion and proceeding to all things?"[187] They can, he replies, because this is proper to God who is "dissimilar to all things [ἀνόμοιος πᾶσιν] . . . who is both fixed and unmoving [ἑστὼς καὶ ἀκίνητος] and enthroned in eternity, yet is also in motion and proceeding to all things."[188] God is he who "ever-moving abides in himself"[189] or who, according to the apophatic formula of the *MT*, is "neither fixed nor in motion."[190] Transcendent with regard to both motion and rest, God grounds both in his own being just as we saw that he grounds both the One and the Many in himself. While this is the paradox, the essential for Dionysius rests in the fact that he is thus enabled to discover in God's Providence the source of both στάσις and κίνησις in the creation: "For [God] is both στάσις and κίνησις for all that which, beyond all rest and motion, establishes each in its proper λόγος and moves each to its proper motion."[191] The two must be read as in a certain sense equivalent in the creature, the fulfilling of whose proper motion equals its proper rest, i.e., the fulfillment of its λόγος—a term to which I return in chapter 3 below—and this ultimately because κίνησις finds in God himself

185. For the philosophers, however, motion is not propert to the One; see Dillon, *Iamblichi*, 44, and Gersh, Κίνησις ἀκίνητος, 2 and 100. Note also the parallels between Dionysius and Maximus the Confessor in their common defense of Providence/Κίνησις as from God; see L. Thunberg, *Microcosm and Mediator* (Lund: Gleerup, 1965), 70 and 73–74.

186. For sources, see esp. Gregory of Nyssa (Golitzin, *Et introibo*, 305–308) and for targets, Origen and Evagrius (*Et introibo*, 274–276 and 324 respectively).

187. *DN* IX.9 916C (213:7–8).

188. *DN* IX.1 909B (208:4–6).

189. *DN* X.1 937B (215:12).

190. *MT* V 1048A (149:5); see also *DN* V.10 825B (189:13).

191. *DN* IV.7 704C (153:1–3); see also V.7 821B (185:22–23) and von Semmelroth, "Aufstieg," 28.

its analog. God *ad extra* is God in motion, motion which is—again quoting at length:

> not mental, nor of the soul, nor physical, but God bringing all things into being and holding them together, and taking forethought for all in every manner of way, and present to all in his boundless embrace and in his providential processions and energies which extend to everything which is. . . . [Divine motion is called] direct, wherein one is to understand . . . the unswerving procession of the energies and the genesis of everything from him; spiral, as the fixed procession, the generative rest; and circular, as both that which embraces the identical, the means, and the extremes, and holds together that which is embraced, and as the return to himself of what has come forth from him.[192]

These, then, are the outlines of Dionysius' Providence, the cycle of love which provides the ground for all that is to follow, both in the *CD* and in my essay.

3. The Names: Notional Icons, Resonances of God as Providence

In his introduction to Proclus' *Platonic Theology*, H. D. Saffrey points to Dionysius as the first to introduce into Christian theology a treatise concerning the names of God.[193] He also specifically dismisses the theological contribution of the Cappadocians as no more than "developments of trinitarian catechesis," notes their distrust of philosophy, and refers his readers finally to Dionysius' debt to Proclus. I, to the contrary, think Saffrey's denial of the Cappadocians' contribution to a theology of the divine names altogether too swift and, in relation to their impact on Dionysius, simply wrong. The Areopagite's debt to Proclus is of course undeniable, whether one chooses to speak of the plan of the *DN*—particularly from chapter 4 onward—as reflecting the Neoplatonists'

192. *DN* IX.9 916CD (213:11–20).
193. Saffrey, *Théol. Plat.*, I.cxci–cxcii.

Parmenides commentaries,[194] or of the "circle" theme whose prominence I have noted, or of the particular names as, for example, the Good in *DN* V, or, in chapters 5–7, the intelligible triad of οὐσία - ζωή - νοῦς that figures so prominently in post-Plotinian and even Plotinian Neoplatonism,[195] or in fact almost every one of the names dealt with in the treatise.[196] Yet I have also noted how widely our author differs from the pagans. He, in Armstrong's phrase, "knocks the philosophical stuffing" out of the hierarchy of names through his denial of any sort of independent or hypostatic reality to that which the names represent.[197] Instead of referring to separate entities, whether divine or merely "intelligible," all of Dionysius' names direct us instead to the single out-flowing or procession of divine love. I use the verb "direct" intentionally, for it leads us to the fourth point of correspondence between the Dionysian and Cappadocian teaching on God's names. I have already shown how closely Dionysius' teaching follows the first three points listed in this chapter's introduction as characteristic of Cappadocian theology, i.e., the priority of the apophatic approach in view of divine transcendence, the positive attributions of God as directing us only to the "penumbra" of his being and, therefore, to his energies or powers rather than to his essence. A fourth point remains. The names serve as "notional icons." They

194. See, however, von Ivanka, *Plato Christianus*, 238–240; Sheldon-Williams, *CambHist*, 462, and von Balthasar, *Herrlichkeit*, 194–195.

195. For its role in Plotinus, see P. Hadot, "Être, Vie, Pensée chez Plotin et avant Plotin," in *Les Sources de Plotin* (1957), 107–141; for Iamblichus, see Dillon, *Iamblichi*, 36–39; and for Proclus, *Elements*, propositions 101ff. (Dodds) 91ff.; *Théol Plat*, III.9ff. (Saffrey/Westerink) 34ff.; Beierwaltes, *Proklos*, 93–117. Dionysius' care to avoid identifying God *in se* (the Trinity) with any aspect of this triad may explain his reluctance to give much prominence to the traditional name, Λόγος, for Christ. It is mentioned once (*DN* VII.4 872C [198:21]), but generally the names "Jesus" or, more rarely, "Christ" are preferred. For background to this consistently apophatic attitude with regard to the Trinity and created triads, particularly ones associated with the Neoplatonist Νοῦς, see Armstrong, "Escape from the One," 86.

196. Corsini, *Il tratto*, 46–57.

197. Armstrong, "Negative Theology," 183.

point us, as one scholar has said in reference to Gregory of Nyssa's theology, "to an appropriate reality in God."[198]

I begin by noting that for Dionysius the names of God are first of all given. They come to us, before all, through the revelation declared in Scripture. It is a point on which he is quite insistent: "One may neither dare to say nor even to conceive anything [about God] aside from the things which have been declared to us in a deiform manner in the sacred Scriptures."[199] God as known, or at all knowable, is God revealed in the sacred utterances (ἱεροῖς λόγοις) of Scripture that he has made the vehicle of his illuminations,[200] and, as Dionysius does allow for elsewhere, in the tradition of the saints.[201] In either case, as one modern theologian writes who might be speaking for both Dionysius and the Cappadocians, "if human forms of thought and speech are to have a transcendent reference to what is really beyond them, this reference must be given to these forms by God himself."[202]

But still, Dionysius asks, how is it possible for us to ascribe names to God given the impossibility of conceiving (ἐννοῆσαι) the Trinity?[203] It is possible, he answers a few chapters later, precisely because it is not the divine essence that is in question, but "the divine names revelatory of Providence [τὰς τῆς προνοίας ἐκφαντορικὰς θεωνυμίας]," of "Providence the creator of good [ἀγαθοποιός] that has revealed itself," and is therefore justly celebrated as "the cause

198. B. Krivochéine, "Simplicité de la nature divine et les distinctions en Dieu selon St. Grégoire de Nysse," *MessPR* 91–92 (1975): 133–158, at 141.

199. *DN* I.2 588C (110:3–4); see also I.1 588A (108:6–8). He does use unbiblical names, though to do so was not original in Christian thought with the *CD*—see, for example, Basil's attitude to ἀγέννητος (Golitzin, *Et introibo*, 300).

200. *DN* I.2 588C (110:4); and see my discussion above (2.2.1., "Procession: A Lesser God?").

201. Thus the teaching of his inspired teacher, the mysterious Hierotheos; see *DN* II.9 648AB (133:13–134:6); III.2 681AB (139:17–140:15); and *DN* IV.14–17 713A–D (160:15–162:5); and, for speculation concerning this personage, von Balthasar, *Herrlichkeit*, 153–154.

202. T. F. Torrance, "The relation of the Incarnation to Space in Nicene Theology," in *The Ecumenical World of Orthodox Civilization: Essays in Honour of Georges Florovsky* (ed. Andrew Blane; Paris: Mouton, 1974), 43–74, at 46.

203. *DN* I.5 593B (116:8–10).

of all good things [πάντων ἀγαθῶν αἰτία].[204] Providence, God in extension, is God as revealed, and God as revealed is revealed as "the reality [ὕπαρξις] of goodness, the cause of everything which is;" therefore, "one must celebrate the Providence of God [τῆς θεαρχίας] as source of good in all its effects [ἐκ πάντων τῶν αἰτιατῶν]."[205] Cause and ground (ὕπαρξις) of all, Providence embraces everything, and everything may therefore be seen as in some sense expressive of it. God may thus be called by any of the names of his creation.[206] His name is every name and no name.[207] Here we have the basis for all three of the Dionysian "theologies" or approaches to the divine: the negative (apophatic), the positive (cataphatic), and the symbolical.[208] As the super-essence, God is beyond any attribute we may conceive while as Providence, in his energies, he leaves no creature without its proper manifestation of the universal ground of being. As Providence he is also the revelation granted in Scripture. Finally, in the person of Jesus, God has granted us that supreme symbol or "cipher" of himself, the worship of the Church, which is empowered to bring us back to the contemplation of his glory.[209] The basic tension, applicable to the "symbolical" theology too, is that of the positive and negative, and the continuous dialectic, a simultaneous affirmation and denial, that Dionysius will bring to bear on every name or symbol discussed in the *CD*. To every symbol, that is, except—and I think most significantly—the ἀκριβὴς εἰκών of the ecclesiastical hierarchy.[210] The dialectic ceases on confronting the Church's liturgy.

204. *DN* V.2 816C (181:12–13).

205. *DN* I.5 593D (117:11–13).

206. *DN* I.7 597A (120:5–8).

207. *DN* I.7 596D–597A (120:3–5).

208. See Roques, "Introduction," xxxix, and "De l'implication des méthodes théologiques chez le Ps.-Denys," *RAM* 30 (1954): 268–274, at 269–270. See also *DN* I.1 588AB.

209. See, for example, *DN* I.8 597A–C (120:9–121:13), and *CH* II.2–5 136D–145C (10:13–17:2) on Scripture; *CH* I.3 (121C–124A [8:14–9:15]) on esp. the Liturgy; and *DN* I.4 592A ff. (113:7ff.) for Christ.

210. *EH* II.3.6 401C (77:8). See also I.2 373B (65:14); I.4 376C (67:14); I.5 376D (67:20); V.1.2 501CD (105:17–21); and *CH* VIII.2 241C (35:22–25).

Let us return to the term manifestation, ἔκφανσις, used above in relation to the creature. We have already encountered it twice, once in reference to the Trinity as "manifestation of the superessential fecundity," and once where God as love is described as becoming the "manifestation of himself."[211] The term appears twice more in contexts relevant to my purpose and both times in parallel with those expressions we have established as denoting God "outside" himself. In *Ep.* IX, Dionysius speaks generally of the "processions, gifts, manifestations, powers of God,"[212] but in *DN* II specifically of the διακρίσεις of the Thearchy (*not* the Trinity) as signifying its "processions and manifestations."[213] Following Lossky here, who bases himself in turn on the *Scholia* of John of Scythopolis,[214] I choose to see a distinction between the usage of "procession" and "manifestation," the former referring to the divine as cause and the latter to the divine as revealed in the creature. According to Lossky,

> the relation between cause and effect is the manifestation: the invisible and secret causes . . . appear visible and knowable in the effect. God reveals himself in his creatures (θεοφάνεια). The relation between the effect and the cause which determines it is that which is termed participation (μέθεξις) or again, imitation (μίμησις), but in virtue of which the effect becomes the image of the cause.[215]

Later in *DN* II we find a discussion of the relationship of created effects to their causes in God which provides a summary of my argument so far: "for there is in the effects no exact likeness [ἀκριβὴς ἐμφέρεια] of the causes, rather the effects have the images [εἰκόνες] of the causes possible to them."[216] The foundation, then, of the theology of the *DN*, the intelligible names of God—as well as of

211. *DN* I.4 592A (113:1) and IV.14 712C (160:8) respectively.
212. *Ep.* IX.1 1105A (195:2–3).
213. *DN* II.2 640D–641A (126:10–11).
214. *PG* IV, 157.
215. Lossky, "Théologie négative," 217.
216. *DN* II.8 645C (132:14–15).

the *CD* generally—lies in that fact that the ἐμφέρεια, that likeness which, however splendid—or lowly[217]—remains ever inadequate to its prototype. The whole unfolding of the *CD* is at least in greater part to be understood as a sequence of imagery, a study in iconography, having as its continuously present corrective—with the singular and vital exception noted above—the apophaticism of the *MT*. Dionysius' vision of the icon is adumbrated elsewhere, in *DN* IX, in his discussion of the intelligible names of "similar" (ὅμοιος) and "unlike" (ἀνόμοιος), with the first indicating the gift of divine imitation to the creature[218] and the second stressing God's absolute distance from creation: there "is nothing whatsoever similar to him."[219] The same chapter finally confirms my argument in its praise of τῶν θεωνυμιῶν ἀγαλμάτων.[220] The intelligible names are notional ἀγάλματα, images of the divine glory which may direct us to the latter's splendor, which are indeed given us to do so but which cannot wholly enclose the brightness of the uncreated.[221] Saffrey is doubtless correct to direct us to Proclus as a source of this teaching,[222] but the groundwork for Dionysius'

217. See *CH* II.1–5 137A–145B (9–17).

218. *DN* IX.6 913D–916A (212:5–8).

219. *DN* IX.7 916A (212:12–15).

220. *DN* IX.1 909B (207:8).

221. See again Torrance, "Relation of the Incarnation to Space," esp. the following from p. 47: "Theological statements operate with essentially open concepts . . . which, though relatively closed on our side of their reference through the connectedness with the space-time structures of our world, on God's side are wide open to the infinite objectivity . . . of His divine being. . . . Conceptuality characteristic of theology is one in which our acts of cognition are formed under the pressure of the transcendent reality they intend to know so that the intelligible content of what is disclosed constantly bursts through the forms we bring to it in order to grasp it." Thus, for Dionysius, we have the *MT*.

222. Saffrey, "Nouveaux liens objectifs," esp. 3–9. His reference is to *Théol. Plat.*, vol. I.I.29, 123–125, for Proclus and the names as ἀγάλματα. While acknowledging the dependence on Proclus, it still seems clear to me that Dionysius uses the word ἄγαλμα throughout his works as simply a synonym for εἰκών, σύμβολον, τύπος, etc. In *CH* II.5 145A he refers to the ἀγάλματα of Scriptures; in III.2 165A the members of the hierarchy are ἀγάλματα of the divine light; in *EH* II.3.3 428D the ἀγάλματα refer to the movements of the bishop;

theologyhere, however much the latter may have seen it converg-
ing with the pagan's teaching, had already been laid by Gregory
of Nyssa particularly, and the brief residue (λείψανον) of divine
fragrance the latter had detected lingering within the high names
we give to—and are given by—God.[223]

4. Summary

God's names are sacraments of his presence, and in the notion
of sacrament we approach the sense not only of the *DN* but of
Dionysius' vision as a whole. We are still only at the periphery
of the Incarnation. Concerning the *DN* itself, it appears to be a
Christian's re-working of pagan philosophy, in light of God's
revelation in Christ and of prior Christian tradition, that fundamentally alters, or redirects, the thrust of pagan Neoplatonist
teaching. The intelligible names are not things, no longer have
reference to objectively and independently existing entities, but
are instead windows opening onto the sense—and reality—of
God present in his powers or energies. While it may be the case
that the particular icons or echoes of his "out-passing" considered
in the *DN* are often rather less the result of scriptural revelation
and more of the philosophical reflections of pagan antiquity than
Dionysius would have us—and perhaps himself—believe,[224] still
the point seems to be clear: they direct us to, and participate in,
the greater sacrament, μυστήριον, of God's self-giving love. The
key to all the *CD* is the nature and all-predominance of that one
divine love. It is God himself who gives himself, opens himself
to participation, enables the same in his creatures, and so leads
them back to himself. The divine names are one case in particular
of that cycle of grace. The participation they grant is real, for God

---

in IV.3.1 473B it is the rite of the μύρον that is an ἄγαλμα of divine beauty and,
476A, of the divine fragrance.

223. See Golitzin, *Et introibo*, 297 and n. 104.

224. But he can and does find justification for all of them in Scripture. See,
for example, Rorem, "The Biblical Allusions and Overlooked Quotations
in the Pseudo-Dionysian Corpus," *SP* 23 (1989): 61–65, on the range and
omnipresence of Scripture in Dionysius.

is truly present in his processions, though at the same time they can but direct us further into the depths of his being. We have thus completed the first stage of our journey into Dionysius' vision of divine-human relations at whose core is the new θεανδρικὴ ἐνέργεια given us through and in Christ. The next stage will be the consideration of the reason-endowed creature as at once participant and image of the divine Providence and then, in chapter 4, of the living worlds of angels and humans as called upon to reflect the light of the divine energies—of God's love—and to conduct their several members back and up to the encounter with their creator. We shall thus be moving increasingly toward Jesus as the center and fulfillment of divine Providence, the point where the worlds meet and whence they—and with them all the treatises of the *CD*—derive their sense and coherence.

Chapter 3

The Mystery of the Creature

Toward the Divine Likeness and Union

Introduction

Let us recall the questions I posed early in the last chapter. If God is forever transcendent how is he then manifested? How are the δυνάμεις participated in by created beings? Where and what is the point of, as it were, intersection between Creator and created? How is it that the creature realizes first of all the reflection of God and Providence and, secondly, how is it given to apprehend and appropriate to itself the knowledge and activity of the uncreated energies? What, finally, is the sense of the creaturely ἔκστασις and in what manner is it of a piece with the whole shape of Dionysius' thought concerning the mutual relations and communion of God with the world? In this chapter I will take a number of the key terms discussed in chapter 2—specifically κίνησις, στάσις, ἔρως, δύναμις, ἐνέργεια, πρόοδος, πρόνοια, ἔκστασις, and ἕνωσις—and see how they are used in reference to the reason-endowed creation, angels and humans, as each of them is individually a potential icon of God and called to union with him. I will then, in chapters 4 and 5, be in a position to consider the created world collectively in the hierarchies—the God-intended world(s) of creation—as both the reflection of God in procession and the ladder of ascents given for our assimilation into participation in his life, i.e., as at once the image of his πρόοδος and the reality of his ἐπιστροφή working our return to him. The last will lead, in chapter 5, to a discussion of Christ in his Church as God's supreme μυστήριον. The movement of my presentation, one which I believe to be Dionysius' own as well, will thus be always toward the Incarnation, as toward that point where the tensions basic to the CD—manifest/unmanifest,[1] exodus/return, icon/archetype, motion/repose, knowing/unknowing, etc.—discover their resolution, coherence, and highest expression.

These tensions are both basic and deliberate. They are not, however, without certain ambiguities. The πρόοδος / ἐπιστροφή language underlying all the CD leads us to at least two serious questions concerning the nature of the Dionysian vision. There is first the notion of creation itself. We must ask if Dionysius truly teaches this doctrine rather than the automatic or unconscious emanationism usually associated with Neoplatonism.[2] Secondly, the cyclic thrust of these two terms calls to mind the timeless round of the pagans' cosmos wherein, for Plotinus as well as for his successors, something very like the Indians' *karma* dictates the perpetual reincarnation of the soul.[3] Regarding the first question I will argue that, while Dionysius' creationism represents perhaps the most ambiguous feature of his thought, the CD is scarcely so distant from received Christian orthodoxy as some would have it. It speaks instead fundamentally of the mystery of God's love. That mystery, and the tensions which are inseparable from it, also serve to shatter the pagans' static and layered ontology.[4] God's loving will, or λόγος, for each creature is reflected in the latter's

---

1. See von Balthasar, *Herrlichkeit*, 167 (emphasis in original): "As *manifestation* of the unmanifest, God's movement is *proodos*, and as manifestation of the *unmanifest . . . epistrophe*."

2. Brons, *Gott und die Seienden*, 192–236, esp. 233–236.

3. For Plotinus, see *Enn.* IV.3.16 (also IV.2.1 and 4.16); for Iamblichus, Dillon, *Iamblichi*, 28–29; and for Proclus, *Elements*, propositions 206 (esp.) and 211 (Dodds) 181 and 185, together with Dodd's commentary, 304–305 and 309–310 respectively, and Beierwaltes, *Proklos*, 192–239, esp. 219–239.

4. *Contra* Brons, *Gott und die Seienden*, 29–77, esp. 72–77.

ἀναλογία, i.e., as the intended reflection of the divine the creature strives ever to become what, in a sense, it is already in God.
The tension or "gap" between the divine will to communicate
itself and the creature's to appropriate the divine gift determines
Dionysius' understanding of creation. He has, I argue, followed
here the lines laid down over a century before him by Gregory of
Nyssa and broken entirely with the philosophers' closed system.
Both "ends" of his cycles meet in God the infinite. The result is a
dynamism or stress on motion, foreign to the pagans, as a progress
or ascent into God that can have no end. The way is thus opened
for an absolute value to be accorded the individual soul, time,
and so to history. This in turn allows for the revelation of God in
Jesus and thus in Christ's body, the Church.[5]

We turn now to consider (1) God the Creator, (2) the creature
as individually the analogue and intended mirror of Providence,
and (3) the meaning of the creature's ἔκστασις and ἕνωσις with
its Creator.

1. God the Creator

1.1. Emanationism?

In an article on creation versus emanationism in Gregory of
Nyssa,[6] H. A. Wolfson sets out the following three points of distinction between pagan and Christian ideas: (1) emanation is
from God—i.e. his substance—while creation is from nothing;
(2) emanationism is an eternal process but creation is in time; (3)
emanationism occurs by nature whereas creation comes to be by
God's will. I must admit straightaway that, if these criteria are
to be accepted without qualification as absolute standards, my
defense of the *CD* will be hard-pressed indeed. Brons has noted
the lack of any mention by Dionysius of the "out of nothing" (ἐξ

5. See the article by Armstrong, "Salvation Plotinian and Christian," *DRev*
75 (1957): 126–139, esp. 136–139 on the Church and community as a particularly Christian, non-Plotinian development.
6. H. A. Wolfson, "The Identification of *Ex Nihilo* with Emanation in Gregory of Nyssa," *HTR* 63 (1970): 53–60, at 54–55.

οὐκ ὄντων),[7] and also that the traditionally Christian language of κτίζω / κτίστης ("to create / creature") appears only in direct quotations from Scripture.[8] The same scholar then points to the essentially metaphysical—therefore pagan—αἴτιος-αἰτιατά vocabulary of the *CD*, particularly as the expression of a timeless Providence signifying the totality of God in relation, as the real Dionysian teaching however "cosmetically" retouched with Christian phrases.[9] I would, for my part, also add such texts as *DN* IV.1, where Dionysius uses the image of the sun as a type (οὕτω) of the Good sending forth its "rays," "neither by deliberation nor by choice" (οὐ λογιζόμενος ἢ προαιρούμενος).[10] Elsewhere he refers to Providence as "without beginning" (ἄναρχος) and "without end" (ἀτελεύτητος).[11] Similarly, we hear of the "eternal circle" (ἀΐδιος κύκλος) of divine love,[12] and of beings sharing in God's gift of Being as the radii share in the monad of the circle's center.[13] Finally, Dionysius tells us that divine love does not allow God to abide in himself without offspring (οὐκ εἴασεν αὐτὸν ἄγονον ἐν ἑαυτῷ μένειν), but came forth instead into creation.[14] Inasmuch as Dionysius uses the divine "fertility" elsewhere in reference to the Trinity,[15] and also speaks of γόνιμος στάσις ("fecund stillness") and of the "overflowing" of God's εἰρηνικῆς γονιμότητος ("peaceful fecundity"),[16] this statement seems to indicate a want of the distinction between nature and will in God which, for example, Georges Florovsky understands as fundamental to the creation theology of Christian patristic lit-

---

7. Brons, *Gott und die Seienden*, 193–194.

8. Brons, *Gott und die Seienden*, 196.

9. Brons, *Gott und die Seienden*, 183–202, 222–231, and, for a convenient summary, Brons, "Πρόνοια," 178–180.

10. *DN* IV.1 693B (144:5); see also IV.4 697B–700C (147:2–148:11) for the analogy with the sun.

11. *Ep.* IX.3 1109B (202:2).

12. *DN* IV.14 712D (160:13).

13. *DN* V.6 821A (185:4–11).

14. *DN* IV.10 708B (155:18–19).

15. *DN* II.1 637B (123:9); II.7 645B (132:2); XIII.3 981A (229:8); *Ep.* IX.1 1104C (194:8); *DN* I.4 592A (113:1).

16. *DN* IX.9 916D (213:17); *DN* IX.2 952A (219:23).

erature.[17] On all three of Wolfson's counts, therefore, Dionysius appears to fail.

While granting the difficulties it poses for its defenders, I do not think the question of creationism versus emanationism in the *CD* can be quite so simply reduced and answered. Indeed, with the exception of an eternal world,[18] this reservation applies even to the pagans themselves. In the previous chapter I pointed to some of the difficulties involved in applying the emanationist metaphor *tout court* to the Neoplatonists' transcendent One and the universe that derives, somehow, from it. The same may be said concerning, specifically, the points bearing on will versus necessity and on the world as drawn from God's substance.[19] Regarding the first, it is true that Plotinus and Proclus both speak of creation as a "by-product (παρακολούθημα)" of divine contemplation[20] and not the result of will—of its nature the Good *must* produce.[21] Yet, Plotinus uses the verb ποιέω on four occasions in reference to the One.[22] He also denies the distinction, as applied to God, between will and essential being.[23] The action of creation, as Rist notes, "seems finally to be wholly mysterious."[24] Turning to the world as of God's substance and again taking Plotinus as our exemplar, we do indeed find the lower levels described as an "issuance [ἐξίτηλον]" of the higher,[25] or as a radiation or a

17. Georges Florovsky, "The Idea of Creation in Christian Philosophy," *ECQ* 8 (1949): 53–77, esp. 54–55 and 66–67. See also his "The Concept of Creation in St. Athanasius," *SP* 6 (1962): 36–57, esp. 54.

18. See, for example, *Enn.* II.9.3 and II.9.7 as a position which holds as well for Plotinus' successors.

19. For the latter point esp., see the article by H. Dörries, "Emanation: Ein unphilosophisches Wort im spätantiken Denken," in *Parusia: Festgabe für Hirschberger* (ed. K. Flasch; Frankfurt am Main: Minerva, 1965), 119–141.

20. Dodds, *Elements*, 290, citing both Plotinus, *Enn.* III.8.4 and Proclus, *In Parm.* 791:14.

21. *Enn.* II.9.3 and 8, and IV.8.6.

22. All are found in *Enn.* VI.8.19.

23. *Enn.* VI.8.13.

24. Rist, *Road to Reality*, 26–27.

25. *Enn.* III.8.5 and V.1.6; see also Proclus, *Elements*, propositions 7 and 25, 8 and 28, together with Dodds' commentary, 193–194.

circumambience of their source.[26] Yet he refuses to identify the
One in any way with the world.[27] The undiminished and un-
moved quality of the cause, which Proclus emphasizes as well,[28]
takes away, as Armstrong observes, "any question of emanation.
What is left is simply an omnipresence of the spiritual."[29] Thus,
again in agreement with the latter scholar,[30] it appears that even
with the pagans there is a certain definite quality of "grace" or
"gift" attaching to the world's origins.

Once more it appears that Dionysius has set out to seize upon
and exploit areas of convergence with Christian doctrine. Let us,
then, take up each of Wolfson's points. With regard to the "of
God" rather than *ex nihilo*,[31] I noted in chapter 2 that Dionysius'
πρόοδοι are not, as with the pagans, synonymous with the next
level of existence down the scale of being. God as Providence,
in his processions, "is given to every thing which is, while yet
transcending [ὑπερέχουσα] the participations [μετουσίαι]."[32] The
"transcending" here must be insisted upon. It is true that the Good
is said both to bring all things into being and to leave nothing
without some trace of itself.[33] "There are," as Lossky writes, "as
many providences as there are beings"[34]—a point, incidentally,
that also serves to set Dionysius apart from, at least, Plotinus.[35]
Yet, the nature of this relationship or link with each creature,
while not without some ambiguity, does not diminish the fact

26. *Enn.* V.1.6; also V.3.10.

27. See esp. *Enn.* V.3.11 where Plotinus denies even immanence to the One.

28. See *Elements*, propositions 26–27, 30–32, and Dodds, 213–214.

29. Armstrong, *The Architecture of the Intelligible Universe in the Philosophy
of Plotinus* (Cambridge: Cambridge University Press, 1940), 60. For similar
sentiments concerning Iamblichus, see Larsen, *Jamblique*, 177f.

30. Armstrong, "Salvation Plotinian and Christian," esp. 130–131.

31. Much stressed by Brons, *Gott und die Seienden*, 193ff.

32. *DN* II.9 649B (135:15).

33. See *DN* IV.20 717D–720A (165:17–166:3) and IV.28 729A (174:8–13) on
matter.

34. Lossky, "La notion des 'analogies,'" 284–285; see also *DN* IV.33 733B.

35. For Plotinus, there are no "personal" Providences; see Armstrong,
"Salvation," 128–129. Note, however, that the power of ἐπιστροφή is a kind
of given or grace (*Enn.* VI.7.31).

that God ἐν ἐκστάσει is still God. That linkage for which Dionysius uses such Platonist commonplaces as μετουσία ("participation"), ἐπιτηδειότης ("fitness," "suitableness"), etc., expresses indeed a certain "intimacy"[36] between the Creator and his creation. It does not, though, signify for our author, as it does for example with Plotinus, that the creature is already and eternally made, a complete and fully accomplished microcosmos covering all the spectra of reality.[37] Instead, as we shall see,[38] the microcosm that is the creature both requires community and awaits fulfillment. The κοινωνία ("communion") to which Dionysius refers in the terms just cited opens onto the, for him, allied expressions of θεοειδής, θεομίμησις, and ἀφομοίωσις, i.e., precisely onto motion or ascent. In other words, the Areopagite's creature is not a "piece of God," a "being," but is rather contingent, fully a creature, having only a power to be or to become and without any stability save in God[39]—or, better, save in ever moving into God. The language of "participation" thus signifies neither a hidden monism nor a timeless *Verhältnis*,[40] but instead a certain double and mysterious—in the broadly sacramental sense—aspect of creaturely being: created being truly shares in divinity while remaining radically other. Like the notional icons of the divine names, the creature itself is at once like, and a revelation of, God, while at the same time permanently "inadequate" to him. On the side of the Creator, transcendence is therefore maintained—in fact it is essential—and the *ex nihilo*, if not clearly stated, must surely be assumed.[41]

36. The expression is von Balthasar's, *Herrlichkeit*, 173.

37. See esp. *Enn.* III.4.3: ἕκαστος κόσμος νοητός and ff. as a key to Plotinus' system and essential to his development of the soul's solitary return to the One. See also W. R. Inge, *The Philosophy of Plotinus* (2 vols.; 3d ed.; London: Longmans, Green & Co., 1929), 1:202–203, together with *Enn.* IV.4.23 and Moreau, "L'idée du monde," 49–50.

38. See below on ἀναλογία, κίνησις, and δύναμις.

39. See Armstrong, "Salvation," 133–134.

40. Brons' view, *Gott und die Seienden*, 195.

41. Indeed, Dionysius "does not argue in defence of the principles of his theology. . . . He simply states them in an affirmative way, widely utilizing a broad range of already established doctrines of Christian theology. . . . The doctrine of creation is one of such concepts. . . . It is plainly acknowledged

Secondly, we have Wolfson's "creation is in time." Here we look first to Dionysius' discussion of time (χρόνος) and eternity (αἰών) in *DN* X.3.[42] Even Florovsky can admit that creation is a "contingent eternity."[43] I believe this expression speaks as well for Dionysius' own view. Not only does the latter argue for God as source or cause of χρόνος and αἰών, as himself pre-eternal (πρὸ αἰώνος), but he is also careful to point out clearly that while angels, the first rank of creation, may be called eternal, theirs in no way is an eternity comparable to the Creator's: "the realities called 'eternal' [τὰ αἰώνια λεγόμενα] are not to be understood as simply coeternal with God, who is preeternal [συναΐδια θεῷ τῷ πρὸ αἰώνος]."[44]

There is, granted, no mention in the *CD* of a "time" when creation was not. But on reflection, how could there be? Both time and αἰών are properly measures of created being. To speak of a creation "in time" seems then logically to place God within time, on a level with the creature. If, though, there is no time or "moment" for his creating, then there is in the *CD* certainly a kind of "before": "God knows the angels before they come to be."[45] Further, there are at least two occasions when the verb παράγω ("to bring forth") is used in the past tense, in the *CH*: "on account of goodness the super-essential divinity, having established the essences of all, brought them into being,"[46] and in *Ep.* VIII, where it is Christ who "makes all things to be and brought [παρήγαγεν] everything into being."[47] We recall also the divine love that "did not suffer

---

by the author without intention to argue for its validity. . . . [this approach] by no means denies that he supported this notion in principle." V. Kharlamov, "The Beauty of the Unity and the Harmony of the Whole: The Concept of Theosis in the Theology of Pseudo-Dionysius the Areopagite" (Ph.D. diss., Drew University, 2006), 291; see also 290–297.

42. *DN* X.3 937C–940A (216–217).

43. Florovsky, "The Idea of Creation," 67.

44. *DN* X.3 940A (216:16–17). See also Bradshaw, "Time and Eternity in the Greek Fathers," *The Thomist* 70 (2006): 311–366, esp. 316–319.

45. *DN* VII.2 869A (196:14–15), πρὶν ἀγγέλους γενέσθαι εἰδὼς καὶ παράγων ἀγγέλους.

46. *CH* IV.1 177C (20.9–11).

47. *Ep.* VIII.1 1085D (174:1).

[εἴασεν]" to remain in itself, but "moved itself [ἐκίνησε αὐτόν]" to create.[48] It would thus appear that Dionysius, in so pointing to *a definite divine act*, is here as well at least "susceptible" to an orthodox interpretation.

The last quotation above brings us back to the third and most difficult issue, that of agency or will in God's creating—or, rather, since it is at least clear that God alone is the agent in the *CD*,[49] of will versus necessity. It may be best to begin by asking what exactly Dionysius is referring to in his "automatic" imagery of light, sun, overflowing, goodness, and so forth. Now it appears clear, to us at least, that the subject of these metaphors is the mystery of God's superabundant love.[50] His goodness (ἀγαθότης), as Dionysius tells us expressly, means his love: God "loves [ἐρᾷ]" all and *is* love. This love which is God in turn moves, must move, to the giving of itself. Does the "must" here involve a necessity that is in contradiction to God's freedom, his will? Let us first recall that element of mystery which even the pagans, particularly Plotinus, had understood as underlying the whole discussion of the creation or derivation of the world from God. That element is certainly no less pronounced in Dionysius, and, surely, his notion of its being rooted in the overflowing of God's love must be taken as both fundamentally Christian in inspiration, and, moreover, fully in accord with, and pointing toward, the supreme act and mystery subsequent to creation, the Incarnation: "For God so loved the world . . ." (John 3:16). Secondly, and still in reference to "mystery," we must keep in mind, as surely Dionysius must have done, the inadequacy of all human-based distinctions such as, exactly, that between will and necessity. At this point the words of Dom Illtyd may shed some light on the apparent difficulty posed by such metaphors as the "sun" imagery, and phrases as the οὐ λογιζόμενος ἢ προαιρούμενος ("neither by deliberation nor by choice") cited above:

48. *DN* IV.10 708B (155:18).
49. Admitted by Brons, *Gott und die Seienden*, 189.
50. *DN* IV.10 708AB (155.14–20).

God is not, if we are to speak properly, free to *choose*. To conceive of him as presented with alternatives offering themselves to him . . . "possible worlds" . . . is anthropomorphic. God's plan for creation is what it is because he is who he is. This is freedom in the fullest, most positive sense where it *coincides* with necessity in the fullest, most positive sense. . . . God is super-generous love. The question of his *not* creating does not arise.[51]

Now, while it may be argued that both Trethowan and Dionysius are somewhat incautious with respect to the issue of creation versus emanation,[52] or freedom versus necessity, it should be equally admitted that (1) they are both theologian-philosophers caught in the toils of a rationally insoluble difficulty, and (2) that their common vision of the divine love "bursting forth" into the creation of the worlds must (if we are not to slip into slander) be read as the fruit of Christian inspiration and Revelation. Theirs is a real feeling, in other words, for the living God of Christian faith rather than the vaguely Christianized poeticizing or tinting of an essentially pagan insistence on the priority of metaphysics. Once again, therefore, I find Wolfson's dichotomy overly simplistic, and hence deceptive.

This is not to say, however, that there is nothing whatever to the distinction between will and nature. I have already noted that Dionysius does distinguish between God's essence and "powers," and, further, that he places the act of creation in the latter: God in relation is God in his πρόοδοι. Neither are specific expressions of God's will wholly lacking in the *CD*. We find the vocabulary of volution—βούλησις, βούλομαι, θέλημα—used seven times directly in reference to God. The divine will (βούλησις) for the salvation of humanity is shared by all three Persons of the Trinity.[53] God's will

---

51. Dom Illtyd Trethowan, "Irrationality in Theology and the Palamite Distinction," *ECR* 10 (1977): 19–26, at 21 (emphasis added).

52. Thus see Gersh's remarks on Dionysius, *From Iamblichus to Eriugena*, 217 and 227.

53. *DN* II.6 644c (130:8–9).

(θέλημα) is, in fact, the salvation of both people and angels.[54] He creates all things and "wills [βούλεται] that they draw near to him and share in him."[55] He enlightens the angels as to his βούλησις.[56] While he did not will [ἠβουλήθη—note again the past tense] to create evil,[57] he still left us free to know his will (θέλημα) and not to do it.[58] It is noteworthy that God's will or willing here is in every case clearly associated with his goodness, that is, his love acting on and for his creation. It is both personal and dynamic—and in these two adjectives we discover at once the Creator of Christian Revelation and, in summary, the argument of this chapter.

1.2. The Divine λόγοι

Dionysius uses two terms in particular to describe the polarity, yet real intersection—"intimacy"—between Creator and created, λόγος and ἀναλογία. Their mutual relation and tension provide the moving force of his system's dynamism. The most important statement regarding the λόγοι comes within his definition of the divine paradigms:

> And we say that the paradigms [παραδείγματα] are the essence-creating *logoi* of all things which pre-subsist unitedly in God, which Scripture calls fore-ordinations, and divine and good wills, the generative causes [ποιητικά] and definitions of beings according to which the super-essential [God] has fore-ordained and brought all things into existence.[59]

The use here of the λόγοι as equivalent to the παραδείγματα—and therewith also to the αἰτίαι ("causes"), ἀρχαί ("sources") and like terms for the divine origins of the creature[60]—*as well as* to the divine will(s)—is surely of great significance. Ronald Hathaway is

---

54. *EH* I.3 373D (66:10–11).
55. *Ep.* VIII.1 1085D (174:2); see also *CH* IV.1 177C (20:12).
56. *EH* I.4 376B (67:4).
57. *DN* IV.18 716A (163:2).
58. *DN* IV.35 736A (179:7).
59. *DN* V.8 821C (188:6–10).
60. See Brons, *Gott und die Seienden*, 144f, as well as *DN* V.5 820B (184:6–7).

doubtless correct to see in Dionysius' λόγος the nature (φύσις) of a given creature,[61] but certainly incorrect to see its derivation coming solely from Proclus. For the latter term, λόγος, serves merely to signify the relations of causes to their effects and so provides the "glue" for his triads.[62] Dionysius' λόγοι, on the other hand, are not "mean terms," but are of God, "supra-mundane."[63] They are the divine models of all things, precisely the paradigms. The notion of divine exemplars, however, does give rise to certain questions. It may suggest static thoughts, ideas within God's essence and so, relatedly, imply a necessary relationship between him and his creature. When taken together with προορισμός ("predetermination"), it could also indicate an element of predestinationism. We shall look briefly at each of these questions.

The term παράδειγμα, in the sense of divine exemplar, is used only once outside of the text cited above. In *DN* VII, Dionysius states that our positive knowledge of God derives from the order (διάταξις) of his creation, insofar as the latter bears certain "likenesses" (ὁμοιώματα) of the paradigms. God in himself, however, abides beyond all knowing (ἐπέκεινα πάντων).[64] This statement must, of course, recall my argument in chapter 2 above: our knowledge of God is obtained uniquely of and through his energies which provide the ground for the "sacramental" presence carried somehow in his "names." The connection, or rather identity, between the "models" of the world and the "creative power of God realizing itself in creation" is rendered specific by Dionysius' identification of the former with the λόγοι.[65] Furthermore, and just as with the δυνάμεις, although the λόγοι discover their origin in

61. Hathaway, *Hierarchy*, 46–47; so see *DN* IV.26 728C (173:10–11) and V.7 821B (185:22), esp. the former for the λόγος as referring to the creature's φύσις.

62. See *Elements*, propositions 21, 23, and 24, 24–18, and Rosán, *Proclus*, 157.

63. *CH* XI.2 284D (42:1).

64. *DN* VII.3 869D–872A (197:22–198:1); also VII.1 865B (193:5–9). For the Good as παραδειγματικόν, see also IV.7 704A (152:6) and IV.10 705D (155.1).

65. See the article by Beierwaltes, "Johannes von Skythopolis und Plotin," *TU* 108 (1972): 3–7, at 5, which I take as opposed to the too-easy contrast Sherwood draws between Maximus and Dionysius on the λόγοι, *The Earlier Ambigua of St. Maximus the Confessor* (Rome: Herder, 1955), 176.

the hidden super-essence, they must be ascribed in their actuality to the οὐσιοποιὸς πρόοδος ("the being-producing procession") whence all derive and in which all participate.[66] God's creative "out-going" (ἔκβασις) is in fact mentioned in the sentence immediately preceding the definition of the παραδείγματα in *DN* V.8. The λόγοι-παραδείγματα are therefore proper to the divine energies rather than to the essence.[67] Gathered or held within the one Providence, we may identify them with the "specific providences" mentioned in the preceding section. The equation λόγοι = δυνάμεις = πρόνοιαι is unmistakable and deliberate.

As for a "necessary relationship," the ambiguity is surely no less—and no greater—here than in my discussion above of will versus necessity in God. In identifying the λόγοι further with the divine θελήματα, Dionysius is clearly drawing attention to the volitional, and thus personal, character of God's relationship with his world. He is also as clearly "rejecting . . . the non-deliberative emanative process which pagan Neoplatonist philosophers . . . had made fundamental to their thought."[68] God's "models" for the world are in fact his wills, his intentions or purposes, for each of his creatures.

Concerning the divine will, I have already shown that it may be known, but not necessarily obeyed. The λόγος of each being is, as it were, the closest approach of the Creator to the created. It is

66. *DN* V.9 825A (188:18); see also *DN* I.4 592D (115:9–10) for the "superessential ray" holding in itself all things. For comment, see Lossky, "La notion des 'analogies,' " 285.
67. This is opposed to the contrast Thunberg draws between Maximus and Dionysius in *Microcosm and Mediator*, 79 and 81. Generally, much of what Thunberg has to say concerning Maximus' δύναμις as revealed in his doctrine (76–83, and more broadly, 63–97) he rightly applies to Dionysius, save the issue above. On the λόγοι, we might also look to Plotinus, whose "formative forces" are much more akin to Dionysius' λόγοι than Proclus' use of the term (see *Enn.* III.2.15; III.8.2; and V.1.6; as well as Armstrong, *Plotinus* [1953] 35), and to the long Christian background of the term (see my discussion on Origen in *Et introibo*, 269–271; also A. Aall, *Geschichte der Logosidee in der griechischen Literatur* [2 vols.; Leipzig: Reisland, 1896], esp. 1:394–450).
68. Gersh, *From Iamblichus to Eriugena*, 265, with, however, the ambiguities in the pagans themselves that I have already noted.

the given creature as it is intended or willed to become by God's creating love. Yet, as Florovsky points out, to see these προορισμοί as inescapable laws of nature is dangerously mistaken.[69] The same love that ordains our being calls us to itself, wills our communion, but this call may be refused. Dionysius' whole argument elsewhere concerning the nature of evil becomes inexplicable unless this refusal is understood as possible.[70] Evil does not find its cause in any λόγος or δύναμις, but rather in the impotence or illness of the rational creature's own will.[71] The λόγοι are thus "predestinations" only, as it were, to beatitude.[72] They in no way include a foreordained fall or damnation. The latter remains the creature's responsibility. It follows that the divine will with regard to each may not be readily apparent in the actual state of any given creature—effectively, of any given human soul—a corollary which has certain repercussions that I will note when considering the nature of the ecclesiastical hierarchy.[73] The λόγοι are therefore our personal and foreordained vocations to which we may or may not choose to become conformed, or better—since they remain transcendent by virtue of their source in God[74]—to which we may choose to be ever in process of becoming conformed in order thus to share, as it were, in the eternal process of our own creation.[75]

At the same time present in each, yet divine and transcendent, the λόγοι thus constitute at once: (1) the creative and originating causes of each being; (2) the closest approach of God to creation

69. Florovsky, "Idea of Creation," 74.

70. *DN* IV.18–35 713D–736A (162–179).

71. *DN* IV.31 732B (176.10–11) and IV.35 733D–736A (179:5–13).

72. See my discussion on the divine θεσμός ("law") in chapter 4 (1.1.2., "By Command of God: A Question of Law").

73. See below, chapter 4, 1.2.3. ("The Apportionment of Knowledge: A Difficulty") and especially chapter 5 (4.1., "Ministers and Ministered," and 4.2.5., "The Resurrection as Fulfillment of the Icon").

74. For example, *DN* II.8 645C (132:15–17): "the causes [τὰ αἴτια] transcend and are established beyond those things of which they are the cause [τῶν αἰτιατῶν]."

75. Florovsky, "The Idea of Creation," 74.

and therefore the objects of our contemplation;[76] and (3) through that same contemplation, the powers gathering the created mind up and toward its foreordained end (τέλος), i.e., the final causes drawing each toward its proper degree of participation in the imparticipable God.

2. The Reason-Endowed Creature as the Mirror or Analog of God's Energies

2.1. "Proper Degree": The Creature's ἀναλογία

The other half of the polarity I spoke of above, the presence as it were of its λόγος within the creature, Dionysius expresses chiefly through the use of the term ἀναλογία. It is, however, true that the two terms do occasionally overlap. In *DN* IV, for example, Dionysius compares the sun's giving "light to all who are capable, in accord with their λόγος for sharing in its light," with the Good's granting of "its rays to all according to their measure [ἀναλόγως]."[77] Elsewhere, again, he describes salvation (σωτηρία) as the divine power "preserving all without battle or conflict, ordered according to the λόγοι proper to each . . . and establishing the ἀναλογίαι of each without their suffering transformation into their opposites."[78] Overlapping, perhaps, but they are not quite synonymous. While the ἀναλογίαι may be seen as occasionally equivalent to the divine wills as paradigms,[79] they are, as is clear even from the quotations above, primarily referred to the creature. They are the very "friction point," or contact between God and creation, whence may derive the slight ambiguity of Dionysius' ἀναλογίαι. We miss, for example, Gregory of Nyssa's clear statement that the creature represents

---

76. See von Semmelroth, "Geeinte Vielheit," 395–396, in relation to *DN* VII.3 869D–872A (197–198) and *MT* I.3 1000D–1001A (144) on the λόγοι as associated with the τόπος θεοῦ; also W. Völker, *Kontemplation und Extase bei Ps.-Dionysius Areopagita* (Wiesbaden: Steiner, 1958), 179.

77. *DN* IV.1 693B (144:5).

78. *DN* VIII.9 897A (206:4–7).

79. See Lossky, "La notion des 'analogies,' " 299–305 and 308. For a view opposed to the ἀναλογία - λόγος overlap, see, however, von Semmelroth, "Geeinte Vielheit," 397ff.

in a sense God's concretized immanence, his "substantialized" will, so that as soon as the procession "solidifies," so to speak, it is a creature and not God.[80] Nonetheless, it still appears to me that the Nyssene's remark offers the most reasonable access into the Dionysian term. God gives to each "according to measure"; he establishes and maintains as unconfused the varied ἀναλογίαι or "proportions" of created beings.[81] A creature's ἀναλογία is thus the "measure" of its share in the Creator—literally, according to its λόγος (ἀνὰ + λόγον). Here we arrive at the "friction point," or tension, that sets Dionysius' use of the term apart from his pagan contemporaries, especially Proclus. Unlike the latter's ἀναλογία,[82] Dionysius' does not denote what is in fact something already accomplished. Our likeness to God, our ἐπιστροφή, is not now fully achieved. Rather, inasmuch as ἀναλογία means the capacity or potential of each for God,[83] that in us which is capable of and open to the answering of God's "word" to us, ἀναλογία necessarily opens onto movement. It denotes not so much what the creature *has* or *is* at any one time, but rather what it is willed to *become*, the level of contemplation—and thus of both activity and being—that it is called upon to realize.[84]

80. *Con. Eunom.* II.548; for comment, see Gaïth, *La liberté chez Grégoire de Nysse*, 33 and 39. For a discussion of this passage in relation to Dionysius, see Golitzin, *Et introibo*, 295. See also Koch, *Beziehungen*, 194.

81. The "variety" is particularly important for Dionysius' notion of a non-uniform creation. See Völker, *Kontemplation*, 162; Golitzin, *Et introibo*, 274–277, 282; and chapter 4 below (1.1., "A Sacred Order: Hierarchy as τάξις"). The variety, though, need not conflict with the infinite ascent.

82. For Proclus on ἀναλογία, see *Elements*, esp. propositions 125, 31–32 (for ἐπιστροφή as already in a sense accomplished) and 195–196, pages 111–113, 34–36, and 168–171 respectively. For commentary, see Dodds, *Elementsi*, 218–219 and 299–300; Gersh, Κίνησις ἀκίνητος, 83–89; and Rosán, *Proclus*, 74–75. The latter scholars, in particular, note the "return" as already fully present. Thus, for the soul as a complete microcosm, see propositions 192 and 195, 169–171. For ἀναλογία in Iamblichus, see Larsen, *Jamblique*, 448.

83. See, for example, *EH* VI.3.6 537C (120:11–12): to each of the orders of the hierarchy, the illumination of the divine ray is bestoyed ἀναλόγως; also *DN* I.1 588A (109:3); I.4 592B (114:1–2).

84. Von Semmelroth, "Die θεολογία συμβολική des Ps.-Dionysius Areopagita," *Schol* 27 (1952): 1–11, at 6. See *DN* IV.2 696C (145:14–15): the souls

The term thus embraces the whole of creaturely being and does so not as a given, static fact but as a process. The division of every creature into οὐσία, δύναμις and ἐνέργεια, "in accordance with the heavenly λόγος which concerns them,"[85] is to be read as three aspects of a single and simultaneous—though not compulsive—evolution. Dionysius elsewhere defines the perfection, τελείωσις, of each created intelligence as "being led up [ἀναχθῆναι] to the imitation of God in accordance with its proper degree [ἀναλογία]."[86] The degree analogy of each is then to be read as comprehending all three of the categories of creaturely being: οὐσία as the expression of the being's creating λόγος, i.e., the sum of its characteristics and ground of being as willed by God; δύναμις as declaring that capacity or potential in the creature for the realization of its ordained degree of participation in God; and ἐνέργεια as, finally, the eternal process itself of that accomplishment. "Eternal realization" leads us to our consideration of motion and repose.

2.1.1. Στάσις: ever-moving repose. We touch here on a point of crucial importance for Dionysius. That each creature finds its

---

are led up (ἀνάγεσθαι) by angelic guidance to the good source of all good things and, according to their capacity (κατὰ τὴν σφῶν ἀναλογίαν), they enter into sharing (ἐν μετουσίᾳ γενέσθαι) the illuminations streaming forth from the source. Note also *DN* IV.5 701A (149:19–20). Dionysius' "entering into" (γενέσθαι), "being received" or called into, and "participation" (μετουσία) is clearly an important point. The term for the Neoplatonists denotes something already present and, if imperfect, then forever so—for example, Proclus, *Elements*, prop. 143, 127. For Christian writers, however, "it is seldom used of a thing's relationship to its constituent form or substance; it is commonly contrasted with οὐσία, and indicates a state or condition, or the fact of enjoying it . . . a gift, not by nature" (C. Stead, *Divine Substance* [Oxford: Clarendon, 1977], 141). Thus we may understand Dionysius' μετουσία in *CH* IV.2 180A (21:3); VII.4 212A (31:16); X.3 273C (41:4); *EH* III.3.14 445A (94:1); and IV.3.3 476D (97:26). God "receives (εἰσδέχεται)" me into it in *EH* II.3.4 400C (75:22); "establishes (καταστήσασα)" me in it by virtue of Christ in *EH* III.3.7 436C (88:4); and, through Jesus, calls me (καλοῦν) to "participation in himself" in *EH* III.3.13 444C (93:20).

85. *CH* XI.2 284D (41:22–42:1).

86. *CH* III.2 165B (18:15). See the note below on Dionysius' use of passive voice.

perfection through participating in God "according to its own degree" implies a structure and tiered universe wherein there is a place for everything, and each is called to its proper place. Within the place foreordained by God, insofar as that place expresses its God-intended reality—λόγος—the creature is to discover its τέλος: to become in its own right and foreordained manner the imitator of God (θεομίμητος), "God's co-worker" (Θεοῦ συνεργὸν γενέσθαι).[87] This is to say that ἀναλογία, according to Dionysius, signifies that each creature—especially each reason-endowed being—is intended to become the reflection of the Godhead as the latter relates to the world, i.e., of Providence: "to show forth the divine ἐνέργεια in oneself according to one's capacity for showing it forth."[88] Becoming the reflection suggests a process or motion— "being lifted up" (ἀναχθῆναι) to godlikeness.[89] The realization of its λόγος/ἀναλογία is for each creature a continuous activity, particularly, as we shall see, a perpetual ascent into knowledge—the ἀναγωγή—and thus, together with this growth in knowing, an ever-increasing participation in the divine θελήματα or "movements" of the Good. Therefore, although the creature fulfills its ἀναλογία through discovering its place in a well-articulated

---

87. *CH* III.2 165B (18:15). Relatedly, humankind is called to become the angels' "concelebrant" (συλλειτουργός), *CH* I.3 124A (9:9); we are to work things divine together with the angels (αὐτοῖς τὰ θεῖα . . . συνεργήσωμεν), "in accordance to the providence of Jesus" (*DN* XI.5 953A [221:7]).

88. *CH* III.2 165B (18:15).

89. *CH* III.2 165B. Note the passive voice. The same predominance of the passive, when the verb applies to the creature, applies to ἀνάγω. Thus, for example, *CH* I.3 121C (8:18); II.1 137B (10:11); IV.1 177C (20:6); *EH* I.2 373A (65:15); III.1 424C (79:5); IV.1 472D (95:6); V.1.4 504C (106:25); *DN* I.3 589C (111:17); III.1 680C (139:5) (we are led up to divine radiance in prayer); V.9 825A (188:17); *MT* I.1 1000A (142:11) (for Timothy to be led up, again in prayer, to the supreme vision of God's mystery); and see *CH* I.3 124A (9:13) for God as the active agent, and *CH* II.3 141A (13:7); IV.2 180B (21:12–14); and V 196C (25:18–19) for the angels as leading me up. Thus, while Rorem, *Symbols*, 111, rightly notes that ἀνάγω/ἀναγωγή is for Dionysius—following Iamblichus—a *terminus technicus* for "spiritual interpretation," still I insist on seeing in the use of the passive an indication that Dionysius is simultaneously—indeed, predominantly—referring to the activity of divine power or grace within us; see chapter 4 (1.2.4, "Knowledge as Cooperation and Ascent").

cosmos,[90] yet that place itself remains always an activity and a progress into God.

Στάσις, repose as the equivalent to the creature's fulfillment of its ἀναλογία, is then far from static. We recall that God as the Good is repose and motion for all, equally the source of both, and that both are mentioned in the same breath in reference to what is "beyond all repose and motion."[91] Dionysius' στάσις is not static because, as the expression of a given creature's ἀναλογία, it is a reflection of the divine Providence. The latter may indeed be termed "repose," as grounding the identity of all things in its own transcendent "reality,"[92] yet it remains first of all God in motion, the "fixed procession and fertile repose."[93] Thus the "repose" of created being in Dionysius' vision can never, as was the case with the Origenists, be conceived of as some ultimate, or both primordial and ultimate, cessation of activity and motion.[94] The creature's repose, precisely its reality and beatitude as a given reflection of the uncreated God *ad extra*, lies in its motion toward, and specific activity in imitation of, the abiding transcendence and unceasing energies of Providence.[95]

2.1.2. Κίνησις. All motion whatever has its origins in God. All repose and motion have their being and meaning "in," "for," "from," and "toward" the Good.[96] All things are moved by the Good,[97] and all, even not-being, are stirred by desire for it (ἐφέσεως

---

90. Indeed in this paragraph I have sketched Dionysius' definition of hierarchy; see *CH* III.1 164D (17:3–9) and chapter 4 (1.1., "A Sacred Order: Hierarchy as τάξις").

91. See esp. *DN* IV.7 704C (152:22–153:2) and also IV.10 705BC (154:7–11).

92. *DN* IX.8 916B (212:16–213:6).

93. *DN* IX.9 916D (213:18).

94. See my argument concerning Origen and Evagrius in *Et introibo*, 274–277 and 324 respectively.

95. For the στάσις/κίνησις tension and its relation to mysticism and deification in the Christian Neoplatonists, including and subsequent to Dionysius, see Gersh, *From Iamblichus to Eriugena*, esp. 243–244.

96. *DN* IV.10 705D (154:20–24).

97. *DN* IV.10 705D (154:20–24).

κίνησις).[98] Drawing its being from Providence, created existence moves to the ἐπιστροφή to its transcendent source, "the creatures endowed with intellection and those having reason, after the manner of knowledge of vital desire."[99] All motion looks to Providence, the Good, for its cause, whether that motion be of intellection, of discursive thought, the surges of irritability[100] or of desire,[101] or the physical round of sun and stars.[102] Similarly, the whole creation looks to Providence for the preservation and ordering of its proper motion in order to accomplish the continuous realization of its being. As Dionysius says of the divine Peace:

> And if the things that are in motion [i.e., all creation] do not keep still [μὴ ἠρεμεῖν], but would rather be moved ever in their proper motion, even this is a desire [ἔφεσις] for the divine and universal Peace, which preserves all things unerringly in themselves and conserves immobile and indefectible the proper life and principle of motion of all, by which all things moved abide at peace with themselves and, ever abiding identical with themselves, accomplish those things that are proper to them.[103]

Motion, i.e., motion as embracing change and progress, is the very expression of created being. Never is the creature without movement or outside of becoming. Existence means motion, change. The motion of our being is called upon to conform itself to the λόγος/ἀναλογία of our nature that remains always in process of a realization never absolutely achieved, ever desired and ever striven after. It is this desire that is the key to and sign of our reflection of the Good. Even in the worst sinners, Dionysius tells us, there remains "a certain movement of desire."[104] The latter

---

98. *DN* IV.23 725B (171:12).

99. *DN* IV.4 700B (148.16–17); see also I.5 593B (116:10–13) and VI.1 856B (191:2–8).

100. *DN* IV.20 720B (167:4) and *CH* II.4 141D (14:7–8).

101. *CH* II.4 141D–144A (14:4).

102. *DN* IV.4 697B (147:15–21).

103. *DN* IX.4 952CD (220:12–17).

104. *DN* IV.23 725B (171:12).

leads us to the point that, while our motion is equivalent to this abiding desire for God, it is also true that it may be perverted out of weakness or ignorance—hence Dionysius' definition of evil in souls as deriving "from disordered and rebellious motion."[105] Evil is an "aversion [παρατροπή] . . . and departure [ἔκβασις] from the things that are proper."[106] Motion therefore comprises both desire and will. It is at the heart of Dionysius' vision of the created universe and of God in relation to that universe. I turn now to take note of the specific modes of motion proper to the created existents, in which creation finds its recapitulation and meaning, the reason-endowed beings, humans and angels.

2.1.2.1. Angelic motion. The movement of the angels is defined in the fourth chapter of the *DN*:

> And the divine minds are said to be moved in a circular manner when they are united to the unoriginate and unending illumination of the Good and Beautiful; directly whenever they proceed to the providence of subordinates, immediately accomplishing all things; and in a spiral manner when, at once taking forethought for their inferiors, they remain without departure in identity, unceasingly dancing around the Good and Beautiful which is the cause of identity.[107]

Angelic motion lies outside of those categories of time and space that affect human beings, who are subject to the exigencies and limitations of corporal being.[108] The angels are the beings "closest"

---

105. ἀτάκτου καὶ πλημμελοῦς κινήσεως, *DN* IV.28 729B (175:1–2).

106. *DN* IV.23 725B (171:14–16).

107. *DN* IV.8 704D-705A (153:4-9).

108. See again Dionysius on αἰών and χρόνος in *DN* X.3 937C–940A (216:2–217:4) and my discussion above. See also Roques, "Introduction," lxxii–lxxv, wherein he notes that, as distinct from our experience of time (χρόνος) and from God who simply takes on the name of αἰών in relation to us, the angels are said to enjoy an αἰώνιος χρόνος, a "durée," knowing eternity although not as God does. Unlike God, they are ever in the process of realizing eternity, hence their motion—a vision significantly different from Plotinus' Νοῦς (*Enn.* V.1.4), which is eternal actuality.

to God—immaterial (ἄϋλοι), bodiless (ἀσώματοι)—in short, the created intelligible world (κόσμος νοητός) of the Dionysian universe. Their motion is therefore purely a matter of the intelligence or, better, of intellection or intuition:

> for it is not from without that God moves them to divine things, but instead intellectively and they are illumined to the most divine counsel from within by means of a pure and immaterial ray.[109]

It is this immaterial, immediate aspect of their motion or knowing—and for Dionysius the latter two, particularly with respect to the reason-endowed beings, are inseparable—which permits our author to speak of the heavenly intelligences as being "united" to the divine illumination. For them there is no break, no hesitation or process of dialectic in attaining to the object of their intellective motion. Instead, in a manner certainly reminiscent of Plotinus' Νοῦς,[110] they are "united to their intellections [ταῖς νοήσεσιν] and to the things that they are in the process of intellecting [τοῖς νοουμένοις]."[111] There is neither complexity nor ambiguity attached to their motion. It proceeds instead directly to "simple intellections [ἁπλαὶ νοήσεις]"; being free from "material multiplicity" and dividedness, the angels enjoy a uniform and all-embracing (ἐνοειδῶς . . . συνοπτική) vision of the divine counsel to which they are joined as being thus above the distinction of knower and known, and, to continue with this passage, to which they are ever in process of being conformed (ἀποτυπουμένη).[112]

The last, of course, is not a pagan sentiment[113] and it merits a brief discussion. Roques, in summing up the characteristics of

---

109. *EH* I.4 376B (67:2–4).

110. Thus see, for example, *Enn.* VI.7.35. Recall, though, that the angels are creatures, not creators. As we see below, their πρόοδος is a principle of spiritual life and not a demiurgic function. Neither are they exclusively real (τὰ κυρίως ὄντα) as is Νοῦς in *Enn.* II.4.16.

111. *DN* XI.2 949C (219:5–6).

112. *DN* VII.2 868B (195:11).

113. For Plotinus the universe stands already "accomplished to the ultimate possibility," *Enn.* IV.8.6.

angelic motion and knowledge, declares there to be "exclusively a progress in the unification of the intelligence, which our notion of time is quite inapt to measure."[114] Progress is not a notion familiar to the pagan philosophers in relation to either νοῦς or ψυχή, and this open-ended aspect of κίνησις reveals the tension inherent in the λόγος/ἀναλογία notion we spoke of above. It breaks up the Neoplatonist cycles. Dionysius speaks in the *CH* of the angels' "ever-moving course towards [ἐπί] the divine" and of their "progression toward [ὁδοποιητικὸν πρός] the heights."[115] Ἀεικινησία ("perpetual movement") is in constant use whenever our author discusses the hosts of heaven.[116] It does not appear to me—and here I stand opposed to de Gandillac[117]—simply as a kind of perpetual revolution about (περί),[118] the knowledge of God, but as well, as is suggested by the usage of ἐπί and πρός and εἰς,[119] a continuing ascent and ever-deepening union into and with the God who is contemplated. Thus the angels "are led up toward the intuitive knowledge of the thing beheld."[120] In what is perhaps his clearest recollection of Gregory of Nyssa's ἐπέκτασις,[121] Dionysius speaks in *DN* IV of human souls "tasting fully [ἀπογευόμενοι] of the divine light and, still desiring more," of their "stretching ever to that which is before."[122] The source of this perpetual motion,

114. Roques, *L'univers*, 164.

115. *CH* XV.3 332C (54:13–15).

116. In addition to the texts just cited, see *CH* VII.1 205BC (27:14–16); VII.4 212A (31:9); XIII.4 305A (47:18); XV.2 329B (52:19); *EH* IV.3.7 481A (100:15); *DN* VI.1 and 856B (190:6) VI.2 856C (191:12); and VIII.4 892B (202:2).

117. Maurice de Gandillac, *Oeuvres complètes du Pseudo-Denys l'Aréopagite* (Paris: Aubier, 1943), 107n. 1.

118. For this preposition in connection with ἀεικινησία, see *CH* VII.4 212A (31:7); XV.9 340A (58:20).

119. See the texts quoted above, together with *CH* VIII.1 240A (33:11–15); and XIII.4 304D–305A (47:18).

120. *CH* XIII.4 305A (47:18–19).

121. For this term and Gregory of Nyssa on κίνησις, see Golitzin, *Et introibo*, 305–308.

122. ἀεὶ ἀνατείνειν αὐτὰς ἐπὶ τὰ πρόσω κατὰ τὴν σφῶν εἰς ἀνάνευσιν ἀναλογίαν, *DN* IV.5 701A (149:17–20). See also von Balthasar, *Herrlichkeit*, 175, on the room existing in Dionysius' notion of fittingness (i.e., ἀναλογία) for "an endless

both for angels and for humans, is the ever-present desire (ἔφεσις) for the Good that they receive from the same gracious Providence, "from the δύναμις which is infinitely good."[123]

Let me stress that "infinite," for here, in God's infinity and in his gift to his creation of unending desire, lies the key at once to Dionysius' alteration of the pagans' perpetual round (and so of their notion of the microcosmos) and his fidelity to patristic tradition as represented particularly by Gregory of Nyssa. First of all, like the latter's God,[124] Dionysius' is unambiguously infinite, ἄπειρος. I say "unambiguously" because the term is not unknown to the Neoplatonists. Plotinus, however, only very reluctantly applied it to the One[125] while, for the later philosophers, it stood specifically below the first principle,[126] whether the dyad πέρας - ἄπειρον (finite - infinite),[127] or the triad πέρας - ἄπειρον - μικτόν (finite - infinite - mixed).[128] While we can indeed find examples in the *CD* paralleling the philosophers' use of the term,[129] as well as others in which ἄπειρον is used to signify "formlessness" or "disorder,"[130] there remain several texts where Dionysius clearly identifies God with the infinite. The divine is, for example, invisible, infinite, and uncontained (ἀόρατον, ἄπειρον, ἀχώρητον), and we can never thus comprehend its boundlesssness (ἀοριστίαν),

---

striving," a "matter of infinite approximation" to the measure laid down by the infinite God in whom we are called to share.

123. *DN* VIII.4 872C (202:3).

124. See Golitzin, *Et introibo*, 292.

125. And that only in relation to the One's δύναμις, *Enn.* V.8.9. For an analysis, see Armstrong, "Plotinus' Doctrine of the Infinite and Christian Thought," *DRev* 73 (1954/5): 47–58, esp. 53.

126. See esp. Proclus, *Elements*, prop. 92, 83. Also, more generally, see propositions 89–92, 83, and Dodds' comment (246–248).

127. In Iamblichus, see Dillon, *Iamblichi*, 31–32; and in Proclus, *Théol. Plat.* III.8 (Saffrey/Westerink), 30–34.

128. See Beierwaltes, *Proklos*, 50–59. See again Lilla, "The Notion of Infinitude," 100–101.

129. See, for example, *DN* IV.10 705C (154:16); V.10 825B (189:9); VIII.2 889D (201:6–8); XIII.1 977B (226:11) and XIII.3 980C (228:20). Also, in relation to the expression ἀπειροδύναμος, *DN* VIII.1 889D (201:4) and VIII.3 892B (201:17).

130. Thus see *DN* IV.31 732B (176:12–13) and IV.32 732D (177:14); XI.1 949A (218:4) and XI.5 953A (220:21).

which is beyond being, ungraspable by the intellect, and ineffable (ὑπερούσιον, ἀννόητον, ἄρρητον).[131] The relation of infinity to the divine incomprehensibility clearly corresponds to the Nyssene.[132] Similarly in line with Gregory, Dionysius also speaks of the divine infinity in which we, the creation, are called to participate: "the infinite and selfless sea of the divine light, ever ready to open itself for all to share."[133] God's gifts, graces, goodness, and love for mankind are thus likewise infinite.[134]

It is then, secondly, in that endless gift of love that we discover the meaning of the angels' perpetual motion and, indeed, of our own beatitude as ἰσάγγελοι ("like the angels").[135] We find that there can therefore be no end to the ascent, and so no cycles. Any creaturely desire for God must remain, eternally, desire. It can never be satisfied, which is to say that it can never, in the face of an infinitely generous Providence, discover an end to God's gift of himself. The angels are therefore said to have an "undiminishing desire" for the Good, to be "ever in a state of desiring."[136] Their (and so, our) enjoyment of God, their contemplation, cannot then be other than an everlasting ascent into knowledge,[137] a perpetual movement into beatitude and union—though the latter

---

131. *CH* II.3 140D–141A (12:15–20).

132. For the notion as related to God's incomprehensibility, see also the κρύφια ἀπειρία ("infinite hiddenness") of *DN* I.1 588C (110:12); to his transcendence (ὑπεροχή), IX.2 909C (208.10) and IX.7 916A (212.14): God is removed from all things "by measures infinite and incomparable" (μέτροις ἀπείροις καὶ ἀσυγκρίτοις). Compare my discussion of Gregory of Nyssa in *Et introibo*, 292 and 304–306.

133. *CH* IX.3 261A (38:11–12); see also Gandillac, 135n. 2.

134. *DN* V.3 817B (182:15): τοῦ . . . ἀπειροδώρου θεοῦ μετέχοντα; *EH* III.3.15 445C (94:17–18): τὰς ἀπείρους τῶν θεουργιῶν [τοῦ Ἰησοῦ] χάριτας; *EH* III.3.11 441A (91:9): ἀπειροτάτη φιλανθρωπία; *DN* III.2 681D (141.9–10): τὴν ἀπειροδύναμον ἀγαθότητα τῆς θεαρχικῆς ἀσθενείας—note the reference to 1 Corinthians and the "weakness" of God in Jesus Christ.

135. *DN* VII.2 868BC (195:12–16).

136. ἀνελάτωτος ἔφεσις . . . ἀεὶ ἐφίεσθαι εἶναι, *DN* VIII.4 892C (202:1–5).

137. Thus see Dionysius' discussion of angelic κάθαρσις as a continuous advance into knowledge, *CH* VII.3 209C (30:19, 23); and Roques, "Introduction," lxxv–lxxvi.

term stands as well, albeit relatedly, for a creaturely experience[138] that is strictly speaking outside the capabilities of created being. I will return to ἕνωσις in my final section below, but for now my point is clear: the pagan cycles are broken by the single "cycle" of the divine procession in which the creature is called to participate. This means in turn that created, intelligent being, as a microcosmos, is far from being an already accomplished reality. It is instead an openness to the divine, a continuous process of assimilation to, and reflection of, the gift and motion of the God whose "ends" vanish in the infinity of his secret being.

In relation to that activity of reflection, and as a prelude to the created microcosmos as requiring community rather than isolation, we turn to the "direct" and "spiral" motions of the angels. As the beings "closest" to God, the "firsts" of creation, the angels most perfectly mirror the divine Providence. They are θεοειδεῖς, or θεομίμητοι, the closest analogs to God who, as Providence, both abides in transcendence and proceeds forth to creation.[139] Thus the angels, established in contemplation about God, also proceed to the providence of those beneath them. Here I may briefly note a point I will return to below, another basic alteration of the Neoplatonists' scheme. The latter see the act of emanation as accomplished in the very act of ἐπιστροφή, with the higher level, as it were, "throwing off" the level beneath it as it returns in contemplation (θεωρία) to its source.[140] Dionysius dismisses the demiurgic function but keeps the ethical aspect[141] as a principle of the spiritual life. The angels' "direct" motion is a function of their turning to God but, instead of becoming thus secondary creators or causes, they become rather revelations of the one cause,[142] images (εἰκόνες) of

138. *DN* VII.1 865C–868A (194:10–15).

139. See esp. *DN* IX.9 916C (213:18–19) and, for comment, Gandillac, 164–165n. 1.

140. See, for example, *Enn.* III.8.3; IV.4.22; and V.1.6.

141. Certainly, the ethical aspect was important for the pagans as well; see *Enn.* I.2.6–7 and E. Bréhier, *The Philosophy of Plotinus* (trans. J. Thomas; Chicago: Chicago University Press, 1958), 88.

142. *CH* X.2 273AB (40:11–14).

the divine power[143] and of a kind of sovereign freedom.[144] They become indeed truly the declarations of their own λόγοι, and powers thereby who lead back and up to the universal source of all in God.[145] Their "spiral" motion is simply a way of stating that the two first forms are simultaneous: in the process of moving toward fulfillment of their λόγος/ἀναλογία, the angels most clearly declare their source and so fulfill as well their providential task of which we, humankind, are the primary beneficiaries.

2.1.2.2. Human motion. The definition of our κίνησις, that of the soul, is also given in *DN* IV. As it will prove of great importance for the rest of my essay, I quote it at length:

> And the motion of the soul is "circular" when the soul enters into itself and away from exterior things, a "rolling-up" of its intellectual powers, as in the manner of a circle returning unerringly to itself away from the multiplicity of things outside of itself, and first gathering itself into itself, then, uniting itself—as having become in the form of the One—to the uniformly united powers [i.e. the angels], it is thus guided to the Good and Beautiful that is beyond all beings, both one and the same, without beginning or end. The soul is moved in a "spiral" form when it, in so far as is proper to it, is illuminated as to divine knowledge, not in a uniform or intellective manner, but rather through reason and discourse, and so in a manner of speaking in mixed and altering operations. Its motion is "direct" whenever it does not enter into itself or is moved by uniform intellection—for this is, as I have said, the circular manner—but rather when it proceeds to the things about it, and from these exterior things, as from certain varied and multiplied symbols, is led up to contemplations that are simple and unified.[146]

143. *CH* VIII.1 240A (33:14).

144. See Dionysius' description of fire, *CH* XV.2 329A–C (52:11–53:5), as a symbol for God and thus for the angels as deiform and moving in imitation of him.

145. *CH* XV.6 333D–336B (55-56); and XV.8 337AB (57:6–22), the latter in reference to the angels holding up the chariot of God in Ezekiel 1.

146. *DN* IV.9 705AB (153:10–154:6).

Here again Dionysius has given priority to the "circular" mode of
motion or knowledge which, as E. Hugueny writes, "preserves,
quite while participating in the mobility of becoming, something
of the uniformity, of the immobility of the divine Eternity. It is also
this movement which is the principle of all the others."[147] As with
the angels, the motions of the human soul are equivalent properly
to the realization of their ἀναλόγιαι. Unlike the angels, however,
we are yet a further step removed from the divine unity at once
transcendent and perfectly present. The human reality is not the
angelic. We are embodied spirits, partaking of both the sensible
and intelligible worlds, and uniting them both in ourselves.[148]
Our mode of knowing is thus "mixed and changing," dependent
on the necessarily limited vision of the intelligible that may be
derived from the discursive and progressively deepening consideration of the "echoes [ἀπηχήματα]" of the divine Wisdom found
in the sensible world, and so our knowledge lacks the spontane-
ity and immediacy of the angelic motion.[149] We require, at least
on this side of the eschaton,[150] the assistance of symbols taken
from the sensible world.[151] To reverse the order given in the text
above, we move out to a consideration of the things about us and,
penetrating as it were their material opacity, circle about them in
growing awareness of their divine content until we are enabled
to return to ourselves—hence the priority of the circle image: out,
about, and back—where, gathering together our perceptions and
refining them, we are ready to be led up to the succeeding stages

147. E. Hugueny, "Circulaire, rectiligne, hélocoïdal, les trois degrès de la
contemplation," *RSTP* 13 (1924): 327–331, at 329. See also Koch, *Beziehungen*,
150–153, and Gersh, *From Iamblichus to Eriugena*, 72–75, for the background
in Proclus of the threefold motion. Gersh notes however that in at least one
instance Proclus is speaking of bodily motions.

148. This is a key point for the ecclesiastical hierarchy as the reality of our
world, the divine within the sensible (vs. Brons, *Gott und die Seienden*, 30–56
esp. 52–56).

149. *DN* VII.2 868BC (195:12–20), and also *EH* I.1 372A (64:2–4).

150. Note Dionysius' promise of the isangelic state to come, *DN* I.4 592C
(115:3–4).

151. *DN* VII.2 868BC (195:12–20); see also *CH* I.3 121Cff. (8:19–9:7); and
EH I.2 373AB (65:11–17).

of knowledge with the angels, of course, acting as our guides. As Dionysius writes elsewhere:

> we make use of elements and symbols and words and writings and reasonings for the sake of the senses, but when our soul is moved by its intellective powers toward intelligible things, the senses together with sensible beings become superfluous as do, indeed, the intellective powers themselves, once the soul, having arrived at the likeness of God, is impelled by an unknown union to the rays of the light unapproachable by means of sightless [lit. "without eyes"] impulsions.[152]

I will return below to this mysterious ἕνωσις. For now I should like to draw attention to two points. First, the mode of human motion or knowing is inferior to the angelic, bound to the world of time, and so of succession, alienation (ἀλλοίωσις), and, implicitly, of mortality.[153] Yet it is inclusive of a certain capacity for knowledge—rather, for "unknowing"—that is paradoxically outside of its proper sphere of being and activity. We are called upon first to imitate the motion of the angels on the plane of the sensible creation, then we are to be led up through this same sensible world, as through a succession of symbols, to the gates of divinity itself—and beyond. Secondly, however, we must ask how all this can be, especially given our mortality and its obvious limitations. How may we achieve the "form" of God here-below and how, truly, know him in the sensible? How, indeed, can we be expected to fulfill the infinite vocation of our λόγος/ἀναλογία? In reply (1) I have already alluded to the eschaton; (2) we can thus already discern as implicit the grand design of the Incarnation, and therefore together with it, of the ecclesiastical hierarchy's simultaneous presence and promise of the world to come. The Incarnation, as the supreme expression of divine love, also directs us toward the nature of those nameless "impulsions" uniting us

---

152. *DN* IV.11 708D (156:14–19).

153. *DN* X.3 937D (216:10–15); note also in this text the promise of a future change in our mode of being.

to God and so to that unique force which enables our imitation of God here below.

2.2. The Power of Love: ἔρως

"The primary motion toward divine things," Dionysius tells us, "is the love [ἀγάπησις] of God."[154] In most cases throughout the CD the term used is ἔρως: "a certain unifying and conserving power . . . moving the superior beings to providence of the inferiors, equals into communion with one another, and finally subordinates towards the return to their superiors."[155] Now this quotation is certainly reminiscent of Proclus,[156] and it is clearly with the latter in mind that Hathaway defines Dionysius' ἔρως as the "ἀνατατικὴ δύναμις that lifts up each being towards its own generic principle [i.e., its λόγος]."[157] The definition is correct, so far as it goes, but it is also misleading. In order to balance it, we must recall that λόγος refers to what is simultaneously the origin of created ἔρως, God's Providence, the divine love, in which "single and simple power"[158] all ἔρως throughout the cosmos discovers its source. God is the first to love or desire in the CD and, in consequence, any "pull" or "tension" that the creature may know in the direction of its origins, the λόγοι located in the divine energies, must be understood as the created analog—together, I ought to note, with the active presence of the divine prototype—of that original and uncreated "tension" which "pulled" the transcendent God into the act of creation and relation with the beings whom he had made. This is the true sense of Hierotheos' three "compressions" found in the

---

154. *EH* II.1 392B (69:4–12); note that Dionysius restricts any real love of, or motion toward, God to the baptized Christians. The "divine birth" is required, since "on the human level it is first necessary that we exist, and then act . . . because that which in no way exists, neither moves nor subsists." See chapter 5 below (3.1.3., "The Contemplation: A Triple Reality and Revelation").

155. *DN* IV.15 713AB (161:2–5).

156. See my discussion above on the divine love and Proclus, chapter 2 (2.3.1., "The Divine ἔρως").

157. Hathaway, *Hierarchy*, 60.

158. *DN* IV.17 715D (162:1–2).

definition of ἔρως in *DN* IV.[159] Beginning with a general description of ἔρως, "whether divine or angelic, whether intellective or of the soul or of physical things," the author moves to a "gathering" or "compression" (συναιροῦντες) of these varied sorts of ἔρως into two fundamental expressions, that which stems, first, from the creature and, second, from the Creator. We arrive finally at the last compression into the one, unique ἔρως, "a single, simple δύναμις" uniting all things and stemming from God's traversal of all creation and return through all of creation back to himself.

It is therefore in the unique ἔρως of God that the love proper to created intelligence—and everything else—must be said to participate. On each level of created being, every creature has its proper reflection, its analog, of the θεῖος ἔρως."[160] Thus, the angels are said to "have the divine ἔρως unceasingly," just as their knowledge comes to them without effort.[161] We, on the other hand, as belonging to a lower plane of being and, moreover, as fallen, may deny or pervert it.[162] In both cases, though, it remains the force, outside of and prior to rational or even intellective thought,[163] that wells up within the created intelligence, impels the latter to motion up the paths of the knowledge of God,[164] and that increasingly shapes the creature's activity in conformity with the divine. Ἔρως, as a

159. *DN* IV.15–17 715A–D (161:1–162:5).

160. Note how often ἔρως is qualified by θεῖος: *CH* II.4 144A (14:12); IV.2 180A (21:7); XV.8 337B (58:1–2); *EH* III.3.7 436B (87:18); IV.3.5 480C (100:2); VI.1.2 532C (116:2–3); VII.3.10 565C (130:10); *DN* IV.12 709C (158:3); IV.13 712A (158:19); VIII.8 869B (205:4); X.1 937A (215:6–7); *Ep.* X 1117B (209:1). In contrast, we hear only twice of an evil ἔρως: the desire of evil which marks the fallen (*EH* II.3.3 400A [74:16]) and which is explained later as a falling away (ἔκπτωσις) from true or divine ἔρως (*DN* IV.12 709C [158:1–2]). Therefore its general characteristic is that it belongs to God as that divine motion—or grace—from which it is still possible for a free creature to "relax" (*EH* II.3.3 400A [74:16]) or "fall away" (*DN* VIII.8 869B [205:4]).

161. *EH* IV.3.5 480C (100:1–2), and *CH* II.4 144A (14:12–16).

162. See on the Fall, *EH* III.3.11 440C–441C (90:11–92:1) and below, chapter 5 (2.1., "Outside the Doors: The Fall and the Devil"). Note also *EH* I.1 372B (64:4–5) where ἔρως is specifically linked with Jesus.

163. See Horn, "Amour et extase," esp. 282–283.

164. See von Semmelroth, "Aufstieg," 33.

process of continuous motion and ascent, is that power enabling the creature to realize its ἀναλογία and so to become truly itself. We become what we are through love of God—or, better, through God loving in us. In seeking to picture this process I propose two very rough images. The first is that of a river system comprising innumerable tributaries joining larger ones—i.e., from φυσικὸς to ψυχικός to νοερὸς ἔρως—until finally all meet in the one, great river whose end and beginning is the sea (τὸ ἄπειρόν τε καὶ ἄφθονον πέλαγος). The reader must bear in mind, though, both that the great river is at once present in and the source of its tributaries, and that the latter never lose their identity in the sea. The second image, one that also bears on Dionysius' alteration of the emanation scheme, is the coalescence of a star from its constituent nebula. That "stuff" from which the soul "condenses," and that comprises its own deepest reality, is ultimately none other than the love, the λόγος, of God directed specifically toward it. In turning toward that source (the ἐπιστροφή) the soul at once accomplishes progressively the realization of its own true being, and increases the intensity of its warmth and light directed to those about it (the πρόοδος).[165] The "gravity" of divine grace, if heeded, compels this concentration and accompanying radiance. We may then rightly speak of "radiation" resulting from the creature's "return," but never of a second-level creation. The image is also useful in that it suggests the divinely willed variation in "magnitude" present in the firmament of created intelligences (1 Cor 15:41), and so, together with the astral families of constellations and galaxies, the orders, ranks, and interlocking dependencies of the hierarchies.

It remains to be noted that ἔρως, as beginning in God, must also have its end in God. The creature in moving to realize its λόγος is compelled to transcend itself: "ἔρως on the part of the creatures, just as with God [is] ecstatic."[166] It is no more than the logical

---

165. For further discussion and examples of creaturely πρόοδος, see below, 2.3.2., "Πρόοδος and Πρόνοια: Procession and Providence."

166. DN IV.13 712A (158:19–159:8). The quotation is from von Semmelroth, "Aufstieg," 33. For an account of the same in Maximus, see Thunberg, Microcosm, esp. 95, and in the Neoplatonists, Gersh, From Iamblichus to Eriugena, 39–40.

outcome of the reason-endowed creature's nature, in as much as that nature is both deiform and theomimetic, that its "vector" or "thrust" should take it ultimately outside of itself.

2.3. Θεοειδής *and* θεομίμησις: *Potential and Realization*

A striking feature of the *CD* is the lack, with one exception, of any reference to the phrase from Genesis describing humans as "in the image and likeness of God." I suggest that Dionysius uses the expressions θεοειδής ("deiform, godlike"), θεομίμησις, and—to be dealt with in the following chapter—ἀφομοίωσις ("assimilation") in place of the biblical terms. Consider how very much akin the usage of θεοειδής is, at DN II.11, to Dionysius' only reference to "image" and "likeness," in the context of a discussion on θέωσις:

> Through the deification [θεώσει] that derives from him, there come to be many gods by means of the deiformity [θεοειδεῖ] proper to the potential of each; there appears and is said to be a differentiation and multiplication of the one God, yet God who is the source of gods and beyond gods . . . is no whit the less . . . unmingled with the many and unmultiplied.[167]
>
> The theologians declare that God "bestows a divine likeness [ὁμοιότητα θείαν] to those who return to him by the imitation, according to the ability of each, of the definition and understanding beyond all. And it is the power of divine likeness [τῆς θείας ὁμοιότητος] to return to the cause all things that have been brought forth. Indeed, one must describe these as being like God [ὅμοια θεῷ] according to a divine image and likeness [κατὰ θείαν εἰκόνα καὶ ὁμοίωσιν]."[168]

The quality of θεοειδής would here appear to be something already existing within the creature—at least in potential. At no time may the θεοειδής be considered a static quality or given. Like ἀναλογία and στάσις to which it is related, the creature's deiformity is something it may realize only in action. As Hornus rightly observes:

167. DN II.11 649C (136:13–17).
168. DN IX.6 913C (211:15–20). The broader context here of the divine ὁμοιότης seems further to bear out my contention.

"It is in an ascending mobility that we become images of God, ever tending more toward our model . . . ever separated from it by the unbridgeable chasm dividing the super-essential from all beings."[169] We therefore discover the term serving most often as an adjective—the above passage from *DN* II.11 constituting in fact one of its rare appearances as a substantive[170]—such that when Dionysius speaks, for example, of the angels' "deiform ranks,"[171] or the "deiform *habitus*" restored by Christ,[172] he is, as reflected particularly in the latter citation, describing rather an activity or process than an established state. For the creature to be in the form of God means to be in his likeness as action, movement. We find thus the angels' "deiform energies"[173] or "motion"[174] "gathering together" the multiplicity of their inferiors "in a providential and deiform manner."[175] We discover the soul's deiformity in process of realization (θεοειδής γενομένη), together with its union through unknowing "with the rays of the unapproachable light."[176] The allied expression, θεομίμησις,[177] seems almost a doublet of the first, although it does tend rather more exclusively toward an emphasis on either action or the potential for action.[178] It is then again equivalent, though more in the direction of actual realization or operation, to ἀναλογία and στάσις/κίνησις. A slight difference

169. Hornus, "Quelques réflexions à propos du pseudo-Denys l'Aréopagite et de la mystique chrétienne en général," *RHPR* 27 (1947): 37–63, at 55.

170. See also *CH* VII.2 208 (28:15), and VIII.1 237C (33:7).

171. *CH* II.2 140B (11:22–12:1).

172. *EH* III.3.12 444B (93:9); see also the "deiform manner of returning good for evil," *Ep.* VIII.1 1085B (173:3).

173. *CH* VIII.1 237D (33:9–10).

174. *CH* VIII.1 240A (33:12).

175. *DN* XII.4 972B (226:4–5).

176. *DN* IV.11 708D (156:17).

177. For their linkage, see *CH* VII.2 208A (28:15); VIII.1 237C (32:16–17), and 240A (33:11–12); XV.2 329C (53:5); and *DN* I.4 589D (112:14).

178. For the term used as an adjective with δύναμις and ἐνέργεια, see *CH* XIII.3 301C (45:20); with ἐνέργεια alone, XIII.3 304A (46:9) and XIII.4 305A (47:22–48:1); with κίνησις, *EH* IV.3.3 477A (98:6); and as a goal, i.e., with ἐπί and substantive θεομίμητον: *CH* III.1 164D (17:5); III.2 165B (18:15); IV.2 180A (21:3); VIII.1 240A (33:11); and, relatedly, *EH* III.3.12 441C (92:2–4).

seems to be indicated, in the manner described, in Dionysius' use of the image of "fire" as revealing the angels' "deiformity and, as far as possible [ὡς ἐκφικτόν], their imitation of God."[179]

These two terms express in fact much of what I have been saying up to this point, and it is under their general rubric that I wish to continue and conclude this final section on creaturely ἔκστασις and ἕνωσις. The likeness or imitation of God cannot but mean, in a system whose God in relation is God in motion, a continuous operation. The following section is also included because it is the proper τέλος of created being, in striving after its transcendent λόγος and thus acting in obedience to its ἀναλογία or potential for deiformity, so to realize itself in the imitation of God as to transcend itself. The theoeidetic or mimetic capacity of the reason-endowed creature is given it to be realized thus in two manners: providentially with regard to its fellow creatures and ecstatically in relation to God. The first is accomplished through the variety of activities given us that lie, given divine cooperation (συνέργεια),[180] within our powers. The second, however, takes us from knowing to unknowing entirely by means of the "impulsions" of divine love working within us. I turn now to a further consideration of the first.

2.3.1. Δύναμις and ἐνέργεια. Together with οὐσία, these terms express the three basic aspects of created existence,[181] i.e., the full range of that which is proper to created beings. I emphasize the latter because, in contradistinction to God whose δύναμις and ἐνέργεια express his action *ad extra*, these expressions in reference to the creature denote the latter as it is in itself, *in se*. We recall, too, that the λόγοι of each are held in the divine procession, and therefore that created being mirrors Providence and not the

179. *CH* XV.2 329C (53:5).

180. For other references to the important term συνέργεια, see *CH* III.3 168A (19:22); VII.4 212A (31:13) where it is coupled with κοινωνία in God; and *EH* II.2.4 393C (71:5) where it is allied with συνεόρτασις. See also Bradshaw, *Aristotle East and West*, 185.

181. For the triad οὐσία - δύναμις - ἐνέργεια, see *CH* XI.2 284D (42:1–2); *DN* IV.1 693B (144:6–7); and IV.23 724C (170:16–17) and 725A (171:1).

super-essence,[182] the "ray" of God's procession "super-essentially pre-contained the bounds of all essential knowledge and capacities [οὐσιωδεῖς γνώσεις καὶ δυνάμεις] by means of its wholly incomprehensible δύναμις."[183] Finally, while in God any distinction between δύναμις and ἐνέργεια may be suggested only very cautiously, in the creature they may be and are distinguished.[184]

I translated δύναμις just above as "capacity" rather than "power" or "virtue" because this expression in created being denotes a faculty or potential for action, and not necessarily an action accomplished or even in process. Dionysius can thus say of Jesus that he has given us the "δύναμις of the sacred priesthood," while it remains for us to "go on to its realization [ἐνέργεια]."[185] Similarly we learn in *DN* VIII that God has given us the δύναμις for deification,[186] but, as implied, the actuality of θέωσις remains at least in part our own responsibility. The whole discussion concerning evil revolves around this distinction, for if the creature has been accorded the potential for the imitation of God, this by no means necessitates the fulfillment of that potential. Evil does not affect the inherent capacity of any given creature for the good (although there is a suggestion in the *CD* that the Fall did mean some sort of inherited debility).[187] It is rather a "falling away [ἀποπτῶσις] from the power conserving perfection," a "closing of one's eyes to the Good,"[188] a "weakness" or "want" of "the natural conditions, activities, and capacities."[189] By this "weakness" or

182. And still less the Trinity; for the same notion of the "image" as of God *ad extra* in Gregory of Nyssa, see above, chapter 2 (2.2.2, "Δύναμις and ἐνέργεια") and Golitzin, *Et introibo*, 307–308.

183. *DN* I.4 592D–593A (115:13–14).

184. For discussion of the same in Maximus, see Sherwood, *Ambigua*, 56–57 and 122.

185. *EH* I.1 372B (64:7); other examples of δύναμις as capacity are too numerous to cite in full, thus—for instance only—see *CH* I.3 124A (9:10–11); *EH* II.3.3 400A (74:16–17); *DN* II.8 645C (132:5); and VIII.7 896B (204:21).

186. *DN* VIII.5 893A (202:22).

187. See my discussion below, chapter 5 (2.1., "Outside the Doors: The Fall and the Devil" and the note on the "weakness" and "lack" of the will).

188. *DN* IV.23 725B (171:15–16).

189. *DN* IV.25 728B (173:7).

"want" Dionysius would appear to mean a failing of the will or, as in *EH* II, an attraction (ἔρως) for evil due to ignorance, mixed with "the capacities [δυνάμεις] for illumination naturally implanted in our capacity for self-determination [αὐτεξουσιότης]."[190] If, then, the capacities of the created being—in our case humanity—are provided for ascent toward the good, we nonetheless have the freedom not to realize them. As I noted above, we must cooperate with, become συνεργοί of, God. The δυνάμεις are then necessarily always good, since they are the potentialities expressed in the λόγοι addressed to each created being. The creature's actions, ἐνέργειαι, or realizations may, however, be either good[191] or bad,[192] although the latter must always be understood as a perversion of the creature's proper activity.[193]

Why a perversion? Because δύναμις and ἐνέργεια, the former per force or per nature and the latter per deliberation, are both dependent on, and ultimately expressions of, the indivisibly multiplied power and operation of God.[194] Each reason-endowed being is called to become the likeness of the divine by means of "grace

190. *EH* II.3.3 400A (74:15–17); see also *CH* IX.3 260C (38:3–5). For the capital importance of this term in the thought of Gregory of Nyssa, see J. Gaith, *La conception de la liberté chez Grégoire de Nysse* (Paris: Vrin, 1943); Golitzin, *Et introibo*, 285–317. Human freedom to refuse God is certainly stressed by both the Nyssene and Dionysius, and for both the choice against God is simultaneously a loss of true freedom which only God can restore—see *EH* II.3.6 401D (77:15–16) for Christ and the restoration of our ἐλευθερία; and, relatedly, *Ep.* VIII.5 1097C (188:13–189.8); *Ep.* X 1117B (208:10–12); and chapter 5 below (2.2., "The Incarnation: The Restoration of Our Being in Jesus and the Ground of the Ecclesiastical Hierarchy") and *Et introibo*, 309–310.

191. *DN* IV.24 728A (172:15) and IV.35 736A (179:8).

192. *DN* IV.30 732A (176:2 and 6) and IV.35 736A (179:8 and 13).

193. See, for example, *DN* IV.25 728B (173:6–7) and 30 732B (176:7–8).

194. In this and the following see the parallels in Maximus, Thunberg, *Microcosm*, 94 and 222–224, and (though he has some misgivings) von Balthasar, *Kosmische Liturgie*, 187–189. The notion of true action and freedom as the willing of one's own being is also, of course, present in Plotinus; see, for example, *En.* III.1.9 and VI.8.4; and, for the comment, R. T. Wallis, *Neoplatonism* (London: Duckworth, 1972), 63–64.

and God-given capacity" (χάριτι καὶ θεοδότῳ δυνάμει)[195] insofar,
again, as each participates in the single "super-essential power
which is creative of power"[196] and which extends throughout
creation. The same applies to the ἐνέργειαι of each: "every sacred
and theomimetic operation is to be referred to God as cause."[197]
There is then a "natural" and proper ἐνέργεια for the human
being: precisely "to will oneself," i.e., to consent to and cooperate with, the unfolding of one's own true nature as God wills it.
Inasmuch as each rational being thus acts toward the fulfillment
of its λόγος/ἀναλογία, it moves toward an increasing conformity
with God's energies containing those same λόγοι, and thus, in its
own contingent being, "shows forth . . . the divine energies."[198]
The true nature of God's processions into and activities within
his creation is love, and the eternal expression of that love is his
Providence. Therefore, created being, in fulfillment of its ἀναλογία
and impelled by the divine ἔρως in which it participates, moves
"naturally" to: πρόοδος and πρόνοια.

2.3.2. Πρόοδος and πρόνοια: procession and providence. These
activities in created beings are directly the result of the love that
moves all toward providence with respect to those below one's
rank, communion with one's equals, and attraction toward one's
superiors.[199] The creature is to become at once the expression and
the agent of the uncreated procession of God that is "revealed and
continuously present . . . in all the hierarchies."[200] We thus find
the angels spoken of frequently in terms relating to providence

195. *CH* III.3 168A (19:23); see also IV.1 177D (20:18–20); XIII.3 304A (46:7–
19) and 304C (47:7–10); and *EH* I.1 372B (64:3–14).

196. *CH* VIII.1 240A (33:13–15).

197. *CH* XIII.3 301A (44:17–18); see also above, chapter 2, and *DN* IX.5 912D
(210:10) and IX.9 916C (213:12–14); XIII.1 977B (226:13–227.1); and *Ep.* IX.3
1109D (203:1–5) on the energies.

198. *CH* III.2 165B (18:16–17); and also *EH* VI.17 508CD (109:22–25).

199. *DN* IV.15 713AB (161:1–5); see also IV.2 696B (144:19–145.1); IV.7 704B
(152:14–18); IV.8 709D (158:13–18); and IV.13 712A (159:1–3).

200. *CH* IX.2 260B (37:11–13).

and procession.[201] The two expressions often occur simultaneously. For example, each level of the angelic hierarchy is said to
be "moved to a generous and providential procession toward its
subordinates."[202] Each level, again, acts as a force to reveal, turn
and lead the lower levels back up to their source in God.[203] The
being and activity of all lie thus in their "participation in [God's]
providential δύναμις through their generous procession to those
below them."[204]

Similarly, humankind too, as "moved by the love of God,"
discovers that its true σωτηρία[205] lies in the assimilation to God's
loving activity: for "the procession [i.e., ours] to the sacred practice
[ἱερουργία] of the divine commandments is the ineffable effecting
[also creation or making: δημιουργία] or our becoming divine."[206]
Here, in the context of the Church's liturgical life, Dionysius is
clearly referring to the evangelical—especially Johannine (e.g.,
John 15:12 and 1 John 4:7-12)—commandments of love. It is thus
during the Eucharist—exiting the altar to cense the entire temple,
reentering the altar, and, later, inviting believers to partake of
the Gifts—that the bishop provides us with an icon of the divine
procession and Providence.[207]

This participation in God's Providence is finally our "natural"—
i.e., true being as intended by God's λόγος for each—sharing in the
activity of Jesus. It is Jesus who stands at the head, as principle

201. See *CH* VIII.2 240C (34:11–14); XV.1 328C (51:18–21); and XV.6 333D
(55:20–22) for πρόνοια, and *CH* XIII.3 301D (46:1–5); XV.5 333B (55:10–11); XV.9
340A (59:1); and *DN* IV.7 704A (152:16) for πρόοδοι.

202. *CH* XV.6 333D (55:22).

203. ἀνάγωγος . . . καὶ ἐπιστρεπτικὴ δύναμις, *CH* XV.5 333B (55:11).

204. *CH* XV.1 328C (51:18–20).

205. See Dionysius' definition of the divine σωτηρία in *DN* VIII.9 896D
(205:16–19) as "preserving and guarding the proper and pure being and order
of each [τὴν ἰδίαν ἑκάστου καὶ καθαράν . . . οὐσίαν καὶ τάξιν ἀποσώζουσα καὶ
φυλάττουσα] from the others," and as the cause (αἴτιον) of each being's proper
activity (ἰδιοπραγία). It is not a definition that rules out the Incarnation, thus
see my remarks following here.

206. *EH* II.1 392B (69:6–7).

207. See esp. *EH* III.3.3 429AB (82:17–83:10).

and enabling power, of every created order.[208] Dionysius then notes that the angels are rendered worthy

> of the communion in Jesus, not by means of sacred images being conformed to the theurgic likeness, but as truly drawing nigh to him through a primary participation in the knowledge of his theurgic lights, and indeed that the imitation of God is given them in a supreme manner, and [that] they share, so far as it is possible for them . . . in his theurgic and beneficent virtues.[209]

This is a summary of what we have been considering so far in our discussion concerning both δύναμις and ἐνέργεια, and θεοειδής/θεομίμησις. It is also worthy of note that the created world's increasing participation in God's Providence is concentrated here specifically in the second Person of the Trinity.

While this mirroring of providential love is a primary aspect of the creature's fulfillment of its ἀναλογία, it is not yet the whole of that fulfillment. Procession and Providence, while proper to the creature as such and declarative of divine Providence, do not express the whole of the creature's activities or motion. They signify, rather, a descent or condescension, the lending of aid and leading up of those below oneself, and as such constitute the expression of a state already in process of attainment. I noted above that the ascent of created ἔρως is a growth into the knowledge of God, and that it is the ever-increasing movement into the contemplation of divinity which has as its fruit, or "radiance," the beneficent activities just now discussed. Our text above therefore continues:

> and at the same time they are initiates, not as being illumined as to an analytic science of varied sacred things [that is, as opposed to human ways of knowing], but as filled with a primary and transcendent deification in accord with the supreme science of the divine operations proper to angels.[210]

---

208. See esp. *CH* II.5 145C (16:17–19), and also IV.4 181C (23:18–24.3).
209. *CH* VII.2 208C (29:9–15).
210. *CH* VII.2 208CD (29:15–18).

I thus move to the last section of my discussion of θεοειδής and θεομίμησις.

2.3.3. Γνῶσις. In discussing created κίνησις, I noted that the activities of reason-endowed creatures are primarily defined in terms of thought, the motions of the intelligence (broadly understood). "Intellectual" (νοητός) or "intellective" (νοερός) in the *DN* thus frequently modify ἐνέργεια[211] when referring to the contemplation of divine things that spills over into action on behalf of one's fellows. What, then, is the context and content of this contemplation, and how is it that both θεοειδής/θεομίμησις and the knowledge (γνῶσις) so obtained are in the form and imitation of God?

Beginning with the latter, I note that, in his discussion of the divine Wisdom, Dionysius declares that God "pre-contains the knowledge of all things in himself, in as much as he is the cause of all"; he thus "does not receive the knowledge of beings from the beings themselves, rather it is he who supplies them with the knowledge both of themselves and of others."[212] God knows the creature as Creator: "before angels came to be he knew them,"[213] and so not "through any science of beings, but rather of himself."[214] The creaturely mode of knowledge is therefore a reflection of God in two respects: (1) any and every act of (true) knowing involves participation in him who "supplies" all knowledge as source and fount of knowing; and (2) just as God knows the creature through the knowledge of himself, so the creature knows God through the knowledge of itself and of its fellows.

In relation to the first point, the angels stand closer to God in knowing the things of, for example, the senses, "not by means of sensible perceptions . . . but in accordance with the proper

---

211. See *DN* I.1 588A (108:4–5); I.4 592D (115:9); II.7 645A (131:4 and 11); IV.1 693B (144:6–7); IV.9 705B (153:17–154:1); IV.11 708D (156:15–16); and VII.2 868B (195:3 and 8).

212. *DN* VII.2 869AB (196:17–20).

213. *DN* VII.2 869AB (196:14).

214. *DN* VII.2 869C (197:13–14).

capacity and nature of a deiform mind."[215] As I have noted, their mode of knowing is immediate and immaterial, and it is through this lack of division, and immateriality, and "unity after a deiform fashion [that they are] conformed to the divine which is beyond wisdom, mind, and reason."[216] It is also thus that they are enabled to express this deiformity through the activity of Providence and procession, the two—i.e., knowing and providential love—being in fact simultaneous, as we recall from Dionysius' definition of the angelic "spiral."

Our knowledge, of course, cannot be so direct. We are forced to ascend through the things of sense[217] to those which are beyond and, even then, "to circle discursively . . . about the truth of beings."[218] Nonetheless, this, too, is a real imitation of God as denoted by the same imagery of circle, spiral, and straight line as was applied to Providence and the angels. Here I should note that Dionysius is unmarked by any contempt for the "merely" sensible as a bearer of knowledge such as, for example, Plotinus occasionally exhibits.[219] Divine Wisdom has "set forth certain images and likenesses [εἰκόνες καὶ ὁμοιώματα] of its divine paradigms" in the sensible world, arranged in a certain order (διάταξις).[220] It is this ordered sequence of images that we are given to ascend in stages, ὁδῷ καὶ τάξει,[221] up to, and in imitation of, God's own Wisdom. The latter indeed includes within its realm, as its "last echo [ἀπηχήμα]," the sensory perceptions

215. *DN* VII.2 869C (197:14–16).
216. *DN* VII.2 868B (195:10–11).
217. *EH* V.1.3 504CD (106:24–107:6).
218. *DN* VII.2 868B (195:12–13).
219. Thus see *Enn.* VI.7.3. Neither, for Dionysius, is the "return" to the supra-sensible understood as a return to one's true self (*Enn.* VI.4.16 and 9.11) and away from the "fall" of separation (*Enn.* VI.5.12). See also Armstrong, *CambHist*, 223; and Bréhier, *Philosophy of Plotinus*, 42. The world under Providence, particularly the sanctified world of the hierarchies, is not for our author a "shadow theater" (*Enn.* III.2.15). Curiously, however, in his truly exalted notion of art as capable of revealing the intelligible λόγοι more clearly than the physical original, Plotinus does somewhat anticipate the *EH* (see *Enn.* V.8.1 and VI.7.22).
220. *DN* VII.3 869CD (197:20–22); see also 872B (198:15–20).
221. *DN* VII.3 869D–872A (198:1).

themselves.[222] These are points of obvious significance for Dionysius' development of the ecclesiastical hierarchy as making present in material symbols the manifestation of divine Wisdom and the angels, its revelators[223]—rather, of Providence and the latter's fulfillment of its "motion" toward us, the Incarnation of Christ.

If, unlike the angels, humans come to knowledge by a process of ascents or degrees, it is still the case for both, with respect to my second point, that knowledge *per se*, whether of the divine or of the creation, is always through the medium of the creature.[224] "All knowledge," Dionysius declares, "is of beings and is limited to beings," while "that which is transcendent to being is also transcendent with regard to all knowledge."[225] Insofar as the creature remains within the sphere of its created powers, it may then know God "by means of participation alone."[226] This is not, of course, to deny that this knowledge does convey something of God in his activities. It has a real content. The reality of every created being lies in its likeness to God and participation in him,[227] in the "measure" of its fulfillment of the divine λόγος addressed to it that it is called upon to reveal or "declare."[228] Beholding the creation, we may then be illumined with regard to the "intentions" of God respecting his creatures, to discern something of his λόγοι,[229] and

222. *DN* VII.2 868C (195:17).

223. See *CH* II.2 140A (11:7–19); XV.4 333A (54:20–23); and *EH* IV.3.7 481A (100:13–23).

224. The sole exception to this would appear to be the first order of the celestial hierarchy who are illumined by the divine γνῶσις itself. This, however, by no means exhausts the object of their knowledge, as is made clear by the "purification" from ignorance which they continually experience (*CH* VII.3 209C [30:17–31:5]).

225. *DN* I.4 593A (115:16–18); see also I.6 596BC (119:5–9).

226. *DN* II.7 645A (131:5–6).

227. For the same in Gregory of Nyssa, see Sheldon-Williams, *CambHist*, 453.

228. For the angels as "declarations" or revelations of God, see my note on ἐκφαίνειν, ἐκφαντορία, ἐκφαντορικός, and ἔκφανσις in chapter 4 (2.1.2., "A Perfected Creation: Our Models for the Life in God").

229. The discernment of the λόγοι of the world is of course a theme familiar to the pagans; see *Enn.* III.2.15 and V.1.3; and for comment, Inge, *The Philosophy of Plotinus* 1:162; and Bréhier, *Philosophy of Plotinus*, 32. For Proclus,

so arrive at the intuition of his energies that irradiate the worlds.[230]
Even so, however, we are still only at the "forecourt"[231] of the truly
divine, the "place [τόπος]" of his abiding, and the indication of
his presence (παρουσία).[232]

Yet, while beginning in the creation, the process of contemplation ends neither there nor in knowledge itself:

> He is hymned from all things which are according to the
> ἀναλογία of all things of which he is cause . . . [but] the most
> divine knowledge of God is knowing through unknowing
> [ἀγνωσία], according to the union [ἕνωσις] that is beyond mind,
> when the mind [νοῦς], leaving behind all things, then abandon-
> ing itself as well, is united to the super-luminary rays, there
> and thence to be shone upon by the unsearchable depth of
> wisdom.[233]

We arrive at the final sense and goal of the θεοειδής, the term—and
beyond—of created being: the movement and gift of ἀγνωσία and
of ἕνωσις.

3. Ἕνωσις: The Creature ἐν ἐκστάσει

In the preceding section I discussed the creature on its own
terms as the reflection and revelation of God in extension, or
Providence. The rational beings particularly, *qua* creatures, are,
in their being, capacity, and activity, their motion, desire, and

---

see Rosán, *Proclus*, 99, esp. 221–222. For the theme in Origen, see Golitzin, *Et
introibo*, 269–271, 275, and 280.

230. Indeed the whole range or "shape" of Providence; see below chapter
4 (1.1.–2., "A Sacred Order: Hierarchy as τάξις" and "The Gift of Light: Hierarchy as Sanctified Knowledge [ἐπιστήμη]").

231. For the use of "forecourt" (προθύροι), see *CH* VII.2 208A (28:21), where
it is the place assigned to the first angels. For the same term in Plotinus as an
expression of Νοῦς, see *Enn.* V.9.3.

232. *MT* I.3 1000D–1001A (144:5–8); for the τόπος theme, see my discussion at the end of chapter 5 (5.1., "A Series of Icons"), and chapter 6 (2.3.,
"Eschatology or Ecstasy? Dionysius and Evagrius on the Experience of God")
on Evagrius.

233. *DN* VII.3 872AB (198:10–15).

knowing, each the image or icon—the angels in the intelligible world and humankind in the sensible realm—of the uncreated God revealed in the "names" declarative of his processions. The mode of created being and motion, though, is such that it does not discover its term or τέλος within its own boundaries. There is a "vector" or "thrust" to the θεοειδής that must, if it is assented to (in the case of people), carry the reason-endowed being up and beyond the categories of created existence. I have touched on this aspect at some length in my discussion of ἔρως, κίνησις, and of λόγος/ἀναλογία. There is a dynamic inherent particularly in the latter two terms which must find its resolution in a state of being that we might call "the creature in the uncreated" in God. The proper end of the rational creation is thus outside itself, ἐν ἐκστάσει, and the name that Dionysius assigns to this final stage of being is union, ἕνωσις.

Vanneste has presented us with a number of valuable studies concerning what he claims to be the false ascription of mysticism to the *Areopagitica*.[234] I am indeed indebted to his illuminating discussion of, especially, the term ἕνωσις. Of the several meanings he distinguishes for the word,[235] one is of primary interest to us here. Placing it at the term of the triad, ἀφαίρεσις - ἀγνωσία - ἕνωσις, which he claims dominates the *MT*—and incidentally which he sees as replacing the "theurgic" triad of κάθαρσις - ἔλλαμψις - τελείωσις—he defines Dionysius' ultimate "union" as a natural faculty of the creature enabling the latter's union with the unknowable and transcendent. As he himself writes:

> on peut raisonnablement admettre, chez le Pseudo-Denys, l'existence d'une faculté (δύναμις) de la connaisssance du Transcendant qu'il appelle ἕνωσις au-delà de l'intelligence . . . nous annonçons ici la doctrine dionysienne: quiconque réussit à ne plus rien connaître (τὸ μὴ γινώσκειν) par l'inconnaissance

234. Vanneste, *Mystère de Dieu*, and related articles: "La théologie mystique du Ps.-Denys," *TU* 80/ *SP* 5 (1962): 401–415; "Is the Mysticism of Ps.-Dionysius Genuine?," *IPQ* 3 (1963): 286–306; "La doctrine des trois voies dans la théologie mystique du Ps.-Denys," *TU* 93/ *SP* 8 (1966): 462–467.

235. Vanneste, *Mystère de Dieu*, esp. 187–189.

(ἀγνωσία)—résultat de l'abstraction abstraite (ἀφαίρεσις)—connaîtra au-delà de l'intelligence (ὑπὲρ νοῦν γνώσκειν) . . . l'union à Dieu . . . tel qu'il est en soi, sera réalisée.[236]

Vanneste, further, sees this "faculty" as realized through the purely personal[237] and willed effort of the human mind: "C'est l'ἀφαίρεσις qui se charge de le [i.e., l'homme] faire aboutir à cette attitude surpassant l'intelligence par la négation de toute détermination, à la simplicité absolue de l'Un transcendent. Là, l'union s'accomplit."[238] It is in accordance with the principle of "like to like" that the ἕνωσις comes into play: through the operation of ἀφαίρεσις humans ascend to unknowing and, as thereby being likened to the unknown (ἄγνωστος), they are enabled to enter into union with the transcendent Unity.[239] Vanneste sees this remarkable symmetry as a particularly strong witness against any claims that might be put forward on behalf of Dionysius' genuinely "mystical" character, and in favor rather of a vision of the Areopagite as metaphysician, advocating a deliberate effort of the will, divorced from any questions of morality and the like,[240] to push the intelligence into conformity with the One.[241]

Now it is clear that Vanneste has hit on certain key elements in the *CD*. He is certainly correct in noting the symmetry of the Dionysian system. Neither is he alone in looking to Dionysius' pagan predecessors for both the sources of the *MT*'s doctrine and its "automatic" or "natural mysticism."[242] The latter is Rist's phrase, and it features prominently in his article contrasting Dionysius' and Proclus' ἕνωσις as a "power to ascend . . . inherent"

---

236. Vanneste, *Mystère de Dieu*, 209 and 210–211.

237. Vanneste, *Mystère de Dieu*, 216–217.

238. Vanneste, *Mystère de Dieu*, 205.

239. Vanneste, *Mystère de Dieu*, particularly 179–181 where Vanneste offers the symmetry ἀγνωσία - ἄγνωστος as the basis for Dionysius' choice of pseudonym.

240. Vanneste, *Mystère de Dieu*, 196–197.

241. Vanneste, "La théologie mistique du Ps-Denys l'Aréopagite," 414.

242. See Koch, *Beziehungen*, 154–155, esp. 159 on the ἄνθος τοῦ νοῦ in Proclus and Dionysius' ἕνωσις.

in humans with Plotinus' mere "capacity to receive (παραδοχὴ)"[243] and consequent mysticism of "grace."[244] Rist's contrasts, however, between even the pagans seem to me a little overdrawn. There are ambiguity and grace in both. Plotinus' rise of "the alone to the alone,"[245] and "not to something alien but to its [one's] very self,"[246] certainly suggests some sort of ontological connection awaiting, as it were, "activation."[247] On the other hand, the ἕνωσις faculty in both Iamblichus[248] and Proclus[249] requires the gracious activity and gift of the gods.[250] Indeed, it was the later Neoplatonists' very distrust of the adequacy of the intellect, unlike Plotinus,[251] that led to their reliance on theurgy—i.e., prayer, among other things—to accomplish the supreme joining.[252] One can certainly not fault Dionysius for taking up whatever themes

243. Rist, "Mysticism and Transcendence in Later Neoplatonism," *Hermes* 92 (1964): 213–225, at 219. Rist is here contrasting *Enn.* VI.7.35 with *DN* VII.1 865C (194.11–12). He might well have added the wonderful passage from *Enn.* V.5.8: "We must not run after It, but fit ourselves for the vision and then wait tranquilly for Its appearance, as the eye waits on the sun's rising" (trans. MacKenna, 56).

244. Rist, "Mysticism and Transcendence in Later Neoplatonism," 224; see also 214 where Rist repeats the assertion that union in Plotinus occurs on the One's "own terms" while at the same time admitting, with regard to *Enn.* VI.9.4, that "there is within Νοῦς a kind of unity derived from the One's transcendence."

245. *Enn.* VI.7.34 and 9.11.

246. *Enn.* VI.9.11.

247. Thus see the following articles: Dodds, "The *Parmenides* of Plato and the Origin of the Neoplatonic One," *ClassQ* 22 (1926): 129–142, at 141 for the "like to like" symmetry of negation and union in Plotinus; R. Arnou, "La contemplation chez les anciens philosophes du monde greco-romain," *DSp* II.1716–1742, at 1727 and 1737; and J. Trouillard, "Raison et Mystique chez Plotin," *REA* 20 (1974): 3–14.

248. See *De myst.* V.26 and I.3; and Larsen, *Jamblique*, 154.

249. See his *In Tim.* 211.24 and Gersh, Κίνησις ἀκίνητος, 34–35.

250. Thus see the ἀφθόνως of the gods' gift in *De myst.* III.17 and, in Proclus, *Theol. Plat.* I.25 (Saffrey/Westerink) 111.

251. See Armstrong, "Escape from the One," 186.

252. See Iamblichus, *De myst.* II.10; III.13; and IV.2; together with Proclus, *Theol. Plat.* I.25, 113; and Beierwaltes' comment, *Proklos*, 393–394, and Zintzen, "Die Wertung von Mystik," 95.

he may have rightly judged here to be in, again, convergence with Christian faith and tradition, and in this case his and the late Neoplatonists' stress on transcendence and prayer.[253]

Of course, that is not all which it is claimed he did take. Vanneste's is the strongest and most developed argument in favor of more sinister pagan borrowings and, for that reason, I should like here to note a few points concerning his essay that, in light of my argument preceding this section, seem to me to be in need of adjustment. In the first place it is not at all clear that the way of negation, while certainly given precedence in both the *DN*[254] and the *MT*[255] over the ascription of positive attributes (καταφάσεις) to God, necessarily and by itself—i.e., as the sort of metaphysical "trampoline" that Vanneste would appear to have us believe it to be—leads to union with the God who is "above both all assertions and all negations."[256] Secondly, and in connection with the "by itself," Vanneste has seemingly overlooked—or failed to explain adequately—the markedly passive terminology Dionysius employs in describing the final leap into union. A notable example of the latter may be found in the description Dionysius gives of his mentor, Hierotheos:

> whether he received [this knowledge] from the sacred theologians, whether he took [it] from the scientific searching of the Scriptures . . . whether indeed he was initiated by a more divine inspiration, not only learning but suffering divine things such that, out of the sympathy he had for these things (if one may so speak), he was perfected in their untaught and mystical unity and faith.[257]

253. Thus see *DN* III.1 680B–D (138:1–139:16): here below we rise to God via πανάγνοις . . . εὐχαῖς (138:8).

254. For example, *DN* XIII.3 981B (230:1–5).

255. *MT* I.2 1000B (143:4–7).

256. *MT* I.2 1000B (143:7).

257. *DN* II.9 648B (133:15–134:4); for the importance of the expression, παθὼν τὰ θεῖα, and its significance as declarative of the divine grace in Maximus Confessor, see Sherwood, *Ambigua*, 153, and Thunberg, *Microcosm*, 431–432 and 450.

This appears to be somewhat distant from the language of a professor of metaphysics. It is noteworthy, too, that elsewhere Dionysius speaks of Hierotheos experiencing God specifically in the context of prayer.[258] To "suffer the divine" suggests, in any case, an active power at work that does not originate within us. This brings me to my third point: Vanneste scarcely mentions, and only then in a sense contrary to the text, the notion of the uncreated energies. For him, the divine "names" of the *DN* refer rather to the "created forms" by which we know God.[259] I have labored to stress the centrality of the essence/energies distinction for the whole of Dionysius' thought.[260] Without this distinction, given instead static, created forms—in short, the Platonist κόσμος νοητός ("intelligible world")—it would indeed be correct to interpret the *CD* in a Neoplatonic sense, and see its "mysticism" as a "natural" one. Such, however, would be alien to its thought. It would eliminate, for one, the συνέργεια that is assumed throughout the corpus, the Dionysian intuition of the ascent and increasing assimilation to God that alone renders meaningful the final leap into ἕνωσις. The real possibility of divine-human compenetration depends on the notion of God's δυνάμεις at work within us and increasingly conforming us to him. The uncreated energies are no less fundamental to the idea of creaturely ἔκστασις and ἕνωσις than we have seen them to be with regard to the whole of created being, activity, and knowledge. At the heart of our ἔκστασις/ἕνωσις, as at the heart of created providence and knowing, lies the dynamism of the Dionysian θεοειδής, the thrust or vector of the ἀναλόγιαι toward their λόγοι in the divine processions, and the power, at once sustaining and drawing us toward itself, of the divine "wills" and love at work within us. The ἔκστασις/ἕνωσις represents, indeed, the meaning and goal of the whole process, and of this chapter.

258. *DN* III.2 681C–684A (141:1–17); and more specifically still, the context here is liturgical prayer—see chapter 5 below (5.1., "A Series of Icons"). Note also the expression κοινωνίαν πάσχων (684A [141:12]).

259. Vanneste, *Mystère de Dieu*, 38–39.

260. See Lossky, *Vision of God*, 102; Bradshaw, *Aristotle East and West*, 179–186.

As such, it merits further discussion. I will proceed in the order of the three points just noted.

3.1. Ἀφαίρεσις - ἀπόφασις: *Impelling Force*

The process of negation, ἀφαίρεσις, cannot be taken in isolation from everything that precedes the final act of union. It is instead a necessary aspect of that process of likening sketched above. Necessary, I hasten to add, not in any involuntary or deterministic sense, but rather that, in the course of its free assent to conformity with the λόγος of God directed to it, the reason-endowed being discovers itself obliged, on the plane of its own powers, to exercise a continual negation of any and all attributes taken from creation and applied to God. Insofar indeed as the "motion" of the rational creature involves a continual ascent, an ever-deepening penetration into the realities undergirding the creation, so, too, it requires a continuous negation, which is the same as to say a progressive abandonment of each successive level of understanding at which it finds itself. Ἀφαίρεσις is a fundamental aspect of the creature's appropriation of the divine from the very beginnings of its ascent. It is therefore present at every stage of the Dionysian anagogy—as may be noted in the text dealing with the properties of human κίνησις: the "circular" movement requires a motion "away" from exterior things and the "direct" proceeds "from" the extrinsic "into" unified contemplation.[261] Roques thus rightly speaks of the necessity of the creature's anagogy corresponding to God's condescension, of all symbol and discourse charged with the divine and, because so charged, pointing beyond itself to the divine reality that surpasses it and is thereby continually schooling the intelligence to press on yet further.[262] Far, then, from being an isolated technique, ἀφαίρεσις/ἀπόφασις—just as the *MT* itself is present at the heart of every treatise in the *CD*[263]—is in

---

261. *DN* IV.9 705AB (153:10–154:6); "away" (153:10–11), "into" (154:5–6).
262. Roques, *L'univers*, 208–209.
263. The *MT* is present in but does not dissolve the symbols; see above, chapter 2 (3, "The Names: Notional Icons, Resonances of God as Providence")

fact the ever-present corrective at all levels of knowing. Rather, it is both corrective and catalyst, or spark or impulsion, compelling us to move ever higher and thus itself essentially partaking of the quality of συνέργεια as almost a synonym for our response to God's mystery, and as indeed suggesting that mystery at work in us. It is for this reason that Dionysius can speak of the sacred writers preferring

> the ascent through negations inasmuch as it takes the soul out [or: drives it out, deprives it of: ἐξιστῶσα] of things akin to it and leads [it] up through all the divine intellections, beyond all of which is that which is above every name and every reason and knowledge, and joins us, so far as we are able to be joined to him.[264]

3.2. Παθὼν τὰ θεῖα: *The Discovery of a Presence*

With the notions of "impulsion" and "being joined"—συνάπτεσθαι: note the passive voice of the verb—I arrive at the second of my three points, and also a second aspect of the ἀφαίρεσις/ἀπόφασις: the markedly passive character of the vocabulary Dionysius employs whenever union with the divine comes under discussion. Ἀφαίρεσις cannot, as I have just hinted, simply be viewed as a philosophical technique or even as wholly an exercise of our created powers. No less than at every other stage of the creatures' ascent, it is a product of that cooperation with God which pervades the Dionysian vision of God and world. It is of a piece with the steady growth into deiformity or, as it were, "transparency" to the divine that I have been outlining.

Horn draws the specific connection between ἀφαίρεσις and ἔρως: "Ne pourrait-on pas schématiser la pensée de Denys à peu près ainsi: ἔρως = ἔκστασις = ἀφαίρεσις = γνόφος? L'amour arrache hors de soi; cet arrachement porte à la négation, qui n'est autre

---

and chapter 1. 6 ("Completing the Context of the *Mystical Theology*: *Epistles I–V* and Christ the 'Sudden'").

264. *DN* XIII.3 981B (230:1–5); see also *CH* II.3 140D–141A (12:17–13:3); and more generally II.1–4 136D–144C (9:16–15:7).

que la ténèbre de l'intelligence, et l'amour pénètre la ténèbre qu'il a engendré."[265] I would add to this statement two qualifications: it is too static and focuses too exclusively on the creature. All of the terms listed have their reference in God as well, the "darkness" (γνόφος) at once to his ineffable presence and supreme unknowability, his "mystery," and the first three all to the same, active power of his love—thus the dynamism which finds, again, its origins in him. Dionysius can therefore speak of God's φιλανθρωπία condescending to us and, "in the manner of a fire, likening the things united by means of the union [ἕνωσις] with himself, in accordance with their capacity for deification [θέωσις]."[266] It is the presence and activity above all of the divine ἔρως working in creation that supports and lends its thrust to the creature's ἀφαίρεσις.[267] Dionysius' call for a "cessation" of our natural activities is to be understood then in the context of God's shining always more radiantly through us. Our energies cease at this point and give way to the "impulsions"[268] of divinity. We then "suffer" God. This is the second and ultimate sense of ἀφαίρεσις. Dionysius therefore insists that "we may apply ourselves [ἐπιβάλλομεν] to the super-essential ray" only through putting to rest, stopping, those intellectual capacities which are natural to us,[269] since those minds that are in process of being united (ἐνούμενοι) to "the light beyond deity" may do so uniquely through this cessation.[270] Far from being a purely logical peeling-away of forms from the transcendently formless, ἀφαίρεσις becomes rather a declaration of

265. Horn, "Amour et extase," 287.

266. *EH* II.2.1 393A (70:6–7).

267. This is precisely the point affirmed by Bernard, "La doctrine mystique de Denys l'Aréopagite," *Greg* 68 (1987): 523–566, esp. 561–563; and denied by Rorem's description of a "loveless" ascent, *Commentary*, 192, 216–222. Rorem is justified in pointing to the fact that ἔρως is not mentioned by name in the *MT*, but he also acknowledges (indeed, drew my attention to) the importance of the passive voice. What else can this passive note indicate other than the ἔρως that Dionysius had earlier (in *DN* IV especially) said was the impelling force of the universe?

268. *DN* IV.11 708D (156:15–19).

269. *DN* I.4 592D (115:9) and II.7 645A (131:3–4).

270. *DN* I.5 593C (116:15–117:1).

praise, the affirmation of a state in process of realization. All the negations of *MT* V are in aid simply of this: that all, everything, must fall away in order to reveal, "suddenly," Christ.[271] Ἀπόφασις is not a "trampoline." It is instead the discovery and declaration of a *presence* surpassing speech. Thus we find that Moses in *MT* I.3, "in accordance with the greater [faculty], being united to the wholly unknowable through a stilling [ἀνενεργεσία] of all knowledge, [and who] even in knowing not at all, knows in manner beyond mind."[272]

3.3. Ἕνωσις: *Present Reality and Future Hope*

3.3.1. In the likeness of the divine ἔκστασις. The "in accordance with the greater [κατὰ τὸ κρείττων]" of the text above brings me to the third point of this chapter: the meaning of that state whose process of realization the "suffering" of God works, our ἕνωσις. At this point let us recall the sense of ἕνωσις in reference to God. It expresses the *in se* of divinity, that unity of God in Trinity which is transcendent to all unities whatsoever, whether of bodies, souls, or of the angels,[273] and which enjoys a certain priority over the unified multiplications of the πρόοδοι or διακρίσεις.[274] If ἕνωσις is then proper to God *in se* and διάκρισις or multiplicity to God *ad extra* or in ἐν ἐκστάσει, then precisely the opposite is the case with created being where multiplicity, however—as with the angels—refined, is the proper, and unity, oneness, the peculiarity of the state ἐν ἐκστάσει. Indeed, here I arrive at an element in the symmetry of the Dionysian scheme which to my knowledge has so far been overlooked: the ἕνωσις or "highest" faculty is precisely the analog in the creature to διάκρισις in God, to his "ecstatic" capacity that gives rise to the divine processions. According to that "faculty," therefore, "we are joined in a manner beyond knowledge and utterance to things unutterable and unknowable in

271. *DN* I.5 593C (116:15–117:1). See chapter 1.6 for ἐξαίφνης.
272. *MT* I.3 1001A (144:13–15).
273. *DN* II.4 641C (128:3–7).
274. *DN* II.11 652A (137:5–6).

accordance with that ἕνωσις which is greater than our faculties of discourse and intellection."[275] Roques is justified in speaking of the "meeting of two ecstasies,"[276] for ἔκστασις is here the common term. Our conformity to God in the imitation of his love, or sharing rather in it, attains thus its term in the sharing of and likeness to his ἔκστασις. Just as he departs from himself in order to enter into relation, so the creature is constrained, in obedience to the very thrust of its being, to transcend itself in union with the "rays of the unapproachable light."[277]

3.3.2. The divine energies and ἕνωσις as our *capax Dei*. The "rays" of God, and the "sightless impulsions" noted already several times, point to another essential feature of the creaturely ἔκστασις/ἕνωσις: it, too, is finally a revelation of, and participation in, the divine energies. It is God who acts in us: from the thearchy, "as a unifying power, we are made one [ἑνιζόμεθα] . . . and gathered together into a deiform unity and unity imitative of God."[278] As opposed to Rist's natural power within the creature, I would say that ἕνωσις signifies rather the capacity or openness of the creature to being filled with the divine δυνάμεις. If the ἕνωσις in the passage just cited might be seen as a wholly natural feature of created being and an expression of the same,[279] it appears to me that there can be little doubt as to its ecstatic nature and the primary role of God in the following:

> One must be aware that our mind has, on the one hand, the faculty of intellection through which it sees the intelligibles,

275. *DN* I.1 585B–588A (108.35); see also VII.1 865C–868A (194.10–15); VII.3 872B (198.12–15); and XI.2 949CD (219:3–11).

276. Roques, "Symbolisme et théologie négative," 112.

277. *DN* IV.11 708D (156:18); for light imagery in this context, see also I.5 593C (116:15–117:3); VII.3 872B (198:14); and *DN* IV.1 693B (144:5). I noted earlier that Dionysius defines the divine darkness as "unapproachable light," "ray," and "super-abundance of light."

278. *DN* I.4 589D (112:12–14).

279. See *DN* II.4 641C (127:16–128:7), where Dionysius speaks of a variety of different "unities" on the planes of body, soul, and intellect (= the angels), all of which constitute participations, according to ἀναλογία, in God's unity.

and, on the other hand, [the ἕνωσις] which transcends the nature of the mind and through which the latter is joined to things beyond itself. It is in this manner, then, that we must conceive divine things, not in a way proper to our own nature, but as completely putting ourselves outside of ourselves and becoming wholly of God, for the highest is of God and not of ourselves.[280]

It is given to each creature, as I noted above, to become the likeness of God through "God-given capacity and grace."[281] Dionysius speaks again elsewhere of there "coming to be many gods" through the deification deriving from the one God by means of a realization of "the potential [δύναμις] for deiformity proper to each."[282] Ἕνωσις is the final actualization—through God's power of deification—of the θεοειδής. It is the ultimate expression of the creature's ἀναλογία become transparent to its divine λόγος: "united with the super-luminary rays,"[283] "super-naturally illumined" by unity with the one God[284]—and I note again the passive constructions. Ἔκστασις/ἕνωσις therefore represents the completion of the "cycle" of divine love that begins in the "unsearchable" unity of the Trinity and concludes—if that is the word we want—in the sharing of created being in that same blessedness. Yet the "cycle" is not forced upon the creature, but depends always upon the latter's assent. At all stages there is the element of cooperation, of the necessity for the creature's agreement to the divine will or movement of love. One must will to become oneself, i.e., one's proper λόγος, from the level of "good works," through the ἀφαίρεσις, to the very gift of oneself in union. One puts aside all things, πάντα ἀφελῶν[285]—including oneself—in obedience to the growing awareness of the reality and presence within oneself of uncreated love. This reality and awareness must finally express itself in union.

280. *DN* VII.1 865C–868A (194:10–15).
281. *CH* III.3 168A (19:23).
282. *DN* II.11 649C (136:13).
283. *DN* VII.3 872B (198:14).
284. *DN* I.5 593C (117:2–3).
285. *MT* I.1 1000A (142:10–11).

3.3.3. The promise. I hesitated over the word "conclude" above because there can be no real conclusion to this process. Dionysius speaks of the "unceasing [ἄσχετος] and absolute departure [ἔκστασις] from oneself and all things in the super-essential ray of the divine darkness."[286] Even ἕνωσις is therefore no absolute repose in God but instead a continuous ascent into his uncreated powers, into the mystery of the divine life. This infinite ascent is, precisely, the mystery of created being, i.e., of our being as the participation in, and hence revelation of, God's mystery, our true "correspondence" to the divine infinity. Immediately I say "our" and an obvious difficulty emerges. As I noted concerning κίνησις above, our ascent, unlike that of the angels, is clearly limited by the constraints of mortality and, as also hinted, of other limitations deriving from our present mode of existence in a world where evil remains a possibility. Whatever glimpses of beatitude we may then enjoy here below can only be momentary and fleeting. If our ἕνωσις is truly to occur, to fulfill itself, then it must also promise some change in the way things presently are. We must look forward to a transfiguration of our present ways of being, toward a more, as it were, angelic estate.[287] The term has thus a necessarily eschatological dimension, and this is in fact exactly what Dionysius does state clearly. If it is the case that now, in this life, we may only taste briefly of blessedness, still:

> Then, when we become immortal and incorruptible and attain to the most blessed and Christ-like condition, "we shall ever," as Scripture says, "be with the Lord," being filled, on the one hand, with the all-pure contemplations of his visible theophany—shining round about us in plainest brilliancies—the same which shone about his disciples in that most divine transfiguration—participating, on the other hand, in his intelligible gift of light through minds grown passionless and immaterial, and finally sharing in the ἕνωσις which is beyond mind through the unknowable and blessed impulsions of the

---

286. *MT* I.1 1000A (142:9–10).
287. Recall my discussion of Dionysius' monks as "angels among men" in chapter 1.1.

super-luminary rays, in more divine imitation of the heavenly minds, for, as the truth of Scripture declares, "We shall be equal to the angels and sons of God, [we] who are sons of the Resurrection."[288]

Here is fulfilled the promise with which I began this chapter, and resolved the "tension" I discussed in λόγος - ἀναλογία. God created all things in love and wills their communion with himself. For us, this motion of God and our own striving to conformity with and in it discover, both, their point of meeting and resolution in Christ. The imperatives of our nature require that God become incarnate.[289]

4. Summary

I have come full circle from the beginnings of chapter 2. Taking as my point of departure the "silence" and "ecstasy" in God's ineffable transcendence, I have followed the course of his descent via his energies into immanence, noted the creation of beings other than himself through his will and Providence, sketched the creature's assent to the reflection of, and growth into, his image that is built into the very depths of created being—the will or intention (λόγος) of God for each—and now find myself at the conclusion of this discussion, having traced the course of those uncreated "vectors" implanted in the rational creation, once again confronted with the same mystery of divine transcendence and creaturely ἔκστασις with which I began.

The circle has indeed closed, but, as compared with the Neoplatonists, it is a circle with a difference, infinite at both its "ends." The mystery of the creature's ἔκστασις and ἕνωσις is the final resolution of a single moving power and a single mystery: the love of God. The divine ἔρως stirs the transcendent into immanence,

288. *DN* I.4 592BC (114:7–115:5). See Golitzin, "On the Other Hand," esp. 310–316 on the eschatological character of this passage, and the experience of beatitude as including all aspects —body and soul—of the human composite.

289. See my earlier remarks at the very end of II. 2.3. ("Πρόνοια: God's Love in Motion") and the article by Bucur, "Foreordained from All Eternity."

establishes the creation and, ever present within the latter, works in and through created beings to maintain and draw them back to itself. It does so by means of that likeness to itself implanted in the creature which must ever seek its source and end in the Creator. This dynamism, inherent in the Dionysian λόγος/ἀναλογία, declares at once the *CD*'s break with its pagan predecessors and its debt to patristic thought, in particular to the writings of Gregory of Nyssa. The created being as icon of the divine, and as microcosmos, is not now fully achieved but looks forward to its τέλος as to an activity always and increasingly in process of realization.

The last statement leads us on to certain further points, and to the chapters following. I have dealt so far with the bare theory of God's descent as Providence, and the properties he has given created existence for the appropriation of that descent. Created being, however, does not exist *in vacuo*. Angels and humans both live in a world, and through their world move to union with the Maker of worlds. This is implicit in the notion of ἀναλογία itself which, as we have seen, points rather to a web of relationships than to splendid isolation. Here, too, I note a departure from the loneliness and self-completeness of Plotinus' microcosmos. I will also, in the succeeding chapters, point to the adaptation which Dionysius has effected here of prior Christian handlings of the micro-macrocosmos theme, chiefly that of the great Origen and his disciple, Evagrius. For the Areopagite, the microcosmos of the particular rational being is both reflected in, and completed by, the macrocosmos of a community of minds—or, rather, of entire planes of existence: for the angels the intelligible sphere, and for humanity the sensible.

At his juncture I must take up the discussion of the hierarchies that constitute the, as it were, "flesh and blood" of Dionysius' vision. The latter phrase I use deliberately in that it recalls that toward which the entire *CD* as sketched so far increasingly moves: the Incarnation of God in Christ. Jesus is the true—or "natural"—end and center of the double motion of God into world, and of world into God. He is also the reply of divine Providence to those needs and wants in our present mode of being that prevent our infinite ascent.

Chapter 4

The Mystery of the Worlds

Hierarchy and the Hierarchies

Introduction

Created being is by its nature contingent being. It depends upon its source in the Creator and exists within a particular context. By context I mean world or universe, since it is in and through its world that each reasonable being receives its definition and attains to the knowledge of itself, of others, and of God. For Dionysius the reality of the created worlds is both realized and revealed in the two hierarchies, the Celestial and Ecclesiastical. The two verbs, *realize* and *reveal*, denote the double and simultaneous function of a given hierarchy: (1) the reason-endowed being, whether human or angel, discovers within its respective hierarchy its own true place or meaning, i.e., its reality; and (2) through or by means of its hierarchy, each is given to rise to the conscious and active apprehension of that same reality and so to the contemplation of the latter's source in God. As both the meaning of the created world and the revelation within that meaning of the Creator, hierarchy represents the "pivot" of the Dionysian system. It is the point in the cycle of love I discussed above at which the descent of God's δυνάμεις into creation becomes the ascent of the creature into God.

I note, again, that in using the word "cycle" I do not intend any sort of eternally realized cosmos. The Dionysian world is fully a dynamic one. It is also one of fundamentally Christian inspiration. Dionysius' hierarchies are not a repetition of Proclus' causal chains (σειραί), a "theory of ratios" or logical sequences.[1] The hierarchies embrace the whole of created being, not merely differing *Seinsstufen*.[2] While Brons points to the various orders of being, i.e., intellective (angels), reasoning (humans), animal, vegetable, and mineral, mentioned in the *DN* as supporting his contention that the ecclesiastical hierarchy applies uniquely to humanity rather than to the entire sub-angelic creation crowned by humanity, we find the same categories of being in patristic writings, especially those of Gregory of Nyssa.[3] The Nyssene's vision of the Church as the presence here and now of the new creation in Christ is not, however, affected.[4] No more do Dionysius' lists limit the role of "our hierarchy," the Church, in his own theology which, as I have already stressed, owes much to the thought of Gregory.

In addition to Gregory of Nyssa, I will also have in mind the thought of Origen and Evagrius, especially their understanding of the created world as at once the providential manifestation of God and the reflection of humanity.[5] For them, as for the Areopagite, hierarchy (the sanctified cosmos) both embraces all and can be embraced by each. "All" and "each" also provide us with a reply to the apparently rigid character of Dionysius' universe and the clue as to how he can maintain both that knowledge comes down uniquely via the sequence of hierarchic ranks and, still, that the direct encounter with God is open to all who participate in the mystery of "our hierarchy." Mystery and icon are once more the keys to the Areopagite's world. Hierarchy is, first, the mystery or sacrament of God's presence and activity on a given plane of being. Secondly, it is for us the image of humanity and, specifi-

---

1. *Contra* Hathaway, *Hierarchy*, 48–50.
2. *Contra* Brons, *Gott und die Seienden*, 36, 76.
3. See Golitzin, *Et introibo*, 305n. 182.
4. Golitzin, *Et introibo*, 304, 310–311.
5. Golitzin, *Et introibo*, 274–277 and 334–338.

cally, of humanity redeemed. Dionysius' vision of a redeemed creation, one in which created being is to become fully obedient to its "natural" calling, is the product, thirdly, of Christian revelation and reflection. The world as sanctified, fully "natural," comes to us uniquely through Christ. Jesus is the τόπος θεοῦ, and in him redeemed humanity and hallowed cosmos at once reflect one another and become "places of meeting" with God.

The points above will, I trust, emerge over the course of this chapter and the following one. I have divided this chapter into two sections: I discuss first the notion of hierarchy in general, taking Dionysius' own definition of the term as order, activity, and knowledge, and, deeply indebted to Roques' analysis in *L'Univers dionysien*, strive to see each in the light of my remarks concerning realization and revelation. I will dwell particularly on the dynamism of the Dionysian world, its source in God's own activity, and at the same time endeavor to point toward the Incarnation as the focus and validation of Dionysius' vision of nature, his φυσιολογία or φυσική θεωρία. I then outline, secondly, the salient characteristics of the angelic and human hierarchies, with particular concentration upon the latter. My discussion of the Church's ordering will lead into chapter 5, my argument concerning the Fall, Incarnation, sacraments, and the Church's order, activity, and knowledge as the image both of humanity and the sacramental icon of God.

1. The Definition of Hierarchy

Dionysius proposes his most important definition of hierarchy in *CH* III.1 164D (17:3–5):

Ἔστι μὲν ἱεραρχία κατ᾿ ἐμὲ τάξις ἱερὰ καὶ ἐπιστήμη καὶ ἐνέργεια πρὸς τὸ θεοειδὲς ὡς ἐφικτὸν ἀφομοιουμένη καὶ πρὸς τὰς ἐνδιδομένας αὐτῇ θεόθεν ἐλλάμψεις ἀναλόγως ἐπὶ τὸ θεομίμητον ἀναγομένη

Hierarchy, in my opinion, is a sacred order, and knowledge, and activity, assimilated, so far as possible, to the divine likeness, and led up in due degree to the illuminations given it from God for the imitation of God.

We find several, as it were, familiar faces. Let me begin with one of the last, ἀναλόγως, in order to approach the first.

1.1. A Sacred Order: Hierarchy as τάξις

1.1.1. The analog of providence and the reality of the created worlds. We recall from my last chapter that ἀναλογία, together with the notion of the λόγοι, occupies a crucial position in Dionysius' vision of created being. Both terms, as we saw, indicate potential and process rather than a fixed state.[6] It is of the utmost importance to bear in mind the dynamic quality inherent in the two terms in order to grasp properly the Dionysian use of the word τάξις when defining the nature of hierarchy. All three terms—ἀναλογία, λόγοι, τάξις—no less with respect to the worlds of creation than to each creature on its own,[7] refer to the same active and sustaining power of the divine will, of God's love at work in creation.

When I declare the sacred τάξις of hierarchy to be the order willed by God for any particular level of being, whether bodiless or incarnate created spirit (i.e., angels or humans), I do not mean to suggest a purely rational σειρά of descending causes and effects, i.e., the sense of τάξις for the late Neoplatonists.[8] The τάξις of Dionysius is indeed grounded on the divine decree or law, θεσμός (an expression to which I will return shortly), and proceeds through a series of triads,[9] but to characterize this in the *CD* as simply the universal law of rational order[10] quite misses the essential in the Areopagite's world. It lacks the element, and

6. For comment here, see von Semmelroth, "Θεολογία συμβολική," 6, and Lossky, "Darkness and Light," 41.

7. For τάξις and the individual creature, see *Ep.* VIII.1 1088C (176:2, 3); VIII.3 1093B (183:3, 6, 7); and VIII.4 1093C (183:15–184:1).

8. For the equivalence of τάξις and σειρά in Proclus, see Gersh, *From Iamblichus to Eriugena*, 141–142.

9. See *CH* X.1 273AB (40:8–18); IV.3 181A (22:18–22); and, for comment, Roques, *L'univers*, 36–39.

10. Hathaway, *Hierarchy*, 38ff.

mystery, of synergy. Neither do "rational principles"[11] do justice to the Dionysian λόγοι which are, more fully, the "intentions" or "purposes" of God active in creation. When λόγος is understood primarily in the latter sense, the following text concerning the hierarchical distribution of creaturely participation in God takes on a character other than logical sequence:

> The ordering principle of all visible and invisible harmony, in accordance with the same purpose of the natural good order, supernaturally manifests the splendor of its own gift of light in radiant outpourings to the highest beings and, through them, the beings after them participate in the divine ray.[12]

The "principle of order," together with its λόγος, expresses less a purely natural law—note the "supernaturally" (ὑπερφύως)—than of God in extension, of the divine purpose for the whole of creation.

The single λόγος of the hierarchies as the ground of their τάξις would thus signify, first, their purpose or meaning, and, secondly, that meaning as equivalent to the same active power of the Good that "above all rest and motion establishes each [creature] in its own λόγος and stirs it to its proper motion."[13] This universal ordering of all creation in accordance with the divine intent for each is not just ascribed to the first name of God as Providence. We also hear it echoed in Dionysius' definition of the divine Δύναμις,[14] Justice,[15] and Salvation, which "preserves all things, as ordered in accord with the λόγοι of each."[16] The names of God are summed up, recapitulated, in the τάξις of the hierarchies. Their single λόγος would in fact appear to be Providence itself, i.e., the whole range of God's activities in relation to the created worlds, God himself in extension. The Trinity can therefore be called the principle of

11. Hathaway, *Hierarchy*, 50.
12. *CH* XIII.3 301C (45:15–18).
13. *DN* IV.7 704C (153:1–3).
14. *DN* VIII.5 892C (202:6–9).
15. *DN* VIII.7 896B (204:18–21).
16. *DN* VIII.9 896D–897A (205:16–206:4).

hierarchy[17] insofar as it is the source of the divine energies. The Trinity in general, but in particular the second Person, must be identified with "Salvation" and "Redemption,"[18] God's action to restore what is lacking and lead his creature back to the state for which it was intended.[19] Jesus is himself "the intent (ἐπίνοια) of every hierarchic revelation,"[20] as well as "the principle, essence and most Thearchic power of all hierarchy, sanctification, and divine work [θεουργία]."[21] I will return in more detail to the role of Christ. For now I wish to stress that hierarchy as a λόγος expresses both the will of God for all of created being, and, in the case of the ecclesiastical hierarchy, of his grace in the divine condescension of Christ. The "principle" of the hierarchies, therefore, is the divine love present in created nature and revealed to humanity in the Incarnation.

If the λόγος of hierarchy is to be identified with God's Providence, what may be said of its ἀναλογία, understanding the latter as the presence of its λόγος in the creature? Clearly, a hierarchy must be the analog of Providence, the entirety of the latter's expression on a given plane of being. Recalling my reference above to the divine Justice, this point emerges clearly in the following:

> The deiform hierarchy is filled with sacred justice, and administers that which each deserves in a saving manner, granting in due time and sacred manner each one's share in divine things in accordance with due measure and analogy.[22]

17. *EH* I.3 373CD (66:6–8). See also Stiglmayr, "Über die Termini Hierarch un Hierarchie," *ZKT* 22 (1898): 182–183.

18. *DN* VIII.9 896D–897C (205–207).

19. See, for example, *DN* I.4 592AB (113:6–12).

20. *CH* II.5 145C (16:17–19).

21. *EH* I.1 372A (63:12–64.2).

22. Ἔστι γὰρ ἡ θεοειδὴς ἱεραρχία δικαιοσύνης ἱερᾶς ἀνάπλεως καὶ τὸ κατ᾽ ἀξίαν ἑκάστῳ σωτηρίως ἀπονέμει, τὴν ἐναρμόνιον ἑκάστου τῶν θείων μέθεξιν ἐν συμμετρίᾳ καὶ ἀναλογίᾳ κατὰ καιρὸν ἱερῶς δωρουμένη, *EH* III.3.6 432C (85:3–6).

As Lossky rightly observes, "it is *analogia* which is the pivot of all hierarchy, of all order" or συμμετρία.[23] Τάξις and ἀναλογία are inseparably linked, and it is indeed ἀναλογία and ἀναλόγως that we find throughout the *CD*, whether included in the definitions of perfection,[24] of the measure of each being's share in the divine wisdom,[25] or of the cooperation with God,[26] the activity of a hierarchy in distributing God's illuminations,[27] or communion,[28] or activities,[29] or knowledge.[30] The "ray" of the uncreated energies proceeds to all creation ἀναλόγως,[31] and thus, ἀναλόγως, do the first ranks of angels receive it[32] and pass it on to those below,[33] such that ultimately it reaches us through "sacred veils"[34] in order that we may enjoy the same divine ray in imitation of the angelic orders[35] through a series of ordered ranks.[36] All is given in accordance with the "thearchic good order [συμμετρία]" of Providence,[37] a "good order" which is reflected, as the notion of analogy, in the very being of the creature as image of Providence[38] or θεοειδής.

---

23. Lossky, "La notion des 'analogies,'" 292. See also von Semmelroth, "Geeinte Vielheit," 399, and "Aufstieg," 26, as well as Roques, *L'univers*, 64.

24. *CH* III.2 165B (18:14–15).

25. *CH* XII.2 293A (43:4–5).

26. *CH* III.3 168A (19:21–22).

27. *EH* II.3.3 400B (75:4–9).

28. *CH* IV.1 177C (20:12–13); see also *EH* IV.3.4 477C (98:25–26).

29. *CH* XIII.4 305C (48:16–18).

30. *CH* XV.3 332B (54:2–4).

31. *CH* I.2 121B (8:9–10); also XIII.3 301A (44:17–21); *EH* III.3.3 429A (82:17–21); VI.3.6 537C (120:10–12); and *DN* IV.33 733C (178:16–17).

32. *CH* VII.3 209C (30:20–22).

33. *CH* X.1 273A (42:11–12); XI.2 285A (42:11–12); and *EH* VI.3.6 537C (120:10–12).

34. *DN* I.4 592B (114:1–4).

35. *CH* I.3 121C (8:17–19), and 124A (9:8–10); *EH* I.2 373A (65:10–13); and I.5 377A (68:2–4).

36. See *EH* IV.3.3 477A (98:3–13); V.1.1 501A (104:11–15); VI.1.3 532D (116:13–14); VI.3.5 536C (119:3–7); and VI.1.6 537C (120:10–12).

37. *EH* IV.3.5 480B (99:21).

38. For συμμετρία see *CH* XIII.3 301A (44:23–24); XIII.4 305A (47:22); XIV 321A (50:7); *EH* I.2 373A (65:12–13); II.1.3 400B (75:8–9); III.3.6 432C (85:5–6); IV.3.8 481B (101:2); V.1.4 504D (107:7–8).

Every divine gift is given in accordance with the hierarchies. As conformed to the likeness of providential activity, hierarchy is itself therefore θεοειδής. A hierarchy's τάξις as the συμμετρία willed and effected by Providence can be nothing less than the ἀναλογία of God's δυνάμεις on a given plane of being, the expression of the divine purpose. Insofar as it is the expression of God's intention for a given level, every hierarchy must also be the reality of creation at that level to which it pertains. Dionysius therefore tells us that "every hierarchy is . . . the entire λόγος of the sacred things [ἱερά] subordinate to it."[39] By "sacred things," I understand both the "instruments" of a hierarchy—in our case, word and sacrament—and the whole realm of being that it acts to sanctify. Τάξις in its broadest sense must then mean the God-intended reality or meaning of creation, and it is thus that I find myself in agreement with Roques: "La hiérarchie n'apparaît pas comme un simple élément de la synthèse dionysienne. Elle est l'univers dionysien lui-même."[40]

The term τάξις is not without problems. Are the variations of creation as defined by the τάξις of a hierarchy declarative of a (particularly Neoplatonic) Dionysian predestinationism? I say that they are not, but express instead the God-intended uniqueness of each being.[41]

1.1.2. By command of God: a question of law. Dionysius insists on the divine θεσμός ("law") underlying the establishment of ranks and orders in creation:

> This is the all-holy law of the Thearchy, that [the beings of the] second [rank] are to be led up to its most divine radiance through [the beings of the] first [rank].[42]

---

39. *EH* I.3 373C (65:22–23).
40. Roques, *L'univers*, 131, vs. Brons, *Gott und die Seienden* 16–17.
41. See *CH* IX.3 260D (38:8–10) on μετουσία. The inequality of created beings is a given of God's will, and there are thus varieties of participation in his gift of light (φωτοδοσία). Note also Lossky's remarks in "Darkness and Light," 41.
42. *EH* V.1.4 504CD (106:24–25). Cf. also *CH* IV.3 181A (22:18–22).

The language of "first" and "seconds" is consistent throughout the
CD.[43] While such language inevitably gives rise to other questions
concerning the possibility of the immediate experience of God,
as well as the centrality of Christ, I will not dwell on them at this
point, save to note here that our full discussion of hierarchy as
the icon of God and of humanity should reveal that Dionysius'
passion for order is not so dangerous to Christian revelation as
might appear from the text just cited. For now, however, we confront two questions with respect to his use of θεσμός. First of all,
does this term signify simply "a translegal and transscriptural
conception of universal nature law"[44] and find its origins in the
speculations of pagan thought? As such it would constitute, in
Gandillac's phrase, "une exigence métaphysique qui s'imposerait
. . . à la volonté créatrice elle-même."[45]

First, τάξις/θεσμός is not a kind of philosophical nemesis overshadowing the action of even divinity itself. In the *DN* we find
θεσμός, together with other terms for order, i.e., τάξις, κόσμος,
ὅρος, subject to the distribution of God's kingship or sovereignty
(βασιλεία).[46] More importantly still, we discover Dionysius denying the possibility of inquiry into the "how" of the Incarnation by
declaring firmly that this took place "by means of a law other than
natural."[47] God is therefore able to overrule at will laws that nor-
mally appear woven into the fabric of the natural order. His will
is sovereign, and I maintain there is a connection between θεσμός
and the divine will in our author's thought that, as with λόγος
and ἀναλογία, makes the philosophical expression a vehicle for
Christian theology. We thus hear, for example, of the "beneficent

43. See, for example, *CH* VIII.2 240D (34:15); XIII.4 305B (48:12–14); *DN*
XII.4 972B (226:2–5); and *Ep*. VIII.3 1093A (182:34). For triads, see also *CH* IV.3
181A (22:16–22); and X.1 273A (40:7–11). See Golitzin, *Et introibo*, 319–348; note
the same use of firsts and seconds in Evagrius (*Et introibo*, 325n. 42), though in
the latter's case indicating the original creation (*firsts*) and then those things
which came to be following the Fall (*seconds*).

44. Hathaway, *Hierarchy*, 45; and generally, 39ff.

45. Gandillac, 159n. 3.

46. *DN* XII.2 969B (224:9–10).

47. ἑτέρῳ παρὰ φύσιν θεσμῷ, *DN* II.9 648A (133:9).

rule [θεσμὸς ἀγαθός]"[48] that foresaw human subjection to the devil and so (by implication) prepared our salvation. Again, the divine θεσμός ordained (ἀπονενέμηκε) the rites of the Church as images of the Thearchy.[49] The θεσμός of our hierarchy "desires [ἐφίησι]" the instruction of penitent and catechumens.[50] Such expressions would seem to indicate that, while we may rightly understand the "rule of the natural good order" as a law or ordinance written into the structures of creation, we must balance this consideration with the qualification that this term stands equally for the God who is beyond the philosophical dichotomies of the One and the Many. The divine θεσμός determines the hierarchic τάξις, but it is also—and no less—the expression of God's sovereign love. So far as human beings are concerned, the θεσμοί determined for people are given in order to lead us up through the things of sense to those of the spirit (τὰ νοητά)[51] and finally to God himself. They—rather, our hierarchy—are not in conflict with, but instead the result of, the Incarnation of Christ who is himself the meaning of hierarchy.

My second question concerns predestinationism. Here I maintain that hierarchic τάξις no more threatens the liberty of the creature than it does that of the Creator. The division of each level of creation into different ranks or orders is first of all expressive simply of the fact that the world made by God is varied. Dionysius describes the activity of the principles of every hierarchy as "multiplying" the simplicity of their participation in God according to the "differences [διαφοράς]" of their subordinates, and as "gathering together" the variety (ποικιλία) of the latter into their own simplicity after the manner of Providence (προνοητικῶς).[52] Does the fact that each being is different and assigned by the will of God to receive its share of the divine through the accomplishment of its proper task (δρᾶν τὰ ἑαυτοῦ), while abiding in its proper

48. *Ep.* VIII.1 1085B (172:10).
49. *EH* V.1.5 505B (107:20–22).
50. *EH* III.3.6 432C (84:25–26).
51. *EH* I.5 377A (67:21–23).
52. *DN* XII.4 972B (226:4–5).

place (ἐν τάξει),[53] mean that each is predestined by Providence to that particular end? Yes, in the sense at least that each has its own unique analog of God to fulfill and therefore its own particular place. There is not, however, any compulsion. The created intelligence is not forced willy-nilly into some arbitrary yet necessary slot in the scheme of things. Dionysius is as much a defender of created freedom as Origen,[54] and the Areopagite's hierarchies answer both to the deepest reality of each being and to the latter's uniqueness. At the same time, hierarchic existence requires active cooperation, συνέργεια. While it is true that hierarchy is not just the intelligible structure of our world but our very reality, it is also true—as I noted in the preceding chapter—that we are still free to refuse assent to our proper τάξις. To do so, however, is to reject God and thus, no less, ourselves.[55] Hierarchy is a "nature law" which presupposes for its fulfillment that which is beyond nature, divine grace. It is indeed "predestination," but a predestination that demands a willing response, one which must be earned.[56] Τάξις as the expression of the providential ordinances directed to creation is finally a reality which, to quote Roques at length, discovers itself

> à la fois dans l'objectivité la plus authentique et dans l'intériorisation progressive des intelligences. Il est à la fois statique et dynamique, sociologique et spirituel . . . l'ordre dionysien vient de Dieu . . . une législation et une organisation dont les termes θεσμός, θεσμοθεσία, θεία πολιτεία, disent l'origine transcendante.[57]

53. See the definitions of divine Justice and Peace, *DN* VIII.9 896D (205:16–19) and IX.4 952CD (220:12–17) respectively. For comment, see Roques, *L'univers*, 100.

54. For Origen on freedom, see Golitzin, *Et introibo*, 275–276.

55. See Roques, *L'univers*, 39 on τάξις/θεσμός as equivalent to our deepest law of being.

56. See Roques, *L'univers*, 61ff. on Dionysius' use of the expression τὰ κατ᾽ ἀξίαν as the active realization, dependent on the creature's will, of the potential inherent in the ἀναλογία. For an example of this, see *Ep.* VIII.3–4 1093B (183:1–11).

57. Roques, *L'univers*, 86.

The above quotation's concluding phrase directs us to a third constituent element, or aspect, of τάξις. As well as being the divinely "legislated" reality of created being, the Dionysian hierarchy is also and at the same time the revelation of that same reality. It is—and here I insist that Dionysius' debt to the Origenist tradition is greater than to the Neoplatonist[58]—the divinely willed manifestation or icon (εἰκών) of God in the created world, and for us the fruit of the Incarnation whose grace it renders present and whose fulfillment it promises.[59]

1.1.3. Ἐικών: hierarchy as revelation and saving presence.

By icon, first of all, we must not understand something purely representational or mimetic. Neither can we take it in the popular sense of symbol (a term which our author also frequently employs) as that which, like an eviscerated notion of sacrament, exists to remind the beholder of something essentially unrelated. Within the system of the *CD*, the icon has "ontological value. It does not obscurely imitate the ideal but rather reveals it."[60] It is a "real presence."

For the pagan Neoplatonists the use of εἰκών or εἴδωλον for the manifestation, at a lower ontological level, of the cause in its effect is also standard practice.[61] When, however, they speak of images, whether created by the hand of an artist[62] or of that icon of the divine which is the universe itself[63] or, more intimately, the human soul,[64] they have in mind something that is either the product of natural human activity or that is inherent in the producer himself

---

58. For the world as revelation of God's Providence in Christ in Origen and Evagrius, see Golitzin, *Et introibo*, 274–279 and 324–326.

59. Recall again the eschatological promise of *DN* I.4 592BC (114:7–115:5).

60. D. N. Koutras, "Ἡ Ἔννοια τῆς εἰκόνος κατὰ τὸν Ψευδο-Διονύσιον Ἀρεοπαγίτην," *Ἐπετηρίς τῆς Ἑταιρείας Βυζαντινῶν Σπουδῶν* 35 (1966/67): 249.

61. Gersh, *From Iamblichus to Eriugena*, 81 and n. 269, citing Proclus, *Elements*, Proposition 65 (Dodds), 62.

62. See Plotinus, *Enn.* I.6.2 and V.8.1.

63. See Plotinus, *Enn.* II.9.8–9; III.2.1 and 3.18; and IV.3.11. See also Iamblichus, *De myst.* III.27 (des Places) 136–137.

64. *Enn.* III.4.3.

and his world.[65] In no case is there any question of grace, of God's free revelation of himself, his energies, and his will. For Dionysius, on the other hand, the free action of God's Providence is precisely the substance of everything constituting hierarchy. The "sacred order" as the icon of God is: (1) the manifestation and presence of the divine here-below; (2) the work of Christ; and (3) limited to the sanctified cosmos of the new creation in Jesus, i.e., the Church.[66] Each of these points calls for elaboration.

Hierarchy, Dionysius tells us, "denotes in general a certain [altogether] holy order, an icon of the Thearchic beauty, sacredly working the mysteries of its proper illumination in ranks and sciences, and, so far as possible, being assimilated to its proper source."[67] All the activities of Providence are summed up or re-presented, i.e., realized or made actual, in a hierarchy whose "sacred operations," hierurgies, are "the perfecting icons of the Thearchic δύναμις."[68] Icon thus signifies an active power, a living and sanctifying reality:

> The purpose . . . of a hierarchy is the assimilation to, and unity with, God, possessing him as guide of every sacred science and activity, and looking as unswervingly as possible to his most divine beauty, both conforming and perfecting its participants as divine images, most transparent mirrors, and unspotted recipients of the primordial light's Thearchic ray who, being filled in sacred manner with the radiance thus

65. See the article by G. Ladner, "The Concept of the Image in the Greek Fathers and the Byzantine Iconoclastic Controversy," *DOP* 7 (1953): 1–34, esp. 8–10.

66. See Ladner, "Concept of the Image in the Greek Fathers," 9; Roques, "Introduction," *CH*, xliv. On this as a typically central Christian transformation of the Neoplatonist κόσμος - εἰκών theme, see Armstrong, "Man in the Cosmos," in *Romanitas et Christianitas* (ed. W. Boer; Amsterdam: North-Holland Publishing, 1973), esp. 99.

67. *CH* III.2 165B (18:11–13).

68. *EH* V.1.5 505B (107:21–22). For hierarchy as the image or images of the divine energies, see also *EH* V.1.7 508C and 508D (109:22 and 110:2).

> bestowed, unselfishly illumine in their turn those who follow
> [them] in accordance with the divine ordinances.[69]

I note the use of ἀγάλματα here as referring not just to the (in our case) material instruments employed by a hierarchy—to which the term can also refer[70]—but as well to the beings themselves who constitute it.[71] Hierarchy as τάξις or εἰκών means that the totality of creation on a given level has been enabled to reflect divine Providence, as a "mirror." It is therefore no surprise to discover the term θεοειδής employed most often in direct connection with the notion of hierarchy. We find, for example, "the deiform and most holy orders" of the hierarchies,[72] their "deiform activities"[73] and "movement;"[74] the "deiform good order of the heavenly hierarchies,"[75] the "deiform hierarch"[76] and, finally, "deiform hierarchy"[77]—in our case the result of Christ coming to restore in us the "deiform *habitus*."[78]

The latter leads me to my second point: "we behold every hierarchy as accomplished in Jesus," who is "the ἀρχή and οὐσία of heavenly hierarchy, sanctification, and divine work."[79] If divine Providence is more or less synonymous with God's love, and if it is that same work of love which is reflected in the hierarchies, then it is supremely to Jesus as the expression of divine love that one must refer when looking for the key and ultimate sense of

---

69. *CH* III.2 165A (17:10–18:6).

70. See *CH* II.5 145A (16:2–3); *EH* III.3.3 428D (82:13–15); and IV.3.1 473B (96:2–4); as well as my section below on the "veils" (2.2.1.) and recall my remarks, at the end of chapter 2, on the intelligible names are notional ἀγάλματα, images, of the divine glory.

71. See also *EH* IV.3.1 476A (96:23–97:1).

72. *CH* II.2 140B (11:22–12:1).

73. *CH* VIII.1 237D (33:9–10).

74. *CH* VIII.1 240A (33:12).

75. *CH* VIII.1 241C (35:21–22).

76. *EH* II.3.6 401C (77:9). See also III.3.6 433B (85:23); V.1.2 501D (105:23); V.3.7 513C (113:23); VI.3.5 536D (119:10); and VII.3.11 568A (131:29) for θεοειδής and the priestly orders.

77. *EH* III.3.6 432C (85:3–4).

78. *EH* III.3.12 444B (93:9).

79. *EH* I.1 372A (63:12–64:2).

the Dionysian universe. All reality, reality in the last and deepest sense, meets, is held in, and proceeds from the "single, theandric" activity of Christ.[80] To speak then, as does one critic, correctly of the icon as in a sense "the incarnation of God," the "bridge leading from earth to heaven,"[81] without allotting so much as a breath to the primacy or even the presence of Jesus, strikes me as singular. The sanctified world, the Church, is the icon of the Incarnation, and the latter is the fulfillment, present now, of the former's promise.

This brings me to my third point, one which, to my knowledge, has not been stressed in recent scholarship: given the εἰκών of hierarchy as at once the reality of the creature and image of Providence, and given that this unity of all creation is concentrated in Jesus, I venture to say that Dionysius is referring to the same reality as that intended by Paul in such texts as Romans 12:4ff., 1 Corinthians 12:12ff., Ephesians 2:15ff., and Colossians 1:18ff. The Church is the one body of Christ, the "new man" and the restored image and likeness of God. Our "deiform ἕξις," given us in Jesus, is then precisely our participation in the single τάξις and unique εἰκών of God that is "our hierarchy"—the Dionysian equivalent to the Pauline "body of Christ." Only within this one, common organism can each soul realize its perfection and deification. This living reality is the reflection in created being of the unknowable Creator whose Providence is at once single in its processions and many in its operation, "the hierarchic εἰκών of divine things" that is naturally divided "into distinct orders and powers" and clearly displays "the theandric energies."[82]

From the notion of icon in Dionysius as the declaration and presence of a higher reality, it follows that a hierarchy, *qua* τάξις,

80. *Ep.* IV 1072C (161:9–10).

81. Koutras, Ἔννοια τῆς εἰκόνος, 256. The same scholar refers to the *CD* as the work of a pagan in "Christian costume" (245).

82. *EH* V.1.7 508D–509A (110:2). I have adopted the variant reading suggested in note 69 of Migne, replacing ἱεραρχικὴ τῶν θείων εἰκόνων with ἱεραρχικὴ τῶν θείων εἰκών. For comment on the "hierarchic icon," see von Semmelroth, "Aufstieg," 44; "Gottes ausstrahlendes Licht," 493.

must also be understood as the carrier of a certain knowledge[83] or, better, as itself the object of contemplation. I move to the second element in Dionysius' definition of hierarchy.

1.2. The Gift of Light: Hierarchy as Sanctified Knowledge (ἐπιστήμη)

1.2.1. The knowledge of creation: the true φυσιολογία. The created universe is made up of both sensible and intelligible components whose meaning and reality are to be discovered in the hierarchies. While that discovery is not a matter given over purely to the exercise of unaided reason, neither would it be true to say that Dionysius preaches a γνῶσις devoid of any connection with the creature and the latter's natural powers. Once again, hierarchic "science" depends on the balance between natural and divine, the cooperation between God and creature. We might indeed speak of a compenetration of Creator with creature that, like the nature of the union insisted upon by the Chalcedonian definition, looks toward a unity at once indivisible and unconfused (ἀσύγχυτος).

> The sensible holy things are representations of the intelligible, and are both instruction and way to the latter; for the intelligible elements of a hierarchy are the principle and science of those perceived by the senses.[84]

The role of the sensible creation as guide to the intelligible is the main burden of the term εἰκών and, still more, of σύμβολον—at least in the more narrowly limited sense of the words.[85] Yet this emphasis on the role of the intelligence in interpreting the signs or

---

83. A knowledge which is surely more than Hathaway's "intelligible nature of the world order," *Hierarchy*, 120.

84. *EH* II.3.2 397C (74:9–11).

85. As I showed in chapter 2 above (3. "The Names: Notional Icons, Resonances of God as Providence"), εἰκών may refer as well to the intelligible names. The angels, too, are called icons: *CH* VIII.1 240A (33:14) and *DN* IV.22 724B (169:22–170:1). Concerning σύμβολον, it would be well to note Koutras, Ἔννοια τῆς εἰκόνος, 250 and 256 (esp. the last page), on symbol as signifying the "putting-together," συμβολή, of different orders of being, of matter and the

symbols presented to it also applies to every level of a hierarchy with respect to the one above it. Each level is a sign or symbol—thus a revelation—to the one below. As Roques observes, this is the Procline distinction between νοητός (intelligible) and νοερός (intelligence in operation).[86] When confronting the hierarchies we are met with a series of contemplations, increasingly refined, that extend from the things of matter to the "gates" of divinity itself. These contemplations, this γνῶσις, brought to us in and through our hierarchy is none other than:

> the knowledge of beings as they truly are; the vision and science of the sacred truth; the inspired participation in the uniform perfection—indeed, so far as possible, in the One himself—the banquet of intelligible vision, nourishing and embracing all who are lifted up to it.[87]

On the basis of this most important statement I wish to make two points. First, that hierarchy is to bring the reason-endowed to the "γνῶσις of beings as they truly are." I noted above[88] that God is "known not from his own nature . . . but from his disposition [διάταξις] of all things."[89] This "disposition" cannot refer to anything other than the hierarchies. They are the analogs of Providence in creation—Providence itself being their λόγος—and embrace thus the ἀναλογίαι of all creatures. Hierarchy is therefore at once the carrier of all true knowledge concerning creation—and so the unique path to knowledge of God—and itself the γνῶσις that it is intended to bear.[90] Through the contemplation of the ἐπιστήμη that may be said to constitute a hierarchy, one is brought to the contemplation of the hierarchy's λόγος, i.e., the uncreated energies of God. Hierarchy is thus the true φυσική θεωρία.[91] Brons is correct: for Dionysius

---

divine or intelligible light. Both terms signify instruction in ascent, and both communicate the power enabling ascent (Koutras, Ἔννοια τῆς εἰκόνος, 257).

86. Roques, "Introduction," *CH*, lxviii.

87. *EH* I.3 376A (66:16–19).

88. Chapter 3 above (2.3.3., "Γνῶσις").

89. *DN* VII.3 869D (197:20–21).

90. See von Semmelroth, "Ausstrahlende Light," 497–498.

91. Roques, *L'univers*, 53.

φυσιολογία is equivalent to theology.[92] This is not, however, a betrayal of Christian teaching. The Areopagite is once again the heir of already long-extant currents in Greek patristic thought.[93]

My second point is the following: for Dionysius there is no separation or distinction to be made between "natural" and revealed truth or theology. All truth, referring again to the quotation above on γνῶσις, is "sacred." The "grace [χάρις] of knowledge"[94] comes to us from above. It is no accident that immediately after the statement on the γνῶσις of beings our author declares that the "essence [οὐσία] of our hierarchy is the divinely given Scripture [τὰ θεοπαράδοτα λόγια]."[95] If the "science" of hierarchy is equivalent to the knowledge of the created universe as intended by God, this must mean knowledge of the creature as sanctified, or redeemed. It follows that, so far as humankind is concerned, there can be no true knowledge of the world apart from that given to us by God through the revelation declared in Scripture and embodied, as it were, in the Church's structure and liturgy. The Scripture reveals theology and theurgy while the liturgy bodies it forth.[96] "Theurgy" recalls, again, the work of Christ, "our most divine Providence."[97] To contemplate

92. Brons, *Gott und die Seienden*, 236.

93. See my discussion in *Et introibo* on Origen (279–282), Gregory of Nyssa (310–313), and Evagrius (333–334). All three of the above had also adopted the Platonist understanding of the world as theophany, seeing the fulfillment of the philosophers' vision as occurring in Christ and—especially for Gregory—in his Church. See again Armstrong, "Man in the Cosmos," 11.

94. *CH* IV.4 181B (22:24–25).

95. *EH* I.3 376B (67:6–7).

96. See *EH* V.3.7 513C (113:21–23) for the Scripture and, for the cult, see my discussion below (2.2.3.2, "Altars to Doors: The Church at Prayer, an Icon of Providence") and in chapter 5 (2., "The Mystery: God's Dispensation in Christ"; 5.1., "A Series of Icons"; 5.2., "Jesus: The Presence of the 'Sudden' ").

97. *EH* III.3.12 441C (92:6–7). See Rorem's remarks on theurgy in *Symbols*, 13–14.

the creation in the hierarchies is ultimately to look upon Jesus,[98] and, in him, the Trinity, that is the goal of knowledge and revelation.[99]

1.2.2. The mind of Christ. The science of hierarchy is closed to those outside the circles of Christian faith: "ineffable and invisible to the many . . . alone revealed to the true lovers of holiness."[100] The accent on love points us toward another aspect of this science: like the divine ἔρως—indeed, part and parcel of it—hierarchic science is something in which the creature is called to participate. We find Dionysius declaring that illumined souls "become participants [μετοχοὺς γενέσθαι] of the perfecting science of the sacred things contemplated,"[101] or, in reference to the first ranks of the angels, that "participation in the Thearchic science [i.e., the direct vision of Providence] is [for them] purification and illumination and perfection."[102] The hierarchic science is not so much something that, albeit divinely given or revealed, we are to apprehend through our own powers as it is, quite simply, a "gift,"[103] a grace, and a perfecting power. It bespeaks, in short, the activity of the divine Pedagogue who is also the content of His own instructions:

Thus even does the all-wise science of the sacred things first hatch them [the initiates of the ecclesiastical hierarchy] through the introductory nourishment of the shaping and life-creating Scriptures, bringing them to perfection through their state of divine generation [i.e., Baptism] and, in due order, granting

98. Recall *DN* I.4 592C (114:9–10) and the θεωρία of the blessed: "in holy contemplations we shall be filled with his [Jesus'] visible manifestation" (τῆς μὲν ὁρατῆς αὐτοῦ ['Ιησοῦ] θεοφανείας ἐν πανάγνοις θεωρίαις ἀποπληρούμενοι).

99. See, for example, *CH* VII.2 208C (29:8–10); *EH* I.3 373C (66:6–7); *DN* II.8 645C (132:6–13); III.1 680B (138:1–6); and *MT* I.1 997A (141:1–3). See also Roques, *L'univers*, 124–125.

100. *Ep.* IX.1 1105C (197:2–4).

101. *CH* III.2 165D (19:13–14).

102. *CH* VII.3 209C (30:23–24).

103. See Gandillac, 116n. 1.

them in saving manner communion with that which is in the
form of light and accomplishes perfection.[104]

The theme of light pervades the *CD*. It is also, as expressed in
the term "illumination [ἔλλαμψις]" in its larger sense[105]—together
with others such as φωτοδοσία ("gift of light") and the like—one
that is inevitably connected with the notion of hierarchic science.[106]
Our initiation into this science introduces us into the knowledge of
God himself in his δυνάμεις. In view of my conclusions concerning
the hierarchic τάξις, it would appear to me that ἱεραρχικὴ ἐπιστήμη
is in fact Dionysius' chosen way of expressing the Pauline *logion*:
"but we have the mind of Christ" (1 Cor 2:16). If the τάξις of hierarchy points to the single organism of the redeemed creation that
is the body of Christ, then its ἐπιστήμη indicates the intelligence of
that same body, the mind of Wisdom incarnate.[107] To participate
in this science is to see and to know the creation as God knows
it, and it is thus one of the essential features of that process that
Dionysius calls deification.[108] Such is the case, for example, in the
priestly orders of "our hierarchy," who in themselves

104. *EH* III.3.6 433AB (85.17–21). See also, again, *CH* VII.3 209CD (30:18–20)
on the Thearchy acting to perfect through its "light" and "science."

105. The narrower sense being the middle term of the triadic activity of
hierarchy: purification – illumination - perfection. See Roques, "Introduction," *CH*, xlvi n. 2, where he observes that, more broadly, ἔλλαμψις stands for
"l'ensemble de la manifestation divine des dons divins," i.e., as the equivalent
of πρόοδος or ἔκφανσις.

106. For a fairly direct connection of light with ἐπιστήμη, see: *CH* III.2 165B
(18:12–14); VII.3 209C (30:21–24); XIII.3 304A (46:13–14); *EH* V.3.8 516B (114:22–
23); VI.1.2 532C (116:2–6) and 3.6 537B (119:24–25). For light and γνῶσις, see:
CH VII.2 208C (29:12–13); *EH* I.2 372B (64:11–14); V.1.3 504C (106:19–20);
DN I.4 592D (115:6–11); IV.6 701B (150:9–14); *Ep.* I 1065A (156–157); and IX.1
1108A (198:7–8).

107. And not, as von Ivanka would have it, a baseless circle without any
substance, *Plato Christianus*, 275–276.

108. See Roques' remarks, "Introduction," *CH*, xxxix–xl. Θέωσις does
not cease with illumination, i.e., sharing in God's knowledge of creation.
There is always the further movement, via self-transcendence and the gift
of grace, into the "ray of the divine darkness" (*MT* I.1 1000A [142:10]), the
passage into the γνῶσις which is the "science of him who is beyond being"

display the ordered illuminations in first and middle and final sacred activities and orders, themselves arranged in hierarchic differentiations, showing forth . . . in themselves the ordered and unconfused nature of the divine energies.[109]

They indeed "perfect those who have already communed in the divine light by means of the perfecting science of those illuminations which they have contemplated."[110]

1.2.3. The apportionment of knowledge: a difficulty. The share of each being in the science of Providence is varied. Each being participates in accordance with its ἀναλογία. There is, as it were, illumination and illumination, depths and, then, depths: "the superior orders have the illuminations and powers of the lower orders, but the latter do not participate in those of the former."[111] Clearly, the hierarchic principle here gives rise to problems which, it must be admitted, Dionysius never adequately answers. That the higher orders should have all the knowledge and "powers" of the lower—and more—sounds dangerously like the causal σειραί of a Proclus.[112] The Areopagite's ranks do not, of course, transmit being to those below, but still what appears to be his identification of advancement into God as coterminus with priestly rank must, from a Christian perspective, be reckoned one of the gravest defects of his system. In his defense I must add that the appearance

---

(*DN* I.1 588A [108:8–10]). This is not contrary to the principle of hierarchy as I understand it. Instead, it is first of all inherent in the promise of Christ whose own Transfiguration is promised us (*DN* I.4 592BC [114:9–11]) because he "took what was ours and exalted it far above us" (*DN* II.10 649A [135:8–9]). As I show below in chapter 5, our hierarchy is at once the "place" of union and itself the icon of the soul in union with God (see esp. my conclusions to chapter 5). For parallels between this understanding of our sanctified world and the systems of Origen and Evagrius, see Golitzin, *Et introibo*, 276–278; 326–340.

109. *EH* V.1.7 508D (109:23–26).

110. *EH* V.1.3 504B (106:11–12).

111. *CH* V 196B (25:9–11).

112. See, for example, *Elements*, propositions 93 and 147 (Dodds), 85 and 129.

here is not quite equivalent to the substance.[113] The Areopagite's supremely idealistic—to say the least—portrait of the Christian clergy[114] is in very great part a function of his vision of the hierarchy as an icon, a sacrament. He is not, however, always clear that the icon, as well as announcing a presence, is also the anticipation of a future fulfillment.

1.2.4. Knowledge as cooperation and ascent.

> Capacities differ, but some share in the deifying science remains open to all: as many of the intelligent and reasonable beings as turn so far as they are wholly able towards unity with it [the Thearchy], and stretch unceasingly forth so far as possible for them toward its divine illuminations are—if it be lawful so to speak—by means of the imitation of God possible to them made worthy even of the name of God.[115]

Open to all, that is, of those who strive after it. We arrive once again at the requirement of our cooperation with grace. If the mark of created being is continual movement, the expression of this principle with regard to hierarchic science is continual ascent, the unceasing and deliberate assent to the activity of the divine illuminations.[116] This willed submission to increasing knowledge of the real and the action of enlightening grace is the root sense of the Dionysian ἀναγωγή.[117] If hierarchy provides—rather, constitutes—the only true knowledge of the created universe and thus the knowledge of Providence itself, such a science must be an

113. See my discussion in chapter 5 below (4.1., "Ministers and Ministered").

114. But not entirely as Meyendorff would have it, his clericalism; see "Notes sur l'influence dionysienne en Orient," *SP* 2 (1957): 547–552. For a more charitable view, see Armstrong, "Negative Theology," 183, and my discussion in chapter 5 (4.1., "Ministers and Ministered").

115. *CH* XII.3 293B (43:16–19). Note the presence again of the infinite ascent.

116. Roques, *L'univers*, 208.

117. Recall the predominantly passive voice of ἀνάγω as noted above. Ἀναγωγή as "uplifting" in the Luibhéid-Rorem translation (see Rorem's remarks in *Symbols*, 99–116). Rorem is quite right to stress the passive voice, but the notes of cooperation and of assent are not adequately covered.

ever-continuing process. Hierarchic science is therefore an ascent into the apprehension of divine Providence, of the mysteries of grace, of divine illumination and transmission, that lie at the core of both the sensible and intelligible worlds: for "this is the all-holy θεσμός of the Thearchy, that the seconds be led up [ἀνάγεσθαι] through the firsts toward its most divine radiance [φέγγος]."[118] The ascent is ordered and, in accordance with a varied creation (and in partial explanation of the difficulties noted above), some are given charge over others:

> that the ascent and conversion toward communion and union with God might be in order; and that the procession from God might be granted commonly and beneficently to all the hierarchies in most sacred good order.[119]

In ἀναγωγή and πρόοδος, creaturely ascent and divine condescension, we again find the cycle of divine love. In this cycle the creature is called to share, and to do so by apprehending through its contemplation the τάξις that is the revealed expression of God's Wisdom, the icon of divine Justice, and reality of his Salvation. The act of participation and apprehension, of assent and ascent, is also an activity, ἐνέργεια, that effects the creature's conformity to God's likeness.

1.3. The Sacred ἐνέργεια: *Hierarchy as the Process of Conformity to Providence*

1.3.1. Hierarchy = θέωσις: a share in God's energies. In the first chapter of the *EH* Dionysius states that

> the thearchic beatitude, divinity by nature, principle of deification . . . bestowed the hierarchy for the salvation and deification of all reasoning [humans] and intuiting [angels] beings.[120]

---

118. *EH* V.1.4 504C (106:24–25).
119. *CH* IX.2 260B (37:10–13).
120. *EH* I.4. 376B (66:20–67:1).

His definition of deification follows directly: "deification is, so far as is allowed, the assimilation to, and union with, God."[121] Concerning this term it is significant first to note that for our author θέωσις is descriptive not of a state of being but rather of an active power. It is "by means of the deification [coming] from himself [τῇ ἐξ ἑαυτοῦ θεώσει]" that God transforms his creatures, according to their capacity, into "many gods."[122] Deification is thus, once again, God's gift of participation in his own energies, such that each (in this text, each order of the hierarchies) is brought up according to measure to "divine cooperation, accomplishing those things by grace and God-given power, being united to the Thearchy both naturally and supernaturally."[123]

The near juxtaposition of hierarchy and deification is, secondly, not accidental. They are one and the same when understood as an activity of God in which the creature shares. Hierarchy, too, "is . . . assimilated [ἀφομοιουμένη], so far as possible, to the divine likeness" and "led up in due degree to the illuminations given it from God for the imitation of God."[124] Both "natural" as the intended realization of the creature's capacity for God, and "supernatural" as wholly dependent upon the grace or δύναμις of Providence whose icon it is—"plainly showing forth the divine energies"[125]—hierarchy is the sacred milieu established by God where divine condescension and creaturely striving, the energies of created and Creator, meet to become "one, new, theandric energy"[126] through and in the unique "philanthropy" of Christ,

> according to which we learn to war no more with ourselves, nor with each other, nor with angels, but rather cooperate in

---

121. ἡ δὲ θέωσίς ἐστιν ἡ πρὸς θεὸν ὡς ἐφικτὸν ἀφομοίωσίς τε καὶ ἕνωσις, *EH* I.3 376 (66:12–13).

122. *DN* II.2 649C (136:13–14).

123. *CH* III.3 168A (19:22–20:1).

124. *CH* III.1 164D (17:4–5).

125. *EH* V.1.7 509A (110:3–5).

126. *Ep.* IV 1072C (161:9–10).

divine things [literally "co-work,"] . . . according to the Providence of Jesus.[127]

We find ourselves, thirdly, yet again confronting the mystery of divine love. The latter finds its center and accomplishment in the person of Jesus, and it works through that series of "compressions" described by Hierotheos[128] to concentrate and gather all up and into itself. Hierarchy represents—indeed, it is—the presence within creation of this "motor" of Providence, and the ἐνέργεια of hierarchy is precisely this sanctification and gathering of creaturely motion up and into the likeness and unity of its source. This activity embraces every holy motion of created intelligence, from the first, feeble turning away from error on the part of sinful humanity to the beatitude of the angels in God's immediate presence. According to Stiglmayr, Dionysius' "whole universe, with all its orders of beings, arranges itself before his eyes into a single channeling ladder."[129]

In a hierarchy, fourthly, creaturely motion or activity becomes the revelation of Providence, of the divine love that moves the superior to care for those below, the latter to those above, and harmony throughout.[130] Dionysius will therefore speak of the angels as moved by God,[131] of the motion granted to the seraphim for the accomplishment of their task, and of the angels as moved from within by God to contemplation. Similarly, it is not of himself (αὐτοκινήτως) that the bishop accomplishes sacerdotal consecrations, but as moved by God in the likeness, indeed, of the High Priest's (Jesus') submission to the Father.[132] In the rites conducted for the dead, the bishop speaks as one moved by the "Spirit who is the principle of every sacrament."[133] Through participation in

---

127. *DN* XI.5 953A (221:6–8).

128. *DN* IV.15–17 715A–D (161:1–162:5).

129. Stiglmayr, "Die Lehre von den Sakramenten und der Kirche nach Ps.-Dionysius," *ZKT* 22 (1898): 246–303, at 253–254.

130. *DN* IV.15 713B (161:3–5).

131. *CH* X.2 273A (40:12–13).

132. *EH* VII.3.7 564 CD (129:3–10).

133. τελεταρχικῷ πνεύματι, *EH* VII.3–7 564B (128:18).

the hierarchic activity—and so in deification—the creature finds itself in process of arrival at its proper goal "to do that which is its own to do,"[134] and in so doing to show forth in itself the single activity of Providence.

1.3.2. Θεομίμησις. This is the sense of the θεομίμησις toward which a hierarchy is ever in process of being conducted. The imitation of God is synonymous with perfection (τελείωσις),[135] and the purpose or goal (σκοπός) of hierarchy is: "to be unfalteringly dependent upon the deiformity imitative of God."[136] It is nothing more nor less than the ministry of love. From the seraphim to whom is given pre-eminently the θεομίμητον,[137] as "made worthy to become ministers [πρωτουργοί] of the theomimetic power and activity,"[138] down through the ranks of angels, "each of whose . . . names reveals the divinely imitative characteristics of their likeness to God,"[139] to the bishop of the Church who acts in imitation of God through illumining the proselyte with Baptism,[140] to the ordinand receiving the seal of the Cross signifying "the life in imitation of God in Jesus Christ,"[141] to the reading of the psalms that teach the θεομίμητον ἀκίνητον with regard to sin,[142] and the Gospels' theomimetic πολιτεία,[143] down to the proselyte himself advancing through Baptism to the θεομίμησις that puts an end to the powers opposed to deification,[144] all participation in hierarchical activity is participation in the single Providence, or love, of God:

134. δρᾶν τὰ ἑαυτοῦ, *DN* X.4 952C (220:17).

135. *CH* III.2 165B (18:14–15).

136. *CH* VII.2 208A (28:14–15). For the use of σκοπός in the Neoplatonists, see Koch, *Beziehungen*, 33–34, esp. Larsen, *Jamblique*, 435–449 and 451–454.

137. *CH* VII.2 208C (29:13).

138. *CH* XIII.3 301C and 304A (45:20–21 and 46:9–11).

139. *CH* VIII.1 237C (32:16–17).

140. *EH* II.3.3 400B (75:6).

141. *EH* V.3.4 512A (111:23–24).

142. *EH* IV.3.4 477A (98:6).

143. *EH* III.3.4 429C (83:21).

144. *EH* II.3.6 404A (77:21–22), and II.3.7 404B (78:9–10).

from which, as from a uniting force, we are united and, our scattered differences concentrated in a manner not of this world, are brought together into a God-like unit and a unity imitative of the divine.[145]

Participating in the ministry of love, angels and humans find their deification. Dionysius' sanctified creature is not a solitary.

The degrees of divinization vary. Stiglmayr spoke of the Dionysian universe as a channeling ladder, and I myself pointed to Hierotheos' "compressions." The text above uses "concentration"—συμπτύσσω—literally, to fold together. The latter verb and, especially, συνάγω are often employed to describe the divine activity and its reflection in the hierarchies.[146] As one moves up the hierarchic ascents there is a gathering or pulling together of faculties and powers, a progressive concentration of activity in God, a kind of acceleration into unity with him, i.e., toward the ἕνωσις which is the τέλος or purpose of created existence. At the same time, we find that this concentration, together with what Stiglmayr describes as the "peeling away [*Losschälung*]" of everything that is opposed to union,[147] does not require the higher ranks to pull away from the lower in the interest of a more perfect contemplation of God. That the contrary is the case is implicit in the θεομίμητον with which the hierarchy seeks conformity. The higher one ascends the scale of a hierarchy, the greater one finds this concentration, the more intense

145. *DN* I.4 589D (112:12–14).

146. For συνάγω, see *EH* III.1 424C (79:10–12), where it is the Eucharist which "gathers together" our several lives into a uniform (ἐνοειδής) deification. Similarly, we find the gathering power of the "kiss of peace" (II.3.8 429A [83:2–3]), of the "philosophy" of monasticism (VI.3.2 533D [118:3]), of the powers of the soul (*DN* IV.9 705A [153:13]), of the "firsts" of the hierarchies (*DN* XII.4 972B [226:4–5]), of the angelic powers (*DN* VII.3 868B [195:3–5]), and finally of the divine ἐνέργεια itself (*DN* I.4 589D [112:14]; IV.4 700B [148:19–20]; IV.6 701B [150:7–10]; IV.7 701D [151:10]; XI.2 949D [219:8–13]; and XIII.3 980B [228:10]). And see "Macarius" on the very similar use of συνάγω (Golitzin, *Et introibo*, 380 and n. 224). For συμπτύσσω, or σύμπτυξις, and the sacred activity of the rites accomplishing this, see *EH* I.1 372B (64:4–5) and III.1 424C (79:11); for our "guides" I.5 376D (67:16–21); and for the monks, VI.1.3 533A (116:18). See also *DN* I.4 589D (112:13–14) and, again in reference to ἔρως, IV.16 713C (161:12).

147. Stiglmayr, "Über die Termini," 183.

the radiance of divine illumination, and consequently the more completely realized is the state of perfection, i.e., the θεομίμησις or participation in Providence. Hierarchy, the ladder of contemplation and love given us for the exclusive and purified contemplation of that which is real, can scarcely do other than engender love. The higher one ascends this ladder, the more intense and greater the scope and field of activity for love's exercise.

1.3.3. Purification - illumination - perfection. The exercise of love in contemplation and providence underlies Dionysius' threefold division of hierarchic activity: "the order of hierarchy is that some are purified and others purify, that some are illumined and others illumine, and that some are perfected and others make perfect."[148] The process is given more detail in the *EH*:

> The first power of those who are being perfected is [the power of] being purified; in the middle and after purification [the power of] being illumined and of contemplating sacred things; finally, and more divine than the others is [the power of] the sacred illuminations, whence is engendered a contemplation illumining as to the perfect science.[149]

Let me note first of all that the passive voice is not limited solely to the ladder's lower rungs, but is proper to all of them. The "perfect science" also recalls the fact that for Dionysius the notions of energy (or motion) and knowledge are inseparable.[150] Hierarchic energy is a business of γνῶσις, leading to, realizing itself in, and proceeding from the "science" that perfects the creature in the image of God. The triple functions of purification, illumination, and perfection correspond, after a certain fashion, to the threefold

---

148. *CH* III.2 165BC (18:17–19:2). For the sources of this triad in the Neoplatonists, see Koch, *Beziehungen*, 174–177, and in the Cappadocians, both Sheldon-Williams, *CambHist*, 445, 451–452 and 454–456, and Gersh, *Iamblichus to Eriugena*, 172–173.

149. *EH* V.1.3 504B (106:12–16).

150. As they are for both Plotinus (see for example *Enn.* III.6.5 and III.8.6, and Wallis, *Neoplatonism*, 85) and Evagrius (Golitzin, *Et introibo*, 329–340).

division of human κίνησις or γνῶσις given in the *DN*.[151] The soul is purified in proceeding from the outward appearance to the inward, intelligible significance of material things or symbols, progressively illumined in circling discursively around this intelligible core, and finally perfected through being gathered into the interior circle of unity. In addition, this correspondence between micro- and macrocosm applies to both human beings and angels:

> in its own fashion each heavenly and human mind has its own first and middle and final orders and powers in relation to the ascents of which we have spoken, which are manifestations— in proportion and after the manner of each—of the hierarchic illuminations according to which each [mind], in accordance with what is lawful and possible for it, comes into participation [μετουσία] of the purification which is beyond because of the super-abundant light, of the perfection which is prior to all perfection.[152]

The references to μετουσία and to God should also recall a third triad, that of ἀφαίρεσις - ἀγνωσία - ἕνωσις, which I discussed above in connection with ἕνωσις, showing that it is at once the necessary complement and simultaneous accompaniment of all sanctified activity.

From first to last throughout the ranks of the hierarchies we find the threefold process. The seraphim know purification as continual liberation (dare I say ἀφαίρεσις) from ignorance, perpetual growth in illumination,[153] and ceaseless motion into the "perfecting science" of God. The lowest orders of the Church's penitents and catechumens knew purification as a turning away from sin and delusion[154] and looking forward to Baptism's illumination

---

151. *DN* IV.9 705AB (153:10–154:6).

152. *CH* X.3 273C (41:1–6).

153. *CH* VII.3 209CD (30:17–31:5).

154. See *EH* II.3.1 397B (73:17–18); III.3.7 436B (87:17–20) vs. Rorem and the idea that Dionysius' purification is purely intellectual.

and the Eucharist's union. At all levels the passive voice marks the process as a participation in God's own activity.[155]

The process is not exclusively passive, however. Each mind in the order of the hierarchies, save the very last of the ecclesiastical hierarchy, must express itself, in accordance with the θεομίμητον, through the active powers of purifying, illumining, and perfecting. Once more we arrive at Dionysius' Christian "baptism" of the Neoplatonist principle of ἐπιστροφή as productive of πρόοδος. The providential love exercised by the created intelligence is the necessary expression of its contemplation of and union with the Beloved.[156] To know and to love God is to become like he is, and so, in the act of returning to him, the activity of the creature "spills over," as it were, in love for its fellows. The higher the order, the greater must be the extent of the "spill." It is in light of this principle that Dionysius attempts to explain how, in Isaiah 6, a seraph is said to have purified the prophet (a technical impossibility in view of hierarchic law):

> For as God purifies all through [his] being cause of all purification, and, to use an example close to hand, the hierarch of our hierarchy through the purifying and illumining of his ministers [deacons] and priests is himself said to purify and illumine—the orders consecrated by him referring to him their proper sacred activities—then the angel effecting the purification of the prophet [Isaiah] refers his proper purifying science and power to God first, as cause, and then to the seraphim as first ministers and hierarchs . . . [as the angel says to Isaiah], "the order of the first beings is hierarch and ruler after God, from which I was initiated in deiform manner into purifying. This, then, is that which purifies thee through me, the same through which the cause and creator brought forth his proper providential energies from the place secret even to us.[157]

155. This is the view of Gersh, *From Iamblichus to Eriugena*, 178–179, in opposition particularly to Koch, *Beziehungen*, 175–176.

156. Roques has expressed this well in *L'univers*, 100.

157. *CH* XIII.4 305C–308A (48:20–49:12).

The same principle is at work in the sacerdotal division of power in our hierarchy.[158] Each order up has the virtue(s) of the one below in addition to its own. There is a certain discrepancy in that, whereas in the angelic hierarchy each accomplishes the full range of operations for the one below, the distribution and order is less tidy in our own. I submit that this is not only due to Dionysius' being "hampered" by the actual existence of a Church order in building his system—the opinion put forward by Roques[159]—but instead, and rather more, to the Christian attendance upon the eschaton. The ecclesiastical hierarchy must exist in a more fluid state inasmuch as its constituents (save the sacraments or at least that which they represent) are themselves fluid, mortal, and the λόγος for any one of them is not readily apparent at any given moment. The hierarchy of human souls awaits its definitive form in the general resurrection.[160] The description of its shape in the present age, however, together with the eternal verities of the angelic hierarchy, brings me to this chapter's second half.

2. The Hierarchies

2.1. The Celestial Hierarchy

2.1.1. The Dionysian "intelligible world." The angelic hierarchy represents the Dionysian κόσμος νοητός ("intelligble world"). The angels are pure intelligences, bodiless (ἀσώματοι) and immaterial (ἄϋλοι), the two adjectives being, in his eyes, necessary complements to an intelligible nature.[161] Their hierarchy also conforms to the scheme of intelligible/intelligent (νοητός/νοερός)

---

158. See *EH* V.1.6–7 508BC (109:3–21) and V.3.8 516BC (114:13–24).

159. Roques, *L'univers*, 198–199.

160. See below, chapter 5 (4.2.5., "The Resurrection as Fulfillment of the Icon").

161. See Roques, *L'univers*, 55.

noted above.[162] There are nine ranks of angels in the *CH*,[163] a traditional number bearing the equally traditional names of seraphim,
cherubim, thrones, dominions, powers, authorities, principalities,
archangels, and angels,[164] arranged, however, in accordance with
a triadic plan that clearly recalls Proclus.[165]

The usual account of the Dionysian hierarchies reads them as
a kind of thinly Christianized adaptation of late Neoplatonist,
triadic ontology.[166] It appears, however, that while the impress
of Procline thought is undeniable,[167] Dionysius also expresses
long-standing Christian speculation about the angelic world.[168] I

162. For more on the νοητός/νοερός distinction or the confusion between
the two, see the discussion following des Places' article, "La religion de Jamblique," *Entretiens Hardt sur l'antiquité classique* 21 (Vandoevres/Geneva:
Fondation Hardt, 1975), 69–94, esp. 95.

163. See *CH* VII.1 205B–IX.2 260B (27:4–37:16) for the listing of the different
ranks and their attributes.

164. See esp. Roques, "Introduction," *CH*, lvii–lxiii, for the biblical and
patristic antecedents of Dionysius' nine orders and their names.

165. See Roques, "Introduction," *CH*, lxivff, and *L'univers*, 135ff. For Proclus, see *In Parm.*, col. 1246–1255.

166. Roques holds that the Areopagite's intelligible world, with its three
triads of orders, is almost exactly that of Proclus' ("Introduction," *CH*, lxvii;
but see also *L'univers*, 78, where Roques notes that Dionysius' angels have
no demiurgic functions). Dodds (*Elements*, 260n. 3) sees the latter's divine
henads simply taken over *en bloc* by our author, while Brons (*Gott und die
Seienden*, esp. 32-33; 44–45) understands Dionysius as having muddled the
Neoplatonist doctrine of the intelligibles (νοητά). See also A. M. Ritter, "Gregor
Palamas als Leser des Dionysios Pseudo-Areopagita," in de Andia, *Denys
l'Aré'opagite* (as above, note 48), 565–579.

167. There are, however, some scholars who do take exception to the specific influence of Proclus; see Sheldon-Williams, "Henads and Angels," in
SP 11 (Berlin: Akademie Verlag, 1972), 65–71, and the same scholar on the
influence of Gregory of Nazianzus, *CambHist*, 442–443.

168. See, for example, Völker, *Kontemplation*, 120–140; Daniélou, *Les anges
et leur mission* (Paris: Éditions de Chevetogne, 1951), 13, 16, 45–46 and 118;
Meyendorff, *Christ in Eastern Christian Thought*, 102; Arthur, *Pseudo-Dionysius
as Polemicist*, 43–69; Bucur, *Angelomorphic Pneumatology: Clement of Alexandria and Other Early Christian Witnesses* (VCSup 95; Leiden/Boston: Brill,
2009), 32–34. Referring to a scholion to *DN* II.9 (PG 4:225, 228; Rorem and
Lamoreaux, *John of Scythopolis and the Dionysian Corpus*, 198), Bucur shows that
it "tried to bring into harmony the Dionysian and the Clementine angelic hier-

argue moreover that the Dionysian hierarchies are based in great part on ascetical traditions, especially of Syrian provenance, and are designed to reconcile the ascetic visionary tradition with the sacramentally based polity of the Church.[169] A striking illustration of this presence of ascetical tradition in the Areopagitica would be to note the description of a chain of divinely inspired teaching, and therefore of successively graced individuals, in terms that recall quite precisely Dionysius' *CH* VIII.2[170] that occurs full-blown a century earlier in Palladius of Heliopolis' letter to Lausus, prefacing the *Lausiac History*: "The first order of beings have their learning from the most high Trinity, the second learns from the first, the third from the second, and so on. . . . Those who are higher in knowledge and virtue teach the lower."[171] Dionysius simply puts the bishop ("hierarch") in the place of the monastic elder, exactly the point of his exegesis here of Isaiah 6:1-7.

---

archies" (33 and n.124). The connection between Clement and Dionysius has been raised by earlier scholarship. Thus, see U. Riedinger, "Eine Paraphrase des Engel-Traktates von Klemens von Alexandreia in den *Erotapokriseis* des Pseudo-Kaisarios," *ZKG* 73 (1962): 253–271, at 262: "Wenn er [Clement] auch in der kirchlichen Hierarchie ein Abbild der himmlischen erblickt (*Strom*. VI, 107, 2; II 485, 24–32) und die einen Engel von anderen 'gerettet' denkt, selber wiederum andere 'rettend' (*Strom*. VII 9, 3; III 8, 17–21), dann bleibt es rätselhaft, das man bisher diese Lehre nicht als Quelle für die Engel-Hierarchien und deren Tätigkeit bei Pseudo-Dionysius erkannt hat." Cf. also Riedinger, "Pseudo-Dionysius Areopagites, Pseudo-Kaisarios und die Akoimeten," *ByzZ* 52 (1959): 276–296.

169. For details see Golitzin, *Et introibo*, 359–392. Arthur accepts the view that "Dionysius adopted a basically Jewish angelology, albeit transmitted via Syrian Christianity," but finds that Dionysius "shows little, if any, interest in encouraging the ascetic lifestyle," setting forth the life of contemplation and the hierarchies as an "alternative means of salvation, provided that one keeps its rules" (*Ps.-Dionysius as Polemicist*, 69; cf. 65; 135–136).

170. *CH* VIII.2 240D (34:14–16): "the all-embracing principle that beings of the second rank receive enlightenment from beings of the first rank" (trans. Luibhéid and Rorem, 168).

171. *Palladius: The Lausiac History* (ACW 34; trans. R. T. Meyer; New York, 1964), 21. For the Greek text see C. Butler, *The Lausiac History of Palladius* (Cambridge: Cambridge University Press, 1904), 2:7.

I note first of all that it is to Jesus that Dionysius accords the title "super-essential cause of the heavenly beings," and his assertion a line below that, in becoming incarnate Jesus did not "overthrow the good order [εὐταξία]," i.e., the hierarchical arrangement of creation, "that had been ordered and chosen by God himself."[172] Jesus is both the sense (ἐπίνοια) of all hierarchies and its beneficent cause, the single, personal reality of the angels' hierarchy fully as much as he is of our own. A second, basic assertion follows: the angelic powers are each, and all equally, creatures. Dionysius is careful to note this at the beginning of the same chapter that deals with Christ as cause. The Thearchy "established all the essences of beings . . . [and] brought them into existence." The same transcendent Creator calls every creature, from the lifeless stones to the immaterial intelligences, into communion (κοινωνία) with himself.[173] There is no source of being, life, or intelligence other than the unique providence of God in Trinity.[174]

What happens, then, to the world of Proclus? That philosopher's vision of the intelligible order, a vision which E. R. Dodds has characterized as "almost the *reductio ad absurdum* of rationalism . . . a doctrine of [Aristotelian] categories . . . transformed into an objectively conceived hierarchy of entities or forces,"[175] is radically altered. Dionysius has eliminated that which tied the whole system together, provided indeed its *raison d'être*: the attempt to portray the sensible and spiritual worlds as a sort of unbroken chain of causes, each level ontologically dependent upon the level or complex of levels immediately above and ontologically prior. Insisting on the God of Christian tradition, and particularly on Jesus as the unique and immediate cause and agent of creation, Dionysius has effectively broken the back of Proclus' σειραί or hierarchies.[176] The beings of the *CH* do not have even any of that association with the maintenance of the physical

---

172. *CH* IV.4 181C (23:12–13).
173. *CH* IV.1 177C (20:10–11). See also *DN* IV.1 693B (144:3–5); VII.2 869A (196:13–16); and *Ep.* VIII.1 1085D (173:14–174:3).
174. A view echoed by Gersh, *From Iamblichus to Eriugena*, 173.
175. *Elements*, xxv.
176. See the argument, too, of von Ivanka, *Plato Christianus*, 255–261.

universe for which there were precedents in Christian tradition.[177] To say, therefore, that the *CD* represents the attempt, however covert, to present the essentials of late Neoplatonist cosmology amounts in effect to an act of eisegesis for which there is simply no support in the text.[178]

2.1.2. A perfected creation: our models for the life in God.

Brons' accusation of "dialectical weariness" is a serious one. If Dionysius' κόσμος νοητός ("intelligble world") is not a hypostatized sequence of generative causes, then we must wonder just what the complex language of hierarchies and triads does signify. While there is a certain quality of the "decorative" to some of Dionysius' writing here, his angelic world cannot be reduced, as does von Ivanka's,[179] to the purely ornamental. The angels have a real function:

> an angel is an εἰκών of God, a manifestation of the unseen light, a pure mirror, most transparent, blameless, undefiled, unsullied, receiving into itself (if it is lawful so to speak) the beauty of the deiform which is the impress of the Good, and, after a manner of speaking reflecting within itself the goodness of the silence in the sanctuary.[180]

Roques, citing Koch, writes: "Le monde des essences intelligible a pour fonction de faire sortir Dieu de son silence . . . par excellence il est l'ordre révélateur."[181] If God, as our author never tires of stressing, is truly hidden and unknowable, yet also made

---

177. See Daniélou, *Les anges*, 11ff. and 37ff.

178. The eisegesis may vary, for example, from Hathaway's declaration that one is obliged to read into the *CD* the doctrine of intermediate generation, compelled to do so indeed by the very logic of the system (*Hierarchy*, xv–xvi), to Koutras' bland assertion, offered without any evidence, that each level of the angels' hierarchy is ontologically dependent on the one above (Έννοια τῆς εἰκόνος, 249).

179. Von Ivanka, *Plato Christianus*, 255–261.

180. *DN* IV.22 724B (169:22–170:5). Cf. my discussion of Ephrem in *Et introibo*, 339.

181. Roques, *L'univers*, 135; Koch, *Beziehungen*, 131.

known in his operations in creation, then it is the function of the
created intelligible world, the unique function of the angels, "to
reveal in themselves the secret goodness and to be messengers
[angels] and declarers of the divine silence . . . manifest lights
and interpreters of him who is in the sanctuary."[182] The angels are
messengers, manifestations, declarers, icons, and revelators of
the uncreated[183] by nature and in very fulfillment of their being.
Fashioned to enjoy prior to the rest of creation direct illumination
as to the λόγοι both of all created beings[184] and of the divine operations (τῶν θεουργιῶν, i.e., the dispensation of Christ),[185] they
are "pre-eminently and in varied fashion the revelators of the
thearchic secrecy."[186] Indeed they are thus the very models of
created intelligence as God wills it to become.

In Dionysius' working of the philosophers' hierarchies to fit
the requirements of Christian revelation and tradition, the heavenly powers are not empowered to hand down being, life, or
even the capacity for intelligence. They may only reveal to those
already so enabled that which they have themselves received:
the first ranks taking directly "from God who moves them and
the rest in due degree [ἀναλόγως] from those who are moved by
God."[187] All things are from God, every illumination from the

182. *DN* IV.2 696B (145:7–9).

183. For the vocabulary of "showing forth" (ἐκφαίνειν, ἐκφαντορία,
ἐκφαντορικός, ἔκφανσις), and its frequency of appearance in the CD, see A.
van den Daele, *Indices Pseudo-Dionysiani auctore* (Louvain: Bibliothèque de
l'Université, 1941), 55. For their particular connection with the angels as the
expression of the divine, see: 1) ἐκφαίνειν: *CH* I.2 121A (7:13); II.2 137C (10:19);
III.3 168A (20:2); VII.3 209D (30:9–10); *EH* IV.3.5 480B (99:17); *DN* IV.2 696B
(145:7); 2) ἐκφαντορικός: *CH* IV.2 180A (21:11); V 196C (25:13–14); VII.1 205B
(27:13); VIII.1 237C (32:18); IX.2 260A (37:9); X.2 273A (40:12); XII.2 293A
(43:11); *EH* IV.3.6–7 481A (100:7 and 13); IV.3.10 481C (101:12); 3) ἐκφαντορία:
CH II.2 137C (10:22); IV.2 180B (21:14); IV.3 180C (22:4–5); 4) ἔκφανσις: *CH* II.5
144C (15:9); *EH* IV.3.9 481D (101:14–16).

184. *DN* IV.1 693C (144:11).

185. *CH* VII.2 209A (29:23–24). Note, however, that the angels were ignorant
of God's Economy in Christ until they were "informed" by him.

186. *CH* IV.2 180B (21:11).

187. *CH* X.2 273A (40:13–14).

"Father of lights"—as Dionysius takes care to quote James 1:17 at the beginning of the *CH*[188]—and the mediatory capacity of his intelligible world is limited strictly to intelligence, to news or informative declaration. In a sense, then, the mediatory function of the κόσμος νοητός ("intelligble world") is no longer a matter of ontology but of grace.

Returning to the angels as models, let us recall our discussion of the hierarchic science and activity as the ever-increasing contemplation of, and participation in, the Providence or love of God. The angels are not models, in the sense of causative paradigms, but instead because they are in process of perfect fulfillment of the measure (ἀναλογία) given each for participation in grace:

> they before all other things have been deemed pre-eminently worthy of the title "angels," in that the thearchic illumination comes to pass first of all in them.[189]

They are the revelation of a perfect universe that, because it is perfect, is fixed in form in a way that our hierarchy, still in a world darkened by the Fall,[190] cannot yet be. In accordance with the will (λόγος) of God for each, theirs is also a varied world, and so a hierarchical one. Each has its own place in the single flow of being, life, and wisdom from the one cause, just as each has its own share in the unique movement of providential love working all in all, and drawing everything back to itself. In contemplating this particular κόσμος νοητός ("intelligble world"), we are not confronted with a ladder of causes or an ascending scale of being. Instead, we discover a vision of grace that reveals a progression of created perfections, an ascent of contemplations each in its own fashion complete, an ordered series of icons, a drawing up and together of increasingly perfect transparencies, a brilliance of serried mirrors reflecting the light of divinity down to us and leading us up "in harmony divine and in due measure [ἀναλογία] to the

188. *CH* I.1 120B (7:3–4).
189. *CH* IV.2 180B (21:12–13).
190. See *EH* III.3.11 440C–441C (90:16–92:1) and my chapter 5 below (2.1., "The Fall and the Devil").

transcendent beginning and end of all good order."[191] Through dependence on its unique cause, Jesus, the Neoplatonist procession of causes becomes instead a single, perfected organism whose several members work to reveal its one source, mover, and τέλος. The angelic song, "holy, holy, holy," as Dionysius tells us twice,[192] echoes throughout the angels' hierarchy and is its single message.

2.1.3. Our photagogues. The angels lead us up to God. As perfected participants in his Providence, they are set over the human world in the role of pedagogues, "illuminators, and guides toward sacred perfection."[193] This is the main burden of the *CH*, a meditation on Scriptures that seeks to show the angelic orders as ". . . rendered worthy of communion in Jesus . . . as truly drawing nigh to him by prior participation in the knowledge of his theurgic lights."[194] The angels "are rendered perfect . . . by the first and transcendent deification, in accordance with the highest science proper to them of the divine operations [τῶν θεουργιῶν]."[195] They are the first to know of the Incarnation,[196] as initiated into the λόγοι of his theurgies.[197] They are—and here Dionysius is more reminiscent of the angelology of Evagrius Ponticus[198]—given charge over the λόγοι of our Providence and thus are involved in every activity pertaining to our salvation. The revelation of God (θεοφάνεια) given in Scripture is based on the vision (ὁράσεις) granted through the agency of the angels to the "theologians," i.e., the inspired writers.[199] Christ himself, in his incarnate manifestation, is subordinate to them.[200] They are set in charge over

191. *CH* X.1 272D–273A (40:9–10).
192. *CH* VIII.2 240C (34:3–9) and X.2 273B (40:19–22).
193. *EH* V.2 501A (104:18–20).
194. *CH* VII.2 208C (29:9–13).
195. *CH* VII.2 208C (29:17–18).
196. *CH* IV.4 181B (22:23–24) and VII.3 209B (30:8–10).
197. *CH* VII.2 208D (29:23–24).
198. See Golitzin, *Et introibo*, 327–328.
199. See esp. *CH* IV.3 180C (22:4–10).
200. *CH* IV.3 181C (23:11–14).

the nations,[201] given authority to punish sinners,[202] purify and illumine the prophets,[203] announce Christ's birth to Mary,[204] and to the shepherds around Bethlehem,[205] render Christ assistance at Gethsemane,[206] and act generally, throughout our history, as "thearchic channels" of the grace whose source lies outside the circles of the created worlds.[207]

While one may note with Gandillac[208] a certain "prépondérance de l'éternel sur l'historique" in, particularly, the final chapter of the *CH*, a concentration on the angels' "rapport contemplatif à la lumière divine," this is not necessarily a tendency in Dionysius' angelology that accords ill with his general picture. I believe the latter to be the portrayal of the intelligible world as in essence an organic and multi-personal reflection of, and participation in, the love of the one universal cause and Providence:

> . . . toward which angelic beauty the good order of our own hierarchy, as pointing towards it in icons, is assimilated so far as possible, and through it molded, and led up towards the super-essential source of order and of hierarchy.[209]

201. *CH* XI.2 260B (37:14–15) and ff. Dionysius reveals himself as something of a philosopher here. He insists that Israel merited its special treatment rather than receiving it as a peculiar grace. See XI.3 260C (37:17–21), together with Gandillac's notes (133nn. 1, 4; 135n. 3), for commentary and comparison with a similar notion in Origen, *Peri Archon* II.9.2.

202. *DN* IV.22 724B (170:6–8). Again, compare Evagrius (Golitzin, *Et introibo*, 327–328).

203. *CH* IV.4 181B (22:24–23:3) for Zechariah, and XIII.1ff. 300B (44:5) for Isaiah.

204. *CH* IV.4 181B (23:3–5).

205. *CH* IV.4 181BC (23:7–9).

206. *CH* IV.4 181CD (23:19–24:1).

207. *CH* XV.9 337C (58:9).

208. Gandillac, 179n. 3.

209. *CH* VIII.2 241C (35:22–25). Note that for Iamblichus the world is also a single ζῷόν; *De myst.* IV.12 (des Places), 155–156. For Dionysius this is true of both the Celestial and Ecclesiastical Hierarchies. The difference lies in the fact that the unity of the Areopagite's worlds, a unity both organic and binding, discovers itself in Christ.

2.2. The Ecclesiastical Hierarchy

Our hierarchy is, first and most obviously, the means given us to know and to share in God. It is the icon of the invisible: "the sacred and perceptible representations of intelligible realities, and both guide [χειραγωγία] and way to these things."[210] As such, it is secondly the God-intended sense or purpose, λόγος, of that entire plane of being that is realized in space, time and matter.[211] Insofar as "the intelligible [the latter applying here to the energies of God] is source and science of the hierarchic things pertaining to the sensible,"[212] our hierarchy makes use of and so consecrates "the sensible things for the more divine ascent from them to the intelligible."[213] Because the structure or our nature and thus of our intellectual or spiritual mode of apprehension is, unlike angelic simplicity, compounded of matter and spirit and therefore dependent upon discursive or "progressive thought,"[214] it follows that

> neither is it possible for the thearchic ray to illumine [us] otherwise than by the variety of sacred veils [with which] it has been veiled in a manner facilitating our ascent and duly furnished by a fatherly Providence in a manner natural to our faculties.[215]

What is the structure of this pedagogy, of the "veils" that are yet intended to reveal?

2.2.1. The veils. The "veils" are the stuff of our universe: matter, physical gesture or motion, and spoken word. Through what Roques

---

210. *EH* II.3.2 397C (74:9–10).

211. *Contra* Brons, *Gott und die Seienden*, 21–41. See esp. 36 and Brons' admission that his interpretation of our hierarchy as applying *only* to humanity is "implicit" in the *CD*, not "explicit."

212. *EH* II.3.2 397C (74:10–11).

213. *EH* I.5 377A (68:3–4). For the physical world as ἀναγωγή in Origen and Evagrius, see Golitzin, *Et introibo*, 274–276 and 324–326 respectively.

214. See *DN* IV.9 705B (153:17–154:1).

215. *CH* I.2 121BC (8:10–13).

terms the "anagogic condescension of the divine activity"[216]—a condescension whose core is the Incarnation—these elements in our world have in our hierarchy become "God-bearing," θεόφορος. The "ray" of the divine energies is capable of appropriating to itself these basics of the sensible world. It "puts-itself-together-with" the universe of matter, motion, and speech. This is the root meaning of the word "symbol" itself: the "putting-together" or "συμ-βολή of different natures."[217]

2.2.1.1. Matter. Nothing in our world is utterly opaque to God's energies. Matter itself bears traces (ἀπηχήματα) of its Creator and thus possesses a potential for leading "up to the immaterial archetypes."[218] Looking again to his favored solar imagery, Dionysius speaks of the diffusion of the divine light through the levels of creation beginning with the "first matter"[219] of the angels:

> the diffusion of the sun's rays traverses without difficulty the first matter, most translucid of all and through it makes its proper radiance shine most plainly, though on encountering the matters that are more opaque, its diffusive manifestation is more reduced, due to the inaptitude of the illumined matters for the transmission of the gift of light, until little by little the action of transmission becomes nearly impossible.[220]

"Nearly," I must stress, but never entirely. It is for this reason that one may speak of participation in God through the medium of material things, of a revelation of the invisible through the

216. Roques, *L'univers*, esp. 299–300. Note, in view of the Incarnation, that Roques adds that this condescension is also "pour restituer à l'unité."

217. Koutras, Ἔννοια τῆς εἰκόνος, 256. See also Larsen, *Jamblique*, 186–187.

218. *CH* II.4 144BC (15:4–5). Dionysius is, to be sure, echoing here sentiments which may be found in such Neoplatonists as Iamblichus; see esp. *De myst.* V.23 (des Places), 178–179 (although not so much for Plotinus: *Enn.* I.8.5 and 6).

219. See Gandillac, 151n. 4, for the explanation that "matter" here—i.e., esp. in reference here to the angels—does not signify "stuff," but instead "leur caractère de créatures."

220. *CH* XIII.3 301AB (45:2–7).

visible.[221] It is thus as Dionysius writes in *CH* I.3, that the matter and form of the Church's liturgy are given us for participation in God and imitation of the heavenly choirs:

> since it would not be possible for our mind to be ordered to that immaterial imitation of the heavenly hierarchies unless it were to make use of the material guide adapted to its nature, reckoning the apparent beauties as copies of the invisible beauty, the sensible perfumes as figures of the intelligible diffusion, the material lights icons of the immaterial gift of light and the discussions of the sacred teachings [images] of the contemplative fullness according to the intellect, the orders of the clerical ranks here below representative of the harmonious *habitus* [of the mind] ordered toward things divine, and the partaking of the divine Eucharist an icon of the participation in Jesus.[222]

This passage, coming early in the *CD*, is perhaps the most crucial of the entire corpus, a summary of the Dionysian project. As I have already noted in chapter 1, it owes directly to Evagrius and, especially, the *Macarian Homilies*.[223] The whole of the sacred μίμησις of our hierarchy rests on the capacity of matter to carry, however much its limitations may obscure, the light of God. Our hierarchy forms, in its entirety, a holy σύμβολον, a figure of the angels' beauty and of God's,[224] a meeting of heaven and earth that takes place at once in the assembly of the Church, and within the human heart or intellect.

---

221. See again Iamblichus, *De myst.* VII.1 (des Places), 188–189. For the pagans, too, the συμπάθεια enabling this participation (*De myst.* V.7, 162–163) also carries with it a certain element of grace (V.9–10, 163–165). See also my discussion of Origen in *Et introibo*, 274–276.

222. *CH* I.3 121C–124A (8:19–9:6). For the Eucharist as icon, see chapter 5 below (3.2.2., "The Recapitulation of Providence, of Christ, and of Humanity").

223. See Golitzin, *Et introibo*, 382–385.

224. And, I add, of the beauty of the individual, human soul; see again chapter 5 below (3.1.3., "The Contemplation: A Triple Reality and Revelation"; 3.2.2., "The Recapitulation of Providence, of Christ, and of Humanity"; 3.2.5., "The Spiral Motion"; 5.1., "A Series of Icons").

2.2.1.2. Motion. Matter is never without motion. The material apparatus of the ecclesiastical hierarchy is set within a context of sacred actions, themselves iconic, of ritual gestures no less essentially symbolic than the "lights," "perfumes," etc., employed in the course of the Church's liturgy. In speaking of Baptism, for example, Dionysius tells us that this, "in symbols, is the sacred initiation of divine birth [θεογένεσις]." Nothing is portrayed that is unsuitable to God. Instead one is given to behold "mysteries [ἀενίγματα] of a contemplation worthy of God represented in mirrors natural and suited to human beings."[225] In coming to contemplate this mystery enacted, the whole of the rite, we strive to look up

> through sacred ascents to the things accomplished [such that], being sacredly initiated into them, we shall know of which character are the things figured, and of what invisible things they are the icons.[226]

Similarly, the rite of the Eucharist is an icon, a symbol:

> For he [the bishop] outlines perceptibly in these things [the rite], as in images, our spiritual life, bringing to view Jesus Christ who, becoming man after our fashion in a manner all pure and unconfused, from the secrecy proper to God took his form beneficently from us.[227]

We are reminded once more of the christological element that underlies the whole *CD*, particularly the *EH*. It cannot be overlooked. It centers and completes Koutras' otherwise apt definition of "icon" in Dionysius as "the Incarnation of God" through which "the sensible world is saved."[228] We are also directed to the

---

225. *EH* II.3.1 397A (73:13–15).

226. *EH* II.3.2 397C (74:5–7). For the use of εἰκών with Baptism, see also II.3.7 404B (78:5–6).

227. *EH* III.3.13 444C (93:14–16).

228. Koutras, Ἔννοια τῆς εἰκόνος, 256.

reality of ritual gesture as a theophany.[229] As a last example, I take
the bishop's initial censing of the Church as a calling to mind, a
symbol, of the circular motion of Providence. The latter departs
from itself to embrace all things and return them to itself, yet it

> abides truly in itself and moves not wholly from its true iden-
> tity; in the same manner the divine mystery of the synaxis,
> even though it possesses its source as inclusive, simple and
> united, is beneficently multiplied in the sacred variety of sym-
> bols and penetrates even to all the thearchic iconography, yet
> is again gathered together in a uniform manner from these
> same into its proper monad, uniting those who in sacred fash-
> ion are led up to it.[230]

This passage also indicates the three levels of application observed
in *CH* I.3 above. It describes an action taking place (1) within the
Church that is also both (2) the depiction of God's action throughout the universe and (3) of the simultaneous return (ἐπιστροφή) of
the soul to communion with God within its procession (πρόοδος)
outward in cooperation (συνέργεια) with Providence.

The forms of the rites are more than a calling to mind of Providence. They are also a participation in God's activity, a true συμ-
βολή of physical form and gesture with divine grace. Thus:

> The whole order of priests, having been gathered in hierarchic
> order, and having communicated in the most divine things,
> pauses with thanksgiving, recognizing in due measure [i.e.,
> in accordance with their respective ranks] and celebrating the
> grace of the divine operations.[231]

On the one hand, it is true that the rites are given us to contemplate:

> that having reflected . . . upon its [the consecration of the
> μύρον] parts according to the sacred icons [rites], we may thus

---

229. See my discussion of this passage and the crucial ὑπ' ὄψιν in chapter
5 below (3.2.4., Ὑπ' ὄψιν: Recognition of a Real Presence).

230. *EH* III.3.3 429A (82:20–83:3).

231. *EH* III.3.15 445B (94:11–13).

be led up through the parts to its unity by means of hierarchic contemplations.[232]

The consecration of the μύρον is indeed an image (ἄγαλμα) of the "deiform virtue," its pattern in accord with the "intelligible beauty" of its prototype."[233] On the other hand, it is also true that the rites are genuinely efficacious modes or channels for the three-fold divine activity of purification, illumination, and perfection. The psalmody sung during the rite thus

> perfectly purifies those wanting in complete purity, leads those who are holy to the divine images and their vision and com-munion, and establishes those who are altogether holy in blessed and spiritual visions, filling that in them which is in the form of the One with the One, and making them one.[234]

2.2.1.3. Word. Psalmody leads us to the third constituent of the veils: the word, spoken or written. The word carries with it the whole human realm of idea or discourse. For Dionysius, the word can only refer to Holy Scripture—together with the oral teachings of the Apostles and saints. One cannot emphasize too much his insistence on revelation and Scripture as divinely given.[235] The

232. *EH* IV.1 472D (95:5–7). See also IV.3.1 473D (96:17–18), where we are directed to go within (εἴσω) the theomimetic veil in order to discover the intellections of the archetype (ἀρχέτυπος νόησις). Dionysius is clearly basing himself here, at least in part, on the Church architecture of his time. For a discussion on the use of sanctuary veils at the time of the *CD*, esp. in order to conceal the altar, see T. F. Mathews, *Early Churches of Constantinople* (University Park, PA: Pennsylvania State University Press, 1971), 162–171; A. M. Schneider, "Liturgie und Kirchenbau in Syrien," *NAG* (1949): 56–68; and particularly C. Schneider, "Καταπέτασμα," *Kyrios* 1 (1936): 57–73.

233. *EH* IV.3.1 473B (96:2–5).

234. *EH* IV.3.3 477A (98:9–13).

235. For the Neoplatonist background to the expressions λόγια and θεοπαράδοτα, see Koch, *Beziehungen*, 38–48. For their appearance in patristic literature, see Lampe, 629, 805–806.

point is repeated at the beginning of each of the *CD*'s four major treatises.[236]

From the opening chapter of the *EH*, for example, we learn that

> that which is given to them [the angels] in a uniform and inclusive manner is vouchsafed to us from the divinely-delivered Scriptures by means of a variety and multiplication of different symbols. For the Scriptures are the essence of our hierarchy. These Scriptures are . . . most august . . . they have been vouchsafed to us from our inspired and sacred consecrators in theological and holy writings and letters, and, furthermore, whatever has come from the same holy men by means of the more immaterial initiation—as indeed to people somehow already neighbors of the Celestial hierarchy—from mind to mind by means of speech, at once bodiless and yet more immaterial as being without writing, by which our holy guides were initiated. Neither did these things come to us from the inspired hierarchs in intuitions obvious to the commonality of the faithful, but were delivered rather in sacred symbols. For not everyone is holy nor, as Scripture says, is knowledge for all.[237]

Let us briefly examine this passage. Once again we find the difference between our mode of apprehension and the angels'. We apprehend the truth through symbols, a term that embraces both the physical and the notional.[238] Every real insight or grace of intellection and comprehension as to the nature of the real discovers its source, "essence," in the symbols transmitted to us via Scripture. What of the revelations or intuitions given us orally by the Apostles and saints that also possess authority? It appears to me that Dionysius is doing two related things here. He is first of all lending expression to the notion of tradition as the saints' continuous witness to the life in God granted us by and in the Church.

---

236. See *CH* I.2 121A (7:11–12); *EH* I.4 376B (67:4–6); *DN* I.1 588A (108:6–8); I.3 589B (111:6–12); I.4 589D (112:7–10); and *MT* I.1 997A (141:2–3).

237. *EH* I.4 376BC (67:4–15).

238. Recall chapter 2 (3., "The Names: Notional Icons, Resonances of God as Providence").

Secondly, he is defending the principle of the *lex orandi*: the public worship of the Church is itself an authoritative expression of divine truth and source of private inspiration and contemplation[239]—indeed, is even more the authoritative image, ἀκριβὴς εἰκών, than the scriptural images, as based upon a "more immaterial initiation."[240]

The final two sentences of the passage might be read as betraying a dangerous esotericism. Dionysius speaks at least once elsewhere[241] of Scripture's "deliberate" concealment of the "hidden truth" from the many, and he concludes again with the passage from Saint Paul concerning the γνῶσις which "is not for all" (cf. 1 Cor 7:7). Gandillac rightly notes a distinction between the Apostle, who "was simply opposing idolaters to people who know Christ," and Dionysius' differentiation between "those who deserve to possess the truth and those who may only receive it under the guise of parables."[242] Nonetheless, it does not appear to me that the Areopagite is doing much more than referring here to a basic fact of the spiritual life. There are degrees of knowledge, of receptivity to truth, and of advancement in it. We have only to recall the distinction drawn in Hebrews 5:13-14 between "milk" and "strong meat," or even that in 1 Corinthians 13:11 between the child and the man. The deepest things of God require sanctity:

> For we must not consider that the appearance of the [sacred] compositions are formed for their own sake, [they] are rather to shield the unspeakable and invisible science from the many, that the all-holy things be not easily grasped by the profane, but instead revealed alone to the true lovers of sanctity who have packed away every childish fantasy concerning the

239. See C. A. Bernard, "Les formes de théologie chez Denys l'Aréopagite," *Greg* 59 (1978): 44.

240. See also Rorem's remarks on the "more immaterial" in *Symbols*, 118–125. Rorem does, however, rather over-emphasize in my view the Neoplatonist preference for the oral to the written. While doubtless a feature of Dionysius' thought, we must also recall the *lex orandi's* singular importance for the patristic writers, as, for example, an Irenaeus or a Basil. See Louth, *Denys*, 26–27.

241. *CH* II.2 140B (11:16–20).

242. Gandillac, 77n. 2.

sacred symbols and are thus capable, through simplicity of
intellect and capacity for contemplative virtue, to cross over
to the simple and supernatural and transcendent truth of the
symbols.[243]

The "sacred veils" that include the word of Scripture and the
forms of the Church's worship are in essence a collection or sequence of contemplations. They embrace an ascending series of
revelations adapted to the believer's progress in love, simplicity,
purification from selfish imagination, and consequent capacity
for contemplation.[244] They are, indeed, more than simply a scale
of θεωρία. The icon that they constitute is "by its very essence
a χειραγωγία."[245] The ecclesiastical hierarchy is therefore (and I
do not here exhaust its significance) that which takes us "by the
hand" to bring us into knowledge of the truth and shape our souls
in accordance with the divine archetype in order that each may
become a faithful image of the divine virtue.

2.2.2. Our symbols and their apprehension. The icon or symbol, and so our hierarchy itself, is of necessity anagogic. It effects
the education, *paideia*, of the believer who is called upon to discern
"within the schemes and images the divine intention underlying

---

243. *Ep.* IX.1 1105C (197:1–8). See also my discussion of Origen in *Et
introibo*, 277–278, for a parallel in patristic literature to Dionysius' insistence
on varying capacities, dependent upon holiness, for the vision of the invisible
reality beneath the apparent, as well as Evagrius on "pure prayer" and his
suspicion of the imagination, Golitzin, *Et introibo*, 331–332. On Macarius see
Et introibo, 377–378.

244. Note that intellectual ability, worldly intelligence, does not constitute
a Dionysian prerequisite for progress in the divine "science."

245. Koutras, Ἔννοια τῆς εἰκόνος, 257. For the χειραγωγία, see Gregory of
Nyssa, *Contra Eunom.* II.417–419 ("the divine δύναμις . . . fashions itself
after the way of man [κατὰ ἄνθρωπον σχηματίζεται] in its varied theophanies
[ποικίλαις θεοφανείαις], and speaks as man, and clothes itself in wrath and
mercy and such like passions, that, through all its accommodations to us,
it may take our infancy by the hand and lead it up through the words of
Providence to touch the nature of God [χειραγωγεῖτο ἡ νηπιώδης ἡμῶν ζωή]")
and my discussion in *Et introibo*, 295–296.

them."[246] By its nature the symbol, a putting-together or indwelling of the divine in matter, gesture, or word, requires this continual effort toward apprehension—as well, of course, as the presence or power of God actively at work in assisting the anagogy. It implies an increasing process of purification, enlightenment, and perfection, a continual affirmation and negation that bears witness both to the nature of a symbol as a meeting of created and uncreated, and to the double aspect of God's own being, at once hidden and revealed. Here we discover a convergence of the three triads of spiritual activity: purification - illumination - perfection, ἀφαίρεσις - ἀγνωσία - ἕνωσις, and direct - spiral - and circular spiritual motion. All three take place simultaneously at different levels, i.e., according to the believer's degree of conformity to the divine. "The sacred and mystical unfoldings [ἀναπτύξεις]"[247] of the symbols constituting the ecclesiastical hierarchy require a continual progress from the sanctified human intelligence. The "science" of our hierarchy is, as Roques notes, "one and the same act which simultaneously attaches, elevates, and liberates the mind."[248] The demand is unceasing and our potential progress without limit, because the depths to which a given symbol points, which are in a sense carried within it, themselves have no end:

> It is thus necessary for us, instead of [resting with] the common suppositions concerning them, to pass within the sacred symbols in a manner befitting holiness, and in no way to esteem them lightly that are the offspring and figures of the divine likenesses, and visible images of the visions that are ineffable and beyond nature. For indeed, it is not just the super-essential lights, and the intelligibles, and—quite simply—divine things that are adorned by the materially figurative symbols, as the super-essential God is said to be "fire," and "burning" the intelligible sayings of God; but, in addition, the deiform dispositions of angels both contemplated and

246. Roques, "Contemplation," *DSp* 2.1887. See also Koutras, Ἔννοια τῆς εἰκόνος, 249–250 and 256, as well as Golitzin, *Et introibo*, 274–279.

247. *DN* IX.5 913A (211:2); also *CH* II.3 141A (12:17–13:3).

248. Roques, *L'univers*, 201.

contemplating are also delineated in varied shapes and in
many forms and fiery figures. And [it is thus also necessary]
to receive the image of "fire" in one way when used in reference to God who is beyond intellection, and in another way
when it refers to his spiritual providences or wills, and in still
another way with respect to the angels . . . to the one [it is
referred] as cause, to the other as existing, and to the last by
participation.[249]

The resonances of the symbols are thus infinite. This brings us
to the fact that our hierarchy represents the whole revelation of
God and the angels. It is the sole means given us for ascent up
and into contemplation of the created intelligible world, then to
the uncreated wills or energies, and ultimately to the darkness
surrounding God as he is in himself. From the first turning away
from error to the highest rapture of the mystic vision, everything,
all ascent, takes place within the forms and activities of the ecclesiastical hierarchy. As was suggested in the quotation from *CH* I.3
above, the whole *CD* leads inward into the altar and the mystery
that the latter represents.[250]

2.2.3. The icon of the ascent: ministers and ministered.

2.2.3.1. Clergy and laity: a spatial and spiritual ordering. The essence of our hierarchy is revealed in Scripture. The first manifestation or flowering of that essence is:

the threefold virtue of the holy rites of the sacraments, the
purification and brilliant illumination of the sacred divine birth
[Baptism] received from Scripture, the perfecting knowledge
and science of the theurgies [given by] the synaxis and the
consecration of the chrism, through which [threefold power]
is accomplished in sacred manner the unifying ascent to, and
blessed communion with, the Thearchy.[251]

---

249. *Ep.* IX.2 1108CD (199:9–200:8).

250. Here is the truth of Rorem's correct insistence that the *Mystical Theology*
is at the center of the *CD* (e.g., *Commentary*, 200ff.), though not as a "solvent"
of Dionysius' Christian pretentions, but in fact as their fulfillment.

251. *EH* V.1.3 504BC (106:17–22).

Our "sacred order" follows this "division of every hierarchical activity into the most divine mysteries" with the participants in those mysteries, "the inspired men who are instructed and initiated in them, and those who are being initiated by them in sacred manner."[252] The full composition of the ecclesiastical hierarchy is thus the scriptural revelation expressed in the triad of sacraments whose saving activity is realized in the subordinate triads of the clergy, the ministers of that activity, and of the laity who receive the clergy's ministrations.

The priestly order of bishop (ἱεράρχης), priest, and deacon (λειτουργός) do, however, represent[253] those among the faithful who have realized in themselves the first stages of the threefold process which is the activity within the created world of divine Providence:

> for it is necessary for those going to the all-pure and sacred
> activity to have been completely cleansed from the last fanta-
> sies of the soul, and, as far as possible, to approach it through
> likeness with it, for thus shall be [the theophanies of the supra-
> mundane rays] more clearly discerned about them. These
> desire that their proper glory should pass through ever more
> completely and more transparently to the splendors of the
> like-formed mirrors [the clergy].[254]

Here again, as Roques notes,[255] and with the same metaphors of sun and fire already encountered in the *DN* and *CH*, "the principle of the diffusion of God's gifts to the superior orders and through them to the inferiors is maintained and illustrated." The clergy are the "mirrors" of the thearchic ray, the media—themselves thus the icons and channels on our plane of being for revelation—through whom the saving and transforming knowledge and activity of God descend finally to us:

252. *EH* V.1.1 501A (104:11–15).

253. See again my discussion above (1.3.3., "Purification - Illumination - Perfection") and in chapter 5 (4.1., "Ministers and Ministered"), 182–187.

254. *EH* III.3.10 440AB (89:21–90:3).

255. Roques, *L'univers*, 197.

for those who, speaking symbolically, are ever present about
the divine altar behold and hear the divine things clearly revealed to them, and, proceeding in the manner of the Good
outside the divine veils [the curtain or screen blocking the
sanctuary], manifest to the obedient monks and to the holy
people and the orders still in a state of purification, in a manner according to the latter's deserts, the sacred things which
they have preserved well and purely.[256]

Among the orders of the laity the monks are those who stand at
the height of knowledge and contemplation. They receive the
names of θεραπευταί or of μοναχοί from their "pure service and
attendance upon God," and their "undivided and unified mode
of life, unifying them through sacred concentration of their divisions into a deiform unity and God-loving perfection."[257] Even
these, though, are assigned places outside the doors and veils of
the altar area because, "in relation to their order and knowledge,"
they are still "closer to the people than to the priestly ranks."[258]
If this applies to the monks, whose τάξις is the one in process
of perfection (τελειουμένη), then it is still more the case with the
middle order, the baptized laity. The latter is the θεωρητικὴ τάξις,
the one in process of illumination as being

purified from every unholy stain and possessing all pure and
unmoving the foundation of its proper spirit, it is brought over
in priestly fashion to the contemplative condition and power,
and communes in the most divine symbols proper to it . . .
and in due measure is winged by their [i.e., the symbols']
anagogic powers towards the divine love of their science.[259]

---

256. *Ep.* VIII.1 1089A (177:3–8).

257. *EH* VI.1.3 532D–533A (116:15–19).

258. *Ep.* VIII.1 1088D–1089A (176:10–177:1); also *EH* VI.1.3 532D–533A
(116:6–23). See my discussion of the monk's role in Evagrius (*Et introibo*,
328–329) and Dionysius' "clericalism" as a possible reaction to it, as well
as the currents in Syrian monasticism, i.e., "Messalianism" in chapter 3.1.,
" 'Singles,' 'Sons of the Covenant,' and 'Messalians.' "

259. *EH* VI.1.2 532BC (115:20–116:4).

In comparison, however, to the hierarch who "is ever led up by the thearchic Spirit to the holy principles [ἀρχαί] of the things accomplished," the contemplative faculty or illumination of the laity is limited to the mere vision of the symbols: "the many only peek [παρακύψαντες] at the divine symbols."[260]

Still more distant, spiritually and physically, is the final order of those who are "being purified." These are the non-baptized together with those under penance or possessed by devils[261]—the latter having failed to conquer the passions and the disordered motions of evil. This group is forbidden attendance at the holiest of the sacred rites.[262] Physically, they are further removed than the laity who occupy the middle or nave of the Church. Instead, they crowd at the doors of the nave in the narthex. Again, spiritually and physically, they represent the last echo of holiness. Beyond them, outside the doors of the Church, lies an existence entirely sunk in deception and enslavement to the "seeming good [δοκοῦσα εὐπάθεια]" of the world, the flesh, and the devil.[263]

2.2.3.2. Altar to doors: the church at prayer, an icon of providence. Reversing the order of progressive distance from the altar, we discover in the very physical arrangement of the Church itself,[264]

---

260. *EH* III.2 428A (81:10–11).

261. See *EH* III.3.6 432C–436D (84:22–88:9).

262. *EH* III.2 425C (80:14–16) and IV.2 473A (95:9–12).

263. *EH* III.3.7 433D–436A (86:17–24).

264. See the article by Bernard, "Les formes de la théologie," 47, where the author notes the reflection of "la contemplation spirituelle" in "la symbolique architecturale ou picturale," both of which, again "se réfèrent à une experience spirituelle." In an earlier note I pointed to the studies by Mathews and Schneider on the background of Church architecture in Dionysius' day. Concerning pictorial art and its presence in the Christian Churches of the pre-iconoclastic period, see: F. Diecamp, *Analecta Patristica: Texte und Abhandlungen zur Griechischen Patristik* (OCA 117; Rome: Pontifical Institutum Orientalium Studiorum, 1938), 107–153; P. J. Alexander, "Hypatius of Ephesus: A Note on Image Worship in the Sixth Century," *HTR* 45 (1952): 177–184; A. H. Armstrong, "Some Comments on the Development of the Theology of Images," *SP* 9 (1963): 123–125; N. H. Baynes, "The Icons before Iconoclasm," *HTR* 44 (1951): esp. 93–95; J. Gouillard, "Hypatios d'Ephèse," *REB* 19 (1961): 63–75; E. Kitzinger, "The Cult of Images in the Age before

and of the orders of laity and clergy, a process of concentration, a gathering and intensification of the mystery at once divine and yet manifest among and through humans and the stuff of their being, at once revealed and yet increasingly hidden as we approach its core and heart. From the world of darkness and error outside the doors, to the purified orders awaiting in the porch the hour of their entry (or re-entry) into the body of the Church and full citizenship in the Christian πολιτεία; to the laity occupying the nave, full participants indeed though still at the first stages of knowledge; to the monks at the gates of the sanctuary in "pure attendance upon God" and the contemplations brought them by the clergy within the enclosure; to the deacons who guard the gates within and without[265] and who are charged with the task of purification; to the priests who illumine the faithful and guide the initiates to the divine visions (i.e., the physical sight) of the sacraments,[266] who within the sanctuary surround the altar and the hierarch as the seraphim stand about the Godhead,[267] and who receive communion from the bishop directly within the holy place;[268] to the hierarch himself, "the inspired and divine man instructed in all sacred knowledge, in whom indeed the whole

---

Iconoclasm," *DOP* 8 (1954): 83–150, esp. 138; and C. Mango, *The Art of the Byzantine Empire* (Englewood Cliffs, NJ: Prentice Hall, 1972), 3–115. There are also the large monographs by H. Koch, *Die altchristliche Bilderfrage nach den literarischen quellen* (Göttingen: Vandenhoeck & Ruprecht, 1917), and W. Elliger, *Die Stellung der alten Christen zu den Bildern in den ersten vier Jahrhunderten* (Leipzig: Dieterich, 1930), 1-98; and *Zur Entstehung und frühen Entwicklung der altchristlichen Bildkunst* (Leipzig: Dieterich, 1934), 1–284. Dionysius is certainly part of, and a contributor toward, the movement in favor of imagery that saw its most momentous development, as Mango (22) notes, in the mass conversions and liturgical development of the fourth century. See also my Concluding Remarks (3.1.) below.

265. *EH* V.1.6 508AB (108:18–109:12).

266. *EH* V.1.6 505D–508A (108:8–13).

267. *EH* IV.3.6 480D (100:9–12).

268. *EH* III.3.14 445A (93:26–94:3).

hierarchy belonging to him [ἡ κατ᾽ αὐτὸν ἱεραρχία] is accomplished and made known,"[269] whose proper:

> essence and ἀναλογία it is to be perfected in divine things and deified, and to transmit to those subordinates according to the merit of each the sacred deification which has come to pass in him from God,[270]

we witness an increasing drawing up and into the altar—and thus into the bishop who stands immediately before it—of all sacred virtue, activity, and knowledge. It is on the altar that the Scriptures, essence of our hierarchy, rest, from it that they are proclaimed, and on it again that the great sacraments of the Church, particularly the Eucharist, are accomplished: the representations of Christ's "theurgy" which itself is the "recapitulation of all theology [i.e., Scripture]."[271] Before the altar stands the bishop in whom the powers[272] and science of the hierarchy are realized, and through whom all the lower clergy and laity participate in those same virtues and knowledge:[273] "he effects [ἐνεργεῖ] the mysteries of our hierarchy through all the sacred orders."[274] It is on his head that the Scriptures are placed inasmuch as he is the recipient of all "perfecting power and science,"[275] "the one who reveals the judgments of the Thearchy."[276] In view of the fact that he quotes

---

269. *EH* I.3 373C (66:5–6). In the phrase ἡ κατ᾽ αὐτὸν ἱεραρχία there is perhaps a double sense. The phrase can mean, and has usually been taken as signifying, the actual (local) Church as summed up in the person of its bishop. On the other hand, it may also indicate the bishop's own inner hierarchy, i.e., the powers of his soul or intellect—precisely what we find disordered in the monk Demophilus (*Ep.* VIII). The bishop is thus himself the temple (ναός) of God (see *EH* III.3.7 433C [86:10–11]).

270. *EH* I.2 372D (65:2–4).

271. *EH* III.3.5 432B (84:14–21).

272. *EH* V.1.7 508C (109:13–18).

273. *EH* V.1.5 505A (107:13–16).

274. *EH* V.1.5 505B (107:19).

275. *EH* VI.3.7 513C (113:18–19).

276. *EH* VII.3.7 561C (127:16–17). See also "angel of the Lord God Almighty" (127:17–18) and 564A, "interpreter [ὑποφύτης] of the thearchic Justice" (128:4–5).

him earlier in the *CD*,[277] it seems likely Dionysius is saying with Ignatius of Antioch: "Where is the bishop, there is also Christ and his Church."[278]

We would maintain that, under the guise of Neoplatonic vocabulary, this is exactly what he is saying. The bishop occupies the place of Christ "in whom every hierarchy is accomplished."[279] Reversing our perspective once again, we may see in the bishop standing before the altar the icon of the Thearchy, "the source of this hierarchy, the fount of life, the essence of goodness, the unique cause of being."[280] Through the bishop, the "threefold virtue" of the sacraments, like the primordial outpouring of the hidden God's energies streaming into creation and extending from the angels to the last traces of being and even of non-being, pour out to penetrate the whole of the ecclesiastical polity, beginning with the priests and, in descending order together with diminishing *éclat*, extending to the deacons, the monks, the laity, and, most obscurely, to the orders of those not yet purified. Finally, it disperses and disappears from view in the night of ignorance and sin outside the doors. It is therefore no mere metaphor on Dionysius' part when he speaks of the powers of the sacraments, flowing out from the bishop at the altar, as "the perfecting icons of the thearchic power,"[281] or of the dispositions of our hierarchy as "icons of the divine energies."[282] The ecclesiastical hierarchy is the "hierarchic icon of the divine,"[283] an active power and living participant in the divine archetype. The original outflowing of God's energies into the darkness of non-being and then of creation is thus re-presented in the initial censing of the bishop whose tour of the Church is a realization of the activity of Providence that it typifies. It is the same energy of God working in and revealed

---

277. *DN* IV.12 709B (157:10–11). See my discussion of Ignatius and Dionysius in *Et introibo*, 242–246.

278. *Ep. ad. Symr.* VIII (PG V, 852A).

279. *EH* V.1.5 505B (107:16–17).

280. *EH* I.3 373C (66:6–7).

281. *EH* V.1.5 505B (107:21–23).

282. *EH* V.1.7 508C (109:22) and 509A (110:3–5).

283. *EH* V.1.7 508D (110:2).

in the bishop here, which established, preserves, and saves the worlds, and that now, "through this inspired and hierarchic harmony," wills that "each participate, so far as he is capable, in him who is . . . Beautiful, Wise, and Good."[284]

2.2.4. A Gnostic vision?

2.2.4.1. The revelation of a divinized cosmos. One scholar speaks of the Areopagite's "symbolic Gnosticism,"[285] perhaps in reference to the picture just drawn of light not of this world, streaming from a hidden center to penetrate the serried ranks of initiates, and finally disappearing into the blackness outside the shrine. Of course, the hallmarks of the dualistic systems commonly labeled "Gnosticism" are in no way a part of the *CD*: Dionysius' God, while supra-mundane, is never "in his ultimate meaning contramundane," nor is his creation "an evil and alien order."[286] The ecclesiastical hierarchy represents instead the divinely granted and sole means of salvation for a creation which, through humanity and the deceit of the demons, has fallen into the "ways of non-being and danger of destruction."[287] It is not set up in opposition to the world. Rather, to cite Otto von Semmelroth, "there is no area on the earth that possesses stability outside of the hierarchically ordered Church."[288] It is not the denial of the sensible world but

---

284. *EH* I.2 373A (65:7–8).

285. J. Meyendorff, *Christ in Eastern Christian Thought* (Washington, DC: Corpus, 1969), 68ff.; idem, *Byzantine Theology*, 119.

286. H. Jonas, *The Gnostic Religion* (2nd ed.; Boston: Beacon, 1963), 250–251. For the problems raised by the term "Gnosticism," see M. Smith, "The History of the Term Gnostikos," in *The Rediscovery of Gnosticism II* (ed. B. Layton; Leiden: Brill, 1981), esp. 796–807; G. A. G. Stroumsa, *Another Seed: Studies in Gnostic Mythology* (Leiden: Brill, 1984), 1–14, esp. 4–5; B. Layton, *The Gnostic Scriptures* (2nd ed.; New York/London: Doubleday, 1995), 5–23 ("Historical Introduction"); idem, "Prolegomena to the Study of Ancient Gnosticism," in *Recent Studies in Early Christianity: Doctrinal Diversity* (ed. E. Ferguson; New York/London: Garland, 1999), 106–122; M. A. Williams, *Rethinking "Gnosticism": An Argument for Dismantling a Dubious Category* (Princeton, NJ: Princeton University Press, 1996).

287. *EH* III.3.11 440D (91:8).

288. Von Semmelroth, "Gottes ausstrahlendes Licht," 493.

instead its divinely revealed meaning, its justification, such that
the sensible becomes a carrier of the divine, "a field of symbols
that can and must introduce human intelligence to the intelligible
world . . . that constitutes the life of the Church, the angelic beings, and the divinity."[289] Through and in our hierarchy, our world
becomes "itself essentially a revelation of God,"[290] a declaration
of, and a sharing in, the Creator:

> we behold our own [hierarchy] adapted to our condition, mul-
> tiplied in the variety of sacred symbols by means of which we
> are hierarchically conducted up in the measure proper to us
> to the deification that is in the form of the One, to both God
> and divine virtue.[291]

The insistence upon virtue is important. Our hierarchy is "something symbolic . . . in manner analogous to us using things
sensible" in order to "lead us up via sensible things to divine
contemplations."[292] Yet the process does not involve knowledge
alone: "[we] do not participate uniformly in him . . . but as the
divine balance distributes to each according to his deserts."[293]

This stress on conformity to divine virtue, on our hierarchy as
an assimilation to God who is "truly good, truly wise, truly beautiful," is the final proof against the accusation of "Gnosticism." The
ecclesiastical hierarchy is a single organism, "the all-embracing
intent [λόγος] of all the holy ones subject to it."[294] Thus:

> By means of the love for the beautiful which stretches forth to
> him [Christ] and lifts us up with it, [it] folds up our many
> differences together and having made them into one divine
> life, condition, and activity, it grants the sacred power of the
> divine priesthood. Arriving at the holy operation of the same
> priesthood, we become ourselves closer to the beings [angels]

289. Roques, *L'univers*, 53.
290. Von Semmelroth, "Gottes ausstrahlendes Licht," 499.
291. *EH* I.2 373A (65:10–13).
292. *EH* I.5 377A (68:2–4).
293. *EH* I.2 373B (65:16–17).
294. *EH* I.3 373C (65:23).

that are above us by means of our assimilation, according to
possibility, to their stable, indefectible, and sacred foundation,
and by this means, having cast our eyes up to Jesus and the
blessed Thearchy itself, and having beheld it so far as it is
possible to see, and having been enlightened with the knowledge of divine visions, being both hallowed and hallowers of
the mystic science, we shall be enabled to take on the form of
light and become workers of divine things, both rendered and
rendering perfect.[295]

To become imitators of God in his active love for creation, θεοειδής,
is to realize here below, in the sensible realm, the perfection of the
angelic world. Our hierarchy binds us to the one living organism
that is theirs. The bishop is thus, for example, rightly called an
"angel" as a sharer in the angels' prophetic faculty and as elevated
to their "revelatory likeness."[296] The imitation of the κόσμος νοητός
("intelligible world"), of the angels' blessed and united life, is,
generally, the gift vouchsafed us in the Church.[297] It is also the
deification of the sensible realm as a whole. The angels' beatitude
is the model of our own, and of our world's.[298] Bound together
with the angels in a single life of grace, and in the person of the
bishop visibly deriving our knowledge, powers, and activity from
a single source, insofar as it is from him at the altar that we receive
the word and the sacraments, we recognize and praise:

the beneficent and gracious source by which were shown forth
our saving sacraments in order to accomplish in holy manner
the sacred deification of those in process of perfection.[299]

2.2.4.2. The reflection and revelation of Jesus. This single source
is typified in the bishop and at the heart of the angelic choirs. It
is the "philanthropy of the thearchic goodness" that has freed
us from sin and "shown us an ascent beyond the world and an

295. *EH* I.1 372B (64:4–14).
296. *CH* XII.2 293A (43:8–11).
297. *CH* I.3 121C (8:14–17).
298. *CH* VIII.2 241C (35:21–25).
299. *EH* III.3.7 436C (87:22–24).

inspired mode of being [πολιτεία]."[300] Jesus is the supreme joining
and reconciliation, the supreme "symbol." His divinity is the transcendent source of all hierarchy,[301] and his is the "new theandric"
reality that informs our life and substance. He is

> the fount of the divine perfumes . . . [which] in thearchic
> proportions, he distributes to the most deiform of the intellects
> . . . [and] in which the minds [=angels] joyfully delight and
> of which sacred perceptions they are made full.[302]

He is also the mystery of the altar realized in the bishop's
ministrations:

> the source and origin, essence, and perfecting power of all our
> theurgic sanctifications . . . Jesus, divinely-worked sanctifica-
> tion . . . our most divine altar, the thearchic consecration of
> the heavenly minds . . . Jesus . . . in whom we, according to
> Scripture, we the saying, being at once consecrated and mysti-
> cally in mystery wholly consumed in sacrifice [lit. become
> whole burnt offerings, ὁλοκαυτώμενοι], have our access
> [προσαγωγή] [to the Father God].[303]

It is a light that streams from the sanctuary to purify, illumine,
perfect, and render us "co-workers" of his divinity. Veiled in the
images of our hierarchy, as once he was veiled in the flesh, he
renders those veils means of participation in, and revelations
of, his glory. Indeed, it is that very flesh that, I venture to say,
we discover now in the form of the ecclesiastical hierarchy: in
the sacraments that render him present, and in the ranks of the
faithful themselves. Our hierarchy is Paul's "one, new man," the
body of Christ whose "fullness fills all in all," the new creation. It
is the gift of the Incarnation and the anticipation of the eschaton,
the icon, and therefore the present reality of the world which is
and is to come.

300. *EH* III.3.11 441BC (91:22–23).
301. *DN* II.10 648CD (134:7–135:1).
302. *EH* IV.3.4 480A (99:10–13).
303. *EH* IV.3.12 484D (103:3–7).

3. Summary

The characteristics of the Dionysian hierarchies may be summarized as follows: (1) hierarchy is the reality intended by God for the two worlds of creation, intelligible (the angels) and sensible (humans), (2) and is thus the full expression of Providence for that world, the analog of God. (3) As the icon of Providence it is necessarily an object of contemplation, because (4) it carries the γνῶσις of God and so communicates a share in his "mind." The mind of God being love, (5) a hierarchy is therefore a community, a single corporate organism bound together by the exercise of a loving and mutual providence whose origins and enabling power come directly from God. (6) This corporate element means that the given creature, angel or human being, discovers its salvation and deification as the member of a community. The path to ἕνωσις lies through and within the hierarchy, not outside of it. Dionysius has no "alone to the alone." His vision is, speaking sociologically, centripetal. There is, though, (7) a place for the individual's enjoyment of union with God in Christ. This is indicated by hierarchy's function as microcosmos.

The next to last point I understand as a rejection both of Plotinus, the lonely philosopher rising above the unfortunate—if necessary—fall into matter and flux, and of the essentially centrifugal character of the Evagrian stress on the perfected anchorite, or the representatives of Syrian "Messalianism." Evagrius' vision of a providential cosmos has, however, been retained, as has the Syrian emphasis on the enlightened saint as "temple of God" (ναὸς θεοῦ).[304] Dionysius has also succeeded in transforming the Neoplatonists' series of causes into a ladder of icons. This has certain important consequences. With respect, first, to the angels' hierarchy, we note that the *CD*'s κόσμος νοητός ("intelligble world") is no longer causally prior to our own, sensible world. The (created) intelligible world has been cut off from the world of the ecclesiastical hierarchy, at least in the sense that the latter is no longer ontologically dependent upon the former. Our models

---

304. See in this respect Golitzin, "The Place of the Presence of God," referred to above.

and guides, the angels are not our creators. The implication is that, while we may grow to become "like" them in the Kingdom to come, we shall never be exactly as they are, i.e., disincarnate. The sensible world is directly dependent upon God and acquires thus a permanent validity.

Concerning our hierarchy I wish to stress two more points. First, I understand the permanent nature of the sensible icon to be a clear indication of Dionysius' Christian inspiration. An icon is, generally, a kind of incarnation. Our hierarchy, realized and revealed to us in the public worship of the Christian assembly, is the icon of God here below. It is thus the present reality of the Incarnation of Jesus Christ. The union of visible with invisible, of matter with spirit, of creature with Creator, that I outlined in the preceding chapter as fundamental to Dionysius' vision of the creature and its destiny, achieves its culmination in the Incarnation, whence is derived the possibility for, the enlightening power of, and the ultimate reality to be discovered within all icons or symbols, all unions. Our hierarchy represents, i.e., makes present, the abiding and active reality of the incarnate Christ. Jesus is the "place of meeting" and face of Providence disclosed to "true lovers of sanctity" within the veils of the Church. The latter is the flesh he has assumed, and its glory awaits the open revelation of the eschaton.[305] He is the truth of our world. Indeed, he is our true world.

Secondly, the Areopagite's Church is therefore not a thing, not an institution—whether teaching body or state. It is instead the continuation of the Incarnation. I repeat: it is *the* icon of God. Thus, before all else, it is an object of contemplation: divine grace is rendered visible in oil and water, bread and wine, order, gesture, and spoken word. While still in a sense incomplete, not yet perfectly achieved, it remains our single reality, the meaning of our universe and the latter's unique hope—and assurance—of stability and final salvation. Outside of it there is nothing save error, darkness, and final loss.

---

305. See *DN* I.4 especially and as well *EH* VII.I ff. on the general resurrection, together with my article, "On the Other Hand."

Whence come the darkness and its threat? How is the person of Jesus truly of a piece with the system of the *CD*? How, finally, is it that our hierarchy is also the icon of the individual, human soul, the macrocosmos reflecting the microcosmos? Each of these questions requires further elaboration. I maintain that the Fall is not an idle element in the Areopagite's vision. I also hold that Jesus is not simply a name to which our author has attached certain "metaphysical" functions. He is rather, for Dionysius as for the NT, the answer given to fallen humanity. He, in his Church, is also the personal reality of every believer. For discussion of these questions, I turn to the next chapter.

Chapter 5

The Mystery and the Mysteries

Christ and the Sacraments as Revelation and Communication of True God and True Man

Introduction

Apart from its opening chapter, the *EH* begins and ends with death. Chapter 2 deals with the catechumen's participation in Christ's death through Baptism while chapter 7 presents us with a meditation on Christian burial. It is also correct, and perhaps more to Dionysius' point, to speak of two births. Baptism is the divine birth (θεία γέννησις) which marks the beginning of Christian existence, the ground of our being in, and growth into, the truly existing.[1] Death and burial, on the other hand, signify for the Christian simply the end of earthly struggles. Toward that end the believer goes in hope of the resurrection of the "members of Christ."[2] The latter is the fulfillment of Baptism's "divine birth," "the sacred re-birth [παλιγγενεσία]"[3] of the general resurrection. Linking the two deaths, the bond of the double birth, we find the journey or way (ὁδοποίησις) of our hierarchy.[4]

1. *EH* II.1 392B (69:7 and 14).
2. *EH* VII.1.1 552D–553B (120:13–121:9, esp. 121:1–7).
3. *EH* VII.1.3 556B (122:15).
4. *EH* II.1 392A (69:2).

The ecclesiastical hierarchy is our context, our world, the place of our strivings and the milieu of our encounter with Christ and, through him, with the angels and finally the divine δυνάμεις. Nothing of any validity or truth may be accomplished outside of our hierarchy. It is by way of illustrating this that I will touch on the Fall and the Incarnation before going on to trace the course of the ascent beginning in Baptism and realized, in accordance with the various ranks of the hierarchy, in the sacraments of the Eucharist and consecration of the Chrism.

Our hierarchy realizes and reveals the reality of all and is also the icon of each. Every stage of sanctified human knowing—and unknowing—is present, and represented, in the icon of the Church at worship. Here is the key both to the unity of the *CD* and to the Christian inspiration of the Dionysian vision as a whole. If the macrocosm of the Church is truly reflected in the microcosm of the redeemed human soul, then the difficulties indicated by Hornus and stressed by Vanneste regarding the *CD*'s unity—especially the problem of the *MT*'s relation to the hierarchies—are largely resolved.[5] In part, Hornus unwittingly points toward the answer to his questions in noting at once the "exteriorization" of grace with respect to the hierarchy

---

5. What, Hornus asks ("Quelques réflexions," 38–44), is the relation, if any, between Dionysius' emphasis on direct, "ecstatic" experience of the deity in the *DN* and *MT* and the elsewhere apparently rigid maintenance of the hierarchies? Are the two approaches wholly separate or, in fact, contradictory? Does the visible, human hierarchy correspond exactly to the invisible realities of grace, i.e., does progress in the spiritual life correspond precisely to the literal ascent of the ecclesiastical hierarchy? Vanneste seeks to explain Dionysius on the knowledge of God solely in terms of the *DN* and *MT* without recourse to those principles of theurgy embodied in the *CH* and *EH*, which, he maintains, constitute an entirely separate mode of knowing (*Mystère de Dieu*, 32–35; 196–197). The unity of the *CD* is not only broken but, thus considered in isolation from the hierarchies rather than embedded in them, the *DN-MT* can safely be approached through the virtually exclusive medium of Proclus' thought, raising grave doubts about Dionysius' Christian inspiration (e.g., *Mystère de Dieu*, 17–19). Deprived of its setting within the Church and liturgy Vanneste finds it reasonable to read into the *MT* a "natural mysticism" devoid of any specifically Christian elements, devoid indeed of Christ (*Mystère de Dieu*, 216–217) and expressive instead of a cold, impersonal rationality, "an autonomous and groping ascent of the human spirit towards the absolute" ("Is the Mysticism of Pseudo-Dionysius Genuine?," 304).

and, later, of the "interiorization" of God in Dionysius' mystical theology.[6] What Hornus terms the "exteriorization of grace" in the hierarchies and the "interiorization of God" in Dionysius' passages dealing with the mystical union, i.e., in the *MT* and *DN*, are not to be separated. Both are held within the single icon of our hierarchy—although, admittedly, not without occasional confusion or ambiguity.[7] If, secondly, the unity of soul and world are discovered in the Church, this means in turn that the unity of all discovers itself in Christ. Jesus is neither a "cipher"[8] nor is the deification wrought by and for us in his Church other than the result of his Incarnation.[9] The *CD* is centered in the *EH*, at the altar, and thus in Christ.

We begin this chapter with a discussion of my first point above, specifically: the place of the *MT*, i.e., the mystic ascent, as within the ecclesiastical hierarchy. Dionysius' use of Moses' ascent of Sinai shall be the basis for this chapter's prologue.

1. Sinai: The Image of the Ascent and Type of the Church

In the first chapter of the *MT* we find the following account:

> The divine Moses is bidden first of all to be purified himself, and then to separate himself from such as have not undergone it, and, after every purification, he hears the many-voiced trumpets, he beholds many lights lightening with pure and many-streaming rays. Then, when he has separated from the many, with the chosen priests, he attains to the summit of the divine ascents. And yet in these he still meets not with God, for he sees not him—since he is not to be seen—but the place where he dwells. And this I believe to mean the highest and most divine of the things which are beheld and intuited, and certain basic λόγοι of the things subordinate to him who

6. Hornus, "Quelques réflexions," 56.

7. See chapter 4 (1.2.3., "The Apportionment of Knowledge: A Difficulty") and below (4.1.2.3., "An Abiding Ambiguity").

8. Brons, *Gott und die Seienden*, 125. For the same opinion of Jesus Christ in the *CD* see also Rorem, "The Uplifting Spirituality of Pseudo-Dionysius," 144, and Meyendorff, *Christ in Eastern Christian Thought*, 75–84.

9. Meyendorff, *Christ in Eastern Christian Thought*, 71.

transcends all things, through which is shown his presence which is beyond every notion and transcends the spiritual summits of his most holy places. And then, abandoning both the things beheld and those beholding them, he enters into the truly secret darkness of unknowing, according to which he renounces all perceptions open to knowledge and comes to have his being in him who is altogether untouchable and invisible and beyond all things, and, belonging to nothing else, whether to himself or to another, he is united according to the greater [faculty] by the cessation of all knowledge to him who is wholly unknowable, and, through knowing not at all, knows in a manner beyond mind.[10]

According to Vanneste, the Moses-Sinai typology as well as other "specifically religious elements," such as the invocation of the Trinity opening the treatise, are without any real significance.[11] Moses serves to introduce the logically rigorous system of negations,[12] and the whole passage takes place on the plane of the abstract: "This biblical image taken from Exodus is only a verbal expression of God's transcendent unknowability."[13] It would in fact scarcely appear to be pushing matters too far to see in Dionysius' use of the already traditional image a deliberate deception, the biblical passage, together with "le manteau du pseudonymat," serving to introduce in disguise "une merveilleuse metaphysique de Premier Principe, qui plonge ses racines dans le neoplatonisme."[14]

I maintain that Vanneste is able to discuss the figure of Moses as inconsequential solely because he has previously declared that the *MT* (and *DN*) are unrelated to the treatises on the hierarchies. The "retour cosmique" of the latter[15] bears no relation to the former's "démarche d'une psychologie individuelle et

10. *MT* I.3 1000D–1001A (143:18–144:15).
11. Vanneste, "Théologie mystique," 405.
12. Vanneste, "Doctrine des trois voies," 465.
13. Vanneste, "Is the Mysticism of Pseudo-Dionysius Genuine?," 301–302.
14. Vanneste, *Mystère de Dieu*, 182.
15. Vanneste, "Théologie mystique," 409–410.

autonome."[16] "Theurgy" and "theology" are entirely separate spheres,[17] and Vanneste thus frees himself to consider *MT* and *DN* by themselves.[18] It is a mistaken freedom, the first error being, generally, the sharp separation between individual and cosmos and the second the specific failure to recognize in the use of the Sinai motif more than simply the casual—or even dishonest—reference to a traditional image. If there is indeed a connection between the *MT* and the hierarchies, if Dionysius' mysticism proceeds "from the vision of the world and the Church that he draws from Scripture and the Liturgy,"[19] then his use of Moses and the ascent of Sinai cannot be fortuitous or merely glib. There must be a discernible relationship between Moses, Exodus, and our hierarchy.[20] The connection appears in the text itself of Exodus. The *MT* passage is based on Exodus 19:16-20; 20:18; 24:9-12; 33:9ff.; and 34:29-35. Of these, Dionysius draws primarily from chapters 19 and 24. I cite both in full from the LXX, beginning with 19:16ff.:

> [the people are purified and warned not to touch the Mountain] . . . it came to pass on the third day, when they had drawn near the Mountain, that there were voices and lightnings and a dark cloud on Mount Sinai, and the voice of the trumpet rang mightily, and all the people were frightened in the camp. And Moses led the people out of the camp to the meeting with God, and they were present beneath the Mount . . . and all the people were exceedingly amazed. And the voices of the trumpets, approaching, grew greatly louder. Moses was speaking and God was answering him with his voice. And the Lord descended on the Mountain, on the peak of Mount Sinai; and the Lord called Moses up to the peak of the Mountain and Moses went up.

16. Vanneste, *Mystère de Dieu*, 27.

17. Vanneste, "Is the Mysticism of Pseudo-Dionysius Genuine?" 302; idem, "Théologie mystique," 409.

18. Vanneste, *Mystère de Dieu*, 34–35.

19. See Roques, "Note sur la notion de THEOLOGIA selon le Pseudo-Denys l'Aréopagite," *RAM* (1949): 200–212, at 212.

20. Noted by Rorem, *Symbols*, 140–142; idem, "Moses as the Paradigm."

Let me note the sequence of actions. The people have purified themselves. They are warned not to touch the holy mountain. They are led up to its foot where they see and hear sights and sounds that they cannot fully comprehend, but which Moses does. God comes down upon the peak in a cloud and calls his chosen one, Moses, who ascends alone into the darkness of the holy place. We continue with Exodus 24:9ff.:

> And Moses ascended with Aaron and Nadab and Abbioud and seventy of the elders of Israel. And there they saw the place [τόπος] where the God of Israel was standing; and the area beneath his feet was, as it were, a work of sapphire brick, in purity as the form of the firmament of Heaven . . . and the Lord said to Moses; "Come up to me in the Mountain. . . ." [vv. 15–16:] And Moses went up to the Mountain, and the cloud hid the Mountain. And the glory of God came down upon [it] . . . and the cloud hid it.

Here we find a new element, the chosen few, the elders (πρεσβύτεροι) of Israel who are allowed access to a certain vision of the holy place, the τόπος where God is, but are not invited to go where Moses goes alone, the peak hidden by the cloud. Of other texts we should also note Exodus 20:18-21 where once more the people are given to hear and see the "voice," the "trumpet," and the "lamps" while remaining "afar off" from the peak that Moses ascends alone. Again, we have Exodus 33:9ff. where the column of cloud rests by Moses' tent while God speaks with him and the people worship from outside. Later in the same chapter (vv. 18–23) we find Moses' vision of God: he is given to see the "back of God," "for my face shall no man see and live." Finally, we point to Exodus 34:29-35 where Moses covers his face with a veil to shield the people from his "glorified" countenance, still bright from his proximity to God.

Where is the connection with the hierarchies? The texts' image of a people purified and rendered witnesses to a theophany clothed with the lights, trumpets, voices, smoke, and cloud of the descent upon Sinai, a theophany whose deepest meanings remain yet veiled for them, a people both chosen and gathered about the frontiers of a holy place yet not granted complete entrance within it—such an image must certainly recall to the reader's mind (and how much more so to a Dionysius) the description of the baptized, i.e., purified and illumined laity, we encountered in the last chapter. There, too, we found a chosen and purified people, the Christian λαός, accorded a certain vision of divine things by virtue of their purification yet still standing outside the gates of the holy places, the altar, "peeking at the divine symbols,"[21] the "sensible perfumes," "material lights," and audible "discussions of the sacred teachings"[22] that have been granted them. We discover in the few who are given access into the holy place, the presbyters of Israel, an unmistakable parallel to the orders of the clergy, particularly the priests, gathered about the altar and the hierarch as the seraphim round God,[23] who "behold and hear the divine things clearly revealed to them."[24] In Moses, of course, we see the hierarch, "the inspired and divine man instructed in every sacred knowledge in whom . . . his own hierarchy is accomplished and made known."[25] The references to the "cloud," the "place" of God, and the "firmament" might recall both the altar itself and, particularly, the choirs of angels who are at once the "places where rests the Thearchy"[26] and the "holy minds who . . . are filled full of the secret light . . . [and] who deliver it to us."[27] The nature of Moses' vision, obscured in the darkness, of God's "back" may very likely (although there is no explicit reference to it in the *CD*) have suggested to Dionysius the union with God that is accomplished in and through the δυνάμεις while leaving the essence hidden.[28] In the prophet's descent with radiant though veiled face, again

21. *EH* III.2 428A (81:10–11).
22. *CH* I.3 121C-124A (8:21–9:7).
23. *EH* IV.3.6 480D (100:8–12).
24. *Ep.* VIII.1 1089A (177:4–5).
25. *EH* I.3 373C (66:5–6).
26. *CH* VII.4 212C (32:7–8); see also VII.2 208A (28:20–21).
27. *CH* XV.6 336A (58:8–9); see also Gandillac, 182n. 1.
28. For Exodus 33:18-23 and the essence/energies distinction in patristic thought, see A. de Halleux, "Palamisme et Tradition," *Ir* 48 (1978): 479–493, at 484.

not referred to explicitly by Dionysius, we are reminded of the delivery of sacred things by "the inspired hierarchs in intuitions not obvious to the commonality of the faithful, but . . . rather in sacred symbols" veiled to the majority.[29]

The texts of Exodus to which Dionysius alludes in the *MT* account of Moses and Sinai provide us with nothing less than a sketch of the ecclesiastical hierarchy. All participation in sacred knowing, and "unknowing," every union with the divine that we may be given to experience here below, all is to be understood as realized within the context of our hierarchy. Recalling the passages from Exodus and their parallels, this in turn means specifically within the frame of the Church's worship. Sinai is a type of the Church within whose liturgy the mystical union here below is signified and accomplished.[30]

Our worship is also both the icon of the soul's union with God and that which uniquely enables the union. Of this union Roques writes that "il doit être rare et bref . . . n'est accessible qu' à une catégorie de chrétiens privilegiée et particulièrement sainte."[31] Here-below, short of the eschaton, it must constitute "un sommet privilegié, un éclair, un instant."[32] The category of "privileged and particularly holy" believers and the "privileged summit" appear to me to refer to—as typified in—the person and office of the hierarch. Moses is identified with the office at least twice. In *EH* V we hear of "those who were sacredly initiated as to that sacred tabernacle [of the OT] by Moses, the first and chief [ἥγεμων] of the hierarchs according to the Law."[33] Again in the

29. *EH* I.4 376C (67:12–14).

30. The texts from Exodus, esp. chapters 19 and 24, are themselves surely connected to and reflect the later worship of Israel at the Temple in Jerusalem. The trumpets recall the shofar and the thick, dark cloud hiding the glory, the darkness within the holy of holies, the place of the *kabod* (cf., e.g., 1 Kgs 8). See M. Noth, *Exodus, a Commentary* (Philadelphia: Westminster, 1962), 11–17, and R. Clement, *The Temple* (Philadelphia: Fortress, 1965), 17–27 and 100–122.

31. Roques, *L'univers*, 328.

32. Roques, "Note sur THEOLOGIA," 211. On the importance of the "instant" or "sudden" for Dionysius, see my discussion of *Ep.* III and the ἐξαίφνης in chapter 1.6.

33. *EH* V.1.2 501C (105:11–12).

same chapter, in a passage discussing the sacrament of ordination and worth quoting at length, we find parallels between our
bishops and both Moses and Christ:

> Declaring the mystery, the hierarch cries aloud the sacred proc-
> lamations of the consecrations and those consecrated, in as
> much as the God-loving initiator into sacred things is declarer
> of divine election, himself leading the ordinands to priestly
> consecration not by his own grace, but moved by God to every
> hierarchic sanctification. Thus Moses, the initiator into the
> sacred things of the Law, neither brought his brother, Aaron,
> to priestly consecration nor deemed him even a lover of God
> or of a priestly nature until he was moved to this by God—by
> God the source of all consecration—and accomplished in sa-
> cred manner the priestly consecration. And indeed our own
> first and thearchic initiator into sacred things—for Jesus, the
> lover of mankind, became even this for our sakes—glorified
> not himself . . . wherefore he also thus led the disciples to
> priestly consecration [calling on the Spirit to act, a citation of
> Acts 1:4ff.].[34]

There are three other texts besides *MT* I which treat of the mystical
vision or union with God, "l'état théopathétique." The first is the
vision of Isaiah in Isaiah 6:1ff. This takes up the whole of *CH* XIII
and seeks to explain the manner whereby the prophet "learned
. . . that the divine is incomparably established above every visible and invisible power"[35]—i.e., precisely above every negation
and affirmation,[36] the vision of Moses. The second text, from the
DN, describes the vision of Dionysius' master, Hierotheos:

> When, as you [Timothy] know, we and he [Hierotheos] and
> many of our holy brothers came together for the sight of the
> life-originating and God-bearing body, both James . . . and
> Peter . . . were there, too. And, after we had seen, it seemed
> good to us for all the hierarchs to hymn the infinite virtue and

34. *EH* V.3.5 512BC (111:26–112:12).
35. *CH* XIII.4 304C (47:4–5).
36. Gandillac, 157–157n. 1.

goodness of the thearchic weakness as each one was able. It was he [Hierotheos] who, second only to the theologians [Apostles] themselves, prevailed over all the other holy initiates, being wholly transported, wholly taken out of himself, suffering communion with the things hymned [in such fashion] that all who heard and saw him, who know him—or, rather, knew him not judged him to be rapt of God.[37]

The third vision is that of Carpus, bishop in Crete, whose tradition it was never to celebrate the liturgy without first having experienced a vision,[38] and who also was provided a vision of Christ "suddenly" during his midnight prayers.[39] Besides the fact that these visions deal with "hierarchs" and concern the same rare experience of God's transcendence, they also have a common context in public worship. They take place within (or, as with Carpus, just before) a "cultic" setting, be the latter that of the OT or of the NT Church. Isaiah is granted a vision of God upon the throne of glory within the Temple of Jerusalem (Isa 6:1-4), just as it is within the Temple that the prophet receives his purification and his ministry (vv. 5-9). Similarly, whether in reference to the Dormition of the Virgin Mary,[40] or, as one scholar would have it, originally to the Eucharist itself,[41] it is clear that Hierotheos' vision takes place within the Church's worship.[42] Carpus' visions take place before the celebration of the Eucharist, but in preparation for it. The Church at prayer is the reality of Sinai. It both typifies the individual soul's union with God—a point to which I return below—and itself constitutes the milieu

37. *DN* III.2 681C–684A (141:5–14).

38. *Ep.* VIII.6 1097BC (188:11–14).

39. *Ep.* VIII.6 1100AF (190:5ff.). Rorem, *Symbols*, and Louth, *Denys*, mention Moses, Hierotheos, and Carpus, though not Isaiah.

40. See the Scholiast, PG IV 236C, and Pachymeres' commentary, PG III 689C.

41. See the article by G. Every, "Dionysius the Pseudo-Areopagite," in *One Yet Two* (ed. B. Pennington; Kalamazoo: Cistercian, 1976), 85ff.

42. See again the Scholiast, PG IV 257BC, and Pachymeres, PG III 689D–692A.

within which that union is made possible.[43] One cannot find in the *CD* any encounter with God that is outside the general frame of the σύμβολον given in our "hierarchy," the meeting place of heaven and earth.

A second point concerns the ὑποθετικοὶ λόγοι that Moses contemplates, the τόπος θεοῦ. Following Lossky,[44] I identify these λόγοι with the divine reasons or wills underlying creation. Furthermore, I understand them as identical to the "holy principles [ἀρχαί] of things accomplished"[45] on and around the Church's altar. Recalling the discussion of λόγος/ἀναλογία, in the preceding chapters, I return to the fact that for Dionysius the true contemplation, the real φυσικὴ θεωρία, consists of the contemplation and science of hierarchy. In our case, this must refer to the Scripture and, yet more clearly, to the rites of the Church. It is through this contemplation that we arrive at the intuition of the angelic hierarchies, the "places" or "forecourts" of God, and finally of the uncreated δυνάμεις that irradiate all creation in order to bring the creature to a share in the Creator. This process finds its fulfillment in the "philanthropy" of Jesus.

Stiglmayr is certainly correct in seeing the Areopagite's mysticism as "on the whole . . . of a sacral character."[46] The mystery of divine love revealed in Christ, the revelation of the single "ray" upholding and penetrating the worlds of humans and angels, is discerned in the forms of the liturgy established by Scripture and adapted to the several capacities of each.[47] The whole mystery is also discovered in each sacred action, in each "mystery" of the Church, although the action may be differently received insofar as each believer's ability (ἀναλογία) or degree of advancement in

---

43. See Roques, *L'univers*, 328.

44. Vanneste, "Théologie mystique," 218; see also von Semmelroth, "Θεολογία συμβολική," 3.

45. *EH* III.2 428A (81:12).

46. Stiglmayr, "Aszese und Mystik des sog. Dionysius Areopagita," *Schol* 2 (1927): 161–207, at 206.

47. See the article by Sheldon-Williams, "The Holy Hierotheos," *SP* 8 (1966): esp. 115.

sacred truth also differs. This principle is spelled out in the following passage concerning the sacrament of the Chrism:

> Neither is the visible consecration of the myron invisible or
> not communicated to those about the hierarch [the clergy] but
> . . . penetrates also unto them, establishing [them in] the con-
> templation which is beyond the many, sacredly veiled by them
> and separated in hierarchic manner from the multitude. For
> the ray of the all-holy things shines purely and immediately
> upon the inspired men, as on ones who are akin to the spiri-
> tual, perfuming in unveiled manner their spiritual percep-
> tions. It does not, however, proceed in a similar manner to the
> subordinates [i.e., laity], but by them [the clergy], as secret
> contemplations of the spiritual . . . it is veiled under winged
> enigmas, through which sacred enigmas the well-ordered
> ranks of the subordinates are led up to the sacred measure
> proper to them.[48]

Again in chapter 5 of the *EH*, we find the same multivalent nature
of the symbols encountered in our hierarchy. Here the reference is
to Scripture as read or sung within the context of liturgical action:

> The scriptural hymns and readings . . . hatch the imperfect
> into life-bearing adoption to sonship, effecting the conversion
> of those who are accursedly poisoned, removing the hostile
> enchantment and terror . . . and giving them to understand
> in appropriate manner the summit of the deiform condition
> and power according to which they instead terrify the oppos-
> ing powers [the demons] and arrive at the healing of others,
> not only possessing the activity of the theomimetic immobility
> with regard to the hostile terrors, but bestowing it as well;
> and, for those who have already passed over from worse
> things to a holy mind, they [Scriptures] instill a holy state of
> being . . . they perfectly purify those still in need of becoming
> altogether pure; and they lead the holy to the divine icons and
> to both contemplation of and communion in them; finally, they
> give feast to the completely holy ones, through blessed and

---

48. *EH* IV.3.2 476BC (97:8–18).

spiritual visions filling full their likeness to the One and making them one.[49]

Acting at once on many levels, their depths revealed to and deifying the few who are capable of and open to further ascent, veiled yet still edifying to the many, in all respects and in every instance realizing divine Providence in the world, the rites and sacred texts of our hierarchy present themselves as an ordered ascent from ignorance and sin into the knowledge of, participation in, and union with God.

The "singleness" of the ascent leads us to a final consideration of Moses' ascent in the *MT*. We discover in the ἀνάβασις of Sinai the type of the individual's ἀναγωγή that our hierarchy both embraces, as our God-given context or world, and reveals as the icon of the perfected human being. Moses first purifies himself and then separates himself from the impure. Secondly, he hears and sees the heavenly voices and lights. He experiences illumination in the vision of the λόγοι underlying creation. Finally, completing the triad, he is taken wholly outside of himself by means of that movement and gift of union with the divine energies with which I dealt in discussing the creature's ἕνωσις, the latter being the deification that is the goal of all hierarchy.[50] Every stage of the individual believer's ascent to God is both typified in, and enabled by, the hierarchy. The "mountain of God" is the Church itself, the "meeting place" of heaven and earth whose ascents, from ignorance to knowledge, from sin to perfection, from separation to union, are the allotted task and sanctifying grace respectively demanded of and bestowed upon every Christian believer.

Summary: Against Vanneste I assert that Dionysius' *Mystical Theology* belongs as much to our hierarchy as the analyses of the sacraments. We hear the words of Scripture and, simultaneously confronted with the moving imagery of the rites, are called upon to cooperate with divine grace in employing at one and the same time the exercise of the symbolical, positive, and negative

49. *EH* IV.3.3 476D–477B (97:28–98:13).
50. See *EH* I.4 376B (66:20–67:6) and *CH* III.1 164D (17:3–5).

theologies[51] in order thus to be led up to "the γνῶσις of beings as they truly are,"[52] to grow conformed to the divine, and ultimately, still within the frame of the Liturgy, to be united with God. The ἀναγωγή moves from the visible world (our hierarchy) to the invisible one (the angels), from the latter to the powers of God discussed in the *DN*, and at last to union with God (the *MT*). At no point, though, do we ever depart from our proper context, our hierarchy. Our journey is at once outward, beyond the realm of sense and finally of creation itself to God, and inward, away from exterior things to the depths of the soul and to the point therein— the "altar"—where the Creator stoops to meet his creature. The whole of the *CD* is an entry that is always directed toward, and always the experience of, the meeting of sensible and intelligible, created and uncreated, realized once for all in the Incarnation, typified and made actual at the altar of the Church.

2. The Mystery: God's Dispensation in Christ

Before dealing specifically with Dionysius on the incarnate Christ, we must first consider briefly what our author believes to be the alternative to our hierarchy. We therefore leave the precincts of the Church.

2.1. Outside the Doors: The Fall and the Devil

The world outside is a shadow reality, fallen. We find Dionysius' main description of the Fall given in chapter 3 of the *EH*:

> The life which is most full of passions and the termination of corrupting death took up human nature after the latter had senselessly fallen away in the beginning from the divine good things. For, consequent to its destructive abandonment of the truly good and the transgression in paradise of the holy ordinance . . . it was given over to its own inclinations and to the

51. See the article by Roques, "Symbolisme et théologie négative," 107–108, and "Introduction," *CH* xxix.
52. *EH* I.3 376A (66:16–19).

bewitching and hostile deceits of the adversary, to those things which are the opposite of the divine good things. Whence it wretchedly received the mortal in place of the eternal, possessing its proper origin in corruptible [i.e., mortal] generations. . . . Rather, indeed, falling away by its own will from the divine and untaught life, it was brought to the opposite extreme, the many-passioned alienation . . . being subordinated to the ruinous and evil-working multiplicities . . . it fell piteously into the danger of destruction and of non-existence.[53]

Let me note the characteristics of the Fall and of fallen existence as outlined in this passage. The Fall took place in "the beginning [ἀρχῆθεν]." It was the result of an act of deliberate choice, an exercise of free will (ἐθελουσίως), and a departure (ἀποστασία) from the truly good which saw as its inevitable result the handing-over of our nature to the dominion of false goods, of lies and deceit, of the rule of the devil and to dissolution and death. At this point, let me recall my discussion of the θεοειδής in chapter 3 (2.3.). The latter is the capacity in created nature for growth into, cooperation, and union with the uncreated. It is the potential for participation (μετουσία) in God's beatitude through the channeling of our energies, our motion, into the single theandric activity of love that is at once the proper use of our natural powers and the reality of grace. In this account of the Fall we discover precisely the opposite: rather than a channelling we find a scattering of powers. "The variableness of many passions" replaces the unifying force of the "motor" of love. Rather than a dependence on the unique source of life and love, of goodness, humanity is given over to brokenness and division, to the clatter of "multiplicities" and factions both inside and outside its being, to an apostasy that ends in the last rejection one may make, that of life itself. The One, and therefore the ἐνοειδής that is given the creature to realize through participation in the One, is being and life. The alternative is the slide into a "multiplicity" that results finally in non-being.

If the last two sentences have a Neoplatonic ring, then it might be well for us to recall, in connection with the theme of

53. *EH* III.3.11 440C–441A (90:16–91:8).

"multiplicity" and its equation here with evil and unreality,[54] the words of the Gadarene demoniac: "My name is legion, for we are many" (Mark 5:9). The biblical passage directs us to an element of the Dionysian scheme quite lacking in the systems of the philosophers.[55] Over and within the rule of the passions and their "many motions,"[56] this is the force that governs in a sense that loss of balance and dissipation of the proper interior ordering of reason (λόγος), irritability (θυμός), and desire (ἐπιθυμία) in the soul,[57] which is an integral part of the post-lapsarian state.[58] This final and personal element is, of course, the devil, the "genius" behind all loss and division, the Adversary, the first of creation to embrace evil as "the desire for that which is not,"[59] to lust for the "seeming good,"[60] and thus to father the lie. They are his "proper inclinations," his "bewitching and destructive deceits" to which we have been given over, his rule or power (κράτος) that prevails against us,[61] that drags us inevitably to death, and from which

54. The term πλῆθος and derivatives are used 53 times in the CD (see van den Daehle, *Indices*, 116) almost invariably in a negative sense; for example, ἡ δαιμόνια πλῆθος of *DN* IV.18 716A. By contrast, the terms ποικιλία (26 times, *Indices*, 117) and ἑτερότης (10 times, *Indices*, 67), as expressive of the providentially intended diversity of creation, carry a positive connotation. The one exception is *DN* XI.5 952D (220:18), a rebellious "otherness" which accords with the sense of "manyness" as a rejection of God and a characteristic of the demons.

55. For the Neoplatonists, evil is generally seen as an inevitable—if regrettable—concomitant of the cosmic "dance," see *Enn.* IV.4.32–33 and 39.

56. *DN* XI.5 953A (220:22–221:2). For Dionysius' invariably negative use of the term πάθος, see also *EH* III.3.11 441B (91:21–22); VII.1.3 556A (122:8); *DN* IV.19 717A (164:10–11); XI.5 953A (221:2); *MT* IV 1040D (148:5); and *Ep.* X 1117B (209:5–6).

57. See esp. *Ep.* VIII.3–4 1093A and C (182:6–8 and 183:11) on Demophilus, the monk whose interior hierarchy (of the soul) is not in order.

58. See particularly the "weakness [ἀσθένεια]" or "lack [ἔλλειψις]" of will and the exercise of will mentioned in *DN* IV.23 725B (171:13–16); IV.24 728A (172:16); IV.31 732B (176:11); IV.32 732D (177:10–15); and esp. IV.35 733D–736A (179:5–13).

59. *DN* IV.23 725C (172:10–11); also IV.34 733D (179:3–4).

60. *DN* IV.20 720C.

61. *EH* III.3.11 441B (91:15–16); see Heb 2:1.

we, powerless, stand in need of redemption. Together with his angels,[62] the "prince of this world" is the last, and necessary, element in the Dionysian sketch of the Fall.

And that sketch is a traditional one. It is the vision of a kind of cosmic disintegration presided over by destructive powers of a "spiritual" nature. We may thus recall the phrasing of Romans 5:12. "As through one man Sin came into the world, and Death through Sin, so Sin spread to all men, on account of which [Death] all have sinned." I insist on the traditional aspects of his scheme as against those of Dionysius' modern critics who see in the Areopagite's version of "original sin" and its consequences an insufficient appreciation for the "radical" change brought by the Fall and thus a dangerous dilution of the Christian Gospel of redemption. This argument is advanced with particular force by Julius Gross, as well as by Stiglmayr, von Semmelroth, Brons, K. P. Wesche, and, more recently, by Arthur and Mazzucchi.[63] The main thrust of Gross' argument lies in his assertion that, for Dionysius, "the soul can only be impaired . . . through mistaken and disordered motions. Mistaken [only because] disordered." In fact, however, nothing "essential" occurred through the fall. Freedom of will remains and thus there is no "inseparable division" between God and humanity. The divine "light" is still there to be grasped through the exercise of will and "a Savior in the Christian sense appears superfluous."[64] Baptism becomes purely a matter of forgiveness of personal sins in the adult while children

62. The terms δαίμων and δαιμόνιος appear 18 times (*Indices*, 42). Another, and often equivalent term for the demonic is ἐναντίος, used over 50 times (*Indices*, 57). See, for example, *EH* I.3 376A (66:15–16); II.3.6 404A (77:21–22); and III.3.11 440C (90:20–21).

63. J. Gross, "Ur- und Erbsünde in der Theosophie des Pseudo-Dionysius Areopagita," *ZRG* 4 (1952): 32–42; Stiglmayr, "Die Lehre von den Sakramenten"; von Semmelroth, "Erlösung und Erlöser," 321–324; Brons, *Gott und die Seienden*, 57–77; K. P. Wesche, "A Reply to Hieromonk Alexander's 'Reply,'" *SVTQ* 34 (1990): 324–327, at 326; Arthur, *Ps.-Dionysius as Polemicist*, 196; Mazzucchi, "Damascio, autore del *Corpus Dionysiacum*," 725.

64. Gross, "Ur- und Erbsünde," 36; 39–40; 37. Cf. Arthur, *Ps.-Dionysius as Polemicist*, 196: "Dionysius . . . more or less eliminated the Incarnation, Cross and Atonement"; Mazzucchi, "Damascio, autore del *Corpus Dionysiacum*,"

are baptized solely (citing *EH* VII.3.11 568C) in order to be raised in the Christian life. Dionysius' optimism, therefore, coupled with his "starkly metaphysical system" (Gross points particularly to the frequency of "sun" and "light" imagery as betokening a kind of metaphysical determinism in the *CD*) amounts to an effective betrayal of the Christian Gospel, a blunting of the "fine edge" of Augustinian pessimism, and so a major contribution to the necessity of the Reformation.[65]

It is clearly with the latter two statements that we arrive at the heart of the problem. Leaving aside the fact that, of course, there was no "Augustinian pessimism" in Dionysius' theological world of discourse to be "blunted"—it is quite possible that the author of the *CD* had never even heard of the great bishop of Hippo; he had certainly never read him—von Semmelroth's complaint that the "weak point" in all Greek patristic writings, "particularly characteristic in Dionysius," lies in the lack of a strong natural/supernatural distinction,[66] sums up the difficulty. This criticism bases itself on a tradition of NT interpretation generally, in particular of Romans 5, that is neither that of our author nor indeed of the Greek (especially Alexandrian) tradition generally. It is neither my intent to comment in detail on the effects of an intepretation of the ἐφ᾿ ᾧ of Romans 5:12 as referring to the person of Adam rather than to death, its nearest antecedent, and the consequent vision of human nature as itself radically fallen, nor the prevailing and very different understandings of the same passage among the Greek Fathers.[67] I do, however, believe it necessary to point to this

---

725: there is no place in the *CD* for the Christian understanding of evil and sin "qui hanno richiesto l'atroce redenzione della croce."

65. Gross, "Ur- und Erbsünde," 42.

66. Von Semmelroth, "Erlösung und Erlöser," 322; see also 324.

67. For a discussion of these matters, see the articles by Romanides, "Original Sin according to St. Paul," *SVSQ* 14 (1955–1956): 5–28; S. Lyonnet, "Le sens de ἐφ᾿ ᾧ en Rom V,12 et l'exegèse des Pères Grecs," *Bib* 36 (1955): 436–456. See also Meyendorff, *Byzantine Theology* (London: Mowbrays, 1974), 143–146. For a more complete analysis, see Romanides, *The Ancestral Sin: A Comparative Study of the Sin of Our Ancestors Adam and Eve According to the Paradigms and Doctrines of the First- and Second-Century Church and the Augustinian Formulation of Original Sin* (Ridgewood, NJ: Zephyr, 2002); D. Weaver, "From Paul

fundamental difference between two long-established currents of interpretation within the Christian tradition in order to arrive at a just evaluation of the *CD*. Dionysius is not an Augustinian, quite so, but to fault him for not being so is unfair. For him there is indeed no strict natural/supernatural distinction, rather nature presupposes grace. To put the matter another way, one which relates to what I have already written concerning the nature of image and symbol, ideally, i.e., as intended by its Maker, creation should be one with revelation. That ontology is not directly transparent, as it were, to theology, is not the result of God's will but of an alien element whose distorting and disruptive activity has broken and obscured the original transparency. It is the vision of this original "state of nature," wherein grace was never a *superadditum* but instead a prerequisite, that Dionysius specifically understands as restored to us in our hierarchy, and in this he shares with other representatives of the Greek Christian tradition. It is unfair to say of his account of the Fall that it is purely a matter of a decision for the "manyness" of the passions rather than the unity of God,[68] or that it requires for its correction simply another act of free will coupled with the aid of an exemplarism provided by the teaching and person of Christ.[69] This is simply to ignore that irrational power of evil, possessing its παρυπόστασις first and primarily in the person of the devil and his angels, to which Dionysius gives due credit as the effectively ruling power of the world "outside the doors," and whose reign he sees (being here perhaps rather more in harmony with Paul than was Augustine) as effectively barring the way to a restoration of our proper and divinely willed participation in God. Salvation is not simply a matter of our choice. The Fall requires our liberation from an active, hostile, and dominating power. While this understanding

---

to Augustine: Romans 5:12 in Early Christian Exegesis," *SVTQ* 27 (1983): 187–206; idem, "The Exegesis of Romans 5:12 among the Greek Fathers and Its Implications for the Doctrine of Original Sin: The 5th–12th Centuries," *SVTQ* 29 (1985): 133–159; 231–257.

68. Von Semmelroth, "Erlösung und Erlöser," 371; see also Stiglmayr, "Die Lehre von den Sakramenten," 302–303.

69. Von Semmelroth, "Erlösung und Erlöser," 375.

of the fallen state is not, save for the passage cited at the beginning of this section, dwelt on at length by Dionysius, it remains nonetheless a fundamental component of his thought.

Let me summarize. What is it that we discover in the world "outside the doors?" We find a slavery to "principalities and powers," whose "deceits" and "spells" hold us bound to passions and "seeming" realities—the "evil-working multiplicities" of our present world—and who thus act to prevent our attainment to any true knowledge or communion in God, and so doom us to diminution and final extinction. What is needed therefore is the revelation of a mode of being, a πολιτεία, which will at once enable us to achieve mastery over our divided inclinations so that, freed from their turbulence, we may gain a clear vision of the truly existing, gather our powers, and follow that "vector" implanted in our nature whose final resting place lies in the transcendent Creator. More than this, we require the introduction of a power superior to the ones now in authority over us, one which is able to break their domination, "loose" the claims of that death to which we have been given over, and so restore us, through the activity of its benevolent rule and universal authority, to that capacity for union with the divine which can never know its fulfillment "outside the doors."

2.2. The Incarnation: The Restoration of Our Being in Jesus and the Ground of the Ecclesiastical Hierarchy

Dionysius' chief account of the Incarnation comes immediately following his account of the Fall:

> The infinite philanthropy of the thearchic Goodness did not abandon the Providence which it benevolently works on our behalf, but entered without sin into a true participation of everything which is ours, and being united with our lowliness . . . bestowed thus communion with itself upon us as upon kin . . . cancelling the power over us not by might, as overpowering it, but, according to the saying mystically delivered to us, by judgment and righteousness . . . it freed the dwelling place of the soul from most accursed passions and corrupting

stains through the complete salvation of our essence which had fallen, showing us a heavenly ascent and an inspired citizenship.[70]

At the very beginning of the *EH* (I.1), Dionysius is careful to stress the unique and all-predominating person and function of Jesus, "the most divine [Θεαρχικότατος] and super-essential mind, source, and essence, and most divine power of every hierarchy, sanctification, and divine work."[71] It is Jesus who, "by means of the love both drawn up towards him and drawing us up," frees us from the powers to which we were subject, gathers together our brokenness, accomplishes perfection in us, grants us imitation of the angels through the exercise of the priesthood, gives the vision of himself and of the Thearchy, and who renders us finally sharers in the knowledge of divine things and makes us both "consecrated and consecrators, in the form of light and workers of divine things, perfected and workers of perfection."[72] It is in the person of Jesus, then, that we discover the answer to those needs just outlined: the introduction into our world of a power superior to the "principalities" of "this world" and able to restore us to communion with ourselves, with the angels, and so finally with God. In Jesus we discover our "approach" or "access [προσαγωγή]" to God.[73]

Why and how Jesus? I return to the passage opening this section. The same "infinite philanthropy" of God that made us has itself entered into the marrow and sinews of our being. The gift of communion with God, and thus the "cancellation" of that power that had assumed command over us through the Fall, can only have come about through the fact that Jesus is, himself, God. Dionysius, as Roques notes,[74] makes no distinction between Jesus and the Word.

---

70. *EH* III.3.11 440C–441C (91:8–23); see in the NT, Heb 4:15.
71. *EH* I.1 372A (63:12–64.2).
72. *EH* I.1 372B (64:13–14).
73. *EH* IV.3.12 484D (103:7); see also *CH* I.1 121A (7:11).
74. Roques, *L'univers*, 320.

> For the one and simple and secret [divinity] of Jesus, the most
> divine Word, through becoming man for our sakes, by means
> of goodness and philanthropy proceeded without change to
> the composite and visible . . . [thus] having united in the
> highest degree the lowly things proper to our mode of being
> to his divine ones . . . we are framed accurately together with
> him [recall Colossians] as members to a body.[75]

While the problem of Dionysius' precise relation to, or perhaps
better, deliberate avoidance of, the christological debates of the
late fifth century[76] does not lie within the scope of my essay, I note
in passing the appearance in this passage of both the Severian
term σύνθετος and of two of the four negative adverbs qualifying
the Chalcedonian definition of the hypostatic union, ἀναλλοιότως
and later on ἀσυγχύτως.[77] These indicate what I take to be Dionysius' consistent effort to steer clear of the impassioned arguments
troubling the Church of his era.[78] The "negative" approach to the
mystery of the Incarnation is his preferred approach, inasmuch
as that mystery is both "ineffable with regard to all discourse and
unknowable to any intelligence, even to the first of the angels,"
and, as he goes on to declare, "we have received his taking-on the
essence of a man in a mystical way . . . and of the other things,
as many as refer to the supernatural physiology of Jesus, we are
ignorant."[79] We are, though, missing the treatises in which Dionysius tells us he deals at greater length with the Incarnation. In

75. *EH* III.3.12 444AB (92:21–93:3).

76. For a discussion of the problem, see Roques, *L'univers*, 315–317.

77. *EH* III.3.12 444A for σύνθετος and ἀναλλοιότως (92:23), and 3.13 444C
(93:16) for ἀσυγχύτως.

78. The degree to which he succeeded may be noted in the fact that both
Chalcedonians and non-Chalcedonians laid claim to him; see Stiglmayr,
"Aufkommen der Ps.-Dionysischen Schriften," 39–63. Strothmann, however, has argued for Dionysius as a Syrian Monophysite on the basis of our
author's insistence on the importance of the sacrament of the Chrism. The
latter was, according to Strothmann, a rite that was considerably stressed by
Monophysite circles as being both of Apostolic origins (hence, perhaps, Dionysius' pseudonym) and an avowal of Jesus' divinity; see esp. Strothmann,
Myron-Weihe, xliii–xlvi and lvi–lx.

79. *DN* II.9 648A (133:5–12).

the case of the passage just cited he refers us to the *Theological Elements*, and elsewhere to the *Outlines of Divinity*.[80]

What does remain clear, however, is his insistence that "Jesus, who is above all things, has been joined to everything human,"[81] to the degree, indeed, that "the super-essential cause of the heavenly beings . . . does not transgress the human good order which he has himself chosen and ordained, but rather obediently submits himself to it," i.e., here to the superior ministry of the angels.[82] "The divinity [θεότης] of Jesus" is unquestionable, the "cause of all,"[83] and yet he who is "beyond essence became essence"[84]:

> above man, having truly become man, henceforward indeed [he] works not the things of God after the manner of God, nor human things after the manner of humanity, but [as] God having become man, he has administered to us [ἡμῖν πεπολιτευμένος] a certain new, divine-human activity.[85]

The brokenness resulting from the Fall and the rule of the foreign power, the devil, have themselves been broken. Through the Incarnation the way is again opened to sharing in the life and activity of divinity, to μετουσία—and it is instructive to note that this term is, on three specific occasions in the *CD*, connected with the name and person of Jesus[86]—and cooperation, συνέργεια.

The new life comes to us through the sacraments. In our hierarchy we find not only the perfecting priesthood that Jesus has established, to which he leads us as our "divine and first consecrator,"[87] but, in addition, within and behind the words and actions coming down to us in his name, we are brought to recognize Jesus himself, "our most divine altar . . . in whom

---

80. E.g., *DN* XI.5 953AB (221:10–12).

81. *Ep.* IV 1072A (160:3–4).

82. *CH* IV.4 181C (23:11–13).

83. *DN* II.9 648C (134:7).

84. *Ep.* IV 1072B (160:9).

85. *Ep.* IV 1072C (161:7–10). I translate the ἡμῖν as "to us" rather than "among us." See my discussion of *Ep.* I–V in chapter 1.6.

86. *CH* I.3 124A (9:5–6); VII.2 208C (29:12–13); and *EH* III.3.13 444C (93:19).

87. *EH* V.3.5 512C (112:8–10).

. . . being consecrated and mystically consumed, we have our approach."[88] "In whom" because he has taken our humanity on himself and "sacrifices [or sanctifies, ἀγιάζει] himself on our behalf." He is our "approach" because the "symbols" of our hierarchy—the sacraments, priesthood, Scripture and ultimately the divinized humanity of Christ himself (of which the former are in fact the extension[89])—render us sharers in the life and grace and activity of his divinity: "but receiving in tranquility the beneficent rays of Christ, who is truly God and beyond Good, let us through them be led up in light to his divine good works."[90]

In the ecclesiastical hierarchy the division worked by the Fall is overcome. United in Christ, we are united to our immediate superiors, the angels, and, together with them, are called to co-operate with God "according to the Providence of Jesus who works all in all and makes Peace ineffable and fore-ordained from eternity, who has both reconciled us to himself and, in himself, to the Father."[91] The reconciliation worked through the Incarnation of Jesus is, as Roques writes, a double one, joining "d'une part, la hiérarchie humaine à la hiérarchie angélique, et qui, de l'autre, récapitule en les achevant . . . toutes les hiérarchies dans l'unité divine. Christ est partout, il fait tout, il éduque, il sanctifie tout."[92]

If our redemption and reconciliation are worked once and for all in Christ and are presently realized here-below through the agency of the ecclesiastical hierarchy that constitutes his presence among us, and if, after the Fall, our "approach to the Father" has been restored to us in Jesus and through his body, the Church, then we should also recognize that for Dionysius, uninterested in the processes of history as he generally is, this reconciliation did not come about immediately. It is the crown of a process of redemption discovered in the sacred history of Israel, a process of which, however briefly and perhaps inadequately, he does take

---

88. *EH* IV.3.12 484D (103:4–7).
89. See *EH* III.3.9 437C (89:6–10) and IV.3.10 484A (102:1–7).
90. *Ep.* VIII.1 1085C (173:11–13).
91. *DN* XI.5 953AB (221:8–10).
92. Roques, *L'univers*, 322.

note.[93] The ecclesiastical hierarchy did not spring full-blown into the darkness of the fallen world. It was anticipated. We find the history of this anticipation noted a number of times in the *EH* in what Dionysius calls the "hierarchy according to the [OT] Law [ἡ κατὰ νόμον ἱεραρχία]." Following Hebrews (κατὰ τὸ λόγιον—note especially Heb 5:12ff. and 10:1ff.), he understands the "dim and unclear" symbols of the legal hierarchy, their particular initiation or sacrament (τελετή), as the preparation (ἀναγωγὴ) for the "spiritual worship" of the ecclesiastical hierarchy. The latter shares in the celestial hierarchy through its "spiritual contemplations" (νοεραὶ θεωρίαι), and in the legal hierarchy in that, like the latter, it is rendered variously in perceptible symbols and through symbols leads to the divine.[94] The "approach" began in the law given by Moses, the "first initiate and leader [ἥγεμων] of the hierarchs according to the Law,"[95] and was fulfilled in Christ, the first hierarch of the ecclesiastical hierarchy and himself the source and bond of all hierarchies. We note as well those passages in the *CH* that Dionysius devotes to the recollection and explanation of elements in the OT dispensation, the tutorial role of the angels and the παιδεία (a term that usually means "discipline"[96]) of the old dispensation. These were given to lead to the revelation given in Jesus and participation in the knowledge of "his theurgic lights." The latter, mediated to us by means of "sensible symbols" and the variety of the sacred Scriptures, are at once the property of angelic being and the reality of our beatitude.[97]

Given the Incarnation and the "approach" to the Father given us in Jesus, how do we actually set about our reconciliation and avail ourselves of this entry? How do we leave the darkness outside to make our way to the light "inside" the doors?

---

93. Brons (*Gott und die Seienden*, 60–64) finds Dionysius totally inadequate on this point.

94. *EH* V.1.2 501BD (105:3–16).

95. *EH* V.1.2 501BD (103:11–12).

96. See esp. *CH* XV.5 333C (55:13–14), and *Ep.* IX.6 1113B (206:11).

97. *CH* VII.2 208BC (29:7–18).

3. The Mysteries: From the Doors to the Altar

The sacraments of Baptism, Eucharist, and the Holy Chrism occupy Dionysius' attention in chapters 2 to 4 of the *EH*. These three mysteries represent a certain progression, beginning with the proselyte outside the Church and concluding with a meditation on the mystery of the altar, and on the heart of that mystery, Jesus Christ. Chapters 5 and 6, on the nature of the priestly ranks and the orders of the laity respectively, follow a descending pattern while at the same time deriving from that central mystery, having their being in it, and looking toward it as their τέλος. At the very beginning of the *EH*, Dionysius notes that this mystery is the whole purpose of our hierarchy. We have been given "the sacred operation of the priesthood" through Jesus in order that

> we may . . . become closer to the beings above us [the angels]
> . . . enabled [by Jesus] to become consecrated and consecra-
> tors . . . in the form of light and workers of divine things,
> perfected and workers of perfection.[98]

It is through the sacraments that we are called to incorporation into, and conformity to, Christ. They are his "mysteries," reflections of his "theurgies."[99] Our hierarchy is designed to bring us

---

98. *EH* I.1 372B.

99. For the term μυστήριον as signifying the Incarnation, see: *CH* IV.4 181B (22:23); *DN* II.3 640C (126:2); and *Ep.* III 1069 (159:9); as meaning the sacraments (esp. the Eucharist), see: *EH* I.1 372A (63:6); II.3.8 404D (78:20); III.1 425A (79:17–21); V.1.5 505B (107:19); VI.2 533C (117:14–15); VI.3.5 536C (119:3); *Ep.* IX.1 1108A (197:15); and as referring generally to the hidden things of God (or of the angels) to which we are directed by means of the Revelation, see: *CH* IV.2 180B (21:19); VI.1 200C (26:5–6); *DN* IV.22 724B (170:8); *Ep.* IX.1 1104B (193:10); and *MT* I.1 997A (142:1). The Eucharist is described specifically as "theurgic" in *Ep.* IX.1 1108A (198:4). Dionysius' theurgy, however, because it is linked to Christ, is not equivalent to the theurgies of Iamblichus. Although the latter emphasizes the free action of the gods (see *De myst.* I.11–12 and III.17–19 [des Places], 60, 62, 122, 125 respectively) at work in the cult which reveals them (I.21, 76), as well as the role of prayer (V.26, 182), the content and philosophical basis of his mysteries are fundamentally different. Their content features ecstatic or mediumistic trances (e.g., III.3 and 14, 102 and 117–118), "ectoplasmic" apparitions (e.g., II.3 and 6, 80 and 86), and mysterious

through the variety of the material symbols to deification and to its source in Jesus. θέωσις is defined in the paragraph immediately following:

> Deification is, so far as possible, the assimilation to and union with God; this is the common limit of every hierarchy: the persistent love for God and for divine things as accomplished in sacred fashion, in a manner both inspired and united, and, indeed, prior to this, the complete and undeviating abandonment of all opposites; the knowledge of things as they truly are, the vision and science of the sacred truth; the inspired participation in the perfection which is in the form of the One—indeed [the participation] in the One himself in so far as it is possible—the feast of vision intelligibly feeding and embracing everyone who stretches himself up to it.[100]

We note three stages in this definition of deification: (1) the persistent love of God, in which we recognize the ἔρως or desire that is basic to the Dionysian vision, coupled with the rejection of evil.

"names" of a preferably foreign and incomprehensible sort (VII.4, 192). To these we might add the sacred stones, herbs, and plants Proclus mentions in his Περὶ τῆς καθ᾽ Ἕλληνας ἱερατικῆς τέχνης (ed. J. Bidez; *Catalogue des manuscrits alchimiques grecs* [Bruxelles: Maurice Lambertin, 1928], 137–151, at 148–149); see also Dodds, "Theurgy," 62–63, and *Theol Plat* I.25 (Saffrey and Westerink), 112–113. The philosophical basis lies at once in the doctrine of "sympathy," the cosmos as a single divine entity (*De myst.* V.7, 162–163), and in the belief that the lower levels of the world, because simpler, also enjoy a more direct connection to their divine sources (see Gersh, *From Iamblichus to Eriugena*, 117 and n. 179, and Rosán, *Proclus*, 78, 86, and 216–217). Dodds is certainly too harsh in simply dismissing the philosophers' attempt to justify their cult as a case of "spineless syncretism" ("Theurgy," 58), and we would do well to heed the more balanced and sympathetic judgments of Festugière ("Proclus et la réligion traditionelle," in *Études de la philosophie grecque* [Paris: Vrin, 1971], 575–584) and Larsen (*Jamblique*, 86–87 and 152–154). Nonetheless, Dionysius' mysteries are clearly different, of a Christian origin, and "not potent in their own right, but . . . the agents of the potency of God" (Sheldon-Williams, *CambHist*, 471–472), as vehicles of—inasmuch as they derive from—the single mystery of Christ. See also Rorem's remarks on θεουργία in Dionysius (*Symbols*, 14–15) as signifying the mighty works of God, specifically in Christ.

100. *EH* I.3 376A.

One must will one's actions in accordance with the true *desidera-tum* and abandon the false. This is the Dionysian purification, or κάθαρσις, whose sign is Baptism. (2) We discover the nature of things as they truly are; the vision of the truth that is given us in the sacrament of the Eucharist. (3) Although the latter holds all the sacraments within itself, Dionysius will choose to use the consecration of the Chrism for his meditation on the final sense of θέωσις: participation in, and contemplation of, the divinity that embraces all, and whose Providence knows its definitive revelation in the person of Jesus.[101]

After beginning "outside the doors" and advancing to gather everything within the mystery of the altar—with regard to "movement," I will have occasion to point out a certain echo of the three spiritual motions, "straight," "spiral," and "circular," in Dionysius' presentation of Baptism, Eucharist and Chrism—we move out from the center in the last three chapters and travel back down the ranks of the clergy and faithful until, in chapter 7 and his discussion of Christian burial, we are led once more outside the enclosure of the Church. This time, however, it is no longer in fear of dissolution and non-existence, but in confident anticipation of the promise of the Resurrection.

3.1. Baptism: The Mystery of Entry and First Stage of the Ascent

If the Fall led to a break-up of unity, and to division as the ruling principle in our world, a ruling principle which further led to a reversal of the natural hierarchy of λόγος, θυμός, and ἐπιθυμία, to the rule of the passions, and at last to dissolution (ἀνυπαρξία), then the order in Dionysius' discussion of Baptism is precisely the reverse. We begin, as it were, in the shades of non-being, the illusory existence of life "outside the doors," and in need therefore of another birth:

101. See *DN* XII.2 969C (224:13–225:3); *Ep.* IX.1 1104C (194:1–4); and *EH* I.3 373C (66:6–8).

For if the divine birth is to be in divine fashion, then neither can one ever know aught of the things divinely delivered, nor in any way accomplish them, who does not possess the mode of existing in divine manner. Or are we not obliged (we speak here in human fashion) first to exist, and then to accomplish the things that are proper to us, in as much as that which in no way exists has neither movement nor existence, but only when something somehow exists does it accomplish or suffer those things which are proper to it.[102]

Only when incorporated into the body of Christ, or "City of God" (ἡ ἔνθεος . . . πολιτεία), can one truly exist and be endowed with the capacity for accomplishing what is proper to nature, i.e., deification. We therefore find a warning concluding the introduction to this chapter, embellished with reminders drawn from grim OT precedents, against permitting any non-initiate (ἀτέλεστος) approach to the sacred things.[103]

3.1.1. The rite. This section begins with a description of the hierarch in the likeness of God and of the divine φιλανθρωπία. God desires all to be saved and to unite "all, in the manner of fire, to himself, according to their aptitude for deification."[104] Having stated the theme of the whole *CD*, Dionysius describes the entry into the τάξις of the Church: (1) outside the Church an "initiate" (layperson) is approached as prospective sponsor by one who "desires . . . salvation." (2) The layperson agrees and leads the catechumen into the Church to the hierarch.[105] (3) Giving thanks for the "one beneficent rule [ἀρχή],"[106] the hierarch salutes the altar and leaves the sanctuary for the body of the nave where the whole assembly gathered in the "sacred space [ἱερὸς χόρος] gives thanks for a man's salvation."[107] (4) The catechumen confesses past godlessness (ἀθειότης), "ignorance [ἀγνωσία] of the truly good,"

102. *EH* II.1 392B (69:7–12).
103. *EH* II.1 392C (69:14–19).
104. *EH* II.2.1 393A (70:6–7).
105. *EH* II.2.2 393B (70:11–19).
106. *EH* II.2.3 393C (71:3).
107. *EH* II.2.4 393C (71:6–7).

and his failure to accomplish (ἀνενεργεσία) anything of "the divine life." (5) The hierarch instructs the catechumen concerning the divine polity to which he (or she) is seeking entry and inscribes him.[108] (6) The rite of Baptism itself begins with the stripping of the candidate by the deacons, his triple renunciation of Satan, and the hierarch's thrice repeated call for him to be "ordered with [συντάξασθαι] Christ."[109] (7) After he has confessed Christ three times, has been blessed by the bishop and anointed with oil by the priests, the candidate is led to the baptismal font. (8) The water is anointed three times with Chrism and the candidate baptized with triple immersion, accompanied by the invocation of the Trinity. (9) He is then vested in white robes, "sealed" with anointing by Chrism, and (10) rendered a communicant of the Eucharist.[110]

3.1.2. Θεωρία and a word on the νοητά. Dionysius now proceeds to his explanation of the rites' significance, their contemplation (θεωρία) being "transferred from things divine to things divine by the divine Spirit."[111] As this is the pattern that he will follow in the course of his discussion of every sacrament, I take the opportunity here to address certain aspects of it.

I note first, following Roques,[112] the "collapsed" or "telescoped" quality of the action just described. The process of entry into the Church is described in a way which leaves the impression that the whole process of initiation takes place within the space of a single day. Inasmuch as Dionysius clearly allows elsewhere[113] for the presence of catechumens in the Church, presumably undergoing the normal procedures of instruction lasting several months, it appears that the "compression" here is deliberate. I believe it is done in order to underscore the unity of action and "direction." Dionysius is always primarily interested in the, as it

---

108. *EH* II.2.5 396A (71:15–18).
109. *EH* II.2.6 396AB (71:20–72:7).
110. *EH* II.2.7 396B–D (72:7–73:7).
111. *EH* II.2.8 397A (73:9–10).
112. Roques, "Le sens du baptême selon le Ps.-Denys," *Ir* 31 (1958): 431.
113. See, for example, *EH* III.2 425C (80:14); IV.2 473A (95:9–10); VII.2.3 556C (123:6–7); and 3.3 557C-560A (124:12–17).

were, "synoptic view." The rite of entry thus appears as a single action, a motion κατ᾽ εὐθείαν, advancing without interruption from "outside the doors" to the midst of the sacred assembly and up to the altar itself, whence the hierarch brings the eucharistic elements to render the neophyte both a member and a communicant of Christ. Details of time and space as they actually occur are never Dionysius' concern. He always looks to the principles, ἀρχαί or νοητά, of which the temporo-spatial is the illustration and revelation.[114] In this case the point of greatest import is the baptismal rite as a movement directly away from the fallen state and into Christ, out of seeming and into truth.

This lack of interest in actual details underlies Roques' observation contrasting the Dionysian treatment of Baptism, and the sacraments generally, with the "typological" approach accorded the Church's rites by, especially, the Fathers of the fourth century: "Les correlatifs *typos* et *aletheia* sont dépouillés de cette note historique . . . le *typos* devient l'un des nombreus synonymes de *symbolon* et de l'*eikon*."[115] While Roques is careful to note that Dionysius does not eliminate history, he does claim that it is nonetheless "attenuated" in favor of θέωσις: "the return to the intelligible which alone and of itself is divine and divinizing."[116] He describes Dionysius' approach as "transhistoric rather than historic" and "always of a vertical orientation,"[117] and concludes that "the truth, according to Dionysius, is by essence the intelligible."[118]

In reply, I offer the following three, cautionary points. First, although there can be no denying Dionysius' "vertical" bias, it would be no less foolish to deny (and Roques, at least, does not entirely) the presence of a certain temporal thrust within the *EH*.

---

114. *EH* II.3.2 397C (74:5–11).

115. Roques, "Baptême," 434–435. But see my discussion of Ephrem of Syria's practically identical treatment of the Syriac equivalents for τύπος, σύμβολον, etc. (Golitzin, *Et introibo*, 360–361). His purpose in doing so is also the same as Dionysius': to witness to the Incarnation.

116. Roques, "Baptême," 443.

117. Roques, "Baptême," 448. See also Sheldon-Williams, *CambHist*, 459; and, opposed, Völker, *Kontemplation*, 18, 59, and 63.

118. Roques, "Baptême," 435.

Dionysius is not fundamentally interested in history, true. I have already pointed (and will again) to a certain quality of "unfinished business" represented by the very imperfections of our hierarchy—i.e., the latter remains, in this age, an inconsistent reflection of the celestial hierarchy.[119] The eschatological is neither wholly lacking nor wholly extraneous to our author's notion of "symbol." I began this chapter by noting that the action of the *EH* unfolds between two deaths or births, with the first birth, Baptism, anticipating the second, the general Resurrection, and I intend to show a real movement within the *EH* from chapter 2 on the mystery of "entry" to the final chapter on the mystery of Christian burial, the sanctified "exit" in sure hope of the age to come. This movement and its associated hope both pervade the *EH* and provide the whole of the *CD* with a certain necessary, "historical" presence.

My second point consists of a reminder concerning the nature of the νοητόν as Dionysius conceives it. The Dionysian κόσμος νοητός ("intelligble world") is not the realm of Platonic ideas, nor the Νοῦς of Plotinus, nor the hypostatized categories of Proclus. At the (secondary) level of created being it is instead a cosmos or world of creatures wholly sanctified and altogether transparent to the Creator, a body or organism deriving its being from, and radiating the being of, its single head or "cause," the "divinity of Jesus." While we may read this as Dionysius' adaptation of the Procline doctrine that all effects are present in the cause, we also recall that it can no less easily be ascribed to the teaching of the NT, as suggested by such texts as Ephesians 1:20-23, Philippians 2:6-11, Hebrews 1:1-4 and 2:8, and, especially, Colossians 1:15ff.

God is the deepest and primary level of the νοητά, the source of the νοητοί. By "divinity" we refer to the Dionysian notion of the λόγοι as outlined above, and to the "names" of God that lend expression to his eternally flowing activities *ad extra*. Again, we encounter here a notion of the "intelligible world" for which I feel the associations conjured up by such expressions as "mind,"

_____

119. See above, chapter 3 (2.1.2.2., "Human Motion") and chapter 4 (concluding paragraph of 1.3.3., "Purification-Illumination-Perfection").

"idea," and "forms" to be dangerously misleading. In employing such terms as λόγοι, ἐνέργειαι, δυνάμεις, Dionysius intends the non-hypostatized activities or wills of God at work in creation. In a word, he means Providence, and Providence in turn refers in general to the Trinity, and specifically to the Second Person of the Three in whom the θεία πρόνοια has acquired a human face: "Who is the *image* (εἰκών) of the invisible God" (Col 1:15).

The third point concerns the Dionysian notion of symbol. I agree with Roques in seeing truth for Dionysius as the "intelligible significance which the purified intelligence discovers in the biblical or sacramental symbols," such that "*typos* becomes another of the numerous synonyms for *symbolon* and *eikon*."[120] Now, let us recall first that for Dionysius both the latter terms refer to a kind of incarnation of the divine in the universe of matter and distension in time, and thus that, secondly, anything "symbolic" must reasonably discover its true source and validation in the supreme instance of divine condescension, the Incarnation proper. The "vision of the sacred truth" or contemplation of the νοητά is then inseparable from the person and activity of Christ. The exercise of the discursive intellect is invalid unless it has first been initiated into the Christian mysteries. As Roques himself observes: ". . . nous ne pouvons rien faire de valable . . . sans l'initiation baptismale . . . la méthode démonstrative doit être insérée au coeur même de la révélation transcendante . . . l'intelligence illuminée."[121] The sense and coherence of the world of humans, our world's soul as it were, must be sought at the altar. Our intellectual powers, given for the apperception of that reality, are of no use to us unless we first "put on Christ."[122]

---

120. Roques, "Baptême," 434–435.

121. Roques, "Note sur THEOLOGIA," 206, commenting on *Ep.* IX 1105.

122. The whole discussion of the intelligibles (νοητά) here might also be applied to Rorem's Luibhéid's consistent rendering of νοητόν and related terms as "conceptual." The latter, in light of my argument, is quite inadequate. Thus, for example, Rorem's characterization of Dionysius as wholly preoccupied with "epistemology" (*Commentary*, 93).

3.1.3. The contemplation: a triple reality and revelation. According to a pattern which he will apply to each of the sacraments of our hierarchy, Dionysius' contemplation of Baptism is threefold. The sacrament is a reflection on: (1) the mystery of the individual believer's purification and its corresponding spiritual motion; (2) on the all-encompassing mystery of Christ; (3) and an illustration of God's activity in relation to His creation. Put another way, the same sacrament at once typifies an aspect of the redeemed soul, is a sharing in Christ, and reveals God's universal Providence. Mutually reinforcing, the different levels of meaning are present simultaneously and without conflict.

3.1.3.1. The soul: direct motion. Baptism is purification,[123] the first stage of deification. The proselyte is moved by desire (ἀγάπησις) for the divine and, simultaneously, becomes aware of his own inadequacy, his own faults. He repents, and his repentance is met by the "divine beatitude" acting through the hierarch to lead him up, in due degrees, to the divinity itself.[124] The repentance, although out of desire for God, is a voluntary departure (ἀποφοίτησις) from evil, as signified by the renunciation of Satan and the exorcisms.[125] It is also a continual process:

> never at any time is there to occur any relaxation of the sacred love for the truth, rather [the neophyte] is, in sacred fashion, to work whole-heartedly, attentively and eternally at stretching himself up to the most perfect things of the Thearchy.[126]

The divine beneficence remains inalterable,[127] but it can be refused. The human "capacity for willed action [αὐθαίρετος αὐτεξουσιότης]"[128] can either "shut up its naturally implanted capacities for illumi-

---

123. See *EH* II.3.1 397B (73:17–19) and II.3.5 401B (76:11–21).
124. *EH* II.3.4 400C (75:12–19).
125. *EH* II.3.5 401B (76:19–20).
126. *EH* II.3.5 401C (77:5–8).
127. *EH* II.3.3 397D (74:12–14).
128. Concerning this term, see my discussion of Gregory of Nyssa (Golitzin, *Et introibo*, 307–308).

nation," be drawn by a "desire for evil" (the "seeming good"), and so remove itself from the light,[129] or else, as in the baptismal sequence, recognize the true goal of desire, repent of the old ways, and strive to persevere in the good in order that, thus implanted in the vision and ways of God, the soul may be, in due order, wholly "cleansed of its [i.e., of the ἐναντίας ζωῆς] fantasies by means of a pure, divine mode of life and desire [ἕξει καὶ ἔρωτι]."[130] The spiritual motion typified by this continual purification is the "straight" or "direct." Thanks to Dionysius' "telescoping" of the action, we see this illustrated in an unbroken, linear progression: from "outside the doors" into the vestibule, then the nave, and finally to the altar itself.

3.1.3.2. Christ. The proselyte is called to repentance, to change his ways,[131] but this happens only through and in Jesus. The neophyte is "called to the contests [ἀγῶνες]" of virtue and

> is placed accordingly under the judge who awards the prize, Christ, since as God he is maker of the games, as wise he has laid down the rules, and as beautiful [καλός] has made the prizes becoming to the victors. And, yet more divine, because he is indeed good, he entered in sacred fashion into the games with them, and struggled with the empire of death and corruption for the sake of their freedom and victory. The initiate, rejoicing, sets forth to the contests as to divine things, abiding by the rules of him who is wise, and according to them, strives without transgression, being certain in the hope of the beautiful prizes and ranged [ranked] under the Good Lord and Ruler of the games. And, when he has set forth upon the footsteps of him who, out of goodness, was first of the athletes, [in] his theomimetic struggles with the activities and beings which wrestle with him against θέωσις, he dies together with Christ in Baptism.[132]

129. *EH* II.3.3 397D–400A (74:15–17).
130. *EH* III.3.7 436B (87:18–19).
131. See the summary by Hornus, "Quelques réflexions," 40.
132. *EH* II.2.6 401D–404A (77:12–23).

It would be difficult to imagine a more traditional presentation. In order properly to exercise our free will and so to conquer πάθος and ἐπιθυμία,[133] to give play thus to the thrust of the "vector" or ἀναλογία that God has implanted in us in order to impel us to participation in himself, we must become partakers of the "theurgies" of Christ.[134] It is his game in every sense that we are called to share.

Thus the necessity of Baptism: we must share in Christ's death to sin. For, as Dionysius tells us in an admittedly rare reference to Christ's death, just as death is the separation of the united body and soul, with the consequent disappearance of the body in the earth and vanishing of the soul "as becoming formless [ἀειδὴ— certainly a curious notion of 'form' for a reputed Neoplatonist] without the body," so is

> the complete veiling through water received as an icon of death and the formlessness of the tomb. The symbolic teaching thus initiates the baptizand, by means of the triple immersion, into the imitation of the divine death and three-day sojourn in the tomb of Jesus, the life-giver.[135]

The vesting in white robes and the anointing with Chrism bears witness to the fact that,

> By means of the courageous and deiform dispassion with regard to the contrary powers, and by earnest inclination towards the One, that which was without beauty is adorned and the formless given form, rendered shining by the life that is wholly in the form of light.[136]

Sharing in Christ's death to sin, Baptism is the birth to life in God. Thus we find the anointing with Chrism, the "sweet savor" of

133. See my discussion of these themes in Evagrius (Golitzi, *Et introibo*, 322–325).

134. See my earlier note about sacraments as Christ's "mysteries" and reflections of his "theurgies."

135. *EH* II.3.7 404B (78:6–9).

136. *EH* II.3.8 404C (78:11–14).

the Holy Spirit, following the immersion: "for the sacred initiation of the divine birth unites the things so consecrated with the thearchic Spirit."[137] Finally, the gift of the Eucharist completes the process of entry, sealing the baptismal purification with illumination and union.

3.1.3.3. Icon of providence. Contemplated as veiling spiritual realities (νοητά), Baptism reveals the same truths concerning uncreated realities and created nature that we encountered earlier. The θεία αγαθότης which sends forth its rays upon all,[138] recalls the solar imagery of the Good pouring out its energies upon all creation that we met in the *DN*: "the unique, beneficent ἀρχή by which all things are called,"[139] and the φιλανθρωπία that seeks the salvation of all.[140] Similarly, the recognition of desire (ἀγάπησις) for the Good that moves the proselyte to seek entry, and the model of the hierarch, recalls the ἔρως that finds its end in God. Yet, as well as revealing the "sacred order" whose source is "the divine," this icon of seeking and receiving, of the candidate's longing and the bishop's gracious reception, is finally a statement that neither repentance and conversion, nor the acceptance exercised on behalf of (or in imitation of) God's philanthropy and rendering it present, is possible outside the Church. If we begin with desire for the good, we must end in Jesus and before his altar. Turning, then, to the consideration of that altar, we proceed to the second mystery of our hierarchy.

3.2. The Eucharist: Illumination and the "Sacrament of Sacraments"

3.2.1. The central mystery. The Eucharist is second of the three main mysteries of the Church considered by Dionysius. It is also the central one, the "sacrament of sacraments [τελετὴ τελετῶν]."[141]

---

137. *EH* II.3.8 404C (78:15–16).
138. *EH* II.3.3 397D (74:12–14).
139. *EH* II.2.3 393C (71:3–4).
140. *EH* II.2.1 393A (70:4–7).
141. *EH* III.1 424C (79:3).

It enjoys this pre-eminence because it is literally, as it were, at the center, and because its activity is precisely "to center," i.e., to gather all back up and into God. We find thus the second of its two names preferred by our author to be σύναξις. Boularand has shown that this term,[142] together with the other name, κοινωνία (less specifically tied than is the former to the sacrament itself[143]), agrees with the tradition of West Syrian usage. Σύναξις, from the verb συνάγω, is also in accord with the whole *CD*.[144] It is, of course, true that every sacrament is in some sense a "gathering" or "rolling-up" into unity. In the following, Dionysius employs both synonyms:

> each holy sacrament both gathers together our disparate lives
> into uniform deification and, by the rolling-up in God-like
> manner of the divisions, grants communion and union with
> the One.[145]

The Eucharist, however, being that action which acts supremely to unite us with the cause (αἰτία) of our and every hierarchy, Christ, remains nonetheless the "gathering-together" or "rolling-up" *par excellence*. As the "chief" or "sum" of all the other sacraments (κεφάλαιον τελετῶν[146]), the whole ecclesiastical hierarchy meets in and depends on it.

> It is not possible for scarcely any consecration to be effected
> without the most divine Eucharist that sacredly works to
> gather the one initiated together into the One and, by means
> of the divinely-delivered gift of the consecrating mysteries, to
> bring to completion his communion with God . . . the goal

---

142. E. Boularand, "L'Eucharistie d'après le ps.-Denys," *BLE* 58 (1957): 193–217; 59 (1958): 129–169; here I am referring to 199–204.

143. Boularand, "L'Eucharistie d'après le ps.-Denys," 198.

144. See Stiglmayr, "Die Lehre von den Sakramenten," 268–269, and my remarks concerning συνάγω and συμπτύσσω in chapter 4 (1.3.2., Θεομίμησις); cf. on "Macarius," Golitzin, *Et introibo*, 380n.224.

145. *EH* III.1 424CD (79:9–12).

146. *EH* VI.3.5 536C (119:3–4).

of every [sacrament] being the communion of the divine mysteries for him who is being initiated [or consecrated].[147]

3.2.2. The recapitulation of Providence, of Christ, and of humanity. It is therefore scarcely surprising to discover both the *CD*'s central themes, the general dispensation of Providence for created being and the culminating act of the Incarnation, most extensively discussed in the *EH*'s contemplation of the σύναξις.[148] These themes are the "holy principles [ἀρχαί]" toward which the bishop is "led up by the thearchic Spirit. . . . in blessed and spiritual visions and purity of deiform ἕξις."[149] At the very beginning of Dionysius' contemplation of the Eucharist and before any discussion of the "theurgies" or specific action of the Incarnation, we are thus introduced to the leitmotif of the Dionysian vision: the triad of μονή - πρόοδος - ἐπιστροφή. Dionysius sees this pattern reflected—better, participated—in the entire action of the Eucharist itself, and here in the specific activity of the bishop beginning the service with a general censing of the Church.

> For the thearchic beatitude which is beyond all things, while indeed going forth in divine goodness for the communion with the holy ones who participate in it, yet departs not from the unmoving στάσις and foundation which it possesses by essence; and it both shines in due measure on the deiform, and . . . swerves not at all from its proper identity. Just so, the divine sacrament of the σύναξις, while possessing its ἀρχή [as] single, simple, and inclusive, is multiplied in philanthropic manner in the sacred variety of the symbols, and travels unto all the thearchic iconography while, at the same time, it is gathered in uniform manner from these into its proper monad, and unifies those who are in sacred fashion led up to it. In the same manner, then, the divine hierarch, while indeed he brings his single science of the hierarchy beneficently down to the subordinate [ranks], making use of the multitude of sacred enigmas, yet he is at the same time, as unconditioned and

147. *EH* III.1 424D–425A (79:14–22).
148. See Boularand, "L'Eucharistie," 213–216.
149. *EH* III.2.1 428A (81:11–13).

unchecked by the lesser, restored without diminishment to
[his] proper ἀρχή, and, having made his spiritual entry to the
One, beholds in pure fashion the uniform λόγοι of the things
accomplished, and makes the limit [accomplishment] of his
philanthropic procession to the δεύτερα his more divine return
to the πρῶτα.[150]

We see repeated on several different levels—on that of the
spiritual-intelligible principle of the Eucharist, of the action of the
rite itself, and of the personal state of the hierarch—the original
principle of the One and the Many held together in God, unity
indivisibly multiplied in its relation to the creature: the themes
of the *DN*! Before objecting that this is simply to make of the
Christian sacrament an illustration of metaphysical principles,
let us take a moment to look more closely at this text. Recalling
the nature of the Fall and its results—loss of unity, brokenness,
false love, and death—and of our restoration through Jesus in
the Incarnation, we should see in this description of the hierarch
less an example of philosophical *dicta* than, in fact, the pattern
of humanity restored. The hierarch's is the pattern of θεομίμησις
made possible for humanity through the Incarnation. Here is the
true sense of the "deiform ἕξις," i.e., the imitation of (and imitation because true participation in) the divine love. I note again the
essentially Christian conversion of the Neoplatonic "procession"
and "return" that Dionysius has accomplished: contemplation of
God in love necessarily means sharing in his love for creation.
Loving means participation in love. The hierarch, as exemplar of
Christian perfection, "realizes his 'return' [as] the accomplishment
[πέρας] of his philanthropic 'procession.'"[151] The love which "suffers the divine" is one and the same with the love that is active in
the world. I ask the reader to note the transition: God is mirrored
by the rite, and the latter in turn is reflected in the man. All three
levels of the mystery are at once present and fully valid. The
Creator is mirrored by the redeemed world, and the macrocosm
of the Church by the microcosm of the holy man.

150. *EH* III.3.3 429AB (82:17–83:10).
151. *EH* III.3.3 429B (83:10).

The mystery is also one. It is to Jesus that we look for the model of the hierarch's actions. Better than model, he is rather the presence working through and in the bishop, the "proper ἀρχή" to which the latter is restored. His "mind" constitutes the hierarch's "single science."[152] The ἀρχή of the σύναξις, and the sacrament's activity, are identical with Jesus' person and "theandric activity." There is nothing in the passage that is at variance with the essentially Christian inspiration and traditional vocabulary found in Dionysius' account of Baptism. Nothing has altered, save here the terminology of the philosophers, as well the stress—perfectly traditional—on the centrality of the Eucharist. The latter both validates and seals the salvific activity of all the Church's mysteries as itself, I should say, peculiarly the sacrament of the Church. Beneath the forms and types we are to discern Jesus who works all in all, and who is made present among us through these same actions and "symbols"—indeed, who unites us to himself through the same. Here is the sense of Dionysius' prayer directed to the Eucharist, i.e., the illumination necessary to recognize the reality hidden in the forms.[153] Here, too, we find a reply in part to the criticisms made of Dionysius' insufficient sacramental realism,[154] a question to which I will return shortly.

3.2.3. The rite. The description Dionysius gives of the service is as follows: (1) the ruling themes of divine condescension and redemption are outlined in the two paragraphs[155] devoted to the interpretation of the psalms and the other readings heard prior to the offertory. We are taught in these readings the "unique concordance" (σύμπνοια), or single thread, of divine intent revealed in the sacred writings (θεολογία) and accomplished in the divine work (θεουργία) of Jesus.[156] (2) We move in the following two

152. See chapter 4 above (1.2.2., "The Mind of Christ").

153. *EH* III.2 428A (81:11–14).

154. See, for example, Brons, *Gott und die Seienden*, 87; Meyendorff, *Byzantine Theology*, 203–204.

155. *EH* III.3.4 and III.3.5 429C–432B (83:11–84:21).

156. *EH* III.3.5 432B (84:20–21).

paragraphs[157] to a consideration of the κάθαρσις of the catechumens and penitents. The former are quite incapable of responding as yet to the greater things and, as illustrating the divine justice of the hierarchy which gives salvation to each according to his ἀναλογία (a clear reference, both here and in that which immediately follows, to the as yet fluid nature of the ecclesiastical hierarchy) and worthiness (ἀξία), are therefore dismissed at the conclusion of the readings.[158] The penitents and possessed are dismissed as being too weak (the former) or altogether "strangers to the vision" of the sacraments (the latter). They also occasion a meditation on the demonic powers and the imprisoned life.[159] (3) Opening the liturgy of the faithful, we find a reference to what must be the Creed[160] and with it a recollection of the grace of the Incarnation that "restored" us to communion with divine things.[161] (4) Dionysius sketches the offertory, kiss of peace, diptychs, and lustration of the clergy prior to the *anaphora*.[162] The diptychs recall the blessed dead, who are not separated from the body of faithful in Christ.[163] With the kiss and the lustration, the theme of purification predominates.[164] The admonitions are more intense and exacting in reference to the clergy's lustration. As they are called to "the most perfect hierurgy," so they must be completely purified from even "the last fantasies of the spirit" in order to be conformed to the likeness of the sacred things they are about to effect, and to be without reproach before Christ.[165] (5) Purified and "united with divine things," the hierarch, "having hymned the sacred hierurgies, sacredly performs the most divine things

157. *EH* III.3.6–7 431C–436D (84:22–88:9).

158. *EH* III.3.6 432C–433B (84:22–85:1).

159. *EH* III.3.7 433D–436A (86:16–24).

160. *EH* III.3.7 436C (87:22). See Boularand, "L'Eucharistie," 144–152.

161. *EH* III.3.7 436CD (87:24–88:9).

162. *EH* III.3.8–10 437A–440B (88:10–90:10).

163. *EH* III.3.9 437B (88:22–27).

164. *EH* III.3.8 437A (88:15–21).

165. *EH* III.3.10 440AB (89:14–90:8).

and brings into sight the things which are hymned."[166] (6) The communion of clergy and laity follow.[167]

3.2.4. Ὑπ᾽ ὄψιν: recognition of a real presence. The phrase ὑπ᾽ ὄψιν ἄγει τὰ ὑμνημένα ("brings into sight the things which are hymned") occurs three times: above as cited, again in paragraph 12 with the addition, "through the symbols sacredly set forth,"[168] and finally in the following paragraph, slightly altered: "bringing into sight, as in images, Jesus Christ our spiritual life, from the secrecy proper to the divine."[169] While Dionysius will continue to repeat the themes bearing on purification throughout these paragraphs,[170] I believe nonetheless to have discovered in the phrase above the crux not only of the Eucharist and the ecclesiastical hierarchy but the heart of the Dionysian vision itself.

What does Dionysius mean by the ὑμνημένα here? As detailed in the whole of *EH* III.3.11, it would appear that the ὑμνημένα refer primarily to the saving acts of the Incarnation. To "hymn" these is, in a sense, to render them present and, with them, to make present Jesus himself: ὑπ᾽ ὄψιν . . . τὰ ὑμνημένα—ὑπ᾽ ὄψιν . . . Ἰησοῦν. But what, precisely, does "present" mean? Following the account of the dispensation and beginning in III.3.12, Dionysius continues:

> And how could the θεομίμητον otherwise come to pass in us, unless the memory of the most sacred hierurgies were being perpetually renewed by both the hierarchical sacred teaching and ministrations . . . wherefore [the hierarch], following the sacred hymns of the theurgies, at once reverently and in hierarchical fashion apologizes for the ministry which is beyond him, crying beforehand [the consecration itself] in holy fashion

166. *EH* III.3.10 440B (90:10).

167. *EH* III.3.14 444D–445B (93:23–94:10).

168. *EH* III.3.12 444A (92:17–18).

169. *EH* III.3.13 444C (93:14–16).

170. See, for example, *EH* III.3.12 444B (93:6–9); III.3.13 444CD (93:20–22); and III.3.14 445A (94:3–6).

to him [Jesus]: "Thou hast said, Do this in remembrance of me."[171]

With the terms "memory [μνήμη]" and "recollection [ἀνάμνησις]" does our author intend simply a "calling to mind," but not a declaration of presence, a "memorial" or "symbolic" action in the modern sense? Such a notion of "symbol" is inadequate to the Dionysian idea of hierarchy generally and thus, all the more, to the "consecratory invocations . . . in which the powers of God are at work."[172] We read that it is the "renewal of memory" alone which enables the θεομίμητον. The latter is nothing more nor less than the participation of the reason-endowed creature in God's energies, which means in turn, for us, in the θεανδρικὴ ἐνέργεια of Jesus. The θεομίμητον is Dionysius' equivalent to the new life in God given or restored in Christ. It is the life of his body, the ecclesiastical hierarchy. In order to share in the new life we require the renewal of the ἀνάμνησις, that re-presentation of the sacred acts of the Incarnation which truly brings those acts, and in them, Jesus, "into sight." Dionysius would certainly appear to be suggesting this, both when he refers to the hierarch's consciousness of his ministry as being "beyond" or "above" his own powers and when he continues:

> Then, having asked to be made worthy of this theomimetic ministry and, by means of the assimilation to Christ himself, to accomplish the things divine and to distribute them in a manner all-pure, and that those participating may do so in a manner befitting them . . . [dividing the "indivisible" bread and portioning the "single" cup] he symbolically multiplies and distributes the unity, accomplishing in these things [his] all-pure ministry.[173]

This passage is followed immediately by a second recollection of the Incarnation and its saving effects, together with an exhortation

---

171. *EH* III.3.12 441C–444A (92:2–14).
172. *EH* VII.3.10 565C (130:6–8).
173. *EH* III.3.12 444A (92:14–21).

to conform ourselves to Jesus; "for it is thus that the communion with the life (τὸ ὅμοιον) will be given in harmonious fashion."[174] This sequence or pattern, and the third ὑπ᾽ ὄψιν, are repeated in the following paragraph:

> These things [i.e., τὰ ὑμνημένα] the hierarch makes manifest in the matters sacredly accomplished, bringing the veiled gifts to sight, dividing their unity into many, and by means of the unity in the highest degree of the things distributed with those which in them come to pass, renders the participants communicants of them. For he sensibly delineates in these things, as in images, our spiritual life, leading into sight from the secrecy proper to the divine Jesus Christ [who], by means of his all perfect and unconfused Incarnation according to our mode of being, as a lover of mankind took form from us and went forth without alteration from the One which is his by nature into our divided existence, and through this beneficent philanthropy calls the race of men to communion with himself and the good things which are his, if indeed we be united to his most divine life through our assimilation . . . to it, and in this manner we shall be truly rendered communicants of God and of divine things. . . . Having participated in and distributed the divine communion, he [the hierarch] finishes with all the sacred fullness of the Church in holy thanksgiving.[175]

Is this an exemplarism pure and simple? To be sure, I find the anagogic function of the hierurgies, but that spiritual atomism—private virtue exercised as the result of a purely individual appreciation of "intelligible truths"[176]—to which an extreme exemplarism must lead remains quite foreign to Dionysius. I said above that with the ὑπ᾽ ὄψιν, echoed in such phrases as ἐμφαίνει and πρὸς τὸ ἐμφανές, we have arrived at the heart of the Dionysian vision. That heart or core is the very nature of symbol and icon: Christ embodied in our hierarchy. The mystery at the heart of things is the union κατ᾽ ἄκραν ("in the highest degree") of the distributed material

174. *EH* III.3.12 444B (93:9–10).
175. *EH* III.3.13–14 444C–445A (93:11–24).
176. See Meyendorff, *Christ*, 79–80, and *Byzantine Theology*, 28.

gifts with "the things which in them come to pass," i.e., which are rendered visible, present. Those things are the "good things" proper to God, to Jesus. They are indeed Jesus himself, μετουσία ἑαυτοῦ. The ἀνάμνησις is a true re-collection of the Incarnation, and because this is the case, the σύναξις is a true "gathering" into Christ. We recall the progression noted above: the "things hymned," the theurgies or Incarnation, are "brought to sight;" they are "brought to sight through the symbols"; and finally, Jesus Christ himself is brought to sight. The mystery is rendered present, visible, yet still awaiting the perfect revelation and complete declaration of the eschaton.[177] The stuff of our world reaches its highest point on the altar. It realizes the Incarnation, and it is the function of the "elect," the "initiates," to recognize the vision of the final reality toward which these types point and which, indeed, is present in them now: the time when Christ will be all in all. This is the sense of the ἀρχή to which we were directed at the beginning of the sacrament's contemplation.

Recognition is the key because, bearing in mind the Dionysian vision as sketched so far, we may say that sacramental realism is in a sense presupposed. We are united through the sacraments to Christ. What we are called to do, and what is done, by each according to capacity is to recognize, become aware of, the mystery that is accomplished. I therefore find Dionysius employing this very term, ἐπιγιγνώσκω (to recognize, become conscious of), when describing the thanksgiving of the ranks of clergy as "having recognized [ἐπιγνοῦσα] and hymned . . . the graces [χάριται] of the theurgies,"[178] and in his remarks concluding this section:

---

177. Certainly, Dionysius' notion is not yet adequate to the distinction between symbol and Eucharist drawn at Nicea II (see Meyendorff, *Byzantine Theology*, 203–204). Nonetheless, his cannot be reduced to a purely symbological interpretation. The Eucharist for him differs supremely in degree, if not in kind, from the other symbols proper to our hierarchy.

178. *EH* III.3.15 445B (94:12–13); for other uses of the verb and its related noun, see: *CH* IX.3 260C (38:1–3); IX.4 261C (39:13–15); XIII.3 301C (45:18–21); *EH* II.2.1 393A (76:1–2); II.3.2 397C (74:5–7); II.3.4 400B (75:10–13); II.3.8 404C (78:16–19) esp.; III.3.15 445C (94:18–22); IV.3.8 481B (101:3–4); and VII.3.6 561B (126:21).

> "Taste," say the Scriptures, "and see": for by the sacred initia-
> tion into the things divine the initiates will recognize their
> munificent graces, and by participation contemplating their
> most divine height and breadth, they will hymn the super-
> heavenly beneficences of the Thearchy.[179]

One does not leave behind the physical elements of the sacraments in becoming truly initiated. We instead become more alive
to the reality of grace informing them. It is now, at the altar and
in Jesus, that we grow aware of the common image and reality
that binds all together. He is "our most divine Providence,"[180] just
as he is the meaning and action of the liturgy, the mystery of the
altar, and the source of the sanctified soul's deification.

3.2.5. The spiral motion. There is a final point with regard to
the Eucharist. Just as this sacrament brings an illumination at once
revealing and making Christ present, so the action or "spiritual
motion" to be associated with it is that of the spiral. We begin at
the altar and follow the bishop out as he moves to include the
whole of the Church in his censing, and then as he returns to the
altar. The instruction of "those being purified" follows with the
readings from Scripture and the outlining of the saving acts. With
the Creed and offertory we enter on a second cycle that concen-
trates on the altar and sanctuary area: the recalling of the dead,
the kiss revealing the unity of the purified and enlightened laity
together with the clergy. We move further up the scale with the
lustration, and concentrate exclusively on the clergy around the
altar. Finally we are present at the great recollection of the Incarnation and the consecration effected by the hierarch, standing
alone before the altar, followed by his communion. The distribution of the consecrated gifts moves down from him to the clergy
and then to the laity. The circle of motion beginning and ending
at the altar grows tighter with each step, and it culminates in the
prayer of the bishop, called to a ministry ὑπὲρ αὐτόν, the ὑπ' ὄψιν

---

179. *EH* III.3.15 445C (94:17–22).
180. *EH* III.3.11 and III.3.12 441A and C (91:8–10 and 92:6–7).

of the *anaphora*. At every stage the altar remains the point where we both begin and conclude.

Dionysius' θεωρία of the sacrament is at once a turning around and a gathering into that unique point, precisely a spiral. It is therefore also an image of the sanctified human intelligence both circling about, and increasingly drawn into, the mystery of God— as into the "still point" of the poet.[181] Inasmuch as it is an image, so it is as well a reality. Contemplating the icon of the σύναξις, and sharing the bread and wine, we are called upon to become aware, according to our ability and degree of holiness, of a reality and presence at once in our midst yet transcending our present sensibilities: Christ, the συμβολή of human and divine. The "validity" of the Eucharist is therefore not denied, rather the intuition of the presence and activities of God (and of the angels) begins and ends at and on the altar. These activities flood the whole complex of sacred actions centered upon the altar, and emanate from it with the light of the world to come.

3.3. The Sacred Chrism: Union

3.3.1. The circular mode. In the sacrament of Chrism we find Dionysius dwelling on the image of union or perfection itself,[182] and thus upon the "circular" mode of spiritual motion. This assertion is borne out by considering the locus of this sacrament's action. Unlike Baptism, which begins "outside" and concludes before the sanctuary, or the Eucharist, which moves from the altar to embrace the whole Church in a series, one might almost say, of "pulses," the sacrament of the Chrism is confined to the space behind the veils of the sanctuary, and it is open alone to the contemplation of the clergy gathered around the altar. There

---

181. T. S. Eliot, "Burnt Norton," in *The Four Quartets* (New York: Oxford University Press, 1973), 16–17: "At the still point of the turning world . . . there the dance is // But neither arrest nor movement. And do not call it fixity // Where past and future are gathered. Neither movement from nor towards // Neither ascent nor decline. Except for the point, the still point // There would be no dance, and there is only the dance."

182. See Stiglmayr, "Die Lehre von den Sakramenten," 283–290 and 291.

is very little action at all by way of actual movement. Nothing obvious happens. Rather, the holy oil is covered with its twelve veils, placed upon the altar by the bishop, and we are asked to contemplate the vessel, the altar, the bishop before the altar, and the priests surrounding it. Yet in this stillness we in fact discover the recapitulation and crown of all that has gone before, exactly that gathering-into-itself and attachment to union that Dionysius describes in the "circular mode" of the soul's motion.[183]

3.3.2. The threefold ascents of the clergy. The purified orders of the ecclesiastical hierarchy are scarcely mentioned at all, being dismissed after the reading of the Scripture.[184] For the laity, only the vision or sight of the veiled mysteries is permitted.[185] The heart of the mystery, indeed, the subject of the action here, is the order of the "all holy," the clergy.

It is with the latter, and with their aptitude for beatitude, that Dionysius is preoccupied in the first four paragraphs of his θεωρία. In the first,[186] rather than the exhortations to perfect purity such as the one accompanying the explanation of lustration, we are given a statement concerning the purity of those who gaze directly on the mystery of the altar. Employing the metaphor of the artist revealing the archetype in the image, dear to Plotinus[187] he writes that since

> the secret and inconceivably sweet-smelling beauties of God are undefiled, they appear indeed only to the spiritual who, according to their virtue, are able to produce the uniform images incorruptible in their souls.[188]

The veils about the perfumed oil suggest, first, the modesty of holy virtue and of its possessors[189] who have conformed themselves

---

183. *DN* IV.9 705A (153:10–16).
184. *EH* IV.2 473A (95:9–12).
185. *EH* IV.3.2 476C (97:17–18).
186. *EH* IV.3.1 473B–476B (95:19–97:3).
187. See *Enn.* I.9.9.
188. *EH* IV.3.1 473B (95:24–96:2).
189. *EH* IV.3.1 473B (95:19–23).

to the "most beautiful imitation [τὸ κάλλιστον μίμημα],"[190] the θεομίμητον in other words. Through their "persistent and un-flinching contemplation," the beholders of the ἀρχέτυπος νόησις are likenesses of the divine:[191]

> Wherefore . . . neither are they lovers of things that vainly seem good and just, but of those which truly are, nor do they look for the glory which is senselessly blessed by the many, but instead, judging in theomimetic manner the good or ill in itself, they are divine images of the most divine sweet savor.[192]

Following purification, we move to the illumination of the clergy. Being true images of the divine "sweet savor" through their exercise of virtue and enlightened discrimination and imitators thus of God, it is to these "inspired ones" that "the ray of the holy things . . . shines purely and without intermediary [ἀμέσως], perfuming their spiritual perceptions [νοεραὶ ἀντιλήψεις] in unveiled manner."[193] Theirs is the illumination (here the "visible consecration of the myron") for which the laity are as yet incapable. And theirs, too, is the call to recognize beneath the visible "the more divine beauty . . . the blessed radiance clearly shining, and filling us with the savor revealed to the spiritual."[194]

Dionysius follows this with a paragraph stating the comparable rank (ὁμοταγῆ) and activity of the myron with the Eucharist, not an untraditional position in Syrian Christian circles.[195] It, too, is the image, and presence, of the last and highest of the triple work

---

190. *EH* IV.3.1 473B (96:2–5).
191. *EH* IV.3.1 473D (96:16–18).
192. *EH* IV.3.1 476A (96:20–97:1).
193. *EH* IV.3.2 476BC (97:12–15).
194. *EH* IV.3.2 476BC (97:6–8).
195. See Strothmann, *Myron-Weihe*, esp. liii–lx. Indeed, the exaltation of the oil of anointing in Syriac Christianity long antedates the controversies over Chalcedon (e.g., Ephrem Syrus: see Golitzin, *Et introibo*, 367–368), though in earlier Syriac writers it is primarily attached to the person of the Holy Spirit and not, as here in Dionysius (and his Syrian contemporaries), to the divinity of Jesus Christ.

of hierarchy and perfection. The bishops and priests within the sanctuary, both purified and illumined, are also called upon to reveal perfection. Just as the myron, a composite of material perfumes, lends its sweetness to those who partake of it,[196] so

> in analogical fashion might one say also that our spiritual powers, being unalterably disposed against the falling-away into evil, and by the natural strengthening of the critical [faculty] in us, come into perception of the divine sweet savor and are filled full of holy joy and most divine nourishment in accordance with the theurgic degrees and the corresponding conversion of the mind to the divine.[197]

With τροφή ("nourishment") we arrive at the term of the ascent, the last phase of the process that we saw Dionysius define at the beginning of the *EH* as θέωσις: "the inspired participation of the uniform perfection, the feast of vision spiritually feeding (τρέφουσα) . . . everyone who stretches up to it."[198] We thus arrive as well at him who is the source of deification: "and we are persuaded that it is the most divine Jesus who is the superessential fragrance filling our spiritual being [τὸ νοερόν] with spiritual distributions of divine delight,"[199] and so finally to the recognition that the "symbolic combination of the myron depicts Jesus himself, who is the font and bliss of all divine and fragrant perceptions."[200] Jesus is the "sweet savor imprinting itself on its true images," the "spiritual food" of the deified, and therefore both the "archetypal νόησις" informing the sacrament and the power enabling the θεομίμητον. Purified, illumined, and perfected (ὡς ἐφικτόν), the clergy about the altar are ravished by his

---

196. *EH* IV.3.4 477C (98:24–26).
197. *EH* IV.3.4 477D–480A (99:3–8).
198. *EH* I.3 376A (66:14–19).
199. *EH* IV.3.4 477C (98:26–99:1).
200. *EH* IV.3.4 480A (99:8–10). See again Strothmann, *Myron-Weihe*, esp. lx: the consecration of the myron "ist ein Bekenntnis zur monophysitischen Christologie: wie nämlich bei der Mischung der Öle der Duft der kleinen Menge des Balsamöls die größere Menge des geruchlosen Olivenöls überdeckt, so durchdringt die Gottheit Christi die Menschheit Jesu."

sweetness, contemplate his light, and so are rendered imitators of his Providence.

3.3.3. The mirror of the angels. Dionysius, having sketched the virtues of the clergy, moves in the succeeding paragraphs[201] to a consideration of the celestial hierarchy, specifically the order of the seraphim. They, too, are established "around Jesus," and their "sacred γνῶσις," both "tireless . . . and unceasingly in possession of divine love," and "lying above every evil and forgetfulness," gives rise in them both to perpetual thanksgiving (an eternal Eucharist) and to the gift of their vision to those subordinate to them in a manner which at once hides, "in fashion undefiled, their supreme vision and participation," and distributes it in a manner "analogous" to the capacity of their dependents in the hierarchy.[202] This is the vision of perfection that has been mediated to us through "sensible images" in the Scripture and which, as Dionysius remarks to his "Timothy,"

> we have shown to your spiritual eyes . . . since indeed those who now surround in holy fashion the hierarch represent for us in brief that supreme order [the seraphim] itself, and now with immaterial eyes we shall see their most deiform splendor.[203]

The seraphim are the models for the clergy gathered around the altar. They are, indeed, more than simply models, but are actually present as well, the intelligible world of created beings invisibly among us—or, rather, visibly so long as we look with "immaterial eyes."[204] Our liturgy is at one with theirs, and it is called upon to become transparent to theirs in proportion to our capacity for

201. *EH* IV.3.5–10 480B–484A (99:15–102:4).

202. *EH* IV.3.5 480BC (99:15–100:5).

203. *EH* IV.3.6 480D (100:9–12).

204. Compare *CH* 121C (18:14–17) and 124A (9:8–15) with *EH* 372AB (64:2–14), and see Stiglmayr, "Die Engellehre des sogenannten Dionysius Aropagita," in *Compte rendu du quatrième Congrès scientifique des Catholiques* (ed. U. Chevalier; Fribourg: Oeuvre de Saint Paul, 1898), 406.

vision, for grace. The latter term brings us again to the one reality pervading, filling, and joining both hierarchies.

3.3.4. Jesus, our bond and consecration. Dionysius moves from consideration of the angelic ranks to their participation in Jesus' dispensation of salvation.[205] Following our author, we descend thus with Christ into our humanity and, with him in the baptismal waters blessed by the myron, into his saving death and Resurrection.[206] From the seraphim about the Presence to the tomb and death, embraced within a single paragraph, is a displacement of prodigious dimensions. Linking both, bond of the visible and invisible worlds, is the person of Jesus. Following the discussion of the clergy, then of the seraphim, and finally of the Incarnation, we find a final "settling," a "descent" that is in fact a coalescence, a resolution and coming together:

> Wherefore the tradition of sacred symbols, in the consecration
> of the divine myron, renders the seraphim present [to us],
> recognizing as unchanged and outlining Christ in his true and
> complete becoming man as we.[207]

The sacrament of the Chrism completes the movement toward the altar and up to God that we began with baptism, and it reveals that movement to have been a circle. What is revealed at the end of our journey from ignorance to knowledge, from sin to purification, from darkness to light, from imperfection to perfection, from earth to the courts of heaven, proves to have been present from the beginning. It is Christ who is the center, circumference, and all within. He is "our most divine altar."[208] Our sanctification, our union with the heavenly powers such that we may contemplate the seraphim in earthly symbols, the bond of heaven and earth, rests finally on and proceeds from the sacrifice of the Incarnation, Cross, and Resurrection, on what Dionysius, "quoting" his

205. *EH* IV.3.10 484A (101:19–102:4).
206. *EH* IV.3.10 484B (102:8–16).
207. *EH* IV.3.10 484A (102:1–4).
208. *EH* IV.3.12 484D (103:4–5 and 7–8).

masters, calls the "sacrament" or "initiation [τελετὴ] of God;" "for
it is his sacrament to be sanctified for us in a manner proper to
men, and in divine fashion both to consecrate all things and to
sanctify the consecrated."[209] Our union, ἕνωσις, and meditation
on that union is nothing more nor less than our sharing here
and now in Christ, in the unique sacrament of his dispensation
made present to us in Baptism, Eucharist, and the consecrating
oil. Sharing in that sacrament or presence, we become sharers in
the liturgy of the angels and are gathered with them about the
throne of God to echo their thanksgiving with the praise which, as
Dionysius tells us on concluding his treatment of the sacraments,
properly befits the works of God.[210]

Summary: We have traced the ascent that began outside the
gates of the Church and concluded within the sanctuary veils
around the altar. We began in the clamor and brokenness of the
fallen world and concluded with the timeless liturgy of the seraphim. We have discovered in all three of the mysteries, in the
"direct" thrust of the baptismal entry and re-birth, in the "spiral"
of the Eucharist gathering all up and into itself, and in the still
"circle" of contemplation at the myron's consecration, that the
Providence which is the source, model, active power, and goal of
these sacraments is one, and moreover, that this one Providence
is revealed in the person and dispensation—the "theurgies"—of
Jesus Christ. Through and in the unique sacrament of Jesus the
Christian is purified, illumined, and perfected, and made a concelebrant of the angels.

4. From the Altar to the Doors

4.1. Ministers and Ministered

4.1.1. The structure. We are required to become like God
through active imitation of him. Conversion requires procession, and to rise to the likeness of light means necessarily that
one must oneself become a light to others. It is not by accident

---

209. *EH* IV.3.12 485A (103:16–18).
210. *EH* IV.3.12 485B (103:19–104:2).

that our author led us to a consideration of the heavenly choirs at the conclusion of the consecration of the myron. Gathered about the Presence and simultaneously the enlighteners of those below them, the seraphim are the models of our clergy who, from meditation on the mystery of the altar, turn to purify, illumine, and perfect those below them. Thus the structure of the treatise, having taken us up to the summits of contemplation, the altar, now, in accordance with the "divine law,"[211] obliges us to retrace our steps back and down the ladder of ascents. From the altar, illumined, we proceed to the doors, and the light that we have traced to its source at the altar is, in the following chapters, discussed in its outward streaming, its radiance at once diminishing according to the degree of each order's participation in it, yet caught and revealed to the contemplative gaze in the operations of purification, illumination and perfection: first and foremost in the priestly orders whose actions body it forth—"the perfecting icons of the thearchic power"[212]—and then as received and contemplated by the laity, in particular by the monastic order.[213] There is a clearly outlined ladder of functions wherein the terms τάξις or διακόσμησις correspond to the English "rank."[214] Unlike the angelic hierarchy, wherein each rank is dependent upon the one immediately above it, in the ecclesiastical hierarchy there is a clear division[215] between the initiating or priestly ranks and those which are subject, both individually and as a group, to the former's ministrations. This same order, however, leads me to confront what is perhaps *the* problem of the Dionysian hierarchies.

4.1.2. Clericalism or charismaticism? John Meyendorff understands the Dionysian hierarchy as either a structure of ranks of "magical efficacy," or else as "charismatic," i.e., with the bishops

211. *EH* V.1.4 504C (106:24–25).

212. *EH* V.1.5 505B (107:21–22).

213. *EH* VI.1.3 532D (115:4–15).

214. See Roques (*L'univers*, 56) on the rough equivalence of τάξις/διάκοσμος.

215. For example, as described in *EH* V.1 (104:3–10).

corresponding to the Evagrian *illuminati* transposed, as it were, onto the sacerdotal ladder.[216] While there is indeed something to be said for an Evagrian connection here,[217] such a tidy dismissal of what Roques has referred to in another context[218] as the Dionysian "antinomies" is neither just nor helpful. The answer is instead in Dionysius' presentation of our hierarchy as an ideal form, a presentation that is linked to his idea of the hierarchy as icon. The difficulty lies largely in his failure to distinguish clearly the function of this icon as the present communication of grace from its role as pointer to a future, eschatological reality.

4.1.2.1. Arguments for a clerical/charismatic interpretation. Three aspects of Dionysius' treatment of our hierarchy appear to argue for this interpretation. The first is the apparent and often repeated[219] legalism of the Areopagite: "the lesser are incapable of leaping over to the greater, in addition to its being contrary to the divine decree [μῆδε θεμιτόν] for them to attempt such an imposture."[220] Again, the monk is on several occasions[221] specifically excluded from priestly functions, or, most explicitly in the *Epistle* to the erring Demophilus, directly forbidden and roundly blasted for having so presumed.[222] As Roques notes: "rien n'habille le moine pour le moindre fonction dans l'Église; il n'y fait en aucune façon figure de chef, mais seulement de fidèle . . . du suivant (ὀπαδός)."[223] The demarcation of function, coupled with a vocabulary that frequently uses terms such as "superiors," "inferiors," etc.,[224] certainly

216. See *Christ*, 78–79 and 82–83.
217. See my discussion in *Et introibo*, 298–299 and 325–327, on the "Messalians."
218. Roques, "Théologie de l'état monastique," 287.
219. See my discussion in chapter 4 above (1.1.2., "By Command of God: A Question of Law").
220. *EH* V.I.7 508C (109:18–20).
221. *EH* VI.1.3 533A and VI.3.1 533C (116:20–23 and 117:17–22).
222. *Ep.* VIII.1 1089B-1092A (177:10–180:3).
223. Roques, "Théologie de l'état monastique," 298.
224. For the frequency of such terms as, for example, δεύτεροι and πρῶτοι, see *Indices*, 42 and 124. See also Golitzin, *Et introibo*, 345 and n. 42, on Evagrius' use of the same vocabulary.

appears to weigh heavily toward a "yes." Secondly, there is the very nature of the lay and priestly ranks as an icon, as the collective image of the celestial hierarchy and the divine energies, and therefore as potentially transparent to that which it represents, i.e., the providential object of our contemplation. The legalism is thus strict so that "the order [διακόσμησις] of our hierarchy" be shown as definitely rejecting "the disordered [ἄτακτον] and confused," while "showing forth in the proportions of its ranks that which is decorous, ordered and steadfast,"[225] qualities that in turn point to our hierarchy as revealing and preserving "in human manner" the dispositions of the celestial hierarchy,[226] and so as finally declarative of the "Thearchy which first purifies, then illumines, then perfects."[227] The ecclesiastical hierarchy is the "hierarchic icon of divine things."[228] Seemingly linking yet more firmly the persons of those occupying the rungs of the hierarchic ladder to their iconic roles, Dionysius' portrait of the Church appears, thirdly, to offer little room for the principle of *ex opere operato*.[229] This appears in his discussion of prayer for the departed[230] wherein he declares that the bishop, as "interpreter of the divine justice," "would never seek that which is unpleasing to God . . . [i.e. pray for a sinner] because he would stray in this from the imperative order."[231]

Even more emphatic are his declarations in *Ep*. VIII, "nearness" to the altar signifies not only physical (τοπικῶς) nearness to God but degrees of "God-receptivity" (θεοδόχος ἐπιτηδειότης); thus,

> if the priestly order is illuminative [φωτισηκή], he has entirely fallen away from the priestly order and virtue who is not illumined.. . . . Such a one is not a priest . . . but a hostile

225. *EH* V.1.1 500D (104:6–10).

226. *EH* VI.3.5 536D–537A (119:12–15).

227. *EH* V.1.7 508CD–509A (109:21–110:5).

228. *EH* V.1.7 508C (110:2).

229. See Roques, *L'univers*, 296–297, and Stiglmayr, "Die Lehre von den Sakramenten," 295–296, but also von Balthasar, *Herrlichkeit*, 177–178.

230. *EH* VII.3.6–7 560C–564D (125:24–129:10).

231. *EH* VII.3.7 561D and 564D (127:16–17; 128:4–5). For this expression in relation to the bishop, see also *CH* XII.2 293A (43:9–11).

element, a deceiver, an entrapper of himself and a wolf set against the holy people.[232]

4.1.2.2. Arguments against a clerical/charismatic interpretation.

Let us consider again the sense of "office" or "function" as revealed in the highest of their respective orders—laity and clergy—the monk and the hierarch. Oppenheim and, following him, Roques[233] have noted the parallelism between monastic tonsure and Baptism present in Dionysius' account of the former. We might also observe a certain, as it were, sacramental intensification. The monk not only rejects the bad for the good as does the neophyte, but, leaving behind "fantasy" as well, strives for the "perfect philosophy," the "science of the unifying commandments"[234]—probably a reference to the evangelical precept of love. So, too, his tonsure is sealed with the Eucharist, the high point (κεφάλαιον) of the hierarchy,[235] which he now approaches with an intensified knowledge (θεία γνῶσις) as compared to the rest of the laity.[236] The monk continues, as Roques notes,[237] the movement from the doors to the altar, from West to East, as is revealed (an apparent Dionysian addition) through his being stationed near or next to the "gates of the sanctuary."[238] Yet he remains a member of the initiated

---

232. *Ep.* VIII.2 1092BC (180.12–181.9).

233. P. Oppenheim, "Mönchsweihe und Taufritus: Ein Kommentar zur Auslegung bei Dionysios dem Areopagiten," in *Miscellanea liturgica in honorem L. Cuniberti Mohlberg* (Rome: Edizioni liturgiche, 1948), 259–282; Roques, "Théologie de l'état monastique," 286–296.

234. *EH* VI.3.2 533D (117:23–25).

235. *EH* VI.3.5 536C (119:3–4); and see Oppenheim, "Mönchweihe und Taufritus," 280.

236. *EH* VI.3.5 536CD (119:4–7).

237. Roques, "Théologie de l'état monastique," 295–296.

238. *Ep.* VIII.1 1088D–1089A (176:12–177:1). Indeed, Dionysius' whole treatment of monastic tonsure is innovative, particularly his equation of it with baptism. His effort is in fact to integrate the monks thus into the structure of the visible Church, very likely in response to the dangers threatening the latter and coming primarily from the monastic enthusiasts ("Messalians") active still in the late fifth century, as well as the implications of Evagrian notions. See Golitzin, *Et introibo*, 319–322 and 355–359, for these points as

orders, subordinate to the clergy and, although taught directly
by the bishop and so led by the latter's "science . . . into most
perfect perfection,"[239] he remains nonetheless one who is led,
a "follower." Does this mean that even the monk cannot participate directly in the mystical union? Such does not appear to
be the case. The monk's activity, in Roques' words, is "stricte-
ment intérieur, consiste à retrouver la stable et sainte unité de la
monade."[240] He is to remain in himself, "in a uniform [μοναδικὴ]
and holy στάσις."[241] Recalling the three modes of spiritual motion and applying them to each of the initiated orders: if the
"motion" of the neophytes is primarily "direct" and equivalent
to purification, while that of the baptized laity is "spiral" and
signifies the illumination they receive from their presence at
the sacraments, then the "motion" of the monks is representative of the "circular" mode, the "motion" or activity proper
to mystical union, and his role or function is thus to stand as
representative of the summit of contemplative—which is here
also to say passive—activity.[242]

What of the bishop? Does he in fact deliver or mediate the
ἕνωσις? Here it might be helpful to take up the suggestions offered
by Orrieux.[243] The latter sees the function of Dionysius' "hierarch"
rooted in the ecclesiastical practice—and even partially the vocabulary[244]—of our author's era. The function of the bishop's
"perfecting" lies in his explanation (catechetical or mystagogical

---

well as for Dionysius' simultaneous attachment in some of his apparent
"innovations" to traditional elements in Syrian Christianity. The physical
placement of the ascetics is one such element.

239. *EH* VI.1.3 532D (116:13–14).

240. Roques, "Théologie de l'état monastique," 298.

241. *EH* VI.1.3 533C (117:20).

242. Note that *Ep.* I and II, on ἀγνωσία and σκότος, are addressed to
monks.

243. L. M. Orrieux, "L'Évêque 'perfectior' selon le Ps.-Denys," in *L'Évêque
dans l'Église du Christ* (Paris: Brouwer, 1962), 237–242.

244. Orrieux, "L'Évêque 'perfectior' selon le Ps.-Denys," 237–238. Orrieux
cites particularly the *Apostolic Constitutions* (PG I, 189, 801–805 and 1149–1153)
as paralleling Dionysius in 165A, 377A, 512B–513A, and our author's stress
on each order of the hierarchy obeying its proper limits.

lectures) of the "symbols" which the neophytes are seeing for the first time, and in the continued explication of doctrine and preaching directed toward the laity.[245] A similar teaching program, on an intensified scale, could thus be envisioned for the monks. The extreme single-mindedness required of their "order," always a group prone to excesses, might also explain the rigor of Dionysius' insistence on the due order of the hierarchy in his *Epistle to Demophilus*. We might then read the ἐπιστήμη of the hierarch as equivalent to the teaching office that was traditionally held to be the peculiar duty of the episcopacy. Transmission of knowledge, rather let me say the magisterium, is limited to the hierarch and, through him, to his clergy. He, and through him his clergy, alone have the right to interpret authoritatively. The *visio Dei*, however, as an experience would be open to others. Thus we might justify Armstrong's understanding of the Areopagite as "a good churchman, who likes to think of God's gifts being distributed decently and in order in heaven and on earth," and who therefore sees to it to stress "that superiors will have their proper function of loving care for their inferiors and transmit the gifts which they have received to them," while "the inferiors will have the proper attitude of receptive humility."[246]

Lastly, in connection with the stress on charity, we might view the hierarch, at the peak of the initiators into the mysteries, as parallel to the monk at the peak of the initiated. The hierarch stands at the summit of the active side or facet of contemplation, of θεομίμησις, while the monk incarnates the passive virtues. All of the active virtue (δύναμις) of the hierarchy rests in the bishop—together, of course, with all of its knowledge or ἐπιστήμη.[247]

4.1.2.3. An abiding ambiguity. Yet this explanation still remains partial. As much as I would like to endorse Armstrong and Orrieux with respect to these matters, I am nonetheless confronted

245. Orrieux, "L'Évêque 'perfectior' selon le Ps.-Denys," 239–242.
246. Armstrong, "Negative Theology," 183–184.
247. For example, *EH* V.3.7 513C (113:18–20); but, see *Ep.* VIII.1 1085Cff. (173:11–175:13) where Demophilus is bidden to look directly to Jesus for both his example of charity and his illumination.

by texts which present the bishop as, both *ex officio* and personally it seems, on a higher level of perfection than everyone else—in "virtue" and in "knowledge." I believe that Dionysius is, in part, just what Armstrong says he is, but it remains to be said that the latter's dismissal of hierarchy as simply "good church order" fails to meet two requirements. I cannot, first of all, use it to reply to such texts as we encounter in, for example, *Ep.* VIII: "each order [διακόσμησις] of those about God [περὶ θεόν] is more deiform than [the one] which is further distant, and both more illumined and more illumining are those that are closer to the true light,"[248] an equation that would clearly place the priestly orders about the altar itself on a higher level, in every sense, than any of the lay ranks.

Am I left with Meyendorff's choice: magic or charismaticism? While I would choose the former as closer to our author's mind[249] if forced, I feel that the "antinomies" uncovered by Roques in his examination of Dionysius' account of the monastic estate are closer to the Dionysian problem. They are:

> L'orientation [du moine] à peu près exclusivement vertical [mais] . . . son obligation de service dans l'Église: la primauté de Christ avec la primauté de l'Un; l'espèce de juridism inhérent aux cadres et aux médiations hiérarchiques avec le "pneumatism" que représentent les exigences de l'union mystique.[250]

The presence, however muted by the arguments of Orrieux and Armstrong, of these antinomies brings me to my second requirement and to the key of the Dionysian tensions regarding the orders, as it were, of law and of grace. The Areopagite has been compelled, both by the intent or thrust of his vision and the very mode or style with which he has chosen to clothe that vision,[251] to present his readers with a markedly—if not extraordinarily—

---

248. *Ep.* VIII.2 1092B (180:12–15).
249. See Golitzin, *Et introibo*, 319–348, esp. 340–341.
250. Roques, "Théologie de l'état monastique," 313.
251. Koch, *Beziehungen*, 92–97.

idealized picture of the Church structure and functioning. It is this idealization that, allowing for the ambiguities noted above, requires the virtual identification of law and grace, of office and person, inasmuch as the latter two "orders" are both expressed by the single "order" (τάξις) of hierarchy. The τάξις of our (or any) hierarchy is, we have seen, more than simply the mode ordained for the orderly transfer of information. It is as well the symbol, icon, or revelation of the very structures of grace. When looking toward the altar of the Church, we are called upon to do more than consider the physical presence of the sacraments, clergy and faithful. We are ultimately asked to discern in these symbols, in the order of their arrangement and in the sequence of the transmission of knowledge about them, the presence of Christ, the stable ranks of the angels, the eternal outflowings of the divine powers, and ourselves. It is in order, I believe, to make this iconic vision clear, to give it exclusive prominence, that Dionysius has chosen his particular—indeed, peculiar—mode of presentation, a mode which excludes nearly all concern for detail fine or otherwise, and avoids any adjustments such as might be required by the intrusions of the actual; for example, the simple fact that not all (rather few, in fact) bishops are "holy." Everything and everyone must fit within the picture.

If the orders of law and grace are completely identical, then this would point to another grave problem in Dionysius' presentation. To use the language of biblical scholarship, he would be preaching a completely "realized eschatology": all is now as it should and will always be. Hornus' judgment of Dionysius' eschatological passages would then be entirely justified: "C'est là une donnée chrétien totalement étrangère à la structure générale du monde dionysien, et plaquée par dessus son système philosophique comme une affirmation de la foi."[252] This is not the case, however. But in order to prove my contention, we must turn to a consideration of chapter 7 of the *EH*.

---

252. Hornus, "Quelques réflexions," 54n. 54.

4.2. The Mystery of Burial: Once Again outside the Doors; Dionysius' Eschatology

In light of what I have said up to this point and in view of Hornus' opinion (which is far from a lonely one) I must ask first if Dionysius' eschatology is truly present; secondly, what he says it to be; and, thirdly, what possible place it can have within his system.

4.2.1. Formally correct. The texts leave us in no doubt as to the affirmation, at least *pro forma*, of the Resurrection and traditional Christian doctrine concerning it. I have already mentioned two references to the Christian hope appearing in the *DN*. Once in the treatise's "Introduction" in connection with the dispensation of symbols as a feature of this age,[253] and again in the sixth chapter, on "Life" mentioning the promise to transfer "our whole selves, both . . . souls and the bodies linked to them, to all-perfect life and immortality."[254] The second reference to the Resurrection in the *DN* occurs in the chapter devoted to "eternity" and time, where Dionysius remarks that, whereas "here-below [ἐνθάδε] the theology [Scripture] says we are bound by time [κατὰ χρόνον ὁριζόμενον], [we shall have] participation in eternity when we have attained to the eternity which is incorruptible and ever the same."[255] Elsewhere, *Ep.* VIII speaks of rewards and punishments in the future life, while *Ep.* IX, at greater length, of the royal banquet [συμπόσια] where the King himself, Jesus, will serve his guests.[256] Half the references are, however, to be found within the *EH* and of these, with one exception,[257] the majority are in turn concentrated in chapter 7, whose first two paragraphs provide us with Dionysius' most complete statement.[258]

---

253. *DN* I.4 592C (114:1–115:8).
254. *DN* VI.2 856D (192:1–5).
255. *DN* X.3 937D (216:11–13).
256. *Ep.* VIII.5 1097AB (187:8–188:6) and IX.5 1112D–1113A (205:8–206:7).
257. *EH* III.3.9 437BC (88:22–89:10).
258. *EH* VII.1.1–2 556A (120:13–122:11); elsewhere: VII.3.1 557AB (123:16–124:7) and VII.3.9 565B (129:23–130:5).

In order to find what the Christian hope is not, we look to the second paragraph of the chapter.[259] Writing against the opinions of the "unholy" (ἀνιεροί), Dionysius lists four unacceptable options. The Resurrection is not: (1) non-existence (ἀνυπαρξία); (2) the severance or permanent "liberation" of the soul from an embodied state which is fundamentally alien (ἀνάρμοστον) to it; (3) the taking-on of another body; (4) an exact repetition of the conditions of the present state of embodied existence, including the need for food and drink. Positively, then, Dionysius argues for a life after death that will be "according to the scriptural promises." This life will entail a resurrection (ἀνάστασις) and therefore an embodied state. Moreover, the resurrection body will be the same body that had been linked to the soul (ὁμόζυγον) and fought the latter's battle together with it (συναθλῆσεν), and which has therefore been "co-inscribed [συναπογραφέν]" with it in the Kingdom. As he notes below, "our life in Christ has already begun,"[260] we have already "become members [μέλη]" of Christ.[261] The body, though, will be changed and share in the soul's "transition . . . to an all-perfect life and incorruption."[262] The vision of the Resurrection as Dionysius depicts it is therefore fully traditional, reminiscent indeed of the eschaton as depicted, for example, in 1 Corinthians 15.

4.2.2. Consistent with the *EH*. Does Dionysius' eschatology play any logical role in his overall vision, or has our author simply tacked it on to the *EH*, and elsewhere, in obedience to the demands of orthodoxy? Looking first to the structure itself, primarily literary, of the *EH*, I feel enabled to say that this doctrine is not a *Fremdkörper*.[263] On the contrary, it is implicit in the treatise's construction and intent. The fairly long chapter (nine full columns, certainly rather a good deal to devote to the funeral rite were it not felt to be important) comes as the required conclusion to the movement that began with the convert's first steps toward the

---

259. *EH* VII.1.2 553B–556A (121:10–122:11).
260. *EH* VII.1.2 553C (121:13–14).
261. *EH* VII.1.1 553B (121:5–7).
262. *DN* VI.2 856D (192:2–3).
263. So Brons, *Gott und die Seienden*, 3.

Church doors. As I think indicated by the discussion on the angels in the final paragraphs of chapter 6,[264] it is, moreover, a conclusion that looks forward to a resolution beyond the confines of the present age. If the ecclesiastical hierarchy is intended to cover and to consecrate all of human existence, "the whole man hallowing and his complete salvation hieratically effecting," it follows that "the Resurrection will be his [man's] most perfect salvation."[265] Recalling that Dionysius has defined σωτηρία as being the preservation of each nature,[266] I wonder how else an embodied spirit would be preserved "according to its proper . . . being and order" unless it were through Resurrection (another example, perhaps, of an essentially Christian understanding informing a Neoplatonic commonplace). The seventh chapter marks the end of the movement from "doors" to altar to "doors," at both ends of which there is a "dying" in Christ and to the world. Dionysius is careful therefore to note the parallels with Baptism: the last kiss and anointing of the body with myron recall the conclusion to the first sacrament,[267] just as the expression "re-birth [παλιγγενεσία]"[268] echoes the "divine birth" of Baptism. The Christian's struggles (ἀγῶνες), of which Baptism marked the beginning[269] and monastic tonsure the intensification,[270] are here portrayed as attaining their conclusion[271] in sure hope of a "cessation of labors . . . and a city divine [πολιτεία ἔνθεος] in the light and land of the living."[272] To reject the transcendent end of the cycle, the overcoming of death, would thus be to reject the cycle as a whole: the Fall, the Incarnation, Baptism, and, between the "ends" toward and from the altar, the progression of sacraments wherein Dionysius has sought to portray "the divine ordinance [θεσμοθεσία]" as "providing

---

264. *EH* VI.3.5–6 537A–537C (119:13–120:12).
265. *EH* VII.3.9 565BC (130:3–5); see also Roques, *L'univers*, 8.
266. *DN* VIII.9 896D (205:16–19).
267. *EH* VII.3.8 565A (129:12–22).
268. *EH* VII.1.1 553A (120:23) and VII.1.3 556B (122:15).
269. See *EH* II.3.5 and II.3.6 401A–404A (76:11–77:23).
270. See *EH* VI.1.3 532D–533A (116:9–19); VI.3.2 533D (117:23–118:5).
271. *EH* VII.1.1 553AB (121:1–4) and VII.3.9 565BC (129:24–130:5).
272. *Ep.* IX.5 1112D–1113A (206:1–3).

communion in the divine to both [soul and body]."[273] The inner consistency of the *EH* would be quite broken.

4.2.3. Consistent with the *CD* as a whole. I have noted the opinion suggested by Roques concerning the discrepancies between the strictly vertical vision of the *CH* and the obviously more fluid, less rigidly fixed, structure of the *EH*. Roques advanced the view that Dionysius was compelled by the presence of an already existing Church structure to adjust his Neoplatonic doctrine and treatment in order to account for it. As I maintain that the *EH* provides us with the unique context within which the other treatises are to be read and their doctrine apprehended, I cannot accept Roques' analysis as adequate. Dionysius looks up to the *CH* (and *DN/MT*) from the *EH*, and not down from the angelic world to ours. He invites us to look up to the vision of a perfect, unfallen world and toward that time when we, too, shall be granted the lineaments of its sure and certain foundation (ἵδρυσις) in God.[274] It is the perspective one takes in treating Dionysius that is crucial. To read him from, as it were, the top downward—as do most of his critics—is inevitably to portray him as primarily a Neoplatonist philosopher with Christian pretensions, whose descent from certain immutable, divine principles grows increasingly more uncertain, and his discourse increasingly spotted with Christian excrescences, until, by the time he has stumbled all the way down to the realm of the phenomenal, i.e., the Church, his vision has grown so riddled with inconsistencies and top-heavy with accretions that it suffers exactly that "shipwreck" that Hornus understood as the outcome of the *CD*.[275] To take, on the other hand, his Christian professions seriously and so begin with him at the "doors" of the Church, and then move toward the altar and up to the latter's significance, will eliminate a great many, if

273. *EH* VII.3.9 565B (129:29).

274. See *DN* I.4 592BC (113:11–115:5); VII.2 865D (194:10–15); *EH* VII.1.1 553A (120:16–22); and *Ep.* IX.5 1112Dff. (205:8ff.).

275. Hornus, "Quelques réflexions," 57–62; idem, "Les recherches dionysiennes de 1955 à 1960: Bibliographie dionysienne 1954–1959," *RHPR* 41 (1961): 22–81, at 80–81.

not all, of the problems which its critics have, particularly in the twentieth century, discovered in the *CD*.

I maintain in any case that this is precisely the case with regard to the "failure" of our hierarchy exactly to parallel the angels'. When we look up through our hierarchy to that of the angels, the same inconsistencies that to the philosopher appeared embarrassing now take on an entirely new dimension, or better, point toward the new age. They become, in short, eschatological indicators. The ecclesiastical hierarchy is indeed a "fluid" organism, its ranks are not fixed insofar as one may move up—and down—among them. The very fact of initiation (Baptism), of hieratic consecration (ordination), of the existence of penitents and others who have fallen from grace (and their possible re-admission), even the want or tenuous nature of the *ex opere operato* principle, and, last and most glaringly of all, the fact of death to which Dionysius devotes considerable space, these all point to, require, a resolution beyond the confines of the present age.

4.2.4. A reply to the problems of law and grace: the nature of an icon. That the ἀναλογία or divine purpose for each particular Christian is not infallibly apparent on examination of the actual composition of the hierarchical ladder at any given time, and that the position of each does not necessarily even correspond to his or her state of personal grace or, even if so, that the possibility of descent or of further ascent (in short, the ἄγων) is always present—all of this renews the questions with which I concluded my last section: the "orders" of law and grace, realized eschatology, and the nature of the icon. If the interior reality of persons in the ecclesiastical hierarchy does not correspond to their exterior rank, and if even a bishop may prove false, then, while the structures of grace and the visible ordering of the ranks of faithful may be virtually identified, they cannot be so completely. There is a manifest tension within the single τάξις of our hierarchy. This tension is limited by, and points toward, death and the resolution of the future age. Dionysius' eschatology therefore cannot be a fully realized one. The ranks and functions embraced by the hierarchical τάξις truly reveal the active power and, as it were, shape of grace, but they are also open. They reveal and demand both a vocation and a hope. This, I maintain, is the very nature of our hierarchy as icon: it is both the reality of grace and the promise of grace, the revelation in fact of him who is present and still to come, ὁ ὢν καὶ ὁ ἐρχόμενος (Rev 4:8; cf. 1:4).

4.2.5. The resurrection as fulfillment of the icon. I return at this point to the idea itself of Resurrection and ask how it fits, if at all, within Dionysius' system as I have described it so far. Central to the notion of Resurrection, as the Christian tradition has proclaimed it, is the insistence on the continuity of the embodied state in the world to come. At the same time, the tradition looks toward a permanent change or transfiguration in the conditions of incarnate being that will enable a communion within God at once far greater—"eye hath not seen" (1 Cor 2:9)—than is possible to us in the present age, and no longer subject to diminishment or falling away. I have shown that Dionysius, too, has both the continuity and the change, i.e., that his formal presentation meets the requirements of orthodoxy. Indeed, but does he mean it? It appears to me that he does, because it answers the requirements and tensions within his presentation of the body, and so by extension of the ecclesiastical hierarchy as icon. The embodied state is one within the "veils" I discussed in my previous chapter, that nexus of matter, form, gesture, and word through and in which the divine dispensation, Christ, acts to reveal himself while remaining hidden. The body is, on the personal level, what our hierarchy is for the whole: the image of the present age, the reality of symbols through which we have been given to discern the lineaments of the age to come "as in a glass darkly" (1 Cor 13:12). The two, our hierarchy and the body, parallel one another in their reflection of the tensions of existence and loyalty to Christ in a world still darkened by the Fall. Where the ecclesiastical hierarchy reflects this in the "fluidity" and consequent tensions I noted above, the incarnate spirit does so in its continued struggle against the "appetites of the flesh,"[276] the

---

276. *EH* V.3.4 512A (111:22).

"corrupting pleasures" and "seeming good"[277] that infect the will and turn it toward sin[278]—in short, the struggle with "the inclinations . . . and deceits of the Adversary [τοῦ ἐναντίου]."[279] Reflecting one another in the ἄγων, they both look forward to the same hope. A Christian death signifies both the end of the struggle and the transition (μετάταξις) to a state of being without change (τὸ ἄτρεπτον).[280] Having shared with the soul in its struggles, the body will share as well "in the soul's inalterable foundation in the divine life [ἐν τῇ ἀτρέπτῳ κατὰ τὴν θείαν ζωὴν ἱδρύσει]."[281] With the end of the struggle, with death and Resurrection, comes the shift from mutable to immutable where, we may assume, the outer and inner realities will correspond, and thus the end of the age of the icon: "they shall see more clearly [ὁρῶσι ἐμφανέστερον]."[282] "*Now*," As Dionysius writes in the crucial text from the *DN* 1.4 592BC, we are obliged to see "through the sacred veils of the philanthropy of Scripture and the hierarchical tradition"; "*now*, as is possible for us . . . we make use of symbols for the divine things." "But *then*," as immortal and incorruptible, "we shall be filled full of his *visible* [ὁρατῇ] theophany, shining round about us in most evident [φανόταται] brilliancies, as about the disciples in that most divine transfiguration"—but then, in another's words, we shall see "face to face."[283]

Both body and soul, both the Christian and the Church, look forward to the day when Christ will be all in all. The icon, as I have stressed, is a notion linked firmly to the Incarnation, the means whereby Christ, and through him, the angels and the "powers" of God, are presently discerned and their presence felt. If it looks,

---

277. *EH* III.3.7 433D–436A (86:21–24) and *DN* XI.5 953A (220:21–221:4).
278. *EH* II.3.3 400A (74:15–19).
279. *EH* III.3.11 440C (90:20–21).
280. *EH* VII.1.1 553A (121:1).
281. *EH* VII.1.1 553A (121:3–47).
282. *EH* VII.1.2 553 (121:24).
283. Note the sequence: νῦν μὲν . . . τότε δὲ . . . νῦν δὲ (114:1; 114:7; 115:6). And see my article "On the Other Hand," esp. 312–316. See also the Scholiast's remark that, in this passage, Dionysius affirms the body's share in the Resurrection (*PG* IV, col. 197C).

then, back to the dispensation of Christ, it must equally anticipate the Resurrection; and, if individual Christians look forward to the resurrection of their own bodies, then it can only be because they have become one with the single body of Christ, "ὡς μέλη χριστοῦ γεγονότα."[284] The ecclesiastical hierarchy is this single body, the present reality of the Incarnation and thus, necessarily, of the Resurrection: "our most divine life in Christ which has already begun [ἀρχθεῖσα ἤδη]."[285]

5. Summary of the *Ecclesiastical Hierarchy* and the *Corpus Dionysiacum*

5.1. *A Series of Icons*

Let me begin my recapitulation with the *EH*. It is an icon. An icon is a place of meeting or joining (συμ-βολή) of different realities. It can be an image in the strict sense, but I understand the term as covering persons as well as things, actions, and mental constructs or ideas. Whatever the particular icon may be, it always carries both a revelation and a vocation, a presence and a promise. The icon which is our hierarchy is one that works at one and the same time on several levels, at once revealing and thus realizing the presence of: (1) Providence; (2) the angels; (3) the Incarnation; (4) our world, i.e., our "context" of space, time, and matter as redeemed; thus (5) our very selves; and finally (6) the mystical union itself. I have discussed (3), (4), and (5) chiefly in connection with *EH*, while (1), (2), and (6) would appear to be properly the subjects of, respectively, the *DN*, *CH*, and *MT*. It has been my thesis, though, that each of the latter three discovers its proper setting or context within the frame of the *EH*. I move, then, to a brief summary of each of these icons.

(1) As outlined in the first section of my preceding chapter, each hierarchy is the complete manifestation of Providence on a given plane of being, the divine *ad extra*, "the icon of the divine

---

284. *EH* VII.1.1 553B (121:5–6).
285. *EH* VII.1.2 553C (121:13).

beauty."[286] The τάξις of hierarchy reveals the uncreated powers at work in the creature, while hierarchic "science" means participation, through contemplation of the τάξις and its content, in the divine wisdom informing those powers, and hierarchic "activity" the sharing in the δυνάμεις themselves—i.e., finally the sharing in the single creative and unifying action of divine love. Hierarchy, generally, is thus the revelation, contemplation of, and participation in God as he "moves out of" himself.

(2) The hierarchies, specifically, are two, corresponding to the two fundamental categories of created being: (1) intelligible (νοητός) and (2) sensible (αἰσθητός), pure spirit and incarnate existence, the worlds of angels and of humans. The former enjoy the priority—a given of the Platonic tradition, it is true, but one no less rooted in Christian patristic tradition and even the NT. As I have noted, the angelic is the model of our own hierarchy. Their perfect and unfallen spiritual world is declared in Scripture, in whose revelation to us they have played a mediatory role,[287] and it is mirrored in the structures of our rites and rankings. Their active presence is, indeed, as much a feature of our cult as it has been in the granting of Scripture. God has made us their "concelebrants."[288] Through our hierarchy we are both linked to theirs and are given to contemplate their presence.

(3) But it was not always thus. The link between human and angelic, between our mode of being and theirs, was disturbed, broken, by the Fall, through which we were given over to the devil and his angels. Even the gift of the Law to Moses and the OT dispensation established only a partial and shadowy reflection of the celestial hierarchy (the νοητά).[289] Thus, we find the ecclesiastical hierarchy as the icon of that specific "procession" of God which re-established us in communion with him and so with the angels: the Incarnation of Jesus Christ. It is through the "theurgies" of Christ that we are rendered concelebrants (συλλειτουργοί) of the

286. *CH* III.2 165B (18:11).
287. *CH* IV.3 180D–181A (22:11–17); and chapter 4 above (2.1.2. "A Perfected Creation: Our Models for the Life in God").
288. See, for example, *CH* I.3 124A (9:9–10).
289. *EH* V.1.2 501CD (105:9–21).

heavenly liturgy. These same theurgies are rendered present to us through the cult. In Christ's presence, now, we discover the presence of both the past and the future, for the ecclesiastical hierarchy is peculiarly the icon of the world to come, sign and presence of the eschaton. The Church which enfolds us in Baptism is the body of his Incarnation, radiant for holy eyes with his divinity.

(4) The "powers," or Providence, bring us back to the notion of τάξις and my discussion in chapter 4. If a hierarchy is the reflection or analog of Providence on a given plane of being, then it follows that it must embrace everything which is real and enduring on that plane, i.e., real and enduring as the expression of the divine will. Our hierarchy is therefore the icon of our world, both the latter's present reality and the revelation of its promised transfiguration. Matter, form, gesture, and spoken word are the "veils" of our hierarchy and the components of human existence. Thus, our hierarchy embraces the whole of the physical world. It is the revelation, consecration, and promise of redemption of the entire sphere of our being, both actualizing (albeit at present "hiddenly") and pointing toward the time when the whole of material creation will become fully transparent to the spiritual and divine. The meaning of our world, the soul, as it were, of the cosmos, discovers itself at the altar.

(5) With the discovery of the world's sense or soul within the sanctuary, comes as well the revelation of one's own soul or being, and of its meaning. The ecclesiastical hierarchy is also the image of humanity, of the individual Christian from birth (in Baptism) to death (being ushered outside of the doors in the sacrament of burial). We find portrayed in between, in the sequence of ranks, the stages of the Christian life: from purification to illumination to contemplative union and then, moving down from the altar, the action of the θεομίμησις—or exercise of love—which must follow communion with God, as represented in the grades of the clergy. I spoke above of the parallel between the individual and the Church, that both bear physical bodies through which they have been given to know and to manifest God. The altar, then, is for both the sign and reality of Christ's presence, of God, and of the promised transfiguration to come. The altar is for our

world the place where it discovers its soul, Christ, and so it is also the type of that "place" within each believer, hidden now by the "veils" of the flesh, where he must turn in order to discover God in himself. The altar is the type of the soul.

(6) We are brought to our last icon: our hierarchy as the type, and so for each the potential fact, of the mystical union itself. Let us, rather, continue our narrowing process and say that the whole Church hierarchy as I have discussed it is the icon of the individual soul. The altar thus answers to that "place" (τόπος) within each soul where God stoops to dwell, the "peak" of the Mountain where, having completed the ascent, the believer encounters the divine darkness. Bearing in mind Dionysius' assertion that each reason-endowed being (Dionysius has νοῦς) has "first, middle, and final powers," powers he further identifies as participation in the divine activities of purification, illumination and perfection,[290] we discover the soul motif as borne out when we recall the parallel I sought to establish beween the three motions of the soul in contemplation[291] and the activities that are proper to each of the primary three sacraments. Furthermore, I tried to indicate the role that each rank of the hierarchy plays as representing one of the three motions in either its passive aspect (the laity) or its active one (the clergy)—hence as well certain of the difficulties in Dionysius' notion of the τάξις.[292] At the heart of this motion or activity, directed toward it in contemplation and proceeding from it in the θεομίμησις, we find the altar, sign in this instance of that place or "faculty" (ἕνωσις[293]) within the human

290. *CH* X.3 273C (41:1–6); and see Gandillac, 141n. 4.

291. *DN* IV.9 705AB (153:10–154:6).

292. See *CH* IX.3 260C (37:17–38:1); and Gandillac, 134n. 4, concerning the term ἀνομοιότης (see also *DN* VIII.9 897BC [206:11–207:5]). The latter is a key notion for the understanding of hierarchy as the divinely willed diversity of the created world. Unlike Origen (*Peri Archon* II.9.2), Dionysius does not admit an original equality of all creatures (see my discussion in *Et introibo*, 274–275). As a result, however, we do discover that undeniable ambiguity in the Dionysian cosmos, "liée à une métaphore unique, qui designe à la fois l'ordre hiérarchique voulu par Dieu et les désordres nés du péché" (Gandillac, 134n. 4).

293. *DN* I.1 585B–588A (108:3–5).

soul which is *capax Dei*. Recalling my discussion above (II.3) of the triad ἀφαίρεσις - ἀγνωσία - ἕνωσις as indivisible from purification - illumination - perfection, we may thus say of the altar that it is the sign of ἔκστασις and union with the divine.

5.2. Jesus: The Presence of the "Sudden"

The divine for Dionysius is not, however, a faceless entity. If in the review of our hierarchy as icon I spoke just now of a "narrowing" process, from the δυνάμεις of God to the angels, to the Incarnation, to our world, to humanity, to the soul and union with God, then at the terminus of these "compressions," at the very point of the intersection of human and divine, we discover Christ: "Jesus, our most divine altar . . . in whom . . . we have access [to God]."[294] It is Jesus who went "forth from the One which is his by nature,"[295] who "took on essence from everything which is truly human,"[296] and, having become human while remaining divine, took "that which is ours and raised it far above us."[297] The humanity, or body, of Christ is the Church that enfolds and incorporates us, the Church typified and rendered actual within the enclosure of the temple and the gathering of the baptized faithful at the mysteries. The "divinity of Jesus which is cause of all things"[298] and "works all things in all"[299] is the goal and term of the ἀναγωγή. It is indeed *the* mystery of the altar, the "darkness" beyond the light that forms the subject of the *MT*.

The themes of Christ, altar, and soul—together with a striking illustration of Dionysius' ability to allude simultaneously to sources in both Christian and Platonist literature—converge in the first five of the *Ep.* that conclude the *CD*, in particular in *Epistle* III. As I have shown in chapter 1.6, *Ep.* I through V work as a kind of chiasm, with V paralleling I, IV picking up on II, and

---

294. *EH* IV.3.10 484D (103:4–7).
295. *EH* III.3.13 444C (93:18).
296. *MT* III 1033A (146:7–8).
297. *DN* II.10 648D–649A (135:3–9).
298. *DN* II.10 648C (134:7).
299. *DN* XI.5 953A (221:8).

Ep. III tying them up and together. To summarize the points made by *Ep.* III, the center and "punchline" of the chiasm: "suddenly" (ἐξαίφνης) each Christian may meet Christ, who is the eternal and infinite in the flesh. The meeting takes place on two levels, in the temple and on the altar of the Church's liturgy, and within the sanctuary of the believer's heart, or νοῦς. This meeting also includes the accompaniment of the heavenly liturgy. Recalling the μεσημβρία, together with the NT allusions and Dionysius' own use of the Transfiguration in *DN* I.4, the meeting appears to be an experience of overpowering light. Creator (στάσις) and creature (κίνησις) are joined, and in order to meet both must have departed from themselves (ἔκστασις), though God remains ever and wholly transcendent (νοούμενον ἄγνωστον) while the human being does not lose his or her humanity. This is, in short, the θεανδρικὴ ἐνέργεια and heavenly polity of the Church, the anticipation of the eschaton in Christ's sacramental and experiential (or mystical) presence. Thus it is not at all surprising to find Dionysius concluding his *Epistles*, and the *CD* as a whole, with a letter to John the Divine in exile on Patmos.[300] This allusion to Revelation, with that book's sharp eschatological anticipation and liturgical tone (in addition to prophetic experience), fits the Dionysian ἐξαίφνης: "Amen. Even so, come Lord Jesus" (Rev 22:20). The visible things, as Dionysius writes the seer, are "manifest images of the invisible" (i.e., of the eschaton), and there are already faithful who, here on earth, have begun to taste of the Kingdom to come.[301]

The Dionysian ascent from the physical realm (the ecclesiastical hierarchy) to the world of created intelligible being (the celestial hierarchy), and thence to the uncreated νοητά or divine Providence (the divine Names), and finally to the hidden divinity is a series of meditations on the ecclesiastical hierarchy and the mystery of the altar. We are called to the θεωρία of the icon which is the Church. It is the icon embracing all icons, the place of our encounter with God and constituted as such by Christ's Incarnation and abiding presence.

300. *Ep.* X 1117A–20A (208–209).
301. *Ep.* X 1117B (208:9 and 209:2).

5.3. *The Unity of the* Corpus Dionysiacum *in the* Ecclesiastical Hierarchy

Turning very briefly to the *CH* and *DN*, we see that the *EH* is also intended to embrace them. In the *CH*, the first three chapters are devoted to themes linking the two hierarchies, i.e., to the notion of hierarchy in general (with special mention of ours as reflecting the angelic one and of the Church as a whole reflecting the ordering of the soul[302]), and to the modes of interpretation of Scripture and its images. The remainder of the treatise is given over to the analysis of angelic characteristics as described by the biblical names for them, and the accounts and nature of their activities. Here as well, however, the connection with the *EH* is not difficult to discern. The angels are described as both exemplars— thus, for example, the first order of the *CH* and its continual "liturgy" of praise in contemplation of God as the "places [τόποι] of the divine rest"[303]—and as active agents in revelation. The first level of created being, the νοητά, are our models and our guides.

The *DN* has as its subject the second and uncreated level of the νοητά—the "intelligible names of God,"[304] his Providence or δυνάμεις. This treatise, too, claims its basis in Scripture.[305] Indeed, but how does this place the *DN* within a liturgical context? As I have had occasion to note, the Scripture is very much in the midst of the *EH*. It is placed upon the altar, its exposition is the particular prerogative of the hierarch;[306] it instructs the faithful in all things;[307] it is read at every service. The liturgical aspect of the *DN* is, in my view, further borne out by the remarkable language Dionysius employs throughout this treatise—as throughout the entire *CD*. Koch devotes considerable space to the influence of the mystery language on our author.[308] I believe that this vocabu-

302. See esp. *CH* I.3 121C–124A (8:14–9:15).

303. *CH* VII.4 212C (32:7–8).

304. *DN* I.1 588A (121:6).

305. See *DN* I.1 588A (108:6–8); I.2 588C (110:2–4); I.3 589B (111:6–12); and I.4 589D (112:7).

306. *EH* V.3.7 513CD (113:17–114:6).

307. *EH* III.3.4 429C-432A (83:13–84:6).

308. Koch, *Beziehungen*, 92ff.

lary, represented by such terms as ὑμνεῖν or ὑμνολογία,[309] points to Dionysius' basic concern to maintain what I might call a "cultic ambience" in all his works.[310] The hush of the sanctuary—recall the frequent injunctions on silence before the uninitiated[311]— prevails throughout the corpus. No less than the angels (rather, more so if anything, inasmuch as they are prior, the source of both hierarchies) are the powers or energies of God at work within our hierarchy and revealed by it. And, a final point, the initiation into the contemplation of the intelligibles, created and then uncreated, begins the moment one crosses the threshold of the Church doors. Indeed and to offer a tentative suggestion, the *DN* might be equated with the first half of the eucharistic σύναξις, the "liturgy of the catechumens," whose particular function it is to read and teach the content of the Scriptures. The *MT*, therefore, as peculiarly the mystery of the altar, would correspond to the eucharistic anaphora and consecration, the realization of the presence.[312]

We return, then, to the final stage of the ascent and to Sinai. Let me take up once more the text I cited in the prologue to this chapter, the ascent of Moses described in the *MT*.[313] I wrote that this description, and the biblical passages on which it is based, amount to an image of the *EH*, and that the stages of purification, illumination, and perfection correspond to Moses' rise to

309. According to van den Daehle (*Indices*, 137–138), ὑμνέω appears in the *DN* sixty-six times, ὑμνός seven times, ὑμνῳδία three times, ὑμνολογία twice, ὑμνητικῶς, ὑμνολόγος, and ὑμνῳδός each once.

310. See also the articles by Jones, "(Mis?)-Reading the Divine Names as a Science"; Bucur, "Dionysius East and West: Unities, Differentiations, and the Exegesis of Biblical Theophanies," 122–123; Graciela L. Ritacco de G., "Los himnos theárquicos," *Teol Vida* 43 (2002): 350–376, esp. 352, 354–356; Arthur, *Ps.-Dionysius as Polemicist*, 166–168.

311. For example, *DN* I.8 597C (121:8–15); compare with *EH* I.1 372A (63:7–11).

312. And to the *DN* we might add the two other, non-extant Dionysian treatises devoted to the exegesis of Scripture, the *Theological Outlines* and *Symbolic Theology*. For a parallel, see my discussion of Macarius, particularly of his *Homily* 52 (I), in *Et introibo*, 382–384.

313. *MT* I.3 1000C–1001A (143:8–144:15).

"the place where God is" (Exod 24:10, LXX). In that "place" he
encounters the "summit of the divine ascents," "the λόγοι underlying the things subordinate to him who transcends all"; and it
is through these that "God's presence, which transcends every
notion, is revealed." I have sought to identify that "place" with
the ecclesiastical hierarchy or, more accurately, to show the ecclesiastical hierarchy and its heart, the altar, to be the σύμβολον or εἰκών
where the worlds of matter and spirit, of humans and angels, of
Creator and creature, meet and join. There, at the altar, the angels
serve. There, too, are revealed the "wills" or "powers" of God *ad
extra*. The ascent in contemplation is threefold. We move toward
the altar, up the hierarchy of being, and into the depths of the soul
until, finally, we attain to that "place" which marks the frontier
of created being. There our own motion ceases and Another's
begins, or better, continues, taking us up out of ourselves and into
himself and the radiant darkness beyond the light of knowledge.
God and human join within the Church. Rather, within the Church
they are already united, and it but remains for each believer to
recognize the divinity that, now in hidden manner, pervades the
body of the Incarnation.

5.4. A Christian Vision

We have come full circle from the beginnings of my exposition. Chapters 2 and 3 began in the divine darkness and traced
the course of the divine processions into creation, God's motion
"outside of" himself and into immanence. Then I took note of
the echoes, as it were, of the δυνάμεις in created being that enable
the latter to move toward its reciprocal act of self-transcendence.
During the course of the last two chapters I have sought to sketch
the outlines of the Dionysian universe, the hierarchies, in which
created intelligences move and have their being, and by means
of which God's Providence leads them back to himself. I have
spoken of the hierarchies in general and, at length, of the ecclesiastical hierarchy. At once the reality of our world and the presence among us of the divine, "our hierarchy" is both the way
of our return and the place of our journey's end: the leap into
ἔκστασις and union.

It has been my intention to portray the Areopagite's vision as consistently a Christian one, and furthermore, coherent. Its coherence rests primarily upon the *EH* as the context within which the whole of the *CD* is to be understood. Indeed, I might note that the vision of Dionysius which I have just sketched, that of the altar as the mystery at the heart of all things—of our world and our souls—and the irradiating reality of Christ's divinity, may be discerned today in the design and iconography of the Churches of Eastern Europe and the Near East. It is the vision which, over a century after our author, Maximus the Confessor would outline explicitly in his description of the Church as a series of icons embracing Providence, creation, man, and the soul.[314] For my present purposes, however, the question lies not so much with Dionysius' effects on his successors as with the matter of his Christian antecedents. Scholars who have stressed the Neoplatonist elements in the *CD* have been compelled to refuse the corpus its fundamental coherence, whether through separating the hierarchies from the *DN/MT* and dismissing the centrality of the former, or by endeavoring to maintain that the Neoplatonist vocabulary and—therefore—its presuppositions result in the "shipwreck" of whatever Christian intent the author may originally have had. To this I reply that there are certainly ambiguities or tensions within the *CD*, a number of which I have already indicated, but that very much rests on whether or not we can set the *CD* within a certain Christian context or tradition.

The essential questions with regard to Dionysius are: (1) did he misjudge the risk and fail to salvage a vision both Christian in fundamental inspiration and, with perhaps certain reservations, generally coherent?; and (2) did he have any predecessors in the Christian tradition to whom he may have looked and from whom he may have taken? I have tried to demonstrate that he did not fail in the broad outlines of his system. If we ask Dionysius, regarding the knowledge of the νοητά and the questions *what? who? where?* and *how?*, we find him replying to the "what" with

314. PG 91, esp. 664D–688B. And see my concluding remarks below (6.1. "On Piety and Ascetic Literature: A Sketch of the Dionysian Trajectory").

the processions of God in love, the ἐνέργειαι; to the "who" with the person of Jesus, who reveals them; to the "where" with the Church and its worship; and, finally, to the "how" with the Revelation given in Scripture. His understanding of Providence is of a piece, and it is rooted in Christ.

Chapter 6

Dionysius' Predecessors

Evagrius and Macarius

Introduction

The five preceding chapters have sought to deal with the CD as a coherent, Christian vision. In what follows I would like to expand upon remarks made in chapter 1, and discuss those elements in the Christian patristic tradition that were most important in the elaboration of the CD. Having offered a broader treatment in my earlier book—the New Testament, pre-Nicene writers, the Cappadocians, the mystagogies of Cyril of Jerusalem, Theodore of Mopsuestia, and John Chrysostom, and finally the Syrian writers of the fourth and fifth centuries—I will here confine my discussion to the Egyptian desert tradition and Evagrius Ponticus, on the one hand, and the Syrian ascetic tradition and the Macarian Homilist, on the other.

1. Dionysius and the Egyptian Desert

The Egyptian desert at the end of the third century and beginning of the fourth was the scene of one of the great revolutions in the history of the Christian Church, the monastic movement. Within a century the face of the Church and of Christianity had been profoundly and permanently altered, and Dionysius is as much the heir of this momentous shift as he is of the rest of the tradition.

Aside from the whole picture of the ascetic saint that emerges from the *Life of Anthony*, traditionally ascribed to Athanasius,[1] two specific passages in the *Life* represent possible points of contact with the *CD*. The first one, concerning the use of ἐξαίφνης, has already been discussed in chapter 1.6. The second passage is the description of Anthony after his twenty years of prayerful solitude and isolation: he emerges, says his biographer, "like an initiate and God-bearer from a kind of sanctuary," and immediately begins a ministry characterized by healings, clairvoyance, and wise counsel as the "physician of all Egypt."[2] Anthony is pictured as the true Spirit-bearer, a man of God clothed with the authority of an Old Testament prophet, and thus as a primary witness to humanity redeemed and transfigured in Christ.[3] He is, indeed, a kind of epiphany of the new creation and, thus, of the Church. Athanasius is quite careful to show that the great ascetic reverenced the clergy,[4] and even how he had gone, at the Archbishop's request, to Alexandria to testify against the Arians.[5] This reverence toward the popularly received (and often undoubted) sanctity of the ascetics and simultaneous care to forestall their potentially disruptive effects bear important affinities to Dionysius' handling of the monks' place in the hierarchy, particularly in *EH* VI and *Ep.* VIII.

1. *PG* XXVI 837A–976B (English, *NPNF* IV, 2d series, 195–221). For recent doubts about Athanasius' authorship and the possibility of a prior Coptic *Life*, under Syrian influence, see T. D. Barnes, "Angel of Light or Mystic Initiate? The Problem of the Life of Anthony," *JTS* 37 (1986): 353–368; Athanasius of Alexandria, *The Life of Antony: The Coptic Life and the Greek Life*, trans. Tim Vivian and Apostolos N. Athanassakis, CS 202 (Kalamazoo, MI: Cistercian Publicatons), xxiii–lxvi.

2. *Life* 14 (865C) for the emergence and beginning of the healings; 57 (925B), 60 (929AB), 66 (937AB), and 86 (964AB) for the clairvoyance; and 87 (965A) for *iatros* of Egypt.

3. He is the ἄνθρωπος θεοῦ (*Life* 70 [941B]), recalling OT figures like Elijah, etc. See, for example, P. Rousseau, *Ascetics, Authority, and the Church* (Oxford: Oxford University Press, 1978), esp. 18–67, for the theme of the prophet.

4. *Life* 67 (937C).

5. *Life* 68–69 (940B–941B).

A similar combination occurs in the other great source book of the early monastic movement, the *Sayings of the Fathers* or *Gerontikon*.[6] There is no evident plan to this collection, though editing doubtless did take place.[7] The words, λόγια, of the elders are presented in apparently artless, alphabetical sequence. Nonetheless, conficts with church authorities, for example, still do appear, as well as questions over the sacraments, in particular the Eucharist. Perhaps the most important conflict, though its target is unstated, occurs over exactly the question that sets the stage for Dionysius' letter to Demophilus: the reconciliation of penitent sinners. In at least three stories in the collection, the prevailing system of rigorous penances set up by the clergy of the day is overruled by the inspired word of one of the elders.[8] This, as it turns out, was but the opening salvo of a centuries-long debate in the Greek (and non-Greek) East over the relative places of charismatic and institutional authority, a debate within which both the *Sayings* and the *CD* represent different episodes.[9]

The second issue of possible relevance to the *CD* concerns, as noted, the Eucharist. A certain brother in Scete is troubled by the thought that the Eucharist is merely a "symbol." He is counseled by three elders not to believe this and advised to pray on it. He

6. Greek text of *Apophthegmata Patrum*, PG LXV 72A–440D (English, *The Desert Christian* [ed. and trans. B. Ward; New York: Macmillan, 1980]).

7. See, for example, G. Bunge, "Évagre le pontique et les deux Macaires," *Ir* 56 (1983): 215–227 and 323–360, for Evagrius' relationship to one of the giants of the early desert, Macarius the Great, and the former's subsequent near disappearance from the collection in the wake of the early Origenist controversies, esp. 352 and 355–356.

8. See Lot 2 (*PG* LXV 256AB, Ward 122), Sisoes 20 (400AB, 217), and especially Poemen 12 (325AB, 169). For an analysis of the fourth-century issue, see H. Dörries, "The Place of Confession in Ancient Monasticism," *SP* 5 (1962): 284–311, esp. 291–297.

9. For a review of the sources from the fourth- through fourteenth-centuries in the Greek East, see the still valuable study by K. Holl, *Enthusiasmus und Bussgewalt beim griechischen Mönchtum* (Leipzig: Hinrichs'sche, 1898), esp. 225–330. For the Syrian equivalent, starting even earlier, see my remarks at the beginning of chapter 6 (3.3.1. "Singles," "Sons of the Covenant," and "Messalians").

does and is rewarded by the vision of an angel pouring the Christ child's blood into the chalice at the time of the consecration.[10] A second monk wonders if his priest is worthy to celebrate the Eucharist. He is given heaven's reply on receiving the vision of an angel descending at the liturgy's beginning in order to clothe the celebrant in a robe of radiant light.[11] The priest's deficiencies are covered over by divine grace in order to assure the sacrament's efficacy. The angelic concelebration, in both visions, is also an interesting parallel to the *CD*. Questions over the necessity and "real presence" of the sacraments, as well as over the worthiness of those in holy orders, point to the existence of a revolt against— or at least indifference to—the importance of the hierarchy, and must therefore have been of concern to Dionysius, particularly given the Messalian controversy (on which more below) concentrated in—though not limited to—Syria. On the other hand, the Areopagite seems to share a number of the monks' views, for example, on the illumining power of the Eucharist,[12] or his opinion, in agreement with Demophilus, that the unillumined priest (ἀφώτιστος ἱερεὺς) is no priest.[13] Nonetheless, and in the same breath, he still insists that Demophilus obey the person in orders, whether worthy or not.

A third area of interest for us, as in the *Vita Antonii*, is the image of the ascetic fathers as Spirit-bearers. The *Sayings* are, at any rate in appearance, quite innocent of Clement of Alexandria's or Origen's philosophical concerns and sophistication. Nonetheless, what we find in them seems precisely to be Clement's Gnostic and Origen's διδάσκαλος incarnated in living men. The temple language is not specifically used, but roughly the same idea seems to be present. Clement had described the perfected Christian as vested with the splendor of Christ's glory, and as a little temple

10. Daniel 7 (156D–160A, 53–54).

11. Mark the Egyptian 1 (304A–C, 151).

12. See Isaac the Theban 2 (241AB, 110) and compare with *EH* III.1 and Dionysius' illumination.

13. 1092C (181:7–10). Compare with Abba Matoes' unwillingness ever to celebrate the liturgy because of his unworthiness, Matoes 9 (292C–293A, 144).

in the large temple that is the Church.[14] In the *Sayings* we find the elders both beholding and radiating the divine δόξα. Arsenius insists on the possibility of seeing God, citing John 14:21, and one of the fathers sees the old man wrapped in heavenly flame.[15] Abba Silvanus has to break off his contemplation of the glory in order to speak with a visitor, and later is seen reflecting it like Moses in Exodus 34.[16] Abba Sisoes dies in its radiance and Abba Joseph's hands are transformed into fire before the startled Abba Lot.[17] The message is clear, and it is the same one that we found in the *Vita Antonii*: here is the fulness of Christianity, the transfigured human being of the age to come. The hierarchy and—but only passively—the monk of the *EH*, Moses' ascent in the *MT*, together with Dionysius' ἐξαίφνης and his mention of the Transfiguration in *DN* I.4, all surely fit into this context. In between Dionysius and the earliest monks, however, stands a figure in whom these themes were given their first systematic articulation.

2. Dionysius and Evagrius Ponticus

Evagrius was an anchorite, a sometime protegé of Gregory of Nazianzus, an early inheritor and perhaps the greatest theoretician of monastic spirituality. He is not often associated with Dionysius save via Maximus the Confessor who, it is argued,[18]

14. E.g., *Strom.* 5.6.40.1 (SC 278:90); *Strom.* 7.13.82.2, 4 (SC 428:250, 252). For details, see my discussion of these passages in reference to Ps-Dionysius, in Golitzin, *Et introibo*, 267–268.

15. Arsenius 10 (89C, 10) for the citation, and 27 (96BC, 13) for the vision.

16. Silvanus 3 and 12 (409A and 412C, 223–224).

17. Sisoes 14 (396BC, 223); Joseph of Panephysis 7 (229CD, 103).

18. See von Balthasar, *Kosmische Liturgie*, 35–45; Dalmais, "Saint Maximus le Confesseur et la crise de l'Origènisme monastique," *TVM*, 411–421, and "L'héritage évagrienne dans la synthèse de Saint Maxime," *SP* 8 (1966): 356–362; Viller, "Aux sources de la spiritualité de Saint Maxime," *RAM* 11 (1930): 156–184 and 239–268; Hausherr, "Contemplation chez les anciens Grecs et autres orientaux chrétiens," *DSp*, 2.1762–1782, and "Les grands courants de la spiritualite Orientale," *OCP* 1 (1935): 114–138; Bornert, *Les Commentaires Byzantins de la Divine Liturgie*, 85; and vs. Lossky, Sherwood, *Ambigua*, 177–178. The latter, however, in an extended footnote (Ibid., note

took from both (previously unrelated) theologians in order to produce his own, original synthesis.

Evagrius' system is a clarification of Origen's that leads to a further radicalization of the latter.[19] Dionysius differs sharply from Evagrius. He emphasizes God's absolute transcendence, rejects the Origenist myth of a first creation, affirms creaturely κίνησις and with it the permanence of change and of variety, i.e., hierarchy, and finally maintains the Incarnation as the true ἐνανθρώπησις of God and therefore at the core of the mystery of human salvation—as, indeed, *the* Mystery now present among us. All this is, of course, simply reaffirming the Cappadocian correction of Origen, of which I believe the Areopagite to have been a faithful student. Yet for all their differences, the parallels between Evagrius and Dionysius are quite striking.[20]

2.1. The Corpus Dionysiacum: *A "Neoplatonized Origenism"?*

I have discussed Evagrius' theological system at length elsewhere.[21] He is both heir and subscriber to the results of the fourth-

---

1, 124–128), has anticipated much of my own argument. Hausherr as well, in a later article ("Pierre l'Iberien," *OCP* 19 [1953]: 247–260), has contributed to my position in favor of an Evagrian link with the *CD*.

19. So sharply so, indeed, that following A. Guillaumont, *Les Kephalia Gnostica d'Évagre le Pontique* (Paris: du Seuil, 1962), there now appears to be little doubt that the "Origen" condemned in 553 was in fact the Alexandrian as filtered through the mind of his disciple. See, however, G. Bunge, "Origenismus–Gnostizismus: Zum geistesgeschichtlichen Standort des Evagrios Pontikos," *VC* 40 (1986): 24–54, for some qualifications of Guillaumont's picture of Evagrius' Origenism and a defense of his trinitarian orthodoxy against a generation of gnostics still active in Egypt. See also Bunge, "Hénade où monade: au sujet de deux notions centrales de la terminologie évagrienne," *Mus* 102 (1989): 69–91, esp. 89–90 for later changes in Evagrius' thought.

20. Other scholars whom I have noted already, von Balthasar and Bouyer, have seen some of these parallels. I should add A. Dempf, "Evagrios Pontikos als Metaphysiker und Mystiker," *PJ* 77 (1970): 297–319. If anything, Dempf exaggerates the likenesses between Evagrius and Dionysius in order to arrive, via both, at Thomas Aquinas (315–316), and even to posit Evagrius as Dionysius' mentor, Hierotheos (317).

21. Golitzin, *Et introibo*, 323–340.

century's debates concerning the Trinity. He accepts and defends the Cappadocian triad of co-eternal and co-equal Persons.[22] He also, particularly in the *Gnostic Centuries*,[23] appears occasionally to refer to the Cappadocian distinction between God's unknowable essence or nature and the energies, which he chooses to call the Divine Wisdom (σοφία).[24] Jesus, who is not the Logos but instead the "first-born" of the νόες and joined by the "unction" of unity with the Word,[25] has "traced" his wisdom in the nature of corporeal being.[26] He is himself the lesson that the secondary worlds have been created to impart. Insofar as they appropriate this lesson to themselves, the *logikoi* realize Christ in themselves and so ascend the ladder. The historical Incarnation is therefore, as in Origen, to be placed within this pattern of universal instruction. It is iconic, presenting us with a paradigm for imitation here below, and in his own person revealing the true "doctrine"[27] of our nature: its ultimate equality with the νοῦς, Jesus Christ.[28]

Evagrius does, though, work a definite development of Origen here. In giving Christ the role of demiurge he not only gets around the difficulties Nicean orthodoxy presents to a strict Origenism but as well makes the Incarnation itself far more of a piece with the overall pattern of pedagogy, as well as the latter's evident focal

22. See R. Melcher, *Der achte Brief des Basilius, ein Werk des Evagrius Ponticus* (Münster: Aschendorff, 1923).

23. I will be referring throughout to the edition and translation of the Syriac text by A. Guillaumont, *Les six centuries des "Kephalia Gnostica" d'Évagre le Pontique* [henceforth *KG*] (*PO* 28; Paris: Firmin-Didot, 1958), and without exception to the second text, "S2," which Guillaumont has established as bearer of the authentic Evagrius.

24. See esp. *KG* V.51; also I.71; II.21; III.82, and, for comment, N. Gendle, "The Apophatic Approach to God in the Early Greek Fathers, with Special Reference to the Alexandrian Tradition" (Ph.D. diss; Oxford University, 1974), 410–411.

25. See *KG* IV.20, and, for the "Chrism" of the "science of unity," IV.18 and 21. We might recall "Jesus our unction" and the importance accorded the consecration of the Chrism in *EH* IV.

26. *KG* III.57.

27. See *Évagre le Pontique: Traité Pratique où le Moine* (trans. Antoine and Claire Guillaumont; 2 vols.; *SC* 170–171; Paris: du Cerf, 1971), 2:498.

28. *KG* VI.89.

point. Christ is author and sense of both the Scriptures and the worlds. He is the mystagogue and summit of the levels of being and contemplation for which he has prepared us, and which he has himself, in himself, revealed in history. He is the action of God's Providence as shaping and directing in time. The picture of the Savior must appear as closely conforming to Dionysius' Jesus, head and maker and sense of the hierarchies, mystery and mystagogue.[29] The differences are equally important. For Dionysius Jesus is also our τέλος. His mystery is the presence of God in our world and not merely of the "beginning." Procession and Providence are not, in the CD, associated strictly with the Fall and its remedying. Dionysius does not therefore require the services of a lesser, and temporary, intermediary. Jesus, for him, is permanent.

Evagrius provides us with a completely traditional spectrum of reason-endowed beings ranging from the angelic hosts, through humankind, and down to the legions of hell. The doctrine of original and final equality rules out, however, any notion of permanent diversity. The Providence of Christ is provisional, and so are the structures he has created for our edification. Abolition of the hierarchies rather than their transfiguration is the Evagrian gospel. They are the reflection of states of being rather than of abiding differences in essence.[30] His τάξεις, the ranks and distinctions proper to the secondary world, are therefore purely functional.[31] They do not reveal the original will or intentions of God with regard to each—i.e., the creative λόγοι—as they do in Dionysius, but instead teach the temporary, pedagogic intent of Christ's Providence. They are to be ascended as steps on the way back to the original γνῶσις, but not as themselves bearing that ultimate science. Nonetheless, however temporary and functional they are, and thus distinguished from the hierarchies of the CD, the effect—indeed, precisely the function—of Evagrius' τάξεις here below remains markedly similar to that of their Dionysian

---

29. See D. B. Evans, "Leontius of Byzantium and Dionysius," *EB* 7 (1980): 1–34 for a suggested connection between Palestinian Evagrianism and Dionysius, 28ff.

30. See, for example, *KG* V.47.

31. Recall Origen, *In Jn.* 2.33 (304); see also Guillaumont, *Les Kephalia*, 106.

equivalent. This is particularly clear with regard to the role he gives the angelic orders. The latter stand on the highest rungs of the world-ladder. Their τάξεις being functional, they are not possessed of a nature essentially different from humanity's. They are also νόες, less fallen than we but still not yet perfected,[32] serving as guides (ὁδηγοῦσιν) of the just.[33] In short, Evagrius' angels fulfill then the same functions as those of Dionysius. They are not themselves creators or demiurges, but they both reflect and assist Christ, the true demiurge, to effect our ἀναγωγή through purifying, illumining, and perfecting.[34]

The admittedly rather curious expression, "Neoplatonized Origenism," that I have chosen to head this sub-section deserves some explanation. Briefly, it seems to me that Evagrius' elaboration and sharpening of Origen's general vision of the creation as providential, as a τάξις bearing the γνῶσις of Christ, as centered on Christ, and finally as the divinely willed image of humanity (= νοῦς) intended to instruct us and bring us back to ourselves, to Christ, and thus to God, are of significance to the creation of the *CD*. The following I would call Dionysius' Origenism: the attempt to portray creation as ἀναγωγή, as the τάξις enabling return (ἐπιστροφή) to God that is given uniquely in and through Christ. As for "Neoplatonized," Dionysius was first of all simply another participant in the long Christian (and pre-Christian, Philo) dialogue with late Platonism that began long before Origen. Regarding specifically Neoplatonic elements, he was, secondly, already the heir of a very important Christian-Platonist exchange, itself involving the modification of Origen, via the Cappadocians. His own particular contribution from late Neoplatonism lay, thirdly, in the introduction of the hierarchies as well as, of course, a great deal of the rather rococo vocabulary whose sources in pagan literature have been so admirably detailed by Koch. Yet, his is an

32. See Hausherr, *Leçons d'un Contemplatif* (Paris: Beauchesne, 1960), 48–49, in comment upon *De Orat.* 30 1173B, and *KG* VI.2.

33. *Ad monachos* 23 (H. Gressman, ed., "Nonnenspiegel und Mönchsspiegel des Evagrius Ponticus," *TU* 39, 4B [1913]: 153–165, at 155.

34. See *KG* IV.25; *KG* VI.86. Recall chapter 3 above (2.1.3, "Our Photagogues").

Origenism—as just defined—that has been "Neoplatonized," and not the reverse. His hierarchies are not temporary, pedagogic devices, true, but even less are they causal chains or successive demiurges. Rather, like those of Evagrius, they are a mystagogy. They proclaim; they reveal; and they initiate into the Mystery that accomplishes our return. As with Evagrius', Dionysius' hierarchies are the work of Christ, and unlike the earlier man's, they will continue to show forth Jesus, who is God, forever. The Incarnation for Dionysius does not cease with the eschaton.

2.2. Dionysius and Evagrius on the Nature of Essential Knowledge: ἔκστασις vs. κατάστασις?

Evagrius has often been contrasted with such advocates of negative theology as Gregory of Nyssa and the Areopagite. Hausherr, for example, opposes Evagrius' "katastatic" theology to the ecstatic interpretation of encounter with God found in Gregory and in the *CD*.[35] The contrast, and particularly that between Evagrius and Dionysius, has been somewhat overdrawn.[36] Nicholas Gendle noted that Evagrius' use of Exodus 24:9-11 indicated a "katastatic" rather than an "ecstatic" experience.[37] However, Gendle also points to certain previously unstressed elements in Evagrius: the presence of the divine οὐσία/δυνάμεις distinction and the need of grace, features that link the disciple to his partially Cappadocian antecedents.[38] I feel they also link him to Dionysius. True, there seems to be no ecstasy, no enraptured transcending of

35. "Contemplation," *DSp*, 2:1827ff.

36. Here once again I follow Gendle, "Apophatic Approach," 410ff. See also his article, "Cappadocian Elements in the Mystical Theology of Evagrius Ponticus," *SP* 16 (1985): 373–384. Gendle does come down, though, finally for a natural—or "restorative"— experience, not the "violent" ecstasy of Dionysius Areopagite (esp. 381–382). I am not so sure the contrast holds. See thus also G. Bunge, "The 'Spiritual Prayer': On the Trinitarian Mysticism of Evagrius of Pontus," *Monastic Studies* 17 (1987): 191–208.

37. Gendle, "Apophatic Approach," 416.

38. Gendle, "Apophatic Approach," 410–411.

creaturely limits in Evagrius' scheme of things,[39] and here I must admit a difference from both the Areopagite and—perhaps even more so—the Nyssene. Evagrius' encounter takes place within the mind, at the τόπος θεοῦ. On the other hand, his stress on the voῦς as "susceptible to God [δεκτικὸς Θεότητος]" and his corresponding remark that the power of "essential knowledge" in which lies the voῦς' proper repose is not at the same time co-natural to it[40] do bring back to mind that δύναμις or faculty of ἕνωσις in Dionysius by which we are united to God beyond intellection, and the CD's insistence that it is always the power or love of God which is the active force within us. Hausherr's contrasting of Evagrian "activité" with Dionysian "passivité" would therefore also appear to be exaggerated.[41] For the monastic theologian, too, there is at the end a "suffering of divine things [παθὼν τὰ θεῖα]."[42] Although one cannot say that Evagrius subsequently follows Moses into the darkness beyond the τόπος θεοῦ ("place of God"), still it does appear that he shares much with the CD.[43]

Yet even here matters are not as clearcut as the usual reading of light (Evagrius) versus darkness (Dionysius) allows. As I noted above in dealing with the "sudden" (chapter 1.6.), and as is also clear elsewhere in the CD, if one were to choose between light and dark as signaling the ultimate for Dionysius, one would have to give the nod to the former. By the same token, Heinrich Bacht has suggested that Evagrius' "gleaming light is at the same time deepest darkness."[44] Bunge has argued at length for the Trinitarian

39. Yet, see the discussion in Sherwood, *Ambigua*, 127–128. And Frankenberg sees fit to include ἔκστασις at one point in his retroversion; chapter 30 (455).

40. *KG* V.77.

41. Hausherr, "Grands courants," 124–125.

42. Dionysis famously describes Hierotheus as not merely learning but experiencing ("suffering") the realities of theology: οὐ μόνον μαθὼν ἀλλὰ καὶ παθὼν τὰ θεῖα (*DN* II.11 648B).

43. Besides Sherwood, Bouyer somewhat anticipates me here; see his *History of Spirituality*, 1:413.

44. H. Bacht, "Evagrius Ponticus und Pachomius von Tabennêsi: Das Vermächtnis des Ursprungs," in *Zeugen christlicher Gotteserfahrung* (ed. J. Sudbrack; Mainz: Matthias-Grünewald Verlag, 1981), 34–63, at 42.

character of Evagrian mysticism,[45] and we recall that the *MT* begins with a Trinitarian invocation. Further, I would underline the fact that for Evagrius the experience of the divine light is not a purely natural state. While the "form of the soul" is indeed in the "likeness of heaven," it is precisely beyond (ὑπέρ) this heaven that "the light of the Trinity shines forth at the time of prayer."[46] The divine light is a gift. It "inclines by grace to the knowledge of the soul," and this is so because the Trinity is not any created thing, but alone and unique is "essential knowledge . . . unsearchable and incomprehensible."[47] It "dawns" or "rises [ἀνατέλλοντος]" in the soul at the time of prayer.[48] The one certain difference that I can find between the anchorite and the Areopagite is that the former sees the beatific vision as the cessation of any and all motion,[49] while the latter does not. This one significant difference points again to Evagrius' debt to Origen's myth and Dionysius' deliberate rejection of it. Together with, and doubtless following, Gregory of Nyssa, Dionysius clearly belongs to the same "family" as Evagrius while just as clearly accepting the Nyssene's correction of the great Alexandrian where the anchorite does not.

2.3. Eschatology or Ecstasy? Dionysius and Evagrius on the Experience of God

With all his insistence on the necessity of disincarnation for the vision of God, Evagrius often suggests that a real experience of God is possible for us here below. This element comes to the fore particularly in his imagery of τόπος, φῶς, etc., and in the "radical apophasis"[50] of "pure prayer" as outlined particularly in *De orat.* 56–78. The tension is comparable—or in fact related—to that which many have remarked in the *CD*, i.e., between the ecstasy of the

---

45. Bunge, "On the Trinitarian Mysticism of Evagrius Ponticus."

46. *Chapter* 4 (Frankenberg 427).

47. *Ep.* 29 (587).

48. *Ep.* 17 (579). Recall Plotinus in *Enn.* V.5.8 awaiting the One's rising like the dawn.

49. See, for example, *Chapters* 45 and esp. 43 (461 and 465).

50. The phrase is Gendle's ("Apophatic Approach," 421).

MT and *DN* and the elsewhere apparently rigid maintenance of the hierarchies. Comparable, too, is the key to its (at least partial) resolution.

The νοῦς, Evagrius tells us,[51] is the temple (ναός) of God whose altar is the contemplation of the Holy Trinity. The latter, when considered in connection with what I have just noted concerning the Evagrian hierarchies as "moments of the knowledge of God," leads me to my solution—and, I believe, very close to Dionysius. The universe, or worlds, of Evagrius is in essence the fallen νοῦς writ large or, after the manner of Dionysius, the icon of humanity. They correspond very nearly indeed to that series of icons constituting the *EH* which I outlined at the conclusion of chapter 5: the images of Providence, of Christ, of humanity, and of the soul. The world(s), to phrase the relationship yet another way, is in a sense Evagrius' Church, the body of Christ, the way of initiation into the mystery of God. The parallels appear to me too striking to be considered accidental.[52]

No less significant, of course, are the differences: that the Evagrian cosmos is not the icon of the divine δυνάμεις, nor of the angels, represents Dionysius' correction via the Cappadocians of the Origenist myth accepted by Evagrius. It is then no surprise to find another point of contact, and a no less significant difference, in their respective understandings of the supreme experience of God possible here below. First of all, both do agree that such is possible. That, for Evagrius, the mind is God's temple whose altar is the contemplation of the Trinity does imply that, even

51. *KG* V.84.

52. Two other resemblances between *CD* and Evagrius deserve mention, at least in a footnote. In his *Epistles* 27 and 56 (583–585 and 605), as well as elsewhere (e.g., *Ep.* 36 [591] and 41 [595]), Evagrius goes back to Moses and David as exemplars of the mystics. Of note for us is his underlining of the meekness (πραότης) of these two figures as the essential prerequisite for the vision of God. Likewise, in Dionysius' *Ep.* VIII, we find the latter pointing out Moses and David (as well as others) to Demophilus as examples, exactly, of the meekness (πραότης) necessary for the approach to God (1084B–5B, 171.3–172.10, "meekness" in 171.4 and 6). For something, secondly, very like the Areopagite's treatment of evil in *DN* IV:18 ff., see *Ep.* 30 (587), 43 (597), and 59 (609).

in the embodied state, some real anticipation of that "ultimate beatitude"[53] may be granted in the present age, that one may—if only momentarily—enter into the temple of one's own being to stand before that altar. The same would apply, in somewhat different form, to Dionysius: the Church both "images" and thereby enables our participation in the vision of the world to come, because it carries the mystery within it even now.

In pursuance of the latter, and turning to the texts printed by Frankenberg in his Greek retroversion from the sixth-century Syriac translation, we find that the parallels multiply.[54] For Evagrius as for the *MT* the key scriptural text is from Exodus, in particular Exodus 24:10, and the vision that the elders of Israel have (in the LXX version) of the "place" of their God. Evagrius returns again and again to this text. Perhaps his most complete statement comes in the following from *Ep.* 39, wherein we may detect echoes not only of the *MT* but of the angelic liturgy as well:

> If then by the grace of God the intellect both turns away from these [the passions] and puts off the old man, then it will as well see its own constitution at the time of prayer like a sapphire or in the color of heaven, which recalls as well what the scripture names the place of God seen by the elders on Mount Sinai. It calls this the place and the vision the peace by which one sees in oneself that peace which surpasses every intellect and which guards our heart. For another heaven [ἄλλος οὐρανός] is imprinted on a pure heart, the vision of which is both light and the spiritual place, because within it are beheld so many [great things]: the meaning of beings and the holy angels who sojourn with the worthy.[55]

---

53. *Pratique*, Prologue 8 (493).

54. W. Frankenberg, *Euagrios Pontikos* (Berlin: Weidmann, 1912), esp. the appended supplement to the *Gnostic Chapters*, 429–465, and the *Letters*, 561–633. For a German translation, with introduction and commentary, of the latter, see G. Bunge, *Briefe aus der Wüste* (Trier: Paulinus, 1986).

55. *Ep.* 39 (Frankenberg 593). For more echoes of Exodus 24:10, see also chapters 2 (425), 4 (427), 21 (441), and 25 (449). For the νοῦς as "altar" of God, see chapter 45 (461), and as temple, chapter 37 (457). Note in chapter 4 (427) that the light beheld is not simply equal to the soul. It is *other*: God's light.

The visionary encounters the whole company of heaven together with the light from above. Turning to other significant biblical images in Evagrius' lexicon, and related to the themes of temple and Sinai so important to Dionysius as well, I note first of all his citation of Psalm 75:3 in order to declare that the soul is the true Zion, God's intended dwelling place (κατοικητήριον).[56] Referring to Genesis 28, the "revelation of the mysteries of God" is the ladder revealed to Jacob which the soul ascends "by degress [ἀναβαθμῶν] of virtue" toward "perfect union [or 'mingling,' σύμμιξις] with God."[57] Babai, Evagrius' Syriac commentator, sees Jacob's ladder as the heavenly hierarchy "by which we ascend to God."[58] For Evagrius, the knowledge of the Trinity is the "spiritual mountain" that is difficult to approach (recall Exod 19), but revealed to the "intellect stripped of the passions."[59] In a work preserved under the name of Nilus of Ancyra, Evagrius both spiritualizes the Eucharistic words of Jesus—the "bread" is a "type" of the intellect—and cites the prophet's vision in Isaiah 6:1ff. for the soul or intellect as "throne" of God: "For it is there that God takes his seat, and there that he is known."[60] Finally, he expresses the following wish to a correspondent:

For a sensitive exploration of Evagrius' exegetical and theological use of "the place of God," see C. Stewart, "Imageless Prayer and the Theological Vision of Evagrius Ponticus," *JECS* 9 (2001): 173–204; W. Harmless, "The Sapphire Light of the Mind: The Skemmata of Evagrius Ponticus," *TS* 62 (2001): 498–529.

56. Chapter 28 (453). See also *KG* V.88 and VI.49 for the Zion motif.

57. Chapter 43 (459).

58. Chapter 43 (460).

59. *Ep.* 58 (607–609). In *Ep.* 25 (583), written probably to one of his acquaintances in Jerusalem, Evagrius proposes a spiritual itinerary, linking the different places associated with the life of Christ to the progress of his interlocutor's soul and concluding with the Mount of Olives.

60. *PG* LXXIX, 1228C. This text, particularly its spiritualization of the Eucharist, was underlined by H. V. Beyer in "Die Lichtlehre der Mönche des vierzehnten und des vierten Jahrhunderts," *XVI Internationaler Byzantinistenkongress* (Wien: Österreichische Akademie der Wissenschaften, 1981), 473–512, esp. 484. The same also rightly notes the impress of the Evagrian heaven within the soul on the blue mandorla of Christ in Paleologan icons depicting the Transfiguration, though oddly he fails to include their prototype in the Sinai mosaic.

May the Lord grant that the noonday [μεσημβρία] of your virtue be radiant, and that your tabernacle [σκηνή] become the
lodging of the holy angels and of our Savior, Jesus Christ.[61]

These texts, together with the temple theme and especially the two
citations concerning the tabernacle and throne, the inhabitation
of Christ and the "noonday" of virtue, call to mind in particular
my discussion of the *CD*'s *Ep.* III and the Dionysian "suddenly."
Neither am I the first to note a correspondence between the Platonist ἐξαίφνης and Evagrius in this regard. In a fascinating article,
Guillaumont took up the Evagrian use of the temple, throne, and
Sinai motifs in order to draw a connection between them and
the "sudden" vision of light described by Plotinus in *Enn.* V.3.17;
5.7; and VI.7.36.[62] Séd followed up on this essay by exploring
Evagrius' treatment of Exodus 24:10 (and Ps 75:3) in relation to
the tradition of the Targums and the Syriac *Peshitta.*[63] Séd's conclusions are striking. According to him, Evagrius in fact follows the
Targums and *Peshitta* in his use of Exodus 24, while at the same
time his "vision of peace" links him closely to the Targumic tradition, even down to the haggadic play on the name "Jerusalem";
his was thus "the first intellectual interiorization of which we
have a written attestation"—i.e., for Evagrius the spiritual Sinai
is within the νοῦς.[64]

The consequence of these insights for a proper accounting of
Dionysius' sources is in my view most significant. First, we note
the internalization of the Sinai motif as having already occurred
in Evagrius. Second, there is the fact that his handling of Sinai and
Zion links him to Aramaic and Syrian traditions, and this, in view

61. *Ep.* 33 (589).

62. Guillaumont, "La vision de l'intellect par lui-même dans la mystique
évagrienne," in *Mélanges de l'Université Saint Joseph* (Beirut: Dar el-Machreq,
1984), 255–262. H. V. Beyer ("Lichtlehre," esp. 478) has also drawn a connection
between Evagrius and Plotinus, though limiting himself to *KG* I.35 alone as
textual support.

63. Séd, "La Shekinta et ses amis araméens."

64. Séd, "La Shekinta et ses amis araméens," 242. As I noted in chapter
1.5, Séd also points to parallels with Ephrem's use of Exodus 19 and 24 in his
Paradise Hymns; I will return to this point later in this chapter.

of the parallels we have already seen between him and Dionysius, seems to provide added weight to the idea of the latter as himself in turn related to Syrian Christianity. Third, the Areopagite's handling of the "sudden" is clearly foreshadowed by Evagrius and, moreover, betrays precisely the same kind of blending of Platonist and biblical allusions as the great ascetic writer had managed over a century before the likely composition of the *CD*. Indeed, in light of the *Vita Antonii*'s own use of the "sudden," Evagrius himself might be part of a tradition antedating his own works, and to which both he and the Areopagite are simply witnesses. Fourth, however, what we might call the ecclesial echoes in Dionysius' "sudden" and his use of Sinai, in particular the background of the liturgy and the Eucharist, are largely missing in Evagrius.

2.4. The Mystery of the Church: Eternal Worship

Dionysius effectively reverses Evagrius' equation of the world with the Church: for the Areopagite, the Church, our hierarchy, is his world. Like the Evagrian, his is a world that is a providential order (τάξις) bearing a knowledge (ἐπιστήμη) and thereby enabling an activity (ἐνέργεια) that in turn effects the soul's purification, illumination, and union with God—in short, the vision of God and likening (ἀφομοίωσις) to him. Evagrius distinguishes Christ from God. Dionysius does not, and therein I contend—above and beyond any talk of late Neoplatonist influence—lies the basic difference informing his alterations of the earlier thinker's system. For the author of the *CD* Christ does not merely reveal the structures of creation he designed after the Fall. Instead, through the Incarnation he constitutes them. In becoming human, Jesus grants us the new, theandric πολιτεία. In a sense, therefore, Dionysius' world is a narrower one than Evagrius'. The angels, for example, remain our instructors and guides, and, through Christ and the newly centered world he brings us, we are joined to their liturgy, but the two worlds of humans and of angels no longer belong to one and the same grand scheme. Our world, that which embraces—and always will embrace—the sensible creation, finds its very being, sense and coherence, in the incarnate Christ, thus in the hierarchy that is his body, and so ultimately at the altar of the Church's Liturgy. Effectively therefore, Dionysius has put the Church and its organized worship in the place of Evagrius' providential cosmos.

In order further to illustrate my point, let me address the following questions to the two writers: What is the Christian to do? Where is the encounter with God? Evagrius would reply in favor of the ἀναχώρησις, of the solitary's ascetic effort, armed with the "data" of Revelation, to master himself and to contemplate the world wherein—i.e., in the mastery and the contemplation—he will meet God. Dionysius, on the other hand, answers: "*the Christian goes to Church.*" I do not, naturally, wish to suggest that the Areopagite intends thereby to deny or belittle ascetic effort—he clearly does not—but he has as clearly altered, as it were, the center of gravity, the locus of encounter. It is at the altar, in and through the celebration of the mysteries as administered by the tiered ranks of the clergy and as received by the ordered masses of the faithful, that the Christian is to find his place in the world and the meaning of the world, the λόγος of his and the world's being, and so the fulfillment of his being through the γνῶσις thus given and obtained. The bishop, albeit remaining a charismatic figure, replaces the anchorite, and he does so most emphatically. Here one might recall the bishop's role in another Syrian, Ignatius of Antioch. In a curious sense, Dionysius has "institutionalized" the Origenist ἀναγωγή—so long, that is, as I do not understand "institution" in a purely hard and legal sense, as simply a formal collective bound by certain rules. Our author is, after all, a species of Origenist and his ἀναγωγή retains the flavor of a fundamentally personal affair, essentially contemplative, and not the basis for a dynamic doctrine of the Church militant or, even, of the magisterium. Nonetheless, it is decidedly centripetal rather than centrifugal. It pulls into the center of a visible, established, and public worship.

Dionysius also expressed this centripetal thrust in such a way that it affirmed the contemplative Christian in his or her silent prayer. His "institutionalizing" takes nothing away from Evagrius' inward ascent. The spiritual mountain is still there, and it remains the calling of every believer to make the climb. But that mountain and its ascent have been superimposed onto the Christian assembly at worship, Clement's "true gnostic" onto the Ignatian bishop, the encounter with Christ in light onto the Church's altar and the consecrated elements, and the structures of the human soul onto the very "geography" of the believers gathered for prayer.[65] Yet this was not to turn Christian worship into "mere" symbol, nor the sacraments into a moving illustration of no further interest once its meaning had been decoded. Perhaps rather than superimposition, with its "Nestorian" ring, we should speak instead of a fusion, a union or a "mingling." The hidden, whether of God or of the soul, is revealed in the manifest without loss or confusion. It permeates the visible. This side of the eschaton it can only be glimpsed, but "then" it will be all in all. The "it" in question has a name, and that name is Jesus. Here is the meaning at once of Dionysius' attraction to Neoplatonism, especially to Iamblichan theurgy, and of the latter's transformation at his hands. The philosopher's longing to meet the needs of a "weak" human soul with the revelation of "unspeakable rites" linking us directly to the gods finds its counterpart, its end and fulfillment, in the presence of the incarnate Christ informing the Church's worship, just as Evagrius' sacramental cosmos discovers its own transformation into the κόσμος of the divine liturgy.[66] The visible world, i.e., the world of the Church, remains fully sacramental. At the same time, it also continues to serve—as did Evagrius' universe and Origen's before him—as the image of the soul. It mediates the "hidden" of Jesus, now in veiled fashion and openly—φανοτάταις μαρμαρυγαῖς—at the eschaton.

---

65. For the last point, see A. Louth, *Denys*, 54–55.

66. For the point on Iamblichus and the role of his theurgy in relation to Dionysius, I am particularly indebted to J. M. Rist, "Pseudo-Dionysius, Neoplatonism, and the Weakness of the Soul," in *From Athens to Chartres: Neoplatonism and Medieval Thought* (ed. H. J. Westra; Leiden: Brill, 1992), 136–161.

2.5. Dionysius and the Origenism of Syria-Palestine

There are several indications that the Origenist debate carried on without break from Origen's condemnation and the expulsion of the Origenist monks from Egypt at the turn of the fifth century to Justinian's condemnation in 543, and even beyond.[67] If we place Dionysius in Syria-Palestine at the end of the fifth century, and further assume his acquaintance with the monastic-ascetic tradition, for which there can be no doubt, then he had to have had an intimate knowledge of both Evagrius and the Evagrian current (as well as a certain amount of sympathy for them). We should thus also be able to situate the main lines of much of his thought as in continuity with the critique of Evagrian and post-Evagrian Origenism as that criticism was expressed both before and after the appearance of the *Areopagitica*. Let us glance first at the critique, and then move on to three figures from the early sixth century who were connected both to Dionysius and to Evagrius: Stephen bar Sudaili, Sergius of Reshaina, and John of Scythopolis.

Elisabeth Clark has done us the service of analyzing the early debate. Several issues that the latter raised go to the heart of the *CD*. There is first of all Ephiphanius of Salamis' complaint that Origen denied the body: "Having allowed itself to be tamed in holiness, then it should not be deprived of a reward along with its soul."[68] We recall particularly *EH* VII.1.1 where Dionysius speaks of the "pure bodies," which, having sweated and struggled with the soul (συναθλήσαντα), are yoked together (ὁμόζυγα) with the souls of the holy ones and receive their just reward;[69] he uses the same language a paragraph later against those who dissolve the

67. See Guillaumont, *Les "Kephalaia,"* esp. 81–135, for this continuity; Sherwood, *The Lesser Ambigua* for its continuation past Justinian; and E. Clark, *The Origenist Controversy: The Cultural Construction of an Early Church Debate* (Princeton: Princeton University Press, 1992), for its beginnings and early ramifications. I would add the articles by Bunge, "Évagre et les deux Macaires," "Hénade où Monade?," and "Origenismus—Gnostizismus," together with D. Evans, "Leontius of Byzantium and Dionysius."

68. Clark, *Origenist Controversy*, 92, summarizing Ephiphanius in *Panarion* 64:71 (*GCS* 31:519).

69. *EH* VII.1.1 553AB (121:2–7).

bond (συζυγία) between body and soul, a critique that is moreover seconded by the Scholiast's specific mention of Origen.[70] Secondly, Clark quotes Jerome's citation of Theophilus of Alexandria's *Festal Letter* of 403 CE. She notes Jerome's critique of the Origenist equation of κίνησις (*motus*) with the Fall, and continues: "The very beauty of the world [κόσμος] depends on its ornamentation with creatures . . . [yet on] Origen's understanding of creation . . . there could be no ranking . . . [among the angels] without a precosmic fall, that is the hierarchy . . . would be the product of sin."[71] Here, therefore, are the very building blocks of the *CD*: motion, beauty (κόσμος) and τάξις—hierarchy, in short. Finally, in the same passage, she also includes Theophilus' complaint against Origen's "slanderous" limitation of God's power, at which point we recall the divine infinity that Dionysius has taken from Nyssa and Clement, and which comprises an essential component of the defense of motion.

Just over a century later we find exactly the same critique, this time specfically against Evagrius, lodged by a Syriac-speaking ecclesiastic and authority on the spiritual life, Philoxenus of Mabboug. The latter, one of the most distinguished spokesmen for the struggle against Chalcedon, criticized particularly Evagrius' lack of a permanent place for variety (κόσμος, I might say), for permanent differences in rank and order (τάξις), or for change and development (κίνησις).[72] Philoxenus may also have been the earliest translator of Evagrius into Syriac.[73] Finally, he had genuine cause to be worried about Evagrian influence, since there were live, Syriac-speaking Origenists in his own area, in particular one

---

70. *EH* 7.1.2 553BC (121:10ff.), and *PG* IV 176A.

71. Clark, *Origenist Controversy*, 115, summarizing Jerome's own summary of Theophilus in the former's *Ep.* 98 (*CSEL* 55:194ff).

72. See G. Harb, "L'attitude de Philoxène de Mabboug à l'égard de la spiritualité 'savante' d'Évagre le pontique," in *Mémorial Mgr Gabriel Khouri-Sarkis* (ed. F. Graffin; Louvain: Imprimerie orientaliste, 1969), 135–156, esp. 142–146; 149; 155. Harb works chiefly from Philoxenus' *Letter to Patricius*.

73. See, however, J. W. Watt, "Philoxenus and the Old Syriac Version of Evagrius," *OC* 64 (1980): 65–87.

Stephen bar Sudaili, to whom the bishop of Mabboug had been obliged to write a very sharp letter.[74]

Stephen brings us to the first of our three figures and unquestionably the most curious. If he is indeed the author of the *Book of the Holy Hierotheos*, and if the present late MSS are relatively untampered with and unadulterated—altogether rather an "iffy" proposal—then we discover a quite extraordinary mingling of Dionysius with Evagrius occurring sometime between 494 and 512, the latter being the years between which Philoxenus wrote his letter.[75] Guillaumont's recovery of the *Kephalaia Gnostica*, together with his own research in the area of Syriac-speaking Christianity, has made more likely Philoxenus' linkage of this strange figure with Evagrius,[76] and Bunge has recently pinpointed some of Stephen's misreadings of Evagrius.[77] But the document itself seeks to link its doctrine, in effect a pantheism with strong Gnostic overtones, to the Areopagite, and to portray Evagrius' temporary hierarchies in the language of Dionysius' permanent ones.[78] In all, it is clearly Evagrius (though the Evagrius of a dream) who predominates, and it is the *CD* that is assimilated to him. Yet the very fact of this juxtaposition and its date, given the qualifications noted above, are significant. Someone else was reading both men before the end of the fifth century and making connections between them, even if those connections were very odd and not altogether coherent.

74. See F. S. Marsh's edition, translation, and introduction to Stephen's work, *The Book of the Holy Hierotheos* (London: Williams & Norgate, 1927), 223–224 for Philoxenus' letter.

75. See Marsh, *Hierotheos*, 191–224, for the MS tradition. There is relatively little scholarly literature on Stephen other than Marsh. Of note are I. Hausherr, "L'influence du *Livre de saint Hierothée*," *OC* 30, no. 3 (1932): 34–69, and D. Bundy, "The Book of the Holy Hierotheos and Manicheanism," *Aug* 26 (1986): 273–280.

76. See his *Les Kephalaia*, 311–332, for particular attention to Stephen.

77. Bunge, "Hénade ou monade," esp. 79.

78. See esp. *Hierotheos*, Discourses I.12 (Marsh 20–25) for the angels; II.3 (28) for the language of the *MT*; 17–18 (39–42) for a mystic Eucharist; 20 (44) for hierarchy; III.1 (64) for Tabor; and 6–7 (77–82) for the νοῦς as true hierarch and Christ as priest celebrating the Eucharist for the angels.

Not so odd, but still quite as interesting, is another figure from the Syriac-speaking world, Sergius of Reshaina (d. 536), Dionysius' earliest translator into Syriac. According to the Ps. Zachary of Mitylene, Sergius was a man "practiced in the reading of many books of the Greeks and of Origen," a onetime student in Alexandria, and a rather indifferent non-Chalcedonian who, in fact, ended his life in Constantinople within the Chalcedonian camp.[79] His translation work, besides including certain of Aristotle's works and Porphyry's *Eisagoge*,[80] included the earliest renderings we know of into Syriac of both Dionysius and Evagrius.[81] That Sergius read the Dionysian corpus in a very Evagrian light, though without reference to the Origenist myth of a precosmic fall, is immediately clear from even a cursory reading of his *Mimro* prefacing the translation. He does, though, admit to having written most of the preface before commencing the translation itself.[82] Nonetheless, his witness to a relation or correlation of some kind between Evagrius and Dionysius, if not the exact equivalence he wishes to establish, should be taken seriously.[83] This is a man, given his simultaneous acquaintance with philosophy, who must have known something about the subject. He thus also fits within a pattern.

The pattern becomes clearer still with John of Scythopolis, bishop of that Palestinian city from 536–548, who has increasingly become a center of scholarly attention as the author of many of

79. Zachary of Mitylene, *The Syrian Chronicle* (trans. Hamilton and Brooks; London: Methuen, 1899), XI.19 (266–268).

80. Ortiz, *Patristica Syriaca* (1965) 110–111.

81. See Sherwood, "Sergius of Reshaina and the Syriac Version of the Pseudo-Denys"; Guillaumont, *Les Kephalaia*, 222–227 (and see 327n. 90, where Guillaumont wonders if Sergius and bar-Sudaili were not possibly linked); Wiessner, "Handschriftüberlieferung."

82. "Mimro de Serge de Rešayna sur la vie spirituelle," 69 (112–113) and 114 (146–147).

83. Thus "Mimro de Serge de Rešayna sur la vie spirituelle," 115–119, with its equation of the *EH* with Evagrius' πράκτικη, the *CH* with the θεωρία of the δεύτερα, the *DN* with that of the πρῶτα, and the *MT* with the θεολογία. The last has a certain cogency, but not so much the first three.

the s*cholia* on Dionysius in *PG* 4.[84] John's proximity to the likely
date of the *CD*'s composition, within no more than two generations and perhaps less, his Palestinian location, and finally his
persistent interest—other than in the christological furor where
much of his energy is concentrated (and where scholarly interest
in him is likely to focus, understandably)—in issues pertaining
to Origenism,[85] all seem to point toward and lend support to my
sense that Dionysius is somehow connected with both the debate
over Origen/Evagrius, and with Christian Palestine. Whatever
John's motives in defending Dionysius and, indeed, seeking to
lay claim to him, it seems clear to me that these included more

84. See now Rorem and Lamoreaux, *John of Scythopolis and the Dionysian Corpus: Annotating the Areopagite*. The earliest work was von Balthasar's "Das Scholienwerk des Johannes von Scythopolis," *Schol* 15 (1940): 31–66, expanded in *Kosmische Liturgie* 644–672, but the most breathtaking results came forty years later in a series of articles by B. M. Suchla, "Die sogenannten Maximus Scholien des Corpus Dionysiacum Areopagiticum," *NAG* (1980): 31–66, and "Eine Redaktion des griechischen Corpus Dionysiacum im Umkreis von Johannes von Scythopolis, des Verfassers von Prolog und Scholien," *NAG* (1985): 1–18. The articles examined the Greek, Latin, and Syriac MSS in order to single out in a clear way John's *Scholia* from other hands. They also demonstrated that the *CD* had been handed down *en bloc* from the earliest. Thus Suchla's very sharp criticism in "Eine Redaktion," 17–18 of Brons' attempts, *Sekundäre Textparteien*, to discover later additions to the Dionysian works on literary-critical grounds. W. Beierwaltes and R. Kannicht have pointed to John's unacknowledged use of Plotinus, thereby demonstrating a familiarity with Neoplatonism, in "Plotin Testimonia bei Johannes von Scythopolis," *Hermes* 96 (1968): 247–251; see the extensive discussion in Rorem and Lamoreaux, *John of Scythopolis and the Dionysian Corpus*, 99–137.

85. Noted by von Balthasar, "Scholienwerk," 22–23; Sherwood, *Ambigua* 75–76; and Rorem and Lamoreaux, "John of Scythopolis," 424–425. Without distinguishing John's hand from the other s*cholia*, and at rough count, we find Origen mentioned nine times and once obliquely. Of those nine references, three bear on the body and the Resurrection (*PG* IV 20CD, 65D [Resurrection], 172C–173B [on the Resurrection and vs. the ἀποκατάστασις], 173CD, 176A, 197C [oblique], 337D, 545C [vs. Origen's defamation of the body], and 549B). Evagrius appears twice expressly, and twice in a way that clearly suggests him, 76D–77A (quoting *KG* II.3), 172A (on the Resurrection, quoting *KG* II.78 and V.19), 252A (oblique, though the language is Evagrian), and 332C (oblique, but in the context of a defense of change, and thus likely vs. Origenism).

than simply an attempt to "co-opt his Monophysite opponents' apostolic witness."[86] I think that he had other irons in the fire, up to and including a possible acquaintance with the mysterious author himself whose writings John clearly admired.

More needs to be said, however, about Dionysius' context and sources. Commentary on the Church's liturgy was a genre already over a century old at the time of the *CD*'s likely composition, and the latter as an example of this genre has been frequently noted. At the same time, the *EH* has been singled out as a very peculiar instance of this type of commentary: "timeless," "allegorical," not only failing to account for the sacraments but actually dissolving them.[87] I will in consequence devote relatively little space to the nascence and character of liturgical commentary, and much more to my investigation of the sources for that "timelessness" and "allegory." This is because Dionysius owes a debt to earlier, primarily fourth-century and Syrian sources for both the genre of his treatise on "our hierarchy," and for his reading of the latter as the soul writ large. In other words, he had the "makings," as it were, of his response to Evagrian Origenism not only in the works of Iamblichus or Proclus but also—and I think even more importantly—in the ascetical literature of his native, Christian Syria.

3. Dionysius' Sources in the Syrian Ascetic Tradition

3.1. "Singles," "Sons of the Covenant," and "Messalians"

No one knows much about Syriac-speaking Christianity before the fourth century and the writings of Aphrahat of Persia (fl. 330s–340s) and Ephrem of Nisibis (d. 373). The mysterious *Odes of Solomon*, dated anywhere from the first to the third centuries, the *Acts of Judas Thomas*, and perhaps the *Gospel of Thomas* are nearly all that we have of these communities' early literature. One feature that does emerge with singular force, especially in the latter two documents, is a remarkable stress on the ascetic life, an emphasis that continues on into the writings of Aphrahat, Ephrem,

---

86. Rorem and Lamoreaux, "John of Scythopolis" 428.
87. Most recently by Rorem, *Commentary*, 91–126, esp.118–126.

and beyond. At the center of this concern we find two technical phrases, the *ihidaya* or "single one" denoting the individual ascetic, and *bnai qeyama* or "sons of the covenant" indicating the ascetics as a group.[88] While the questions and speculations around these *termini technici* are genuinely fascinating, in particular their possible connections to first century Palestine (perhaps tying in somehow with those roots in the Targums and OT *Peshitta* that we saw above in Evagrius' use of the Sinai motif), I will limit myself to a few observations concerning their bearing on the *CD* and Dionysius' background.

The first term, *ihidaya*, derives from the Syriac for "one" (*hd*) and "appears five times in the [Syriac] New Testament to describe Jesus as God's 'single son,'" i.e., as the μονογενής.[89] It thus carried the natural implication of a "special relationship" with Christ, the ascetic as having been particularly assimilated to the person of the Only-Begotten in a public ceremony of commitment.[90] As discerned by Robert Murray, two other senses flowed from the latter: the imitation of Christ's celibacy and becoming "single minded," simple, i.e., uniquely and exclusively focused on Jesus and the things of God.[91] This concentration on deliberate simplification is in turn seen as restoring the ascetic to something like

88. See Vööbus, *History of Asceticism in the Syrian Orient*, vol. 1: *The Origins of Asceticism* (Louvain: Peeters, 1958), 14–30 for speculations about the origins of this system in the Qumran community, and 98–108; G. Nedungatt, "The Covenanters of the Early Syriac-Speaking Church," *OCP* 39 (1973): 191–215; 419–444; Murray, *Symbols* 7–17; S. Brock, "Early Syrian Asceticism," *Numen* 20 (1973): 1–19; and for a recent and sober review of the literature, S. Griffith, "Monks, 'Singles,' and the 'Sons of the Covenant': Reflections on Syriac Ascetic Terminology," in *Eulogema: Studies in Honor of Robert Taft SJ* (ed. E. Carr et al.; Rome: Pontificio Ateneo S. Anselmo, 1993), 141–160.

89. Griffith, "Monks, Singles, Sons of the Covenant," 143–144.

90. Griffith, "Monks, Singles, Sons of the Covenant," 143–145.

91. R. Murray, *Symbols*, 16. See also, for example, I. H. Dalmais, "La vie monastique comme ascèse vigiliale d'après saint Ephrem et les traditions liturgiques syriennes," in *Liturgie, conversion, et vie monastique: Conférence Saint-Serge, 35e semaine d'études liturgiques, Paris, 28e juin-1er juillet 1988* (ed. A.M. Triacca and C. Andronikof; Rome: CLV-Edizioni liturgiche, 1989), 73-86, esp. 77 on *hd - ihidaya* as meaning "to be one": "C'est bien là . . . le sens fondamental du *monachos*: celui qui est un, unique, unifié . . . l'idéal primitif

the status of primeval man, Adam before the Fall.[92] The ascetics' single-minded vigilance connects them with the eternal vigil, or liturgy we might say, of the angels, the "watchers" of Syriac Christian parlance.[93] The Syrian holy man, *qaddisha*, thus emerges as the *pneumatophore* or Spirit-bearer *par excellence* in the communities of Oriental Christians, in other words quite what we saw in the *Vita Antonii* and Egyptian Desert tradition, save that this Syrian expression of the same idea may in fact be the older and original one.[94]

These elements—celibacy, oneness, simplicity (ἁπλότης), concentration, together with the tie to the angels and the effective claim to spiritual authority—are all to the fore in Dionysius' handling of the monks in *EH* VI and *Ep.* VIII.[95] He affirms all of them, save the last for which he makes special provision and warning. He calls the monks μοναχοί, and it seems clear to me that he felt he could do so without any obvious anachronism because of the already ancient tradition of the Syrian *ihidaya*.[96] The monks are called to a state of celibacy, "complete purity,"[97]

---

du μοναχός a des attachés profondes avec cette vertue judaeo-chrétienne du 'simplicité' (ἁπλότης)."

92. See Brock, "Early Syrian Asceticism," 12.

93. Dalmais, "Vie monastique," 74–75.

94. Brock, "Early Syrian Asceticism," 10–11 and 18. For Syria as the original home of the "man of God" in Christianity, see H. Drijvers, "Die Legende des heiligen Alexius and der Typus des Gottesmannes im syrischen Christentum," in *Typus, Symbol, Allegorie bei den östlichen Vätern und ihren Parallelen im Mittelalter* (ed. M. Schmidt, C. F. Geyer [Regensburg: Pustet, 1982]), 187–217, and esp. his article "Hellenistic and Oriental Origins" in *The Byzantine Saint* (ed. S. Hackel; London: Sobornost, 1981), 25–33.

95. Louth, *Denys*, 70, has touched on the Syrian connection here, while Roques ("Éléments pour une théologie de l'état monastique selon Denys l'Aréopagite") has described Dionysius' understanding of the monk very much in the same terms, but quite without reference to its background in Christian Syria.

96. The one other expression Dionysius uses for the ascetics is θεραπευταί, a clear borrowing from another first-century writer, Philo, as pointed out by the scholiast, *PG* IV 528A, and at much greater length by Pachymeres, *PG* III 433A–436C, who quotes the relevant passages from Philo at length.

97. *EH* VI.1.3 532D (116:9).

and their life is to be "simple [lit. 'without parts,' ἀμέριστος] and uniform," "being made one in deiform unity [μονάς] and God-loving perfection."⁹⁸ Dionysius concludes the chapter by reflecting on the likeness of our hierarchy to the heavenly one, and includes a final paragraph on the purified orders among the angels.⁹⁹ All the salient and traditional elements of the *ihidaya* are therefore present. What sets the *EH*'s portrayal of the monk apart, however, is the Areopagite's insistence on the role of the ordained clergy, in particular of the hierarchs, as the ascetics' guides and directors.¹⁰⁰ The monks are not leaders, he repeats, but called to be followers, and obedient ones at that.

I will return shortly to the tensions that clearly underlie this insistence. For now, though, I would like to turn to the other technical term denoting Syrian ascetics, the *bnai qeyama*. The key term in the latter is the Syriac root, *qwm*, meaning "to rise" or "stand." Sidney Griffith has noted a number of possible associations with the latter that go beyond the most commonly accepted one of "covenant." These include the idea of resurrection (thus "sons of the Resurrection"), of community with the "standing ones," or "watchers" (the angels), or simply of a "station" or "status" beyond the normal requirements of the community of believers.¹⁰¹ Once again Dionysius appears at one point or another to reflect each of these possible renderings. In *DN* I.4's passage on the eschaton there may be an echo of the allusion to the resurrection in the phrase, *bnai qeyama*, when the relevant section concludes by noting that "we shall be sons of God who are sons of the Resurrection [υἱοὶ τῆς ἀναστάσεως ὄντες]."¹⁰² Back in *EH* VI we find the Areopagite declaring that the "monastic taxis" is not to be leader of others, but to "remain [lit. 'stand'] in itself in a unified and holy standing [or 'station,' στάσις]."¹⁰³ Finally, in the following paragraph, he notes that the monks are called to a more perfectly

98. *EH* VI.1.3 533A (116:16–17), also *EH* VI.1.2 533D (118:2–3).
99. *EH* VI.3.5 536D–7A (119:12–15); *EH* VI.3.6 537A–C (119:16–120:7).
100. See *EH* VI.1.3 532D (116:11–14); *EH* VI.3.1 533C (117:18–22).
101. Griffith, "Monks, Singles, Sons of the Covenant," 148–153; 158–160.
102. *DN* I.4 592C (115:4–5).
103. *EH* VI.3.2 533C (117:19–20).

unified life, even to a denial of fantasy (recall Evagrius' struggle against the λογισμοί), than the rest of the baptized laity, i.e., precisely to a higher station or status.[104]

The scholiast's comment on the last citation leads us to Dionysius' emphasis on the leading role of the ordained clergy. Unlike the Areopagite's insistence on the rigors of monastic withdrawal, the commentator observes, "those Messalians" observe a limited ascesis of three years and then do whatever they want.[105] With "Messalianism" (from the Syriac "to pray") we arrive at the native Syrian equivalent to those tensions between the holy man and the Church hierarchy, between personal charisma and sacramental authority, that we saw alluded to in the stories of the Egyptian monks. I do not intend to elucidate the ups and downs and scholarly confusions of the Messalian controversy, where until recently there has been much smoke and little light. Having already broached this subject in chapter 1.1–2., I simply want to point out the following four points: (1) the controversy stemmed from and continued to embroil the Syrian East from the late fourth through at least the fifth centuries; (2) it must clearly have featured certain extreme claims to charismatic authority (to which I will return momentarily), but (3) the same extremism prompted a reponse, beginning in the late fourth century, from within the ascetic community itself; and (4) Dionysius himself is to be placed within both the swirl of controversy and the continuum of response that it had begun to elicit over a century before the apparition of the *CD*.

That Dionysius was consciously involved in the controversy is affirmed by a second clue in *EH* VI on the monks, as well as in his *Ep.* VIII to the turbulent Demophilus. This second clue—second in addition to the Scholiast's reference to Messalianism—comes at the end of *EH* VI.1.3. The divine ordinance (θεσμοθεσία) has expressly given a special consecrating invocation to the monks,

104. *EH* VI.3.2 533D (117:23–118:3).
105. *PG* IV 169D–172A. Note also the long passage vs. Origen, Evagrius, and their putative angelism and ἀποκατάστασις, that accompanies Dionysius' comment on the angels in *EH* VI.3.6; *PG* IV 172C–173B.

i.e., that service of monastic consecration that we saw above is probably Dionysius' own invention.[106] The term ordinance, with its reference to the divine law (θεσμός) of hierarchy that I sketched in chapter 3 above, also echoes one of the earliest critiques of Messalianism. At the close of the fourth century, Epiphanius of Salamis had complained that the ascetic wild men were quite without θεσμός and νομοθεσία, "law and order" we might say.[107] Dionysius is quite as clearly interested in providing them with just that.

Before turning to my points three and four above, we might then take a moment in this section's conclusion to note the nature of the disturbances that Dionysius was facing. Arthur Vööbus has provided us with a series of portraits of noted Syrian ascetic heroes of the fourth and fifth centuries. I underline in particular his picture of Alexander Akoimetos (d. 432).[108] The latter was a canonized saint whose way of life appears even in his official *Life* to have been characterized by continual struggles with church authorities, accusations of "Messalianism," and an emphasis on his own inspiration by the Spirit. As early as the second- or third-century, a text such as *Acts of Judas Thomas* may display one theme that Dionysius approves, and a second that his exchange with Demophilus was designed to counter:

> Blessed are the bodies of the holy ones which are worthy to become clear temples [lit. "houses"] that the Christ may dwell in them. Blessed are you, holy ones, for you are empowered to forgive sins.[109]

The very antiquity of this view, perhaps even including the idea that the ascetic life "makes the anchorites not only members of the Church, but actually makes them priests,"[110]rooted as it was in

106. *EH* VI.1.3 533A (116:19–20).
107. Epiphanius, *Panarion* 80.3.3 cited by Stewart, *Working the Earth of the Heart*, 18–20.
108. Vööbus, *History of Asceticism* II:185–195.
109. Vööbus, *History of Asceticism* I:96, note 133.
110. Vööbus, *History of Asceticism* II.10.

"certain ideas which went back to . . . immemorial traditions,"[111] might well point to a good reason why Dionysius would have wanted to pick a pen name from the origins of Christianity: in order to offer a countervailing antiquity to very old ideas in the Syrian Christian milieu. That these ideas were also very much alive at the time of the *CD*'s composition is no less evident. Once again I go to Vööbus while at the time same recalling both the precise "geographical" positon allotted the monks in Dionysius' *Ep*. VIII (just outside the "gates of the sanctuary" but closer to it than the rest of the laity),[112] and Demophilus' having snatched up the consecrated gifts (τὰ ἅγια) in order to guard them.[113] Vööbus points to canons issued under the authority of Rabbula of Edessa (d. 436), one of which forbids the ascetics "to ascend the raised floor of the altar,"[114] while another declares that "no one of the brothers, if he is not a priest, shall dare give the Eucharist."[115] Finally, the same scholar observes that "wherever an enumeration of the different ranks of the members of the congregation appears, the *qeiama* is always placed behind the deacons."[116] Do we not find in this a corroboration of the physical ordering of the congregation and celebrants that Dionysius insists upon? In any case, the Messalian issue was still aboil during the period up to the composition of the *CD*, and indeed appears to have been around for some time afterward.[117]

---

111. Vööbus, *History of Asceticism* 131.

112. 1088D–1089A (176:12–177:1 and 177:5–8).

113. 1088B and D (175:9–13 and 176:9–12).

114. Vööbus, *History of Asceticism* II:334, citing Canon 58 of Rabbula.

115. Vööbus, *History of Asceticism* II:182, citing Canon 20. See also II:I:276, citing Canon 13 of Seleucia-Ctesiphon, 410 CE, on the same issue.

116. Vööbus, *History of Asceticism* II:207.

117. See Stewart, *Working the Earth of the Heart*, 12–51, and the lists of Messalian propositions compiled as late as John of Damascus, 52–53. The issue continued, in fact, up to the end of the Byzantine era. See Fitschen, *Messalianismus und Antimessalianismus*; J. Gouillard for the tenth through twelfth centuries, "Quatre procès de mystiques à Byzance (vers 960–1143)," *REB* 36 (1978): 5–81, and the Hesychast controversy of the fourteenth, as evidenced in the reaction against accusations of Messalianism in the *Hagioretic Tome*, *PG* CL 1225–1231.

At the same time as Dionysius was responding to a movement originating in Syrian asceticism, he was also taking from its literature in order to frame his reply both to the challenges that it posed to Church order and to the problems of Evagrian Origenism.

3.2. *The* Liber Graduum

Written in Persia sometime in the latter half of the fourth century and never translated from Syriac into Greek, the *Liber Graduum* or *Book of Steps* seems to have been the first work in either language to have advanced a clear and deliberate coordination between "the Church—its ministry . . . its priesthood, eucharistic sacrifice, altar, baptism, catechesis"—and the life of (inward) prayer at three levels: "that which is visible and public (*qalya*), that which is hidden or secret (*kasya*) in the heart, and that which is above (*l`el*) or heavenly (*šmayyana*)."[118] I believe that these three levels—the heavenly church, the visible one, and the "church of the heart"—correspond more or less exactly with the Dionysian plan of the celestial and ecclesiastical hierarchies, together with the latter as the inner human writ large. I also think that the reason for the composition of both the *Liber* and the *CD* was much the same. Murray speaks of the *Liber*'s insistence on "the divine origin, lawfulness, and importance of the public 'level' with what seems an undertone of defensiveness."[119] The author was writing in a situation where he, or at least his particular views, were under criticism, if not attack. This accords with the Messalian crisis that we have observed obtained in the East from the end of the fourth century onward, and in fact the *Liber* was, on its first printing earlier this century, called a "Messalian" work, though that label seems happily to have been rejected by more exacting scholarship.[120] Vööbus' remarks sum up the response: "There is not only

118. Murray, *Symbols*, 263. For the text in Syriac and Latin translation, Kmosko, *PS* 3, esp. 285–304 for the key *Discourse* XII.

119. Murray, *Symbols*, 263; see also 129.

120. See Kmosko's *Praefatio* for the accusation, and for the rebuttal, Vööbus, *History of Asceticism* I:178–184, and A. Guillaumont, "Situation et significance du *Liber Graduum* dans la spiritualité syriaque," in *Symposium Syriacum*

nothing of the doctrine and views ascribed to the Messalian movement, but positively the document unfolds a theological structure which leaves no room for Messalian teachings."[121] On the other hand, it is worth noting that Guillaumont, who shares Vööbus' general views, still sees in the *Liber*'s division of Christians into the "perfect" (i.e., ascetics who have renounced the world) and the "just" (the baptized laity) as, at the least, susceptible to the creation of "a tension, not to say a conflict, between the perfect and the ecclesiastical hierarchy."[122] It betrays, in other words, something of that tension that I have noted was latent and not infrequently expressed in the monastic movement, and with regard to which we find Dionysius laboring to reply.[123]

Nonetheless, the *Liber*'s conscious effort at the coordination of the heavenly, earthly, and inner realities of the Christian dispensation does mark a new and most significant step on the way toward my understanding of the *CD*. In *Discourse* XII the anonymous author writes:

> For our Lord . . . did not erect in vain the Church and the altar and baptism, all of which are visible to physical eyes. It is through these visible things, however, that we shall be in these heavenly things, which are invisible to eyes of flesh, our bodies becoming temples and our hearts altars.[124]

1972 (*OCA* 197; Rome: Pontificium Institum Orientalium Studiorum, 1974), 311–325.

121. Vööbus, *History of Asceticism* I:183.

122. Guillaumont, "Situation et significance," 321. See also A. Persic, "La Chiesa di Siria e i 'gradi' della vita Christiana," in *Per foramen acus: Il cristianesimo antico di fronte alla pericope evangelica del 'giovane ricco'* (ed. G. Vissona et al.; Milan: Vita e pensiero, 1986), 208–263, esp. 214–222.

123. Perhaps of some note, given my focus on Evagrius above, is Vööbus' observation that the *Liber* appears often to have circulated under Evagrius' name, *History of Asceticism* I:184, note 31. Other people, it seems, were also and early drawing a parallel between the ascetic from Pontus and the advocate of the "little church."

124. *Book of Steps* XII.2 (Kitchen-Parmentier, 122).

To find oneself into the celestial counterpart and model of the earthly church[125] (recall Dionysius' εἰκών, ὁμοίωμα, ἄγαλμα, etc.) occurs even while still in the visible church[126] on condition that our bodies become temples and our hearts altars. And it is the earthly Church alone, with its priesthood and rites, that makes this transformation possible: in Baptism "this church . . . gives birth to people as infants," then she enables them to make "their bodies temples and their hearts altars . . . until they become Perfect and truly eat our Lord,"[127] so as to set them forth as "good examples"—Dionysius would say εἰκόνες or ἀγάλματα—for their education and ascetic life in Christ.[128]

Briefly put, "without this visible church a person will not live in that [church] of the heart and in that higher [church]."[129] If we hold the visible Church in contempt, the author continues,[130] "our body will not become a temple, nor will our heart become an altar" and "that higher church and its altar, its light and its priesthood will not be revealed to us."[131] Indeed, even the saints who luxuriate in the light of the heavenly church "do not treat with contempt this blessed nurse who gives birth everyday and

125. *Book of Steps* XII.4 (Kitchen-Parmentier 122): "From that heavenly church originates everything that is beautiful and from there the light shines on us on all sides. . . . Its image was the church on earth and its priests and its altar. Whither are gathered all the saints who are pure in their heart . . . and luxuriate in its light." See also the description of those made perfect in *Discourse* VI (Kitchen-Parmentier, 62): "while living in the flesh on earth, his mind daily dwells in Eden in the Spirit, that is, in the heavenly Jerusalem."

126. "When . . . a person is diligent in this visible church, he is living in that church of the heart and in that higher [church]" (*Book of Steps* XII.4, Kitchen-Parmentier, 122); "that heavenly church and spiritual altar will be revealed to us and we will sacrifice praise upon it . . . while believing in this visible altar and this priesthood" (*Book of Steps* XII.2; Kitchen-Parmentier, 120).

127. *Book of Steps* XII.3 (Kitchen-Parmentier, 121–122).

128. *Book of Steps* XII.2 (Kitchen-Parmentier, 120).

129. *Book of Steps* XII.4 (Kitchen-Parmentier, 122–123).

130. The author seems to have in mind the more extreme representatives of Syrian asceticism. See also *Discourse* XII.4 (Kitchen-Parmentier, 123): "If a person has separated himself from [the church] and has served on the mountain, he will be guilty or lost."

131. *Book of Steps* XII.2 (Kitchen-Parmentier, 121).

educates good envoys and sends [them] to that great church in heaven."[132] Hence, the exhortation:

> Let us open [the door] and enter into this visible church with its priesthood and its worship so that [our bodies] may become good examples to all people to imitate [the church] in the vigils and fasting and patience of our Lord and his preachers.[133]

There are therefore, the *Liber* declares, three churches, and "there is life in each of the three churches and their ministries."[134] All three Churches, all three liturgies, are thus necessary, although only the second (the heart) and the third (the heavenly original) will abide in the eschaton. It is there alone that "our Lord shines openly" and "is clearly visible."[135] The heavenly church is, thus, none other than "the mountain of the Lord" mentioned in Psalm 24:3-5.[136] Implicitly, we may surely recall Sinai and Tabor as well. Now let us recall *CH* I.3, *DN* I.4 and *MT* I.3: the liturgy as the image both of heaven and of the "deiform *habitus* [ἕξις]," the "now" of symbols and the "then" of the eschaton foreshadowed in the Transfiguration, and the ascent of the "mountain" into the cloud and before the Presence. The "mountain" for both the *Liber* and the *CD* is an image at once of the eschaton, the liturgical assembly, and the mystical encounter. The parallels are striking, indeed, and I think in addition that the historical context that produced them—i.e., the tension between ascetic experience and ecclesiastical authority—is much the same as well.

3.3. *The* Macarian Homilies

The "three Churches" of the *Liber* and the adumbration thus of the *CD* acquire a still sharper focus in the late fourth-century body of writings traditionally ascribed to Macarius the Great of

132. *Book of Steps* XII.2 (Kitchen-Parmentier, 121).
133. *Book of Steps* XII.2 (Kitchen-Parmentier, 122).
134. *Book of Steps* XII.4 (Kitchen-Parmentier, 122).
135. *Book of Steps* XII.7 (Kitchen-Parmentier, 125).
136. *Book of Steps* XII.7 (Kitchen-Parmentier, 125–126).

Scete, but since credited to an unknown author, imbued with the traditions of Syriac Christianity, but writing in Greek from somewhere in Roman Mesopotamia near the Persian frontier.

The *Macarian Homilies* were destined to have an influence as great as their contemporary, Evagrius, in both the Greek "West" and the Syrian "East" from the fifth through the fifteenth centuries, and beyond. That influence must often have been clandestine, since it seems that "Macarius" was nearly as controversial in Greek ecclesiastical circles as was Evagrius.[137] That aura of controversy is perhaps the reason why these writings do not appear in the patristic library cited by Dionysius' scholiasts.[138] Yet it is clear to me that Macarius and Dionysius have more in common than anyone has heretofore thought fit to see in them.

The whole thrust of the *Macarian Homilies* is in effect "the soul as throne of God" or temple.[139] This *leitmotif* is perhaps most forcefully expressed in Macarius' famous allegorization of Ezekiel's vision of the *Merkabah*, the divine chariot, that begins *Homily* 1 in the collection of fifty: "For he [the prophet] beheld a mystery of the soul that is going to receive its Lord and become the throne of his glory."[140] Rather as Evagrius appears to have been the first to internalize Sinai, so does Macarius turn the long-established tradition of *Merkabah* speculation into an inner experience.[141] The

---

137. Thus see the offical lists of "Messalian" tenets held up for official condemnation that Stewart has compiled and analyzed in his *Working the Earth of the Heart*, 52–68. Many of the propositions condemned are lifted directly from the homilies, though they as often appear to have been misconstrued.

138. Though the Scholiast does mention the Messalians twice, *PG* IV 169D–172A and 557B. There may also be an unacknowledged debt to Macarius in his use of *plerophoreo* in the context of mystical union with Christ (353D). For the special association of this term with mystical union as one of Macarius' signature themes, see again Stewart, *Working the Earth of the Heart*, 97–116.

139. See Florovsky, *The Byzantine Ascetic and Spiritual Fathers* (Belmont, MA: Notable & Academic, 1987), 154.

140. (II) 1.2 (Dörries 1–2); cf. also 1.12 (19–20).

141. See G. Scholem, *Major Trends in Jewish Mysticism* (3d rev. ed.; New York: Schocken, 1973), 40–79, for the *Merkabah* tradition in Jewish mysticism of the first centuries C.E. He also singles out Macarius as a "mystical reinterpretation of the Merkabah," 79.

experience—and Macarius is nothing if not emphatic about its experiential character[142]—is known in the form of light:

> [The soul] is illumined by the beauty of his [the Lord's] ineffable glory . . . she becomes all light . . . the ineffable beauty of the glory of the light of Christ who ascends and takes his throne upon her.[143]

While his use of Ezekiel 1 is clearly in the context of the eschaton, Macarius is very clear elsewhere that the believer may experience the glory of the Kingdom "while still in [this] world," within the temple of the heart or νοῦς.[144] He provides testimony of his own personal experiences in the following, remarkable passage from *Homily* 8 (II):

> To certain persons the sign of the cross appeared as light and plunged itself deep into the inner man. At another time a man entered into ecstasy while in prayer and found himself standing in a church before an altar, and three breads were offered him as it were leavened by oil, [and] as he ate the more he increased . . . another time again a kind of robe of light [appeared] such as there does not exist on earth in this age . . . at yet another time this light shining as it were in his heart opened [onto] the more inward and deeper and hidden light, such that the whole man was swallowed up in that sweetness.[145]

Specifically and on several occasions he links this experience of light with the scriptural account of the Transfiguration, for example:

---

142. See the article of P. Miquel, "Les caractéres de l'experience spirituelle selon le Pseudo-Macaire," *Irénikon* 31 (1966): 497–513; and, tracing the tradition of πεῖρα, idem, *Le vocabulaire de l'experience spirituelle dans la tradition patristique grecque du IVe au XIVe siècle* (Paris: Beauchesne, 1991).

143. (II) 1.2 (1–2).

144. (I) 10.3.2 (138:15).

145. (II) 8.3 (78–80).

As the body of the Lord was glorified when he ascended the mountain and was transfigured into the divine glory and the infinite light, so, too, are the bodies of the saints glorified . . . and [while now] the power of Christ is within [ἔσωθεν] the saints, on that day it will overflow into the bodies outside [ἔξωθεν]. For even now [ἀπὸ τοῦ νῦν] they partake in their intellect [νοῦς] of his essence and nature.[146]

Likewise Moses on Sinai appears frequently as the OT type of the glory both present and to come.[147] The same passages featuring Moses, together with still others, make use of a "now . . . then" (νῦν . . . τότε) construction that clearly recalls the use of the same adverbs in an identical context in *DN* I.4. For example: "For what the soul now [νῦν] has treasured up within [ἔνδον], will then [τότε] be revealed and appear outside [ἔξωθεν] the body,"[148] and: "For what dwells now within the soul will then go outside and effect the resurrection of the body."[149] The glory of God, through the gift and indwelling of Christ, is therefore a present possibility as well as the eschatological consummation. The one difference is that now it is available hiddenly, i.e., within the "temple of the body" and so in the "inner man" or soul.[150] Yet this is the same glory that shone from Moses' face coming down from Sinai, that was hidden behind the veil of the temple, and that stunned the disciples on Tabor.

146. (II) 15.38 (149–50). For other Transfiguration references, see also (II) 4.13 (37), 8.3 (79), and (I) 10.3.1 (138:4 ff.). The last contains a phrase that rather strikingly recalls *DN* I.4: "As the sun . . . one sees the brilliance of his rays [τὰς μαρμαρυγὰς τῶν ἀκτίνων] . . . [so] they shall see the ineffable variety of the inexpressible glory, how it is transfigured 'from glory to glory.'"

147. See, for example, (II) 5.10 (62), 12.14 (114), 38.2 (272), and 47.1 (304).

148. (II) 5.8 (60), 5.9 (61).

149. (II) 11.1 (96). See also the Moses texts cited just above, together with (II) 32.2 (252) and 34.2 (261). Macarius, like Dionysius, seems also to be responding to doubts concerning the resurrection of the body, perhaps against something like the Origenist opinion. See in this regard, for example, (II) 15.10 (132–3): "All the members are raised . . . [they] are not, as some say, dissolved and turned into fire, [such that] the nature [of the physical world] should no longer exist." We recall both *DN* I.4 and *EH* VII.1 ff.

150. See the *Great Letter* 9 (Jaeger, 45).

Christ is the key. All the OT images of God's dwelling with Israel—Sinai, tabernacle, Jerusalem, temple—are summed up in him. He is himself the "true world [κόσμος ἀληθινὸς] and living bread, and fruit-bearing vine, and bread of life, and living water."[151] He becomes thus for his holy ones "their house and tabernacle and city . . . their dwelling not made with hands."[152] This dwelling and city, this heavenly Jerusalem[153] is of course the Church, the new creation,[154] and it binds together angels and humans, heaven and earth: "For thus was God well pleased, that those below and those in heaven might become one Church in a single bond of love."[155] Holding all together in a single living community, their head and soul, is Christ: "For they are his limbs and body, the whole church of the saints, and he is the head of the Church as a soul is in all its body."[156] As with Origen and—to a certain degree—with Ephrem as well, all the types of the OT, such as Passover and Exodus together with Jerusalem and the temple, become

> mysteries [μυστήρια] . . . of the soul. . . . Glory to him who delivered the soul from the slavery of Pharaoh and established it as [his] house and temple and pure bride, and has brought it into the kingdom of everlasting life while it is even still in this world.[157]

Heaven and earth, hidden and manifest, the world to come and this world coexist in the Church on earth and, in particular, in the Christian soul.

Before turning to Macarius' development of the soul/church parallel, I should like to set the stage a little further while touching on a number (sadly, not all) of his terminological similarities

---

151. (II) 34.1 (260).
152. (II) 34.2 (261).
153. (II) 38.3 (272).
154. *Great Letter* 13 (Jaeger, 251–252).
155. (I) 1 (74:11–16).
156. (II) 52.4 (Marriott 26).
157. (II) 42.15 (310).

with the CD. These will have a bearing on the notion of the soul
as church, and they will also serve at once to expand the parallels with Dionysius regarding this central theme, and to indicate
certain sources that the two writers may have had in common.
The similarities are: (1) the notion of the church/soul as "world"
and especially "city" (πόλις); (2) the stress on motion and repose
(στάσις, μονή, ἐπιστροφή); and finally (3) the soul's perpetual ascent
into God's infinity (ἐπέκτασις, ἀπειρία).

Let me begin with the last. Macarius' God is infinite, ἄπειρος.
He has "made himself small" in his Incarnation in order that "the
soul might be able to live in and perceive the divinity."[158] God's
infinity squeezing itself into a human body, on the one hand, is
reciprocated, on the other hand, by the soul's perpetual expansion into the Godhead—which is to say that Macarius advocates
something very like Gregory of Nyssa's ἐπέκτασις.[159] As the eye
of the "inner man" opens up and begins to see:

> Doors are opened to him and he enters into many mansions
> [μοναί], and as many as he enters [so many] again are opened
> to him . . . from one hundred mansions into another hundred
> mansions; and he is made wealthy, and as much as he is made
> wealthy, yet again other, newer wonders are shown to him.[160]

The "motor" of this eternal increase, as with the CD, is the impulsion of a love or yearning (ἔρως) that is both a feature of
created nature and a gift of grace.[161] In speaking of this ascent
Macarius repeats often that the saint's yearning or love is "insatiable" (ἀκόρεστως), as in the following: "The enjoyment of God
is insatiable, and as much of it as one may come to and eat, the

---

158. (II) 4.9–10 (33–4).
159. See, for example, (II) 8.6 (83); 10.1 and 4 (93 and 95); and 15.37 (149).
160. (II) 8.6 (83).
161. See *Great Letter*, 23 (Jaeger, 271): "divine ἔρως" and the "wound of
love" are our possession. We receive "heavenly ἔρως" from above. The latter
is also the gift of prayer. See also (II) 5.5 (50), where ἔρως and ἀγάπη are the
"new creation" of the Christians, and 14.9 (88) where the ἔρως of the ἀγάπη of
God is the "heavenly fire" that Christ came to shed on the earth.

more one hungers."[162] It is difficult not to catch in this word especially some echo of Nyssa's effort to respond to Origen's finite God, as well as to the Alexandrian's notion of the original fall.

Turning toward God with a yearning that is both natural and supernatural at once requires and elicits a particular spiritual condition: repentance and humility, or meekness (πραότης). Whoever is visited by the "abyss of the grace of light, to that degree [that he does possess it] he knows himself poor and wretched."[163] In *Homily* 37 (II), Macarius points to much the same OT examples of meekness as Evagrius and Dionysius,[164] and then presents this virtue as the precondition for entry "within the veil" in order to behold "the future things with certainty."[165] Allied thus with the ascent through ἔρως and meekness is the process of conversion, and in Macarius' lexicon the latter occasionally carries the name of return, ἐπιστροφή.[166] On at least one occasion he uses μονή for the repose and indwelling of Christ.[167] Now, this is not to say that he is aware of Neoplatonist philosophy and a terminological predecessor of Dionysius in the strict sense. Both ἐπιστροφή and μονή were in the air of the time, and both appear in the Greek scriptures. What it does do, though, is remind us at the least that these words had certain resonances, other than to a strictly metaphysical depiction of the cycle of being, and that these associations may also have been at work for the Areopagite even as he was quoting or paraphrasing his pagan sources—μονή with its echo of John's Gospel and ἐπιστροφή carrying the force both of repentance and of return to our home in God. Even repose or stillness, στάσις, finds a place in the Macarian corpus. The soul is called to "mirror the eternal good things"—we recall the hierarchies

---

162. (II) 15.37 (149). See also 10.4 (95): "insatiable yearning for the Lord," "immeasurable and insatiable ἀγάπη," and the adverb *insatiably* twice here and twice again earlier in 10.1 (93).

163. (II) 16.12 (164).

164. (II) 37.1 (265).

165. (II) 37.5 (266–267).

166. See (II) 4.17 (39) and 24 (43), and esp. (I) 3.5.6–8 (39:8–29, esp. 8–16). Note also the latter's use of ἐπίγνωσις together with ἕνωσις and ἐνόω.

167. (II) 29.9 (246), quoting John 14.

as "mirrors" of God—and to "attain to repose [στάσις] and sure
foundation [ἑδραιότης] and untroubledness [ἀταραξία] . . . in the
peace of Christ,"[168] because Christianity is "another world [ἕτερος
κόσμος]" than this.[169] We might recall here the language of *DN* XI
and the divine peace and σωτηρία.

The reference to the "other world" of Christians brings us to
Macarius' use of the ideas of world (κόσμος), city (πόλις), and citizenship or polity (πολίτευμα, πολιτεία) with respect to the Church
and the Christian. Christ is himself the true κόσμος of the Christians.[170] He is their πόλις,[171] and both the way to the city and
its portal.[172] The heavenly city is the Christians' real home and
goal,[173] and their world.[174] It is even in this life the dwelling place
of the inner man.[175] It is identical with the heavenly Church,[176]
and possessed of ranks and degrees—hierarchy—like any city.[177]
The city of the King and of the first-born, an echo of Hebrews 12,[178]
it is there that we have our true citizenship, πολίτευμα,[179] while our
way of life here below, our πολιτεία, is in imitation of it.[180] Indeed,
through the monastic life in particular one may already breathe
that city's air and partake of the life of the angels.[181]

There is certainly nothing new in all of this. I noted the echo
of Hebrews, and I might add the Revelation as well. But once
more, the echoes of this same, peculiarly Christian (and perhaps
especially monastic) "politics" seem to me to constitute part and

---

168. (II) 5.4 (49).
169. (II) 5.1 (46–47).
170. (II) 34.1 (260).
171. (II) 34.2 (261).
172. (I) 3.3 (31).
173. (II) 12.4 (109); 15.3 (132); 16.8 (163); and (I) 6.3 (86).
174. (II) 16.3 (163).
175. (I) 5.2 (77–78).
176. (II) 38.3 (272).
177. (II) 36.2 (264).
178. (II) 43.4 (287); 44.6 (294).
179. (II) 31.6 (250).
180. (II) 43.9 (290).
181. *Great Letter* 30 and 34 (Jaeger, 285 and 290).

parcel of the atmosphere of the *CD* as well.[182] Both men look for the kingdom to come, and the imitation of its eternity in the life of the church (and monastery) here below.

Macarius is not a man without, or insensitive to, community. His attention to and concern for the workings and harmony of his congregation of ascetics is evident from the *Great Letter* alone.[183] Murray remarks justly that there "is no tension here between the public church and that in the heart, and the eschatological language is strikingly 'realized' in the ordinary liturgical life of the Church."[184] All the same, however, Macarius is not without his own opposition (as we shall see shortly), nor—and relatedly—is his primary attention focused on ecclesiastical structures and the liturgy. Both the latter figure importantly in his thought but, as with the *Liber Graduum*, their function is to illustrate and mediate betwen the heavenly church and the soul.[185] The latter is Macarius' true interest. It is for the sake of the soul that the Word took flesh and "hid his divinity so that he might save the like [τὸ ὅμοιον] through the like," and both Christ and all the heavenly host minister to and with the soul.[186] The center of the human being, the heart (καρδία), is therefore spacious indeed. It is the home of good and evil (ἡ ἐναντία).[187] Heaven and hell are within,[188] and there Christ seeks to make his throne together with his angels and establish his kingdom.[189] The "inner man," heart or intellect,

182. I am reminded of Hathaway's analysis of the political language of, especially, *Ep.* VIII, and in particular his (rather disgusted?) conclusion (*Hierarchy*, 124) that the Areopagite's system is simply non-political, "devoid of citizenship." This is true, at least so far as participation in the political process of the state—or Roman empire—goes. But then that is not the empire or kingdom that either Dionysius or Macarius is looking toward.

183. *Great Letter*, esp. 15–35 (Jaeger, 256–292).

184. Murray, *Symbols*, 274.

185. See Murray, *Symbols*, 275.

186. (II) 25.44 (153).

187. (II) 15.30 (146).

188. (II) 43.7 (289).

189. (II) 15.33 (146); and also 6.5 (68–69) for the νοῦς as throne of divinity, together with 33.2 (258–259) on Ezekiel 1 and the soul. See, in addition, 7.7–8 (75–76) for Macarius' definition of the soul as the "inner man," like an angel

is the "site" of the heavenly city where the Lord and the angels
come to dwell "as into their homeland,"[190] and so where he reigns
and the vision of him in glory occurs.[191] The soul is the place of
the heavenly Jerusalem:

> And he [Christ], on the throne of his majesty in the highest in
> the heavenly city, comes down and is wholly with her [the soul]
> in her body. For he established her image [εἰκών] on high in the
> heavenly city, [in] the Jerusalem of the saints, and the same
> image [ἡ ἴδια εἰκών] of the ineffable glory of his divinity he es-
> tablished in her body. He himself ministers to her in the city of
> her body, and she in turn ministers to him in the heavenly city.[192]

This language of service or ministry, διακονέω, has something of
a liturgical ring to it. That echo of the Church's worship is hardly
unique. Elsewhere Macarius speaks of a process of gathering,
συναγωγή, in a way reminiscent of Dionysius in the *EH*, particularly of course regarding the σύναξις of the Eucharist. The soul
is to gather, συνάγει, her wandering thoughts "into the house
of her body," in order that Christ may "gather her unto himself
and make her thoughts divine . . . heavenly, and teach her true
prayer"; the gathering and the prayer are a double process. While
they depend on human action, it is finally Christ who "by his
own will comes to you and makes his abode [μονή] with you."[193]
We find in other words something very like Dionysius' ἐπιστροφή
and ἀναγωγή as accomplished or imaged through the rites of the
earthly church.

The echo of liturgical and especially Eucharistic imagery is
especially marked in *Homily* 44 (II). Whoever, Macarius begins,
wishes to become Christ's minister, literally one who stands be-
side his throne (πάρεδρος), must be transformed, μεταβληθῆναι.

(ὁμοία . . . τῷ ἀγγέλῳ) in inward reality, and the νοῦς as the "eye" of the
"inner man."

190. (II) 16.13 (165).

191. (II) 17.3–4 (168).

192. (II) 44.4 (303).

193. (I) 4.7.1 (48:27–49:4). On συνάγω, see my earlier note in chapter 6 (1.3.2,
Θεομίμησις).

The latter is a verb with definite Eucharistic overtones.[194] The associations become more specific as he continues:

> For our Lord came for this reason, that he might change [ἀλλάξαι] and transform [μεταβαλεῖν] and renew and recreate the soul that had been overturned by the passions . . . mingling [κεράσας] with it his own Spirit of divinity [an echo of the epiclesis?] . . . he came in short to make new men, anointing them with his own light of knowledge, that he might put [in them] the new wine which is his Spirit.[195]

Again, in the following paragraph: "He who changes [μεταβάλλων] the nature of the five breads into many . . . the same can change . . . this soul . . . into his own goodness by the Spirit of the promise."[196]

The change effected by Christ is the exercise of his eternal priesthood: "the true priest of the future good things . . . entered into the tabernacle of their bodies, and he ministers to and heals the passions."[197] Those in whom Christ has exercised his priesthood appear thus as "the vessels in whom God is well pleased and bestows his grace"; they themselves in turn "receive the sanctifying power [ἁγιαστικὴ δύναμις]" without which no teaching carries authority.[198] The priesthood and liturgy of Christ is thus manifested in those who are inspired and holy. At this point we have obviously arrived at the language and thinking that underlay much of the Messalian controversy, and that could have easily been "seen as a threat to hard-won church order."[199] That Macarius took steps to avoid a "de-emphasis of sacramental and

---

194. See Lampe, 848 for μεταβολή and 850 for μεταβάλλω as terms used in connection with the change of the eucharistic elements from the time of Justin Martyr.

195. (II) 44.1 (291).

196. (II) 44.2 (292).

197. (II) 44.4 (293). For continued use of μεταβάλλω, see (II) 44.8–9 (295). See also (II) 4.11 (36) for a suggestion of similar sacramental imagery.

198. (II) 15.52 (157).

199. Stewart, *Working the Earth of the Heart*, 238.

official ministers,"[200] and in such a way that he anticipated the *CD*, we shall see momentarily.

If the worship of the Christian Church is reflected in—or better, reflects—the working of grace in the believer's soul, then it follows that the Church itself discovers its true analogue in the same. In the following passage we recall 1 Corinthians 3:16, Evagrius in the *Kephalaia Gnostica*, together of course with the *CD*:

> The body of the human being is a temple of God . . . and the human heart is an altar of the Holy Spirit. . . . With the temple of the Lord let us also sanctify the altar, that he may light our lamps, and that we may enter into his bridal chamber.[201]

The work of sanctifying the heart/altar and body/temple means that purity and order, διακόσμησις (certainly an important term for Dionysius), must prevail within in order that the whole company of heaven may take up its residence there. As the householder prepares his or her home for the arrival of a royal guest, so:

> How much more so does the house of the soul, in which the Lord takes his rest, need much order [διακόσμησις] so that he who is without spot or stain may be able to enter therein and rest. For it is in such a heart that God and all the Church of heaven take their rest.[202]

It is within the soul, as for Ephrem in his *Paradise Hymns*, that Christ has planted the "all-spendid paradise of the Holy Spirit"[203] and, again in a recollection of eucharistic imagery, it is only through Christ that the soul may receive "mingling [μῖξις] and communion [κοινωνία] of the heavenly nature" in order to become

---

200. Stewart, *Working the Earth of the Heart*, 238.

201. (I) 7.18.3 (114:11ff.). See also 5.2.7 (78:4–9) and (II) 28.1 (231) for a parallel between the soul and the Jerusalem temple, and (II) 31.5 (249–250) for the body/soul as altar of the heavenly fire in a recollection of Elijah calling down fire on Mt Carmel, 1 Kings 18:30-40.

202. (II) 15.45 (153–154).

203. (II) 28.3 (232).

"the temple and dwelling place of God."[204] Macarius can thus appeal quite directly to the principle of microcosm and macrocosm:

> "Church" is therefore said with regard both to the many and to the single soul. For that soul which gathers [συνάγει] all its thoughts is also the Church of God . . . and this term [therefore] applies in the case both of many [people] and of one [person].[205]

But what precisely is the relation of the one soul to the many, and especially to the community of the faithful here on earth who gather to celebrate the sacraments? In what I have so far described, I note not only parallels or at least affinities with the *CD* but also the potential for several of the same accusations that have been lodged against Dionysius. Macarius, as a "Messalian," has also been accused of exhibiting more Neoplatonism than Christianity and thus, *inter alia*, of evacuating the Christian sacraments of any real content by turning them into mere illustrations of inner experience.[206] The answer he offers to such charges, since it does appear that he was faced with a double opposition—advocates of both an extremely "spiritualizing" position, on one hand, and angry or suspicious ecclesiastics, on the other—bears a singular resemblance to key elements in the *CD* of a century later. That answer is developed most fully in *Homily* 52 (I).[207] The principle that governs it is, as with Dionysius in *Ep.* X of the *CD*, simply that "all visible things are types [τύποι] and likenesses [ὁμοιώματα] and images [εἰκόνες] of the invisible."[208] The visible Church is the providentially given icon here below of both the Church in heaven

204. (II) 32.6 (255), citing 1 Cor 6:19-20.

205. (II) 21.5 (115–116), and see also 37.8–9 (268–269).

206. See most recently H.-V. Beyer, "Lichtlehre," 504 for the Neoplatonist charge, and 509 for Macarius vs. the Eucharist.

207. See the references to this homily in Stewart, *Working the Earth of the Heart*, 218–220, developing Murray's remarks on the "little church" in *Symbols*, 262–276. In what follows here, I will essentially be repeating material published in a second article, "Hierarchy versus Anarchy?" *SVTQ* 38, no. 2 (1994): 131–179, esp. 157–160.

208. (I) 3.3.10 (7); cf. Dionysius, 1117B (208.9–10).

and the inner man. This is therefore the note on which Macarius begins *Homily* 52 (I):

> The whole visible arrangement [φαινομένη ὀικονομία] of the Church of God came to pass for the sake of the living and intelligible being [νοερὰ οὐσία] of the rational soul that was made according to the image of God, and that is the living and true Church of God. . . . For the Church of Christ and temple of God and true altar and living sacrifice is the man of God.[209]

Just as the Old Testament was the shadow of the New, he continues, "so is the present and visible Church a shadow of the rational and true inner man."[210] Macarius does not, however, mean that the visible Church is "merely" a symbol. He seems indeed to have been accused of this very thing by "many who are nurslings in the faith," and who, "for the sake of the similarity and statutes of names and of worship . . . trust alone in the statutes of the flesh."[211] Such trust in the purely outward and visible is misplaced, first and foremost, because "the living activity of the Holy Spirit is to be sought from God in living hearts," and therefore because only the latter will endure the eschaton, while "all the present arrangement [of the Church] will pass away."[212] Secondly, though, and on this side of the eschaton, the visible rites do carry a "real presence": "The Savior granted through the Apostles that the Comforter Spirit should be present and take part in all the liturgy of the holy Church of God."[213] The same Spirit is genuinely communicated to the faithful through the sacraments, although

209. (I) 52.1 (138:1–8).

210. (I) 52.2 (10–11).

211. (I) 52.3 (138:18–32). The reference to "names" is intriguing, the more so as Macarius has just noted that "things that are bodily and without soul were honored with names similar to the rational . . . and heavenly beings" (138:4–6), by God's economy. We naturally recall Dionysius against the literalists in *CH* II–IV.

212. (I) 52.6 (139:27–29).

213. (I) 52.4 (139:7–9).

it does stay "far away from the unworthy [ἀνάξιοι]."[214] The true function, thirdly, of the visible Church is therefore as an icon, in the full, sacramental sense of the term. It is indeed, Macarius says, for this reason that the Saviour came and that we have:

> the whole formation [διατύπωσις] of the icon [εἰκών] of the Church, that the intelligible beings [νοεραὶ οὐσίαι] of faithful souls might . . . be made again and renewed and, having accepted transformation [μεταβολή], be enabled to inherit life everlasting.[215]

Once again, and in quite unmistakeable form, we find the parallel between the Christian soul and the Eucharistic liturgy. The consecration, μεταβολή, of the sacred elements is an anticipation of the eschatological transformation of the believer.

We thus find Macarius turning his attention next to the shape of the eucharistic liturgy itself. He begins by restating his point in a way that reminds me very much of Dionysius' remarks in *CH* I.3:

> Because visible things are the type and shadow of hidden ones, and the visible temple [a type] of the temple of the heart, and the priest [a type] of the true priest of the grace of Christ, and all the rest of the sequence [ἀκολουθία] of the visible arrangement [a type] of the rational and hidden matters of the inner man, we receive the manifest arrangement and administration [τὴν καταφαινομένην οἰκονομίαν καὶ διοίκησιν] of the Church as an illustration [ὑπόδειγμα] of [what is] at work in the soul by grace.[216]

By sequence and arrangement, ἀκολουθία and οἰκονομία, Macarius means, respectively, the sequence of the liturgy and the hierarchical ordering of the faithful and clergy. Beginning with the first, he observes that the two parts of the Eucharistic liturgy, the σύναξις (liturgy of the word) and ἀναφορά (offertory, consecration with the invocation of the Spirit, and communion), are incomplete without

214. (I) 52.5 (139:26–27).
215. (I) 52.6 (139:30–140:2).
216. (I) 52.2.1 (140:3–8), and cf. *CH* I.3 121C–4A (8:18–9:6).

each other. The whole rule (κανών) of the first must be completed in order for the consecration to follow and, conversely, the σύναξις is "incomplete and in vain" without sacramental communion.[217] Just so, he argues, is it the case for the individual Christian. The latter must have the full complement of "fasting, vigil, prayer, ascesis, and every virtue" for the "mystical activity of the Spirit" to be "accomplished by grace on the altar of the heart."[218] This interior order (κόσμος) of the Spirit's activity (ἐνέργεια) corresponds thus to the visible order and glory of the sacrament.[219]

Turning to the order of the Church's hierarchy, Macarius' remarks bring very sharply back to mind what Dionysius had to say to Demophilus about the physical place of each of the Church's ranks of believers and celebrants. Those faithful, Macarius says, who "do not sin and who make progress . . . come to the priesthood, and they are transferred from some outer place [ἀπὸ τόπου τινὸς ἐξωτέρου]"—by the latter referring presumably to the narthex or nave—"up to the altar [ἐπὶ τὸ θυσιαστήριον] so that they may be God's ministers and assistants [λειτουργοὶ καὶ πάρεδροι]."[220] We have come across πάρεδροι already, and shall again shortly below. Here it is quite clearly referring to those around the throne, ἕδρα of Christ, just as the clergy would be seated around the bishop's throne in the σύνθρονος in the apse of Macarius' local church. As he did with the liturgy's sequence, Macarius then takes and applies this spatial arrangement of clergy and laity to those "Christians who are moved by grace."[221] Whoever sins must repent and confess in order to come again under the "oversight"—ἐπισκοπῆς, an evident play on ἐπίσκοπος—of the Spirit.[222] As for the soul that makes continual progress in the struggle for the virtues:

217. (I) 52.2.2 (140:8–19).

218. (I) 52.2.3 (141:2–3).

219. (I) 52.2.3 (141:2–3). Note the use of κόσμος, simultaneously here both order/adornment and world, and recall my description of the Dionysian τάξις in chapter 4 above, 95ff.

220. (I) 52.2.5 (141:13–15). Cf. Dionysius, *Ep.* VIII, esp. 1088D–1089A (176:9–177:8).

221. (I) 52.2.5 (141:16).

222. (I) 52.2.7 (142:1).

> It is made worthy of promotion [μετάθεσις] and of spiritual
> rank [ἀξίωμα], and of being transferred from divine to heav-
> enly mysteries . . . and thus, having reached the perfect mea-
> sure of Christianity through both her own freely willed ordeal
> and help from on high, the soul will be inscribed in the King-
> dom among the perfect workers and with the blameless min-
> isters and assistants [λειτουργοὶ καὶ πάρεδροι] of Christ.[223]

The spatial ordering of clergy and laity is the icon of both the
τάξις of heaven and of the illumined soul. Here, a hundred years
before the composition of the *CD*, we find the core of its portrayal
of hierarchy. Macarius' development of the soul as throne of God
and little church is the foundation upon which Dionysius would
build his synthesis, his correction of Evagrius and the Origenists,
and his incorporation of those elements in late Neoplatonism that
he felt were compatible with the Christian tradition.

3.4. Between Macarius and the Corpus Dionysiacum: Fifth- and Sixth-Century Notices of the "Little Church"

Macarius by himself (especially his fifty-second *Homily*) would
be enough to show that Dionysius was not as original with respect
to his hierarchies as almost all scholars have read him to date. Taken
together with the *Liber Graduum*, and even earlier known traditions, he clearly stands in continuity with a tradition alive and
well in the late fourth century. These writings, however, together
with the "Messalianism" that inspired—or provoked—at least
Macarius and the *Liber*, continued on well past the fourth century.
The theme of the "little church" in particular appears continuously thereafter in Syrian literature, at least into the eighth century. I will therefore take two examples each from Syriac writers

---

223. (I) 52.2.8 (142:9–16). On the transference from "divine to heavenly
mysteries," Macarius seems to have in mind moving from the sacraments
here below to the experience directly of the Kingdom. So recall Dionysius to
John at Patmos: there are some in this life who already partake of the one to
come (*Ep.* X 1117B [208:13–9:2]).

in the fifth and sixth centuries in order to illustrate the continuum within which I maintain the *CD* belongs.

One of our fifth-century examples mentions the "little church" notion specifically. This is the homily traditionally ascribed to Ephrem, "On Hermits and Desert Dwellers."[224] Its anonymous author describes the utter poverty and labors of the ascetics with words and ideas that by now are quite familiar to us:

> They stay very late at service, and they rise early for service. The whole day and night, their occupation is the service. Instead of incense, which they do not have, their purity is reconciliation. And instead of a church building, they become temples of the Holy Spirit. Instead of altars, [they have] their minds. And as oblations, their prayers are offered to the Godhead, pleasing him at all times.[225]

The body of the holy man is the Church in its fulness, the place where sacrifice to God is accomplished.

The second example comes from a little later in the same century. It is the Syriac *Life* of Symeon Stylites, composed around 473.[226] The saint was honored by two other *Lives*, one while he still lived written by Theodoret of Cyrrhus, and the other shortly after his death in 459 by a monk of his monastery, Antinous.[227] The latter two, both in Greek, present portraits of the saint quite

224. English translation by J. Amar, "On Hermits and Desert Dwellers," in *Ascetic Behavior in Greco-Roman Antiquity: A Sourcebook* (ed. W. L. Wimbush; Minneapolis: Fortress, 1990), 66–80.

225. "On Hermits and Desert Dwellers," in *Ascetic Behavior*, 79:481–496. See also 72:181–184 and 73:229–232. Amar's introduction provides the provenance and dating of the text (early fifth century), and notes the Evagrian influences at work in the ascetic traditions of Syria in this period (67–68).

226. See R. Doran's introduction to *The Lives of Simeon Stylites* (introd. and trans. R. Doran; Kalamazoo: Cistercian, 1992). My references to the *Life* will be taken exclusively from Doran's translation, the numbered paragraphs of the *Life* followed by page numbers in parentheses. On the Syriac text that he chose, see *Lives of Simeon Stylites*, 45–51.

227. *Lives of Simeon Stylites*, 36–34. See also Susan Ashbrook Harvey's analysis of all three *Lives* in "The Sense of a Stylite: Perspectives on Symeon the Elder," *VC* 42 (1988): 376–394.

different from the Syriac account. Theodoret in particular looks at Symeon with very "Greek" eyes, reading him as a model of the ascetic's mastery over the body, a paradigm of the will's triumph over the flesh.[228] By contrast, the Syriac *Life* is much longer and significantly different in emphasis. Although it does not specifically mention the theme I have been pursuing, it points in exactly the same direction. Several features recall as well still other points that I have raised in connection with the *CD*.

Let me begin by looking at a couple of those other features. The *Life* mentions the Eucharist no less than fourteen times, as opposed to once only in the Greek accounts.[229] A heavenly Eucharist begins the saint's career.[230] It is his sole nourishment during Lent early in his asceticism,[231] marks the end of his periods of abstinence and various ordeals,[232] banishes a plague,[233] ends a drought,[234] stops a moving mountain,[235] and marks the holy man's communion with the angels.[236] Another interesting feature is that, while the unordained Symeon is himself referred to several times as a priest,[237] the regular clergy of the region—bishops, priests, and deacons—appear with remarkable frequency. Time and again local and pilgrim priests from the countryside show up before his column, often together with their flocks, and receive confirmation

228. Harvey, "Sense of a Stylite," 379–380.

229. *Syriac Life*: 5 (107), 10 (110), 18 (113), 24 (116), 28 (118), 29 (119), 54 (135), 61 (141), 85 (165), 86 (166), 87 (167), 98 (171), 99 (172), and 101 (173). *Theodoret's Life*: 7 (73).

230. *Syriac Life* 5 (107).

231. *Syriac Life* 10 (110).

232. E.g., *Syriac Life* 18 (113), 24 (116), 28 (118), 29 (119), 101 (173), and after a vision in 54 (135).

233. *Syriac Life* 61 (141).

234. *Syriac Life* 85 (165).

235. *Syriac Life* 86 (166).

236. See again *Life* 5 (107), together with *Syriac Life* 98–99 (171–172); 112 (181).

237. The *Syriac Life* calls him "overseer" (bishop?) in 3 (105), "priest of the Holy Spirit" in 45 (129), and "anointed priest" in 130 (195).

in their authority.[238] Symeon, in short and not to make a pun, is
represented as a pillar and support of the hierarchy. Thus in one
of the climactic moments of his life, featuring a vision of Elijah
in the glory of the heavenly chariot and with overtones of the
Transfiguration, the saint is given an express commission by the
prophet:

> You should be concerned about God's priests and that the
> laws of the Church be observed. You should make sure that
> no one depises or scorns the priesthood. You should order
> everyone to obey the priests and their superiors.[239]

It is difficult not to see in this emphasis on the Eucharist and the
authority of the clergy a deliberate effort on the part of the *Life*'s
author. We are, in other words, in the same territory as Athanasius'
desire to portray Anthony as a supporter of ecclesiastical order, or
Bishop Rabbula's canons legislating discipline in the monasteries,
or the *Liber*'s and Macarius' efforts to harmonize the charismatic
with the institutional, or finally—and only a generation or so later
than Symeon's *Life*—Dionysius' *Ep.* VIII to Demophilus. The *Life*
certainly does not want to deny its saint's charismatic authority,
but it is just as clearly laboring to situate this remarkable figure as
firmly as possible within the context of the Church's hierarchical
structure and sacramental life. Such concerns do not arise without
cause, and we may be sure that the same concerns were around
when Dionysius took up his pen twenty or so years later.

Perhaps even more interesting than these parallels are certain other recurring elements in the *Life*. Susan Harvey's article
singles out in particular the overall theme of "transformation,"
and within it the supporting themes of Sinai and Tabor, Moses
and Elijah, sacred high place and altar, Eucharist and incense

---

238. See *Syriac Life* 14 (112) where a bishop calls the holy man a "chosen
vessel," together with *Syriac Life* 38 (122); 50 (132); 69 (150–151); 76 (158);
79 (159); 81 (162); 85-86 (165); 87 (166-167); 90 (168); 92 (169); 120 (189); 124
(191) on the saint embracing all the priests and "as a father to them"; 125–126
(192–193), honored by all the clergy.

239. *Syriac Life* 43 (127).

offering.[240] At the center of these different themes, and thus approaching the idea I have been stressing of the little church, is the figure of the stylite himself. Symeon's pillar becomes at once the altar and the mountain of God, and the saint in his own person the oblation of incense and even, in a way, a personification or manifestation of the Eucharistic presence itself.[241] He is called "to reorder God's world, to be a new Moses dispensing from his new Mount Sinai the New Law."[242] "The ultimate image of Christ," Harvey continues, "that rests behind this portrait of Symeon" is the "high mountain apart" on which "Christ was transfigured before his apostles,"[243] and therefore the stylite is portrayed as transfigured, like Christ himself, "in the presence of Moses and Elijah."[244] Symeon thus both sees the light of Christ on several occasions,[245] and in turn reveals the glory of divinity to those who encounter him.[246] He is himself the place of encounter, the τόπος θεοῦ.

Turning to the early sixth century, we find two poems, both of them written for the occasion of the consecration of a church: the sermon by the chorepiscopus Balai for the church at Qenneŝrin (Chalcis), and by the bishop Babai for the cathedral at Edessa. Robert Murray has provided us with a near complete translation of the first, and K. McVey of the second.[247] Balai makes clear reference to the theme of the little church in stanzas 20–21:

240. Harvey, "Sense of a Stylite," 381–386.

241. Harvey, "Sense of a Stylite," 384–385.

242. Harvey, "Sense of a Stylite," 382. We recall Moses in *MT* I.3 as well as in *EH* V.1.2 as a type of the Christian hierarch, and the latter in turn in *EH* I.3 as the summation or even epiphany of the whole hierarchy, i.e., of the Church. Symeon, in short, is a hierarch in something very like the Dionysian sense.

243. Harvey, "Sense of a Stylite," 384.

244. Harvey, "Sense of a Stylite," 386. See *Life* 41–43 (127).

245. *Syriac Life* 23 (114); 24 (115); 52 (134).

246. *Syriac Life* 68 (148–149); 75 (157).

247. For Balai, see Murray, *Symbols*, 271–274, and for Babai, McVey, "The Domed Church as Microcosm: Literary Roots of an Architectural Symbol," *DOP* 39 (1983): 91–121 (text: 91–94; translation: 95; commentary: 96–106; analysis 106–121).

> Three [gathered] in thy name are [already] a church . . . for
> they have toiled on the church of the heart and brought it to
> the holy temple, built in thy name. May the church that is
> inward be as fair as the church that is outward is splendid.
> Mayst thou dwell in the inner and keep the outer, for [both]
> heart and church are sealed by thy name.[248]

The poem moves on to the figure of the priest of the church in
stanzas 24–26. Here we find something like the Dionysian hierarch, the holy man of illumined heart:

> May his soul surpass in hidden beauty the visible adornment
> which the house displays. Since his heart carries the temple
> of his Lord . . . this visible house proclaims concerning the
> mind of him who built it, that the inward heart is illumined
> and fair.[249]

Babai's poem, on the other hand, lacks the note of the "inner
church" that we have found in Balai, Macarius, etc.[250] It does, however, refer its reader to Exodus and the traditions of the tabernacle
and divine presence in Israel that I have touched upon often.[251] Its
ruling theme, that of the church building as a microcosm of the
universe, is itself of interest in light of my analysis of Dionysius'
Ecclesiastical Hierarchy in chapter 4 above, i.e., of the Church as
his true world. Both Babai and Balai are in any case witnesses to
the fact that these two ideas, the ecclesiastical microcosm and the
individual believer as microcosm of the Church, were flourishing
in the Christian Syria of the early sixth century. Indeed, given
that these two men were also ranking church officers, hierarchs,
I might even say that this play on the theme of macrocosm/mi-
crocosm was practically official teaching in the generations immediately after the likely apparition of the *CD*. I do not mean by
this that Dionysius was the cause of its appearance, but rather that
he was himself within a continuum that began well before him

---

248. Murray, *Symbols*, 272.
249. Murray, *Symbols*, 273.
250. See McVey's comment on this in "The Domed Church," 120–121.
251. McVey, "The Domed Church," 95:1–3, and commentary, 96–98.

and carried on afterward. Here, too, we also begin to approach the matter of the *CD*'s swift reception in the Greek (and Syriac) East.

Summary

Important elements in the Dionysian corpus certainly have key affinities with traditional themes and emphases of Syriac-speaking Christianity, beginning with the ancient tradition of the ascetic "single one" and running up to and through the fourth- and fifth-century emergence of the idea of the sanctified believer as the "little church." These two ideas are furthermore connected to each other. The latter owes its articulation at least in part to the need for a response to extreme elements within Syrian asceticism whose emphais on their "singleness" threatened the maintenance of traditional church order—the leadership of the sacramental ministers—and sacramental practice. Dionysius reflects the same concern, and he adds to it his desire to reply both to the late Neoplatonist thinkers, whom he admired, and to Evagrius and the Origenists of the late fifth century, to whom he was also indebted. The result is the *CD*, in particular its hierarchies, and the seemingly curious version of the genre of liturgical commentary that the *EH* presents.

Modern scholarship has usually seen in the Dionysian application of liturgical commentary something strange and quite without precedent in Christian literature. The explanation for it has therefore looked primarily to his dependence on Iamblichus and Proclus, together with a nod in the direction of Christian Alexandria.[252] Rorem sums up this view as follows:

> When it comes to precedents for the Areopagite's interest in the liturgical actions as timeless allegory, as opposed to Theodore's typology of Christ's passion or Cyril's exegesis of the liturgical texts, there are no credible candidates within

---

252. See Bornert, *Les commentaires*, 48–71 for the Alexandrians and Dionysius, and esp. 66–69.

Christianity. There is, however, a methodological similarity to
Iamblichus regarding the rituals of later Neoplatonism.[253]

Aside from the fact that Dionysius' "allegories" are not perfectly
timeless but linked instead to his eschatology and christology, it
also appears to be the case, in light of the Syrian ascetic tradition I
have just outlined, that his version of mystagogy is after all neither
curious nor without precedent. His interest in and exposition of the
Church's worship owes more to Macarius, in short, than to either
Cyril of Jerusalem or to Theodore of Mopsuestia (though it does
have notable affinities to both the latter, especially to the last). This
is so because his concerns are likewise similar to Macarius', just
as his roots are in the same ascetical tradition. Here is the source
of that "timeless" and "allegorical" character of his treatment of
the Church and its sacraments. Iamblichan theurgy is doubtless a
contributing element, but more important still is the long tradition,
beginning with the NT itself and running through the Alexandria
of Philo and Clement, of the believer as the ναὸς θεοῦ. The same
tradition in Syria, arriving there doubtless from the same Palestinian
(?) sources as had inspired the Alexandrians, received if anything
greater emphasis than elsewhere in the Chrisian world. We saw it
alluded to in the passage quoted above from the *Acts of Judas Thomas*,
and developed at some length in Ephrem's treatment of the Paradise Mountain (discussed in chapter 1.2.). It then reaches a kind of
bloom in the *Liber Graduum* and Macarius, after whom it remains a
constant feature of even official—i.e., clerical—Syrian Christianity.
The clerical interest, if I may put it that way, is clear even in the *Life*
of so prominent an ascetic as the famous stylite, Symeon.

I do something of an injustice, though, to this interest in church
order and the sacraments by labeling it simply "clerical," since
it was also and primarily rooted in ascetic practice and thought.
Its most powerful exponent prior to Dionysius, Macarius was
clearly himself a monk and anxious to affirm the harmony of
Christianity's institutional worship with the faith's subjective
appropriation. Dionysius stands in this same continuum, pre-

253. Rorem, *Commentary*, 121.

dominantly ascetic and Syrian inspired. It is only thus, I believe, that the success of his corpus could have been so immediate, powerful, and long lasting. He was received, in sum because his readers (in particular the monks) recognized, beneath the unusual vocabulary and baroque syntax, themes and concerns, together with a testimony to experience, that they held in common with the Areopagite and that everyone involved wholly approved. Were they not monks who commissioned that mosaic adorning the apse of Saint Catherine's church at Mt. Sinai? Were not people like John of Scythopolis, Severus of Antioch (even Stephen bar Sudaili) monks as well, before at least they became bishops?

Christian Syria, in short, supplies a vital and up to now entirely missing piece in the puzzle not only of Dionysius' Christian background but as well both of his swift reception and of the great authority that he would enjoy in the Christian East ever afterward. Even much of his apparently novel way of treating the names of God, Christology and triadology, together with his understanding of the role of language, scripture, and sacrament, discovers surprising affinities in the writings of an Ephrem Syrus.[254] Given this "Syrian connection," and within the context of those concerns that run through Syrian Christian literature from its beginnings, the main lines of the *CD* take on a new and hitherto unsuspected familiarity. Neither Dionysius' *Divine Names* nor his *Mystical Theology*, for which patristic precedents have been admitted by modern scholarship, nor even and especially his treatises on the hierarchies were all that new and different. They all belong to a continuum. Perhaps, though, it is better to say that there are various *continua* that converge in the *CD*. The great frame that enables this convergence is the explication of "our hierarchy," and that, too, as we have just seen, finds its roots in a long-established way of reading the paradoxical relationship between the Christian's life in this world and his or her hope of the age to come.

---

254. Aside from the remarks on Ephrem and Dionysius in chapter 1.2, see the more extensive treatment in Golitzin, *Et introibo*, 359–371.

Final Summary and Concluding Remarks

Ὁ καθόλου θεῖος ἀνὴρ ὁ τῶν θείων ἄξιος κοινωνὸς . . .ναὸς δὲ ἅμα καὶ ὀπαδὸς . . . τοῦ θεαρχικοῦ πνεύματος ἔσται . . . καὶ ἑτέροις ἰατρὸς ὀφθήσεται (*EH* III.3.7 433C)

1. Recognition of the Church: The *Corpus Dionysiacum*'s Reception

Over the course of this study I have sought to show that Dionysius was rooted in a community of belief, a continuum, and that this evaluation—as scholars such as Lossky, von Balthasar, and Bouyer have recognized—has all along been that of the ecclesiastical tradition. From the beginning the Church, in particular the ascetic community, recognized that the *CD* articulated its own experience, in however new and unfamiliar an idiom.

But was that idiom really so new, so very unfamiliar? How, as has occasionally been suggested, could the Dionysian pseudonym alone have persuaded the trained and not uncritical minds that were around "even" in the sixth century to accept a body of writings which was entirely—or even just mostly—alien to the Christian faith? As Florovsky once remarked, "It hardly seems possible that the patent anachronism of the document could have remained unnoticed . . . historical memory at the time was not *that* weak."[1]

---

1. Florovsky, *Byzantine Ascetic and Spiritual Writers*, 204. See also Mazzucchi, "Damascio, autore del *Corpus Dionysiacum*," 725–729. For similar questions, at

The suggestion is too great a strain on credulity. Jaroslav Pelikan's observation is surely to the point here: "Pseudonymity usually succeeds only if it manages to set down on paper what everyone will recognize as commonly received truth."[2] We do not need to follow Pelikan, though, in seeing the work of John of Scythopolis and Maximus Confessor in the following century as necessary to facilitate Dionysius' "odyssey from the heretical [Monophysite] East to the Orthodox [Chalcedonian] East."[3] Pelikan is voicing a widespread opinion, namely that the Dionysian corpus was sufficiently alien to the *esse* of Christian tradition as to require "christological" and other "correctives."[4] The need for such "correctives" has been much exaggerated. Severus of Antioch, John of Scythopolis, or John Philoponus, and later on Maximus, Germanos of Constantinople, and John Damascene—indeed, noted representatives of especially the ascetic tradition down to the very end of the Byzantine era (to whom I will return below)—felt entirely free to promote the Areopagitica, and even, in the case of the earlier writers, perhaps to participate consciously in the pious fiction of the pseudonym. They must have done so not because they were fooled by the forgery, but because they recognized in the "divine Dionysius" someone whose central concerns mirrored

---

least implied, regarding John of Scythopolis, see P. Rorem and J. Lamoreaux, "John of Scythopolis" esp. 482, and with respect to John Philoponus, Rist, "Pseudo-Dionysius, Neoplatonism, and the Weakness of the Soul," 136n. 7.

2. Pelikan, "The Odyssey of Dionysian Spirituality," in *Pseudo-Dionysius: The Complete Works*, 23.

3. Pelikan, "The Odyssey of Dionysian Spirituality," in *Pseudo-Dionysius: The Complete Works*, 23.

4. For examples of this opinion, see J. Meyendorff on Gregory Palamas' use of the Areopagite in *Introduction to Gregory Palamas* (trans. G. A. Lawrence; London: Faith, 1964), 187–192; 204–209; K. P. Wesche, "Christological Doctrine and Liturgical Interpretation in Pseudo-Dionysius," *SVTQ* 33 (1989): 53–73, and his "Reply to Hieromonk Alexander's Reply." For a reply in particular to Meyendorff on this issue, see Romanides, "Notes on the Palamite Controversy and Related Topics," *GOTR* 9 (1963/64): esp. 250–262; Golitzin, "Dionysius Areopagites in the Works of Saint Gregory Palamas: On the Question of A 'Christological Corrective' and Related Matters," *SVTQ* 46 (2002): 163–190; Louth, "The Reception of Dionysius in the Byzantine World: Maximus to Palamas," in *Re-Thinking Dionysius*, 55–69, esp. 61, 67.

their own convictions, and whose witness to those concerns they felt was important and even necessary.

I cannot believe that the practically instantaneous and over-whelming success of the word "hierarchy," which Dionysius invented in order to express his system, owed exclusively to the fact that sixth-century society was stratified (though more on that below, too). If the Dionysian hierarchy provided a sociological expression in tune with the times, it also and more importantly answered to a need within the Christian Church, and was more-over perceived by the latter to have articulated basic givens of Christian experience: κόσμος and τάξις as foundational to the life in Christ of both the community and the individual soul. Dionysius' hierarchy bound the two together. It wedded the ecclesial once and for all to the mystical, the sacramental to the experiential, and it was enabled both to do so and to be recognized as such because it built on themes already long established in the Eastern Christian tradition, in particular of the ascetics.

As for the leaders of the Christian Church and Empire, Hypatius of Ephesus provides us with an example of the sort of episcopal readership that would receive the *CD*. This is the metropolitan who headed the colloquium that the Emperor Justinian convoked in 532/533 in order to reconcile the different parties in contention over Chalcedon. The dissidents quoted Dionysius on the θεανδρικὴ ἐνέργεια in support of their position. Hypatius refused to counte-nance the citation, pointing out that none of the earlier fathers—Athanasius, Cyril—had ever referred to this body of writings.[5] Yet practically within days of this refusal, we find him writing to a suffragan in order to defend the use and veneration of images, and doing so in language that is highly reminiscent of the Areopagite. This does not necessarily mean that he had read the *CD*, but his letter surely provides us with the example of a bishop who could easily have accepted the corpus as "a leader's manual or guide, intended not for the immediate use of all the faithful, but for the

5. *Acta Concilium Oecumenicorum* IV.2: *Concilium Universale Constantinopo-litanum sub Iustiniano habitum* 2.173:13–18.

guidance of the hierarch who in turn leads others."[6] If anything, Hypatius is a good deal more the snob, more a confirmed elitist, than Dionysius.[7] In any case, as Louth notes, "Hypatius' suggestion that, had Athanasius and Cyril known the Dionysian passage cited (*DN* I.4, 113, 6–12), they would have used it, requires that he found nothing unorthodox in the passage."[8]

Moving to other figures of the early sixth century, we come to Severus of Antioch, John of Scythopolis, Stephen bar Sudaili, and Sergius of Reshaina—to whom I might add Leontius of Byzantium.[9] What strikes me about their attitude to the *CD* is far less any effort to defend it (though John does note,[10] it is true, that some questions were being raised) than precisely a strenuous attempt *to lay claim to it*—whether for the non-Chalcedonian camp (Severus), or for the Chalcedonian definition (John), or for a reading in harmony with Evagrius (Sergius), or for a particular, strange brand of pantheism (Stephen). While Hypatius indicates that the fight over the *CD* had spread to the capital, the main battle was being played out in Syria-Palestine (Leontius' home ground as well). It is out of the latter region that the reading of the *CD* would come which would subsequently influence the Eastern Church to the present.

6. Rorem, *Symbols*, 149.

7. For the letter, see F. Diecamp, "Letter to Julius of Atramytion," in *Analecta Patristica* (OCA 117; Rome: Pontifical Institutum Orientalium Studiorum, 1938), 127–129, and 107ff. for Diecamp's introduction to Hypatius. P. J. Alexander provides a translation and discussion of the letter in "Hypatius of Ephesus: A Note on Image Worship in the Sixth Century," *HTR* 45 (1952): 177–184. J. Gouillard, in "Hypatios d'Ephèse, ou de Pseudo-Denys à Théodore Studite," *REB* 19 (1961): 63–75, argues for Hypatius' having read the *CD*. S. Gero, "Hypatius and the Cult of Images," in *Christianity, Judaism, and Other Greco-Roman Cults: Studies for Morton Smith* (Leiden: Brill, 1975), 208–216, argues more convincingly to the contrary.

8. Louth, "The Reception of Dionysius up to Maximus the Confessor," in *Re-Thinking Dionysius*, 43–53, at 45; Rorem and Lamoreaux, *Annotating the Areopagite*, 18.

9. So see D. B. Evans, "Leontius of Byzantium and Dionysius the Areopagite," *EB* 7 (1980): 1–34.

10. *PG* IV 20AB.

2. The Elements of the Dionysian Synthesis

That element of the Dionysian synthesis which has been most to the fore in the scholarship of the past century is the matter of the *CD*'s relationship to Neoplatonism. Here we confront a shibboleth that has long troubled the investigation of Christian thought from its beginnings down to the Middle Ages: that is, the assumption that the Platonic tradition and Christianity are mutually exclusive. It should be clear that Platonic thought was part of the mental "furniture" of the earliest Christian documents.[11] The same applies to all the writers that came after, from Irenaeus through Clement, Origen, the Cappadocians, Evagrius, and including the Syrians. Ephrem's dialectic and Macarius' use of the micro-macrocosm motif, together with the latter's emphasis on the "inner man," are as much the product of the Hellenistic and—yes—Platonist background of late antique thought as are the perhaps more obvious (or at least more generally acknowledged) debts that Origen and Nyssa owed to the philosophers. Indeed, Macarius' development of the idea of the "little church" seems to me to point to something very interesting and hitherto unremarked. His *Homilies*, together with the *Liber Graduum* and Evagrius, are only some two or three generations removed from Iamblichus' *De mysteriis*. An inquiry into whether any relationship can be establishd between these exemplars of the ascetic tradition and Iamblichus and his school might bear interesting fruit. They are all, including Iamblichus, fourth-century writers; all represent themes that hark back to first-century themes; and all are writing out of the same general area, Syria-Palestine, from which Dionysius would emerge a century later. Is it then so surprising that the Areopagite was recognized and welcomed? The mingling and confluence of scriptural (if I may speak so generally) and Platonist—even strictly Neoplatonist—themes had already

---

11. The same applies to first-century Jewish thought. See, for example, M. Hengel, *Jews, Greeks, and Barbarians: Aspects of the Hellenization of Judaism in the Pre-Christian Period* (trans. J. Bowden; Philadelphia: Fortress, 1980), esp. his conclusions at 125–126.

been underway a long time, and that in directions which clearly foreshadowed the *CD*'s ruling themes.

Of course Dionysius borrowed from the Neoplatonists. We must recognize as a constituent element—and not an inconsiderable one—of the *CD* the ruling metaphor of Plotinus: the microcosm is the reality of the macrocosm. Reality itself is finally the great analog of mind, of levels of thought or θεωρία. Yet this is also an element that we encounter front and center in Origen, no less a contributor to the *CD*, and more clearly still in Evagrius. The world-levels are stages of contemplation providentially arranged to mirror our true being that we, in ascending, recognize again as our own. Dionysius' "great imaginative effort" was to take from both the sources of pagan and Christian Platonism,[12] and to re-cast them both. He did so through incorporating them with other elements: (1) the Iamblichan theurgy that sought to establish communion via grace between gods and humans, intelligible and sensible; with (2) the fourth-century Church's new emphasis on mystagogy that stressed the Liturgy as type and presence of the age to come; and (3) the triadic ontology and the theological language of Proclus as reinterpreted in the light of (4) the Cappadocian discussion of the "Names" of God and Gregory of Nyssa's development of the Pauline mystical body of Christ, and (5) the writings of Ephrem and the *Macarian Homilies*, in particular the theme of the "little church." The result was the *CD*: a vision of the world redeemed in the Church, itself the εἰκών—presence—here below of Heaven (God and the angels) given us in Jesus Christ, itself as well the image of our own true being, of humanity both corporate and individual: the body of Christ and unique locus of the encounter and union of God with his creature.

I now turn to Dionysius' Christ and the notion of the icon.

---

12. G. Every, "Dionysius the Pseuo-Areopagite," *One Yet Two: Monastic Tradition East and West* (Kalamazoo, MI: Cistercian Publications, 1976), 81–94, at 83.

3. The Icon of the Mystery

3.1. Transfiguration of the Sensible

Harl remarked that Origen's Christ fulfills his function insofar as he becomes disincarnate. However valuable he might declare the value of icons, Origen was therefore the prototypical iconoclast.[13] All symbols, all images, because rooted precisely in a concrete and historical person, must finally be abandoned. Dionysius, on the other hand—as evidenced by Hypatius' letter—anticipates the iconodules.[14] The humanity of Jesus crowns and embraces the whole of the ecclesiastical hierarchy. That humanity clothes his divinity, the mystery hidden within the veils. Contemplating Jesus within the ecclesiastical hierarchy (and the Church within Jesus), the worshipper is led up through him to the vision of the angelic hosts, beyond whom, again, he encounters Jesus, God, lighting creation with the presence of his δυνάμεις. Jesus' humanity joins us to the angels and renders possible our knowledge of God and so our θέωσις. This is not unlike Origen, save that in the *CD* there is no ascent through time and worlds to God. Jesus' humanity, his body, is so to speak our permanent "envelope." One can never move through and beyond him to disincarnation. There is no "beyond," and motion is therefore always into him, the infinite center. Neither, then, are the "veils" ever to be wholly dissolved. The eschaton promises their transfiguration rather than their abolition. Everything is truly present *now*, and the succession of worlds—or moments of contemplation—have all been folded up and into our hierarchy, into the One who lives "forevermore." We can thus say that for Dionysius the icon, even while it looks forward to a more perfect transparency in the age to come, carries a certain permanent validity, and its validity is rooted exactly in

13. See the article by G. Florovsky, "Origen, Eusebius, and the Iconoclastic Controversy," *CH* 19 (1950): 77–96, esp. 86ff. and 94–95 for the iconoclastic tendencies also present in Plotinus.

14. See Kitzinger, "Cult of Images," esp. 138; and also Armstrong, "Some Comments on the Development of the Theology of Images," *SP* 9 (1963): 117–126, at 123, on the Christian emphasis on humans as shifting the balance of religion away from "cosmic religion" to the image.

the Incarnation, in Jesus who is our permanent bond with the νοητά both created and uncreated.

3.2. An "Open" Cycle

All is present now, all in a sense already accomplished. Yet it would be a mistake to say that the Dionysian cosmos is a frozen one. Quite to the contrary, the impression that the reader takes away from it is one of constant motion, of the universal dance of providential grace descending, and of love ascending as purified desire, and of everything again turning around and in to the Incarnate God. Motion is the key to the *CD*. Motion and its "refinement," its unceasing conformity to the divine—and for us that also means to the angels and to Christ—is the reality of contemplation and salvation. Do we find this in the Neoplatonists? We do. It is none other than the cycle of πρόοδος—ἐπιστροφή. Dionysius has, however, shorn it of its demiurgic functions—save in the case of God alone. Neither does it refer any longer primarily to the structures of thought, or even to the psychology of mystical union. It has instead been personalized, made to depend on God's grace realizing itself in creation through Christ. And this, furthermore, is the result of a long process of transformation that can be traced in Origen, Evagrius, the Cappadocians—especially the Nyssene—and the Syrians. In Plotinus and his successors the cycle comprises the sum of reality which necessarily ever was and will ever be: thought is πρόοδος—ἐπιστροφή, is being, is forever. The Origenist system adapted the cycle to signify the Fall, Providence, and the return to the "beginning." Dionysius took from and corrected both in order to say that our ἐπιστροφή is the realization of God's loving πρόοδος (or πρόνοια), the making actual of what he has ever willed us to become. We effect God's ἐπιστροφή to himself and in so doing come increasingly to mirror his πρόοδος in love. The pagans' cycle of being becomes Dionysius' round of love. And another transformation: our motion is a striving to become ourselves, to possess what is ours in God, but, because God is the infinitely transcendent, our movement toward possession is necessarily without end. Here is the heritage of Irenaeus,

Gregory of Nyssa, and Macarius. The cycle is still there, indeed, and both its "ends," ἀρχή and τέλος, still meet in God, but one can no longer describe it as "closed." For Gregory, as for Dionysius, to say that the "ends meet" in God is to say nothing at all—or, rather, it is to say everything and more than everything, since where, so far as human thought can comprehend, is there "meeting" in infinity? We still have the cycle, but cycles there can never be. No repetitions are possible where the "return" is endless, ἀφομοίωσις unceasing, and where the "beginnings" disappear together with the "end" into transcendence. And, because change, growth, or becoming are permanent, then so do our history, our world, our mode of being acquire a lasting importance and validity.

3.3. Christ the Infinite Center

Once again we arrive at Christ, and to another point Dionysius owes to Gregory of Nyssa's development of the New Testament revelation: the "infinity within a span of the Incarnation."[15] Jesus is God's mystery; in him the "ends" have already "met"; in him our "return" has already been accomplished. The cycle begins and ends in him, and he is the inexhaustible center of the ecclesiastical hierarchy through and into whom we grow forever. Any analysis of the *CD* that neglects or loses sight of Christ's true centrality will see the system at once collapse into incoherence. For without that center the *MT* must inevitably dominate and dissolve the *EH*.[16] The logic of negation, of transcending the symbol through the ἀναγωγή, would insist upon this dissolution, and we should be

15. Gendle's fine phrase ("Apophatic Approach," 375) points to Gregory's insistence on God's transcendence and infinity, paving the way toward a neat complete reevaluation of creation, Incarnation, anagogy, the knowledge of God and union with him. Everything becomes, as it were, "infected" with infinity. Centered on Christ, the mysteries of creation and revelation, contemplation and ascent, God and humanity are all found to turn on deeper paradoxes, on antinomies, and to insist upon unceasing appropriation, to be ever in motion around and into Christ, the center. "Infinity within a span" thus also points toward the new theandric reality at the core of the Dionysian vision, and so toward the mystery of the icon.

16. This is exactly the argument of Rorem (see esp. *Commentary*, 207–209).

left with either a cosmetically Christianized pagan or else a species of vertically oriented Origenist: in both cases a most unsat-
isfactory result, and an untrue one, since it would be to miss the
heart of the *CD* and the tensions that are vital to it. With regard
to the anagogy of the *EH*, I point to the following: (1) Dionysius'
symbols carry a "real presence" while at the same time they are
multi-valued, require continual transcendence through ascending
negation; (2) Christ is truly present in the ecclesiastical hierarchy
that is his body, yet that presence must be discerned and the discernment reveals levels of apprehension; (3) we must therefore
always ascend, ever further, ever deeper, yet—and here is the
essential—*we never depart from the "place" where we began.* We are
continually in motion about the same altar, the same Jesus Christ
in whom our union with God is accomplished and present now.
Von Balthasar has put the matter well: "In the Church's Liturgy
the Platonic dialogue of the image is to a certain extent stilled:
its emphasis on the 'holy myth' and its destruction for the sake
of pure concept."[17]

4. An Inherited Inadequacy

Dionysius knows no "pure concept," only Jesus Christ. I touch
here on a dilemma that was quite as much a part of his Christian inheritance as it was of his pagan learning. The αἰσθητός/
νοητός language he employed was frankly inadequate to the several meanings he required of it: the multivalency of his symbols,
the angelic world, and the Person of the Incarnate One whose
Providence works all in all. He was, though, precisely heir to the
ambiguities inherent in any attempt to articulate the biblical revelation in Platonistic language, that attempt which, together with
certain of its difficulties, can be traced back to the first century,
to Philo and even, to a certain degree, the Pauline corpus itself.
While not denying this, and other tensions stretched nearly to
breaking-point—e.g., presence now and eschaton, hierarchy itself and immediate vision, "legal" and "charismatic," subjective

17. Von Balthasar, *Herrlichkeit*, 2:187.

and objective—all of which are related and all of which, again, I believe to be at least as dependent on the limitations of human thought as on the inadequacies of Dionysius as a thinker, I still maintain that our author was more successful in avoiding serious traps than many—if not most—of his predecessors.

Concluding my citation from von Balthasar, I feel that he "saved the whole spiritual energy of the Alexandrians and Cappadocians and at the same time definitely banished the tendency to threaten the Incarnation, the visible Church, and the resurrection of the flesh."[18]

5. A Prevailing Fidelity

Dionysius, as Vanneste has suggested, may well have been influenced in his choice of a pseudonym by Acts 17:23 and the relevance of the ἄγνωστος θεός to his own endeavor, i.e., according to Vanneste, the exploration and use of pagan metaphysics to describe the encounter with the unknown and unknowable God.[19] For my part, though, I would choose to see in his chosen name a conscious declaration of faithfulness to the Pauline tradition, just as in his concluding "Letter" to Saint John on Patmos, he both acknowledges and affirms his debt to the Johannine. In all, I feel that Dionysius' contribution to a long tradition of Christian faith and witness is such that the "pseudo" attached to his pen name by generations of scholars pre-judges him unfairly, that von Balthasar is quite correct to note that "one speaks rightly of a deutero- and trito-Isaiah, but not of a pseudo-Isaiah."[20] The honesty and justice of his claims to be both a disciple of Saint Paul and a Christian theologian basing himself upon Scripture should be given serious and sympathetic consideration.[21]

---

18. Von Balthasar, *Herrlichkeit*, 2:187.

19. Vanneste, "Théologie mystique," 187.

20. Von Balthasar, *Herrlichkeit*, 2:152–153; see also Larsen, *Jamblique* 157, on Iamblichus' use of a pseudonym in *De mysteriis*.

21. See also Riordan, *Divine Light*, 149. For an extended argument, see my *Et introibo*, 233–253.

It is my contention that the main lines of the *CD* as, of course, I have outlined it, are already present in embryo in the NT texts, especially in those which have traditionally been ascribed to the Apostle Paul. These main lines are: (1) that God is forever transcendent and unknowable in his own being; (2) that he is or rather by his own will has become, nonetheless participable, sharing his "glory," or "light," or "love" or other of his "names" and attributes with his creatures; (3) that, to the fallen world, this sharing in the divine is made possible uniquely through Jesus, who is God in the flesh and whose risen body (4) embraces the whole of created existence, material and immaterial; (5) which—in Dionysius' phrase—"new, theandric" reality is the Church whose presence, while still "hidden" in the present age, is yet realized and discernable in the baptized faithful, and (6) especially within and through their coming together in the Eucharistic assembly. Lastly, (7) the light and glory of Christ also reside within, rest upon the "altar" of, the individual Christian soul which is led to this discovery through its contemplation of, and participation in, the sacraments of the Church.

Let us then review once again that faithfulness I maintain is a feature of "Deutero-Dionysius" by working backward from the seven points I singled out above. The treatises of the *CD* (*CH*, *DN*, and *MT*) are all in fact meditations on the (7) the soul as typified by the *EH*, thus on (6) the mystery of the altar. Dionysius, as he tells us himself, began at the center of the Church's life, at Christ given and received in the Eucharist.[22] Jesus is made known in the "breaking of bread," and this "initiation of initiations [τελετὴ τελετῶν]" in turn opens one's eyes to (5) the "theandric" reality of the Church which, although "hidden" in the present age, is still realized and discernable by and in the baptized faithful gathered for worship. Growing in faith and prayer and love, the believer arrives then at the apprehension of (4) this new reality as embracing the totality of created being, that he concelebrates with the angels to whose hosts he has been joined through the risen body of Jesus, who (3) has, in coming to a fallen world, dying, and ris-

---

22. *EH* III.1 425AB (79:18–80:4).

ing again, enabled humanity to share even in God. Then (2) the initiate rises still higher in contemplation of the unique mystery to touch and sense the light of God himself, and (1) to "know" him in the darkness of his unattainable glory. Here together we discover united the biblical-Alexandrian-Cappadocian tradition, and finally the late Platonist milieu in which the Fathers—and certain authors found in Scripture—lived and wrote. In point seven we find the inheritance of Ephrem, Evagrius, and the *Macarian Homilies*, while in six we discern the echoes of the fourth-century mystagogues as well as of Scripture; in points five, four and three the Origenists, Cappadocians and New Testament as well as elements borrowed from the Neoplatonist equations of mind-humankind-world and their theurgists; and finally in two and one a tradition of speech about God that, while it takes and ultimately derives from the Neoplatonist and prior Hellenistic sources, still finds a basis as well in Scripture and, decidedly, in that treatment of the "Names" of God whose roots extend through the Cappadocians and Ephrem back to Clement and Philo.

6. An Enduring Influence

Vanneste was far from alone when he characterized the Areopagitica as a "lonely meteorite in the spiritual life of the Eastern Church" whose influence, "aside from the acceptance of a few scattered notions . . . was not decisive."[23] Others are willing to accord Dionysius a certain influence, often a regrettable one, on Byzantine piety,[24] and even on the art and church architecture

---

23. Vanneste, "Is the Mysticism of Pseudo-Dionysius Genuine?" 288–289. See also René Bornert, *Les commentaires byzantins de la Divine Liturgie du VIIe au XVe siècle* (Paris: Institut Français d' études byzantines, 1966), 268; Hausherr, "Contemplation," *DSp* 2.317–318; idem, "Les grands courants de la spiritualité orientale" *OCP* 1 (1935): 114–138, at 125.

24. E.g., Meyendorff, *Christ in Eastern Christian Thought*, 83; Koch, *Pseudo-Dionysius*, 94 and 195–200; M. Lot-Borodine, "Initiation à la mystique sacramentaire de l'Orient," *RSPT* 24 (1935): 664–675, esp. 674n. 1; von Balthasar in *Kosmische Liturgie*, 24.

of the Byzantine middle ages.[25] There is certainly something to
be said for these views. In our own day, for example, a Roman
Catholic scholar can, without a single mention of Dionysius, write
a general introduction to Orthodox worship whose tone is un-
mistakeably Dionysian,[26] while an American student of architecture, innocent of any acquaintance with the *CD*, can be found
describing a Russian-American cathedral in ways that recall my
analysis of the hierarchical vision in chapter 4 above.[27] I might add
as perhaps early examples of Dionysian influence both the com-
missioning of the Sinai mosaic I discussed in chapter 1.8 and the
addition to the Constantinopolitan liturgy of the offertory hymn
of the Cherubikon, "let us, who mystically represent-as-icons
(μυστικῶς εἰκονίζοντες) the Cherubim . . . "[28]

Yet true as these views may be, in contradistinction to Vanneste
and others, neither side in my opinion touches the quick of the
matter, and each can easily counter the other. Architecturally,
musically, iconographically, theologically, and spiritually, it would
be quite true to say that the main lines of Eastern thought and
practice had been set well before the appearance of the *CD*. Likewise, the traditions of hieratic iconography were certainly in place,
or at least acquiring their definitive form, by the middle years of
Justinian's reign. Even more so does this apply to the triadology,
soteriology, and Christology (less, of course, the catastrophically
violent quarrel over details) of the East. These had long been established by, in particular, the contribution of the Cappadocians.
The two great fountainheads of ascetic spirituality, Evagrius and
Macarius, had also been written over a century before the *CD*. Finally, society and, together with it, the Christian Church had been

25. For example, H.-J. Schulz, *The Byzantine Liturgy* (trans. M. J. O'Connell;
New York: Pueblo, 1986), 33, and P. Scazzoso, *Ricerche sulla struttura del linguaggio dello Pseudo-Dionigi Areopagita* (Milan: Vita e pensiero, 1967), 133–138.

26. R. Taft, "The Spirit of Eastern Worship," *Diakonia* 12 (1977): 103–120.

27. F. West, "The Conquest of Space: Sacred Space at Holy Trinity Russian
Orthodox Cathedral, Chicago, Illinois," *SVSQ* 22 (1978): 153–167.

28. E. Wellesz, *A History of Byzantine Music and Hymnography* (Oxford:
Clarendon, 1961), 166, dates the hymn at 574. See also his discussion of Dionysian influence, 57–60.

set in hierarchical ways for centuries. What then did Dionysius have to add? Thus typically Vanneste, for whom the *CD* was a fundamentally pagan irruption, can write that the corpus had no real effect—Byzantine Christianity being securely Christian by the sixth century—other than perhaps an occasional twitch in the vocabulary of subsequent generations. On the other hand, even those scholars who do admit a particular Dionysian impact do so, as it were (with some exceptions, e.g., von Balthasar and Lossky), in ways that are frankly piecemeal, partial.

As I have shown extensively elsewhere,[29] Athens and Jerusalem, Alexandria, Cappadocia, the Egyptian Desert and the traditions of Syrian-inspired mystagogy and ascetical literature all meet in the Dionysian Corpus in a way that they had never met before. They were gathered into a unitary vision that was grounded on the double altar of the worshiping church and the individual, Christian soul. It is in this confluence that the power of the *CD* lies, and thus as well its genuine ability to shape the thought, prayer, art, liturgy, and indeed architecture of subsequent generations. It is perhaps no exaggeration to say that Dionysius marks the beginning of Byzantine theology proper. His is the framework within which everyone afterward, from Maximus Confessor to Symeon the New Theologian to Gregory Palamas and Nicholas Cabasilas, would think and pray. This is a bold statement, and it demands some explanation. In what follows I will try to give a thumbnail sketch of the Dionysian trajectory that stretches from 500 CE to the fall of Byzantium, and even beyond.

6.1. On Piety and Ascetic Literature: A Sketch of the Dionysian Trajectory

Let us begin with the Greek ascetic literature, for it is there I believe that the Dionysian trajectory is primarily to be traced. We recall that Syria-Palestine was the region whence the *CD* has long been thought to have come, and that the same area also saw

29. Golitzin, *Et introibo*, 233–392.

the corpus' earliest commentators, claimants, and translators. Again, we remember that all of the latter (save Severus of Antioch, though he too began his career in a monastery and retained his links with the ascetic tradition) were connected in one way or another, whether as approving or disapproving, with the thought of Evagrius of Pontus. The next step in tracing the reception will take us to the first half of the seventh century and to Maximus the Confessor.

The connection between the Confessor and the Areopagite is well known, though Maximus is usually given the entire credit for accomplishing the synthesis that had in good part been effected first by Dionysius.[30] Thus, while most have taken it as expressing quite a different interpretation of the Church's worship, I believe that Maximus' *Mystagogy* covers in fact the exact same ground as our account of the *CD*, in particular of the *EH*.[31] He presents the Church as a series of images or icons that represent, in the following order, God, the world, the human being, and the soul. The interpretation, furthermore, builds on the physical division of the church building into nave and sanctuary. Thus, for example, in *Mystagogy* 4, Maximus speaks of the human body as the nave, the soul as the sanctuary, and the νοῦς as altar.[32] Everything meets ultimately in the one mystery of the latter,[33] at which we discover the anticipation of the Resurrection.[34] The remaining and larger part of the commentary then goes through the liturgy from the entry of the clergy to communion,[35] and builds on the opening passages in order to portray the Church's common worship as an

30. See, just for example, Meyendorff, *Christ in Eastern Christian Thought*, 83–84 and 99.

31. See my analysis in chapter 5 above (5.1, "A Series of Icons"). For texts of the *Mystagogy*, I will be citing *PG* 91:657C–717D, and in parentheses the English translation by G. Berthold in *Maximus Confessor: Selected Writings* (New York: Paulist, 1985), 186–197. For the standard interpretation of the *Mystagogy*, particularly as distinct from the *CD*, see Bornert, *Les commentaires*, 83–104, summarized by Rorem, *Commentary*, 121–122.

32. *PG* 91:672BC (Berthold 189–190).

33. *Myst.* 5, *PG* 91:681D–684A (195).

34. *Myst.* 7, *PG* 91:685BC (197).

35. *Myst.* 8-24, *PG* 91:688B–717D (198–214).

image—and communication—of the soul's encounter with and growth into Christ. In short, there is very little in Maximus' account that is new, i.e., that we have not met in our analysis of the *EH*. The binding thread of his *Mystagogy* is the assumption that the liturgy of the earthly church serves as the image at once of heaven and of the soul, and mediates between them. We certainly do hear the echoes of both Evagrius and Macarius, but my points are, first, that the latter have already met in the Areopagitica and, second, that Maximus is consciously in continuity with Dionysius' fusion of the two. The only thing un-Dionysian about the *Mystagogy* is the perfect absence of the Areopagite's repeated emphasis on the hierarch. Maximus has quietly dropped it. This, too, will be typical of the ascetical literature subsequent to the *CD*.

I also believe that we get a glimpse of the transmission of a tradition in the *Mystagogy*'s opening lines, a tradition moreover that probably takes us back to Palestine. Maximus opens by doing obeisance to the Areopagite. He does not, he tells us, intend to repeat what the "divine Dionysius" had said so wonderfully, but will instead write about what the latter had, out of kindness, left for future generations to say.[36] This remark has led most scholars to the conclusion that the Confessor, having made the requisite bow to an authority, intended to go on to write something quite different.[37] I disagree, and think instead that Maximus assumes what we might call an interpretive context for the Areopagitica, and that that context is none other than, broadly speaking, the idea of the "little church" and of the νοῦς as altar that we found in Dionysius' two unsung contributors, Macarius and Evagrius respectively. I suggest, further, that this context was one that had been handed down in at least some of the monasteries of the East, and in particular those of Christian Palestine.

---

36. *Myst.* I, *PG* 91:660D–661B (184).

37. See again Rorem, *Commentary*, 121–122, and at greater length on the differences between Maximus and Dionysius, L. Thunberg, *Man and the Cosmos: The Vision of St. Maximus the Confessor* (Crestwood, NY: St Vladimir's Seminary Press, 1985), 149–173.

The latter region is especially inviting because, if Maximus himself was not born there,[38] then he certainly came into contact with it through his mentor, Sophronius, later Patriarch of Jerusalem, who had himself been the disciple in Palestine of his fellow Damascene, the sainted ascetic John Moschus.[39] These two men take us back to mid-sixth century, that is, rather interestingly, to just about the time of the construction of the Sinai mosaic. Maximus is perhaps referring to one or the other of them when, just before and after his reference to Dionysius, he tells us of the "blessed elder," μακάριος γέρων, who had taught him and whose wisdom he intends to pass on to his reader.[40] The insights of the elder's wisdom are, precisely, the *Mystagogy* itself. I see no reason to assume that Maximus is doing anything else here than witnessing to a monastically based tradition of interpretation of the Church's communal worship. To be sure, he adds the grace of his own genius, but what he has to say is very clearly of the same shape as my account of the Dionysian mystagogy. His reference to the latter is perfectly natural, and there is nothing disingenuous

---

38. According to the Syriac *Life* of the Confessor discovered by S. Brock, though, he was a native of the area. See Brock's "An Early Syriac Life of Maximus the Confessor," *AnBoll* 91 (1973): 299–346.

39. On Sophronius and Moschus, see C. von Schönborn, *Sophrone de Jérusalem: Vie monastique et confession dogmatique* (Paris: Beauchesne, 1972), 57ff. For Moschus himself, see his *Pratum spirituale*, PG 87:2851ff., and in English, *The Spiritual Meadow* (trans. J. Wortley; Kalamazoo, MI: Cistercian, 1992), and Wortley's "Introduction," ix–xx. Of some note is the fact that the Eucharist and affirmations of its power occur with some frequency in the *Meadow*. For example, see *Meadow* 25 (PG 2869D–2872A; Wortley, 17) for the rule that only the ordained may offer the Eucharist, but 96 (2953B–2956A; 77–78) for the prayers of a holy (non-ordained?) ascetic as effecting the consecration; also the vision of the Holy Spirit's descent at the epiclesis in 150 (1873C; 122–124); the sacraments' connection with fire from heaven in 196 (3081B; 172–174); and the concelebration of the angels in 199 (3088AB; 177–178).

40. *Myst.*, Introduction, PG 91:657C and 661BC (183 and 184–185). See also in *Mystagogy* 1, PG 91:664D (186) and following through chapter 12, PG 91:689D (199) that the "old man" is quoted at the beginning of each chapter, and again beginning chapter 24, PG 91:701D (206). For discussion on the identity of the elder, see T. Nicolaou, "Zur Identität des μακάριος γέρων in der Mystagogie von Maximus der Bekenner," *OCP* 49 (1983): 407–418.

about it. He understands the Areopagite, first of all, as part of a continuum that includes Evagrius and Macarius. Secondly, he has himself been initiated into this tradition by a man or men who have read both the *CD* and its two predecessors (i.e., Macarius and Evagrius) in the same way. Thirdly, Sophronius and Moschus, if the one or the other is the "blessed elder," take us back again to Palestine.[41]

Palestine is also the monastic homeland of another major figure and conduit of the Dionysian inheritance, John of Damascus, a monk of Mar Sabbas. The impress of the Areopagite is particularly clear in the opening chapters of John's handbook of doctrine, *De fide orthodoxa*, which takes especially from the *DN*.[42] His Homily on the Transfiguration[43] also reflects a number of the corpus' central themes: the Transfiguration itself, of course, and with it the *CD*'s emphasis on light as associated with the experience of divinity. While John does not, to my knowledge, touch on the specific subject of our inquiry, his *Apologies in Defense of the Images*, certainly a subject related to worship and thus to Dionysius, make notable use of the *CD*.[44]

Between the Confessor and the Damascene, however, we also find a writer at the imperial capital who makes use of the *CD* in the early decades of the eighth century in his interpretation of the liturgy. Patriarch Germanus of Constantinople's *Historia Ecclesiastica* "was for centuries the quasi-official explanation of the Divine

---

41. I should note that Nicolaou ("Identität des μακάριος γέρων," 417) places the elder in Chrysopolis.

42. See *Johannes von Damaskos: Die Schriften* (ed. B. Kotter; Berlin: de Gruyter, 1973), II:7–44; *NPNF* IX:1–18.

43. Kotter V:436–451. See esp. 438 and 448.

44. See Kotter III:84–85, 127–128, and 144–145. English translation by C. Roth, *St. John of Damascus on the Divine Images* (Crestwood, NY: St Vladimir's Seminary Press, 1980), 19–20, 34–35, 76, and 79. See also, for example, Meyendorff, *Christ in Eastern Christian Thought* and *Byzantine Theology*; Pelikan, *The Spirit of Eastern Christianity* (Chicago: University of Chicago Press, 1974), 120; idem, *Imago Dei: The Byzantine Apologia for Icons* (Princeton: Princeton University Press, 1990), esp. 153–182; Louth, "St Denys the Areopagite and the Iconoclast Controversy," in *Denys l'Aréopagite et sa posterité*, 329–339.

Liturgy for the Byzantines."[45] The composition is of interest for us in its dual approach. It juxtaposes an account of the liturgy as the earthly expression of heavenly realities, *à la* Dionysius, with the rite as a symbolical reenactment of salvation history in the style of Theodore of Mopsuestia. The "little church" aspect of the CD is, on the whole, absent, although something of the ascetic tradition's emphasis on experience does show up later in the treatise. Germanus is clearly striving to incorporate a more "Platonist" reading of the liturgy with an emphasis on the events of Christ's life—his birth, suffering, death and resurrection—and is probably doing so in response to the first rumblings of the imperial iconoclasm that would break out at the end of his patriarchate and, in fact, force him into exile.[46] Thus, for example, the altar in his acount emerges as both a sign of Christ's tomb (the historical emphasis) and of the "heavenly and spiritual altar" where the earthly clergy represent the "immaterial and celestial powers" (Dionysius).[47] If the liturgy as symbol of the inner experience is not present, still we find a clear echo of Dionysius' *MT* in Germanus' portrayal of the celebrating bishop. The latter, at the time of the consecration, stands before the altar and throne of God as Moses stood before him on Sinai:

> God truly spoke invisibly to Moses and Moses to God. So now the priest [i.e., bishop], standing between the two cherubim in the sanctuary and bowing on account of the dreadful and uncontemplable glory and brightness of the Godhead . . . is initiated even into the splendor of the life-giving Trinity.[48]

At the beginning of the anaphora, the bishop leads "everyone into the heavenly Jerusalem, to his holy Mountain,"[49] and, after the

45. Meyendorff, "Introduction," in *St. Germanus of Constantinople: On the Divine Liturgy* (trans. P. Meyendorff; Crestwood, NY: St Vladimir's Seminary Press, 1984), 10.

46. See Meyendorff, "Introduction," in *Germanus of Constantinople*, 42–52.

47. Germanus of Constantinople, *On the Divine Liturgy* 6:60–61, and Meyendorff's comment ("Introduction," 43).

48. Germanus of Constantinople, *On the Divine Liturgy* 41:90–93.

49. Germanus of Constantinople, *On the Divine Liturgy* 41:90–91.

consecration, takes the sacred elements into his hands as Isaiah's seraph took the coal from the heavenly altar.[50] We inevitably recall Dionysius on Isaiah 6:1ff. in *CH* XIII, and quite especially the portrait of Moses as hierarch in *MT* I.3. As might be expected of a ruling bishop, Germanus thus preserves, among other things, just that emphasis on hierarchy and the hierarchy that we saw Maximus ignore. At the same time, the liturgy as icon of the "inner church" disappears. It would show up later in the Greek tradition, though, and would do so not only because Maximus and Dionysius were still being read in the monasteries (as they assuredly were) but also through a new infusion, once again via Palestine, of the current of Syriac spirituality that the Confessor and Areopagite both articulated.

Sometime in the tenth century and through (probably) the translating efforts of the monks of Mar Sabbas, Greek-speaking Christianity received part of the corpus of Isaac of Nineveh, and together with and under his name, treatises of other Syriac mystics, including Philoxenus of Mabboug and the remarkable John of Dalyatha.[51] In these writers, whose concerns (especially John's) anticipate in striking ways the leading themes of later Byzantine Hesychasm, the Syrian tradition of the "little church" lived on.[52] One might argue that it is Macarius, or the *Liber Graduum*, who simply lives on in these authors together with Evagrius, but that Dionysius has nothing to say to them. I disagree. Macarius and Evagrius were, indeed, perhaps the most important contributors

---

50. Germanus of Constantinople, *On the Divine Liturgy* 41:94–97.

51. For Isaac's corpus and the procession of transition, see the "Introduction" to *The Ascetical Homilies of Saint Isaac the Syrian* (trans. D. Miller; Boston: Holy Transfiguration Monastery, 1984), lxxiv–xciv. For the inclusion of Philoxenus' "Letter to Symeon" and *Homilies* 15–17 and 31 by John, see xci.

52. See on John of Dalyatha the article by R. Beulay, "Formes de lumière et lumière sans forme: Le thème de la lumière dans la mystique de Jean de Dalyatha," *COr* 20 (1988): 131–141, and with specific reference to his anticipation of the Hesychasts, idem, *L'enseignement spirituel de Jean de Dalyatha, mystique syro-oriental de VIIIe siècle* (Paris: Beauchesne, 1990), 440–461.

to later Syriac spirituality,[53] but we have seen that these lines had already come together in the *CD*, and we know that Dionysius was both translated and read by later Syriac authors.[54] Thus, in the following passage from Isaac on Christ, I pick out the Dionysian themes of silence, ineffability, and the dark cloud:

> O glorious God who dwells in ineffable silence. You have built for my renewal a tabernacle of love on earth where it is your good pleasure to rest, a temple made of flesh . . . Then you filled it with your holy presence so that worship might be fulfilled in it . . . an ineffable mystery. . . . In wonder at it the angelic beings are submerged in silences, awed at the dark cloud of this eternal glory and at the flood of glory which issues from within this source of wonder, for it receives worship in the sphere of silence.[55]

Isaac then turns shortly afterward to the microcosm, or inner temple, and the note of hiddenness:

> You have made my nature a sanctuary for your hiddenness and a tabernacle for your mysteries, a place where you can dwell, and a holy temple for your divinity.[56]

In John of Dalyatha we find the same echoes of Sinai (and the *MT*?) and Zion, together again with hiddenness, temple, cloud, glory, and the microcosm:

> You who are hidden and concealed within me, reveal within me your hidden mystery; manifest to me your beauty that is within me; O you who have built me as a temple for you to dwell in, cause the cloud of your glory to overshadow inside your temple.[57]

---

53. See, for example, R. Beulay, "Lumière sans forme," 94, and S. Brock, *Spirituality in the Syriac Tradition* (Kottayam: Ephrem Ecumencial Research Institute, 1989), 9–17.

54. See again Brock, *Spirituality*, 11–12 and 30–31.

55. S. Brock, *The Syrian Fathers on Prayer*, 349.

56. S. Brock, *The Syrian Fathers on Prayer*, 350.

57. S. Brock, *The Syrian Fathers on Prayer*, 362.

Arriving at Constantinople perhaps sometime around the date of his birth in 949, the corpus of Isaac's writings and a new emphasis on the "interior" or "ascetic"—and I would say proper—reading of the *CD* shows up with striking force in perhaps the greatest of Byzantine mystics, Symeon the New Theologian (949–1022), and continues in his disciple and biographer, Nicetas Stethatos (d. ca. 1090). Both the New Theologian and Nicetas work quite hard in defense of the "interior" reading of the *CD*, and are largely in harmony with Dionysius' own intentions, and certainly in concert with the tradition out of which the corpus came and within which it continued to be read in the ascetic milieu.[58]

Appreciation for Dionysius' influence on Symeon the New Theologian has grown somewhat in recent years, but to date no one has looked for the impress of the *CD*'s treatises on the hierarchies in a writer who was famed as a thorn in the side of church officials and a fervent advocate of charismatic authority.[59] Yet this impress is very clear. Symeon paraphrases *CH* I.3 in his fifteenth *Ethical Discourse*,[60] borrows from the *CH* again, together with *DN* III, to describe the "golden chain" of—not episcopal, but—charismatic succession,[61] and defends the principle of the

58. See the extensive discussion in Golitzin, "Hierarchy versus Anarchy?"; idem, "Earthly Angels and Heavenly Men"; idem, "The Body of Christ: Saint Symeon the New Theologian on Spiritual Life and the Hierarchical Church," in *The Theophaneia School: Jewish Roots of Eastern Christian Mysticism* (Piscataway, NJ: Gorgias, 2009), 106–127.

59. Compare, for example, K. Holl, *Enthusiasmus und Bussgewalt*, 99n. 2, who declared a century ago that Symeon had "keine direkte Kenntnis" of the *CD*, with B. Fraigneau-Julien, *Les sens spirituels selon Syméon le Nouveau Théologien* (Paris: Beauchesne, 1985), 171–180, who admits to a considerable presence of the *DN* and *MT*. For the influence of the *CH/EH* on the New Theologian, see my "Hierarchy versus Anarchy," esp. 134–152; Perczel, "Denys l'Aréopagite et Syméon le Nouveau Théologien," in *Denys l'Aréopagite et sa posterité*, 341–357.

60. *Traités ethiques* (SC 129; ed. and trans. J. Darrouzès; Paris: Cerf, 1966), 424–443; and see "Hierarchy versus Anarchy," 149–152.

61. See *Chapitres théologiques, gnostiques, et pratiques* III.4., ed. and trans. J. Darrouzès, SC 51, 81; and compare *CH* IV.3 (181A), V (196B), and *DN* III (680C).

holy man's authority to forgive sins in his *Letter on Confession*.[62] In
the New Theologian's account of the mystical marriage there is
clearly an interweaving of the ecclesial and the mystical: Church
and believer, altar and heart, confirm and reflect one another,
and each is, as it were, the icon or sacramental image of the
other through which the presence of the Word enfleshed is communicated. A crucial text in this regard is the fourteenth *Ethical
Discourse*, "On the Feasts and their Celebration." The setting he
appears to have in mind is the solemn, liturgical celebration of one
of the decisive moments in the history of salvation—the Nativity,
the Ascension, or the Descent of the Spirit at Pentecost, etc.—or
else, perhaps, the commemoration in vigil and liturgy of one of the
great saints, or indeed his own instituted veneration of Symeon
the Pious. His overall purpose is to remind his readers of the intent and meaning of liturgical worship. That purpose is nothing
earthly. Symeon begins by questioning ecclesiastical solemnities.
These things are all earthly, "here today," he says, "and tomorrow
gone." The one who is wise therefore looks to what is not visible,
"the future [i.e., eschatological] events which are present in the
rites being celebrated," and, doing so, such a person will celebrate
the feast "in the Holy Spirit . . . with those who celebrate . . . in
heaven."[63] No reckoning of feasts or splendor in decoration suf-
fices if one does not realize that the latter do not comprise "the
true feast, but are rather symbols of the feast." Without that realization, he concludes, there is neither "gain nor joy."[64] The New
Theologian certainly does not discourage liturgical solemnities:
"God forbid!," he exclaims, and goes on to insist: "On the contrary,
I indeed both advise and encourage you to do these things, and to
do so lavishly!" He does, though, want to explain what the things
done "in types and symbols really mean"[65] and to emphasize that
each Christian is called to participate in the celestial liturgy. For

62. Text of the Letter in Holl, *Enthusiasmus*, 110–127. Compare in Dionysius' *Ep.* VIII, as well as *EH* VII.3.7 (561B), and see again "Hierarchy versus
Anarchy," 134–142.

63. *Ethical Discourses* XIV, 35–44.

64. *Ethical Discourses* XIV, 54–78.

65. *Ethical Discourses* XIV, 87–89.

him, as for Dionysius, the Church at worship is an icon at once of heaven and of the new man transfigured in Christ.

It is no surprise to find Symeon's disciple, Nicetas, elaborating on the parallels between the New Theologian and the "divine Dionysius" in his "Preface" to the Hymns,[66] or in his own treatises, *On the Soul, On Paradise,* and especially *On Hierarchy,* advocating almost exactly the micro-macrocosm reading of hierarchy that I sketched above in chapters 2–5.[67] Nicetas' entire treatise, *Contemplation of Paradise,* is devoted to the sighting of the spiritual (νοητός) and eternal paradise of heaven within the sanctified soul. As he remarks at the conclusion of the treatise, it is there, within the soul, that one is to find the presence of the Holy Spirit and so the reality of the third heaven to which Saint Paul says he ascended in 2 Corinthians 12:2-4. This interior and more spacious paradise, the "great world in the small," is the "palace [παλάτιον] of Christ.[68] Thus, too, the hallowed intellect is "the altar within us," the "throne of God."[69] The inner altar as "throne of God" suggests, furthermore, the liturgy of heaven. In *Century* 3.16, to cite one example, Nicetas spells this out:

> So long as the nature of the powers within us is in a state of inner discord, we do not participate in God's supernatural gifts. And if we do not participate in these gifts, we are also far from the mystical liturgy [lit., "priestly work," ἱερουργία] of the heavenly altar, celebrated by the intellect through its spiritual activity . . . [but, once the intellect has been purified through ascesis and prayer] we participate in the ineffable blessings of God, and worthily, together with God and God

66. See *Syméon le nouveau théologien: Hymnes,* ed. and trans. J. Koder, *SC* 156, 106–132.

67. See *Nicetas Stethatos: Epitres et opuscules,* ed. and trans. J. Darrouzès, *SC* 81; esp. *On the Soul* III.4.16 and 27 (76–78 and 88–90); *On Paradise* II.19 (176); and *On Hierarchy,* "Introduction" (300); IV.38–39 (340–342) and 36 (338).

68. *Contemplation of Paradise,* 8.53 (SC 81:216) for the "palace of Christ"; 2.19 (SC 81:176) for the "greater world" and inner "paradise," and for "the great world in the small," *On the Soul* 27 (SC 81:88).

69. *Ep.* 6.8–10 (SC 81:268–272), on the "inner paradise" and "throne of the Trinity," in the course of a discussion of 2 Cor 12:2-4.

the Word, offer up the divine mysteries of the intellect's spiritual [νοερόν] altar as initiates [ἐπόται] and priests [ἱερεῖς] of His mysteries."[70]

It must be admitted, however, both that this was not the only way the Byzantine Church read Dionysius and that neither Symeon nor Nicetas was absolutely in agreement with the *CD*'s intentions. Turning first to the latter point, Nicetas' characterization of the "true bishop" as the "man whose intellect . . . has been purified . . . illumined . . . and perfected into the perfect man,"[71] while it catches the greater part of the Dionysian hierarch, just as obviously dismisses the Areopagite's attempt to underline and support the offical role of the sacramental ministry. Nicetas, like Maximus before him and Macarius in the fourth century, is talking about the charismatic saint, the "blessed elder" or "man of God." The ambiguities in Dionysius' portrait of the clergy are resolved by going back to the picture of the Christian "Gnostic" first sketched by Clement of Alexandria and then embodied in the Desert Fathers. It is frankly difficult to see how the monks could have done otherwise. On the one hand, they embraced Dionysius' account of the soul writ large in the physical church and liturgy, the meeting of personal experience and corporate adoration at the altars of church and heart, but they could not, on the other hand, accept what was obviously untrue, i.e., that all bishops are holy virtually *ex officio*. What Freudians used to refer to as the "reality principle" got in the way. Yet I still feel that the *CD* largely succeeded in its mission. It played a crucial role, I believe, in securing a unity between sacramental practice and mystical experience. It could not, however, resolve the tensions between the Church's life in this world and its anticipation of the eschaton. No one ever has, nor can. Symeon and Nicetas were content with the tension.

Not everyone was, though. Certainly, during the nearly three centuries that stand between Symeon's death and the rise of the Hesychast Movement, the Byzantine Church authorities made

70. C 3.16 (*Φιλοκαλία τῶν Ἱερῶν Νηπτικῶν* 3:330); *Philokalia* 4:144, slightly altered.

71. *On Hierarchy* IV.38 (340).

a rather determined effort to put a damper on the influence of charismatics like the New Theologian. Tidy government was the order of the day, especially during the dynasty of the Comnenoi, and this emphasis had a decided effect on at least the official life of the Church.[72] It is in the context of this assertion of hierarchical authority (in the sense that I understand that phrase in modern English) that we find Metropolitan John of Ephesus appealing to the *CD*, and particularly to Dionysius' *Ep.* VIII, as a support for institutional structures, and especially as opposed to the claims lodged by uppity monks.[73] John's message is clear. God and the "divine Dionysius" intended that everyone have a place in the Church, but that place—and the monks' place in particular—is most emphatically under the authority of the bishop.

The Hesychast Movement of the fourteenth century brings the ascetic and, I believe, more genuine reading of the Areopagitica back into the forefront, where it has very much remained to the present day. Gregory of Sinai (and note the geography of his name) is one of the earliest representatives of the movement, often indeed credited with sparking it. Remarkably, the ascetic or "interior" reading of the *CD*'s hierarchy appears—if not prominently, then at least—unambiguously in two of his *Profitable Chapters*. Chapter 112 speaks of the "spiritual priesthood" as the "sacred working [ἱερουργία]" of the intellect within the "altar of the soul."[74] In chapter 43, though, we find an even more explicit joining of the *EH* with the *MT*, and quite in the sense that I understand Dionysius himself to have intended:

---

72. For an overview of the period, see J. M. Hussey, *Church and Learning in the Byzantine Empire: 867–1185* (London: Humphrey Milford, 1937); and specifically for anti-charismatic attitudes on the part of the hierarchy, see the articles by P. Magdalinos, "The Byzantine Holy Man in the Twelfth Century" in *The Byzantine Saint* (ed. S. Hackel; London: Fellowship of St. Alban and St. Sergius, 1980), 51–66, and J. Gouillard, "Quatre procès de mystique à Byzance," *REB* 19 (1961): 5–81.

73. See J. Darrouzès, *Documents inédits d'ecclésiologie byzantine* (Paris: Institut Français d'Études Byzantines, 1966), esp. 351, 371, 384, and 390.

74. *Φιλοκαλία τῶν Ἱερῶν Νηπτικῶν* 4:51; *Philokalia* 4:237.

According to the Mosaic Law, the Kingdom of Heaven is likened to a tabernacle pitched by God, possessing the age to come behind two veils. And, while all who are priests of grace shall come into the first tabernacle, only as many as have hierarchically celebrated the Trinity here-below in the darkness of theology [shall enter] into the second. [These are the ones] who, before everything else, possess Jesus as their consecrator and hierarch with respect to the Trinity. Entering into the tabernacle that he has pitched, they are the more manifestly illumined by his radiance.[75]

Let us note the vocabulary and its associations with Sinai and Exodus: the "darkness [γνόφος] of theology," light or "radiance," "hierarchically," "consecrator [τελετάρχης] and hierarch." Implicit, as it is explicit in the first citation, is the thought that this is the inner liturgy of the soul. Dionysius is assimilated to Evagrius and Macarius, and that is exactly where I believe that he belongs.

In the later struggles of the Hesychasts against the opposition and ridicule of Barlaam of Calabria, Gregory Palamas emerged as the champion of the former. His articulation of the ascetic tradition was confirmed at the Constantinopolitan councils of 1341, 1347, and 1351. I have touched often enough on the essence-energies distinction, its importance in Dionysius and its defense by Gregory, not to have to go over the territory again. Suffice it to say here that, first, Palamas was engaged in the defense of a tradition, both of theology and of ascetic praxis, that long antedated him; second, that Dionysius was himself an inheritor and contributor to the same tradition. Barlaam appreciated neither fact.[76] The heart of the struggle, moreover, was very much focused on the proper interpretation of the *CD*. Gregory himself draws

---

75. *Φιλοκαλία τῶν Ἱερῶν Νηπτικῶν* 4: 37; *Philokalia* 4:220.

76. It is the great merit of J. Meyendorff's work on Gregory, esp. his "Introduction," to have demonstrated Palamas' continuity with his predecessors. On the other hand, Meyendorff did not accord Dionysius the same regard. Thus see Romanides, "Aspects," esp. 250–262, who is helpful in redressing the balance.

the connection between Macarius' light and Dionysius',[77] stresses the Areopagite's ἕνωσις as an experience beyond knowledge,[78] turns to *DN* I.4 in particular and at several points for the glory of Tabor,[79] and refers Barlaam to *DN* V.8 and XI.6 for his celebrated distinction between essence and energies.[80] These are but a few examples of a ubiquitous Dionysian presence. With regard to our particular theme of the inner and outer church, Palamas does not express himself much. I do note, though, his understanding of the Dionysian hierarchy as primarily concerned with the inner life and assimilation to God,[81] and his passing observation that the saint is true temple of God.[82]

The inner and outer church in the context of the *EH* do, however, appear in the two classic books by Nicholas Cabasilas (d. ca. 1390), *A Commentary on the Divine Liturgy* and *On the Life in Christ*, with which I will conclude my sketch of the Dionysian trajectory.[83] In his *Commentary*, Nicholas states that "the whole celebration of the mystery is like a unique portrayal of a single body, which is the work of the Savior."[84] He stresses, together with the "real presence," that the liturgy is iconic. The celebration seeks "to set before us the divine plan, that by looking upon it our souls may be sanctified"—recall Dionysius' θεωρία of the

77. See Palamas, *Défense des saints hésychastes* (trans. J. Meyendorff; Louvain: Universite Catholique de Louvain, 1959), I.3.3 (111–113).

78. E.g., Palamas, *Défense des saints hésychastes* I.3.20–29 (153–173) and II.5.68–69 (529–533).

79. E.g., Palamas, *Défense des saints hésychastes* I.3.35 (185–189) and 43 (205–207); II.3.20 (429), 23 (433), 25 (437), and 32 (451–453).

80. Palamas, *Défense des saints hésychastes* III.2.18-24 (675–683).

81. See Palamas, *Défense des saints hésychastes* II.3.73–74 (539–543).

82. Palamas, *Défense des saints hésychastes* III.1.31 (617–619); and cf. 38–40 (633–639).

83. For the critical editions, see *Explication de la divine liturgie* (ed. S. Salaville; SC 46bis; Paris: Cerf, 1967) and *La Vie en Christ*, Books I–IV (ed. M.-H. Congordeau; SC 355; Paris: Cerf, 1989), and V–VII in (SC 361; Paris: Cerf, 1990). For English translations, see *A Commentary on the Divine Liturgy* (trans. J. M. Hussey and P. A. McNulty; London: SPCK, 1960; repr., 1983) and *The Life in Christ* (trans. C. J. de Catanzaro; 2d ed.; Crestwood, NY: St Vladimir's Seminary Press, 1982).

84. Cabasilas, *Explication de la divine liturgie*, 62 (Hussey, 27).

sacraments—since "an idea is more deeply impressed upon us if we can see it depicted."[85] In commenting on Baptism in the *Life of Christ*, he recalls *EH* II's emphasis on this sacrament as the beginning of genuine existence. Here the Christian begins "to be," and "until these things, we do not yet live."[86] This sacrament thus marks the beginning as well of our infinite ascent toward the fulfillment of the desire (ἐπιθυμία) that God has implanted in our nature.[87] Nicholas then splits up *EH* IV's meditation on the myron into a chapter on the Chrism and anointing following Baptism and another, after his consideration of the Eucharist, on the consecration of the altar. In both he recalls Dionysius' earlier work. The first, chapter 3, concludes with the reflection that the Church's true priest and altar are one and the same. Christ is the offerer, the altar, and the sacrifice offered.[88] The Eucharist, as in *EH* III, is the greatest of the sacraments, their completion, their true context and activation.[89] Turning to the consecration of the altar, Cabasilas first, as in the pattern of the *EH*, describes the ceremony and then ponders its meaning. The latter is, quite simply, the burden of my argument concerning the *CD*. The hierarch approaching the altar in order to consecrate it is, Nicholas tells us:

> a vested type and image of the altar, which is man himself. If
> a man, as David says, "wash away all wickedness and become
> whiter than snow," and recollects himself and bends in on
> himself and bows down, that makes God truly dwell in the
> soul and makes the heart an altar. The ceremonies are the signs

85. Cabasilas, *Explication de la divine liturgie*, 64 and 68 (Hussey, 28 and 30).

86. Cabasilas, *Life in Christ* II.2 and 4 (SC 355:138–140, 156; de Catanzaro, 67–68, 73).

87. Cabasilas, *Life in Christ* II.19 (SC 355:218; de Catanzaro, 96); cf. also *Life in Christ* VII (SC 361:180; de Catanzaro, 214).

88. Cabasilas, *Life in Christ* III.7 (SC 355:258–260; de Catanzaro, 111–112).

89. Cabasilas, *Life in Christ* IV.1 (SC 355:262–264, 270–272; de Catanzaro, 113–114, 116). See also Cabasilas' quotation of *EH* III.1 in *Life of Christ* IV (SC 355:284; de Catanzaro, 121).

of these things . . . [the bishop] exhibits the altar in himself before he enters the sanctuary.[90]

The bishop, as "exemplar of the altar," is moreover the sign "that human nature, alone of all things visible, is truly capable of becoming a temple of God and an altar."[91]

The last two chapters of the book are devoted to the preservation of sacramental grace in the Christian life, and finally to a picture of the perfected believer. Once again, Nicholas touches on the heart as temple, and does so in such a way as to join the Church's public worship with the personal and private "liturgy" of the believer at prayer.[92] Boris Bobrinskoy summarizes these chapters as follows:

> At the heart of his teaching on mental prayer, Cabasilas would unite that interior Eucharist which is the uninterrupted invocation of the Name, with the frequent partaking of the heavenly Bread which is the sacramental root of the presence of Christ in the believer's heart . . . the "real presence" of Christ both by invocation of the name and by communion.[93]

While the tradition of the "Jesus Prayer," to which both Cabasilas and Bobrinskoy are alluding, was something that we do not find in Dionysius, the union between the inward and the outward liturgy is, and I believe that Nicholas takes it up in direct and conscious continuity with the Areopagite. In doing so, he is simply a witness to the uninterrupted tradition that long preceded the *CD*, provided the context to which Dionysius also gave conscious expression, and within which—as I have tried to indicate—he continued to be interpreted up to and including Cabasilas himself. The latter finishes up his treatise by recalling, at least to my mind, the concluding lines from the *CD*'s *Ep.* X. We may see and

90. Cabasilas, *Life in Christ* V (SC 361:18; de Catanzaro, 151).
91. Cabasilas, *Life in Christ* V (SC 361:20; de Catanzaro, 152).
92. See *Life in Christ* VI (SC 361:124–130; de Catanzaro, 191–193) and *Life in Christ* VII (SC 361:152–156; de Catanzaro, 203–204).
93. B. Bobrinskoy, "Introduction," *Life in Christ*, 33.

know God in Christ even in this life, though he yet remains partly hidden and partly revealed. This glimpse of the glory at once concealed and manifested in works of love is indeed the substance of the Christian life: to manifest the One who is love and who through love moves in us.[94]

Dionysius was always, in both his own mind and in his readers', simply part of and a contributor to the tradition. He does not stand out, nor does he constitute in any significant way a break, interruption, or departure from the tradition. He did, indeed, contribute to it, as I noted above, and his was an important contribution that found a ready and welcoming readership. Those readers were primarily monks, who embraced the corpus because they recognized it as in harmony with their own concerns and emphases. If they added any "correctives" to the divine Dionysius, those came chiefly by way of quietly dropping the Areopagite's effective identification of the bishop with the perfected ascetic saint. This corrective was, admittedly, a necessary one. Dionysius had attempted the impossible, and the attempt did not meet the test of reality. But the corpus as a whole did, and it succeeded in its primary aim, i.e., the wedding of the ecclesial and the mystical which has ever since served to protect the Eastern Church from those divisions between the charismatic and institutional aspects of Christian life that have continued to trouble, on occasion, the Church of the West. As for Dionysius' christology and triadology, these were perfectly orthodox. A Maximus Confessor did no more, with regard to the christological issue, than turn the knob a little to adjust the focus. Neither was the Confessor the first to blend Evagrius and Macarius with the Cappadocians. Dionysius had done it before him. Maximus recognized this, and he summed it up perhaps most brilliantly in his *Mystagogy*.

We are not yet quite finished. Not all of the readers of the *CD* were monks. We have already noticed a slightly different "spin" on the corpus coming from bishops. Thus it is also the case that the Areopagitica, perhaps more by way of side effect than anything else, did have a certain influence on the shape of Christian society

---

94. Cabasilas, *Life in Christ* VII.15 (SC 361:219–220, de Catanzaro, 227).

in the Eastern Empire. My penultimate remarks will therefore turn briefly to that question.

6.2. On the Self-Identity of the Christian Oikoumene

The following is admittedly speculative, but I suggest that Dionysius more or less inadvertently made a contribution to the identification of the Christian Faith as the divinely established sense and sacred order of the world, i.e., the world of the Eastern Roman Empire of the late fifth century. His was a time when the theology underlying the ancient order of pagan Rome had become a vanishing gleam in the eyes of lonely philosophers, while, on the other hand, the shape of the Christian oikoumene had more than begun to emerge. The hierarchical vision embodied in the *CD* helped perhaps to bridge the gap between the pagan and Christian social τάξεις, and so to aid in the latter's establishment.

A few words are in order on the pagan background. Jaeger tells us that from the earliest period of classical culture "the Greek polis was both state and church," and that the latter was particularly accentuated at the hands of Plato.[95] The *Republic* saw the elaboration of the city as the soul of man writ large,[96] the image indeed of absolute reality.[97] With the rise of Empire to embrace the greater part of the known inhabited world this notion was duly expanded in keeping with the nature of the new cosmopolis. According to Cochrane,[98] the state came to be present as the fulfillment of the divine logos in history, as truly a kind of theophany: "the *religio* of this world,"[99] a realized image of eternity itself "immune from the flux . . . [i.e.] mere movement."[100] This exaltation above time and change, together with an increasingly rigid social stratification,

---

95. W. Jaeger, *In Search of the Divine Centre* (vol. 2 of *Paideia*; Oxford: Blackwell, 1944), 158.

96. Jaeger, *In Search of the Divine Centre*, 240–241.

97. Jaeger, *In Search of the Divine Centre*, 355.

98. C. Cochrane, *Christianity and Classical Culture* (New York: Oxford University Press, 1957), 63.

99. Cochrane, *Christianity and Classical Culture*, 73.

100. Cochrane, *Christianity and Classical Culture*, 82.

reached its peak (interestingly enough) at the end of the fourth century. Citing the *Codex theodosianus* (VI.5.2) Cochrane remarks that "the apotheosis of the state was revealed as the apotheosis of immobility itself."[101] This deified social structure may well have been influenced by—as well as influencing—the strictly determined tiers of being analyzed by the later Neoplatonists.[102]

It is my feeling that Dionysius, too, contributed to that identification of Imperium with Ecclesia which von Ivanka points to as occurring already in Eusebius.[103] With his development of the notion of hierarchy and his exclusive centering upon the altar—the "centripetal" force of his whole system—he may well have acted to place the capstone on an edifice already in the building. While I do not at all agree that an analysis of the *CD* after the method of a Durkheim or Weber, as Goltz has attempted,[104] is adequate to the Dionysian vision, there is still no denying that the corpus as read from a certain, narrow angle could not but reinforce the social and political status quo. As much as the idea itself of hierarchy, this must have been the effect (so powerful because so natural in that society) of that Dionysian focus on eternity. The work of our hierarchy continues as now until the consummation of the Age, but the Church's presence between the two Advents constitutes a kind of pause. It is filled, certainly, with the presence of Heaven and the activity of salvation, but it is no less essentially a pause, a hush. True, it is not difficult to see why Hathaway declared this system non-political, "devoid of citizenship."[105] Our author

101. Cochrane, *Christianity and Classical Culture*, 323.

102. The view, at least, of A. C. Lloyd, "The Later Neoplatonists," *Camb-Hist*, 274.

103. Von Ivanka, *Rhomäerreich und Gottesvolk* (Freiburg: Alber, 1968), 58; see also F. E. Cranz, "Kingdom and Polity in Eusebius of Caesarea," *HTR* 45 (1952): 48–66; and G. Kretschmar, *Studien zur frühchristlichen Trinitätstheologie* (Tübingen: Mohr, 1956), 8. For Eusebius himself, see, for example, *De laudibus Constantini*, PG XX 1316–1440; for an extended discussion of the Eusebian contribution and those following him, F. Dvornik, *Early Christian and Byzantine Political Philosophy* (2 vols.; Washington, DC: Dumbarton Oaks Center for Byzantine Studies, 1966), 2:611–850.

104. Goltz, *Hiera Mesitea*; see Golitzin, *Et introibo*, 35.

105. Hathaway, *Hierarchy*, 124.

had no interest whatever in the forms and forces of human society and history. Everything outside the sanctified sphere of the hierarchy remains, in a sense, unreal—*extra ecclesiam nulla salus.* Yet it would be no less correct to say that, in the manner of a side effect, his could not help but be a markedly political statement. The elaborate apparatus of worship that the *EH* assumes belonged properly within the basilicas and cathedrals of late Roman cities. How, in those buildings, in that society, and given the "eternalist" bias and "centripetal" thrust of the Dionysian system, could the *CD* have done otherwise in such a setting than to appear to lend support—if not ultimate sanction—to the forms, and so by extension to the existence itself, of the later Empire? The immense Church of Holy Wisdom, built by Justinian not long in fact after the appearance of the *Areopagitica*, would come more and more to be regarded as the true heart of the Empire and its society, the latter depending on the central mystery hierarchically enacted round that great altar for its justification, and seeing in the sacred action accomplished there both the paradigm of its own life, and reassurance in the hope that, given this God-instituted and protected center, it would itself abide until the end of time. Dionysius may therefore be read as having caught and perfectly expressed the mind of an age at once Christian, yet still carrying the ancient dream of a society whose polity would reflect, so far as possible in the realm of flux, the city of the gods.

7. A Last Word and a Little Speculation

By way of concluding the long journey of this book, I cannot resist some mild speculation, or at least a few questions. What kind of man, I wonder, could have written this corpus? He obviously had to have been connected somehow with monasticism and the ascetic tradition. He was just as obviously associated with and concerned for the organized worship and officers of the Christian Church, and quite (even overly?) sensitive to the dangers that an untrammeled, ascetic charismaticism posed for ecclesial unity and sacramental life. Let us therefore assume that he was both a monk and a bishop. Further, he was someone who was intimately familiar with a very considerable library of pagan philosophy and Christian literature. From Plato to Proclus among the Hellenes, from the Scriptures through the Cappadocians, Evagrius, and the Syrian writers, he moves with ease and assurance. Nor does he simply juxtapose his sources, but he integrates them and puts them to work in the service of a single, integrated and comprehensive vision. As we saw when I treated his use of the "sudden," he was fully capable of taking a single word or phrase and, through it, alluding not just to one source or set of sources but to several—in the case of the ἐξαίφνης to Platonism, the Scriptures, the ascetic writings of an Evagrius, and even perhaps to a work like the *Life* of the first stylite—and make all of them resonate in harmony with his purpose. It seems to me that this ability argues not merely for a writer of singular intelligence, spiritual depth, and wide reading, but also for someone who has lived with and pondered his sources for many years. I therefore suggest that the *CD* is not the product of a young man, or even one of middle years, but of someone nearing the end of his life—though still in command of all of his intellectual powers.

The picture of "Dionysius" that comes to my mind is therefore of an aging monk-bishop sitting before his writing table in the quiet of his residence, perhaps a monastery, putting the impressions of his long study together with the fruits of his ascetical and (yes) mystical experience, and seeking to set them down in such a way as to focus attention as much as possible on the ideas he wants to emphasize and, since the glitter of worldly fame and influence no longer attracts him, as little as possible on himself.[106] He admires the Platonists, holds Origen and the other Alexandrians in high regard,[107] and is devoted to Paul and to John the Divine. He is the product of the trinitarian debates that produced the Cappadocians' response, and equally of the ascetic traditions that led to Evagrius and Macarius, though extreme tendencies

---

106. See Larsen's remarks on the use of pseudonymity (*Jamblique*, 157).

107. See Rist, "The Weakness of the Soul," 160, on Dionysius' perhaps deliberate echo in *Ep.* VII (1080AB) of the charge, recorded by Eusebius (*E.H.* VI.19), that Porphyry leveled against Origen.

among some of the monks also trouble him deeply. He abhors the alarms and violence of the christological controversies, and—who could blame him?—wants no part of them.[108] The Emperor Zeno's *Henotikon* is the offical line of the imperial church at the time our author is writing and, since the decree was after all promulgated in order to keep the peace by avoiding controversy, it suits our old man just fine.

What better vehicle, therefore, might he have found to carry his particular purposes in writing than the pseudonym that he did in fact choose? Dionysius was an associate of Saint Paul and a philosopher. He was also a witness to the apostolic beginnings of Christianity and, as such, at least equal in antiquity—and thus in authority—to the ancient tradition of the *ihidaya*.[109] Finally, Dionysius was converted before the altar of the "unknown God" who, as Saint Paul's sermon in Acts 17 sought to demonstrate, had been definitively revealed in the person of Jesus of Nazareth, the Christ and Word of the Father. It was an admirable choice, and it worked very well indeed. Perhaps, too, my supposition that "Dionysius" was an old man might help in replying to the question of the *CD*'s missing treatises. The answer could be quite simply that he did not live to write them.

Now, I grant that everything about this portrait is merely plausible surmise and in no way "proof" of anything, but it does seem to fit with my reading at least of the *CD*. It also matches up rather well, I think, with one (and only one) of the candidates for the corpus' authorship that I noted above in the opening pages of my introduction. This is Peter the Iberian, whose case was first put forward by E. Honigmann in the 1950s and reopened

108. See esp. his *Ep.* VI (1077B).

109. I point, again, to Stang's suggestion that the very act of writing as Dionysius is "an ecstatic devotional practice." Like Chrysostom summoning and "channelling" St. Paul in the very act of composing his homilies, our anonymous fifth-century author is mystically refashioning himself into a disciple and imitator of the Apostle, thus illustrating the very topic of divine inhabitation, of which he is writing.

by M. van Esbroeck.[110] Both Honigmann and van Esbroeck mar-
shall complex arguments involving esoteric details of calendrical
calculation and the analysis of episcopal sees in the late fifth
century. These are frankly beyond my competence.[111] What does
catch my eye is the way in which Peter, as presented by the
Syriac *Life* that we still possess,[112] and as summarized by both
Honigmann and van Esbroeck, seems to pull together in his
person and in his circumstances nearly all of the features of my
little portrait. Born and raised in Georgia until his thirteenth
year,[113] he came from a church that had been evangelized and
greatly shaped by Syrian monastics.[114] Raised for eight years in
the court of the devout Theodosius II,[115] he had surely the occasion to acquire some familiarity with at least a smattering of the
theology current in Constantinople, perhaps especially of the
Cappadocians—such as Gregory Nazianzus, the one-time bishop
of the city. He could as well have been initiated into late Neoplatonism there. The Empress Eudocia, with whom he was very
close,[116] was a native of Athens and a convert from the cultivated
paganism (read Neoplatonism) of the ancient city.[117] Interestingly, the Empress is reported to have been deeply influenced

110. E. Honigmann, *Pierre l'Iberien* (1952), and M. van Esbroeck, "Peter
the Iberian and Dionysius the Areopagite," *OCP* 59 (1993): 217–227.

111. I might note, though, that van Esbroeck ("Peter the Iberian and Dionysius," 222–223) responds not unimpressively to Hausherr's critique of
Honigmann on the christological issue. See the latter's "Le Pseudo-Denys
est-il Pierre l'Iberien?" *OCP* 19 (1953): 247–260, and also R. Roques, "Pierre
l'Iberien et le corpus dionysien," *RHR* 114 (1954): 69–98.

112. See "The Life of Peter the Iberian," in *Lives and Legends of the Georgian Saints* (trans. D. M. Lang; London: Allen & Unwin, 1956; repr., London:
Mowbrays, 1976), 58–80.

113. "The Life of Peter the Iberian," 58–59.

114. See A. Vööbus, *History of Asceticism in the Syrian Orient*, vol. 2: *Early
Monasticism in Mesopotamia and Syria* (Louvain: Peeters, 1960), 354–360.

115. "The Life of Peter the Iberian," 60–64.

116. "The Life of Peter the Iberian," 60 and 67.

117. See van Esbroeck, "Peter the Iberian," 220, citing in particular the
Church History of Nicephorus Xanthopoulos, PG CXLVI 1129–1132; 1223–1240
(esp. 1237A).

late in life by Symeon Stylites.[118] Peter then travels to Palestine in the company of his friend and mentor, another Georgian named John Mithridates,[119] in order to frequent the venerable ascetics of the Holy Land and there embrace the monastic life. On arrival in Jerusalem, he and his companion are warmly welcomed by Melanie the Younger, granddaughter of Evagrius' correspondent and Rufinus' patron.[120] In 452 he returns to the holy city to be consecrated bishop by the Monophysite patriarch, Theodosius, and is assigned to the town of Mayuma near Gaza where he had previously been residing in monastic retreat.[121] Peter's proximity to Gaza is itself of interest since the city boasted a soon-to-be-thriving school of Christian Neoplatonism.[122] Peter spends some time shortly afterward in Alexandria and the surrounding desert of the ascetics in support of the opposition to Chalcedon,[123] and returns to the Holy Land to complete his life in 491 on the coast near Jamnia, at a resort that "was crown property, and had once been the residence of the Empress Eudocia."[124] Among his dying words, according to his biographer, was the advice to "meditate on the writings of the saintly bishop, Basil [the Great], concerning the ascetic life."[125]

Two more items, among the several miracles that the *Life* reports, draw my attention. The first occurs during Peter's stay in Constantinople. While struggling over the mystery of the Trinity, he prays for help and heaven sends it. He has a vision of the Apostle Peter leading him up "to a high place" where he sees the Trinity in the form of three lights, "inaccessible and incomprehensible . . . one essence, one nature, one glory, one light, one

118. Van Esbroeck, "Peter the Iberian," 221.
119. "The Life of Peter the Iberian," 64–65.
120. "The Life of Peter the Iberian," 64–65.
121. "The Life of Peter the Iberian," 69.
122. See the introduction to this unsung center of Christian life in Palestine by G. Downey, *Gaza in the Sixth Century* (Norman, OK: University of Oklahoma Press, 1963), esp. 106–116. The town was also a melting pot, a center where Greek and Aramaic cultures and languages converged, 50–51.
123. "The Life of Peter the Iberian," 71–73.
124. "The Life of Peter the Iberian," 77.
125. "The Life of Peter the Iberian," 78.

Godhead in three hypostases," with the middle light carrying in its center "the features of the Nazarene."[126] We are reminded of the discussion of the Trinity in, especially, *DN* II.4 and 7, the "lamps" and "superessential lights" respectively. We might also recall the appearance of Jesus in light to Paul on the road to Damascus that I argued was part of the background to *Ep.* III and the ἐξαίφνης. Our second passage from the *Life* is quite reminiscent of another important theme in the *CD*. Peter, we learn, at first sought to escape the burden of episcopacy by doing himself severe injury (falling off of a cliff), but was prevented by a divine voice calling him instead to the task. He submitted and was consecrated but, as his biographer tells us, "he would not perform any church services until he had been admonished by the voice of God."[127] Here it is difficult not to recall both Carpus' refusal in *Ep.* VIII to celebrate the Eucharist without a vision first, and Dionysius' remarks in *EH* VII.3.6–7 on the hierarch as the interpreter of the divine judgement because moved by the "divine spirit."

Taken in a sympathetic spirit, there is little in my portrait that does not find some correspondence, or at least potential for correspondence, in Peter's *Life* and the people associated with it. He must have been acquainted with the Syrian tradition if only via his native Georgia, though as bishop of Mayuma it must also have been the case that he had Aramaic speakers among his flock. He specifically mentions Basil the Great, and it is hard to see how he could have avoided the other Cappadocians after having lived in the imperial capital. Not only does he meet Melanie, but his whole life in Palestine—not to mention the years spent in Egypt—places him in the regions where the Evagrian and other ascetic writings were circulating. His see is close to a burgeoning center of Neoplatonist studies, to which philosophy the Empress herself could also have introduced him some time before. Even Symeon Stylites makes an appearance. His vision of the Trinity and experience of the heavenly voice recall similar notes in the *CD*. Finally, it is from

126. "The Life of Peter the Iberian," 62.
127. "The Life of Peter the Iberian," 70.

Palestine that we receive the earliest commentary on Dionysius, John of Scythopolis' *Scholia*.

Unfortunately, there is still little that we can do with all this, and certainly nothing that would pin Peter down as the author of the *Areopagitica*. The lack of extant works under the ascetic bishop's own name presents the greatest obstacle to a definitive "yea" or "nay." Thus again, while we may talk of possibilities, the lack of hard evidence rules out any end to the quest for Dionysius' identity. If he was Peter, he guarded his anonymity very well. On the other hand, I feel that even if Peter was not the ellusive Dionysius, the author of the *CD* must have been someone very like the Iberian bishop. We might remember John of Scythopolis' and John Philoponus' defense of the apostolic origins of the corpus, along with Severus of Antioch's efforts to keep "our Dionysius" out of the hands of the Chalcedonians. Whoever the author was, he had the respect of his contemporaries. If he was not on the Chalcedonian side, then it would certainly have suited John of Scythopolis to affirm the pseudonym, just as the latter was pushed by Severus and Philoponus in order to support their cause. Both sides were playing the same game, and if Severus knew that the author was one of his own, it is easy to see why he might have felt frustrated at seeing the wrong party lay claim to him. All three men mentioned, together with a Sergius of Reshaina, could very likely have known the author, or at least known of him. Peter the Iberian was a holy man, someone in whom all the combatants could have recognized their own deepest convictions about the Christian life. How many sainted monk bishops, one wonders, were there in the region? And how many of those might have possessed the requisite learning and intellect?

We are left with questions. Still, I think that the questions we are left with may point in directions at least as fruitful as much of the discussion over the past century. The Syrian tradition, for one, should certainly be explored in connection with Dionysius, and especially that confluence of late Platonism and Christian asceticism that I picked out already at work in Macarius—and Evagrius, too, for that matter. Christian Palestine should take center stage. The Merkabah tradition began there. So did the speculations about the Sinai theophany we find, for example, in the Qumran documents. The New Testament is carrying on local traditions that we pick up later in the Christian ascetics and finally Dionysius. Palestine produces the earliest commentaries, and it continues to be a center, if my considerations of Maximus' *Mystagogy* are at all on the mark, while there is no guesswork at all about where John Damascene did his theology. Palestine is the center, a meeting point from New Testament times and before of Greek and Jew. It is therefore altogether appropriate that half a millenium after it had given birth to Christianity, already a fusion of Hellenic and Semitic elements, the Holy Land should have produced a still nameless Syrian (or Oriental of some kind) who claimed the patrimony of Greece and the mantle of the Apostles in the service of the Word made flesh.

> καὶ ἐσκήνωσεν ἐν ἡμῖν, καὶ ἐθεασάμεθα
> τὴν δόξαν αὐτοῦ, δόξαν ὡς μονογενοῦς
> παρὰ πατρός, πλήρης χάριτος καὶ ἀληθέιας.
> John 1:14

> καὶ ναὸν οὐκ εἶδον ἐν αὐτῇ. ὁ γὰρ
> κύριος . . . ὁ παντοκράτωρ ναὸς αὐτῆς ἐστιν,
> καὶ τὸ ἀρνίον. καὶ ἡ πόλις οὐ χρείαν
> ἔχει τοῦ ἡλίου . . . ἡ γὰρ δόξα τοῦ
> θεοῦ ἐφώτισεν αὐτήν.
> Revelation 21:22-23

Bibliography

Primary Sources

[Evagrius Ponticus]

Evagrius Ponticus. *Evagriana: Extrait de la revue Le Muséon*, vol. 42, *augmenté de nouveaux fragments grecs inédits*. Edited by J. Muyldermans. Paris: Paul Guethner, 1931.

———. *Evagrios Pontikos: Briefe aus der Wüste*. Translated by G. Bunge. Trier: Paulinus-Verlag, 1986.

———. "Evagrios Pontikos: Der Prolog des *Antirrhetikos*." Translated by G. Bunge. *Studia Monastica* 39 (1997): 77–105.

———. *Evagrius of Pontus: The Greek Ascetic Corpus*. Translated by R. E. Sinkewicz. Oxford: Oxford University Press, 2003.

———. *Evagrius Ponticus*. Edited and translated by W. Frankenberg. Abhandlungen der königlichen Gesellschaft der Wissenschaften zu Göttingen, Philologisch-historische Klasse: Neue Folge. Vol. 13, no. 2. Berlin: Weidmann, 1912.

———. "Evagrius Ponticus, *Antirrheticus* (Selections)." Translated by M. O'Laughlin. Pages 243–62 in *Ascetic Behavior in Greco-Roman Antiquity: A Sourcebook*. Edited by Vincent L. Wimbush. Minneapolis: Fortress, 1990.

———. *Evagrius Ponticus: Praktikos and De oratione*. Translated by S. Tugwell. Oxford: Faculty of Theology, 1987.

———. *Le Gnostique ou celui qui est devenu digne de la science*. Edited and translated by A. and C. Guillaumont. SCh 356. Paris: du Cerf, 1989.

———. *Les six centuries des "Kephalaia Gnostica" d'Évagre le Pontique*. Edited and translated by A. Guillaumont. PO 28. Paris: Firmin-Didot, 1958.

————. "Le Traité de l'Oraison D'Évagre le Pontique (Pseudo-Nil)." Translated by I. Hausherr. *Revue d'ascétique et de mystique* 15 (1934): 42–93 and 113–169.

————. *Letter to Melanie I.* Edited and translated by M. Parmentier. *Tidjschrift voor Philosophie en Theologie* 46 (1985): 2–38.

————. *Nonnenspiegel und Mönchsspiegel des Euagrios Pontikos: zum ersten Male in der Urschrift herausgegeben von D. Dr. Hugo Gressmann.* Edited by H. Gressmann. TU 39, no. 4. Leipzig: J. C. Hinrichs, 1913.

————. *The Praktikos and Chapters on Prayer.* Translated by J. E. Bamberger. Spencer, MA: Cistercian Publications, 1970.

————. *Praktikos and on Prayer.* Translated by S. Tugwell. Oxford: Faculty of Theology, 1987.

————. *Scholies a L'Ecclésiaste.* Edited and translated by P. Géhin. *SCh* 397. Paris: du Cerf, 1993.

————. *Scholies aux Proverbes.* Edited and translated by P. Géhin. *SCh* 340. Paris: du Cerf, 1987.

————. *Seconde partie du Traité, qui passe sous le nom de "La grande lettre d'Évagre le Pontique à Mélanie l'Ancienne."* Edited by G. Vitestam. Scripta Minora Regiae Societatis Humaniorum Litterarum Lundensis 1963–1964, no. 3. Lund: Gleerup, 1964.

————. *Sur Les Pensées.* Edited and translated by Paul Géhin. *SCh* 438. Paris: du Cerf, 1998.

————. *Traité Pratique ou le Moine.* Edited and translated by A. and C. Guillaumont. *SCh* 170. Paris: du Cerf, 1971.

Géhin, P. "Evagriana d'un Manuscrit Basilien (*Vaticanus Gr. 2028; olim Basilianus 67*)." *Le Muséon* 109 (1996): 59–85.

Gould, G. "An Ancient Monastic Writing Giving Advice to Spiritual Directors (Evagrius of Pontus, *On Teachers and Disciples*)." Translated by G. Gould. *Hallell* 22 (1997): 96–103.

Hausherr, I. "Nouveaux fragments grecs d'Evagre le Pontique." *OCP* 5 (1939): 229–233.

Muyldermans, J., ed. "'À Travers la Tradition Manuscrite d'Èvagre le Pontique." *Bibliothèque du Muséon* 3 (1933): 74, 85, 89, 93.

————. "Evagriana." *Le Muséon* 44 (1931): 37–68, 369–383.

————. "Evagriana de la Vaticane." *Le Muséon* 54 (1941): 4–7, 9.

————. "Le De Magistris et Discipulis de S. Nil, Quelques Corrections Textuelles." *Le Muséon* 55 (1942): 93–96.

————. "Le Vatic. Barb. Graec 515." *Le Muséon* 51 (1938): 198–204.

————. "Sur les Séraphins et sur les Chérubins d'Évagre le Pontique dans les versions Syriaque et Arménienne." *Le Muséon* 59 (1946): 371–375.

Van den Veld, P. "Un opuscule inédit attribué à S. Nil." Pages 73–81 in volume 2 of *Mélanges Godefroid Kurth.* Liège: Vaillant-Carmanne, 1908.

[Liber Graduum]

Kitchen, R. A., and M. Parmentier, eds. *The Book of Steps*. Edited and translated by R. A. Kitchen and M. Parmentier. Kalamazoo: Cistercian Publications, 2004.

Kmosko, M., ed. *Liber Graduum*. PS 3. Paris: Firmin-Didot, 1926.

[Pseudo-Dionysius]

Pseudo-Dionysius. *Corpus Dionysiacum I: Pseudo-Dionysius Areopagita, De divinis nominibus*. Edited by B. R. Suchla. PTS 33. Berlin: Walter de Gruyter, 1990.

———. *Corpus Dionysiacum II: Pseudo-Dionysius Areopagita, De coelesti hierarchia, de ecclesiastica hierarchia, de mystica theologia, epistulae*. Edited by G. Heil and A. M. Ritter. PTS 36. Berlin: Walter de Gruyter, 1991.

———. *The Divine Names and Mystical Theology*. Translated by C. E. Rolt. London: SPCK, 1940.

———. *Pseudo-Dionsysius Areopagita: The Divine Names and Mystical Theology*. Translated by J. D. Jones. Milwaukee, WI: Marquette University Press, 1980.

———. *Pseudo-Dionysius: The Complete Works*. Translated by C. Luibheid. New York: Paulist Press, 1987.

[Pseudo-Macarius]

Gregory of Nyssa and Pseudo-Macarius. *Two Rediscovered Works of Ancient Christian Literature: Gregory of Nyssa and Macarius*. Edited by W. Jaeger. Leiden: Brill, 1965.

Pseudo-Macarius. *Die 50 geistlichen Homilien des Makarios*. Edited by H. Dörries, E. Klostermann, and M. Kröger. PTS 6. Berlin: de Gruyter, 1964.

———. *Macarii Anecdota: Seven Unpublished Homilies of Macarius*. Edited by G. L. Marriott. Cambridge, MA: Harvard University Press, 1918.

———. *Makarios/Symeon, Reden und Briefe: Die Sammlung I des Vaticanus Graecus 694B*. 2 vols. GCS. Berlin: Akademie-Verlag, 1973.

———. *Pseudo-Macaire: Oeuvres spirituelles I. Homélies propres à la Collection III*. Translated by V. Desprez. SCh 275. Paris: Cerf, 1980.

———. *Pseudo-Macarius: The Fifty Spiritual Homilies and the Great Letter*. Translated by G. Maloney. New York: Paulist Press, 1991.

[Basil of Caesarea]

Saint Basil the Great. *Lettres*. Edited and translated by Y. Courtonne. 3 vols. Paris: Les Belles Lettres, 1957–1966.

[Philokalia]

Nicodemus and Makarios. *The Complete Text*. Vol. 1 of *The Philokalia*. Edited by G. E. H. Palmer, P. Sherrard, and K. Ware. London: Faber, 1979.

Secondary Sources

Aall, A. *Geschichte der Logosidee in der griechischen Literatur*. Leipzig: Reisland, 1896.

Acerbi, A. *L'Ascensione di Isaia: Cristologia e profetismo in Siria nei primi decenni del II secolo*. Milan: Vita e pensiero, 1989.

Alexander, P. J. "Hypatius of Ephesus: A Note on Image Worship in the Sixth Century." *HTR* 45 (1952): 177–184.

Amar, J. "On Hermits and Desert Dwellers." Pages 66–80 in *Ascetic Behavior in Greco-Roman Antiquity: A Sourcebook*. Edited by W. L. Wimbush. Minneapolis: Fortress, 1990.

Andreopoulos, A. *Metamorphosis: The Transfiguration in Byzantine Theology and Iconography*. Crestwood, NY: St Vladimir's Seminary Press, 2005.

Armstrong, A. H. *The Architecture of the Intelligible Universe in the Philosophy of Plotinus*. Cambridge: Cambridge University Press, 1940.

———. "Emanation in Plotinus." *Mind* 46 (1937): 61–66.

———. "The Escape of the One: An Investigation of Some Possibilities of Apophatic Theology Imperfectly Realized in the West." *TU* 116 (1971): 77–87.

———. "Eternity, Life, and Movement in Plotinus' Accounts of *Nous*." Pages 67–74 in *Le Néoplatonisme*. Edited by C. J. de Vogel. Paris: Centre National de la Recherche Scientifique, 1971.

———. "Man in the Cosmos." Pages 5–14 in *Romanitas et Christianitas*. Edited by W. Boer. Amsterdam: North-Holland Publishing, 1973.

———. "Platonic Eros and Christian Agape." *DRev* 79 (1961): 105–121.

———. "Plotinus' Doctrine of the Infinite and Christian Thought." *DRev* 73 (1954–1955): 47–58.

———. "Salvation Plotinian and Christian." *DRev* 75 (1957): 126–139.

———. "Some Comments on the Development of the Theology of Images." *SP* 9 (1963): 117–126.

Arnou, R. "La contemplation chez les anciens philosophes du monde greco-romain." Pages 1716–1742 in vol. 2 of *Dictionnaire de Spiritualité*. 17 vols. Paris: Beauchesne, 1932–1995.

Arthur, R. A. *Pseudo-Dionysius as Polemicist: The Development and Purpose of the Angelic Hierarchy in Sixth-Century Syria*. London: Ashgate, 2008.

Bacht, H. "Evagrius Ponticus ünd Pachomius von Tabennêsi: Das Vermächtnis des Ursprungs." Pages 34–63 in *Zeugen christlicher Gotteserfahrung*. Edited by J. Sudbrack. Mainz: Matthias-Grünewald Verlag, 1981.

Baker, A. "The Gospel of Thomas and the Syriac *Liber Graduum*." NTS 12 (1965): 49–55.

———. "Pseudo-Macarius and the Gospel of Thomas." *VC* 18 (1964): 214–225.

Barker, M. *On Earth as It Is in Heaven: Temple Symbolism in the New Testament*. Edinburgh: T&T Clark, 1995.

Barnes, M. R. *The Power of God: Δύναμις in Gregory of Nyssa's Trinitarian Theology*. Washington, DC: Catholic University of America Press, 2001.

Barnes, T. D. "Angel of Light or Mystic Initiate? The Problem of the Life of Anthony." *JTS* 37 (1986): 353–368.

Baynes, N. H. "The Icons before Iconoclasm." *HTR* 44 (1951): 93–106.

Beck, E. ed. *Des heiligen Ephraem des Syrers: Hymnen de Paradiso*. CSCO 174. Louvain: Secretariat du Corpus SCO, 1957.

———. "Symbolum-Mysterium bei Aphrahat und Ephräm." *OC* 42 (1958): 19–40.

Beierwaltes, W. "*Exaiphnes*, oder die Paradoxie des Augenblicks." *PhJ* 84 (1966/67): 271–282.

———. "Johannes von Skythopolis und Plotin." *TU* 108 (1972): 3–7.

———. *Platonismus im Christentum*. Frankfurt am Main: Klostermann, 2001.

———. *Proklos: Grundzüge seiner Metaphysik*. Frankfurt am Main: Klostermann, 1965.

———. "Pronoia und Freiheit in der Philosophie des Proklos." *FZPT* 24 (1977): 88–111.

Beierwaltes, W., and R. Kannicht. "Plotin Testimonia bei Johannes von Scythopolis." *Hermes* 96 (1968): 247–251.

Bellini, E. "Saggio introduttivo." Pages 33–73 in *Dionigi Areopagita: Tutte le opere. Testo greco a fronte*. Translated by P. Scazzoso and I. Ramelli. Milan: Bompiani, 2009.

Beneševi, V. "Sur la date de la mosaïque de la Transfiguration au Mont Sinai." *Byz* 1 (1924): 145–172.

Bernard, C. A. "La doctrine mystique de Denys l'Aréopagite." *Greg* 68 (1987): 523–566.

———. "Formes de la theologie chez Denys l'Aréopagite." *Greg* 59 (1978): 39–69.

Beulay, R. "Formes de lumière et lumière sans forme: Le thème de la lumière dans la mystique de Jean de Dalyatha." *COr* 20 (1988): 131–141.

———. *L'enseignement spirituel de Jean de Dalyatha, mystique syro-oriental de VIIIe siècle.* Paris: Beauchesne, 1990.

Blank, J. "Gnosis und Agape: Zur christologischen Struktur paulinischer Mystik." Pages 1–13 in *Grundfragen christlicher Mystik.* Edited by M. Schmidt and D. R. Bauer. Stuttgart: Fromann-Holzboog, 1987.

Blowers, P. M. *Exegesis and Spiritual Pedagogy in Maximus the Confessor: An Investigation of the Quaestiones ad Thalassium.* Notre Dame: University of Notre Dame Press, 1991.

Bornert, René. *Les commentaires byzantins de la Divine Liturgie du VIIe au XVe siècle.* Paris: Institut Français d' études byzantines, 1966.

Boularand, E. "L'Eucharistie d'après le ps.-Denys." *BLE* 58 (1957): 193–217.

Bouyer, L. *The Spirituality of the New Testament and the Fathers.* New York: Seabury, 1982.

Boyance, P. "Théurgie et télèstique néoplatonicienne." *RHR* 247 (1955): 189–209.

Bradshaw, D. *Aristotle East and West: Metaphysics and the Division of Christendom.* Cambridge: Cambridge University Press, 2004.

———. "Time and Eternity in the Greek Fathers." *Thomist* 70 (2006): 311–366.

Bréhier, E. *The Philosophy of Plotinus.* Translated by J. Thomas. Chicago: Chicago University Press, 1958.

Brock, S. "An Early Syriac Life of Maximus the Confessor." *AnBoll* 91 (1973): 299–346.

———. "Early Syrian Asceticism." *Numen* 20 (1973): 1–19.

———. *Spirituality in the Syriac Tradition.* Kottayam: Ephrem Ecumencial Research Institute, 1989.

Brons, B. "Πρόνοια und das Verhältnis von Metaphysik und Geschichte bei Dionysius Areopagita." *FZPT* 24 (1977): 165–186.

Brown, P. "The Rise and Function of the Holy Man in Late Antiquity." *JRS* 62 (1971): 80–101.

Brox, N. *Pseudepigraphie in der heidnischen und jüdisch-christlichen Antike.* Darmstadt: Wissenchaftliche Buchgesellschaft, 1977.

Bucur, B. G. *Angelomorphic Pneumatology: Clement of Alexandria and Other Early Christian Witnesses.* Leiden: Brill, 2009.

———. "Foreordained from All Eternity: The Mystery of the Incarnation according to Some Early Christian and Byzantine Writers." *DOP* 62 (2008): 199–215.

———. "The Mountain of the Lord: Sinai, Zion, and Eden in Byzantine Hymnographic Exegesis." Pages 139–182 in *Symbola Caelestis: Le symbolisme liturgique et paraliturgique dans le monde chrétien.* Edited by B. Lourié and A. Orlov. Piscataway, NJ: Gorgias, 2009.

———. "The Theological Reception of Dionysian Apophatism in the Christian East and West: Thomas Aquinas and Gregory Palamas." *DRev* 125 (2007): 131–146.

Bundy, D. "The Book of the Holy Hierotheos and Manicheanism." *Aug* 26 (1986): 273–280.

Bunge, G. *Briefe aus der Wüste.* Trier: Paulinus, 1986.

———. "Évagre le pontique et les deux Macaires." *Ir* 56 (1983): 215–227.

———. *Geistliche Vaterschaft: Christliche Gnosis bei Evagrios Pontikos.* Regensburg: Friedrich Pustet, 1988.

———. "Hénade où monade: au sujet de deux notions centrales de la terminologie évagrienne." *Mus* 102 (1989): 69–91.

———. "Nach dem Intellekt leben? Zum sogennanten 'Intellektualismus' der Evagrianischen Spiritualität." Pages 95–109 in *Simandron, der Wachklopfer: Gedenkschrift für Klaus Gamber.* Edited by W. Nyssen. Cologne: Luthe, 1989.

———. "Origenismus–Gnostizismus: Zum geistesgeschichtlichen Standort des Evagrios Pontikos." *VC* 40 (1986): 24–54.

———. "Palladiana II: La version copte de l'*Histoire Lausiaque.*" *StMon* 33 (1991): 117–118.

———. "The 'Spiritual Prayer': On the Trinitarian Mysticism of Evagrius of Pontus." *Monastic Studies* 17 (1987): 191–208.

Burrell, D., and I. Moulin. "Albert, Aquinas, and Dionysius." Pages 103–119 in *Re-Thinking Dionysius the Areopagite.* Edited by S. Coakley and C. M. Stang. Malden, MA: Wiley-Blackwell, 2009.

Burrows, M. S. "On the Visibility of God in the Holy Man: A Reconsideration of the Role of the Apa in the Pachomian *Vitae.*" *VC* 41 (1987): 11–33.

Burton-Christie, D. *The Word in the Desert: Scripture and the Quest for Holiness in Early Christian Monasticism.* New York: Oxford University Press, 1993.

Butler, C. *The Lausiac History of Palladius.* Cambridge: Cambridge University Press, 1904.

Casarella, P. J. "Cusanus on Dionysius: The Turn to Speculative Theology." Pages 667–678 in *Re-Thinking Dionysius the Areopagite.* Edited by S. Coakley and C. M. Stang. Malden, MA: Wiley-Blackwell, 2009.

Charlesworth, J. H., ed. *The Old Testament Pseudepigrapha*. Garden City, NY: Doubleday, 1985.

Chernus, I. *Mysticism in Rabbinic Judaism: Studies in the History of Midrash*. Berlin: de Gruyter, 1982.

Chestnut, R. *Three Monophysite Christologies: Severus of Antioch, Philoxenus of Mabbug and Jacob of Sarug*. Oxford: Oxford University Press, 1976.

Clark, E. *The Origenist Controversy: The Cultural Construction of an Early Church Debate*. Princeton: Princeton University Press, 1992.

Clements, R. E. *God and the Temple*. Philadelphia: Fortress, 1965.

Cochrane, C. *Christianity and Classical Culture*. New York: Oxford University Press, 1957.

Coolman, B. T. "The Medieval Affective Dionysian Tradition." Pages 85–102 in *Re-Thinking Dionysius the Areopagite*. Edited by S. Coakley and C. M. Stang. Malden, MA: Wiley-Blackwell, 2009.

Corsini, E. *Il trattato "De divinis nominibus" dello Pseudo-Dionigi e i commenti neoplatonici al Parmenide*. Torino: Giappichelli, 1962.

Cranz, F. E. "Kingdom and Polity in Eusebius of Caesarea." *HTR* 45 (1952): 48–66.

Dalmais, I. H. "Saint Maximus le Confesseur et la crise de l'Origènisme monastique." Pages 411–421 in *Théologie de la vie monastique: études sur la tradition patristique*. Études publiées sous la direction de la faculté de théologie S. J. de Lyon-Fourvière. Paris: Aubier, 1961.

———. "La vie monastique comme ascèse vigiliale d'après saint Ephrem et les traditions liturgiques syriennes." Pages 73–86 in *Liturgie, conversion, et vie monastique: Conférence Saint-Serge, 35e semaine d'études liturgiques, Paris, 28e juin-1er juillet 1988*. Edited by A. M. Triacca and C. Andronikof. Rome: CLV-Edizioni liturgiche, 1989.

Darrouzès, J. *Documents inédits d'ecclésiologie byzantine*. Paris: Institut Français d'Études Byzantines, 1966.

De Andia, Y. *Henôsis: L'union à Dieu chez Denys l'Aréopagite*. Leiden: Brill, 1996.

———. "Transfiguration et théologie négative chez Maxime le Confesseur et Denys l'Aréopagite." Pages 293–328 in *Denys l'Aréopagite et sa posterité en orient et en occident: actes du colloque international, Paris 21–24 septembre 1994*. Edited by Y. de Andia. Paris: Études Augustiniennes, 1997.

DeConick, A. *Seek to See Him: Ascent and Vision Mysticism in the Gospel of Thomas*. Leiden: Brill, 1996.

De Gayoso, G. L. Ritacco. "Los himnos theárquicos." *Teol Vida* 43 (2002): 350–376.

De Halleux, A. "Palamisme et Tradition." *Ir* 48 (1978): 479–493.

Dempf, A. "Evagrios Pontikos als Metaphysiker und Mystiker." *PJ* 77 (1970): 297–319.

De Vogel, C. J. "Greek Cosmic Love and the Christian Love of God." *VC* 35 (1981): 57–81.

Diecamp, F. *Analecta Patristica: Texte und Abhandlungen zur Griechischen Patristik.* OCA 117. Rome: Pontifical Institutum Orientalium Studiorum, 1938.

———. "Letter to Julius of Atramytion." Pages 127–129 in *Analecta Patristica.* OCA 117. Rome: Pontifical Institutum Orientalium Studiorum, 1938.

Dodds, E. R. *Elements of Theology.* Oxford: Clarendon, 1963.

———. *Pagan and Christian in an Age of Anxiety.* Cambridge: Cambridge University Press, 1965.

———. "The *Parmenides* of Plato and the Origin of the Neoplatonic One." *ClassQ* 22 (1926): 129–142.

———. "Theurgy and Its Relation to Neoplatonism." *JRS* 37 (1947): 55–69.

Dondaine, H. F. *Le corpus dionysien de l'université de Paris au XIII· siècle.* Rome: Storia e letteratura, 1953.

———. "Emanation: Ein unphilosophisches Wort im spätantiken Denken." Pages 119–141 in *Parusia: Festgabe für Hirschberger.* Edited by K. Flasch. Frankfurt am Main: Minerva, 1965.

Dörries, H. "The Place of Confession in Ancient Monasticism." *SP* 5 (1962): 284–311.

———. "Ὑπόστασις: Wort- und Bedeutungsgeschichte." *NAWG* 3 (1955): 35–92.

Downey, G. *Gaza in the Sixth Century.* Norman, OK: University of Oklahoma Press, 1963.

Drijvers, H. "Die Legende des heiligen Alexius and der Typus des Gottesmannes im syrischen Christentum." Pages 187–217 in *Typus, Symbol, Allegorie bei den östlichen Vätern und ihren Parallelen im Mittelalter.* Edited by M. Schmidt, C. F. Geyer. Regensburg: Pustet, 1982.

———. "Hellenistic and Oriental Origins." Pages 25–33 in *The Byzantine Saint.* Edited by S. Hackel. London: Sobornost, 1981.

Dvornik, F. *Early Christian and Byzantine Political Philosophy.* Washington, DC: Dumbarton Oaks Center for Byzantine Studies, 1966.

Elior, R. *The Three Temples: On the Emergence of Jewish Mysticism in Late Antiquity.* Oxford: Littman Library of Jewish Civilization, 2005.

Eliot, T. S. *The Four Quartets.* New York: Oxford University Press, 1973.

Elliger, W. *Die Stellung der alten Christen zu den Bildern in den ersten vier Jahrhunderten.* Leipzig: Dieterich, 1930.

———. *Zur Entstehung und frühen Entwicklung der altchristlichen Bildkunst.* Leipzig: Dieterich, 1934.

Elsner J. *Art and the Roman Viewer*. Cambridge: Cambridge University Press, 1995.

Escalon, P. *Monachisme et église, le monachisme syrien du IVe au VIe siècle: un monachisme charismatique*. Paris: Beauchesne, 1999.

Evans, D. B. "Leontius of Byzantium and Dionysius the Areopagite." *EB* 7 (1980): 1–34.

Every, G. "Dionysius the Pseudo-Areopagite." Pages 81–94 in *One Yet Two: Monastic Tradition East and West*. Kalamazoo, MI: Cistercian Publications, 1976.

Ewbank, M. B. "Diverse Orderings of Dionysius's *triplex via* by St. Thomas Aquinas." *MS* 52 (1990): 82–109.

Fekkes III, J. *Isaiah and the Prophetic Traditions in the Book of Revelation: Visionary Antecedents and Their Development*. Sheffield: JSOT Press, 1994.

Fitschen, K. *Messalianismus und Antimessalianismus: Ein Beispiel ostkirchlicher Ketzergeschichte*. Göttingen: Vandenhoeck & Ruprecht, 1998.

Fitzmeyer, J. A. "Glory Reflected in the Face of Christ (2 Cor 3:7–4:6) and a Palestinian Jewish Motif." *TS* 42 (1981): 630–644.

Florovsky, G. *The Byzantine Ascetic and Spiritual Fathers*. Belmont, MA: Notable & Academic, 1987.

———. "The Concept of Creation in St. Athanasius." *SP* 6 (1962): 36–57.

———. "The Idea of Creation in Christian Philosophy." *ECQ* 8 (1949): 53–77.

Fossum, J. P. "Glory." Pages 348–352 in *Dictionary of Deities and Demons in the Bible*. Edited by K. van der Toorn, B. Becking, and P. W. van der Horst. 2nd ed. Leiden: Brill, 1999.

———. "Partes Posteriori Dei: The Transfiguration of Jesus in the *Acts of John*." Pages 95–108 in *The Image of the Invisible God: Essays on the Influence of Jewish Mysticism on Early Christology*. Edited by J. Fossum. Freiburg: Universitätsverl, 1995.

Fraigneau-Julien, B. *Les sens spirituels selon Syméon le Nouveau Théologien*. Paris: Beauchesne, 1985.

Frank, P. Suso. *Angelikos Bios: Begriffsanalytische und begriffsgeschichtliche Untersuchung zum "engelgleichen Leben" im frühen Mönchtum*. Münster: Aschendorff, 1964.

Frankenberg, W., ed. *Euagrios Pontikos*. Berlin: Weidmann, 1912.

Froehlich, K. "*Pseudo-Dionysius and the Reformation of the Sixteenth Century*." Pages 33–46 in *Pseudo-Dionysius: The Complete Works*. Translated by C. Luibhéid and P. E. Rorem. New York: Paulist, 1987.

Gaith, J. *La conception de la liberté chez Grégoire de Nysse*. Paris: Vrin, 1943.

Géhin, P. "Manuscrits sinaïtiques dispersés, I: Les fragments syriaques et arabes de Paris." *OC* 90 (2006): 23–43.

Gendle, N. "The Apophatic Approach to God in the Early Greek Fathers, with special reference to the Alexandrian Tradition." Ph.D. diss., Oxford University, 1974.

———. "Cappadocian Elements in the Mystical Theology of Evagrius Ponticus." *SP* 16 (1985): 373–384.

Gero, S. "Hypatius and the Cult of Images." Pages 208–216 in *Christianity, Judaism, and Other Greco-Roman Cults: Studies for Morton Smith.* Edited by J. Neusner. Leiden: Brill, 1975.

Gersh, S. *From Iamblichus to Eriugena: An Investigation of the Prehistory and Evolution of the Pseudo-Dionysian Tradition.* Leiden: Brill, 1978.

———. Κίνησις ἀκίνητος: *A Study of Spiritual Motion in the Philosophy of Proclus.* Leiden: Brill, 1973.

Giron-Negron, L. M. "Dionysian Thought in Sixteenth-Century Spanish Mystical Theology." Pages 163–176 in *Re-Thinking Dionysius the Areopagite.* Edited by S. Coakley and C. M. Stang. Malden, MA: Wiley-Blackwell, 2009.

Goldberg, A. M. *Untersuchungen über die Vorstellung der Shekinah in der frühen rabbinischen Literatur.* Berlin: de Gruyter, 1969.

Golitzin, Alexander. "Adam, Eve, and Seth: Pneumatological Reflections on an Unusual Image in Gregory of Nanzianus's Fifth Theological Oration." *AThR* 83 (2001): 537–546.

———. "Anathema! Some Historical Perspectives on the Athonite Statement of May 1995." *St. Nersess Theological Review* 3 (1998): 103–117.

———. "The Body of Christ: Saint Symeon the New Theologian on Spiritual Life and the Hierarchical Church." Pages 106–127 in *The Theophaneia School: Jewish Roots of Eastern Christian Mysticism.* Edited by B. Lourie. Saint Petersburg: Byzantinorossica, 2007. A later edition, edited by A. Orloy and B. Lourié, was published in 2009 by Gorgias Press.

———. "Christian Mysticism over Two Millennia." Pages 17–33 in *The Theophaneia School: Jewish Roots of Christian Mysticism.* Edited by A. Orlov and B. Lurié. Saint Petersburg: Byzantino-rossica, 2007.

———. "'A Contemplative and a Liturgist': Father Georges Florovsky on the Corpus Dionysiacum." *SVTQ* 43 (1999): 131–161.

———. "The Demons Suggest an Illusion of God's Glory in a Form: Controversy over the Divine Body and Vision of Glory in Some Late Fourth, Early Fifth Century Monastic Literature." *Studia Monastica* 44 (2002): 13–44.

———. "Dionysius Areopagita: A Christian Mysticism?" *ProEccl* 12 (2003): 161–212.

———. "Dionysius Areopagites in the Works of Saint Gregory Palamas: On the Question of a 'Christological Corrective' and Related Matters." *SVTQ* 46 (2002): 163–190.

————. "Earthly Angels and Heavenly Men: The Old Testament Pseude-pigrapha, Nicetas Stethatos, and the Tradition of Interiorized Apocalyptic in Eastern Christian Ascetical and Mystical Literature." *DOP* 55 (2001): 125–153.

————. *Et introibo ad altare Dei: The Mystagogy of Dionysius Areopagita*. Thessalonica: Patriarchal Institute, 1994.

————. "Heavenly Mysteries: Themes from Apocalyptic Literature in the Macarian Homilies and Selected Other Fourth Century Ascetical Writers." Pages 174–192 in *Apocalyptic Themes in Early Christianity*. Edited by R. Daly. Grand Rapids: Baker Academic, 2009.

————. "Hierarchy versus Anarchy?" *SVTQ* 38, no. 2 (1994): 131–179.

————. "Hierarchy versus Anarchy: Dionysius Areopagita, Symeon the New Theologian, Nicetas Stethatos, and Their Common Roots in the Ascetical Tradition." *SVTQ* 38 (1994): 131–179.

————. "Il corpo di Cristo: Simeone il Nuovo Teologo sulla vita spirituale e la chiesa gerarchica." Pages 255–288 in *Simeone il Nuovo Teologo e il monachesimo a Costantinopoli*. Edited by S. Chialà, L. Cremaschi, and I. Hieromonk. Qiqajon: Monastero di Bose, 2003.

————. "The Image and Glory of God in Jacob of Serug's Homily, on That Chariot That Ezekiel the Prophet Saw." *SVTQ* 46 (2003): 323–364.

————. "Liturgy and Mysticism: The Experience of God in Eastern Orthodox Christianity." *ProEccl* 8 (1999): 159–186.

————. *"Making the Inside like the Outside*: Toward a Monastic Sitz im Leben for the Syriac Apocalypse of Daniel." In *To Train His Soul in Books: Syriac Asceticism in Early Christianity*. Edited by R. D. Young and M. J. Blanchard. Washington, DC: CUA Press, 2011.

————. "The Mysticism of Dionysius Areopagita: Platonist or Christian?" *Mystics Quarterly* 19 (1993): 98–114.

————. " 'On the Other Hand': A Response to Father Paul Wesche's Recent Article on Dionysius." *SVTQ* 34 (1990): 305–323.

————. "The Place of the Presence of God: Aphrahat of Persia's Portrait of the Christian Holy Man." Pages 391–447 in *ΣΥΝΑΞΙΣ ΕΥΧΑΡΙΣΤΙΑΣ: Studies in Honor of Archimandrite Aimilianos of Simonos Petras, Mount Athos*. Athens: Indiktos, 2003.

————. "Revisiting the 'Sudden': Epistle III in the Corpus Dionysiacum." *StPatr* 37 (2001): 482–491.

————. " 'Suddenly, Christ': The Place of Negative Theology in the Mystagogy of Dionysius Areopagites." Pages 8–37 in *Mystics: Presence and Aporia*. Edited by M. Kessler and C. Shepherd. Chicago: University of Chicago Press, 2003.

————. "A Testimony to Christianity as Transfiguration: The Macarian Homilies and Orthodox Spirituality." Pages 129–156 in *Orthodox and*

Wesleyan Spirituality. Edited by S. T. Kimbrough. Crestwood, NY: St. Vladimir's Seminary Press, 2002.

———. "Theophaneia: Forum on the Jewish Roots of Orthodox Spirituality." Pages xvii–xx in *The Theophaneia School: Jewish Roots of Eastern Christian Mysticism.* Edited by B. Lourie. Saint Petersburg: Byzantinorossica, 2007

———. "The Vision of God and the Form of Glory: More Reflections on the Anthropomorphite Controversy of AD 399." Pages 273–297 in *Abba: The Tradition of Orthodoxy in the West: FS Kallistos Ware.* Edited by K. Ware, J. Behr, A. Louth, and D. E. Conomos. Crestwood, NY: St Vladimir's Seminary Press, 2007.

Gouillard, J. "Hypatios d'Ephèse, ou de Pseudo-Denys à Théodore Studite." *REB* 19 (1961): 63–75.

———. "Quatre procès de mystique à Byzance (vers 960–1143)." *REB* 36 (1978): 5–81.

Gould, G. *The Desert Fathers on Monastic Community.* Oxford: Clarendon, 1993.

Goulder, M. "The Pastor's Wolves: Jewish-Christian Visionaries behind the Pastoral Epistles." *NT* 38 (1996): 242–256.

———. "Sophia in 1 Corinthians." *NTS* 37 (1991): 516–534.

———. "Vision and Knowledge." *JSNT* 46 (1994): 53–71.

———. "The Visionaries of Laodicea." *JSNT* 43 (1991): 15–39.

Griffith, R. "Neo-Platonism and Christianity: Pseudo-Dionysius and Damascius." *SP* 29 (1997): 238–243.

Griffith, S. "Asceticism in the Church of Syria: The Hermeneutics of Early Syrian Monasticism." Pages 220–245 in *Asceticism.* Edited by V. L. Wimbush and R. Valantasis. New York: Oxford University Press, 1995.

———. "Monks, 'Singles,' and the 'Sons of the Covenant': Reflections on Syriac Ascetic Terminology." Pages 141–160 in *Eulogema: Studies in Honor of Robert Taft SJ.* Edited by E. Carr et al. Rome: Pontificio Ateneo S. Anselmo, 1993.

Gross, J. "Ur- und Erbsünde in der Theosophie des Pseudo-Dionysius Areopagita." *ZRG* 4 (1952): 32–42.

Gruenwald, I. *Apocalyptic and Merkabah Mysticism.* Leiden: Brill, 1980.

———. *Les Kephalia Gnostica d'Évagre le Pontique.* Paris: du Seuil, 1962.

Guillaumont, A. "La vision de l'intellect par lui-même dans la mystique évagrienne." *Mélanges de l'Université Saint Joseph* 50 (1984): 255–262.

———. *Les six centuries des "Kephalia Gnostica" d'Évagre le Pontique.* PO 28. Paris: Firmin-Didot, 1958.

———. "Situation et significance du *Liber Graduum* dans la spiritualité syriaque." Pages 311–325 in *Symposium Syriacum 1972.* OCA 197. Rome: Pontificium Institum Orientalium Studiorum, 1974.

———. "Une inscription Copte sur la prière de Jésus." *OCP* 8 (1977): 187–203.

Hägg, H. F. *Clement of Alexandria and the Beginnings of Christian Apophaticism.* Oxford: Oxford University Press, 2006.

Hankey, W. J. "Dionysian Hierarchy in Thomas Aquinas." Pages 405–438 in *Denys l'Aréopagite et sa posterité en orient et en occident: actes du colloque international, Paris 21–24 septembre 1994.* Edited by Y. de Andia. Paris: Études Augustiniennes.

Harb, G. "L'attitude de Philoxène de Mabboug à l'égard de la spiritualité 'savante' d'Évagre le pontique." Pages 135–156 in *Mémorial Mgr Gabriel Khouri-Sarkis.* Edited by F. Graffin. Louvain: Imprimerie orientaliste, 1969.

Harl, M. "À propos du *Logia* de Jésus: le sens du mot μοναχός." *REG* 73 (1960): 464–474.

Harmless, W. "The Sapphire Light of the Mind: The Skemmata of Evagrius Ponticus." *TS* 62 (2001): 498–529.

Harrington, L. M. *A Thirteenth-Century Textbook of Mystical Theology at the University of Paris.* Leuven: Peeters, 2004.

Harrison, V. "Perichoresis in the Greek Fathers." *SVTQ* 35 (1991): 53–65.

Harvey, S. A. "Incense Offerings in the Syriac *Transitus Mariae*: Ritual and Knowledge in Ancient Christianity." Pages 175–191 in *The Early Church in Its Context: Essays in Honor of Everett Ferguson.* Edited by A. J. Malherbe, F. W. Norris, and J. W. Thornton. Leiden: Brill, 1998.

———. "The Sense of a Stylite: Perspectives on Symeon the Elder." *VC* 42 (1988): 376–394.

Hathaway, R. *Hierarchy and the Definition of Order in the Letters of Pseudo-Dionysius: A Study in the Form and Meaning of the Pseudo-Dionysian Writings.* The Hague: Nijhoff, 1970.

Hausherr, I. "Contemplation chez les ancients Grecs et autres orientaux chrétiens." Pages 1762–1782 in vol. 2 of *Dictionnaire de Spiritualité.* 17 vols. Paris: Beauchesne, 1932–1995.

———. "Le Pseudo-Denys est-il Pierre l'Iberien?" *OCP* 19 (1953): 247–260.

———. *Leçons d'un Contemplatif.* Paris: Beauchesne, 1960.

———. "Les grands courants de la spiritualite Orientale." *OCP* 1 (1935): 114–138.

———. "L'influence du *Livre de saint Hierothée.*" *OC* 30, no. 3 (1932): 34–69.

———. "Pierre l'Iberien." *OCP* 19, 1953: 247–260.

———. *Spiritual Direction in the Early Christian East.* Translated by A. Gythiel. Kalamazoo, MI: Cistercian Publications, 1990.

Hengel, M. *Jews, Greeks, and Barbarians: Aspects of the Hellenization of Judaism in the Pre-Christian Period.* Translated by J. Bowden. Philadelphia: Fortress, 1980.

———. "'Setzte dich zu meiner Rechten!' Die Intronisation Christi zur Rechten Gottes und Psalmen 110:1." Pages 108–194 in *Le trône de Dieu*. Edited by M. Philonenko. Tübingen: Mohr, 1993.

Himmelfarb, M. *Ascent to Heaven in Jewish and Christian Apocalypses.* New York: Oxford University Press, 1993.

Hofer, A. "Dionysian Elements in Thomas Aquinas's Christology: A Case of the Authority and Ambiguity of Pseudo-Dionysius." *Thomist* 72 (2009): 409–442.

Holl, K. *Enthusiasmus und Bussgewalt beim Griechischen Mönchtum: Eine Studie zum Symeon dem Neuen Theologen.* Leipzig: Hinrichs, 1898.

Honigmann, E. *Pierre l'Ibérien et les ecrits du Pseudo-Denys l'Areopagita.* Brussels: Académie Royale de Belgique, 1952.

Horn, G. "Amour et extase d'après Denys l'Aréopagite." *RAM* 6 (1925): 278–289.

Hornus, J. M. "Le corpus dionysien en Syriaque." *ParOr* 1 (1970): 69–93.

———. "Les recherches dionysiennes de 1955 à 1960: Bibliographie dionysienne 1954–1959." *RHPR* 41 (1961): 22–81.

———. "Quelques réflexions à propos du pseudo-Denys l'Aréopagite et de la mystique chrétienne en général." *RHPR* 27 (1947): 37–63.

Humbrecht, T. D. "Noms divins: les sources de saint Thomas au XIIIe siècle." *RT* 105 (2005): 411–434, 551–594.

Hussey, J. M. *Church and Learning in the Byzantine Empire: 867–1185.* London: Humphrey Milford, 1937.

Inge, W. R. *The Philosophy of Plotinus.* 3rd ed. London: Longmans, Green & Co., 1929.

Jaeger, W. *In Search of the Divine Centre.* Vol. 2 of *Paideia.* Oxford: Blackwell, 1944.

———. *Two Rediscovered Works of Ancient Christian Literature: Gregory of Nyssa and Macarius.* Leiden: Brill, 1965.

Joest, C. "Die Bedeutung von *Akedia* und *Apatheia* bei Evagrios Pontikos." *Studia Monastica* 35, no. 1 (1993): 48–53.

Jonas, H. *The Gnostic Religion.* 2nd ed. Boston: Beacon, 1963.

Jones, J. D. "An Absolutely Simple God? Frameworks for Reading Pseudo-Dionysius Areopagite." *Thomist* 69 (2005): 371–406.

———. "Reading the Divine Names as a Science: Aquinas' Interpretation of the Divine Names of (Pseudo) Dionysius Areopagite." *SVTQ* 52 (2008): 143–172.

Kalaitzidis P. "*Theologia*: Discours sur Dieu et science théologique chez Denys l'Aréopagite et Thomas d'Aquin." Pages 457–487 in *Denys l'Aréopagite et sa posterité en orient et en occident: actes du colloque international, Paris 21–24 septembre 1994.* Edited by Y. de Andia. Paris: Études Augustiniennes, 1997.

Kharlamov, V. "The Beauty of the Unity and the Harmony of the Whole: Concept of Theosis in the Theology of Pseudo-Dionysius the Areopagite." Ph.D. diss., Drew University, 2006.

Kitzinger, E. *Byzantine Art in the Making*. Cambridge, MA: Faber & Faber, 1977.

————. "The Cult of Images in the Age before Iconoclasm." *DOP* 8 (1954): 83–150.

————. *Die altchristliche Bilderfrage nach den literarischen quellen*. Göttingen: Vandenhoeck & Ruprecht, 1917.

Koch, H. "Proklus als Quelle des Pseudo-Dionysius Areopagita in der Lehre vom Bösen." *Ph* 54 (1895): 438–454.

————. *Pseudo-Dionysius Areopagita in seinen Beziehungen zum Neuplatonismus und Mysterienwesen*. Mainz: Kirschheim, 1900.

Koester, C. R. *The Dwelling of God: The Tabernacle in the Old Testament, Intertestamental Literature, and the New Testament*. Washington, DC: Catholic Biblical Association of America, 1989.

Koutras, D. N. "Ἡ Ἔννοια τῆς εἰκόνος κατὰ τὸν Ψευδο-Διονύσιον Ἀρεοπαγίτην." *Ἐπετηρὶς τῆς Ἑταιρείας Βυζαντινῶν Σπουδῶν* 35 (1966/67): 249.

Kretschmar, G. *Studien zur frühchristlichen Trinitätstheologie*. Tübingen: Mohr, 1956.

Krivochéine, B. "Simplicité de la nature divine et les distinctions en Dieu selon St. Grégoire de Nysse." *MessPR* 91–92 (1975): 133–158.

Ladner, G. "The Concept of the Image in the Greek Fathers and the Byzantine Iconoclastic Controversy." *DOP* 7 (1953): 1–34.

Lampe, G. W. H. *A Patristic Greek Lexicon*. Oxford: Clarendon, 1972.

Larsen, B. D. *Jamblique de Chalcis, exégète et philosophe*. Aarhus: Universitetsforlaget I Aarhus, 1972.

Layton, B. *The Gnostic Scriptures*. 2nd ed. New York: Doubleday, 1995.

————. "Prolegomena to the Study of Ancient Gnosticism." Pages 106–122 in *Recent Studies in Early Christianity: Doctrinal Diversity*. Edited by E. Ferguson. New York: Garland, 1999.

Leclercq, J. "Influence and Noninfluence of Dionysius in the Western Middle Ages." Pages 25–34 in *Pseudo-Dionysius: The Complete Works*. Edited by C. Luibhéid and P. Rorem. New York: Paulist Press, 1987.

Levenson, J. D. "The Jerusalem Temple in Devotional and Visionary Experience." Pages 32–59 in *From the Bible Through the Middle Ages*. Volume 1 of *Jewish Spirituality*. Edited by Arthur Green. 2 vols. New York: Crossroad, 1986.

————. *Sinai and Zion: An Entry into the Jewish Bible*. Minneapolis: Winston, 1985.

Lewy, H., and M. Tardieu. *The Chaldaean Oracles and Theurgy: Mysticism, Magic, and Platonism in the Later Roman Empire*. Rev. ed. Paris: Études Augustiniennes, 1978.

Lilla, S. "The Notion of Infinitude in Pseudo-Dionysius Areopagita." *JTS* 31 (1980): 93–103.

—. "Pseudo-Denys l'Aréopagite, Porphyre, et Damascius." Pages 117–152 in *Denys l'Aréopagite et sa posterité en orient et en occident: actes du colloque international, Paris 21–24 septembre 1994*. Edited by Y. de Andia. Paris: Études Augustiniennes, 1997.

Lloyd, A. C. "The Later Neoplatonists." Pages 161–277 in *The Cambridge History of Later Greek and Early Medieval Philosophy*. Edited by A. H. Armstrong. Cambridge: Cambridge University Press, 1967.

Lossky, V. N. "Apophasis and Trinitarian Theology." Pages 13–29 in *The Image and Likeness of God*. Edited and translated by J. Erickson and T. E. Bird. Crestwood, NY: St Vladimir's Seminary Press, 1974.

—. "Darkness and Light in the Knowledge of God." Pages 31–43 in *The Image and Likeness of God*. Edited and translated by J. Erickson and T. E. Bird. Crestwood, NY: St Vladimir's Seminary Press, 1974.

—. "La notion des 'analogies' chez Denys le pseudo-Aréopagite." *AHDL* 5 (1931): 179–209.

—. "La théologie négative dans la doctrine de Denys l'Aréopagite." *RSPT* 28 (1939): 204–221.

—. *The Mystical Theology of the Eastern Church*. Cambridge: Clarke, 1968.

Lot-Borodine, M. "Initiation à la mystique sacramentaire de l'Orient." *RSPT* 24 (1935): 664–675.

Louth, A. *Denys the Areopagite*. Wilton, CT: Morehouse-Barlow, 1989.

—. "The Influence of Denys the Areopagite on Eastern and Western Spirituality in the 14th Century." *Sob/ECR* 4 (1982): 185–200.

—. "Mysticism: Name and Thing." *Archaeus* 9 (2005): 9–21.

—. *The Origins of the Christian Mystical Tradition: From Plato to Denys*. Oxford: Clarendon, 1981.

—. "Pagan Theurgy and Christian Sacramentalism in Denys the Areopagite." *JTS* 37 (1986): 432–438.

—. "St Denys the Areopagite and the Iconoclast Controversy." Pages 329–339 in *Denys l'Aréopagite et sa posterité en orient et en occident: actes du colloque international, Paris 21–24 septembre 1994*. Edited by Y. de Andia. Paris: Études Augustiniennes, 1997.

—. "St Denys the Areopagite and St Maximus the Confessor: A Question of Influence." *SP* 27 (1993): 166–174.

————. *Wisdom of the Byzantine Church: Evagrios of Pontos and Maximus the Confessor.* 1997 Paine Lectures in Religion. Columbia, MO: University of Missouri-Colombia, 1998.

Luck, G. "Theurgy and Forms of Worship in Neoplatonism." Pages 185–228 in *Religion, Science, and Magic: In Concert and in Conflict.* Edited by J. Neusner, et al. Oxford: Oxford University Press, 1989.

Lyonnet, S. "Le sens de ἐφ᾽ ᾧ en Rom V,12 et l'exegèse des Pères Grecs." *Bib* 36 (1955): 436–456.

Magdalinos, P. "The Byzantine Holy Man in the Twelfth Century." Pages 51–66 in *The Byzantine Saint.* Edited by S. Hackel. London: Fellowship of St. Alban and St. Sergius, 1980.

Maloney, G. *Pseudo-Macarius: The Fifty Spiritual Homilies and the Great Letter.* New York: Paulist, 1991.

Mango, C. *The Art of the Byzantine Empire.* Englewood Cliffs, NJ: Prentice Hall, 1972.

Marriott, G. L. *Macarii Anecdota: Seven Unpublished Homilies of Macarius.* Cambridge, MA: Harvard University Press, 1918.

Mathews, T. F. *Early Churches of Constantinople.* University Park, PA: Pennsylvania State University Press, 1971.

McGinn, B. *The Foundations of Christian Mysticism: Origins to the Fifth Century.* New York: Crossroad, 1991.

McGuckin, J. *The Transfiguration of Christ in Scripture and in Tradition.* Lewistown: Mellen, 1986.

McVey, Babai. "The Domed Church as Microcosm: Literary Roots of an Architectural Symbol." *DOP* 39 (1983): 91–121.

Melcher, R. *Der achte Brief des Basilius, ein Werk des Evagrius Ponticus.* Münster: Aschendorff, 1923.

Mettinger, T. D. N. *The Dethronement of Sabaoth: Studies in the Shem and Kabod Theologies.* Lund: CWK Gleerup, 1982.

Meyendorff, J. *Byzantine Theology.* London: Mowbrays, 1974.

————. *Christ in Eastern Christian Thought.* Washington, DC: Corpus, 1969.

————. *Introduction to Gregory Palamas.* Translated by G. A. Lawrence. London: Faith, 1964.

————. "Notes sur l'influence dionysienne en Orient." *SP* 2 (1957): 547–552.

————. *St. Germanus of Constantinople: On the Divine Liturgy.* Translated by P. Meyendorff. Crestwood, NY: St. Vladimir's Seminary Press, 1984.

Miquel, P. "Les caractéres de l'experience spirituelle selon le Pseudo-Macaire." *Irénikon* 31 (1966): 497–513.

————. *Le vocabulaire de l'experience spirituelle dans la tradition patristique grecque du IVe au XIVe siècle.* Paris: Beauchesne, 1991.

Morard, F. E. "Monachos, Moine: Histoire du terme grecque jusqu'au IVe siècle." *ZPhTh* 20 (1973): 332–411.

Moreau, J. *L'idée d'univers dans la pensée antique.* Turin: Societa editrice internazionale, 1953.

Morray-Jones, C. R. A. "Paradise Revisited (2 Cor 12:1-12): The Jewish Mystical Background of Paul's Apostolate." *HTR* 86 (1993): 177–217; 265–292.

———. "Transformational Mysticism in the Apocalyptic-Merkabah Tradition." *JJS* 43 (1992): 1–31.

Mortley, R. *From Word to Silence.* Bonn: Hanstein, 1986.

Müller, H. F. "Plotinos über die Vorsehung." *Philog* 26 (1913): 338–357.

Muñoz-Leon, D. *Gloria de la Shekina en los targumim de Pentateuco.* Madrid: Consejo Superior de Investigaciones Científicas, 1977.

Murray, R. "An Exhortation to Candidates for Ascetical Vows at Baptism in the Ancient Syrian Church." *NTS* 21 (1974): 59–80.

———. *Symbols of Church and Kingdom: A Study of Early Syriac Tradition.* London: Cambridge University Press, 1975.

———. "The Theory of Symbolism in St. Ephrem's Theology." *ParOr* 6–7 (1975/76): 1–20.

Nedungatt, G. "The Covenanters of the Early Syriac-Speaking Church." *OCP* 39 (1973): 191–215; 419–444.

Nicolaou, T. "Zur Identität des μακάριος γέρων in der Mystagogie von Maximus der Bekenner." *OCP* 49 (1983): 407–418.

Noth, M. *Exodus: A Commentary.* Philadelphia: Westminster, 1962.

Nygren, A. *Agape and Eros.* Translated by P. S. Watson. Rev. ed. Philadelphia: Westminster, 1953.

Oppenheim, P. "Mönchsweihe und Taufritus: Ein Kommentar zur Auslegung bei Dionysios dem Areopagiten." Pages 259–282 in *Miscellanea liturgica in honorem L. Cuniberti Mohlberg.* 2 vols. Rome: Edizioni liturgiche, 1948.

Orlov, A., and A. Golitzin. "Many Lamps Are Lightened from the One: Paradigms of the Transformational Vision in the Macarian Homilies." *VC* 55 (2001): 281–298.

O'Rourke, F. *Pseudo-Dionysius and the Metaphysics of Aquinas.* Leiden: Brill, 1992.

Orrieux, L. M. "L'Évêque 'état de perfection' selon le Ps.-Denys." Pages 237–242 in *L'Évêque dans l'Église du Christ.* Edited by H. Bousse and A. Mandonge. Paris: Desclée de Brouwer, 1963.

Palmer, A., and I. Perczel. "A New Testimony from India to the Syriac Version of Pseudo-Dionysius (Pampakuda, Konat Collection, Ms. 239)." *Iran & the Caucasus* 6 (2002): 11–26.

Parmentier, M. "Evagrius of Pontus and the 'Letter to Melania.'" *Bijdragen, tijdschrift voor filosofie en theologie* 46 (1985): 2–38.

Patai, R. *Man and Temple in Ancient Jewish Myth and Ritual.* 2nd ed. New York: Ktav, 1967.

Pelikan, J. *Imago Dei: The Byzantine Apologia for Icons.* Princeton: Princeton University Press, 1990.

———. *The Spirit of Eastern Christianity.* Chicago: University of Chicago Press, 1974.

Pépin, J. *Théologie cosmique et théologie chrétienne.* Paris: PUF, 1964.

Pera, C. "Denys le mystique et la *theomachia.*" *RSR* 25 (1936): 5–75.

Perczel, I. "The Christology of Pseudo-Dionysius the Areopagite: The Fourth Letter in Its Indirect and Direct Text Traditions." *Mus* 117 (2004): 409–446.

———. "The Earliest Syriac Reception of Dionysius." Pages 27–41 in *Re-Thinking Dionysius the Areopagite.* Edited by S. Coakley and C. M. Stang. Malden, MA: Wiley-Blackwell, 2009.

———. "Le Pseudo-Denys, lecteur d'Origène." Pages 674–710 in *Origeniana Septima: Origenes in den Auseinandersetzungen des vierten Jahrhunderts.* Edited by W. A. Bienert and U. Kühneweg. Leuven: Peeters, 1999.

———. "Once Again on Dionysius the Areopagite and Leontius of Byzantium." Pages 41–85 in *Die Dionysius-Rezeption im Mittelalter: Internationales Kolloquium in Sofia vom 8. bis 11. April 1999 unter der Schirmherrschaft der Société internationale pour l'étude de la philosophie médiévale.* Edited by T. Boiadjiev, G. Kapriev, and A. Speer. Turnhout: Brepols, 2000.

———. "Pseudo-Dionysius and Palestinian Origenism." Pages 261–282 in *The Sabbaite Heritage in the Orthodox Church from the Fifth Century to the Present.* Edited by J. Patrich. Leuven: Peeters, 2001.

———. "Sergius of Reshaina's Syriac Translation of the Dionysian Corpus: Some Preliminary Remarks." Pages 79–94 in *La diffusione dell'eredità classica nell'età tardo-antica e medievale: Filologia, storia, dottrina: Atti del Seminario nazionale di studio, Napoli-Sorrento, 29–31 ottobre 1998.* Edited by C. Baffioni. Alessandria: Edizioni dell'Orso, 2000.

———. "'Théologiens' et 'magiciens' dans le Corpus dionysien." *Adamantius* 7 (2001): 55–75.

———. "Une théologie de la lumière: Denys l'Aréopagite et Évagre le Pontique." *REAug* 45 (1999): 79–120.

Persic, A. "La Chiesa di Siria e i 'gradi' della vita Christiana." Pages in 208–263 *Per foramen acus: Il cristianesimo antico di fronte alla pericope evangelica del "giovane ricco."* Edited by G. Vissona, et al. Milan: Vita e pensiero, 1986.

Plested, M. *The Macarian Legacy: The Place of Macarius-Symeon in the Eastern Christian Tradition*. Oxford: Oxford University Press, 2004.

Prigent, P. *Apocalypse et liturgie*. Neuchâtel: Delachaux et Niestlé, 1964.

Quaschning-Kirsch, M. "Ein weiterer Textzeuge für die syrische Version des Corpus Dionysiacum Areopagiticum: Paris B.N. Syr. 378." *Mus* 113 (2000): 115–124.

Quispel, G. *Makarius, das Thomasevangelium, und das Lied von der Perle*. Leiden: Brill, 1967.

———. "The Syrian Thomas and the Syrian Macarius." *VC* 18 (1964): 226–235.

Reale, G. "Introduzione: Il *Corpus Dionysiacum* e i grandi problem che suscita per la sua interpretazione." Pages 11–29 in *Dionigi Areopagita: Tutte le opere. Testo greco a fronte*. Translated by P. Scazzoso and I. Ramelli. Milan: Bompiani, 2009.

Reeves, J. C. *Heralds of that Good Realm: Syro-Mesopotamian Gnosis and Jewish Traditions*. Leiden: Brill, 1996.

Riedinger, U. "Eine Paraphrase des Engel-Traktates von Klemens von Alexandreia in den *Erotapokriseis* des Pseudo-Kaisarios." *ZKG* 73 (1962): 253–271.

———. "Pseudo-Dionysius Areopagites, Pseudo-Kaisarios und die Akoimeten." *ByzZ* 52 (1959): 276–296.

Riordan, W. *Divine Light: The Theology of Denys the Areopagite*. San Francisco, CA: Ignatius, 2008.

Rist, J. M. "A Note on Eros and Agape in Ps.-Dionysius." *VC* 20 (1966): 235–243.

———. *Eros and Psyche: Studies in Plato, Plotinus, and Origen*. London: Oxford University Press, 1964.

———. "Mysticism and Transcendence in Later Neoplatonism." *Hermes* 92 (1964): 213–225.

———. *Plotinus: The Road to Reality*. Cambridge: Cambridge University Press, 1963.

———. "Pseudo-Dionysius, Neoplatonism, and the Weakness of the Soul." Pages 135–161 in *From Athens to Chartres, Neoplatonism and Medieval Thought*. Edited by H. J. Westra. Leiden: Brill, 1992.

Ritter, A. M. "Gregor Palamas als Leser des Dionysios Pseudo-Areopagita." Pages 565–579 in *Denys l'Aréopagite et sa posterité en orient et en occident: actes du colloque international, Paris 21–24 septembre 1994*. Edited by Y. de Andia. Paris: Études Augustiniennes, 1997.

Romanides, J. *The Ancestral Sin: A Comparative Study of the Sin of Our Ancestors Adam and Eve according to the Paradigms and Doctrines of the First- and Second-Century Church and the Augustinian Formulation of Original Sin*. Ridgewood, NJ: Zephyr, 2002.

————. "Notes on the Palamite Controversy and Related Topics." *GOTR* 6 (1960/61): 186–205; 9 (1963/64): 225–270.

————. "Original Sin according to St. Paul." *SVTQ* 14 (1955–1956): 5–28.

Roques, R. "De l'implication des méthodes théologiques chez le Ps.-Denys." *RAM* 30 (1954): 268–274.

————. "Éléments pour une théologie de l'état monastique chez Denys l'Aréopagite." Pages 283–314 in *Théologie de la vie monastique: Études sur la tradition patristique.* Edited by G. Lemaître. Paris: Aubier, 1961.

————. "Le sens du baptême selon le Ps.-Denys." *Ir* 31 (1958): 431.

————. *L'univers dionysien.* Paris: Aubier, 1954.

————. "Note sur la notion de THEOLOGIA selon le Pseudo-Denys l'Aréopagite." *RAM* 25 (1949): 200–212.

————. "Pierre l'Ibérien et le Corpus Dionysien." *RHR* 114 (1954): 69–98.

————. "Symbolisme et théologie négative chez le Pseudo-Denys." *BAGB* 1 (1957): 97–112.

Rorem, P. E. "The Biblical Allusions and Overlooked Quotations in the Pseudo-Dionysian Corpus." *SP* 23 (1989): 61–65.

————. *Biblical and Liturgical Symbols within the Pseudo-Dionysian Synthesis.* Toronto: Pontifical Institute of Mediaeval Studies, 1984.

————. "The Early Latin Dionysius: Eriugena and Hugh of St. Victor." Pages 71–84 in *Re-Thinking Dionysius the Areopagite.* Edited by S. Coakley and C. M. Stang. Malden, MA: Wiley-Blackwell, 2009.

————. "Empathy and Evaluation in Medieval Church History and Pastoral Ministry: A Lutheran Reading of Pseudo-Dionysius." *PSB* 19 (1998): 99–115.

————. "Iamblichus and the Anagogical Method in Pseudo-Dionysius' Liturgical Theology." *SP* 18 (1979): 543–560.

————. "Martin Luther's Christocentric Critique of Pseudo-Dionysian Spirituality." *LuthQ* 11 (1997): 291–307.

————. "Moses as the Paradigm for the Liturgical Spirituality of Pseudo-Dionysius." *SP* 18 (1989): 275–279.

————. "The Place of *The Mystical Theology* in the Pseudo-Dionysian Corpus." *Dionysius* 4 (1980): 87–98.

————. *Pseudo-Dionysius: A Commentary to the Texts and an Introduction to Their Influence.* Oxford: Oxford University Press, 1993.

————. "The Uplifting Spirituality of Pseudo-Dionysius." Pages 132–151 in *Origins to the Twelfth Century.* Vol. 1 of *Christian Spirituality.* Edited by B. McGinn, J. Meyendorff, and J. Leclercq. New York: Crossroad, 1988.

Rorem, P. E., and J. C. Lamoreaux. *John of Scythopolis and the Dionysian Corpus: Annotating the Areopagite.* Oxford: Oxford University Press, 1998.

———. "John of Scythopolis on Apollinarian Christology and the Pseudo-Dionysius' True Identity." *ChH* 62 (1993): 469–482.

Rosán, J. *The Philosophy of Proclus.* New York: Cosmos, 1949.

Roth, C. *St. John of Damascus on the Divine Images.* Crestwood, NY: St Vladimir's Seminary Press, 1980.

Rousseau, P. *Ascetics, Authority, and the Church.* Oxford: Oxford University Press, 1978.

Rowland, C. *The Open Heaven: A Study of Apocalyptic in Judaism and Early Christianity.* New York: Crossroad, 1982.

———. "The Visions of God in Apocalyptic Literature." *JSJ* 10 (1979): 137–154.

Ruh, K. "Die 'Mystica Theologia' des Dionysius Pseudo-Areopagita im Lichte mittelalterlicher Kommentatoren." *ZFDA* 122 (1993): 127–145.

Saffrey, H. D. *Le néoplatonisme après Plotin.* Paris: Vrin, 2000.

———. "Nouveaux liens objectifs entre le Pseudo-Denys et Proclus." *RSPT* 63 (1979): 3–16.

———. "Un lien objectif entre le Pseudo-Denys et Proclus." *SP* 9 (1966): 98–105.

Scazzoso, P. *Ricerche sulla struttura del linguaggio dello Pseudo-Dionigi Areopagita.* Milan: Vita e pensiero, 1967.

Schäfer, C. *The Philosophy of Dionysius the Areopagite: An Introduction to the Structure and the Content of the Treatise on the Divine Names.* Leiden/Boston: Brill, 2006.

Schmidt, M. "Alttestamentliche Typologien in Paradies Hymnen von Ephräm der Syrer." Pages 55–81 in *Paradeigmata: Literarische Typologie des Alten Testaments.* Edited by F. Link. Berlin: Duncker & Humboldt, 1989.

Schneider, A. M. "Liturgie und Kirchenbau in Syrien." *NAWG* (1949): 56–68.

Scholem, G. *Jewish Gnosticism, Merkabah Mysticism, and Talmudic Tradition.* New York: Jewish Theological Seminary of America, 1960.

———. *Major Trends in Jewish Mysticism.* 3rd ed. New York: Schocken, 1973.

Schultze, B. "Grundfragen des theologischen Palamismus." *OS* 24 (1975): 105–135.

Schulz, H.-J. *The Byzantine Liturgy.* Translated by M. J. O'Connell. New York: Pueblo, 1986.

Scott, J. M. "The Triumph of God in 2 Cor 2:14: Additional Evidence of Merkabah Mysticism in Paul." *NTS* 42 (1996): 260–281.

Séd, N. "La Shekinta et ses amis araméens." *COr* 20 (1988): 230–242.

———. "Les *Hymnes sur le paradis* de saint Ephrem et les traditions juives." *Mus* (1968): 455–501.

Segal, A. *Paul the Convert: The Apostolate and Apostasy of Saul the Pharisee.* New Haven: Yale University Press, 1990.

Shaw, G. "Neoplatonic Theurgy and Dionysius the Areopagite." *JECS* 7 (1999): 573–599.

———. *Theurgy and the Soul: The Neoplatonism of Iamblichus.* University Park, PA: Pennsylvania State University Press, 1995.

Sheldon-Williams, I. P. "The ps.-Dionysius and the Holy Hierotheos." *SP* 8 (1966): 108–117.

Sherwood, P. "Mimro de Serge de Rešayna sur la vie spirituelle." *OrSyr* 5 (1960): 433–457; 6 (1961): 95–115; 121–156.

———. "Sergius of Reshaina and the Syriac Versions of the Pseudo-Dionysius." *SE* 4 (1952): 174–184.

Skoyles Jarkins, S. K. *Aphrahat the Persian Sage and the Temple of God: A Study of Early Syriac Theological Anthropology.* Piscataway, NJ: Gorgias, 2008.

Smelik, W. F. "On the Mystical Transformation of the Righteous into Light in Judaism." *JSJ* 27 (1995): 122–144.

Smith, J. Payne. *A Compendious Syriac Dictionary.* Oxford: Clarendon, 1903; Repr., 1990.

Smith, M. S. "The History of the Term Gnostikos." Pages 796–807 in *The Rediscovery of Gnosticism II.* Edited by B. Layton. Leiden: Brill, 1981.

———. "Seeing God in the Psalms: The Background to the Beatific Vision in the Bible." *CBQ* 50 (1988): 171–183.

Stang, C. *Apophasis and Pseudonymity in Dionysius the Areopagite: "No Longer I."* Oxford: Oxford University Press, 2012.

———. "Dionysius, Paul and the Significance of the Pseudonym." Pages 11–25 in *Re-Thinking Dionysius the Areopagite.* Edited by S. Coakley and C. M. Stang. Malden, MA: Wiley-Blackwell, 2009.

Stead, C. *Divine Substance.* Oxford: Clarendon, 1977.

Steel, C. "Proclus et Denys: de l'existence du mal." Pages 89–116 in *Denys l'Aréopagite et sa posterité en orient et en occident: actes du colloque international, Paris 21–24 septembre 1994.* Edited by Y. de Andia. Paris: Études Augustiniennes, 1997.

Stewart, C. "Imageless Prayer and the Theological Vision of Evagrius Ponticus." *JECS* 9 (2001): 173–204.

———. *Working the Earth of the Heart: The Messalian Controversy in History, Texts, and Language to A.D. 431.* Oxford: Clarendon, 1991.

Stiglmayr, J. "Aszese und Mystik des sog. Dionysius Areopagita." *Schol* 2 (1927): 161–207.

———. "Das Aufkommen der ps.-dionysischen Schriften und ihr Eindringen in die christliche Literatur bis zum Lateranconcil 649: Ein zweiter Beitrag zur Dionysios-Frage." *Jahresbericht des öffentlichen Privatgymnasiums an der Stella matutina zu Feldkirch* 4 (1895): 3–96.

———. "Der Neuplatoniker Proklos als Vorlage des sog. Dionysius Areopagita in der Lehre vom Übel." *HJ* 16 (1895): 253–273, 721–748.

———. "Die Engellehre des sogenannten Dionysius Aropagita." Page 406 in *Compte rendu du quatrième Congrès scientifique des Catholiques*. Edited by U. Chevalier. Fribourg: Oeuvre de Saint Paul, 1898.

———. "Die Lehre von den Sakramenten und der Kirche nach Ps.-Dionysius." *ZKT* 22 (1898): 246–303.

———. "Über die Termini Hierarch und Hierarchia." *ZKT* 22 (1898): 180–187.

Strothmann, W. *Das Sakrament der Myron-Weihe in der Schrift de ecclesiastica hierarchia des Pseudo-Dionysios in syrischen Übersetzungen und Kommentaren*. Wiesbaden: Harrassowitz, 1978.

Stroumsa, G. A. G. *Another Seed: Studies in Gnostic Mythology*. Leiden: Brill, 1984.

———. "Form(s) of God: Some Notes on Metatron and Christ." *HTR* 76, no. 3 (1983): 269–288.

Suchla, B. R. "Die sogenannten Maximus Scholien des Corpus Dionysiacum Areopagiticum." *NAWG* (1980): 31–66.

———. *Eine Redaktion des griechischen Corpus Dionysiacum im Umkreis des Johannes von Skythopolis, des Verfassers von Prolog und Scholien: Ein dritter Beitrag zur Überlieferungsgeschichte des Corpus Dionysiacum*. Göttingen: Vandenhoeck & Ruprecht, 1985.

Tabor, J. *Things Unutterable: Paul's Ascent to Heaven in its Greco-Roman, Judaic, and Early Christian Contexts*. Lanham, MA: University Press of America, 1986.

Taft, R. "The Spirit of Eastern Worship." *Diakonia* 12 (1977): 103–120.

Taylor, C. "The Cloud-Author's Remaking of the Pseudo-Dionysius' Mystical Theology." *MAev* 75 (2006): 202–218.

Termini, C. *Le potenze di Dio: Studio su δύναμις in Filon di Alessandria*. Rome: Institutum Patristicum Augustinianum, 2000.

Thunberg, L. *Man and the Cosmos: The Vision of St. Maximus the Confessor*. Crestwood, NY: St Vladimir's Seminary Press, 1985.

———. *Microcosm and Mediator: The Theological Anthropology of Maximus the Confessor*. 2nd ed. Chicago: Open Court, 1995.

Torrance, T. F. "The relation of the Incarnation to Space in Nicene Theology." Pages 43–74 in *The Ecumenical World of Orthodox Civilization: Essays in Honour of Georges Florovsky*. Edited by Andrew Blane. Paris: Mouton, 1974.

Trethowan, Dom Illtyd. "Irrationality in Theology and the Palamite Distinction." *ECR* 10 (1977): 19–26.

Trouillard, J. "Raison et Mystique chez Plotin." *REA* 20 (1974): 3–14.

Turner, D. "Dionysius and Some Late Medieval Mystical Theologians of Northern Europe." Pages 121–135 in *Re-Thinking Dionysius the Areopagite*. Edited by S. Coakley and C. M. Stang. Malden, MA: Wiley-Blackwell, 2009.

Turner, H. J. M. *St. Symeon the New Theologian and Spiritual Fatherhood.* Leiden: Brill, 1990.

Twetten, D. B. "Aquinas's Aristotelian and Dionysian Definition of 'God.' " *Thomist* 69 (2005): 203–250.

———. "Dionysius East and West: Unities, Differentiations, and the Exegesis of Biblical Theophanies." *Dionysius* 26 (2008): 115–138.

Van den Daele, A. *Indices Pseudo-Dionysiani auctore.* Louvain: Bibliothèque de l'Université, 1941.

Van Esbroeck, M. "Peter the Iberian and Dionysius the Areopagite: Honigmann's Thesis Revisited." *OCP* 59 (1993): 217–227.

Vanneste, J. "Is the Mysticism of Pseudo-Dionysius Genuine?" 288–289.

———. "La doctrine des trois voies dans la théologie mystique du Ps.-Denys." *TU* 93/*SP* 8 (1966): 462–467.

———. "La théologie mystique du Ps.-Denys." *TU* 80/*SP* 5 (1962): 401–415.

———. *Le Mystère de Dieu.* Bruges: Desclée de Brouwer, 1959.

Van Parys, M. "La liturgie du coeur selon saint Grégoire le Sinaïte." *Ir* 51 (1978): 312–337.

Viller, M. "Aux sources de la spiritualité de Saint Maxime." *RAM* 11 (1930): 156–184 and 239–268.

Vincent, J. M. "Aspekte der Begegnung mit Gott im alten Testament: Die Erfahrung der göttlichen Gegenwart im Schauen Gottes." *RB* 103 (1996): 5–39.

———. "Is the Mysticism of Pseudo-Dionysius Genuine?" *IPQ* 3 (1963): 286–306.

Völker, W. *Kontemplation und Extase bei Ps.-Dionysius Areopagita.* Wiesbaden: Steiner, 1958.

Von Balthasar, H. "Das Scholienwerk des Johannes von Scythopolis." *Schol* 15 (1940): 31–66.

———. *Herrlichkeit: Eine theologische Ästhetik.* Einsiedeln: Johannes, 1964.

———. *Kosmische Liturgie.* 2nd ed. Einsiedeln: Johannes-Verlag, 1961.

———. "L'héritage évagrienne dans la synthèse de Saint Maxime." *SP* 8 (1966): 356–362.

Von Fritz, K. *Pseudepigrapha I: Pseudopythagorica, lettres de Platon, littérature pseudépigraphique juive.* Geneva: Fondation Hardt, 1971.

Von Ivanka, E. *Plato Christianus: Übernahme und Umgestaltung des Platonismus durch die Väter.* Einsiedeln: Johannes Verlag, 1964.

―――. *Rhomäerreich und Gottesvolk*. Freiburg: Alber, 1968.

Von Schönborn, C. *Sophrone de Jérusalem: Vie monastique et confession dogmatique*. Paris: Beauchesne, 1972.

Von Semmelroth, O. "Die Lehre des Pseudo-Dionysius Areopagita vom Aufstieg der Kreatur zum göttlichen Licht." *Schol* 29 (1954): 24–52.

―――. "Erlösung und Erlöser im System des Ps.-Dionysius Areopagita." *Schol* 20–24 (1949): 367–379.

―――. "Geeinte Vielheit: Zur Gotteslehre des Pseudo-Dionysius Areopagita." *Schol* 25 (1950): 389–407.

―――. "Gottes ausstrahlendes Licht: Zur Schöpfungs- und Offenbarungslehre des Pseudo-Dionysius Areopagita." *Schol* 28 (1953): 481–503.

―――. "Gottes überwesentliche Einheit: Zur Gotteslehre des Pseudo-Dionysius Areopagita." *Schol* 25 (1950): 209–234.

Vööbus, A. *Early Monasticism in Mesopotamia and Syria*. Vol. 2 of *History of Asceticism in the Syrian Orient*. Louvain: Peeters, 1960.

―――. *The Origins of Asceticism*. Vol. 1 of *History of Asceticism in the Syrian Orient*. Louvain: Peeters, 1958.

Wallis, R. T. *Neoplatonism*. London: Duckworth, 1972.

Watt, J. W. "Philoxenus and the Old Syriac Version of Evagrius." *OC* 64 (1980): 65–87.

Weaver, D. "The Exegesis of Romans 5:12 among the Greek Fathers and Its Implications for the Doctrine of Original Sin: The 5th–12th Centuries." *SVTQ* 29 (1985): 133–159; 231–257.

―――. "From Paul to Augustine: Romans 5:12 in Early Christian Exegesis." *SVTQ* 27 (1983): 187-206.

Weber, E.-H. "L'apophatisme dionysien chez Albert le Grand et dans son école." Pages 379–403 in *Denys l'Aréopagite et sa posterité en orient et en occident: actes du colloque international, Paris 21–24 septembre 1994*. Edited by Y. de Andia. Paris: Études Augustiniennes, 1997.

Wellesz, E. *A History of Byzantine Music and Hymnography*. Oxford: Clarendon, 1961.

Wesche, K. P. "Christological Doctrine and Liturgical Interpretation in Pseudo-Dionysius." *SVTQ* 33 (1989): 53–73.

―――. "A Reply to Hieromonk Alexander's 'Reply.'" *SVTQ* 34 (1990): 324–327.

West, F. "The Conquest of Space: Sacred Space at Holy Trinity Russian Orthodox Cathedral, Chicago, Illinois." *SVTQ* 22 (1978): 153–167.

Wiessner, G. "Zur Handschriftüberlieferung des syrischen Fassung des Corpus Dionysiacum." *NAWG* (1972): 165–216.

Will, M. J. "Dionysian Neoplatonism and the Theology of the Cloud, Author I; Author II." *DRev* 379 (1992): 98–109; 380 (1992): 184–194.

Williams, M. A. *Rethinking "Gnosticism": An Argument for Dismantling a Dubious Category*. Princeton, NJ: Princeton University Press, 1996.

Williams, R. D. "The Philosophical Structures of Palamism." *ECR* 9 (1977): 23–44.

Wolfson, H. A. "The Identification of *Ex Nihilo* with Emanation in Gregory of Nyssa." *HTR* 63 (1970): 53–60.

Young, R. D. *In Procession before the World: Martyrdom as Public Liturgy in Early Christianity*. Milwaukee: Marquette University Press, 2001.

Zintzen, C. "Die Wertung von Mystik und Magie in der neuplatonischer Philosophie." *RM* 108 (1965): 71–100.

Zöckler, O. "Evagrius Pontikus. Seine Stellung in der altchristliche Literatur- und Dogmengeschichte." Pages 105–125 in *Biblische and kirchenhistorische Studien von Dr. O. Zöckler*. Munich: C. H. Beck, 1893.

Biblical Index

Dionysius Index

Celestial Hierarchy

Mystical Theology

Divine Names

Epistles

Bibliographic Index

451